THE LONGING FOR MYTH IN GERMANY

THE LONGING FOR MYTH IN GERMANY

Religion and Aesthetic Culture
from Romanticism to Nietzsche

GEORGE S. WILLIAMSON

THE UNIVERSITY OF CHICAGO PRESS
CHICAGO AND LONDON

George S. Williamson is assistant professor of history at the University of Alabama.

The University of Chicago Press, Chicago 60637
The University of Chicago Press, Ltd., London
© 2004 by The University of Chicago
All rights reserved. Published 2004
Printed in the United States of America
13 12 11 10 09 08 07 06 05 04   5 4 3 2 1

ISBN (cloth): 0-226-89945-4
ISBN (paper): 0-226-89946-2

Library of Congress Cataloging-in-Publication Data

Williamson, George S.
    The longing for myth in Germany : religion and aesthetic culture from
    Romanticism to Nietzsche / George S. Williamson
        p   cm.
    ISBN 0-226-89945-4 (cloth : alk. paper) — ISBN 0-226-89946-2 (pbk. : alk. paper)
    1. National characteristics, German.   2. Myth — Political aspects.
    3. Germany — Historiography— History — 19th century.   4. Germany —
    Intellectual life — 19th century.   5. Literature and myth.   I. Title.
    DD204.W47   2004
    943'.0072—DC22

                                                            2003023127

For Joan and Samuel

CONTENTS

ACKNOWLEDGMENTS

In those moments of frustration, blockage, or sheer laziness that accompany every scholarly project, writers sometimes console themselves by drafting their acknowledgments. Recalling the many individuals whose counsel, patience, and good humor have made a book possible evokes a sense of strength in numbers, as well as of obligation for debts incurred. It gives me great pleasure now to give my thanks in print, as this book, so long in preparation, reaches completion.

The origins of this study go back to the Religious Studies program at Brown University, where I first began to grapple with the ambiguities of modern European religious thought. In Wendell Dietrich I found a mentor whose dedication to careful and conscientious scholarship was balanced by a quiet passion for undergraduate teaching. To his mild distress, I switched fields and entered the graduate program in history at Yale University. There I had the good fortune to work with two first-class historians of European cultural and intellectual history, who oversaw the development of my initial ideas into a Ph.D. thesis. Frank M. Turner directed the dissertation, helping me formulate the project and then guiding me through the inevitable (and, in my case, rather frequent) dissertation crises. Peter Gay read my chapters with great care and saved me from numerous pitfalls with his encyclopedic grasp of cultural history and his keen sense of style. Along the way, I received helpful advice from Louis Dupré, Cyrus Hamlin, Mark Micale, Jeffrey Sammons, and Henry Ashby Turner. Among my former graduate student colleagues, I especially thank Cyrus Vakil, who commented on numerous drafts of the dissertation, and Firoozeh Kashani-Sabet, who provided thoughtful criticism and much-needed encouragement along the way.

The process of transforming the dissertation into a publishable manuscript began after I joined the history department at the University of Alabama in 1997. In Tuscaloosa, I have enjoyed the friendship and encouragement of colleagues both inside and outside the history department. In addition, I have benefited from interactions with scholars at other institutions in the United States and Germany. Since I contacted her six years ago with a tentative e-mail, Suzanne Marchand has shown boundless generosity toward this project, commenting on various drafts of the manuscript, inviting me to conferences, helping to secure grants, and all the while inspiring me with the example of her own scholarship. Helmut Walser Smith, Jeffrey Myers, and Brian Vick took the time to read the manuscript in its entirety, offering helpful advice and judicious criticism. Jonathan Hess, Scott O'Bryan, and Paul Hagenloh probed the arguments of the introduction, Timothy Murphy commented on the Nietzsche chapter, Tuska Benes shared her considerable knowledge of the history of linguistics, Rasma Lazda lent her expertise on medieval German literature, and Thomas Howard helped me avoid several errors in the sections on biblical criticism. For their help and advice concerning various iterations of this project, I would also like to thank Wolfgang Burgdorf, Wolfgang Hardtwig, and Christoph Jamme.

This project has been supported by generous grants from Yale University, the Mellon Foundation, the Institute for European History in Mainz, the German Academic Exchange Service, the University of Alabama's Research Advisory Council, and Harvard University's Minda de Gunzburg Center for European Studies. Without the efforts of dedicated individuals, however, such institutional support would have gone for naught. Karl von Aretin, Andreas Kunz, Ralph Melville, Claus Scharf, and Martin Vogt facilitated my stay in Mainz in 1992 and introduced me there to a jolly community of historians. During my fellowship year at Harvard in 2000–2001, I benefited from conversations and exchanges with David Blackbourn, Neil Brenner, Jean-Marc Dreyfus, John Gillingham, Christina von Hodenberg, Peter Kraus, Regula Ludi, Anne Simonin, and Michael Werz. I would also like to thank the librarians and staff of the Yale University Library, the Harvard University Library, the Staatsbibliothek zu Berlin Preußischer Kulturbesitz, and the Gorgas Library at the University of Alabama for their assistance and professionalism. Among the many librarians whose patience I have tested, I owe a special debt of gratitude to Sue Armentrout, Jim Dunkly, and John Janeway of the duPont Library at the University of the South. I also thank Teresa Golson of the University of Alabama's Faculty Resource Center for her careful work preparing the book's illustrations.

The University of Chicago Press did a superb job shepherding the manuscript from submission to publication. I am grateful to my editor, Douglas Mitchell, as well as Robert Devens and Timothy McGovern, for taking an interest in the book and then pushing its author along with a series of cheerful but insistent missives. Warren Breckman and the other outside reader for the Press urged me to clarify my arguments and offered their insights on numerous points of fact and interpretation. The copyediting of Pamela Bruton has been thorough and professional. Needless to say, all mistakes remain my own.

Without my family and friends, this book would not have been written. In Tuscaloosa I would especially like to thank Jerry Rosiek and Alison Schmitke, who plied me with food, friendship, and late-night theorizing, and Lucy Pickering, who reminded me of the need for humor and perspective. I am grateful to Thad Williamson, Adria Scharf, Treeby Williamson Brown, and Robert Brown for their friendship, love, and support, and I thank Frances and Wallace for simply being there. Finally, I thank my parents, Joan and Samuel Williamson, who have lived with this book for so many years. They have been an unfailing source of encouragement, advice, wisdom, and inspiration. I dedicate this book to them.

GGS   Joseph Görres. *Gesammelte Schriften.* Edited by Wilhelm Schellberg. 16 vols. to date. Cologne: Gilde, 1926–.

HSW   Johann Gottfried Herder. *Sämmtliche Werke.* Edited by Bernhard Suphan. 33 vols. Berlin: Weidmann, 1877–1913.

KFSA   Friedrich Schlegel. *Kritische Friedrich-Schlegel Ausgabe.* Edited by Ernst Behler. 35 vols. Paderborn: Schöningh, 1958–.

NBW   Friedrich Nietzsche. *Briefwechsel: Kritische Gesamtausgabe.* Edited by Giorgio Colli and Mazzino Montinari. 18 vols. to date. Berlin: de Gruyter, 1975–.

NKGA   Friedrich Nietzsche. *Werke: Kritische Gesamtausgabe.* Edited by Giorgio Colli and Mazzino Montinari. 31 vols. to date. Berlin: de Gruyter, 1967–.

NKSA   Friedrich Nietzsche. *Sämtliche Werke: Kritische Studienausgabe.* Edited by Giorgio Colli and Mazzino Montinari. 15 vols. Berlin: de Gruyter, 1988.

Plitt   Friedrich Schelling. *Aus Schellings Leben: In Briefen.* Edited by G. L. Plitt. 3 vols. Leipzig: S. Hirzel, 1869–70.

RWGSB   Richard Wagner. *Gesammelte Schriften und Briefen.* Edited by Julius Kapp. 14 vols. Leipzig: Hesse und Becker, 1914.

RWGSD   Richard Wagner. *Gesammelte Schriften und Dichtungen.* 10 vols. Leipzig: Fritzsch, 1871–83.

SBD   Friedrich Schelling. *Briefe und Dokumente.* Edited by Horst Fuhrmans. 3 vols. Bonn: Bouvier, 1962–75.

SSW   Friedrich Schelling. *Sämmtliche Werke.* Edited by K. F. A. Schelling. 14 vols. Stuttgart and Augsburg: Cotta, 1856–61.

WSB   Richard Wagner. *Sämtliche Briefe.* Edited by Gertrud Strobel and Werner Wolf. 12 vols. to date. Leipzig: Deutscher Verlag für Musik, 1967–.

ZfVp   *Zeitschrift für Völkerpsychologie und Sprachwissenschaft.* 1860–90.

> The poetry of the ancients was that of possession; ours is that of
> longing. The former stands firmly on the soil of the present; the
> latter sways between memory and anticipation.
>
> August Wilhelm Schlegel,
> *Vorlesungen über dramatische Kunst und Literatur*

In 1940, the novelist Thomas Mann identified what he viewed as the fundamental difference between German culture and that of the West. Whereas British and French writers produced art rooted in social and political reality, the Germans had dedicated themselves to the "pure humanity of the mythical age," which was based in nature itself rather than the circumstances of any historical era. "The essential and characteristic national distinction is that between the social instinct of the French work and the mythical, primitive, poetic spirit of the German. With the appreciation of this difference, the intricate old question: 'What is German?' perhaps finds its tersest answer."[1] Mann was no disinterested observer in these matters. He intended to show that precisely those qualities that had given rise to Germany's greatest art (including his own) had also led it into the grip of National Socialism. In that respect, his comments are significant less as an analysis of national differences or historical trajectories than as evidence of a widespread belief among German intellectuals that the fate of their nation's culture depended on a continuing engagement with the world of myth.

The roots of this belief lie in the late eighteenth century, when Johann Gottfried Herder and other scholars developed a concept of myth as a distinctive fusion of poetry and religion that expressed the essential spirit of a nation. In Herder's view, every people had at one time possessed its own mythology, which served as the basis for its literature, religion, customs, and law. Building on these arguments, early Romantic writers called in the 1790s for a "new mythology," which would supplant both the biblical and classical mythologies and transform a fragmented modern society into a unified whole. According to the philosopher Friedrich Schelling, this mythology would be "the creation, not of some individual author, but of a new race personifying, as it were, one single poet."[2] Other writers envisioned a specifically national mythology, rooted in the history and experiences of the German "nation." In the decades after 1800, scholars and amateurs alike scoured through medieval verse, church libraries, and peasant villages for evidence of forgotten Germanic deities or lost knightly epics. Jacob and Wilhelm Grimm (among others) collected fairy tales and produced huge tomes on German folklore and mythology. Artists and poets exploited this research, publishing popular versions of legends and painting frescoes of the medieval *Nibelungenlied*. In the same spirit, the Bavarian king Ludwig I built a monumental pantheon overlooking the Danube River, which he named "Walhalla" after the mythical home of the Nordic gods.

This fascination with myth persisted and intensified during the second half of the nineteenth century. Inspired by the growth of comparative philology, scholars debated the merits of ancient "Aryan" and "Hebrew" mythologies. Meanwhile, the composer Richard Wagner populated his operas with heroes and gods from the *Edda* and built a festival theater in Bayreuth to perform them. During the Wilhelmine era, individuals and organizations associated with the *völkische Bewegung* (folkish movement) attempted to revive an actual form of Germanic religious practice, which they construed as either a pagan nature cult or a particularly Aryan prototype of Christianity. Yet however impressive their scope and conception, these artifacts of "mythology" were unable to fulfill the hopes attached to them. The dreams of a society infused by myth remained unsatisfied, mired instead in the religious and political divisions of nineteenth-century intellectual life.

The persistent gap between mythical hope and prosaic reality gave rise to that most Romantic of emotions: longing *(Sehnsucht)*. For Immanuel Kant, longing represented the "empty wish to overcome the time between the desire and the acquisition of the desired object" and was directed toward "objects for whose production the subject feels himself inadequate."[3] For August Wilhelm Schlegel, longing characterized the modern condition, in which poetry "sways between memory and anticipation," and the movement of history precluded fulfillment in any single moment. Sentiments of nostalgia, longing, or exile were indeed a common feature of European culture in the decades following the French Revolution, as writers sensed the profound distance that divided them from the world of their childhood and, by extension, from the seemingly unified and tradition-bound societies of the distant past.[4] In Germany, such cultural tropes fed into a discourse on "myth," which became a means of expressing just what had been lost in the transition to modernity, as well as a means for imagining the eventual reintegration of aesthetic, religious, and public life in some future society. A "longing for myth" would animate the thought of the early Romantics, the Grimm brothers, Wagner, Nietzsche, and a host of lesser-known writers, artists, and scholars, and it would remain a feature of German culture well into the twentieth century.[5]

This phenomenon has not gone unnoticed, of course. Even before World War I, literary scholars had begun to document what already appeared as a particularly intense and productive engagement in Germany with ancient and medieval mythologies.[6] But this tradition came under sharper scrutiny in light of the Third Reich, as historians attempted to explain the intellectual origins of National Socialism. A number of scholars interpreted the Romantic passion for myth as evidence of a deep-seated irrationalism in German culture or as the symptom of a peculiarly German cultural disorder.[7] In response, Thomas Mann attempted to emphasize the humanistic strand within German mythical thought. What both defenders and detractors of this tradition tended to overlook, however, were the considerable differences in content and context between late-eighteenth-century theories of myth and the later writings of Wagner or Nietzsche—not to mention their twentieth-century followers. Further, they frequently assumed that the fascination with myth had distracted German intellectuals from some normative path of progress leading from the Enlightenment to liberalism and culminating in a scientific or rationalistic worldview.

By the 1970s, however, the authority of such historical models had been called into question by various modernist and postmodernist critiques of reason. This led in turn to a reevaluation of Romantic thought on myth.[8] In an important series of lectures, the philosopher Manfred Frank argued that the project of a "new mythology"—far from plunging Germany into barbarism—represented an attempt to found a public sphere that would preserve the ineffable qualities of individuality and freedom.[9] Frank's work inspired a slew of articles and monographs investigating various aspects of mythical thought in the nineteenth century.[10] Such studies have done much to rescue Romanticism from oversimplification and one-sided polemic, but they have sometimes underplayed the more problematic aspects of that tradition, including its relationship to radical nationalism and anti-Semitism.[11] Moreover, none of these studies has systematically examined the links between intellectual attitudes toward myth and the social, political, and religious contexts in

which they emerged.[12] Yet it is only through the reconstruction of those contexts that it becomes possible to avoid the false choice of treating German
mythical thought either as a legitimate response to secular modernity or as
the manifestation of a reactionary "irrationalism."

The present work offers an intellectual history of mythical thought in
nineteenth-century Germany. Focusing on the trope of a "new mythology,"
it examines the influence of a persistent discourse on myth from the era of
early Romanticism *(Frühromantik)* up through the later thought of Friedrich
Nietzsche.[13] In doing so, it traces debates about ancient and modern mythologies across a range of scholarly disciplines, including biblical theology,
classical philology, Germanic philology, and comparative philology, which
dealt with the historical cultures of ancient Israel, ancient Greece, medieval
Germany, and a broadly defined "Orient." Sources from literature, music, and
the realm of *Publizistik* (journalism) are also considered, especially as they
influenced the ongoing debate in Germany concerning what Nietzsche once
termed the "use and abuse" of "myth."[14] This intellectual discussion of myth
is in turn linked to the social pressures, cultural ambitions, and theological
concerns of the (primarily Protestant) educated classes as they evolved over
the course of the eighteenth and nineteenth centuries.

As I argue here, it was the postrevolutionary experience of historical rup-
ture and religious crisis, interpreted in the light of neohumanist *Bildung*,
that led the early Romantics to call for a "new mythology" and encouraged
certain nationalist writers to construct a specifically "German" mythology.
But whereas the *Frühromantik* project of a new mythology was conceived as
an outcome of historical processes generated within modern (Christian) society, over the course of the nineteenth century the discourse on myth came
to be deployed in ever starker opposition to Christian modernity. By demonstrating the power and appeal of a concept of myth in German intellectual
culture, this study emphasizes the degree to which the supposedly secular
realms of nineteenth-century art and scholarship were infused with the
rhetoric, narratives, and assumptions of Christian theology. Indeed, I maintain in this study that the longing for myth is best understood, not as a
secularization of traditional religion or as a form of "secular religion," but
rather as a development *within* Christian (especially German Protestant)
culture, as it confronted the cultural and political challenges of European
modernity.

In elucidating this history, the present work does not start out from a particular definition of "myth." Instead, it is concerned with the meanings, expectations, and attitudes that converged around the word *"Mythos"* and its vari-

ants *"Mythus"* and *"Mythologie."* This approach immediately sets it off
from studies that seek to investigate the construction and significance of
"historical myths" or "political myths" in modern German history. Such
works typically rely on an anthropological or sociological definition of
"myth," applying it to such historical phenomena as the cult of Queen Luise
or the veneration of Bismarck.[15] While these studies have helped to illumi-
nate numerous features of German literary and political culture, they face
the difficulty that their categories of analysis are inseparable from their sub-
jects of analysis. In other words, nineteenth-century intellectuals were aware
of a deficit of "myth" in their society and sought, quite self-consciously, to
fill this gap through the products of their art, scholarship, and imagination.
As a result, the term "myth" itself became a factor within German culture,
pushing it in directions it might not have followed otherwise.

The standpoint adopted here reflects recent theoretical discussions
within the field of religious studies. In the past decade, the fundamental categories of religious studies, including "religion," the "sacred," and especially
"myth," have been subject to a widespread and searching critique.[16] For Ivan
Strenski, myth is best described as "an 'illusion'—an appearance conjured or
'construct' created by artists and intellectuals toiling in the workshops of the
myth industry."[17] Likewise, Bruce Lincoln has argued that there is nothing
intrinsic to a given narrative that makes it a "myth": rather, it is simply a category that has been used to "fetishize or deride certain kinds of stories."[18]
These writers are sharply critical of some of the dominant theories of myth
in the twentieth century, according to which myth is an "important" or functional story (Malinowski), a "sacred story of creation" (Eliade), or a "strongly
structured" story (Lévi-Strauss). Not only have these theories been called
into question as descriptions of myth, but some of their authors (including
Carl Jung, Mircea Eliade, and Georges Dumézil) have been linked to the fascist and anti-Semitic movements of the early twentieth century.

Yet while the new critical history of mythography has focused primarily
on the twentieth century, the origins of the modern discourse on myth lie to
a large extent in eighteenth- and early-nineteenth-century Germany. Here
the brand name "myth" acquired a value quite independent of the stories to
which it was assigned—indeed, the very labeling of artifacts as "myth" can
be seen as a product of this discourse. Part of this had to do with the word
"Mythos" itself, which was a direct transliteration of the Greek and retained
a dark sensuous quality that appealed to the Romantic and subsequent generations. Writing at midcentury, Edgar Quinet maintained that this word had
no direct equivalent in the French language.[19] Likewise, the English "myth"
did not achieve an iconic status among British or American writers until the

end of the nineteenth century. Until that time, the intense and heavily charged discourse on myth remained preeminently a German phenomenon.

Although the meaning of the word "myth" *(Mythos)* was notoriously unstable, nineteenth-century intellectuals used it primarily to denote a sacred narrative (or, in some cases, a body of sacred narratives) that reflected the religious beliefs of a preliterate society or nation. "Mythology" *(Mythologie)*, on the other hand, denoted a broader system of mythical images, narratives, and rituals. By and large, myth was seen as a pagan phenomenon, indicative of a pre-Christian stage of culture. Yet these terms could also be applied to the stories of the Bible insofar as they were seen as products of a pre-Christian or preliterate mind-set. In this respect, the modern concept of myth was intimately wrapped up with notions of history and progress that had become increasingly normative in European culture since the Enlightenment. The close and somewhat ambiguous linking of cultural and religious evolution embedded in this term helps to explain its polemical force for nineteenth-century Germans. Over time, it would be applied to an ever wider array of objects, including many that were seemingly modern or secular in nature.

For the purposes of this book, however, the term "myth" will be used as a generic category to denote a sacred narrative of gods, heroes, or cosmogony that reflects the fundamental values and beliefs of a community or nation. Using the word in this way seems preferable to abandoning it altogether or placing it in quotation marks every time it appears in this text. Nonetheless, it should be emphasized that this definition is derived from nineteenth-century usage and implies no endorsement on my part of a particular theory of myth. In a similar manner, the term "mythology" will denote a system of sacred images, narratives, and rituals that reflects the values of a community or nation. Following from this, the adjectives "mythical" and "mythological" will be used to refer to practices or discourses that deal with myth or mythology in these particular senses. By contrast, these terms will *not* be used to ascribe a "mythical" status to the cultural products or phenomena of eighteenth- or nineteenth-century Europe.

That still leaves the problem of labeling the scholarly study of myth. This is particularly difficult for the nineteenth century, since mythological research typically was conducted under the rubric of theology or philology rather than within its own separate discipline. Further, when scholars of myth attempted to describe their work, they often simply used the term "mythology," which gave that word the same double reference to subject and field of study characteristic of the word "history." To avoid such confusion, I will make occasional use of the more modern "mythography" when referring to scholarship on myth. In general, however, mythological research will be examined in the context of the particular discipline (theology, philology, philosophy, etc.) in which it was conducted, even though disciplinary boundaries were not as airtight in the early nineteenth century as they have subsequently become.

The premise of this book, however, is that the nineteenth-century discourse on myth is significant, not simply for what it reveals about the origins of modern scholarship, but also for what it says about German cultural and intellectual life in the late eighteenth and nineteenth centuries. Indeed, the debates and discussions about myth shed light on a number of issues and debates that have preoccupied historians of late. These include the neohumanist veneration of ancient Greece, the emergence of a public sphere, national identity and the formation of collective memory, and the persistence of confessional and theological modes of thought in the modern era. Before proceeding further, it will be useful to elucidate some of these contexts in more detail.

"Myth" was originally a Greek word (μύθος). While scholars dispute its exact meaning for Homer and Hesiod, by the fourth century B.C. it had come to signify a kind of authoritative speech that philosophers like Plato could criticize as immoral and at the same time exploit for their own purposes. "Mythology," as a coherent system of narratives that legitimated the religious and political traditions of a polis, was a retrospective invention, born of an era in which pious and impious skepticism had already begun to undermine belief in the old tribal stories."[20] The Greek origins of "myth" are crucial to its career in Germany, because it was largely through the study of Greek literature and philosophy that scholars developed an image of what myth was and how it functioned in ancient societies. Indeed, the rise of a discourse on myth coincided more or less directly with the establishment of the institutions of neohumanist *Bildung* in the second half of the eighteenth century. For intellectuals like Goethe, Schiller, and Wilhelm von Humboldt, Greek art represented an absolute standard of beauty, as well as the foundation of individual self-cultivation. In subsequent years, these neohumanist ideals of beauty as well as *Bildung* would be preserved through the institutions of the gymnasium and the philological seminar, which encouraged a regimen of study and scholarship that Suzanne Marchand has aptly characterized as "aesthetic asceticism."[21]

Neohumanism was preeminently a philosophy of the educated middle classes, or *Bildungsbürgertum*.[22] This tiny but influential group, whom Hans-Ulrich Wehler has described as a "state intelligentsia," had no direct parallel elsewhere in Europe.[23] The status of its members was based on talent and education, characteristics that set it off from both the commercial middle classes and the aristocracy, not to mention artisans and the peasantry. Over the course of the eighteenth century, the growth of state bureaucracies had shifted the weight of prestige and numbers within the *Bildungsbürgertum* away from the clergy and toward secular bureaucrats, which led to a corresponding shift in emphasis within universities from the faculties of theology toward the faculties of medicine, law, and especially philosophy. In that context, neohumanism seemed to offer a progressive alternative to an older, Latin-based curriculum, which was associated both with an aristocratic classicism and with the ecclesiastical traditions of the Roman Catholic Church. For that reason, it was ideally suited to Protestant middle-class intellectuals eager to align themselves with the emerging political and cultural ideals of freedom and individuality.

The neohumanist admiration for Greek culture was grounded in historicist principles of scholarship that had been articulated in the 1760s by Johann J. Winckelmann and Johann Gottfried Herder. These writers saw Greece as an autonomous and unique historical culture, in which language, art, religion, and politics merged together in a coherent whole.[24] At the same time, this viewpoint reflected an awareness of the historical distance that separated antiquity from modern (Christian) civilization. Following on the heels of the earlier dispute between the "ancients and moderns," historicism entailed a new attitude toward classical mythology. No longer could artists borrow confidently from the iconography of ancient Greece or Rome, as they had during the Renaissance and Baroque periods. The stories of Apollo or Hercules could not be plumbed for their timeless allegorical meaning or their anticipations of Christian doctrine. Instead, these myths were treated as part of a culture that was both foreign and distinctly premodern. But historicism also undermined the positions of such early-eighteenth-century philosophes as Pierre Bayle and Bernard de Fontenelle, who had dismissed ancient religion as superstition and fraud as part of a campaign against the practices and beliefs of the Christian churches.[25]

Instead, myth came to be treated as the product of a necessary first stage of human culture, similar to that reported by European explorers of the New World. This was the approach of the classicist Christian Gottlob Heyne, the first important theorist of myth in Germany and the founder of the influential philological seminar at Göttingen. Heyne's arguments were developed and extended by Herder, who treated myth as the expression of the spirit of a nation, or *Volk*. Myth for Herder was an irreplaceable cultural substrate, which bound the language, literature, religion, and customs of ancient societies into an organic whole. The image of Greece as a society infused with myth exercised a profound influence on the early Romantics, who contrasted the beauty and "publicness" engendered by Greek religion with the hieratic and divided Christian churches of their own day. Even after scholarship in classical philology had begun to undermine this holistic view of ancient Greece, it was preserved in art museums, popular literature, and gymnasium classrooms. Moreover, the succeeding decades would give rise to new philologies—based in the German language or the study of Sanskrit—with their own varieties of myth scholarship. These disciplines would increasingly come into competition—not only with each other but also with biblical theology—as they vied for status as the caretakers of sacred religious narrative.

A number of recent works have examined aspects of the German neohumanist tradition, including its fascination with ancient myth.[26] But these studies have largely overlooked the intimate connection between attitudes toward ancient Greek myth and developments within Christian (and especially Protestant) theology. Historically, the eighteenth and nineteenth centuries have been viewed as an era of secularization, in which religious worldviews were gradually replaced by those grounded in reason and science. There was indeed an important structural change in religious life in Germany during these years. Among Protestant urban elites, in particular, church attendance declined consistently, even as it remained steady or even surged in other confessional and social milieus. This was accompanied by a gradual shift away from orthodox doctrine and an increased individualization of religious belief and practice.[27]

Yet a change in the structure of religious life did not necessarily entail an abandonment of religious belief.[28] Historians have long noted the role of Ultramontanism and Neo-Pietism in mobilizing Catholic and Protestant orthodoxy between 1815 and 1848. In addition, however, the various enlightened and liberal reform movements were often the bearers of powerful religious emotions (and prejudices).[29] Catholic, Protestant, and Jewish reformers attempted to simplify religious liturgies, eliminate or de-emphasize outdated doctrines, and emphasize the centrality of morality—not in order to weaken their confessions but to make them stronger and more viable. Further, while some reformers challengeded traditional beliefs and practices, others introduced theological rhetoric and modes of thought into the emerging institutions of art, scholarship, and politics, resulting in what Anthony La Vopa describes as the "reformulation of the sacred within a desacralized discourse."[30] Such influences could flow in both directions, however, and in some cases a reformulated concept of the sacred was reimported from secular disciplines like aesthetics, philosophy, or philology back into the field of theology. The upshot of this was not a unidirectional secularization but

rather a process in which nonecclesiastical institutions and individuals competed with the churches and clergy to address the central theological and religious concerns of the German educated classes.

The recent scholarship on religious and confessional life in Germany
suggests a new way of viewing late-eighteenth- and nineteenth-century intellectual life, especially the area of religious thought. In his seminal study *The
Eclipse of Biblical Narrative*, Hans Frei presented theological developments
in these years as leading to a steady hollowing out of Protestant Christianity.[31] Luther and Calvin had originally posited a biblical narrative that began
in the Old Testament, carried into the New Testament, and encompassed the
present-day community of the faithful. This narrative was accepted as literally true, but it was held together by a "figural interpretation" that treated
the stories of the Old Testament as anticipations of events in the Gospels or
of the later fortunes of the Christian Church. By the eighteenth century,
however, belief in the orthodox biblical narrative had begun to break down,
as many intellectuals questioned the literal truth of the Bible, especially its
accounts of miracles. English and French deists, who usually stood outside
their respective national churches, were inclined to dismiss those stories as
lies. In Germany, however, many of the leading Aufklärer (proponents of the
Enlightenment) were Protestant clergymen, who served either in individual
pastorates or in university faculties of theology. As a consequence, they were
inclined to seek a mediating position on this issue, describing the stories in
question as either distorted history or as "myth." Over time, the scope of this
"mythical interpretation" grew ever wider, culminating in David Friedrich
Strauss's claim in *Das Leben Jesu* that the Gospel life of Jesus was a myth. For
Frei, this marked the end of an authentic (i.e., revelation-based) Christianity,
and he largely concurs with Marx's assessment of 1843 that "for Germany
the criticism of religion is in the main complete."[32]

There are reasons to be skeptical of Frei's account, however. Just as a
restructuring of ecclesiastical life did not lead necessarily to a collapse of religious belief, so the critique of biblical narrative was carried out (in the main)
with a sense of moral and theological seriousness. Moreover, the very categories of biblical criticism offered new possibilities for a revitalized Christian
(or Jewish) theology. This was especially the case with the term "myth." The
interpretation of the Old and New Testaments as myth had rendered these
narratives distant and foreign, so that it was no longer possible for educated
Germans to identify reflexively with the travails of the Hebrew people or to
see themselves as part of the "children of Israel" or the "new Jerusalem."[33]
Yet the historicist interpretation also suggested the possibility that myth
could be deployed "positively," that is, on behalf of religion. This could func-

tion in two ways. On the one hand, it was possible to replace the Old Testament with a pagan mythical substrate grounded in ancient Greece, Germany, or the Orient, which would then provide the basis for the move to Christianity. On the other hand, it became possible to envision a specifically modern mythology, which would be the basis of either a revitalized Christianity or a new, post-Christian religion. The result—*pace* Frei—was a series of "mythical" narratives that attempted to explain the historical relationships of old or new mythologies to modern society. The locus for such narratives was typically not theology but rather the newer disciplines of philological scholarship in Germany or the popular scholarship of writers like Heinrich Heine and Richard Wagner. Further, unlike the traditional biblical narrative, their vectors could point both forward to a new mythical era and backward to the lost mythologies of the past.[34] Such historical ambivalence was typical of the Romantic longing for myth.

While neohumanism and Protestant theological culture provided much of the language of myth discourse, the desire for a new sacred narrative was also encouraged by fundamental concerns among the educated elites about their relationship to the rest of civil society.[35] The growth of the institutions of the public sphere in the eighteenth century—newspapers, reading societies, and an expanded commercial book market—had seemed at first to promise a transformation of society and the state on Enlightenment principles. But by the 1780s, the profusion of lowbrow and "sensual" literature and the intransigence of the absolutist state had led many intellectuals to question the merits of a market-based civil society and an Aufklärung (Enlightenment) grounded in utilitarian philosophy. This uncertainty inspired a new emphasis on moral and aesthetic autonomy in the writings of late-eighteenth-century intellectuals. Goethe, Schiller, and Wilhelm von Humboldt found such autonomy exemplified in the culture of neohumanism, while Immanuel Kant emphasized not just aesthetic judgment but also a religion of morality. In both cases, however, these late-eighteenth-century writers emphasized the distance between an interior realm of reason, art, or individuality and the machinery of civil society, the state, and the various churches.

The early Romantics, inspired by the French Revolution and committed to the premises of philosophical idealism, were not content to maintain the aesthetic distance from the world predicated by the neohumanists.[36] They demanded instead that the aesthetic and philosophical principles of idealism be infused into society and politics by means of a "new religion" or a "new mythology," a goal that they articulated in their programmatic writings of 1796–1800. This move has been interpreted (by Thomas Mann and Hans Frei, among others) as contributing to a shift away from properly political or social interests toward the apolitical realm of the ideal. Yet for the Romantics, it was precisely this aggressive move onto the terrain of the churches that constituted genuine revolution. Schelling, in particular, viewed the fundamental problems of modernity—a market economy, the absolutist state, and the lack of a vibrant public culture *(Oeffentlichkeit)*—as manifestations of Christianity's essential religious orientation. The new mythology was intended not only to bridge the divide between a philosophical elite and the broad mass of the people but also to overcome the rift within the modern (Christian) self between freedom and nature, consciousness and the unconscious, infinite and finite.

The attempt to infuse the public sphere with mythical meaning quickly brought the Romantics onto the terrain of liturgy, a category that in the last few years has received increased attention from cultural historians and others. Whereas many scholars still treat any notion of public ritual as an atavism inherently opposed to the "open society," others emphasize the degree to which ritual was a constitutive force in the very societies and institutions that are most associated with liberalism and progress in the nineteenth century.[37] In this book, however, the concern is not so much with the ritual quality of historical phenomena as with the function of a notion of liturgy (often rendered as *Gottesdienst* or *Cultus)* within the broader discourse on myth. In calling for a new mythology, for example, Schelling envisioned the emergence of not only a new set of aesthetic symbols but also a series of rituals and festivals that would be the foundation of a reinvigorated culture of "publicness" *(Oeffentlichkeit)* and an alternative to the purely "private" cultures of the dynastic state, the literary market, and the established churches. Yet rather than allowing this public religious culture to be imposed from above, the Romantics saw it as emerging from the autonomous institutions of art, scholarship, and civil society.

This interest in the cultic embodiment of religion would remain a key feature of the German discourse on myth, animating both scholarship on ancient religious practices and proposals by nationalist writers for liturgies and rituals grounded in the experience of the *Volk*. Previous studies have largely neglected the liturgical dimensions of German mythical thought.[38] In particular, there has been little work done to link these phenomena with broader concerns within Christian and Jewish culture about the relationship between religion and the public sphere. Yet this was an era when the decline of traditional worship seemed to threaten not only the churches and their clergy but the very fabric of social life. Indeed, in questions of liturgy most advocates of myth envisioned less a total break with Christianity than an extension and fulfillment of its ideals within the realm of nonecclesiastical culture.

For all of its appeal, the German discourse on myth contained several fundamental ambiguities, which carried over into scholarly discussions of ancient and medieval mythology. Four issues, in particular, proved vexing to nineteenth-century scholars and critics: first, the relative importance of the individual artist as opposed to the community or nation in creating myth; second (and closely related), the weight that should be given to "aesthetic," as opposed to properly "religious," factors in explicating myth; third, the relative autochthony of a given national mythology vis-à-vis the mythologies of other nations; and fourth, the relationship of non-Christian mythologies to Protestantism, Catholicism, and Judaism. In this book, the debates around these issues are explored as they shaped research in a number of fields, including classical philology, biblical theology, Germanic philology, and comparative philology. This approach departs somewhat from the recent emphasis on viewing academic disciplines as professions in the making, concerned primarily with their own internal development. To the contrary, the small size of philosophical faculties and the multiple teaching responsibilities of philologists in the nineteenth-century German university ensured considerable cross-pollination between research fields that would now be considered separate. In this situation, it was not unusual for a single individual to gain recognition in several different areas. The philologist Karl Lachmann, for example, made influential contributions to the study of the *Nibelungenlied*, the Homeric epic, and the textual history of the New Testament. This wide-ranging research program was indicative of the implicitly comparative nature of most myth scholarship, which thrived on establishing parallels and connections between apparently disparate cultural phenomena.

The concern among nineteenth-century scholars with issues of cultural influence and autochthony, including the relationship between Christianity and its non-Christian "others," touches on issues that have become central in recent years to the emerging field of postcolonial studies. In his study *Orientalism*, Edward Said explored the relationship between nineteenth-century European scholarship on the "Orient" and broader processes of colonialism and domination in the Middle East and Asia.[39] While Said focuses on English and French scholarship, other scholars have discovered important traditions of Orientalism within German culture. Jonathan Hess and Susannah Heschel have argued that a key site for such Orientalism was biblical theology, as Christianity adopted an implicitly "colonial" stance toward the "Jewish" Bible and generated scholarship on both ancient Israel and the Near

East in order to preserve its dominant status.[40] In this context, neohumanism can be seen as a response not only to the dominance of Roman models but also to the "oriental" nature of Jewish and Christian culture, an attitude that is reflected in the rhetoric of early Philhellenists like Humboldt and Schiller. The "anti-oriental" tendency in neohumanism helps to explain the vehement reaction among some classical philologists to the expansion after 1800 of a nonecclesiastical Orientalism grounded in the study of ancient India and Persia, a conflict that came to a head in the bitter controversy surrounding Friedrich Creuzer's *Symbolik und Mythologie der alten Völker* (1810–12). In this debate, questions of Greek cultural autochthony intersected with theological-political concerns about the relative importance of religious doctrines, priests, and rituals for the formation of ancient civilization and, by implication, modern German society. The outcome of the Creuzer controversy also sheds light on the development of scholarly attitudes in Germany toward ancient Egypt, an issue raised by Martin Bernal in his important but deeply flawed *Black Athena*.[41] The *Symbolik und Mythologie* affair would be cited repeatedly in subsequent philological and theological disputes, and its legacy forms a key theme of the present study.

A similar intersection of concerns influenced the attempt to recover a "national" mythology. The historicist logic that had led Herder to classify the Bible as the work of a foreign people brought him to the conclusion that the ancient Germans must at one time have possessed their own deities and myths. In the context of the Napoleonic wars, the "postcolonial" aspects of this argument had special salience for nationalist scholars like Jacob Grimm, who treated (ecclesiastical) Christianity as an occupying power on an originally pagan German soil. Grimm was opposed by scholars like August Wilhelm Schlegel, who emphasized a medieval mythology that fused Christianity with the knightly virtues of loyalty, piety, and bravery. But by the 1830s, Grimm's views had carried the day both within *Germanistik* and with the educated public at large, and it became generally accepted that the ancient Germans had possessed a *Götterlehre* (system of gods) that was of a piece with their language, literature, and legal customs. The figures of Wotan, Brünhild, and Hertha became the subject of poems, paintings, and plays and were made central characters in Richard Wagner's *Ring* cycle. Comparative philologists attempted to trace the origin of these deities to an earlier "Aryan" mythology with roots in India, and even the folk psychologist Heymann Steinthal, who was critical of the unbridled praise lavished on Germanic paganism, did not challenge its existence but sought instead to prove the relative superiority of a competing "Hebrew" mythology.

These debates were fraught with implications for the ongoing theological and confessional conflicts that characterized much of nineteenth-century German intellectual life.[42] In appealing to a notion of "myth," Romantics like Schelling, Friedrich Schlegel, and Creuzer engaged in a double move vis-à-vis their confessional "others." For as they distanced themselves from rationalist traditions within Protestantism, they found themselves drawn to the ("oriental") imagery, liturgy, and festivals of Baroque Catholicism. Such confessional ambivalence opened them up to charges of "crypto-Catholicism" and "Jesuitism" on the part of enlightened or rationalist critics, who viewed the turn to myth as a danger to the freedom and autonomy established by Protestantism. In a similar manner, advocates of a specifically "national" mythology were drawn to the example of the Hebrew Bible, even if they ultimately rejected its imagery as inappropriate to the German people and its experiences. Both dynamics were at work in the writings of Richard Wagner, whose music dramas and theoretical writings popularized the characters and stories of German national mythology and whose creation of the Bayreuth Festival in 1876 guaranteed that mythology a permanent place in German cultural life.

In examining Wagner's operas and other artifacts of the modern discourse on myth, some historians claim to have found evidence of a "political religion."[43] This assumes that by the end of the eighteenth century Christianity was in hopeless decline, thus creating a need for various secular "faiths."[44] But, as I have suggested already, the disentanglement of German intellectual culture from the rhetoric, narratives, and assumptions of Christian theology was a long, protracted, and ultimately incomplete process, which stretched across the nineteenth century. This applies doubly in the case of the scholarship and literature based on "myth." Even when advocates of ancient or "new" mythologies challenged the most fundamental doctrines of Christianity, what they offered was more a reworking of biblical narrative than a complete and utter break from the Christian figural tradition. In the new "mythical" narratives, Greek, Germanic, or Aryan mythologies supplemented or replaced the biblical Old Testament, either to herald the arrival of a new religion or to mourn the death of the old faith. Yet by reworking the biblical narrative in this manner, the advocates of myth implied that the true site of modern religiosity lay not in the churches but in art, literature, or scholarship. It was in institutions that have been traditionally classified as secular that the modern discourse on myth emerged and made its claim to sacred status.

The same arguments also have implications for the burgeoning literature on "memory" in Germany.[45] In recent years, scholars have turned to the concept of collective memory to explain how ordinary citizens internalized a sense of nationhood away from the coercive propaganda of state governments and, to a degree, beyond the conflicts of parties, social classes, or other interest groups. In emphasizing the role of "framing strategies" and "historical gazes" in producing past-consciousness, the new literature on memory provides an important alternative to an earlier emphasis on the "invention of tradition."[46] What is striking, however, is that these studies have largely ignored the role of religion—especially the Christian religion—in the formation of cultural memory in the nineteenth century. Indeed, these scholars assume the possibility of a purely secular memory, even as they acknowledge the necessity of certain religious forms (ritual, mythology, symbols, etc.) for giving that memory social force. To be sure, identities and memories could be multiple, and so it is possible to imagine a "national memory" that existed alongside several different "religious" memories. But, in most cases, the understanding of the national past was framed within a narrative that built on, transformed, or inverted traditional Protestant, Catholic, or Jewish self-understandings.

This emphasis on the persistence of Christian rhetoric and language within institutions traditionally understood as secular suggests the need for a modified understanding of "religion." Religions have often been seen as integrated wholes, with a coherent identity and a definable essence. Yet a closer look shows that they consist of multiple elements—symbols, rituals, narrative traditions, ethical systems—that are often internally contradictory and that can persist, to some degree at least, in isolation from each other. In nineteenth-century Germany, the frequent claims by intellectuals to have created "new religions" often masked the persistence in their thought of elements and assumptions derived from Judaism and/or Christianity. This is not to say that what resulted was a "secularized" form of these religions. Many elements of Protestant theology, for example, were altered or abandoned in the confrontation with modern institutions of aesthetic culture, scholarship, and politics. Rather, it suggests the need for an expanded notion of what constitutes Christian (or Jewish) culture, emphasizing in the case of nineteenth-century mythical thought the persistence of narratives derived from figural history, conventions of religious experience and practice, and traditions of confessional and religious hostility. This straddling of traditions is what gave mythical thought in nineteenth-century Germany its enormous creativity, variety, and influence, as well as its potential to accelerate and exacerbate inherited legacies of religious intolerance and conflict.

The themes and standpoints I have sketched out in this Introduction are developed in more detail over the course of this book. The opening chapter examines early Romantic attitudes toward myth, focusing on the writings of Friedrich Schelling and Friedrich Schlegel. It details the religious and theological situation in late-eighteenth-century Germany, when Aufklärung theology was challenged by revolutionary unrest in France, the growth of philosophical idealism, and a renewed openness to theological language and ritual among educated elites. After placing the Jena Romantic circle in this context, this chapter concludes by analyzing the proposals of Friedrich Schelling and Friedrich Schlegel for a "new mythology." That project was marked by a deep ambivalence concerning the possibilities of myth in a modern world defined by Christianity and its attendant notions of history, moral freedom, and private salvation. The second chapter investigates the efforts in the early nineteenth century to create a properly "national" mythology. It focuses on the attempts by A. W. Schlegel, Joseph Görres, Jacob Grimm, Heinrich Heine, and others to define the relationship between the authentic "German" mythology and Christianity. In doing so, it analyzes debates over the *Nibelungenlied*, the nature and origin of Germanic paganism, and the relationship of the ancient *Götterlehre* to Protestantism, Catholicism, and Judaism.

To complete the picture of early-nineteenth-century mythography, the next two chapters examine debates in classical philology and in biblical theology. Chapter 3 focuses on the controversy in the 1820s surrounding Friedrich Creuzer's *Symbolik und Mythologie der alten Völker*. The Creuzer affair combined issues of sexuality, race, and religion, as the Greek gods were linked to the seemingly grotesque world of Egyptian or oriental deities, and liberal Philhellenists battled a philology that was both theologically heterodox and politically conservative. Chapter 4 traces discussions within Protestant biblical theology, focusing on the thought of David Friedrich Strauss and his opponent Christian Hermann Weisse. Both Strauss and Weisse detected echoes of the earlier Creuzer affair in the debate over *Das Leben Jesu* (1835–36). At the same time, they linked their own Christologies to the contemporary "cult of genius," in which a quasi-religious status had been granted to such heroes of Protestant bourgeois culture as Goethe, Schiller, and Beethoven.

The decades after 1840 witnessed a shift in the human sciences away from idealism and Romanticism, resulting in a de-emphasis of myth as a central category of cultural analysis. Indeed, over the next three decades many of the most important exponents of myth emerged from outside the German university system. That certainly applies to Richard Wagner, whose music dramas and theoretical writings both popularized and transformed the Romantic project of a "new mythology." Chapter 5 illustrates the influence of the Grimms, Heine, and radical *Vormärz* theology on Wagner's version of neohumanism and his theory of musical myth. At the heart of the chapter is an extensive analysis of his programmatic piece *Oper und Drama*, which is linked both to Romantic discussions of mythology and to Wagner's distinctive views of ancient Greece, Christianity, and Judaism.

Chapter 6 takes up the theme of "Aryan" and "Semitic" myth, which emerged as a topic of discussion in the 1850s in the context of comparative philology. It focuses on the efforts of the "folk psychologist" Heymann Steinthal to rehabilitate monotheistic myth in the face of scholarly critics like Ernest Renan and Friedrich Max Müller. In doing so, Steinthal called into question many of the key assumptions of Romantic mythography without abandoning the category of "myth" itself. Chapter 7 discusses the thought of Friedrich Nietzsche, examining his relationship both to Richard Wagner and to the intellectual culture of the Kaiserreich. It discusses his earlier justification of Wagnerism and then shows how his encounter with newer scholarship in anthropology, ethnology, and archaeology facilitated a break from Bayreuth, allowing him to formulate a new, post-Romantic epic centered on the figure of Zarathustra. A brief epilogue considers the continuing influence of mythological ideas in twentieth-century German history, including the rise of National Socialism.[47]

The intertwining of aesthetic, religious, and political categories implied in the discourse on myth was by no means an exclusively German phenomenon. A quick look at nineteenth-century France, England, or the United States reveals a profusion of new cults and movements, many overtly political in nature and most reflecting a dissatisfaction with the dominant theological traditions within Christianity.[48] Moreover, by the end of the century many of the premises of German Romantic mythography had begun to be adopted by non-German writers, some of whom would go on to lay the groundwork for the modern study of religion.[49] But for most observers, the fascination with myth as a "specific force" remained a preeminently German phenomenon.[50] It was in Germany that the Protestant traditions of neohumanist aestheticism and historicist criticism of the Bible had given rise to this discourse on myth, which would be used both to critique European modernity and to express the demand for autonomy in both religious and national life. An analysis of this discourse and its implications for intellectual culture in Germany forms the subject of this book.

CHAPTER ONE

Theophany and Revolution:
The Romantics Turn to Myth

In the spring of 1796, at the age of twenty-one, Friedrich Schelling left his native Württemberg to see the world. Although he had just completed five years of theological training at the Tübingen *Stift* (seminary), he had no intention of becoming a clergyman. Instead, with several publications to his name, Schelling was well on his way to establishing himself as one of the brightest philosophical minds in Germany. That did not guarantee him an income, however, and so he had accepted a tutoring position secured for him by his father, Josef, a respected pastor and Old Testament scholar. Schelling would accompany two young barons, Hermann and Wilhelm von Riedsel, from Stuttgart to Leipzig in order to oversee their university education. Their guardian had sweetened the offer with the promise of trips to France and England; only later did he add that these excursions would not occur unless France restored the Bourbon monarchy and made peace with Great Britain.[1]

Now, as he set off on his tour, Schelling headed for destinations that by the late eighteenth century had already become German landmarks. He reveled in Heidelberg's "Romantic" scenery, especially the castle ruins that surveyed the Neckar River ("paradise before you, destruction and wilderness behind you").[2] He visited Mannheim and its famous Antiquities Chamber, where he gazed at plaster copies of the Medicis' Venus, the Vatican's Apollo, and the Laocoön. But he was also confronted by more disturbing sights—razed buildings, broken battlements, dead horses—caused by four years of war between France and the Austrian-Prussian coalition. Much of this fighting had occurred up and down the Rhine River. "For the first time . . . I greeted this river, which recently—perhaps as the future border of the two halves of our Europe—has become so noteworthy."[3] Schelling's political sympathies were clear, for only republican France could unite the European continent.

The trip also led to Schelling's first encounters with a social world beyond the university and the church. A child of the *Bildungsbürgertum*, Schelling harbored deep prejudices against other classes.[4] When his brother Karl briefly considered a career in business, Schelling warned his parents that Karl would soon think of nothing but "self-interest and profit."[5] After much prodding from his older brother, Karl switched to an academic career in medicine. Schelling also expressed distaste for the manners and customs of the aristocracy: French spoken at the dinner table, meals served to the hostess first and the guests last. Based on a brief stay in the Landgraviate of Hesse-Darmstadt, he concluded that the aristocracy fostered ignorance, laziness, and drunkenness. "In general one observes everywhere here the same thing that one can observe in all states where an aristocratic sensibility is dominant—contempt for all thorough scholarship, an insurmountable horror of all exertion, complete slackening of all spiritual powers, etc."[6]

In turn, Schelling found himself the object of suspicion and distrust. A baroness in Heilbronn worried aloud about the politics of young tutors, who seemed eager to infect their charges with French revolutionary propaganda.[7] Schelling brushed off these comments with a laugh but found it rather more troublesome when Berlin's most influential Aufklärer, Friedrich Nicolai, publicly lambasted him as a philosophical crank *(Querkopf)* and warned against the corrupting effect of idealism on Germany's youth.[8] Nonetheless, Schelling retained his employers' confidence; indeed, the boys' guardians seemed eager to suppress all signs of aristocratic pretension in the youths by exposing them to a talented young academic. For his part, Schelling believed that he belonged to an ascendant class, whose superior talent and education would eventually overcome the dominance of the aristocracy.[9]

At the end of April 1796 the party reached Leipzig, where Schelling began the comprehensive study of physics, chemistry, and medicine that would form the foundation of his *Naturphilosophie.* He also continued to oversee the barons' education, accompanying them to lectures and joining them on excursions outside the city. It was one such excursion that brought Schelling to the remarkable English garden of Wörlitz. The park was the creation of Prince Leopold Friedrich Franz of Anhalt-Dessau, a devotee of Rousseau and the English "back-to-nature" movement. Franz had traveled throughout Europe in order to gather ideas and impressions for his project: to Britain, where he viewed the landscapes of Stourhead and Kew Gardens; to Italy, where he hired Johann Jacob Winckelmann to tutor him in art history; and to France, where he discussed philosophy with Jean-Jacques Rousseau. Construction on the park had begun in 1764 and would be largely complete by 1800. By that

The Venus Temple at Wörlitz. Watercolor by Karl Kuntz (1797).
Source: *Der Englische Garten zu Wörlitz* (Berlin: Verlag für Bauwesen, 1987), 199.

time, Wörlitz had become the subject of numerous travel accounts and a favorite destination for tourists.[10]

A visitor to Wörlitz was expected not simply to enjoy its sights but to undergo a kind of initiation. The garden opened with a labyrinth, which contained various signs urging the wanderer to maintain courage and watch out for danger. This led into a small tunnel, which opened finally onto a clearing that was called the "Elysian fields." In a letter to his parents, Schelling described the site as a "round place overshadowed by high elms and planted with acacias and plane trees, where one perceives no sound—all is quiet—and where one would gladly forget life's worries if they did not violently pursue one. In fact, this is the one thing that reminds the traveler that he is not yet in the true Elysium."[11] Schelling marveled at the other sections of Wörlitz, which were separated by a series of lakes, ponds, and canals. Near the water stood statues of bathing nymphs and naiads, fauns, and other mythological beings. Paths through the garden opened suddenly onto antique temples, dedicated to deities like Apollo, Flora, and Venus. To the visitor walking these grounds for the first time, Wörlitz offered new and unexpected delights around every corner.

The "Stone" at Wörlitz. Schelling described this as the "Temple of the Night Goddess." Watercolor by Karl Kuntz (1797).
Source: *Der Englische Garten zu Wörlitz* (Berlin: Verlag für Bauwesen, 1987), 191.

The selection of buildings and monuments at Wörlitz was not restricted to classical antiquity; a Jewish synagogue, a Chinese teahouse, a Gothic house, and a Christian church all dotted the landscape. In addition, the interior of a Pantheon suggested the origins of Greek art from the soil of Egypt: "below stand the mute Egyptian deities," Schelling commented, "above, nearer heaven—in purer light—the gods of Greece." All of these buildings seemed to culminate in a final structure. "Far across the water—beyond the ocean as it were—rises the Temple of the Night with terrifying majesty."[12] A dark spiral staircase led up to a tower constructed of black stone. At night, sparks and flames spewed forth from its top, giving the impression of a volcano or, as Schelling suggested, the fiery meal of the night goddess. Deep in the heart of the structure lay her shrine, completely black save the ceiling, where constellations glowed. "You can easily imagine how much pleasure I had during this visit," Schelling wrote later. "We stayed . . . two days. They were among the most enjoyable of my life."[13]

In many respects, the English garden at Wörlitz embodied the tastes and sentiments of late Enlightenment classicism. Over the course of the eighteenth century the English fascination with the primitive and the archaic had spread to Germany, where it spurred a reaction against French neoclassical and Baroque styles of art. For the archaeologist Winckelmann, Greek (as opposed to Roman) art embodied the free, natural, and uninhibited life of the polis. The statues of the Greek gods reflected a timeless archetype of beauty already present in the bodies of the Greeks themselves. Such ideas were reinforced by Christoph Martin Wieland, who found in antiquity a well-developed harmony between the needs of the body and the needs of the mind. In his novel *Agathon* (1766–67), he portrayed the education of a young Greek man who undergoes a series of trials before being initiated into the mysteries of Pythagoras. Such notions fed the late eighteenth century's zeal for pedagogy while shaping Prince Franz's fantasy landscape at Wörlitz.

But if Wörlitz reflected eighteenth-century attitudes toward classical antiquity and its myths, it also served to distinguish that era from what followed. For Wieland or Prince Franz, the experience of the ancient gods was a kind of aesthetic idyll, with no direct connection to the wider world. Over the next few years, however, the Jena Romantics would develop a vision of mythology that was at once more political, more religious, and more ambitious than anything seen in the Aufklärung. The key figure in this effort would be Schelling, who placed the longing for myth at the heart of his philosophical system. Drawing on the ideas of his fellow Romantics, from older contemporaries like Herder, Schiller, Goethe, and Karl Philipp Moritz, and from his own theological training, Schelling articulated an ideal of a "new mythology," in other words a system of natural symbols and narratives that would provide the basis for a unified aesthetic, religious, and public life, while overcoming the fragmentation and divisions of modern Christian society. This idea of a "new mythology" would exercise a powerful influence on German Romantic culture and offer a resource for later generations of intellectuals seeking an alternative to the positivist and historicist trends of the nineteenth century.

The early Romantic turn to "myth" has been debated extensively over the past two centuries.[14] For many commentators, it represents the thin edge of an emerging aesthetic ideology that served to distract intellectuals from the political and social issues of their day while buttressing their status as hierophants of a religion of art. On this interpretation, Romanticism was an essentially conservative or apolitical movement, which diverted the energies of the French Revolution into the by-channels of cultural life.[15] Other scholars, however, stress the emancipatory and democratic dimensions of Romanticism, especially in its earliest phase of 1796–1800. In calling for a "new mythology," they argue, Schelling and Friedrich Schlegel sought to address a legitimation crisis in modern society and to prepare the ground for a public life that would foster genuine individuality.[16] Most recently, scholars influenced by poststructuralism have focused on the irony and paradox at the heart of much Romantic thought. In their view, early Romanticism was neither a utopian nor a systematic project but sought instead to demystify the pretensions of philosophy to any kind of totality.[17]

The wide range in scholarly opinion about Romanticism reflects not only the divergent methodologies (and ideologies) of its interpreters but also long-standing disagreements about which writers should be included in the Romantic canon, the exact temporal parameters of this movement, and its relationship to the religious, cultural, and scholarly institutions of the eighteenth century. Those who have interpreted Romanticism as either a revolutionary movement or as a precursor to deconstruction have often based their claims on a limited range of texts (typically those written by Friedrich Schlegel and Novalis), as well as a narrow time frame (beginning around 1796 and ending no later than 1800). Yet to define Romanticism in this way is to overlook or ignore the later evolution of Romantic thought, as it spread beyond Jena and Berlin to shape such early nineteenth-century phenomena as nationalism, liberal Protestantism, and conservative Catholicism. Here it was the writings and lectures of August Wilhelm Schlegel and Schelling, rather than those of Friedrich Schlegel or Novalis, that exercised the predominant influence.

The shift in focus suggested here does not entail a return to older interpretations of Romanticism, which have often treated the turn to myth as an illegitimate incursion of religious discourse onto the previously secular fields of philosophy and aesthetics, which was motivated by political conservativism or merely the wish to appropriate the label "sacred" in a competitive literary market. Without discounting the role of politics and the public sphere, this chapter focuses on how the Romantic notion of a "new mythology" addressed long-standing problems in Aufklärung theology concerning biblical revelation, religious liturgy, and the nature of God. For Schelling, as for other early Romantic writers, such a mythology offered a nonbiblical source of sacred symbolism and narrative, which had the potential to rejuvenate aesthetic and religious life and overcome the divisions of modern society.

To understand how Schelling arrived at these views, it will be necessary to survey the varied contexts of Protestant intellectual life in the late eighteenth century. This chapter begins by examining developments in Protestant theology, focusing on the development of biblical criticism and its implications for Christian thought and practice. It turns next to the tradition of Philhellenist neohumanism, showing how an idealized image of Greece—created in certain respects as a counter-image to Christianity—shaped attitudes among intellectuals toward the function of myth in ancient society. After detailing Schelling's turn from theology to philosophical idealism during his years at the Tübingen *Stift*, the chapter considers the religious thought of the Jena Romantics. The final section examines the proposals by Schelling and Friedrich Schlegel for a "new mythology," focusing in particular on Schelling's 1802–3 lectures on the philosophy of art. What follows, however, is not an in-depth explication of idealist philosophy but rather a broader analysis that uses Schelling's early life and career to reconstruct the historical situation in which a discourse on myth rose to prominence in Germany and became a key factor in debates over aesthetics, religion, and the public sphere.

REREADING THE BIBLICAL NARRATIVE

In his pathbreaking study of eighteenth- and nineteenth-century hermeneutics, the theologian Hans Frei argued that the three centuries after the Reformation witnessed a gradual "eclipse of biblical narrative" within German Protestant theology.[18] According to Frei, Martin Luther and Jean Calvin constructed their theologies on the premise that the Bible offered a literal and self-sufficient narrative of humanity's creation, fall, and ultimate redemption through Christ. The coherence of this narrative and the unity of the biblical canon were secured through the use of what was known as "figural interpretation." Figural interpretation assumed that the Bible revealed a divine plan, such that one event could foreshadow another event without losing its own significance. The resulting "biblical narrative" incorporated not only the Old and New Testaments but also the contemporary religious community in its scheme of universal history. As a result, Protestant believers were able to place themselves within a story that had begun among the ancient Hebrews, turned on Christ's birth and Resurrection, and pointed forward to a coming Kingdom of God. No recourse to historical scholarship or to church tradition was necessary to understand this sacred history, for its meaning was conveyed directly in the words of the Bible.

The "precritical interpretation" of the Bible developed by Luther and Calvin reflected their belief that biblical revelation—as opposed to the Catholic Church tradition—was the sole source of religious authority. But in his analysis of this hermeneutical tradition, Frei understates the fragility of its intellectual and institutional foundations. After all, the claim that the biblical narrative should define the world rather than vice versa could remain plausible only insofar as Protestant intellectual life was defined solely by the church and its theology. But with the rise of the absolutist state and the onset of the scientific revolution, the self-sufficiency of the Bible as a source of historical meaning could no longer be assured. Moreover, the precritical "biblical narrative" assumed that Christian congregations saw themselves reflexively as part of "Israel"—that is, as legitimate heirs of an Old Testament that unfolded in ancient Israel, was written in the Hebrew language, and was claimed simultaneously by Judaism. The development of historicist approaches to the Bible would make such identification increasingly difficult, thereby undermining a central assumption of Protestant theology.

This process began as early as the seventeenth century.[19] The incorporation of the Protestant churches into the apparatus of the state reinforced the development of theological orthodoxies, which used arguments derived from the pagan philosopher Aristotle to form the Lutheran and Reformed confessions into coherent systems of doctrine.[20] Produced in universities like Jena and Wittenberg, the new scholastic theology often took the form of a *Symbolik*, that is, an explication of doctrine that was directed especially against Catholicism or one of the other Protestant confessions. The rise of such orthodox systems had the effect of binding the biblical revelation to an external philosophical system while granting university theologians a unique role in interpreting the word of God and, potentially, locating the source of its meaning outside the text of the Bible. After the Thirty Years' War, however, this state of affairs was challenged by the monarchs of Germany's larger states, who were opposed to the exclusive dominance of a single confession. Since 1613 the Calvinist Hohenzollerns had ruled Lutheran Prussia, whereas the ruling dynasty of Protestant Württemberg converted to Catholicism in 1733. As a result, the state came to constitute a quasi-secular sphere of power, which was often more interested in promoting a measure of religious toleration rather than strict confessional orthodoxy.[21]

By the eighteenth century the perceived stagnancy of orthodox theology had given rise to two major impulses for the reform of Protestantism: Pietism and the Aufklärung. Pietism originated as a reform movement within the established Protestant *Landeskirchen* (territorial churches).[22] Building on contemplative and mystical strains within Protestantism and Catholicism, Pietists stressed inward spirituality and the practical realization of Christian ideals. Further, they de-emphasized the doctrinal controversies that had divided Calvinists and Lutherans and instead promoted a Christianity centered on individual rebirth, spiritual fellowship, and the biblical word. A reform of the Protestant churches, it was hoped, would bring about "better times" on earth, which would include the formation of a "thousand-year *Reich*," the fall of the pope in Rome, and, ultimately, the conversion of the Jews. Pietism was able to achieve a particular predominance in Brandenburg-Prussia, where Hohenzollern support ensured that Halle became a center for Pietist theology and charitable activity, and in Württemberg, where it fused with the reigning orthodoxy to become the prevailing theology among the clerically dominated upper bourgeoisie, or *Ehrbarkeit*.[23]

Although Pietism began as a movement for reform within the churches, separatist strains soon began to appear. The Moravians who gathered on Nicholas Zinzendorf's Silesian estate in the 1720s refused to be bound by the dictates of either Calvinist or Lutheran doctrine and soon formed an independent religious community at Herrnhut. The Moravians became famous for their singing, their celebration of common meals, or "love feasts," and their emphasis on the felt experience of the Holy Spirit, and their influence soon spread into the Baltics and into the Rhineland. A common notion among the more radical Pietists was that the church was in a fallen state, which could be redeemed only by a gathering together of the pilgrims in preparation for the Second Coming of Christ. In Württemberg, the growth among peasants and artisans of a popular form of Pietism led to a series of independent movements that challenged the authority of the Protestant Church and the entrenched power of the *Ehrbarkeit*.[24] By the end of the eighteenth century, these movements helped to create a sense of religious renewal and imminent change within south German Protestantism.

If Pietism emerged as a reform movement both within and outside the established Lutheran and Reformed Churches, the same could also be said of the Aufklärung. Many of the most important exponents of the Enlightenment in Germany were university professors, who sought to adapt Christian doctrine and practice to values of reason and autonomy rooted in the social experience of the educated middle classes.[25] This applied in particular to the "Neologists," who came to particular prominence in the late eighteenth century. The Neologists sought a "middle path" between the Lutheran belief in revelation and deistic notions of "natural religion," treating Christ primarily as a moral teacher rather than as a performer of miracles but still holding on to belief in the Resurrection.[26] The Halle theologian Johann Salomo Semler (1725–91) described his ideal as a "private religion," which would not be dependent on "official prestige or symbolic books" but would instead be fostered by the reading of devotional literature and obedience to the moral law.[27] This, he maintained, was what Martin Luther had meant when he spoke of the "freedom of a Christian," a doctrine he contrasted with the dogmas and superstitions of the Catholics.[28] As contemporaries were quick to note, Neology meshed well with cameralist conceptions of a market-based civil society and an emerging bourgeois public sphere. Indeed, Neology was embraced most wholeheartedly by those in the educated middle classes who associated their interests with the emerging civil society of eighteenth-century Germany.

Just as Pietism earlier won the sponsorship of the Hohenzollern dynasty, so the Aufklärung attracted the support of reform-minded heads of state.[29] One by one, absolutist rulers of both confessions reduced their support for the privileges and prerogatives of the established churches, emphasizing instead the development of efficient bureaucracies and the expansion of trade. In Prussia, Frederick the Great encouraged peaceful coexistence among the confessions, housed Voltaire in Potsdam, and supported Neology as a quasi-official state theology. In Catholic Austria, Joseph II extended religious toleration to Protestants, banned the Jesuit order, and withdrew protection from the ecclesiastical territories of the Holy Roman Empire. Moderate steps were also taken toward toleration for Jews, although the scope of these should not be exaggerated. Frederick II (the Great) viewed Judaism as emblematic of a religious orthodoxy that he despised, and he permitted Jews to reside in Prussia only under onerous restrictions that included ceding governance of their communities to the state. Ironically, it was precisely this weakening of traditional rabbinical authority that allowed Berlin to become a center for the Jewish Enlightenment. The philosopher Moses Mendelssohn promoted an engagement with secular culture, conducting learned polemics with Christian critics of Judaism and developing ties with gentile Aufklärer like Gottholm Ephraim Lessing. In 1781, following Mendelssohn's suggestion, the Prussian bureaucrat Christian Wilhelm Dohm called for a removal of legal disabilities against Jews as the key to their "civic improvement," a plea that was met partially by Joseph II's Patents of Toleration (1781–82).[30]

A favorite project of enlightened clergy and statesmen was the reform of religious worship.[31] "The higher a nation rises in enlightenment, and the more its understanding widens," argued a Catholic Aufklärer, "the simpler and more limited its worship service will become."[32] Reformers urged that the number of holidays and festivals (as many as 100 a year in some places) be slashed, that pilgrimages be curtailed, and that devotions to the saints and to the Virgin Mary be restricted. In their place, they promoted a German-language service consisting simply of the Eucharist and a sermon. The motivations of the Catholic reformers varied. Many argued that the only genuine "service to God" (Gottesdienst) was an ethical life and that the goal of public worship was therefore to promote morality. A number of clergymen aspired to the role of civil servant and recommended that the sermon be used to impart useful information on medical practices or agricultural techniques (such as the benefits of animal inoculation).[33] With these arguments in hand, reformers were able to make some inroads during the late eighteenth century. In Austria, for example, Joseph II decreed in 1782 that German, not Latin, hymns would be used at mass, a move that prefigured Ignaz von Wessenberg's later efforts to introduce a German-language vespers in the Diocese of Constance.[34]

In Protestant Germany, the issue was viewed somewhat differently. Since 1750, there had been a marked decline in church attendance among urban Protestants, especially men.[35] In Berlin, admittedly an extreme example, the average annual number of church communions for every 100 church members fell from 150 in 1739, to 100 in 1780, down to 40 in 1800. Similar patterns can be observed in Hamburg, Dresden, Nuremberg, and Hanover; in one church in Hanover participation dropped from 115 in 1750, to 95 in 1760, to 23 in 1810.[36] As one pastor wrote: "It is impossible to deny that the churches are gradually becoming emptier, and in cities especially it is only the smaller portion that attends church services with assiduity and an apparent desire for salvation. . . . Without doubt the result will be that in several decades the outward cultus of Christianity will simply cease by itself."[37] In an effort to win back churchgoers, some clergy proposed that the worship service be used to impart commonsense information as part of a campaign of public enlightenment *(Volksaufklärung)*.[38] There were also calls for new hymnals and more stimulating orders of worship. A few states introduced entirely new prayerbooks, while in some cases maverick clergy altered individual ceremonies to reflect their own enlightened tastes.[39] In general, however, such efforts did little to halt the trend toward the Neologists' "private" religion or to improve the declining status of the clergy.

These practical concerns within Protestantism were reflected in the ongoing debate about the status of the biblical revelation.[40] The terms of this debate had been defined early on by the Dutch-Jewish philosopher Baruch Spinoza in his *Tractatus Theologico-Politicus* (1670). Spinoza operated from the assumption that the Bible was written by human beings and not by God. Examining the Old Testament, he found numerous incidents that seemed implausible, miraculous, or ridiculous. The true purpose of these stories could not have been to depict history; instead, they were intended to fire the imagination of the Hebrew people and turn their hearts toward the true universal and rational religion. The whole notion of miracle, Spinoza maintained, was grounded in the false assumption that God and the world were distinct from each other, giving rise to the notion that God had intervened in history in contravention of his own laws.[41]

After long resistance, German theologians began to engage the critical methods of Spinoza in the second half of the eighteenth century. By this time models of textual criticism and historicist analysis developed within aesthetics, classical philology, and secular history had begun to be applied to the Bible. In addition, scholars had begun to exploit a growing travel literature from the Middle East to suggest fundamental differences between "Western" and "oriental" (including Jewish) mentalities. In an era of growing enlightenment, the notions of geographical (and chronological) remoteness helped to explain the profusion of the miraculous and seemingly prerational in the biblical record. The Neologist Semler came to abandon the idea that the Bible was a single document and instead sought to understand its different books as products of their individual historical contexts.[42] In the process, he dismissed large sections of the Old and New Testaments as accommodations to the superstitions, prejudices, and local institutions of the Jewish people, even if they were inspired ultimately by God's word. In Semler's view, Christianity was in a process of "perfection" (leading to the moral message of his own theology), and so it could not be bound to the cultural framework of any past era.

The "Orientalist" approach to the Bible was even more pronounced in the work of the Göttingen scholar Johann David Michaelis (the future father-in-law of Schelling).[43] In his six-volume *Mosaic Law* (1770–75), Michaelis argued that Moses had imposed a legal code derived from Egypt onto a more primitive layer of Hebrew customary law to produce what would emerge as the Mosaic law. This borrowing had left its mark in other areas of the Bible: the Genesis story of creation, for example, could be traced to an Egyptian polytheistic cosmology. In Michaelis's view, the Jewish law marked a definite advance over the barbarous practices of the neighboring Canaanites, but it had been superseded by modern law, which was grounded in the principle of universality rather than separateness. In the debate over Jewish "civic improvement," he contended that the Jews' continued adherence to their law, along with alleged racial differences, made them unfit for full citizenship rights.

The most radical approach to the Bible was that of the deist Hermann Samuel Reimarus, whose notorious "Fragments" (1774–77) were published posthumously by Lessing. Reimarus affirmed the scientific impossibility of the Exodus story of the Israelites' crossing of the Red Sea. Even more seriously, however, he declared the Resurrection a hoax, perpetrated after Jesus' death by a band of disappointed disciples.[44] Lessing sympathized to a degree with this approach, viewing revelation as a useful, if ultimately dispensable, aid in the "education of the human race." But the *Fragments* was rejected vehemently by Semler and the Neologists. These men saw themselves as

Christians and continued to uphold the Bible (at least the New Testament) as a document of revelation. Contrasting the Neologists with both English and French deists, Hans Frei complains of the "conservatism of the German Enlightenment."[45] But such a stance was to be expected: after all, the Neologists were clergymen in the employ of the state and had little desire to render themselves irrelevant; further, Protestant self-definition vis-à-vis Catholicism still depended on an identification (no matter how attenuated) with the Bible.

The equivocal stance of Protestant Aufklärer toward both revelation and the churches can be seen in the work of Immanuel Kant. In his moral philosophy, Kant had argued that an ethical system defined in terms of free obedience to the moral law required not only freedom of the will but also the ideas of God and immortality of the soul as necessary "postulates of practical reason." In *Religion within the Limits of Mere Reason* (1792–93), however, he expanded the scope of religion beyond these postulates. Starting from a thesis of "radical evil" in human nature, Kant attempted to demonstrate the utility if not necessity of a visible church for the formation of an ethical community. Such a church would have to be founded on a written revelation, since scripture commanded immediate respect "even among those (indeed, among these most of all) who do not read it."[46] The church could also employ liturgy, provided this was not confused with true service to God *(Gottesdienst)*. Kant seems to have envisioned an enlightened version of Protestantism, which would offer an ethical alternative to the superstition and ritualism of both the Catholic Church and Protestant orthodoxy. Yet he was equally forceful in distinguishing Christianity from Judaism, which he dismissed as a "political faith" established in the service of Jewish theocracy.[47] Four years earlier, Friedrich Wilhelm II had issued his notorious Edict on Religion, which attempted to roll back the gains of the Neologists and enforce theological orthodoxy on clergy and professors in Prussia. In this context, Kant's critique of Judaism as a "political faith" was directed (in part, at least) at the Prussian monarchy.[48] Yet what struck many observers at the time was the relative moderation of his stance regarding institutional religion and the biblical revelation.

While these disputes raged into the 1790s, another approach to the Bible based on a critical concept of "myth" was beginning to emerge. Christians had traditionally maintained a stark distinction between the Judeo-Christian "revelation" and nonbiblical "mythologies." In his First Epistle to Timothy, the apostle Paul contrasted the "godless and silly myths" of the Greeks and Romans with the Christian "logos." During the patristic era, Clement of

Alexandria and Irenaeus attacked the stories of the Greek and Roman gods as lies, fables, or the work of demons and delighted in digging up evidence of immoral practices associated with their worship.[49] With the triumph of Christianity assured, interest in pagan myth among European scholars remained relatively dormant during the Middle Ages. But beginning in the fifteenth century, scholars and artists again became interested in the figural uses of pagan mythology and its relationship to Christianity. In general, Renaissance writers viewed the gods either as allegories of higher Christian truths or as distortions of the original biblical revelation. They attempted to demonstrate these connections by means of etymology or by comparing pagan myths with Old and New Testament stories, a project that gave rise to some of the first mythographies in modern Europe. But by the early eighteenth century this approach had come under serious challenge, as philosophes began to interpret the stories of the pagan gods as the product of delusion, priestly fraud, or poetic invention. For Pierre Bayle and Bernard de Fontenelle, for example, lampooning ancient pagan religion offered a convenient means of attacking contemporary religious orthodoxy.[50]

The Göttingen philologist Christian Gottlob Heyne (1729–1812) departed from this pattern by arguing that myth was not the invention of individual poets or priests but rather a natural and necessary mode of expression during the "childhood of the human race."[51] In a series of studies published beginning in the 1760s, he introduced the concept of a "sermo mythicus seu symbolicus" into classical philology. Like his early Enlightenment predecessors, Heyne was deeply impressed by contemporary travel literature concerning indigenous peoples in Africa and North America and compared their situation with that of the earliest Greeks. But rather than condemning mythical thinking as the product of fear or ignorance, he integrated it into a broader theory of cultural evolution. In the mythical age ("aetas mythica"), humans suffered from a "poverty of language" and thus lacked the ability to think abstractly or in terms of general causes.[52] As a result, they attributed events like lightning, flood, and even victory in battle to the intervention of divine persons—the gods. In their earliest form, the Homeric stories were either philosophical myths that encoded ideas about nature and morality (so-called *philosophemes*) or historical myths that elaborated on real persons and events. So behind the artistic polish of the *Iliad* and the *Odyssey* lurked the primitive reasoning of the earliest Greeks.

In their *Urgeschichte* (1779, 2nd ed. 1790–93), the Jena and Göttingen theologians Johann Gottfried Eichhorn and Johann Philipp Gabler applied Heyne's theory of myth to the Book of Genesis.[53] Rather than viewing the Garden of Eden narrative or other fantastic stories of the Old Testament as either history or poetry, they identified them as philosophical myths. For Eichhorn and Gabler, the "mythical" approach offered a useful alternative to the more negative methods of the Neologists or the deists. Miraculous events in the Bible no longer needed to be interpreted as accommodations to Jewish "superstition" (Semler) or outright lies (Reimarus). Instead, they could be seen as the natural products of an earlier, more childlike stage of humanity. As Eichhorn wrote later, "Forget the century in which you live and the knowledge that it offers you. If you cannot, do not dream that you will enjoy the book [of Genesis] in the spirit of its origin."[54] This incipient historicist approach to the Bible, which drew a clear distinction between the mental world of the Bible and that of modernity, defined the cutting edge of biblical theology in the 1780s and 1790s.

It was in this context of enlightened criticism and an emerging mythical hermeneutic that Johann Gottfried Herder (1744–1803) developed his own distinctive approach to the Bible.[55] During his lifetime Herder came into contact with almost all the major intellectual movements of his age, studying under Hamann and Kant in Königsberg, participating in the Ossian fad and the Gothic revival, befriending Goethe, and finally taking a position as court preacher in Weimar. More than any of his contemporaries, he helped to rehabilitate ancient mythology as a document of both art and religion. At the center of Herder's approach stood his concept of the *Volk* (folk, people, nation), which he viewed as the basic unit of human history. Echoing Rousseau, he maintained that a *Volk* was most aesthetically creative and religiously vital during its youth, before it slipped into the evils of luxury and civilization. Far from suffering from a poverty of language, primitive people enjoyed an unusual richness of language, because they exercised speech at the moment of its creation, when it stood closest to nature and was thus most full of poetic—and mythopoetic—potential. The mythology of a *Volk* contained *in nucio* the seeds of its future development: its poetry, its art, its customs, its religion, its laws. Because it embodied a particular way of viewing nature and the world at large, this mythology was a nation's most precious possession. Herder would dedicate much of his career to collecting and recovering myths, songs, and folk poetry from around the world, although he paid special attention to his native Germany.

Herder's understanding of language and myth informed his approach to the Bible. In *Aelteste Urkunde des Menschengeschlechts* (1774) and *Vom Geist der ebräischen Poesie* (1782), he attempted to locate the Old Testament within a broader context of oriental *(morgenländisch)* poetry. In particular, he sought to evoke the sense of the divine that overcame the Hebrews as they contemplated the sunrise and that they expressed in the rich imagery of Genesis, Job, and the Psalms. "Poetry is a language of the gods, but not so that we can know through it what the Elohim actually said and felt. What it gave to the most godly men, even through higher influences, was human."[56] The Bible was the work of humans, albeit humans acting in the role of sacred poets. In describing its narratives, Herder avoided the term "myth," preferring instead the words "fable" *(Fabel)*, "poetry" *(Dichtung)*, and "legend" *(Sage)*.[57] By identifying stories such as the Garden of Eden narrative as "legends" rather than "myths" he linked them to a certain historical substrate while avoiding any overt identification of the Bible with the imaginative stories of Homer or Hesiod.

The notion of "divine poetry" also allowed Herder to defend the Old Testament as an aesthetic document against deist charges of immorality and classicist claims that it lacked beauty. In contrast to critics like Michaelis, he celebrated the ancient Hebrews as a "free nation" worshiping a "national God" in a steady stream of festivals and ceremonies.[58] With this positive vision of Hebrew religion, Herder offered a note of nostalgia in the face of the contemporary trend toward "private religion" and a purely secular public life. As in the case of Winckelmann's Greece, Herder's depiction of the Old Testament as an object of aesthetic contemplation was the inverse of what Reinhart Koselleck describes as "temporality," in which figural theology was replaced with a concept of chronology grounded in notions of progress.[59] In the long term, however, this historicist approach had the effect of potentially undermining the ability of educated Germans to identify with the stories and figures of the Old Testament narrative. By linking the biblical poetry to the "national" qualities of the ancient Hebrews or to broader characteristics of the "oriental" spirit, Herder rendered the Bible more beautiful but also more distant, more foreign, and, in a sense, more "Jewish."[60]

Herder himself never abandoned the term "revelation" *(Offenbarung)* when referring to the Bible. But his theory of a divine poetry, in which the sacred was expressed by means of metaphor, imagery, and fable, militated against the miraculous intervention of a transcendent deity into the course of history or the writing of biblical Scripture. This purely immanent concept of the "divine" in turn called into question the notion of a personal God. In his *Ethica* (1677), Spinoza had argued that God and nature were of the same material substance, a determinist system that critics condemned as "pantheism." That system came to the fore in the 1780s "Pantheism Controversy," which revolved around the question of whether Lessing had been a Spinozist. In the midst of this dispute Herder published *Gott: Einige Gespräche* (1787), in which he reformulated the basic elements of the Spinozist theory, treating God not as dead substance but rather as a living power that inhabited the entire universe. As Frederick Beiser notes, "by injecting life into Spinoza's static universe, Herder made Spinozism into an appealing doctrine for the post-Kantian generation."[61] Thanks to the Spinoza "renaissance" of the 1780s, it became possible to conceive of a "Christian pantheism" grounded in living nature rather than dead matter.

Herder and Kant—rivals in the fields of history and anthropology—can also be seen as representing two opposing poles in Protestant Aufklärung theology with respect to the nature of revelation.[62] Kant defined religion in terms of obedience to a moral law that had its source in a transcendent realm defined by God, freedom, and immortality. Revelation and the church were necessary in this scheme as initial means for overcoming the radical evil intrinsic to human nature, but ultimately they had no value in themselves. Herder, by contrast, attempted to establish a form of Christian pantheism in which God revealed himself not in the transcendent realm of morality but in the phenomena of nature, art, and history. In his view, the Bible was a crucial but by no means exclusive moment in the divine revelation, which incorporated not just the ancient Hebrews but all the nations of the earth. For all his fascination with myth, art, and liturgy, however, Herder shared Kant's view that religion should be primarily a private affair, and he never advocated a drastic response to the perceived crisis of the late-eighteenth-century Protestant churches. Such radicalism would require the youthful experience of revolution, as mediated through the language and imagery of ancient Greece.

THE GODS OF GREECE

The veneration of ancient Greece as a cultural ideal began in Germany during the last half of the eighteenth century.[63] In his *Geschichte der Kunst des Altertums* (1764), Winckelmann described the naked, white forms of Greek sculpture as the embodiment of nature, linking their beauty to the freedom of the polis.[64] In particular, he lauded the Periclean age of Athens as an era of superior civic culture and economic prosperity. It was in these years that Phidias rose to fame as a sculptor and in which some of the great monuments of Greek art were erected.[65] This art revolved above all around the gods, who according to Winckelmann offered a direct intuition of the divine. They were portrayed by combining the best anatomical features of several models into an ideal of human form, which was then represented in statues such as the Apollo Belvedere. In general, however, Winckelmann was less interested in the religious or cultic aspects of Greek art than in what he took as its purely human content. He was, as Henry Hatfield says, an "aesthetic pagan," al-

The Apollo Belvedere: Winckelmann's paragon of Greek beauty, but some
commentators found the snake equally interesting. Vatican Museum, Rome.
Source: David Bindman, *Ape to Apollo: Aesthetics and the Idea of Race in the
Eighteenth Century* (London: Reaktion, 2002).

though the superiority of Greece to modern Christendom was assumed
rather than explicitly stated in his writings.[66]

If Winckelmann promoted a republican image of Athenian life, scholars
of Homer tended to emphasize the archaic roots of Greek culture. For much
of the eighteenth century, Virgil had been held in higher esteem than his
Greek predecessor, a view summed up in Frederick the Great's laconic "Vir-
gile m'amuse, mais Homère m'ennuye."[67] The impetus to reverse this judg-

ment arose from the English back-to-nature movement, in which Homer came to be seen not as a source of timeless allegory but rather as a solitary bard wandering through the temperate climes and warlike societies of early Greece. Robert Wood, in his *Essay on the Original Genius and Writings of Homer* (1767), refuted the prevailing view that Homer had borrowed his myths from the Egyptians and instead linked them to the details of Greek geography and history. This view of Homer suited the Pietist nationalist poet Friedrich Gottlob Klopstock, as well as the poets of the "Göttingen Grove," who came of age in the 1770s as patriotic opponents of French neoclassicism and Latin culture more generally. The most famous of the Göttingen poets, Johann Heinrich Voss, was inspired to translate Homer's *Odyssey* (1781) and *Iliad* (1793) into a stylistically pleasing German, making the Homeric epic accessible to a large portion of the German reading public.

The fascination with all things Greek might have remained a passing fad had it not acquired institutional roots in the German educational system. Göttingen, in particular, emerged as a center for research and teaching in classical philology.[68] Founded in 1734, the university was encouraged by the Hanoverian government to develop the "lower" faculties, especially law and philosophy, in order to provide civil servants for the expanding state bureaucracy. Under the leadership of Christian Gottlob Heyne, who served as a professor from 1763 until 1812, philology was able to shed its status as a *Hilfsstudium* and emerge as a discipline in its own right. Heyne insisted on a mastery of Greek language and texts as a means to penetrate the lived reality of ancient Greece, including its art, architecture, and mythology. He taught this approach to antiquity in his influential philological seminar, which became a model for the supervision and sponsorship of scholarly research. In addition, he encouraged individual gymnasiums to adopt a neohumanist curriculum centered on Greek, rather than Latin, language and literature, foreshadowing the efforts of Wilhelm von Humboldt. Finally, it was Heyne who developed the theory of ancient mythology as "sermo mythicus seu symbolicus." In this respect, the introduction of a historicist concept of "myth" in German philological and theological scholarship coincided directly with the establishment of neohumanism and the rise of the educated middle classes to prominence in German society.[69]

If Göttingen was the capital of neohumanist scholarship, the capital of neohumanist aesthetics was Weimar, home to the literary giants Johann Wolfgang von Goethe and Friedrich Schiller. In "Die Götter Griechenlands" (1788), Schiller expressed his nostalgia for the lost world of Greek polytheism. Who could measure the poverty of a civilization that saw in the sun only a burning sphere and not, as the Greeks had, Helios and his chariot?

For Schiller, Greece was a land of fables, where humans intermingled freely with gods and life was enriched by an endless series of festivals. But that era had now disappeared. "In order to enrich one above all others, this world of gods had to pass away."[70] With the rise of monotheism, the earth was ruled by a cold and distant deity according to the rigid laws of natural science. As a result, the divine had become less human, and humans less divine.

Schiller's poem unleashed a storm of criticism. The poet Friedrich Leopold Graf zu Stolberg maintained that the sublime representations of the Christian religion were far nobler than those of Greek polytheism and that to suggest otherwise amounted to blasphemy. "I would rather be the subject of universal scorn than to have created such a poem, even if such a poem could bring me the fame of the dear, great Homer."[71] Stolberg's polemic was just one in a series of articles, poems, and reviews that addressed the relative merits of monotheism and polytheism as well as the limits of artistic freedom.[72] Despite the notoriety of "Die Götter Griechenlands," however, Schiller's commitment to the Greeks was rather equivocal. In the words of Henry Hatfield, Schiller maintained only a "semblance of paganism," and he valued aesthetic appearance as a supplement rather than an alternative to Christian morality. Instead, it was Goethe who embraced the pagan ethic, fleeing Weimar in 1786 for the antiquities, monuments, and carnal pleasures of Italy. Rejecting (for a time) the Christian climes of northern Europe, he exalted the classical gods as archetypes of natural beauty and unrestrained sensuality.[73]

Perhaps the purest expression of Philhellenist aestheticism came from the pen of Karl Philipp Moritz, who had met and befriended Goethe on his Italian journey. In his *Götterlehre* (1791), Moritz combined an interpretation of the Greek pantheon with a scattering of poems by Goethe and a striking series of engravings by Asmus Jakob Carstens based on Greek and Roman cameos. Moritz rejected the allegorical and euhemerist interpretations of myth, according to which the gods represented either philosophical ideas or distant echoes of forgotten heroes. Instead, he offered an aesthetic interpretation of Greek mythology, in which the "meaning" of the gods was precisely the human imaginative faculty that had created them. For Moritz, "Jupiter" meant "Jupiter" and not some higher lesson of physics. "Since the entire religion of the ancients was a religion of imagination and not of understanding, its *Götterlehre* is a beautiful dream that certainly has much meaning and cohesion and sometimes provides sublime views but from which one must not demand the exactness and definitude of ideas in a wakeful state."[74] Moritz's interpretation of the gods proved formative for Goethe's distinction between

Cameo images of Perseus by Asmus Jacob Carstens. Richard Wagner said, "All my
subsequent feelings about the ugliness of our present-day world come from looking
at illustrations in Moritz's *Mythology.*"
Source: Karl Philipp Moritz, *Götterlehre, oder Mythologische Dichtungen der Alten,*
ed. Horst Günther (Frankfurt a.M.: Insel, 1999), 157.

the "symbolic" and the "allegorical," and it would play a central role in
Schelling's *Philosophy of Art.*[75]

For Moritz, the Olympians' defeat of the Titans was a triumph of measure
and proportion over the inherent monstrosity and boundlessness of nature. It
was thus crucial that none of the Greek deities acquired "God-like" om-
nipotence, for that would have eliminated the possibility for true creativity.
Instead, even Jupiter stood under the continual threat of the "infinite," which
took the form of the Goddess of Night. Moreover, none of the gods was
"good" in any conventional sense; rather, they stood sublimely over all con-

cepts of morality. Thus, Apollo could be both the beautiful god of youth and
the merciless destroyer of the old with no apparent pangs of conscience. The
chief purpose of the Greek liturgy was neither sacrifice nor pedagogy but
rather aesthetic effect, or *"Schauspiel,"* a phenomenon exemplified by the
wild festivals in honor of Bacchus.[76] Throughout the *Götterlehre,* Moritz
evinced little interest in the origins of Greek aesthetic culture or its relationship to political, social, or cultural life. In this respect, his conception of
Greek mythology resisted the historicism of Heyne or Herder. What was crucial to Moritz, as for Goethe, was the timeless significance of the gods as
symbols of a universal human poetic capacity.

Moritz's interpretation of the Greek gods can be seen as part of a wider attempt in these years to define an independent space for art against the claims
of not only monotheistic religion but also the state and consumer taste. Enlightened theorists had urged that artists encourage morality, either by being
consciously didactical or by "moving" their audiences to right behavior.
With the expansion of the commercial book market, however, the paying
public played an increasing role in determining the content of art. In response
to these trends, a number of theorists had begun to insist on the autonomy
of the aesthetic realm from all external criteria, whether religious, moral, or
utilitarian.[77] In his *Kritik der Urteilskraft* (1790), Kant argued that true art
exhibited a "purposiveness without purpose," which could not be reduced to
any concrete goal or interest but served rather as a "symbol of morality."
Schiller would take up this claim after the French Revolution, arguing for an
"aesthetic education" as the basis for harmony in the individual and in society. Moritz, however, pushed aesthetic autonomy in a more radical direction
by insisting that the gods formed a self-sufficient "world" or a "totality," with
no connection to either Christianity or conventional schemes of morality.

By the 1790s, neohumanism had coalesced into a comprehensive cultural
program in which the contemplation of Greek art and literature became the
foundation of individual cultivation *(Bildung).* The key figure in this development was the Prussian nobleman Wilhelm von Humboldt, a student of
Schiller at Jena who went on to promote the study of Greek culture as a
holistic and progressive alternative to both the Latin curriculum of the
church and philanthropic utilitarianism. Starting in 1812, Humboldt would
oversee the establishment of a system of neohumanist gymnasiums in Prussia, a move anticipated by the Bavarian monarchy in 1808. By this time, Philhellenist ideals had been taken up by ever-larger segments of the educated
middle classes, especially secondary-school teachers and university professors. Meanwhile, philology was developed at Halle into a self-sufficient *Altertumswissenschaft* by Heyne's student Friedrich August Wolf, who would

bring this approach to Berlin after the refounding of the university there in 1810.[78]

Yet from the beginning, neohumanism suffered from a number of internal tensions. As numerous scholars have emphasized, the ideal of Greek culture as an organic and sensual whole coexisted uneasily with the detailed, highly specialized research of scholars determined to demonstrate their "originality."[79] The research imperative led scholars to new sources and new interpretations, which complicated or contradicted the Philhellenist image of Greece. Beyond this, however, there was a fundamental ambivalence within neohumanism concerning its relationship to the wider Christian culture. In the 1790s, philology still remained in a subordinate position vis-à-vis theology within the university and in society as a whole. But while Goethe and Moritz were content to preserve their own rather ahistorical form of aesthetic paganism, others envisioned (and welcomed) a confrontation between ancient Greek religion and Christianity, which would dethrone the biblical revelation from its position of power and privilege and establish the groundwork for a republican public life and aesthetic culture. That confrontation, barely conceivable before the French Revolution, would be the task of Friedrich Schelling and the *Frühromantik*.

YOUNG SCHELLING: FROM REVELATION TO *NATURPHILOSOPHIE*

The Tübingen *Stift* was founded in 1536 to train Protestant clergymen for service in the Duchy of Württemberg. For two and a half centuries, it had educated, housed, and fed promising theology students, on the condition that after graduation they serve the duchy in either the church or the state bureaucracy. During their years at the *Stift*, students were subject to a strict system of discipline, which included mandatory church attendance and the wearing of clerical garb.[80] Whatever their outward manifestations of poverty, however, by the end of the eighteenth century the vast majority of these students came from well-established clerical or bureaucratic families.[81] Because Württemberg had no independent aristocratic estate, the clerically dominated *Ehrbarkeit* presided over social and political life in the duchy.[82] So when Friedrich Schelling matriculated into the Tübingen *Stift* in 1790, he did so with the expectation that he would soon be joining Württemberg's intellectual and cultural elite.

But Schelling had other reasons to feel entitled. Gifted in the study of ancient languages and pushed ahead by an admiring father (who was himself a respected Orientalist), Schelling had completed his preparatory schooling by the age of fifteen. Thus, he entered the *Stift* three years younger than the rest of his soon-to-be legendary cohort, which included Friedrich Hölderlin and G. W. F. Hegel. Nonetheless, it was Schelling who won the accolades at Tübingen and who impressed the teachers with his characteristic combination of energy, intelligence, and arrogance. In his academic work he combined a radical interpretation of Kantian philosophy with a thorough command of enlightened biblical criticism. Indeed, throughout his first three years at the *Stift* Schelling appeared destined for a brilliant career as a theologian.

Yet events would conspire to divert Schelling from this goal. He could not ignore, for example, the extraordinary happenings in France. Although stories of Schelling and Hegel planting liberty trees and translating the "Marseillaise" are probably apocryphal, sympathy for the French Revolution among students and many of the tutors at the *Stift* was quite real. In 1792 a student named August Wetzel ran off, became involved in a Jacobin organization in Strasbourg, and then returned to Tübingen several weeks later to found a prorevolutionary political club. Schelling, who with Hegel and Hölderlin was active in this club, found himself fending off accusations of improper associations in May 1793, just as Duke Carl Eugen of Württemberg was about to visit Tübingen and announce a new, stricter regime of discipline for the *Stift*.[83] The Catholic duke was despised by many Protestants in Württemberg, including Schelling, who saw him as the embodiment of a moral-theological despotism that contradicted both the revolution and the Enlightenment.[84] Throughout his years at the *Stift,* Schelling would interpret his efforts on behalf of theological enlightenment as a struggle against political despotism.

During Schelling's years in the *Stift,* its dominant theological trends were shaped by a conservative reading of Kant. Inspired by F. H. Jacobi and the Pantheism Controversy, many theologians saw Kant's critical philosophy as creating an expanded realm for faith. In *Annotationes quaedam theologicae ad philosophicam Kantii de religione doctrinam* (1793), the Tübingen theologian and *Stift* superintendent Gottlob Christian Storr extended Kant's "postulates of practical reason" to encompass most of the traditional Lutheran dogmas, including a literal belief in the Bible. Storr was especially concerned to secure the authority of the biblical revelation against those Neologists or rationalists who might dismiss certain passages or even books of the Bible as the product of "Jewish ideas."[85] As Schelling noted, Storr and his ally Johann Friedrich Flatt "believe that the essence of Kantianism . . . consists of letting in again through the back door (of the practical postulates) what was kicked out of philosophy through the front door."[86] To Schelling's distress, Storr's "supernaturalist" theology enjoyed a dominant position in the *Stift* at this

time. Given Storr's relatively young age (he was just forty-seven when he published the *Annotationes*), his influence was likely to persist for some time
to come.

So Schelling had ample reason to feel ambivalent about the implications
of the Kantian philosophical "revolution" for his chosen field of theology. To
be sure, Kant had raised philosophy to a new height, establishing a system
based on the principles of freedom and criticism. Yet the danger also existed
that Kant's philosophy might be used to undermine or render irrelevant the
historical-critical investigation of the Bible. Schelling believed that Storr in
particular had sought an illegitimate combination of theology and critical
philosophy in order to rule out questions of historical evidence a priori. In an
unpublished essay from 1793, he labeled this a "Coalition System," a reference no doubt to the coalition formed by Austria, Prussia, and Great Britain
that year to fight the French.[87] To preserve the cause of Enlightenment, he
concluded, historical truth could be demonstrated only on the terrain of history.[88] As a result, Schelling became a devotee of the mythical approach, publishing a master's dissertation on the Garden of Eden narrative while drafting
a study of myths in the Gospel accounts of Jesus' birth.[89]

Schelling spelled out his conception of the origin and function of ancient
myth in the essay "Ueber Mythen, historische Sagen und Philosopheme der
ältesten Welt" (1793), published when he was just eighteen. A story was
"mythical," he argued, if it came from a preliterate era and was passed on by
word of mouth. The basis of that story might be a philosophical idea, a historical event, or simple poetic invention, but when combined with the "sensual" quality of language in the "childhood of a nation," it took on the
"miraculous" features associated with myth. This argument squared closely
with Heyne's and Eichhorn's conception of a "sermo mythicus seu symbolicus." Yet Schelling evinced an affinity for myth that departed sharply from
Göttingen and veered instead toward Weimar. Since entering the *Stift*, he had
become an ardent Philhellenist, idealizing not only Greek art and philosophy
but also Greek religion as uniquely republican and popular. He was joined in
these sentiments by Hegel and especially Hölderlin, whose early poems celebrate the Greek deities as guarantors of freedom and civic harmony. "In the
faces of the gods, you resolved to found your kingdom on love," Hölderlin
wrote in 1790. "All the heavenly beings marveled at this. The Thunderer
[Zeus] inclined his royal head down to you for a brotherly embrace."[90] Schelling did not go quite this far in his enthusiasm for ancient religion, but in
"Ueber Mythen" he described with evident approval how myths were trans-
mitted to sons from their fathers, who recounted the heroic deeds of the past
and the courage of their ancestors. As part of a broader tradition, myth

brought "unformed masses of people into harmony and unity. It became a gentle bond through which the society of one family was joined to one doctrine, one faith, and one activity."[91]

At several points in this essay, Schelling suggested that myth offered a form of thinking superior to that conveyed through "abstractions and dead concepts."[92] He ridiculed the "alphabet men" *(Buchstabenmenschen)*, who attempted to reduce myth to history or allegory, an argument that echoed Moritz's *Götterlehre*.[93] Like Moritz, Schelling attributed the quality of myth to the need by "sensual man" to feel "at home" in the sensible manifold of nature. Through myth "all of nature is for him an image, through which, so to speak, he assimilates his ego."[94] But while Moritz traced the meaning of myth to the aesthetic imagination, Schelling sought a higher *philosopheme* in what he called "transcendental myths." As an example, he cited the Garden of Eden narrative. Rather than interpret this myth as an illustration of "radical evil" (as Kant had), Schelling argued that it depicted the feeling of nostalgia that overcame humanity after the first exercise of its freedom. In this respect, the Genesis story paralleled the myth of Pandora's box, which signified the suffering that inevitably accompanied the human striving for "higher dignity."[95] By eliminating any conception of "original sin" or "radical evil" from his interpretation, Schelling suggested that human striving was necessary for, rather than antithetical to, the "kingdom of God" prophesied by the Swabian Pietists and now conceived by the *Stiftler* (seminarians) as a revolutionary republic. Further, by treating a Greek myth and an Old Testament narrative as essentially identical in terms of form and content, he undermined the unique status of the biblical revelation. Indeed, Schelling would soon reject the very concept of revelation as part of a coercive system of theological and political dogmatism that was inimical to the cause of human freedom.

Schelling was spurred to these conclusions by his encounter with Johann Gottlieb Fichte.[96] The son of a ribbon-maker, a devotee of Kant, and a radical of the first order, Fichte first became known to Schelling through his political and theological writings. While in Königsberg, he had published *Versuch einer Kritik aller Offenbarung* (1792), in which he went even further than Kant in questioning the necessity of religious revelation before concluding that the concept was not incompatible with moral religion. Revelation, he argued, served those people who had an undeveloped sense of morality and thus required some sort of external aid to act according to the ethical law.[97] Shortly thereafter, in his *Beitrag zur Berichtigung der Urteile des Publikums über die französischen Revolution* (1793), Fichte challenged the value of a visible church. In a clear allusion to the situation in Prussia created by the 1788

Edict on Religion, he argued that any visible church would be led by its very nature to impose orthodoxy on its members. Thus, it was incompatible with a moral religion grounded in human autonomy.[98] With his reputation as a radical already well established, Fichte visited the Tübingen *Stift* in June 1793, where it is likely that he met Schelling.[99]

Given the coincidence of their political and theological views, Schelling was uniquely disposed to appreciate Fichte's *Wissenschaftslehre* when it appeared in 1794.[100] In a series of dense and often maddeningly difficult writings, Fichte argued that the free activity of self-consciousness must be the first principle of all philosophy. The acquisition of theoretical knowledge did not involve a passive reception of data from the senses but rather a continual striving by the self to overcome its own limitations. The key faculty here was what Fichte called the "productive imagination," which involved a continuous interplay of the finite and the infinite within the self. This dynamic gave rise to a "striving" through which the self literally created the world according to its own moral ideal.[101] This striving had no end point; instead, it involved a process of infinite approximation toward an ideal of "absolute ego." Making the connection with politics explicit, Fichte suggested that this ideal could be realized only in an ethical commonwealth, in which all individuals strove toward this common end.[102]

For the nineteen-year-old Schelling, the encounter with Fichte's philosophy was a life-transforming experience. His rapid and unequivocal embrace of idealism was facilitated by his support for Fichte the radical publicist. Yet it also reflected the degree to which the *Wissenschaftslehre* solved or rendered moot many of the theological questions that had troubled him since his arrival in Tübingen. By ascribing all knowledge to the practical activity of the ego, Fichte closed the epistemological gaps in critical philosophy into which both Kant and his more supernaturalist readers had inserted God, the soul, the Kingdom of Heaven, and every other imaginable dogma. In particular, this new system abolished the notion that "revelation" was a postulate of practical reason. From that point forward, Schelling saw little point in continuing his historical studies of the Bible. "Who wants to bury himself in the dust of antiquity when the movement of *his* day repeatedly grabs him and carries him forward," Schelling wrote Hegel.[103] Instead, he plunged into philosophy, writing and publishing a series of short studies examining the fundamental concepts of Fichte's philosophy.[104]

These articles were dedicated to overcoming certain ambiguities in Fichte's notion of the "absolute." In the 1794 version of his *Wissenschaftslehre*, Fichte had located the absolute in the spontaneous activity of the self. This was not an empirical self but rather the continuous "I think" that allowed different representations to be constructed in the mind. As such, it could not be known empirically; one became aware of it only through an act of "intellectual intuition." Schelling argued, however, that any activity that could be an object of consciousness—even Fichte's a priori "I think"—was inherently conditioned and thus not the absolute. He therefore took a step backward, positing an original, unconscious "being" whose original division had led to the beginning of self-consciousness. "My ego contains a being that precedes all thinking and representation," Schelling wrote at one point.[105] In his scheme, the goal of striving was less a conquest of being by the ego than a merger or transformation *(Uebergang)* of the ego into the realm of being.[106]

This move from consciousness to the "being" behind self-consciousness eventually led Schelling onto the terrain of *Naturphilosophie.* This term was used in the late eighteenth century to denote a series of parallel pursuits in medicine and physics that sought to overturn the mechanistic view of nature passed down from Newton and Descartes and still embraced by Spinoza.[107] Schelling began research in these sciences shortly after arriving in Leipzig, and armed with the new tools of the critical philosophy he made rapid progress. In *Ideen zu einer Naturphilosophie* (1797), Schelling attempted to present nature as an organic system, that is, a developing process animated by spirit rather than an interlocking set of parts. At the heart of nature was an interplay of forces, expressed most basically in the opposition between light and gravity (or "night").[108] Schelling would later define this opposition in terms of a polarity of the sexes: the female was identified with gravity, or the "real" element in nature; the male was identified with light, or the "ideal" element in nature. The procreative principle of male and female interaction drove nature forward in an endless cycle of diremption and return.

In the hands of Schelling, *Naturphilosophie* became a kind of Spinozism with soul, a unification of spirit and substance whose absolute principle Schelling described as the *Weltseele* (world soul). In this way, he overcame the division between ideal and material realms that was the premise of Kant's epistemology, as well as the basis for the Christian dogmas of God, the soul, and revelation. Schelling's investigations inspired the work of numerous contemporaries, and over the next two decades *Naturphilosophie* would become the dominant theory in some faculties of medicine, influencing both research and therapy.[109] For his part, Schelling maintained that his doctrine of nature as "visible mind" recovered at the level of freedom a wisdom once possessed instinctively by the ancients (most notably the Greeks). This truth was invisible to the Cartesian philosophy of "reflection," which Schelling saw as the source of a "spiritual sickness in mankind." But it had been antici-

Friedrich Schelling in 1801, at the height of his youthful confidence.
Source: Xavier Tilliette, ed., *Schelling im Spiegel seiner Zeitgenossen* (Turin: Bottega d'Erasmo, 1974).

pated in creative imagination, which had begun to discover the "symbolic language" needed to describe the true identity between humanity and the world.[110]

By plunging into the heart of nature, Schelling took the *Wissenschafts-lehre* in a direction that its creator neither understood nor approved. While the split between the two men did not become open until years later, one can detect already in 1795 a basic willingness on the part of Schelling to reconcile philosophy with the ground of being and avoid Fichte's stringent moral critique of the world. Rather than call for an overhaul of Germany's political, religious, and economic institutions, Schelling emphasized the need for a "gentle bond" that would unite a free society and overcome the divisions between philosopher and people, spirit and nature, the ideal and the real. The key to such a reform, he increasingly concluded, would be not ethical exhortation or political revolution but rather a fusion of religion and aesthetic culture akin to what had existed in ancient Greece but was missing from modern Christendom.

ROMANTICISM AND RELIGION

In June 1798, after much prodding and with noticeable reluctance, Goethe arranged for Schelling to receive an appointment as extraordinary professor of philosophy in Jena. With both Schiller and Fichte on its faculty, the university stood at the peak of its reputation as a center of post-Kantian innovation. Yet Goethe was little impressed by Schelling's *Naturphilosophie*, which seemed to him to reduce nature to a series of mental processes. His opinion changed only after a meeting with the young philosopher at the home of Schiller: "he is a very clear and energetic head, organized according to the latest fashion. I detected in him no sign of the sansculotte youth; to the contrary he seems to be in every sense modest and refined."[111] Schelling, Goethe eventually concluded, would bring the university further renown and might also assist in his own scientific investigations. For his part, Schelling jumped at this opportunity, spurning his father's attempts to secure a theological appointment in Tübingen, for which he was "no longer suited."[112] He accepted the offer and arrived in Jena in October 1798.

There Schelling joined an intellectual community without parallel in Europe. Goethe and Schiller became his frequent conversation partners, and he would spend New Year's Eve 1799–1800 in their company. There was also his mentor Fichte, struggling against a philosophical faculty that viewed him with suspicion and an unruly band of student fraternities who resisted his pleas for moral reform. Finally, there were the various scholars and writers who would form the Jena Romantic circle: August Wilhelm Schlegel and his wife, Caroline, Friedrich Schlegel and his wife, Dorothea, Friedrich von Hardenberg (Novalis), and Ludwig Tieck. Schelling had met August Wilhelm Schlegel in Leipzig, and he formed a strong bond with him during a visit to the art galleries in Dresden. A poet, translator, and literary critic, Schlegel had studied with Heyne in Göttingen for five years and spent several years in France and Holland before taking a position in Jena as extraordinary professor. During the trip to Dresden, Schelling also met August Wilhelm's younger brother, Friedrich. Relations between Friedrich Schlegel and Schelling can be described as frosty at best, and the two would coexist uneasily within the shifting circle of conversations that was Jena Romanticism.

The conflict between Schelling and Friedrich Schlegel was in part a matter of social background.[113] Although both were from clerical families, Schlegel had grown up in the commercial center of Leipzig and had originally intended a career in banking. Only at age eighteen did he begin a serious study of Greek and Latin literature, but he progressed rapidly enough to begin publishing monographs on this topic in 1795. During a brief and tumultuous stay in Jena he succeeded in alienating a potential benefactor, Friedrich Schiller, by publishing negative reviews of his journal *Die Horen*. In the summer of 1797 he headed to Berlin, where he became a fixture in the Jewish salon of Henriette Herz, coming into contact with Wilhelm von Humboldt and the Protestant pastor Friedrich Schleiermacher. Cosmopolitan in his tastes and disposition, Schlegel moved relatively easily between the intellectual worlds of Christianity and Jewry. He shared an apartment with Schleiermacher from December 1797 until the summer of 1798, exchanging ideas with him about Greek philosophy and religion. At the same time, he engaged in a scandalous love affair with a married Jewish woman named Dorothea Veit, which formed the basis for his erotic novel *Lucinde* (1799). In these respects, Schlegel differed drastically from the Swabian Schelling, who had been repulsed by Berlin salon life on his visit to that city in 1796, complaining especially of its intellectuals: "the vermin of young scholars and writers, especially among the Jews, cannot be endured at all."[114] Indeed, the threat of anti-Semitism clouded relations between Friedrich Schlegel, Dorothea Veit, and Schelling. In the short term, however, Schlegel confined his complaints to Schelling's "rawness" and infelicity in conversation.[115]

Despite these differences in character and background, Schelling found much to draw him to the Schlegel brothers and Novalis. Not only did they share his veneration for the Greeks, but they also sensed the importance of Goethe and Fichte for contemporary culture. In addition, they were gradually disengaging from their youthful enthusiasm for the French Revolution. In 1796, the French army had invaded southwest Germany as part of its war against the coalition powers. Schelling, whose younger brother was serving in the Austrian army, argued to his parents that the best fate for him would be to be taken prisoner by the French—an implicit declaration of sympathy for the French government. Two years later, however, while he still expected a republican transformation of Württemberg, he hoped that it would be accomplished from within rather than imposed by invading French armies—a sign that he had lost faith in the Directory.[116] Friedrich Schlegel and Novalis underwent a similar change in their political thinking, adopting an ironic distance toward both monarchy and democracy as forms of government. This shift has often been taken as a slide from "liberalism" into "conservatism," but that misconstrues both the context and the content of the early Romantics' political thought. As Gerald Izenberg has argued, it was precisely Friedrich Schlegel's demand for radical autonomy and "infinite individuality" that led him to challenge the ideal of harmony embedded in Greek (or French) forms of republicanism.[117] Schelling, by contrast, remained enamored of republican ideals, but he was increasingly convinced that achieving the harmony and beauty found in ancient Greece required abandoning what he saw as the Revolution's one-sided emphasis on natural rights, civil society, and democracy.[118]

The Romantics' response to the French Revolution was shaped in many respects by their reading of Friedrich Schiller's *Briefe über die ästhetische Erziehung des Menschen* (1795). In the opening letters of this work, Schiller bemoaned the inability of his contemporaries to seize the opportunity for a genuine transformation of political life according to the moral law. There seemed to be a *"physical* possibility of setting law upon the throne," but the *"moral* possibility is lacking, and a moment so prodigal of opportunity finds a generation unprepared to receive it."[119] Surveying what he saw as the lethargy and sloth of contemporary society, he drew a direct contrast with the ancient Greeks, who had merged ethical and aesthetic life into a seamless whole. "The Greeks put us to shame not only by a simplicity to which our age is a stranger; they are at the same time our rivals—indeed often our models—in those very excellences with which we often console ourselves for the unnaturalness of our manners."[120] Schiller especially praised the Greeks for the humanity of their deities, which he contrasted with the "monstrous divinity of the Oriental."[121] In his view, the Greeks' polytheism reflected their overall harmonization of the ethical and sensual faculties within the realm of the aesthetic. Likewise, the Greek polis was a magnificent organism, far more satisfactory than the "ingenious clockwork" of the modern state.[122]

In the face of this situation, Schiller offered aesthetic politics: "if man is ever to solve the problem of politics in practice he will have to approach it through the problem of the aesthetic, because it is only through beauty that man makes his way to freedom."[123] An aesthetic education of the citizenry would offer a bridge between the sensual realm and the demands of the moral law, accomplishing through the senses what the (Kantian) Enlightenment had demanded simply as duty. It was through art and art alone, Schiller maintained, that harmony could be restored both within the individual and in society as a whole. Yet Schiller seemed even within the *Briefe* to back away from the possibility that this ideal could be realized in the contemporary world. Here, as in the essay *Ueber naïve und sentimentalische Dichtung* (1795), Schiller depicted a modern civilization under the sway of an "idealism" that he associated with modern science, economic rationalism, and Christianity's otherworldly theology. Meanwhile, those who belonged to the aesthetic state, like those who belonged to the "pure church" or the "pure republic," were to be found only in "some few chosen circles."[124]

The notion that the chosen few constituted a "pure" or "invisible church" found heightened expression among the early Romantics, who, as followers of Fichte, were even more isolated than the Kantians. In their private and public writings they often referred to the Eleusinian mysteries as a model of religious-philosophical education that could be confined to a few philosophical adepts. "I believe that mysteries belong to any national education, in which the youth is initiated step by step," Schelling wrote to the theologian J. H. Obereit in 1796. This sounded to Obereit like a new Masonry. The difference, Schelling insisted, was that the Masonic secret was "empirical," whereas philosophical "mysteries" were open to anyone with the ability to attain intellectual intuition. Still, he admitted, the obstacles to establishing such an institution were enormous. "[G]iven the flood of our literature through which everything is exposed to a wide public this is impossible. The best writers can do nothing more than give their presentation so much worth, severity, and sublimity of delivery that every page cries out to the profane: *procul, procul esto* [away, stay away]!"[125]

Schelling's allusions to a threatening "flood" of literature reflected concerns common to Goethe, Schiller, and the early Romantics about the quality of contemporary literary culture. By the 1790s, the expansion of the reading public to almost 25 percent of the German population and the resulting increase in demand for secular literature had given rise to a much expanded book market for novels and plays. To cite just one statistic, while 189 new plays were published in the decade 1761–1770, 1002 new plays appeared in the decade 1791–1800.[126] Pundits complained of a "reading frenzy" *(Lesewut)*, especially among female readers, and a general fear persisted that the new literature might have a radicalizing effect on the population.[127] Yet the expanding public sphere was threatening not only to aesthetic autonomy, as Schiller feared, but also to the development of the new philosophy. From the beginning, the Fichtean philosophy had been subject to violent attacks by prolific critics like the *Popularphilosoph* Nicolai and the Kantians of the *Jenaische allgemeine Literatur-Zeitung.*[128] In this context, Schelling and the other Romantics found themselves drawn to a communicative structure that was based more on ritual than open debate and that could be insulated from the whims and tastes of those who had not mastered the *Wissenschaftslehre.*

These social and literary pressures, which were magnified by the scale of their own ambitions, helped push the Romantics to envision their common project as a "new" religion. "Perhaps you have the choice, my friend," Friedrich Schlegel wrote Novalis in December 1798, "to be either the last Christian, the Brutus of the old religion, or the Christ of a new gospel."[129] Over the next three years, Friedrich Schlegel, Novalis, Schleiermacher, and Hölderlin would repeatedly describe their work in terms of the creation of a new religion or a new Christianity. To some extent this was a purely rhetorical stance, as the Romantics ascribed sacred qualities to aesthetic and intellectual modes of intuition. Nonetheless, it is also clear that they conceived the "new religion" as competing not only with other philosophical or aesthetic schools but also with the established faiths of Catholicism, Protestantism, and Judaism.

That a tiny circle of poets and philosophers could imagine themselves to be legislators of a "new religion" was stark testimony to the religious innovation and upheaval of the late eighteenth century. Since the 1780s, Strict Observance Masonry had offered a heterodox form of Christianity, which was celebrated with obscure symbols and elaborate rituals that promised gnostic forms of enlightenment. In addition, numerous popular prophets appeared on the scene, sometimes adopting the mantle of traditional religion and other times, as in the case of Mesmer or Cagliostro, promising redemption through "magnetism" or "Egyptian" rites.[130] In France, the de-Christianization campaign of 1793–94 had given rise to a series of extravagant revolutionary cults, which were conceived as replacements for a decaying Catholic faith. Even after the fall of Robespierre, the Directory regime maintained a hostile stance toward Christianity, while encouraging the spread of Theophilanthropy, a modest worship of the supreme being that spread through France and beyond into cities like Berlin and Amsterdam. Nonetheless, the end of official repression in 1795 allowed Catholics to freely worship once again, generating a powerful religious revival whose influence was felt not only in France but also in the German Rhineland.[131]

The new vitality of Catholicism and the rise of various nontraditional religiosities only highlighted the relatively stagnant situation in the established Protestant churches. Between 1780 and 1820, some 120 different books or pamphlets appeared proposing solutions to what was widely seen as a "decline of religiosity."[132] The symptoms of this problem included a continuing decline in attendance at Sunday services, the fading of traditional Christian customs such as Bible readings and family prayers, a shrinking number of students interested in studying theology, complaints about the enlightened or Kantian nature of the theology being taught in seminaries, and the declining social standing of the clergy. A large number of the complaints were directed at the nature of Protestant worship services, which seemed to be hamstrung by boring sermons and a general lack of aesthetic appeal. Indeed, a number of writers looked longingly to the Catholic liturgy, which appeared to offer a feast for the senses not available in Protestantism. As one clergyman wrote later, "the education of the understanding that is predominant [in the Protestant liturgy] has the unavoidable result that it neglects the religious feeling."[133] For most commentators, the dangers of this situation were obvious: a weakened sense of social order, increasing lawlessness and immorality, and vulnerability to anarchy and revolution.

The complaints about Protestant religious "decline," when linked to the growing political reaction against the French Revolution, placed advocates of philosophical and religious enlightenment in a vulnerable position. It also conditioned their negative reaction to transcendental idealism, which came to a head in the so-called Atheism Controversy. In October 1798, Fichte published an article in the *Philosophisches Journal* in which he more or less equated God with the moral world order. Although this argument was consistent with the standpoint of his earlier writings, it elicited a series of denunciations in which Fichte was charged with "atheism." As Anthony La Vopa notes, the attack was spearheaded by a number of Aufklärer worried about the implications of Fichte's philosophy for Kantian or rationalist forms of Christianity in a time of growing political conservatism.[134] Fichte struck an initial tone of defiance in the face of these charges, but by the end of 1799 he had lost his professorship. The next year he left Jena for Berlin.

For Schelling, the problem was not Fichte's "atheism" but rather the timidity of the Aufklärung in dispensing with the heteronomous structures of traditional Christianity, including the biblical revelation. In *The Conflict of the Faculties* (1798), Kant had conceded to theologians the task of interpreting the Bible, provided that they did not impinge on the intellectual freedom of the philosopher or undermine the concept of true (i.e., moral) religion.[135] But Schelling viewed such a division as not only hypocritical but fraudulent. In "Ueber Offenbarung und Volksunterricht" (1798), he attacked precisely those enlightened theologians who wanted to preserve a discredited notion of revelation just to have an instrument of authority to wield against the public. "What gives you the right to raise yourselves above your brothers? Perhaps because they were not at educated schools or have not memorized oriental languages or some philosophical compendium?" Instead of the Enlightenment's "double path," which separated ("oriental") religion from (Greek) philosophy, Schelling called for a new "highway"—set up under the sign of the Absolute—that would be traveled in the future by all citizens of the state.[136]

Yet it was not Schelling, but rather Schleiermacher, Novalis, and Friedrich Schlegel, who spoke at this time of "religion." As a rule, these three writers were generally less interested than the Tübingen *Stiftler* in democratic popular education and tended to view the new religion as primarily an affair of elites. Rejecting Schiller's claim that antiquity had been informed by a

naïve holism, Schlegel called instead for "divine egoism," which would allow
the artist to realize the highest form of individuality. In his view, the true
artists constituted a race of clerics, Brahmins, or geniuses who should form a
quasi-Masonic alliance independent of the state. Their task would be to nur-
ture the "religion of people and artists that is sprouting up everywhere."[137]
This was a language favored also by Schleiermacher, who in *On Religion:
Speeches to Its Cultured Despisers* (1799) alluded to a "higher priesthood
that proclaims the inner meaning of all spiritual secrets and speaks down
from the Kingdom of God."[138] By speaking the language of mystery in a public form, the Romantics made a claim for their status as a new priesthood.[139]

In general, the early Romantics sought to define religion, not in terms of
ethics or belief in dogma, but rather as an intuition of the infinite within the
particular. "Nothing is more indispensable to true religiosity than a mediator that binds us to the divine," Novalis wrote in 1798. "In no respect can man
stand in an immediate relation to the divine." But this mediator could not
be imposed from outside by either the state or the church: it had to be freely
chosen. The "least coercion" created a situation of heterodoxy and dogmatism that destroyed religion.[140] In a similar manner, Schleiermacher in his
Speeches (1799) defined religion as an intuition or feeling of the infinite
within the individual, whether it took the form of nature, art, humanity, or
history.[141] Finally, Friedrich Schlegel's "Ideen" (1800) described religion as a
relationship of a person to the infinite, but with the infinite defined in terms
of individuality rather than universality.[142] For Novalis, Schleiermacher, and
Schlegel, religion involved a free relationship of the individual with the divine, which did not need to rely on inherited dogmas or revelations for its
symbols but instead had the power to create its own.

In their definitions of religion, Schlegel, Novalis, and Schleiermacher
placed overweening emphasis on the aesthetic realm, presenting religion not
as conformity to a static set of dogmas but rather as a creative mediation between the individual and an unseen infinite. But despite their affinity for
Greek culture, this was neither "aesthetic paganism" nor even a "religion of
art." For one, the emphasis on "feeling" and "intuition" showed considerable
continuity with the Moravian Pietist tradition, which had shaped the early
religious views of both Schleiermacher and Novalis. In addition, the early Romantics saw their perspective as an outgrowth of historical processes initiated by Christianity, especially the expansion of freedom beyond the narrow
limits of the polis and the opening up of intellectual life to conceive of an
infinite beyond the visible world.[143] Thus, they sought to justify these new religions within the historical framework defined by Christianity, while adapt-

ing its key terms ("church," "prayer," *"Gottesdienst"*) to their new philosophical perspective. Novalis went the farthest in this regard, calling in his unpublished essay "Christianity or Europa?" (1799) for a new Christianity that would move beyond the Protestant Reformation and its natural successors, the Enlightenment and the French Revolution.[144] But similar language could be found in Friedrich Schlegel and Schleiermacher.

Just as the Christian and universalist aspirations of the early Romantics ruled out a return to the Greeks, they also excluded a purely "nationalist" imagery. Since the 1770s, an increasing number of nationalist intellectuals had contemplated a revival of the Nordic gods as the basis for a new "German" aesthetic-religious imagery. In "Iduna, oder der Apfel der Verjüngung" (1796), Herder created an imaginary dialogue in which the advantages and disadvantages of the Eddic mythology were debated.[145] But while Herder evinced a mild skepticism toward this project, the early Romantics rejected it categorically. "Not Hermann and Wotan but instead art and science are the national gods of the Germans," Schlegel wrote. "Think about Kepler, Dürer, Luther, Böhme; and then about Lessing, Winckelmann, Goethe, Fichte."[146] The new religion would only arise out of the modern world and its most progressive forces.

In formulating this project, Friedrich Schlegel spoke at times of creating a "new Bible." The early Romantics showed little interest in the narratives or stories of the actual Bible, which they rejected on both aesthetic and philosophical grounds. In "Christianity or Europa?" Novalis expressed an aversion to the Bible "philology" of contemporary Protestantism, while Schleiermacher described the Bible as a "mausoleum of religion."[147] What Friedrich Schlegel had in mind was rather the "new gospel" that Lessing had invoked two decades earlier in "The Education of the Human Race" (1780).[148] In October 1798, he wrote to Novalis expressing his desire "to write a new Bible and to wander in the footsteps of Mohammed and Luther."[149] In the "Ideen," Schlegel described this Bible not as a single book but as an infinite idea that would unify all of art, philosophy, and experience. Just as Greek poetry and literature had formed an organic whole, the new Bible would draw all of modern knowledge together in a single living compendium.[150]

During these years, Schelling remained skeptical if not hostile toward this fascination with religion. Friedrich Schlegel complained of his "irreligion," which he hoped might be relieved by a newfound interest in poetry.[151] Instead, Schelling applied his poetic skills to satirize the religious views of his fellow Romantics. In the "Epikurisch Glaubensbekenntnis Heinz Widerporstens" (1799), he wrote:

My only religion is this,
That I love a pretty knee,
Full breast and slender hips,
As well as flowers with pretty scents.
To all desires, ample feeding,
To all my loves, ample heeding.
For that, there should be a religion
(But if not, I can live without one).[152]

As Schelling saw it, Friedrich Schlegel, Schleiermacher, and Novalis were attempting to throw an idealistic, feminine veil over nature with their talk of
religion.[153] He presented himself as a defender of the material world in the
spirit of Goethe, with whom he had spent considerable time since arriving in
Jena.[154] He had little patience for Schlegel's notion that nature was an image
of the infinite, poetry the mediator of an unseen and unknowable deity, and
the "critic" the high priest of the modern world. In Schelling's philosophy,
the absolute and the world were one and the same.

The Call for a New Mythology

Given their differences in temperament and philosophy, it is telling that
Schelling's and Friedrich Schlegel's thoughts should have converged on so
epochal a notion as the "new mythology." Yet in the spring of 1800, both published works that expressed the need for a new mythology: Schlegel in his
"Gespräch über die Poesie" and Schelling in the closing section of his System des transcendentalen Idealismus. This similarity of thinking can be
traced in part to the communal nature of Romantic philosophizing in 1799–
1800, as the Schlegels and Schelling met together regularly to exchange
ideas, criticism, and—by the end—insults. At the same time, it reflected the
confluence of the factors discussed above: the historicist critique of the Bible,
which had rendered it foreign and out of date for German educated elites; the
idealization of Greek poetry and religion; a disenchantment of intellectuals
with the existing public sphere; a perceived crisis in the church, which
seemed to require new religious and aesthetic institutions; and the French
Revolution itself, which seemed to guarantee the historical momentum to
bring about such a transformation.

Where and when the idea of a "new mythology" first arose has been a
matter of considerable dispute among literary historians and philosophers.
Much of this debate turns on the provenance of the so-called "Oldest System
Program of German Idealism," a two-page manuscript in Hegel's handwriting

that was first published in 1917 by Franz Rosenzweig and attributed at first to Schelling. The document, which appears to have been written in 1796 or 1797, begins by speaking of a new "Ethics" (perhaps an idealist counterpart to Spinoza's *Ethica*), which would connect the Fichtean absolute to the soil of nature or "physics." It turns next to the state, which is described as a "mechanical" creation that must be superseded. From there it briefly examines the "ideas of a moral world," rejecting the Kantian postulates of God and immortality as "superstitions" of the clergy and calling instead for an "absolute freedom of all spirits." Finally, it speaks of the "idea that unites them all, the idea of beauty." Philosophy, the author asserts, must become aesthetic if it is to unite the realms of truth and goodness and if it is to reach those who "understand no ideas." In this way, poetry would "become again what it was in the beginning, a teacher of humanity."[155] Merging Fichte's idealist metaphysics with Schiller's ideas about the pedagogical role of aesthetics, the anonymous author raised art to the highest principle of philosophy.

At this point, the text turns to the issue of religion. "[W]e hear so often that the masses must have a *sensual religion*. Not only the great masses, but also the philosophers need it. Monotheism of reason and the heart, polytheism of imagination and art, that is what we need! First I will speak here of an idea that, so far as I know, has not yet occurred to anyone: we must have a new mythology. But this mythology must stand in the service of ideas: it must be a mythology of *reason*." For the author, such a mythology would bridge the deep divide between the unenlightened and the enlightened. "Then finally there would be eternal unity among us. No longer the blind shivering of the people before its wise man and priests. Only then would there be equal development of all powers, of the single person as well as of all individuals." This alone would be the basis for the perpetual peace desired by Kant and others. But it was difficult to fathom where this mythology would come from. "A higher spirit sent from heaven must establish this new religion among us. It will be the last, great work of humanity."[156] In two short pages, the "System Program" offered a stirring vision of a society united by a common mythology, which would be grounded not in revelation or dogma but in reason itself.

The power and appeal of this short text help to explain the extensive and long-running debate over its author. For while Rosenzweig confidently assigned the "System Program" to Schelling, others felt Hölderlin or Hegel was the more likely author. In recent years, however, a consensus seems to have developed around Hegel.[157] Unlike Schelling, in the years 1796–97 Hegel devoted his writings to the issues of religion and mythology, including Herder's proposals to revive a national mythology. Moreover, the document is written in Hegel's hand, and the proposed scenarios by which he might have transcribed the thoughts of Hölderlin or Schelling do not seem particularly plausible. What is more likely is that Schelling picked up some of these ideas from conversations with his Tübingen friends and then carried them with him to Jena, where they became common currency among the Romantics. In the process, however, individual writers infused them with their own particular concerns.

This can be seen in Friedrich Schlegel's *Gespräch über die Poesie* (1800), a dialogue devoted to expounding the implications of his poetic theory. After a section summarizing the history of poetry from Homer to German Romantic criticism, one of the characters, Ludoviko, proclaims his confidence in a "new dawn, the new poetry," in which philosophy will fuse with art, and the glory of the Greeks will be recaptured at a higher level. What was first required, however, was the emergence of "a new mythology." Greek culture, he argued, possessed a "maternal soil," from which all art, religion, and thought had grown.[158] That maternal soil was their mythology. In the modern era, by contrast, all creation sprang from the hidden sources of the self. If humanity were ever to reexperience the political and aesthetic harmony that the Greeks had enjoyed, a new center *(Mittelpunkt)*, that is, a new mythology, would have to be found.

While Herder had suggested a revival of the Eddic gods, Schlegel maintained that a new mythology could only arise from the wellspring of the modern era, which was free self-determination. Thus, it could not attempt to capture the naïve condition of earliest humanity but instead would build on the efforts of Dante, Shakespeare, and Goethe. As such, the new mythology would have to be "the most artificial of all artworks, because it has to encompass all others, a new bed and container for the ancient eternal source of poetry, and itself the infinite poem, which contains the seed of all other poems."[159] In this respect, Schlegel's notion of a new mythology paralleled his earlier ideas of a Bible that would encompass all written books within it. It also retained a wide capacity for individual creativity and "artificiality," which Schlegel saw as the inescapable condition of modern life and thought.

The initial attempts to create the new mythology were bound to remain incomplete and isolated, Schlegel noted. But now a new science of the self had arisen, transcendental idealism, that would transform every realm of human endeavor, from poetry, to criticism, to natural science. This development was only a part of that wider revolution, the "phenomenon of all phenomena," through which humanity struggled to discover its internal laws and secret hidden powers. As this process came to fruition, idealism would give forth a "new realism" that would itself be a source of the new mythology. Indeed, the signs for such a development could already be seen in "modern physics"—that is, *Naturphilosophie*. For Schlegel/Ludoviko, therefore, it seemed just a short step from this "reenchantment of the world" to the emergence of a beautiful but believable mythology.[160] The growth and spread of the new physics would lead to a fully realistic and yet idealistic poetry and, with it, a mode of communication that transcended the present-day economy of needs. This was the great task of the new age, Schlegel maintained, for it would reveal the principles of "eternal revolution" and provide the basis of a common understanding between people. "And so let us then—by light and life!—delay no longer, but everyone according to his disposition speed the great development to which we are called."[161]

For all its similarities with the "System Program," Schlegel's description of a new mythology departed in significant respects from its predecessor. Whereas the earlier document emphasized the creation of a common language between the educated and the uneducated as part of the creation of a republican politics and a new religion, Ludoviko stressed the centrality of the new mythology as an aesthetic phenomenon, which would be the most "artificial of all artworks." Nor was it necessary to wait for a "higher spirit" to institute this new mythology; instead, it could be the collective project of all educated persons. In January 1800, Friedrich Schlegel read his "Rede über die Mythologie" to his brother to great effect.[162] In a letter written in February, Dorothea commented, "Friedrich is looking over and beyond us and is thinking with such a profound expression that one would swear that he is thinking about the new mythology."[163] Meanwhile, however, Schelling was about to publish a work that would place the concept of mythology at the center of his philosophical system.

The *System des transcendentalen Idealismus* (1800) was Schelling's first attempt at a systematic philosophy and the most "Romantic" of his works. Here he returned to the concerns of his first philosophical writings, the genesis of self-consciousness and its relation to the absolute, but now drawing on insights from his *Naturphilosophie*. In the *System*, Schelling narrated the progressive education of the self until the absolute became an object for the self. The end point of this journey was neither a philosophy nor a polity but a work of art. Only in the work of art did conscious and unconscious forces unite in a single individual, a finite form through which the infinite could be intuited. "[T]hat which the philosopher allows to be divided even in the primary act of consciousness, and which would otherwise be inaccessible to any intuition, comes, through the miracle of art, to be radiated back from the products thereof."[164] The artistic genius, Schelling argued, combined a conscious poetic intelligence with an innate unconscious power to create an artwork that appeared as the product of both freedom and necessity, the infinite and the finite.[165]

The discovery of the role of art as a "universal organum of philosophy" carried with it a cultural imperative. For if science were to inform art, philosophy would have to return to the poetic sources from which it originally flowed. The model for such a synthesis of philosophy and poetry was already available in the mythology of the Greeks, but the conditions that had given rise to Greek myth could not be duplicated. What was needed, therefore, was a new mythology. "But how a new mythology is itself to arise, which shall be the creation, not of some individual author, but of a new race [Geschlecht], personifying, as it were, one single poet—that is a problem whose solution can be looked for only in the future destinies of the world, and in the course of history to come."[166] The new mythology would not be forged simply through the common efforts of philosophers and artists. Instead, it would require an entirely new "race."[167]

Schelling elaborated on these remarks in his *Philosophy of Art* lectures, which he gave in Jena in the winter semester of 1802–3.[168] Since the halcyon days of 1799 the Romantic circle of Jena had dispersed. Novalis had died in 1801. The marriage of August Wilhelm and Caroline Schlegel had collapsed, and Schlegel had left his professorial post for Berlin. Schelling and Caroline Schlegel used this opportunity to develop their friendship into something more conjugal, eventually marrying in 1803. Friedrich Schlegel, disgusted with his brother, his sister-in-law, and Schelling, began a peripatetic journey that would take him to Cologne, where he converted to Roman Catholicism in 1808. Remarkably, August Wilhelm Schlegel and Schelling maintained a friendly correspondence during these years, exchanging notes on Wilhelm's Berlin lectures on the "Kunstlehre" and the Spanish dramatist Calderón.[169] This interaction proved crucial for the development of Schelling's thought on myth. After 1800 he became attracted to the idea of "religion" articulated by Schleiermacher in his *Speeches*. August Wilhelm Schlegel's Berlin lectures showed how he might integrate this definition of religion into a theory of mythology that incorporated both Greek antiquity and Christian modernity.

In his lectures on the philosophy of art, Schelling argued that the ancient Greek gods were neither poetic fictions nor philosophical allegories but "real" in themselves. This argument had been anticipated in Moritz's *Götterlehre*, but Schelling now gave it a metaphysical foundation. According to the terms of his "identity" philosophy (1801–4), the ideal and the real were bound together in a fundamental identity. As a result, there could be no separation between the absolute (or God, as Schelling now referred to it) and the universe. "God" and the "universe" were simply different ways of looking at the same phenomenon.[170] Likewise, each particular thing was a manifestation of the absolute and contained in itself a synthesis of the ideal and the real. Thus, the purpose of art was to portray things, not as they appeared in the empirical world, but according to their ideal form or "archetype" *(Urbild)*. From an ideal or Platonic perspective, the archetypes might be described as the "ideas," but from a real or "aesthetic" perspective, they were the "gods." In other words, Zeus, Poseidon, and Aphrodite did not simply represent thunder, the sea, and love: they *were* those powers.

The defining characteristic of the Greek gods, Schelling argued, was self-limitation. Represented as perfect human bodies, the gods were essentially amoral beings, who acted solely in accordance with their eternal and unchanging natures. This limitation of form raised the Olympian gods high above their counterparts in Persia or India, as well as above their misshapen predecessors, the Titans. Hesiod's *Theogony* had described how the Greek gods emerged from Night, the "mother of the gods."[171] "As the common seed of gods and men, the absolute chaos is night, darkness, and the first shapes that fantasy allows to be born within it are also still formless. A world of malformed and hideous shapes [the Titans] must perish before the mild realm of blessed and eternal gods can arrive."[172] Even after Zeus and his retinue of bright deities had established their dominance in Olympus, the Titans continued to reside in Tartarus, the home of Pluto. This god was "the Stygian Jupiter, ruler in the kingdom of night or of gravity."[173]

The world of Greek mythology was a higher manifestation of the universe, and Hesiod's theogony showed how the ideas or gods of the world had issued from the absolute idea or God. One could even interpret the individual gods according to the potences of nature, so long as one did not lose sight of the fact that there was no essential difference between the idea and its image. This was what Schelling called "symbolic representation," which he carefully distinguished from allegorical representation.[174] In allegory, a universal was represented by means of the particular. In the symbol, however, the particular did not merely represent the universal, it *was* the universal. The forms of the Greek gods thus offered an aesthetic intuition of the universe, whose meaning was made perfectly manifest in its external form.

Schelling's notion of symbolic representation broke sharply from David Hume's theory that the gods were the product of fear or superstitions, such as those found among the primitive peoples of North and South America. It also marked a distancing from his own earlier reliance on Heyne and the Göttingen school. A year after Schelling published "Ueber Mythen," the poet Johann Heinrich Voss issued *Mythologische Briefe* (1794), in which he accused Heyne of intentional obfuscation in his theory of a "sermo mythicus seu symbolicus."[175] While Voss agreed that the gods might at one point have represented natural forces, he rejected any strict linking of the gods to elements "according to the rigid constraint of a duty of office."[176] Voss also objected to Heyne's claim that the gods had originally taken the form of hermaphroditic or half-animal beings. Instead, he insisted on the basic humanity of the Greek gods and their myths. By the time he delivered his lectures on the philosophy of art, Schelling had adopted this view as well. Overlooking his earlier reliance on Heyne's theory, he declared that "the inner spiritual void of such an idea spares us the need for any refutation."[177]

Schelling's discussion of Greek mythology also forced him to address the "Homer question." The long-running debate over the origins and composition of the Homeric epics had come to the fore in recent years thanks to the publication of Friedrich August Wolf's *Prolegomena ad Homerum* (1795).[178] Citing evidence from Greek art, mythology, and architecture, the Halle philologist argued that writing had not yet been introduced into Greece at the time of Homer and that the Homeric epics could not have been written by a single individual. In Wolf's view, one major poet, along with several secondary poets, had composed a series of poems that were passed down orally by various schools of rhapsodes. In the sixth century B.C., editors, or *"diaskeuasts,"* had woven these poems together into the epic forms of the *Odyssey* and the *Iliad.* During the Hellenistic period, the epics underwent further revisions, additions, and polishing at the hands of the Alexandrian scholars.[179] Thus, the *Iliad* was not the product of a single author or even of a single era but the collective work of an entire culture over a long period of time. This last conclusion, while not completely original, was presented by Wolf as a revolutionary new discovery, with much chest thumping about the virtues of scholarly diligence and hard work. Indeed, the *Prolegomena* became a manifesto for the increasingly ascendant discipline of classical philology and established Wolf's reputation as the dominant philologist of his generation.[180]

In the wake of the *Prolegomena,* it was increasingly difficult to claim that the *Iliad* or *Odyssey* had been written by a single individual named Homer. But while Schelling acknowledged Wolf's significance, he proposed a different solution to the Homer question. "Mythology can be neither the work of a single person nor of a species nor of a race (so far as this is only a collection of individuals) but only of a race insofar as it is an individual and identical with a single person."[181] Schelling concluded from his reading of the *Prolegomena* that a people could be led by a guiding spirit to give their common work the character of individuality. This interpretation could make "the universal residing perhaps in [Wolf's] own conception clear and evident."[182]

Further, whatever was said about Homeric poetry applied equally to Greek mythology as a whole, for in their unified character and harmony both displayed the character of an individual.

The collective individuality symbolized by Homer had provided the basis for the remarkable public life of ancient Greece. In his *Method of Academic Study* lectures (1803), Schelling described Greek mythology as "exoteric"—in other words, its meaning lay on the surface and in sight of the public. Because they did not need their religion to be explained by exegetes or priests, the ancient Greeks could forgo institutions like the church. Consequently, Greek religiosity did not stand in opposition to the polis but instead was exercised in full view of the community. The "universal festivals, immortal monuments, dramatic performances, and all actions of public life were only various branches of one universal, objective, and living work of art," Schelling wrote.[183] The Greek gods, in other words, provided the basis for a fully unified and harmonious public life *(Oeffentlichkeit)*, in which there was no inherent division between church and state or between art and religion.

The Homeric world of the Olympian gods did not reflect the totality of Greek religious experience, however. "As in the symbols of nature, so in Greek poetry, the intellectual world lay hidden as if in a bud, concealed in the object and unspoken in subject."[184] Here Schelling referred to the cults of Demeter and Dionysus, in which initiates underwent a series of ritual purifications as they learned a symbolic doctrine of the creation. Friedrich Schlegel had discussed these mysteries extensively in his *Geschichte der Poesie der Griechen und Römer* (1798), tracing them to a desire among the Greeks for more immediate contact with the "divine ideas" than that offered in the public cultus. The mysteries must have emerged in the republican age, Schlegel argued, because philosophy and the republic were both expressions of a striving for "free self-determination."[185] In his lectures on the philosophy of art, Schelling followed Schlegel in linking the mysteries to the republican era. But whereas Schlegel saw the mysteries as a natural outgrowth of Greek culture, Schelling described the interest in the infinite as inherently un-Greek, having been brought in from the Orient.[186] Here he leaned toward Schlegel's rival Schiller, who had drawn a firm distinction between the "Greek" and the "Asiatic" (i.e., Jewish and Christian) worlds.

Christianity brought the world of ancient mythology crashing down. Unlike Greek mythology, the new religion was predicated on a disunion of the ideal and the real worlds, good and evil. Christian doctrine demanded that the infinite moral law be enacted in the world or, as Schelling would say, that the finite be taken up into the infinite.[187] This moral imperative shattered the permanence of Mount Olympus, for it shifted the realm of the divine from nature to history. "The absolute relationship is this, that in Christianity the universe is viewed on the whole as *history*, as a moral empire, and that this universal intuition constitutes its basic character. . . . What the Greek religion had as simultaneity, Christianity has as succession."[188] By intuiting the universe as history, Christianity transcended its status as religion and became the foundation of modernity.[189] This had not occurred as a gradual process but as a sudden "overturning" *(Umkehrung)*, which August Wilhelm Schlegel would describe as the "most remarkable revolution of the human spirit."[190]

The historical significance of Christianity was revealed in the figure of Jesus Christ. Like the pagan gods, Christ embodied both the infinite and the finite, but unlike the pagan gods, Christ's human form was only transitory. In the manner of an allegory, his finite existence was subordinate to his infinite nature, and his suffering and death represented the nullification of the finite before God. Once he had entered heaven, Christ sent not his person but his spirit to lead humanity toward the infinite. "It is as if Christ, as the infinite that has entered the finite and sacrificed itself to God in his own human form, marks the end of antiquity. He is there simply to draw the boundary— the last god."[191] This image had a particularly strong appeal for Hölderlin, whose poem "Bread and Wine" (1804) described Christ as bringing the feast of the ancient deities to an end.[192] According to Schelling, it was no longer possible after Christ to create a timeless collection of archetypes, because no single moment could embody the infinitude of the historical world. The divine could enter the world only from outside, in the form of miracles, prophecies, or scriptural revelation. This left little scope for a permanent or long-lasting mythology.

Schelling contended that this lack of a mythology had had a devastating effect on public life. "Christianity . . . is the revealed mystery, and whereas paganism is inherently exoteric, Christianity is inherently esoteric."[193] In paganism, the state and its public mythology could be seen as manifestations of the infinite in the real. In Christianity, the public mythology disappeared and religion (as an intuition of the absolute) retreated to the sanctuary of the church. Monarchy now controlled the state as a private possession, and public life was dominated by the finite ends of civil society.[194] "Where all public life collapses into the particulars and dullness of private life," Schelling argued, "poetry sinks more or less into this same indifferent sphere."[195]

Schelling presented this change as a shift from the masculine to the feminine. Antiquity had been governed by male friendship and manly virtues, exercised in the open light of the Greek polis. Christian modernity, by contrast, witnessed a privatization and feminization of culture.[196] From the first images of the Virgin and child, through the chivalric romances of the High

Middle Ages, from Dante's *Divine Comedy*, and onto Goethe's *Faust*, modern art had revolved around the search for female love and (private) domestic bliss. As the church lost its hold on public life in the wake of the Protestant Reformation, this impulse toward privatization and feminization had accelerated (the modern novel was a prominent example of this trend). In recent times, the striving for love depicted in modern art had merged with the acquisitive drives that dominated the commercial sector. Thus, for Schelling, the problems of late-eighteenth-century civil society—the disappearance of tradition, the drive for profit, the tendency to despotism, and the privatization of moral, religious, and aesthetic life—could all be traced back to the original transition from paganism to modernity.

The nature of Christian revelation rendered the task of creating a modern mythology particularly difficult. In the Bible, the ideal philosophical principle represented by Christ coexisted uneasily with the Jewish "mother religion" in which it was born.[197] Foreshadowing David Friedrich Strauss, Schelling argued that the Gospels were based essentially on Jewish fables, invented in the wake of Christ's Resurrection on the basis of Old Testament prophecies.[198] The writers of the Gospels were convinced a priori that these stories had to have happened. "In relation to them one can say: Christ is a historical personage whose biography was already written before his birth."[199] As a result, the gospel narrative never transcended the context in which it was written and instead reflected the grimy reality of first-century Palestine. "Just as Christianity originally drew its adherents from the mass of miserable and despised people, thus demonstrating from the very beginning democratic characteristics, so also did it continue to seek to maintain this popularity."[200] It was precisely this prosaic, "realistic" quality of the Gospels that Schelling disliked, just as he rejected the bourgeois realism of the modern novel and the everyday realm of journalism in favor of aesthetic models derived from classical antiquity.

For these reasons, the Bible offered little promise as the basis for a modern mythology. To be sure, Milton and Klopstock had attempted epic poems based on Genesis or the life of the Messiah, but these were seen by the early Romantics as ambitious failures. In the end, Schelling believed that the realism of the Bible was incompatible with the truths of idealism. Its narratives were too prosaic and too rooted in the ugly details of social reality (the crippled, the lame, the poor) to serve as the basis of a healthy public and artistic life. Moreover, the Bible was the document of a foreign people and had no intrinsic connection to modern German life. In sum, Schelling combined a theological argument with an aesthetic argument: on the one hand, he sought to distance himself from both Judaism and the "Bible religion" of the

Protestant churches; on the other hand, he rejected the "realism" of the biblical narrative as incompatible with good taste.

While Schelling dismissed the Bible as a source of mythology, he was
more favorably disposed to the imagery and practices of the Catholic Church.
Breaking with a long tradition of enlightened anti-Catholicism, Wilhelm
Wackenroder, Ludwig Tieck, and Novalis had evoked the aesthetic qualities
of Catholic liturgy and festivals in their poems and prose writings.[201] In his
Berlin lectures on the *Kunstlehre*, August Wilhelm Schlegel had identified
these sacraments and ceremonies as the authentic Christian symbolism.[202]
In a similar vein, Schelling described the liturgy as a genuine mythological
realm within Christianity. While the Greeks had possessed their gods as
timeless and perfect symbols, the spirit of Christianity was the spirit of history, in which the divine manifested itself across time rather than in a single,
perfect moment. In such a world, there could be no symbols, only symbolic
acts. This is what the Catholic Church offered in its sacraments of baptism
and Eucharist. "The public life of the church was . . . alone able to be symbolic, and its cult a living work of art, a kind of spiritual drama in which each
member had a part."[203] Contrary to the claims of "our imbecilic representa-
tives of Enlightenment," there was a genius in these symbols that could not
be re-created once they were lost.[204]

As such barbed comments suggest, Schelling's esteem for liturgy—
whether in the form of the Catholic liturgy or a modern-day mystery cult—
identified him as an enemy of enlightened liturgical reform. He ridiculed the
attempt by the Aufklärer to transform the sermon into a public-service announcement. "Why stop at recommending vaccination from the pulpit?" he
asked, alluding to earlier reform efforts. "Why not instruct the faithful on the
best method of raising potatoes?"[205] Likewise, while advocates of the Catholic Enlightenment called for teaching in the vernacular, Schelling suggested
that it might have been better if the Catholic Church had carried out the proposal that the reading of the Bible be banned.[206] Finally, while enlightened reformers had suggested that an overabundance of festival days had harmed the
economies of Catholic regions, Schelling proposed an expansion of festival
life. After his move to the Baroque city of Würzburg in 1804, Schelling would
distinguish himself as an advocate of—if not a convert to—Catholicism, but
only so long as it retained its preliterate and premodern quality.[207]

As striking as Schelling's affinity for Catholicism was his relative silence
regarding Protestantism. Certainly he acknowledged the historical necessity
of the Lutheran Reformation, since it had established the principle of freedom in scholarship and theology. But he had no patience for the Lutheran or
the more recent rationalist fascination with the Bible. "Living authority [has]

given way to the authority of books written in dead languages," Schelling complained. "[A]s this latter authority, by its very nature, could not be binding, the result was a . . . kind of slavery, namely dependence on symbols founded upon merely human prestige."[208] The Protestant obsession with the Gospels and the so-called early church ignored the fundamentally historical and developmental character of Christianity.

A new mythology could rest on neither the Bible nor the Roman Church, Schelling concluded. Instead, it would have to express the totality of the modern experience. For this reason, he was suspicious of attempts by Wackenroder and others to revive the old Catholic mythology. "Catholicism is a necessary element of modern poetry and mythology, but it is not the whole of it. In the designs of the world spirit, it undoubtedly constitutes only a portion of the whole."[209] Christian mythology, Schelling maintained, had ultimately collapsed for a reason, and there was little sense in reviving it. This applied doubly to what Schelling called the "Nordic-barbaric mythology of the ancient Germans and the Scandinavians."[210] He disapproved of the attempt by Klopstock and Herder to exhume the dead gods of Walhalla. (Not only were these beings unmodern, they were also ugly.) In Schelling's view, the new poesy would have to be "poesy for the entire species and be generated out of the material of the entire history of this species with all its multifarious colors and tones."[211] The result would be, not simply a "German" phenomenon, but a cultural world that was valid for all Europeans.

These factors also militated against a purely political mythology, such as the French had created in their cults and festivals. August Wilhelm Schlegel had opined that "[o]utside of the sheer violence of its creators, the recent crazy attempt in France to suddenly establish a new republican mythology had to fail . . . on the grounds that the French lack imagination and they proceeded from pure, allegorized concepts of reason."[212] Although Schelling did not echo these comments explicitly, they were consistent with his belief that a genuine mythology had to emerge from the totality of the species and not just from the political demands of a single state. Yet such a "universal" poetry seemed impossibly distant, for it depended on an understanding of the world that would be possible only after history had reached its conclusion.

In the meantime, it was up to the individual poet to grasp and express, in poetic form, the entire content of a particular era. "The necessary law of modern poesy, up to that point in an indeterminable future when the great epic of the modern age emerges as a self-enclosed totality, an epic that until now has announced itself only rhapsodically and in individual phenomena, is: that the individual should form into a whole that part of the world that is revealed to him, and from the subject matter of his own age, its history and its science, create his own mythology."[213] In the modern era, in other words, poets could not assume a stable situation from which to develop their art. Rather, they had to re-create the "closed circle" for themselves through an original act of poetic imagination, by which the people and events of a particular era acquired the character of universality. Here Schelling uncoupled the concept of "mythology" from antiquity or the primitive and suggested it might be applied to modern literature.

Creating such a modern mythology was a tall order, however, and Schelling believed that only a few poets had lived up to it. Dante, in his *Divine Comedy*, had fused the entire religious and scientific knowledge of medieval Europe in a work that for Schelling was the prototype of modern art. In a similar way, Shakespeare had re-created the full range of social life, from the king down to the shepherd boy, in his tragedies. "If our world were ever lost," Schelling commented, "one could recreate it from the series of his works."[214] The Catholic Shakespeare was Calderón, whose *La devoción de la cruz* (1640) revealed an authentic Catholic mythology. Finally, Schelling exalted Goethe, his friend and patron but also the most problematic author in this group. Goethe's works were deeply suggestive and yet maddeningly fragmentary and incomplete. Nonetheless, Schelling praised the *Faust* fragment (1790) as a uniquely modern interweaving of science and poetry with the mythical material of old Germany. Schelling foresaw correctly that despite the desperate ending of the first fragment (in which Gretchen dies insane), the trajectory of the poem was essentially comedic and would resolve itself in a "higher realm of authority."[215]

Schelling praised these as "partial" mythologies, but viewed them ultimately as only foreshadowing the "new mythology," which would transcend the limited standpoints of its predecessors. In the present age, he noted, there was a certain "hunger for material," which would only be resolved by the emergence of an aesthetic content that was scientific but that also embodied a "symbolic view of nature." In the absence of this, most art would either succumb to the rawness of its material or float out in the realm of abstract ideas.[216] The answer to this problem lay in *Naturphilosophie*, for this science had shown how to view the realm of nature from the perspective of the idea. "I will not hide my conviction that in *Naturphilosophie*, as it has developed from the idealistic principle, the first distant foundation of that future symbolism and its mythology has been laid. It will not be the creation of an individual but of an entire age."[217]

Yet, as Schelling made clear, a truly new mythology would have to go beyond the simple application of divine properties to nature.[218] The fundamental characteristic of the modern world was its vision of the universe as history, as an arena for individual striving toward the infinite or God. The deities of the modern world, Schelling argued, would have to emerge from this historical realm and plant themselves, as it were, back into nature. In other words, the modern mythology would be an inversion of the mythology of ancient Greece.

> [The gods of Greece] were originally *natural beings*. These nature gods had to extricate themselves from their origin and become historical beings in order to become truly independent, poetic beings. . . . Precisely the opposite will be the case in modern culture. It views the universe as history, as a moral realm, and to that extent it manifests itself as antithesis. The polytheism possible within it is possible only through delimitation in *time*, through historical delimitation. Its gods are gods of history. *They* will not be able to become truly gods, living, independent, and poetic, until they have taken possession of nature, or until they have become nature gods.[219]

Such a deification of history would be the final, logical extension of the move to rediscover the divine within the empirical realm. Once philosophy grasped the inner workings of history as well as it grasped the inner workings of nature, it would be possible to view the totality of events as "the greatest and most marvelous drama, which only an infinite mind could have composed."[220]

In the end, Schelling maintained, the new mythology would arise as part of a general rebirth of society as an ethical and religious totality, in other words, a "nation." "Only out of the spiritual unity of a people, from a truly public life, can the true and universally valid poetry arise—just as science and religion only find their objectivity in the spiritual and political unity of a people."[221] The locus of that unity, he concluded, was the state. Here he meant neither the rationalist absolutism of the Enlightenment nor a parliamentary democracy of the type attempted in France but presumably some republican form of monarchy. By 1803 Schelling had emerged as a critic of what he dismissively rejected as "so-called civil freedom" and "so-called natural rights."[222] Instead, he desired an "ethical totality" in which art, science, and religion were fused with the needs and rhythms of public life. The polarities of contemporary civil society and Christianity would then disappear, to be replaced by a state that resembled a work of art. At that point, philosophy would no longer be mere science but life itself, and Plato's dream of a "republic" would finally be achieved.

The moment of the "new mythology" would be short-lived. By the time he delivered his Jena lectures on the philosophy of art, Schelling's situation had grown intolerable thanks to a nasty squabble with the *Jenaische allgemeine Literatur-Zeitung* and continued rumors surrounding his marriage. In 1803 he accepted a position to teach in Würzburg, now a part of the Kingdom of Bavaria, where he immediately fell into conflict with advocates of the Catholic Aufklärung, which was then reaching the peak of its influence.[223] In reviews and pamphlets they accused this northern carpetbagger of attempting to set up a new form of mystery-mongering, Rosicrucianism, or Jesuitism.[224] This was a criticism echoed by others, notably the Protestant neo-Kantian philosopher Jakob Friedrich Fries, who in his *Neue Kritik der Vernunft* (1807) accused Schelling and the early Romantics of dragging Christianity down to the level of an "oriental" paganism. By this time, Schelling had begun to rethink some of his basic assumptions concerning the nature of religion, philosophy, and the state, turning away from the identity philosophy of 1801–4 toward a system that emphasized the primacy of the Fall and the limitations of human reason. With the world now seen as corrupted by evil, it became impossible to imagine a reenchantment of nature or public life. After 1804, Schelling came to view religion as primarily esoteric, dropping the revolutionary demands for a new mythology in a favor of a philosophical form of Christianity.

If the Jena Romantics veered toward conservatism after 1804, however, their idea of a new mythology would retain its appeal for generations to come. The institution of neohumanism within the German academic system guaranteed that large numbers of intellectuals would idealize ancient Greek culture as an unsurpassed fusion of religious, aesthetic, and public life. For them, the creation of a new body of sacred narrative and imagery promised a way beyond the fragmentation and simple bad taste of contemporary life, while granting a major role to intellectuals and artists in the society to come. All the world could become Wörlitz, and Wörlitz could become all the world. The notion of a new mythology was not simply a product of Philhellenist aestheticism, however. For, in addition, it was a powerful challenge to the symbols and dogmas of a Protestant Christianity that appeared to be in decline. Three previous decades of enlightened criticism of the Old and New Testaments had not only undermined belief in miracles but also rendered the Bible a document of a foreign but still proximate people (the Jews). In this situation, many educated elites came to see true religion as residing outside the church and its doctrines. But whereas the Neologists identified religiosity as moral behavior within civil society, the early Romantics sought religion, defined as an appearance of the divine, or "theophany," in the realm of individual human creativity.

Despite their rhetoric of a "new religion," the early Romantics' attitude toward Christianity was marked by considerable ambivalence. Although they rejected the Christian dogmas of God, original sin, and the immortality of the soul, they still saw Christianity as constitutive of their own philosophical and critical standpoint. Schelling and August Wilhelm Schlegel, in particular, relied in their writings on a historical scheme that echoed certain features of the earlier biblical narrative, but now with the transition from Old to New Testaments replaced by the shift from pagan antiquity to Christian modernity. Starting from an organic view of Greek society, Schelling traced the collapse of this culture in the face of an "oriental" or "feminine" ideal that found its historical expression in Christianity. In this scheme, Judaism and the Bible were essentially outward shells of an inward ideal content. As a result, there was no reason to expect their images or narratives to play a role in the new mythology, which would be constituted under the sign of *Naturphilosophie*. Schelling's "classicist" standpoint, with its close affinities to the thought of Schiller and Moritz, divided him from Friedrich Schlegel, whose affirmation of reflection, subjectivity, and the "nonclassical" was far less guarded and whose historical vision has been aptly described as one of "infinite perfectibility."[225] Schlegel was thus far less sanguine than Schelling about a possible return of paganism and the holistic society it seemed to imply. Rather than fighting off the "infinite" as a monstrous Titan, he sought to incorporate it into his understanding of religion and his vision of a new mythology.

In the end, however, it was Schelling's vision of an organic mythological society that would exercise the more profound influence on later generations of Romantics, including Jacob Grimm, Heinrich Heine, Richard Wagner, and the early Nietzsche. To a greater or lesser extent, each would accept the fundamental dichotomy between naïve paganism and a supposed "oriental" longing for the infinite, a division that often translated into an opposition between Hellenism and Judaism or, as circumstances dictated, Protestantism and Catholicism. Such views would not go unchallenged, however, as other scholars sought to deconstruct this rigid narrative by complicating the image of either antiquity or modernity. This fundamental debate, with its merger of confessional, theological, and aesthetic categories, would come to the fore in the next three decades, as the discourse on myth was taken up by advocates of the nationalist cause.

CHAPTER TWO

The Construction of a National Mythology:
The Romantic and *Vormärz* Eras

Christianity has emptied Walhalla, felled the sacred groves, extirpated the national imagery as a shameful superstition, as a devilish poison, and given us instead the imagery of a nation whose climate, laws, culture, and interests are strange to us and whose history has no connection whatever with our own. A David or a Solomon lives in our popular imagination, but our country's own heroes slumber in learned history books, and, for the scholars who write them, Alexander or Caesar is as interesting as the story of Charlemagne or Frederick Barbarossa. Except perhaps for Luther in the eyes of Protestants, what heroes could we have had, we who were never a nation? . . . [W]e are without any religious imagery *[Phantasie]* which is homegrown or linked with our history, and we are without any political imagery whatever; all that we have is the remains of an imagery of our own, lurking amid the common people under the name of superstition.[1]

So wrote Georg Wilhelm Friedrich Hegel in 1796. As a private tutor in Berne, he had witnessed from afar as the National Convention in France launched its campaign against the Catholic Church in 1793, staging the most audacious festivals in honor of a non-Christian deity since the fall of paganism. To some observers, the time seemed to have arrived when the European nations would abandon Christianity and turn to a religion like that of ancient Athens, whose yearly festivities commemorated the history and myths of the city's past. But Hegel surveyed the prospects for a national imagery in Germany and found them bleak. "The old German imagery has nothing in our day to connect or adapt itself to; it stands as cut off from the whole circle of our ideas, opinions, and beliefs, and is as strange to us as the imagery of Ossian or of India."[2] The Nordic myths of the *Edda* seemed too remote from the lives of modern Germans to experience a resurgence. Only the foreign heroes of the Hebrew Bible enjoyed a general familiarity among the population.

Somehow, Hegel believed, a new religious imagery would have to arise that would link local geography to the popular memory of uniquely German heroes, myths, and legends. "For the vulgar, familiarity with a place is generally . . . the most certain proof that the story told of it is true."[3] Such a mythology had existed among the ancient Hebrews, whose holy books resounded with the names of such familiar landmarks as Jerusalem, Hebron, and Mount Sinai. A similar mythology could also be found in Catholic Germany, where the lives of local saints and tales of nearby miracles had brought towns and villages into the heart of the Catholic faith far more effectively than the Old and New Testaments. The problem for Protestant Germany lay in establishing a "homegrown" imagery without relying on either the foreign myths of the Bible or the outmoded "superstitions" of Roman Catholicism.

Hegel was not the first German writer to identify this problem: it had been addressed as early as the 1760s by both Klopstock and Herder, and it was of common concern to Schelling and Hölderlin during their years in the *Stift*. Faced with this dilemma, the early Romantics had proposed a "new mythology" grounded in modernity itself rather than in the experience of any single people. But with the upsurge in nationalist sentiment during the French revolutionary and Napoleonic wars, an increasing number of scholars and writers insisted on a mythology that would be unmistakably "national." Undaunted by the paucity of sources, they attempted to recover the traces of a lost Germanic mythology, translating the medieval epics, gathering folk songs and fairy tales, excavating pagan burial mounds, and reinterpreting the Nordic gods in such a way that they became evidence of an earlier, pre-Christian religion. These scholars were guided in this project by the Herderian-Romantic discourse on myth, which posited an organic and necessary connection between the art, religion, and folklife of past nations. The result was a kind of "recovered memory"—therapeutic and self-affirming but based to only a limited extent on the historical record. Nonetheless, the themes and motives of this national mythology—the Rhine River, Wotan, Siegfried, Barbarossa—would eventually join such bourgeois culture heroes as Luther, Beethoven, Schiller, and Goethe in the canon of German literature.

The field of national mythology would remain deeply contested, however. Aside from those orthodox and enlightened critics who rejected the project entirely, advocates of a national mythology disagreed among themselves about its origins, nature, and cultural implications. Some commentators, such as August Wilhelm Schlegel, stressed the Christian quality of medieval epics and legends, whereas others, notably Jacob Grimm, viewed them as signs of an earlier Germanic paganism, whose legacy had persisted through the Middle Ages and survived in the customs and practices of contemporary folklife.[4] To a certain extent this conflict reflected a divergence between the literary-aesthetic perspective of early Romanticism and the scholarly concerns of a nascent Germanic philology. But it also pointed to the fundamental theological problem of how best to reconfigure the Christian religious narrative without relying on the Bible.[5] As in early Romanticism, the nexus of concern remained the transition from paganism to Catholicism, which was viewed alternatively as a spiritual triumph or as a moment of tragic loss. But now this history was explained in national terms, with the recovery of myth seen as a decisive moment in the self-assertion of the German *Volk*.

Voices of the *Vorzeit*: Folk Book and *Nibelungenlied*

For most scholars and writers, the path to a national mythology led through the forgotten texts and scattered remnants of the German past, or *Vorzeit*. In general, the term *Vorzeit* referred to the premodern era, which was seen as lasting from antiquity through the Reformation. But the very ambiguity of this word (translated literally as "pre-time") suggested a space outside the process of historical change. In the minds of most commentators, the *Vorzeit* seemed simpler, more pious, and more organically unified than the fragmented and disjointed contemporary world. For some, it was the inspiration for a future German community based on the principle of nationality. For others, however, the demands for a revolutionary transformation of the present gave way to a scholarly imperative that wedded reverence for the past with a rigorous attention to sources.

The fascination with things "old German" *(Altdeutsch)* was not new, of course.[6] Since the fifteenth century, there had been isolated attempts by humanist scholars to generate enthusiasm for the worlds depicted in Tacitus's *Germania* (A.D. 98) and in the poetic works of the High Middle Ages. By the seventeenth century, noble and private collectors had begun to assemble documents, weapons, and other artifacts from the pagan and medieval pasts.[7] But the decisive impulses toward a reevaluation of old German literature came in the wake of the English back-to-nature movement and the accompanying Homer craze. Having rediscovered the author of the *Iliad* as an illiterate bard, scholars in Britain sought to recover their own early poetic traditions. In Scotland, James MacPherson published the epic poem *Fingal* (1762), which he attributed to a Gaelic bard named "Ossian." It was eventually shown that *Fingal* was a creative forgery, but not before this epic had fired the imaginations of scholars and poets alike.

The search for an indigenous bardic tradition preoccupied German-speaking intellectuals as well. During the 1750s, the Zurich grammar-school teacher Johann Jakob Bodmer published a series of old German texts, including a manuscript of the *Nibelungenlied* and a collection of medieval love poems, or "Minnelieder." Over the next two decades, Friedrich Gottlob Klopstock and the Göttingen Grove poets (Johann Heinrich Voss, Ludwig C. H. Hölty, and the brothers Christian and Friedrich Graf zu Stolberg) produced a number of works based on the "old German" motifs found in medieval poetry, Nordic mythology, or the life of the pagan general Arminius (Hermann), who crushed Augustus's legions at the battle of the Teutoburg Forest in A.D. 9. These projects reflected the hope for a German equivalent to Homer, as well as a frustration with the dominance of French and Italian classicism in aristocratic and courtly culture. As such, they testified to a growing assertiveness among middle-class writers, as well as an emerging Protestant nationalism that, while still isolated, could take quite virulent form.[8]

The most wide-ranging and influential advocate of a German "national" poetry was Herder, whose historicist interpretation of the Old Testament formed just one aspect of a larger program to elevate the aesthetic status of nonclassical literatures.[9] Herder was an early and influential proponent of medieval "folk poetry," which he tried to disseminate to a broad German public. He described his *Alte Volkslieder* (1774) as a collection "not for the scholar . . . but for the nation! People! A body called fatherland," and hoped it would inspire the creation of a new national literature.[10] Herder was not interested in reviving the Middle Ages as a social or religious ideal, and like most Aufklärer he saw this era as suffering under an authoritarian clergy and an exploitative social and political system.[11] The value of medieval poetry lay rather in its evidence of a prior folk culture, akin to that which had produced Homer or Ossian. Herder viewed the roots of that culture as pre-Christian, and he regretted the Catholic Church's campaign against the pagan "legends, songs, customs, temples, and monuments," on "which the spirit of the people had [once] hung."[12]

The initiatives of Herder and other scholars notwithstanding, it was the French revolutionary and Napoleonic wars that transformed the study of Old High German literature from the pursuit of isolated intellectuals into a genuine aesthetic and scholarly movement.[13] Already in 1791, the gymnasium director and Herder enthusiast Friedrich David Gräter had founded *Bragur: Ein litterarisches Magazin der deutschen und nordischen Vorzeit*. Gräter described his journal as growing from a "love for our native antiquity and the desire to research the national spirit of our fathers through its literary remains and to share the resulting knowledge with our contemporaries."[14] Over its twenty-one-year existence, *Bragur* (named after the Nordic god of poetry) published not only scholarly investigations but also poems and stories based on the narratives and deities of old "German" mythology. In all of this, a distinct anti-French tone was unmistakable. Responding to critics who found the old German stories too coarse for modern tastes, Gräter commented that for sheer barbarity "Paris's human slaughter bench" outstripped any ancient mythology.[15]

In addition to fostering an interest in "national" myths, the French Revolution helped to spur a search for new sources of the German *Vorzeit*. As it turned out, not a single previously unknown Old High German or Middle High German poem was discovered after 1800.[16] What changed, however, was the level of interest in such manuscripts and the number of scholars and amateurs who sought them out. In addition, Napoleon's encroachments onto German territory and the subsequent secularization of church properties freed up a bounty of new texts for use. This resulted in a publication "mania," as scholars raced often insignificant or obscure fragments into print. Librarians and archivists opened the bindings of modern books and peered between their pages in the hope of discovering some literary-historical treasure.[17] "The sources, the sources are better than all your historical works of artifice," wrote one Germanist.[18] Taken together these sources were seen as constituting the cultural patrimony of the German nation.[19]

The rise of myth as a category of cultural analysis provided a crucial framework for understanding these texts. In the *Vorzeit*, it was maintained, the German heroic myth had supplied a psychological substrate, filling each phase of life with religious significance. Since then, however, it had split into a thousand fragments, which were now scattered across the German landscape. Each scrap of evidence was a potential piece of the lost mythology and thus worthy of collection and preservation. This understanding of myth allowed scholars to articulate and, to a certain extent, justify the sense of nostalgia that had attached to the old German past in the wake of the French Revolution.[20] In the works of the Grimm brothers, however, this feeling of loss shaded into something like postrevolutionary guilt, a mood increasingly shared by Romantic intellectuals. In his short treatise *Philosophie und Religion* (1804), Friedrich Schelling insisted on the fallen state of the world, while the Catholic philosopher Franz von Baader maintained in his writings that the devil was alive and well in the modern world. Such sentiments seemed confirmed in 1806, when Napoleon devastated the armies of Prussia and Austria, occupied Berlin, and brought an end to the Holy Roman Empire. For many Germanists, the recovery of old myths came to be seen less as the basis for a literary revival than as penance for an era that had elevated individual human reason to the supreme arbiter of nature and society. Such sentiments helped inspire the advocates of German national mythology in these years, even as they divided on the question of whether that mythology was Christian or pre-Christian.

Among literary scholars, August Wilhelm Schlegel forms a crucial link between the Jena circle of Romantics and the emerging discussion of national mythology.[21] Since 1801 he had become increasingly active in Berlin, where he held a series of lectures that promoted medieval German poetry as the expression of a specific knightly mythology *(Rittermythologie)*. In "Ueber das Mittelalter" (1803), A. W. Schlegel rejected received notions of a medieval barbarism, arguing that this was an era of physical and spiritual greatness for the German races. "The knightly spirit emerged from the combination of the robust and honest bravery of the German North with a completely spiritual religion coming from the Orient—Christianity, an occurrence that was not just brilliant but truly enchanting, and hitherto without parallel in human history."[22] In organizations like the Knights Templar, the spirit of knighthood fused with that of monasticism, giving rise to a Christian mythology that centered on brave saints, bold quests, and crusading wars of religion.

According to Schlegel, the Middle Ages had suffered too long from the condescension of later generations. This was an era in which women were honored and esteemed by knights and poets alike. Feudalism, often condemned as the height of despotism, was actually well suited to the needs of a military "republic," in which the strong not only ruled over the weak but served them as defenders and warriors. The duel—long criticized by enlightened reformers—was an integral component of the old system of honor and a worthy inheritance from the *Vorzeit*. The launching of the Crusades, seen by critics as the height of barbarism, in fact represented a triumph of the monotheistic idea over the people's natural instinct for self-preservation. "The tolerance of modern Europe—what is it other than disguised indifference, self-satisfied glorification of slackness?" Schlegel asked. Taking aim at the enlightened theologies of his day, he criticized the attempt to strip Christianity of any sense of "rage against iniquity" and praised the clear sense of good and evil that animated the medieval romance.[23]

In Schlegel's view, the stories celebrated in knightly mythology were based on actual historical events. Even accounts of a single knight killing a thousand men in battle could not be dismissed simply because of the "present-day disbelief in the *Vorzeit.*"[24] The earliest race of German heroes, especially those who lived before the era of Charlemagne, were braver, stronger, and physically larger than the men they fought and the generations that succeeded them.[25] Their deeds formed the basis of the *Nibelungenlied, Parsifal,* and the *Heldenbuch,* as well as the legends of King Arthur and the Round Table. If Europe was to acquire greatness once again, the medieval era would have to be redeemed in the eyes of the present. "Those giant shadows, which appear to us as through a fog, must again acquire firm outlines, and the image of the *Vorzeit* must once more be animated by its own unique soul."[26] In this way, present-day culture would turn against an enlightenment that had robbed it of its religious and spiritual mission, leaving it vulnerable to the forces of "financial trickery" and political despotism. For A. W. Schlegel, therefore, the revival of medieval Christian mythology formed part of a program of "European patriotism," which would displace the harmful legacy of the French revolutionary wars and eventually unite the continent.[27]

The exaltation of the Middle Ages was given even more grandiloquent expression in the writings of Joseph Görres.[28] Born in the Catholic city of Koblenz, Görres was an enthusiastic Jacobin until a trip to Paris in 1799— just as Napoleon was seizing power—left him disillusioned with the French republic and its occupation of the Rhineland. Withdrawing into study, Görres mastered the *Naturphilosophie* of Baader and Schelling before turning to mythology. His works on this theme, which he wrote in Heidelberg between 1805 and 1810, combined historical erudition with the drunken gaze of a mystic. They also attracted the allegiance of his Heidelberg colleagues Archim von Arnim and Clemens Brentano, who behaved around him "like traveling schoolboys."[29] While these two poets reworked the folk songs that would form *Des Knaben Wunderhorn* (1806), Görres turned to a set of popular stories, romances, and tales dating from the sixteenth century, which he published in 1807 as *Die teutschen Volksbücher.*

Görres's preface set the tone. The narrator is wandering along a brook, trying to fathom its sounds, when he meets an old monk who leads him into an ancient cathedral. "We came, deep in the base of the cathedral, into the glimmering chapel where Friedrich Barbarossa sat. His beard had grown through the table. Around him crowded all the old heroes." They included Reinhold, Siegfried, Hagen, Charlemagne, Octavian, Wolfdieterich, and others. "Barbarossa looked up. 'What do you seek among the dead, stranger?' 'I am seeking life. In a drought one must dig the wells deep before one comes upon the sources.'"[30] It was an apt metaphor for the Romantic mythographer, for while Görres did not have to travel far to acquire the *Volksbücher* (most were pro-

Joseph Görres at work. Drawing by Wilhelm von Kaulbach.
Source: Joseph Görres, *Ausgewählte Werke und Briefe*, ed. Wilhelm Schellberg
(Mepten and Munich: Kösel, 1911), frontispiece.

vided to him by Brentano), he believed they offered access to the deepest sources of German folklife. "The writings that we are discussing constitute nothing less than the entire real mass of the *Volk* in its sphere of action. Literature has never won a greater range or broader dissemination than when it left the closed circle of the higher estates and broke through to the lower classes, lived among them, became with the *Volk* a part of the *Volk*, flesh from its flesh, life from its life."[31] The *Volksbücher* were the written memory of a mythical tradition that had once penetrated every estate and every nation of Europe, forming a common cycle of folk songs and legends.

Whereas A. W. Schlegel had drawn a firm distinction between ancient and Christian mythologies, Görres stressed the continuity of myth across history. The homeland of myth lay in India, whence it had spread to Persia, Egypt, Greece, and, eventually, northern Europe. "Every young age, when it was born, found its crib surrounded with gifts that the wise men from the Orient [Morgen], the center [Mittag], and the West [Abendlande] brought to it."[32] This theory of the Asian origins of European culture had roots in the Edda but had recently acquired a more scholarly grounding in the linguistic studies of William Jones. Over the next decade it would be developed in greater detail by Friedrich Schlegel, the Heidelberg philologist Friedrich Creuzer, and Görres himself in the massive Mythengeschichte der asiatischen Welt (1810).[33]

According to Görres, German art achieved its most perfect expression during the High Middle Ages, when the Crusades led to an intermingling of the Christian poetic tradition with those of Asia, inspiring the Minnelieder and epics of German Romance. As he buried his readers under images of sweet aromas, fulsome blossoms, and pompous grandeur, Görres exalted medieval art, religion, and society. Christianity had triumphed over the sensualism of paganism; prayer had lifted hearts toward the invisible and the ideal; as poets discovered Romantic love, sexual relations took on a symbolic importance beyond mere biology; heroes were inspired to noble deeds; and art experienced a transfiguration as it rose to meet the new God. But even after the victory of Christianity, the Middle Ages were shot through with a festival life that recalled pagan antiquity. "[N]ow follows a crowd and a festive parade from all estates. Priests, laypeople, kings, dukes, knights, women, all join in the dithyramb. As if a magic wand had touched the entire race, all act in beautiful enthusiasm. The choirs marched jubilantly, swinging the thyrsus for two centuries through the forests, castles, cities."[34] All distinctions of class, gender, and rank disappeared in an ecstasy of harmony, free from the destructive gaze of pedants and journalists.

This vision of medieval mythology reflected a deep nostalgia for the Reich that had gone under the previous year. Citing the Holy Roman Empire's "special constitution," Görres celebrated the multiplicity of the old imperial political structure, with its intermingling of dynastic principalities, Hanseatic towns, and knightly estates, "never monotony and ruling force, the whole invented in total freedom and artfully joined together."[35] A reign of poetry rather than political uniformity had held the Holy Roman Empire together, and no European nation was excluded from its "festival of life."[36] By contrast, Görres spoke harshly of the twin demands of "gold" and "iron" that marked the modern age.[37] He complained of a market-driven modern literature, which he blamed on the upper classes' taste for foreign fashions and the failure of journals and newspapers to create an authentic "public opinion" in Germany.[38] Yet Görres was equally dismissive of attempts to produce poetry according to standards dictated by classical philology's "industrial *Spinnschulen*" ("spinning," but also "crazy," schools).[39] Instead, modern art would have to develop its own forms, based on the characteristics of the present, Christian era. "Trusting in ourselves, we should develop our own particularity as they developed theirs . . . : then the gods will be gracious and send better times."[40]

A rather different view of national mythology was offered by Jacob Grimm (1785–1863).[41] Grimm's father, a judicial official in Hanau, died when he and his younger siblings were still children, leaving Jacob the task of supporting his family even as he worked to establish his own career. He and his younger brother Wilhelm (1786–1859) would eventually choose law, studying in Marburg under the legal historian Friedrich Karl von Savigny. Savigny was instrumental in the intellectual development of the Grimms, providing them with stipends, sharing his library, and infecting them with a zeal for old German history. Savigny also introduced the brothers to some of the key figures in the emerging Heidelberg school of Romanticism, including Arnim, Brentano, and Friedrich Creuzer. In 1805, Jacob accepted the first of a series of government posts in Cassel, which involved serving first the Electorate of Hesse-Cassel, then the Napoleonic Kingdom of Westphalia, and after 1813 the restored Grand Duchy of Hesse. Through much of this time Grimm worked as a librarian, which allowed him time to research and write about German literature while cultivating the circle of friends and fellow scholars that helped secure his preeminence within the emerging field of Germanic philology.[42] Only in 1830 did he accept a university position in Göttingen.

From early on, Jacob Grimm departed from the assumptions that had guided A. W. Schlegel and, to a lesser extent, Görres in their discussions of medieval mythology. Grimm viewed myth as the poetic embodiment of a revelation given by God to all peoples. "The mythical is the pure water that the earth drank from the very beginning, at every appearance new and fresh," Grimm wrote Savigny.[43] Thus, myth could not be reduced to history or to a scientific cosmology without evaporating its inner essence. Instead, it was best grasped as a living phenomenon, which resided in the soul of an entire nation rather than in the experience of any single individual. This view of myth, as Otfrid Ehrisman has noted, owed much to Schelling's philosophies of nature and art. Just as Schelling described nature as a poem "that lies concealed in a secret, miraculous script," Grimm viewed myth as a form of

Naturpoesie that proceeded from the unconsciousness of the *Volk* rather than from the pen of a single writer.[44]

Grimm traced the origins of Germanic mythology to the period of the great migrations, when the peoples and languages of the earth had begun to spread from the East.[45] But while he accepted the possibility of similarities between different mythical traditions, Grimm refused to see them as simply transferable from one nation to another. In his view, Germanic myth was intimately bound up with the language, customs, and peculiar history of the Germanic peoples. Moreover, Grimm drew a sharp distinction between this mythology and the beliefs and doctrines of Christianity. He rejected Schlegel's notion of a *Rittermythologie,* arguing that what was living and vital in the medieval tradition was derived from a submerged pre-Christian paganism rather than Roman Catholicism or knightly culture. "[O]ne only has to understand existing legends and poems mythically in order to discover in them elements and components quite similar to those in Greek religion."[46] This involved penetrating beneath the political and social context of the Middle Ages, which Grimm had no interest in vindicating, and exposing the hidden sources of language and folklife.

Grimm's understanding of myth entailed a new understanding of medieval epic poetry. He maintained that epic was the result of the merger of a divine element (myth) with a real, historical element (a deed). While the historical event provided the occasion for the epic, the mythical substrate determined its narrative form. This could be seen in the legend of William Tell, which had numerous parallels in the German tradition and whose main character was related etymologically to earlier and later heroes. "[W]hat a growth of epic life lies between the divine idea and succeeding ages, in which it enters reborn a thousand times into human history! Poetry, the epic is exactly this nourishing medium, this earthly happiness, within which we live and breathe, this bread of life, wider and freer than the present (history, a past present), narrower and more limited than revelation (the timeless origin)."[47] Rather than confining the epic tradition to the Middle Ages, Jacob Grimm suggested a much deeper mythical tradition, which had originated in the earliest encounters of the Germanic peoples with the geography of central Europe and persisted now in fragmentary form in the sayings and customs of the common people, most notably in the fairy tales that he and Wilhelm published as the *Kinder- und Hausmärchen* (1812–15).

Despite Grimm's early affinity for the highly speculative philologies of Görres, Creuzer, and Johann Arnold Kanne, he was able to achieve a position of respect and influence in the emerging scholarly discipline of *Germanistik.* He did so not by obtaining a university professorship but instead by estab-

Jacob Grimm in 1814. Copper engraving by O. Felsing.
Source: *Archim von Arnim und die ihm nahe standen,* ed. Reinhold Steig (Stuttgart and Berlin: Cotta, 1904), vol. 3, frontispiece.

lishing a circle of scholars who claimed the title of "science" for the work they did and dismissed the efforts of competitors as amateurish or "popular." In the absence of conferences, colloquia, or a central scholarly journal, the Grimm brothers relied on letters to cement their relationships with scholars like G. F. Benecke and Karl Lachmann, who strove to found a genuine "Germanic philology." Meanwhile, they used book reviews to denigrate the work of scholars who did not meet their standards of science, including Gräter, A. W. Schlegel, and Friedrich von der Hagen.[48] In doing so, they identified themselves with the (Protestant) scholarly ethos articulated by Friedrich August Wolf in his *Prolegomena ad Homerum* (1795), which was based on diligence, hard work, and attention to the sources. With classical philology as the model, it was unsurprising that the early Germanists became embroiled in their own version of the "Homer question": the debate concerning the origins and authorship of the *Nibelungenlied*.

The *Nibelungenlied* was poorly suited for the role it was chosen to play in German history. Scholars generally agree that the extant version of the poem was composed around 1200 for performance at a royal court, probably in the Danube region of central Europe.[49] But it drew on traditions of myth, legend, and poetry that dated back as early as the fifth century A.D. One set of legends was based on the fall of the Kingdom of Burgundy in 437 to a combined army of Romans and Huns, the latter thought (wrongly) to have been led by Attila. These songs were at some point combined with a set of Norse traditions concerning the dragon-slayer Sigurd and his bride Brünhild. In its final form, the *Nibelungenlied* offered a sweeping epic in which greed, lust, and treachery predominate and God is strangely absent.[50]

The story begins with Siegfried, son of King Siegmund of the Netherlands, leaving his home to visit Gunther, king of Burgundy, in Worms. The impetuous hero has already garnered fame by killing a dragon and conquering the treasure of the Nibelungen, a race of men living in the North. In Worms, Siegfried falls in love with Gunther's sister Kriemhild, "so fair that none in any land could be fairer."[51] In order to win permission to marry Kriemhild, Siegfried agrees to help Gunther wed the queen of Iceland, Brünhild. This is no easy task because any suitor for Brünhild's hand must defeat her in a medieval triathlon consisting of the javelin throw, a rock throw, and the long jump. If the suitor fails to win her hand, he loses his head. Gunther does not have much confidence in his abilities, and not wanting to lose his head he arranges that Siegfried accompany him to Iceland disguised as a vassal. There, rendered invisible by a magic cloak, Siegfried wins the contest with Brünhild, while Gunther merely goes through the motions. With the Icelandic queen bound to Gunther, Siegfried faces one final task: subduing Brünhild, who has fought off Gunther's advances on their wedding night. Under cover of darkness, Siegfried overcomes Brünhild, stealing her ring and girdle in the process.

With Brünhild reconciled to living with Gunther, Siegfried takes Kriemhild back home to the Netherlands. All seems fine until Siegfried and Kriemhild pay a visit to Worms. There, during a spat between Kriemhild and Brünhild over who has higher status, Kriemhild shows Brünhild the ring and reveals the true story behind her marriage to Gunther. Enraged, Brünhild hatches a plot for Siegfried's destruction, to which Gunther accedes. On a hunt in the forest, Gunther's vassal Hagen plunges a spear into the back of

Siegfried. Hagen and Gunther's betrayal of Siegfried transforms Kriemhild into a vengeful Fury, and she becomes further enraged when Gunther and Hagen steal Siegfried's treasure and hide it in the Rhine River. The second half of the *Nibelungenlied* describes Kriemhild's plot to exact revenge on Gunther and Hagen. First, she marries Etzel (Attila), the king of the Huns. Then she invites her relatives to visit her new home in Etzelburg. Gunther accepts the offer but Hagen is suspicious, and he convinces his king to bring along one thousand warriors. Once the guests arrive, Kriemhild orders that they be attacked, and a long and frightful battle ensues between the Burgundians and the Huns. At the end of the fighting, Gunther and Hagen are captured and taken to Kriemhild. With her antagonists at her mercy, she kills Gunther and then, when he refuses to divulge the location of the treasure, Hagen. Kriemhild's murderous deeds stir another knight into such a fury that he hacks the queen to pieces.

This unsavory tale corresponded only imperfectly with the aesthetic standards of early or later Romanticism. The story was not especially Christian, nor was it especially pagan. The Nordic deities made no appearance, and only the superhuman characters of Siegfried and Brünhild touched on the properly mythical realm. The tragic confrontation of divine and mortal that drove Homeric epic was all but absent: where the text was not obviously a patchwork most of the action could be explained by purely human motives. Further, the poem failed to embody the "German values" of its modern-day champions. Through much of the epic, fearsome women and bellicose men engage in a sometimes mindless bloodfest. The characters of Brünhild and Kriemhild hardly conformed to the womanly ideals so praised by A. W. Schlegel and Joseph Görres. Further, the aristocratic quality of loyalty *(Treue)*, while frequently invoked, seemed to be undermined—even mocked—by the cruel actions it was used to justify.

These defects did not prevent German scholars from launching a campaign to raise the visibility and importance of the *Nibelungenlied* in German culture.[52] Though stories of Siegfried were familiar from the *Volksbücher*, it was not until 1755 that a full manuscript of the *Nibelungenlied* was discovered; two years later it was published by Johann Jakob Bodmer. During the 1780s, a center of Nibelungen research sprang up in Cassel around the historian Johannes von Müller, who proposed that this epic become a German version of the *Iliad*.[53] But these efforts remained isolated and without impact. It was not until the first decade of the nineteenth century that the reception of the *Nibelungenlied* gained momentum as both a scholarly and a national enterprise.

The center of this activity was Berlin. Already in 1803, A. W. Schlegel

devoted a series of lectures to the *Nibelungenlied*.[54] Schlegel dated the poem
back to the fifth century and treated at least its last half as an accurate reflection of history. He esteemed the poetic quality of the *Nibelungenlied* as
superior in some ways to the *Iliad*, a fact he ascribed to the greater convictions and truer passions of the earliest Germans.[55] Moreover, while the epic
contained elements derived from pagan myth, Schlegel maintained that its
overall character was Christian, in the spirit of medieval knighthood. This
Christian character determined the *Nibelungenlied*'s overarching sense of
justice. Each character's demise could be traced to a certain fatal flaw, be it
egoism or hubris. Further, the entire story turned on the original theft of the
treasure, which disappeared into the river once its mischief had been completed.[56] This tragic element made the *Nibelungenlied* particularly suitable
for a dramatic reworking. "If our national mythology is ever successfully renewed, a number of narrower, more limited dramatic works could be developed out of this epic tragedy. After we have roamed all corners of the earth,
we should finally begin to use our indigenous poetry."[57] Schlegel thus made
it his goal to turn the *Nibelungenlied* into a central book of the German
people, proposing that the *Nibelungenlied* and the *Heldenbuch* be read in
schools as "holy texts": "The latter would be our *Odyssey* and the former our
Iliad."[58]

Between 1807 and 1813, the *Nibelungenlied* became by all accounts
quite fashionable in the salon culture of Berlin, a fad encouraged by the
wearying conditions of French occupation and the surge of nationalist sentiment among educated elites.[59] In 1807, Friedrich von der Hagen issued a
popular reworking of the epic, and within a few years five different editions
of the *Nibelungenlied* had been published or announced. For his efforts von
der Hagen was appointed in 1810 to the first chair of German philology, at the
newly founded Friedrich Wilhelm University. Two years later, August Zeune
held a series of public lectures on the *Nibelungenlied* before an audience of
about three hundred. Here he demanded that the epic serve as the basis of a
national education, which would reduce the preeminence of French culture
and lay the groundwork for eventual political unification.[60] Meanwhile, numerous groups sponsored public readings of the epic. Schlegel believed that
these efforts, combined with efforts by poets to imitate the *Nibelungenlied*,
marked a "return to the womb of the *Vorzeit*, the great means for a rebirth of
an original language that has never been separated from its roots."[61] But while
the warlike character of the epic and its emphasis on revenge proved useful
in stirring up dreams of retaliation against France, it did not provide a vision
of the national community once vengeance had been taken.[62]

The ambiguous morality of the *Nibelungenlied* haunted most attempts to rework it in a strictly Christian spirit. In 1808, Baron Friedrich de la Motte Fouqué published *Sigurd, der Schlangentödter*, the first drama of his Nibelungen trilogy *Der Held des Nordens*. A scion of Huguenot nobles and a veteran of the revolutionary wars, Fouqué had returned in 1803 to his wife's estate near Berlin, where he became active in the literary and cultural life of the city. In 1810, he would become a founding a member of the Christlich-deutsche Tischgesellschaft, an organization dedicated to the "Christian" rebirth of Germany. Fouqué took up the *Nibelungenlied* at the suggestion of Schlegel, who in an 1806 letter had emphasized Germany's need for an "alert, immediate, energetic, and especially a patriotic poetry."[63] Like Schlegel, Fouqué saw the epic as the raw material for a Christian tragedy, but he was also interested in placing it within a wider context of Nordic mythology. Such links were already available in "Der gehörnte Siegfried" in Görres's *Volksbücher*, the Icelandic *Volsungssaga* (ca. 1270), and earlier Eddic lays on the life and death of Siegfried.

In his reworking of the *Nibelungenlied*, Fouqué anticipated Richard Wagner's *Ring* in several particulars. For example, he conceived of the *Nibelungenlied* as a trilogy on the model of Aeschylus.[64] Further, he introduced the Norns at the beginning of the play, which symbolized the three ages of the world: past, present, and future. Fouqué was the first to raise the iconic significance of Gramur, Siegfried's sword, tracing it back to the confrontation between Siegmund (Siegfried's father) and Wotan. He was also the first to portray the relationship of Siegfried ("Sigurd" in this play) to a treacherous dwarf, who relates the story of the theft of the Nibelungen treasure just as he is dying. "Protect yourself from the marvelous treasure! Watch out for Andwar's ring. A curse threatens it and will seize you after Reigen's [the dwarf's] and Faffner's demise."[65]

Sigurd also brought Brünhild into the center of the action. Unlike the thirteenth-century version of the epic, in Fouqué's drama Brünhild and Siegfried have already been lovers before they meet in the famous Icelandic competition. Well before meeting Gunther, Siegfried, "the hero who never knew fear," climbs through a circle of fire to reach Brünhild.[66] The two remain happily married until a love potion mixed by Gunther's mother causes Siegfried to forget Brünhild and fall in love with Gudrun (Kriemhild). When Brünhild learns of her betrayal by Siegfried, she becomes a frightful and more than slightly insane figure, who speaks in riddles but skillfully manipulates the weaknesses and sexual lusts of Gunther and his brother to bring about Siegfried's death. Then, after stabbing herself with Gramur, she demands that Gunther arrange a "death marriage" on Siegfried's funeral pyre. With the fire lit, Brünhild throws herself on the flames in order to die next to her hero.

In his effort to create a "Christian" epic, Fouqué highlighted the elements of sin, guilt, and the erotic in the *Nibelungenlied*. The driving figures in *Sigurd* are women like Brünhild, who use their sexual and magical influence over men to carry out the work of fate. Schlegel had already argued that in a Christian epic, magic was to be seen as a manifestation of evil and prophecy as a "message from Hell."[67] By rending Siegfried's marriage to Brünhild asunder and causing Gunther to abandon his oath to Siegfried, these forces undermined the principle of personal loyalty on which the feudal world rested. But by linking evil to female sexuality, Fouqué seemed to invert Schlegel's conception of a *Rittermythologie,* in which love—rather than hatred—of women drives the poetic process. Further, although this Siegfried possessed a Christian sense of guilt and an awareness of the powers bearing down upon him, in Fouqué's trilogy, as in the epic itself, salvation comes to no one.[68] That, too, squared uneasily with the idea of a "Christian mythology."

Many of Fouqué's Berlin peers, including Jean Paul Richter, E. T. A. Hoffmann, Friedrich von der Hagen, and Rahel Levin, greeted *Sigurd* warmly.[69] But others observed the revival of the *Nibelungenlied* with a measure of apprehension. Wilhelm Grimm, who viewed Berlin as the "pinnacle of all modern, bright, glossy, and elegant cities," published an ambivalent but generally negative review in the *Heidelberger Jahrbücher.*[70] Clemens Brentano reported that, when asked by Fouqué how he had liked the play, he had replied, "not only not at all but less than his other things, which I also didn't like."[71] But the most principled opponent was Jacob Grimm, who wrote Wilhelm that he would have criticized *Sigurd* much more harshly than his brother had. "I see in the whole work nothing but poetic cleverness, . . . nothing to bring the legend closer to the human heart."[72]

Jacob Grimm's critique of Fouqué reflected his discomfort with the growing demand for explicitly "national" art. "I don't understand how one can demand from modern poets, in other words dramatic poets, that they work in the direction of nationality, when a certain national essence always and unavoidably appears on its own."[73] This national essence could not be fostered or invented; instead, it would take form through its own inward power, which individual artists should not attempt to steer. Passionate in his insistence that the past be past, Jacob Grimm disapproved of all attempts to renew or rework the old mythology into a form that might make it easier for the public to comprehend.[74] He disliked von der Hagen's "popular" translation of the *Nibelungenlied* and even rejected Arnim and Brentano's *Wunderhorn* as a needless accommodation to contemporary tastes. "Just as foreign, noble animals cannot wander from their native territory onto another without suffering and dying, so the majesty of the old poetry cannot be resurrected universally, i.e., poetically. It can be enjoyed undisturbed only historically. Whoever wants to meet the miserable kangaroos must travel to Australia; captured lions and tigers must always be caged and go around and around in a sad figure eight."[75] German myth belonged to a pagan past and distant terrain that could not be made present—except in the quiet hours of study. This attitude helped determine Jacob Grimm's stance in the controversy surrounding the authorship of the *Nibelungenlied*. For the German epic had no Homer, and this set scholars off on a hunt through the annals of medieval literature for clues to its origin.

Many of these scholars took their cue from Friedrich August Wolf's *Prolegomena ad Homerum* (1795), which had overturned the notion that a single author wrote the *Iliad*. Already in his Berlin lectures, A. W. Schlegel had begun to apply aspects of Wolf's approach to the *Nibelungenlied*. "It is perhaps fruitless, as it is in regards to the Greek epics, to ask for a first single indivisible author of the song of the Nibelungen. Such a work is too great for one person, it is the product of the entire power of an age."[76] Schlegel even suggested the idea of German *diaskeuasts*, who had stitched together various poetic fragments into a larger whole. Still, he recognized in the poem earmarks of unity and craftsmanship that could not have come about randomly or in the work of a group. Instead, the poem must have been brought into its final form by some single individual. In an 1812 article, Schlegel proposed Heinrich von Ofterdingen, best known as a character in the thirteenth-century poem "Der Wartburgkrieg," as the "final author" of the *Nibelungenlied*.[77]

By identifying a single individual with the *Nibelungenlied*, Schlegel wandered into the crosshairs of the Grimm brothers. They were already upset by Schlegel's review of their journal *Altdeutsche Wälder* (1813–15), which had offered a devastating (and largely justified) critique of the brothers' historical and philological methodology.[78] If Ofterdingen were the author of the *Nibelungenlied*, Jacob now argued, he could only be a "mythical" author in the way that Homer was the mythical author of the *Iliad*. Further, there could be no talk of final copyists or last poets: "as we possess it, the *Nibelungen* is nothing other than the living reworking of the poem as it emerged inwardly and necessarily from popular poetry. There is no decisive external or internal reason to ascribe it to Heinrich von Ofterdingen."[79] The spontaneous and unconscious process that had given rise to myth itself had also shaped the final form of the *Nibelungenlied*. The epic's dramatic power and subtle characterizations, which Schlegel believed to be the mark of a poet, were instead brought forth from the soul of the nation.

In terms of the "facts" of this matter, the positions of A. W. Schlegel and

Jacob Grimm were actually quite close; both agreed that the *Nibelungenlied* had emerged from a series of earlier lays and songs and had reached its final form only in the twelfth century. At the heart of their dispute lay a tension within the Romantic discourse of myth concerning the relative weight that should be placed on individual reflection versus unconscious forces within nature or the *Volk* in describing the origin of myth. This ambiguity was already present in *Frühromantik* proposals for a "new mythology": while Friedrich Schlegel emphasized the ability of conscious creativity to bring forth a new system of narratives and symbols, Schelling stressed the role of a new "race" that would be generated from the internal processes of history. In the context of the *Nibelungenlied* dispute, A. W. Schlegel maintained that it was possible for a poet to generate an epic in a dialectical relationship with the unconscious material produced by the people. This might take place in different stages, but it remained the process by which poetry was generated. Jacob Grimm, by contrast, believed that there was essentially one mythical power, which operated behind and within human history but could not be possessed by it. This power had brought forth the *Nibelungenlied:* first as *Naturpoesie,* later as epic poetry. "As God becomes man, so also the divine stories appear again as human," Grimm explained.[80] It was thus impossible for a single individual to claim access to myth or any of its derivatives: legend, epic, or the fairy tale.

The question of the authorship of the *Nibelungenlied* was bound up with a further dispute concerning the religious nature of medieval epic. Schlegel's insistence on a *Rittermythologie,* which was grounded not just in the particularities of the German races but also in the experience of Catholic Christianity, affirmed hopes for a poetic rebirth within modernity. The Christian era had already brought forth the works of Dante, Shakespeare, and Calderón. If Europe returned to its Christian foundations while breaking free of the tyranny of commerce in its public life, Schlegel suggested, a similar poetic renaissance might be possible. Jacob Grimm, by stressing the pre-Christian origins of the medieval epic, seemed to deny the possibility of mythical art within the conditions of Christian modernity. The best one could hope for was a reappropriation of that mythical essence via scholarship, which for Grimm became the privileged medium of access to the divine revelation.

In the end, the dispute over the authorship of the *Nibelungenlied* was resolved by neither Schlegel nor Grimm, but by Karl Lachmann (1793–1851), generally regarded as one of the founders of scientific *Germanistik*. In *Ueber die ursprüngliche Gestalt des Gedichts von der Nibelungen Noth* (1816), Lachmann abandoned the notion of a final author. Using form criticism, he proposed a series of sixteen Wolfian song-units, which were combined together by medieval *diaskeuasts* to form the twelfth-century version of the epic.[81] Lachmann knew he was walking into a potential minefield, and he initially attempted to mediate the positions of Grimm and Schlegel.[82] Eventually, however, he aligned himself with the Grimms, accepting their view that the origin of the *Nibelungenlied* lay in legend, not history. Yet, as Lothar Bluhm has noted, this represented more of a tactical alliance than a real meeting of minds. Both scholars rejected a *telos* of mythography that ended anywhere beyond scholarship itself (e.g., in literature), but while Grimm was interested primarily in the cultural milieu that produced the medieval epic, Lachmann confined his studies to the texts themselves. This difference in emphasis paralleled the emerging struggle within classical philology between *Sachphilologie* and *Wortphilologie*.[83] In the end, it was Lachmann's type of scholarship, including his approach to the *Nibelungenlied*, that would become entrenched within *Germanistik* faculties once they were established in the 1840s.

But by 1816, the year of Lachmann's major work, the Nibelungen fad had already peaked. The revival had been limited to a relatively small population in a restricted geographical area (Berlin). Moreover, the revival had always had its critics: August von Kotzebue, the most successful playwright in the German language at this time, saw in Siegfried the model of a plundering Napoleonic despot.[84] The Jewish publicist Saul Ascher viewed Schlegel's proposals concerning the *Nibelungenlied* as part of an attempt to rid Germany of all foreign influence, including that of Greek antiquity.[85] Hegel, increasingly skeptical of Romanticism and its pretensions, would describe the epic as suffering from "hardness, wildness, and ferocity" while comparing its characters to "wooden figures."[86] With the elimination of Napoleon and the founding of the Holy Alliance in 1815, nationalist enthusiasm for the *Nibelungenlied* began to appear aesthetically vulgar and politically dangerous. More conservative Germanists increasingly played down the poem's potential pagan overtones. In *Die Nibelungen: Ihre Bedeutung für die Gegenwart und für immer* (1819), Friedrich von der Hagen celebrated the end of the "dark empire of the goddess of reason" and the arrival of a new Middle Ages.[87] While the *Nibelungenlied* would play a part in this process, this did not signal any threat to conventional Christianity. "[T]he Nibelungen are in no way our Homer or our *Iliad*. Because we have something higher, sublime beyond comparison, the Gospel and the Bible."[88] Instead, the role of the *Nibelungenlied* was to show the penetration of Christianity into all aspects of medieval German life, thereby providing inspiration for the Restoration.[89]

In light of such remarks, later commentators have come to view the revival of the *Nibelungenlied* as simply an attempt to defend feudalism before the onslaught of progress. "The question of whether the *Nibelungen-lied* could have been interpreted in a politically progressive sense must be answered with a 'no,'" writes one historian.[90] Yet the *Nibelungenlied* was embraced by nationalists of all political stripes, including restorationist conservatives, moderate liberals, and radical republicans, even when the correspondence between epic and ideology was ill-fitting at best. This points to the peculiar nature of the poem's reception in Germany, which began first as a patriotic attempt to find a German counterpart to Homer but developed after 1800 into a search for a mythical substrate for the emerging "nation." Throughout this time, advocates of the *Nibelungenlied* willfully ignored the gap between the content of the poem and the role they intended it to play in German cultural life. For while the epic did describe the end of a certain pagan feudalism, it offered neither the deities, nature myths, and cosmologies associated with Homeric poetry nor the moral and theological doctrines of Christianity. In the end, the epic would be useful as a poem of catastrophe, signaling the fall of one order and the rise of a new one. But it did not promise that what came after would be any better than what came before.

MYTH, NATION, AND LITURGY IN THE NAPOLEONIC ERA

While writers like Grimm and A. W. Schlegel attempted through their scholarly efforts to reconstruct the outlines of a national mythology, others sought a more immediate role for myth in Germany. In particular, a number of the more radical intellectuals in the early nationalist movement—Friedrich Ludwig Jahn, Jakob Friedrich Fries, and Wilhelm Martin Leberecht de Wette—demanded a religious imagery that would form the basis for a revitalized Protestant liturgy and a unified public life. Such proposals echoed the Jena Romantics' calls for a "new mythology," even though their authors typically rejected an increasingly conservative Romantic movement on both political and philosophical grounds. While the dreams of a national liturgy were never fulfilled, they highlighted the aspirations of the early nationalists for a radical reconstruction of religious and cultural life in Germany.

Liturgy had been a subject of almost continual discussion in Germany since the 1780s, whether it concerned the rituals of the various Masonic societies or the worship services of the churches. Shortly after his accession in 1797, the Prussian king Friedrich Wilhelm III had appointed a commission to develop a new liturgy for the Protestant Church as part of an anticipated union of the Reformed and Lutheran confessions. But with the collapse of Prussia in 1806 and the onset of the Stein-Hardenberg reforms, state officials and theologians began to envision a full-scale reworking of the Protestant churches.[91] In this spirit of reform, numerous plans were advanced for an overhaul of the liturgy, including several that reflected the desire for a "civil religion" along the lines described by Rousseau and realized to varying degrees during the French Revolution. Unlike their French prototypes, however, the plans developed in Germany during the Napoleonic wars generally remained within the rhetorical framework of Protestant Christianity.

Among those theologians who rediscovered the value of the church liturgy in these years was Friedrich Schleiermacher.[92] In *On Religion: Speeches to Its Cultured Despisers* (1799), Schleiermacher had been critical of the existing confessions, suggesting that true religious communion could take place only outside the church.[93] After 1800, however, Schleiermacher adopted a more pragmatic view of the church and its liturgy. A worship service, he now argued, offered moral teaching unadulterated by niceties of conversation or the scruples of friendship, producing a society in which rank and order did not matter, as all bowed down before God.[94] By 1804, he had developed a set of proposals to make the liturgy both aesthetically pleasing and socially relevant. While insisting that the initiative be left to local parishes, Schleiermacher suggested that a religious dimension could be added to such public holidays as New Year's Day, the Days of Repentance (Buß- und Bettage), and the harvest festival, while traditional religious festivals such as baptism and first communion took on a more social function.[95] By expanding the influence of religion beyond the walls of the church, Schleiermacher hoped, these festivals would awaken the religious spirit of even those who were not religious.

Schleiermacher's vision of a liturgy that would fuse religious worship with the needs of civic life was recast in specifically nationalist terms in the years 1806–15.[96] Friedrich Ludwig Jahn, the Prussian schoolteacher and future founder of the gymnastics associations *(Turnvereine)*, laid out his gruff vision of German nationality in *Deutsches Volkstum* (1810). After surveying Germany's political and social situation, Jahn turned to the condition of the Protestant Lutheran Church, which he described as suffering "more from its outward existence than its inward essence." On the one hand, he criticized the misbegotten attempts by "false enlighteners" and state officials to crush superstition; on the other hand, he bemoaned the dominance of a tradition that had become mere "love of custom."[97] In particular, Jahn found the present physical state of the churches loathsome: filled to their ceilings with musty sculptures, the corpses of the dead, and sparrows' nests, spiders, and bats, they were increasingly empty on Sunday mornings. Meanwhile, the clergy, poorly paid by the government and dependent on patrons for their employment, lived in a state of near poverty.

Jahn maintained a fervent allegiance to Protestantism, but he valued Martin Luther less for his doctrine of "justification by faith" than for his translation of the New Testament into German. In Jahn's view, salvation could be found only in a church that was fused with the interests of the nation. In particular, Jahn called for a series of national festivals, which would offer an "elevation over common life, an escape from everyday banality, an unshackling of the spirit from bodily burdens. . . . The man stands free as a being who has a public and inalienable right to joy and can taste it not merely surreptitiously, inebriating himself slavishly and greedily in a corner."[98] These festivals would eschew such "mythological caricatures" as the French goddess of reason ("grabbed out of the public brothels") or the immoral gods of classical antiquity.[99] Instead, ordinary Germans would gravitate toward an imagery grounded in their own history, religion, and mythology. To this end, Jahn made a list of "German" books that still needed to be written, including national histories and heroic poems to rival the *Iliad* and the *Odyssey*. (Strikingly, he made no mention here of the *Nibelungenlied*).

At the height of the War of Liberation, the historian and propagandist Ernst Moritz Arndt developed his own plan for a national liturgy in his "Entwurf einer deutschen Gesellschaft" (1814). Arndt envisioned a society that would be dedicated to the preservation of the "German race and sensibility," the awakening of "German power," the purification of the German language, and the memory of great moments in German history.[100] At the end of the "Entwurf," Arndt proposed a series of festivals that would accompany the meetings of the German Society. These included a commemoration of Hermann's victory over the Romans in the Teutoburg Forest, a festival for the battle of Leipzig, and a festival in remembrance of those who had fallen in service to the fatherland. Like Schleiermacher's harvest festival, the Hermann festival would coincide with an existing holiday—in this case Saint John's Day, the longest day of the year. Each festival would have its particular costume: during the Hermann festival citizens would wear oak leaves on their hats; on the Day of the Fallen they would wear a small crucifix.[101] Like Jahn, Arndt saw these festivals as complementing the traditional Christian cycle of holidays, and in formulating them he drew extensively on the language and symbolism of the Christian churches.[102]

Yet although Jahn and Arndt alluded to the need for some sort of national poetry or imagery, Fries and de Wette were the first to link the project of national liturgy to a concept of "myth." Fries, a philosopher at the Universities of Heidelberg and Jena, adopted a neo-Kantian epistemology that distinguished sharply between unknowable religious ideas and their mythical image.[103] He rejected both Romantic and idealist claims that the Absolute could be apprehended through either aesthetic or intellectual intuition. Nonetheless, he granted an important role to "symbols," because they offered at least an indirect presentiment of God.[104] In particular, he extolled the ancient Greek myths, which represented the religious ideas of the mysteries. In his philosophical novel *Julius und Evagoras* (1814) he called for a national poetry that would symbolize the ineffable truths of Christianity but be grounded in the experiences of German history.

> Philanthes: It is only on the foundation of a distinctive, patriotically culti-
> vated, rich, great and beautiful cycle of myths that new and powerful
> creations in the spheres of painting, sculpture, and all epic and dramatic
> literature can grow and flourish with luxuriance and with true signifi-
> cance for the history of a nation. How would it be . . . [if] like the Greeks,
> we should entrust our poets with the unique and great task of creating
> for us a great cycle of myths, myths about angels and spirits for the
> women and children, myths about heroes and demigods for the boys, and
> historical myths for the youths approaching manhood?
> Woldemar: What a great and splendid achievement that would be! I see an
> aesthetic public life, such as history has never seen, emerging from the
> union of the pure truth of faith and love with the power of poetry.[105]

Despite his call for a new national imagery, Fries warned that these symbols should not be mistaken for religious truth itself. That had been the error of Schelling and his school, and it had had the effect of compromising intellectual freedom, promoting religious obscurantism, and easing the way for political reaction.

With its emphasis on manly action, political freedom, and Protestant piety, Fries's philosophy proved deeply attractive to nationalist students during and after the War of Liberation.[106] It also was formative for the theologian Wilhelm Martin Leberecht de Wette. An Old Testament specialist, de Wette turned that field on its head in 1806 when he asserted that the Pentateuch was a national mythology of the Hebrew people.[107] In 1810, he arrived at the newly founded Friedrich-Wilhelm University in Berlin, where he befriended Arndt and, after some initial difficulty, Schleiermacher. While in Berlin, he published a series of studies in which he attempted to reconstruct Christian dogma using Fries's philosophy. But where Fries demanded a sanctification of public and political life through national festivals and ceremonies, de Wette emphasized a nationalization of the existing Protestant worship service.

In *Ueber Religion und Theologie* (1815), de Wette argued that the great task of the day was the construction of a Protestant mythology, which he re-

ferred to as an "ecclesiastical aesthetic."[108] Like the early Romantics, de
Wette was attracted by the aesthetic richness of Catholic liturgy and iconol-
ogy. The worship of the "Mother of God," the church music, and the architecture of Catholicism testified to the same "enthusiasm" that had inspired
Greek natural mythology. Yet de Wette mixed equal parts praise and wither-
ing critique in his account of this religion. In his view, the abundant symbolism of Catholicism frequently slipped into base sensuality, a materialism
that confused the Kingdom of God with the church and that insisted on the
doctrine of transubstantiation. In this sense Catholicism was both a "Christian paganism" and "a Christianity that has sunk to Judaism."[109] From the
perspective of Protestantism, Catholicism (like Judaism) had to be entirely
superseded before its aesthetic qualities could be imitated.

Protestantism, according to de Wette, possessed a critical dynamic that
had brought about a new attitude toward the traditional doctrines of the
church. Just as the radical reformers had treated bread and wine as symbols
of God's presence, the most recent scholarship suggested that Jesus was the
vehicle of a religious idea rather than the miracle worker portrayed in the
Gospels. Given this, de Wette recommended that artists adopt a poetic relationship to Christian dogma. "When Protestant criticism has achieved the
goal of research and the still existing oppositions are dissolved, it will be
allowed once again into the holy area. Then a mythology, higher than that of
the Catholics, will form and draw a circle of free poetry around the holy center of religious life."[110] This Protestant mythology would not grow out of the
visual arts, as it had in Catholicism, but from media more befitting the spiritual and inward nature of Protestantism: music and lyric poetry. Further, the
material for that mythology would be taken not from the existing narratives
of the church but from the history of the German nation.

De Wette maintained that this transformation could be accomplished
within the bounds of the existing Protestant churches. "[T]he true basis on
which every authentic church rests is the aesthetic symbolic cultus," he
noted. "We believe that the Protestant Church is on the way to liberating itself from the bonds of dogma and reshaping itself aesthetically."[111] The result
would be a liturgy that appealed to the senses while fostering patriotism
within the community. To that end, de Wette proposed a transformation of
the traditional church calendar. Christmas, for example, would now become
a festival of children, recognizing the people's hopes for the future. Easter, as
a memorial of victorious sacrifice, would become a festival of martyrs and
heroes of the church and the fatherland. Pentecost, the day on which most
children received their first communion, would be used to initiate children
into the community and to grant them the responsibility of defending it by

force of arms. "Should one be frightened of this connection of the worldly and the religious, think about the religious initiation of the old knights and the holy orders of knights, which were certainly not the worst institutions of the Catholic Middle Ages."[112]

De Wette also envisioned a transformation of the sacraments. All baptisms would take place in public, and they would serve to commemorate the purification of both child and adult. Following the practice of the early church, the Eucharist would become once again a love feast. In this way, the new Protestant community would release itself from the bounds of orthodox dogma and pave the way for a reunification with the Catholic Church. In a time of internal reform and nationalist upheaval such changes seemed possible, and de Wette alluded to the current efforts to rework the Protestant liturgy in Prussia. But he insisted that such changes be made an initiative of the church membership rather than being dictated by government officials or high-ranking clergy.[113]

The writings of Fries and de Wette exercised a considerable influence on the nationalist fraternities, or *Burschenschaften*, that were formed in Jena, Heidelberg, and elsewhere after 1815. In addition, however, their attacks against both the Jewish religion and the tentative steps in Prussia and elsewhere toward Jewish emancipation encouraged an insidious strain of anti-Semitism within the German student movement.[114] For student veterans of the Napoleonic wars, frustrated with the failure of the Congress of Vienna to deliver political reforms commensurate with their sacrifices on the battlefield, this proved a heady mixture. In 1819, the Jena student Karl Sand, a student of theology and *Burschenschaft* member, murdered the conservative playwright August von Kotzebue in protest against what he saw as the immorality, corruption, and tyranny of Restoration Germany.[115] A devoted follower of both Fries and de Wette, Sand imagined that the removal of the popular but bawdy Kotzebue would clear the path for the emergence of a new national art. Instead, this event provided the occasion for the Carlsbad Decrees, which resulted in the arrest and imprisonment of Jahn and Görres, the dismissal of Fries and de Wette, the suspension of Arndt, and the widespread repression of nationalist organizations throughout Germany.

The events of 1819 also dashed the hopes of those who had desired a reworking of the church and its liturgy along nationalist lines. In 1821, the Prussian Section for Cultus and Instruction issued its plan for a new "agenda" for the united Reformed and Lutheran confessions. The liturgy reflected the shift in Friedrich Wilhelm III's tastes away from Enlightenment simplicity and toward a more elaborate and aesthetically sumptuous form of worship. It called for genuflection during baptism, the use of a choir and

candles, and the placing of the sermon at the end of the service.[116] The agenda
was greeted with indignation on the part of liberal Protestants—especially
Schleiermacher, who attacked it as a Catholicization, even paganization, of
the cultus. In the face of this criticism, the Prussian government was forced
to show some flexibility, allowing each church district to adopt the agenda as
it saw fit. In any case, it was clear by this time that the tide had shifted toward
theological and political restoration and away from a reconstruction of religious and public life along liberal or nationalist lines.

Taken together, the efforts toward a national liturgy demonstrate the
close connection between the emerging culture of festival life, Protestant
theology, and the discourse on myth. While numerous historians, notably
George Mosse, have noted the early nationalists' fascination with liturgy,
they have often interpreted it as constituting a "political religion" and thus
an illegitimate incursion of the sacred onto a previously secular realm of politics.[117] In many respects, however, the "political" in Germany—especially in
its liberal form—developed from existing trends within enlightened and Romantic Protestant theology. Schleiermacher, Arndt, Fries, and de Wette
viewed the establishment of a national liturgy as a continuation of both Reformation and then later Aufklärung efforts to elevate and simplify the Christian religion. For these writers, Protestantism defined the national community just as surely as the national community defined Protestantism. But
given their attenuated relationship to Lutheran orthodoxy, they tended to define Protestantism in terms of an affirmation of the values of freedom and
criticism and a rejection of Catholicism and (somewhat less emphatically)
Judaism.[118] This complex of theological and political motives would inform
not only the calls for a national liturgy, however, but also the scholarly efforts
to reconstruct the "lost" Germanic mythology.

RECONSTRUCTING GERMANIC RELIGION: GRIMM'S *DEUTSCHE MYTHOLOGIE*

The desire among Protestant intellectuals for a revitalized and explicitly national mode of worship was reflected and reinforced by a growing fascination
with the earliest forms of religious belief in Germany. This interest first became evident in the eighteenth century, as a handful of scholars began to
treat the pagan practices of their ancestors with a measure of sympathy, viewing them as an example of a "natural religion" that was superior in some respects to the ecclesiastical orthodoxies of Protestantism and Catholicism.
Klopstock's play *Hermanns Schlacht* (1769) depicted a pagan Germanic worship service, which combined animal sacrifice with noble singing modeled

on the biblical Psalms.[119] The decades after 1800, however, witnessed the rise of a considerable body of scholarship that attempted to address the fundamental questions concerning ancient Germanic religion. Did the Germans have a mythology? If so, where did it come from? Was there a liturgy, and was it conducted by priests? In reconstructing the Germanic mythology, these authors were interested not only in recovering the national past but in creating a meaningful religious narrative that would link that past to the problems and concerns of the present.

The search for a Germanic mythology presented patriots and scholars with a knotty problem, for there was and still is very little evidence describing the nature of Germanic myth and religion.[120] The two main sources, Tacitus's *Germania* and the Icelandic *Edda*s (Snorri Sturluson's *Prose Edda*, ca. 1222; the *Poetic Edda*, eighth to eleventh centuries), stemmed from different eras and painted quite different pictures of northern European religion. In fact, none of the names of the German gods recorded by Tacitus match those found in the Nordic pantheon. Given this lack of evidence, the efforts of Jacob Grimm and others to reconstruct the religion of the old Germans were truly monumental.[121] But as we shall see, this triumph was only won through a selective and highly speculative interpretation of both medieval sources and contemporary folklore.

The key source for scholars of Germanic religion was the *Prose Edda*. According to Snorri, the Asen, the race of deities that lived in Asgard, had originally come from Troy. Claims of descent from Priam's city were not unusual in medieval literature, but those who wished to view the *Edda* as a testament to pagan belief and not a creation of Christian humanism had to take Snorri's claims seriously. These statements, combined with the discoveries of kinship between the German language and Sanskrit, as well as parallels between Nordic and Persian mythologies, led many scholars to the conclusion that the home of Germanic mythology lay in Asia, and that a wandering race of priests who called themselves the Asen had established their form of nature mythology in Asgard, in the cold reaches of the North.

Herder cited the "Asen doctrine" in his dialogue "Iduna" (1796), in which he suggested that the Nordic gods serve as the basis for a new national literature (rejecting the imagery of both Greece and the Orient).[122] The Asen theory was developed in a more literal sense by Joseph Görres. In an article for Friedrich Schlegel's *Deutsches Museum*, Görres argued that after the destruction of Troy a group of Asian priests had migrated into northern Europe.[123] There they had set up temples and organized a cult of Wotan, whose main elements encoded a *Naturphilosophie* similar to that found in the Greek mystery religions. Deep in the forests of Germany, priests had dressed

C. F. Müller, *Sacrificial Altar of the Ancient Germans* (1819). Lithograph by
C. F. Müller.
Source: Wilhelm Dorow, *Opferstätte und Grabhügel der Germanen und Römer am
Rhein* (Wiesbaden: Schellenberg, 1819), vol. 1, frontispiece. By permission of the
Houghton Library, Harvard University.

as women, led orgies, and carried phalluses in Bacchic rites exactly like those
found in Asia Minor. The Grimm brothers largely accepted the thesis of the
Asian origin of Germanic mythology, but they saw this mythology as proceeding not from a group of priests but out of the unconscious of the *Volk* in
its encounter with the climate and geography of central Europe.

Yet the validity of the *Edda*s as a source of "Germanic" myth was not accepted by everyone. In his *Aelteste Geschichte der Deutschen* (1806), the

Aufklärer Johann Christoph Adelung contended that the *Edda*s were written by Christian clerics. The Berlin historian Friedrich Rühs, an associate of Fries and de Wette, echoed these views.[124] In *Ueber den Ursprung der isländischen Poesie* (1813), he argued that the Eddic myths were derived from Anglo-Saxon sources rather than from an indigenous tradition. Because the *Edda*s were written by Christians, they revealed nothing about the pagan beliefs of the people.[125] Rühs therefore dismissed the views of Görres and the Grimms as so much wishful thinking. "The brothers have learned the art of baking bread from wind, and I fear that they have once again mistaken a wind-harp for the wind."[126]

Adelung and Rühs soon came under attack from a number of directions. In 1811, the Danish theologian Peter Erasmus Müller published a defense of the historicity of the "Asen doctrine," which was quickly translated into German.[127] Wilhelm Grimm seized on this study in his reviews of Rühs's work, henceforth taking the authenticity of the *Edda*s as a proven fact.[128] Jacob Grimm would later disparage Rühs, Adelung, and all those who "have sinned against their native history."[129] This was clearly a misrepresentation—Rühs was no less a nationalist than Grimm—but it suggests an important fault line within the field of national mythology. On one side stood the more radical Protestant nationalists, such as Fries, Rühs, and de Wette, who were grounded in a neo-Kantian Protestant theology and sought an immediate reform of Germany's political and religious institutions. This group embraced the notion of a national mythology akin to that of the Greeks but insisted on the malleability of aesthetic and religious symbolism and its eventual subordination to individual autonomy. On the other side stood moderate liberal figures like Jacob Grimm, who believed that change should be slow and organic, building on principles of nationality, law, and honor. For Grimm, the concept of "myth" suggested a permanent source of religious tradition and authority that was grounded in the experience of the nation and that had provided the foundation for German Protestantism. Both of these groups were opposed by more conservative writers like A. W. Schlegel or Friedrich von der Hagen, who envisioned a return to the values of medieval (Catholic) Christianity as part of a restoration of political and religious life throughout Europe.

Given the appeal of the Nordic gods in these years for bourgeois writers and intellectuals, those who rejected the validity of the *Prose Edda* were fighting an uphill battle.[130] Between 1812 and 1815, Friedrich von der Hagen, Friedrich Rühs, and the Grimms all published competing editions of the *Prose Edda*.[131] Meanwhile, a number of commentators proposed that the Nordic deities become the basis for a national cult. Writing in the *Vossische*

Zeitung, one individual denied the need for books in "foreign languages."
"For the holy and everything that has its roots in it, the German has nothing
to do but turn to the *Edda*." In this way, Germans would avoid relying on a
(Jewish) past that was "not of the German type and for that reason must age
and die."[132] Although Hegel would complain of the efforts to revive the "misshapen and barbaric representations" of the *Edda* at the expense of modern
culture, he did not doubt their basic link to German nationality.[133] By 1829
Karl Rosenkranz could confidently assert that "the self-sufficiency of Nordic
religion as independent of clerical knowledge of Graeco-Roman mythology
and Christian ideas has been sufficiently proven against Adelung, Rühs, and
the rest."[134]

The *Edda*s provided the key text for Franz Josef Mone's two-volume
Geschichte des Heidenthums im nördlichen Europa (1822–23).[135] Mone, a
librarian and historian at Heidelberg and also a Catholic, was a student of
the classical philologist Friedrich Creuzer.[136] Like Creuzer, Mone developed
a theory of mythology based on the primacy of the symbol, arguing that all
of pagan mythology was derived from an earlier theological symbolism
whose roots lay in India. This symbolism (which in Germany took the form
of runes) had originally encoded a kind of Neoplatonic emanation theology,
but the symbols had subsequently become the basis for a series of religious
narratives, including the stories of the *Edda*.[137] Mone's most striking claim,
however, was that this mythology had actually determined the course of subsequent German history. Thus, the emanation theory was not merely a reflection but the cause of the great migrations, in which the various nations
split off from their geographical center (located in the Caucasus region) like
divinities falling from the godhead. This thesis ran directly contrary to the argument of scholars like Karl Göttling, who in his study of the *Nibelungenlied* had attempted to ground the poem in its twelfth-century political context—in particular the dispute between the pro-papal Guelphs and the
pro-kaiser Ghibellines (Ghibelline = Waiblingen = Nibelungen). By contrast,
Mone proposed that metaphysical tensions within nature and myth had
actually brought about these historical conflicts.[138] In his view, the metaphysics encoded in German mythology explained even such latter-day developments as the Reformation and the persistence of confessional tensions
within Germany.[139]

For Mone, it was a given that religious factors drove history and that conflicts between nations were merely the expression of religious differences. "It
thereby follows that the history of nations, if it should embody that idea,
must be viewed and interpreted according to the spirit of religion, and that it
[history] is only the substrate of the idea, therefore only the image and not

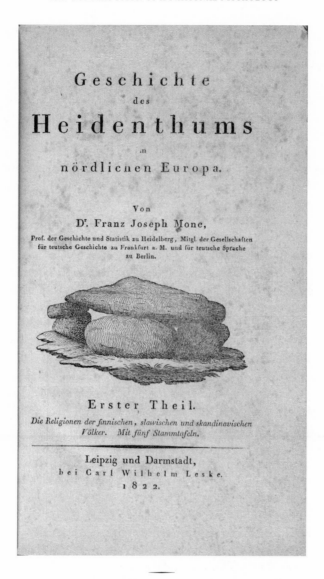

Title page of Franz Joseph Mone, *Geschichte des Heidenthums im nördlichen Europa*, vol. 1.

the essence."[140] These were consciously mystical ideas, written in the most enthusiastic years of the post-1815 religious awakening, and Mone viewed them as directly opposed to a liberalism that had abandoned its stated principle of toleration and instead condemned all religious ideas that did not conform to the "enlightenment of the nineteenth century."[141] His ultimate goal was to reinterpret pagan antiquity so that it might serve as the basis for a re-configured religious narrative. In such a scheme, the conversion to Catholicism would represent a logical and necessary fulfillment of the Nordic "pagan" spirit.

Jacob Grimm greeted Mone's study with a fair degree of skepticism. He noted that Mone suffered from a tendency "to dash off his results as if finished right from the beginning, whether they are tenable or untenable, mature or immature."[142] Further, while he accepted the argument that Germanic mythology could be traced back to Asia, he disagreed with Mone's tendency simply to equate German gods and heroes with their counterparts in India or Greece.[143] Finally, Mone's theory of the symbol (which Schelling would have derided as "allegorical") seemed to imply that idealist philosophy or Neoplatonist mysticism were prior to or superior to mythology. Grimm, by contrast, insisted on the autonomy and superiority of Germanic mythology as a way of knowing and living in the world.[144] In the realm of myth, practice and thought were not divided by the logic of reflection but merged in a single continuum; once that world was lost, no modern culture or religion could ever replace it. More important, however, Mone's study appeared just as Grimm was shifting away from the "Heidelberg" standpoint that had dominated his work from roughly 1805 to 1815, when he had aligned himself with such scholars as Arnim, Creuzer, and Görres.[145] As the Heidelberg Romantics turned toward political restoration or Ultramontanist Catholicism, Grimm embraced a conception of "Germanic mythology" that was self-consciously bourgeois, liberal, and Protestant.

In the *Deutsche Mythologie* (1835), Grimm set out to describe the religion of the oldest Germans. Unlike previous commentators, who focused on the gods and their myths, Grimm examined the totality of Germanic religious experience, from the creation narratives of the *Prose Edda* to the superstitions of the German peasant. "Our mythology . . . has been taken away forever. I turn to the sources that remain of it, which are partly written artifacts and partly the ever-flowing river of living custom and legend. The former can reach high, but they show themselves broken and torn, while present-day popular traditions hang on threads that connect them directly with antiquity."[146] Thus, for Grimm, the laws, sayings, and stories of contemporary folklife were repositories of a lost mythology. Even Christian festivals and holidays contained customs and practices originally derived from ancient beliefs about Wotan, Hertha, or Mother Holla. So while Mone viewed Neoplatonic theology as the key to understanding paganism, Grimm treated ancient paganism as the key to understanding Christianity, at least as it was practiced in Germany.

According to Grimm, the earliest religion in Germany was the cult of Wotan. Wotan (superseded in Norse mythology by Odin) was the god of thunder and the leader of the Asen. He had only one good eye, wore a broad hat and a coat, and carried a spear that he used to grant heroes victory in battle. In the face of contradictory evidence, Grimm maintained that the cult of Wotan had been widespread throughout Germany.[147] He acknowledged that Wotan worship was strongest in northern Germany and Scandinavia, as place-names like Gudensberg, Othänshyllä, Wodenesweg, and Wodenesberg seemingly confirmed, while it had to share prominence with other cults in southern Germany. Nonetheless, Wotan preserved the status of a near monotheistic deity in Grimm's system. "Monotheism is something so necessary and essential that almost all pagans in their colorful swarm of gods start out, consciously or unconsciously, by recognizing a highest god."[148] In the oldest German religion, Wotan was not only an anthropomorphic god of thunder but a metaphysical power, giving shape to the creatures of the earth, granting fertility to fields, inspiring poets, and granting wishes and good luck. Like Mone, Grimm maintained that the other gods were simply emanations of Wotan.

The purpose of pagan liturgy, Grimm argued, was to thank the gods or to assuage their anger. To this end, the ancients had offered a sacrifice, sometimes of fruits, vegetables, or flowers but most often of animals. Occasionally humans—even children—were sacrificed. In certain sacraments, the blood of the sacrificed was collected, mixed with beer, and drunk by the people, a ritual that foreshadowed the Christian Eucharist. Many of these sacrificial practices lived on in contemporary customs, such as the practices of leaving food at the table for an absent guest, drinking to the Virgin Mary or Saint John, and bringing flowers to a tree or a river on particular religious holidays.

Despite the occasional child sacrifice, Grimm's Germanic religion looked remarkably like an enlightened or liberal form of Protestantism.[149] In ancient Germany, he argued, the priests existed as a separate class, but with far fewer powers than their Gallic and Celtic counterparts. The head of a household could conduct religious ceremonies in his own home, and in the earliest times symbolic practices were exercised without the intervention of a priest.[150] Few if any temples were built; instead, rites took place in an open wood, identified by a special holy tree. These trees were decorated with flowers or the carcasses of animals, and sometimes images were carved into their trunks. Such practices gave rise to the "Irminsul": "[a] great wooden column . . . set up and worshiped under the free heavens. Its name meant universal, all-bearing column."[151] During the conversion of Saxony in 772,

Alfred Rethel, study for *The Destruction of the Irminsul* (1848). This painting,
part of a series on the life of Charlemagne in the Aachen Town Hall, preserved the
sense of both triumph and loss in the conversion of the Saxons to Christianity.
Source: Stiftung museum kunst palast, Düsseldorf. By permission.

Charlemagne ordered the Irminsul chopped down before forcing the Saxon
king Wittekind to convert.[152] This paradigmatic event, whose sexual symbolism could not be more explicit, marked the end of open pagan worship in
Germany. Afterward, the Christians built their churches on pagan holy sites
in order to preserve them as sacred spaces.

The Christian conversion, which Grimm described in the most tragic
terms, had forcibly rooted out Wotan and the other Germanic deities. Never-
theless, important remnants of Wotan worship had been preserved. "The
people," Grimm argued, "whose belief was destroyed, saved parts of it when
they transferred their veneration to a new, unpersecuted object."[153] During
the harvest in southern Germany, for example, peasants left a bundle of grain
in the field for Wotan's horse. Near the Steinhuder Lake, boys celebrated the
harvest by running up a hill, lighting a fire, and yelling "Wauden, Wauden!"[154]

Even everyday expressions had their roots in Wotan worship. The space between the thumb and forefinger was named the *Woedensspanne,* thus the
origin of the expression "the game runs on his thumbs," when someone had
good luck in cards or dice.[155] These speculative connections marked the real
innovation of the *Deutsche Mythologie.* For by connecting such superstitions and practices to a forgotten pagan religion, Grimm managed to bestow
on a vanishing rural culture the aura of the sacred. Such a strategy would
prove highly effective, for it linked the discourse of myth to existing concerns
about the disappearance of preindustrial society and a growing fascination
with the folk cultures of Germany.

While Wotan ruled the sky, another deity ruled the earth. In *Germania,*
Tacitus had described the worship of Nerthus (Hertha), the Earth Mother:

> In an island of the ocean there is a sacred grove, and within it a consecrated
> chariot, covered over with a garment. Only one priest is permitted to touch
> it. *He* can perceive the presence of the goddess in this sacred recess, and
> walks by her side with the utmost reverence as she is drawn along by heifers.
> . . . Afterwards the car, the vestments, and, if you like to believe it, the divin-
> ity herself are purified in a secret lake. Slaves perform the rite and are in-
> stantly swallowed up by its waters. Hence arises a mysterious terror and a
> pious ignorance concerning the nature of that which is seen only by men
> doomed to die.[156]

Although there were no references to Hertha or her cult in the *Edda*s and
scant evidence for the presence of the cult in other sources, this story was
simply too intriguing to be thrown out by Grimm or his contemporaries.[157]
In scholarly monographs and literary journals, writers offered paeans to
Hertha, speculated on the origin and nature of her cult, and debated whether
it was authentically German.[158] The question that most excited academics,
however, was where exactly this rite took place. The island of Rügen, Hel-
goland, the Harz lake region, and an island off the coast of Holstein were all
proposed as possible locales.[159]

Grimm did not attempt to identify the exact location of the cult of
Hertha. Like many scholars (including Mone), he believed that Hertha was
only one incarnation of a fertility goddess that was worshiped throughout the
ancient world. "The widespread veneration of the procreative, nourishing
earth without a doubt inspired many appellations among our forefathers, just
as the worship of Gaia and her daughter Rhea was mixed with that of the
Mother Goddess, of Ceres and Cybele. What seems to me especially remarkable is the similarity between the cult of Nerthus and that of the Phrygian

God-Mother."[160] In Germanic lore, this goddess appeared in various guises, but usually as a figure that roamed the countryside, going from town to town. Freya, the head of the Valkyries, rode in a wagon pulled by cats. Mother Holda, who also had a wagon, liked to wait in springs and lakes, snapping up unbaptized children. Frau Perchta, an ugly, witchlike being, typically appeared in towns on Twelfth Night, rewarding those who helped her but taking vengeance on those who did not. After the triumph of Christianity, many of the positive characteristics of motherhood associated with Holda or Freya were transferred to the cult of the Virgin Mary, while the more frightful connotations expressed in Perchta lived on in superstitions and folktales.

Besides Hertha and Wotan, a variety of elves, sprites, and demons personified different aspects of nature. Because they did not challenge the main tenets of Christian theology, these deities were among the last elements of paganism to die out. Grimm described a "water cultus" associated with lakes, rivers, and springs. Each body of water had its own genie, which was usually female. The banks of rivers and streams were seen as magical places, and the local water genie was liable to pop out at any moment. These water demons liked to pull little children underwater and drown them, and the rivers were rumored to be especially dangerous on the summer solstice. "The water spirit demands his yearly sacrifice," the people would say.[161] In other cases, these water nymphs would marry human men, as in the case of Fouqué's popular fairy tale *Undine* (1811), only to disappear should their true identity be spoken out loud.

The myth of Walhalla grew out of ancient German beliefs concerning death and the afterlife. According to the *Prose Edda,* the Valkyries, semidivine female warriors, swooped over the battlefield to carry the dead heroes to Walhalla. There, the heroes enjoyed games of combat and enough food and drink to last an eternity. Grimm linked this rowdy myth to a common religious belief in the migration of the soul out of the body after death. Death arrived via a special genie or messenger, who would carry the soul to God. This notion of death as a messenger helped explain medieval representations of the "Dance of Death" and numerous tales based on the premise that Death could be tricked or misled. According to one story, a doctor asked Death to appear at the head of a bed if the patient were to die and the foot of the bed if the patient were to live. When Death's back was turned, the doctor would sometimes switch the patient around to save him from death.[162]

These ancient beliefs in the transmigration of the soul helped to explain much of the lore surrounding the imperial emperor. In the *Deutsche Sagen* (1816–18), the Grimm brothers reported the legend that Friedrich Barbarossa (the Red Beard) slept on his throne deep in a cave within Kyffhäuser Mountain in Thuringia.[163] He had slept so long that his beard had twice wrapped it-self around the table in front him. When it reached a third time around, Bar-barossa would climb out of the cave and hang his shield on a dying tree, which would immediately begin to bloom. His return would coincide with the arrival of the Antichrist, and the battle of the apocalypse would ensue.[164] By the time Jacob Grimm wrote *Deutsche Mythologie*, patriotic poets and writers had resurrected these narratives in drama and poetry.[165]

For Grimm, the Barbarossa legend marked one manifestation of a typi-cally German fascination with *Entrückung* (being carried off or whisked away). Popular lore related similar tales about Charlemagne, Siegfried, Frau Venus, and Dietrich. In some cases the legends simply referred to a treasure buried in a mountain or, in the case of the Nibelung treasure, buried at the bottom of the Rhine. The return of the heroes or the discovery of these trea-sures was in turn linked to ideas of the apocalypse. The *Prose Edda* prophe-sied the time of Ragnarok, when the creatures of Hel would invade Asgard and defeat the gods, after which a new and better earth would rise from the sea.

> As past and future, the lost and the expected paradise, meld together in the imagination of the people, so they believe in the awakening from the moun-tain sleep of their beloved kings and heroes: Friedrich and Karl, Siegfried and perhaps also Dietrich. That is the real sign of the epic, that it secures eternal and imperishable permanence for its figures. But Siegfried is also Wotan, Dietrich is Wotan, Karl is Wotan, and according to the Muspilli [a ninth-century Bavarian poem], Wotan returns to the world a rejuvenated, reawak-ened god.[166]

Thus, according to Grimm, medieval legends of the coming apocalypse were derived neither from the Investiture Crisis nor from the Book of Revelation but instead manifested the continuing power of the cult of Wotan and the Germanic belief in a "twilight of the gods."

Grimm insisted that the Nordic myths stood closer to the original Indo-Germanic sources than the Christian-Jewish myths emanating from the Ori-ent, which he described as "distorted" and "torn" from their original con-text.[167] Thus, he attributed the popular and familiar elements of Christianity to the lost Germanic religion, while he blamed unfamiliar dogmas and insti-tutions on the work of foreign missionaries and priests. Christianity, in Grimm's view, was never "popular" *(volksmäßig)*. "It came from a foreign land and wanted to repress the old handed-down indigenous gods that the land honored and loved."[168] In their reverence for their own gods, the people had secretly preserved them, transferring their attributes to Catholic saints and continuing their cult under the rubric of Catholic festivals and holidays. Indeed, even as Grimm unearthed legends about Mary and described festivals to Saint John, he insisted that they were only masks of the earlier pagan religion.

Grimm's description of the ancient Germans struggling against the "foreign" Christian power drew much of its rhetorical force from its parallels with both the French occupation and overseas imperialism. As Susanne Zantop has noted, a "postcolonial" moment can be identified in German nationalist discourse already in the 1790s.[169] In his *Briefe zu Beförderung der Humanität* (1793–97), Herder decried the violent imposition of one people's culture on another, whether by the French revolutionary armies or by the forces of European colonialism. "Even Christianity, insofar as it works as the state machine of foreign peoples, oppresses them terribly. Among some it mutilates their unique character, so that even one and a half millennia cannot make it right. Don't we wish that the spirit of Nordic peoples, the Germans, the Gauls, the Celts, the Slavs, etc. had been able to spring forth pure and undisturbed out of themselves?"[170] Jacob Grimm had experienced French imperialism even more directly as a subject of the puppet Kingdom of Westphalia, where he was forced to wear a foreign uniform as part of his official duties. In the *Deutsche Mythologie*, he spun a tale not only of occupation but of resistance, as the lowest ranks of society—peasants, women, and country folk—held onto the old religion under the outward trappings of Christianity.

That resistance broke into the open during the Reformation. "It was not an accident but a necessity that the Reformation began in Germany," Grimm wrote in an 1844 preface. Germany "would long ago have accepted it without division, had there not been foreign intrigues against it."[171] Martin Luther had suggested a faith without churches, priests, and imagery—in other words a religion that matched the traditional "Germanic" affinity for the sublime. The Germans, as well as the English, the Scandinavians, and the French Huguenots, had accepted the Reformation because they had all participated in the old German faith. "As in language and myth, so in the religious leanings among the peoples there is something indestructible," Grimm wrote.[172] In this sense, the subsequent progression of Protestantism toward a sublime natural religion marked a return to the original beliefs of the old Germans.

The strident Protestantism of Grimm's 1844 preface reflected the evolution in his political and religious thought over the previous twenty-five years. In 1830, the revolution in France had sparked widespread unrest in German towns and cities and forced several states to introduce liberal reforms.

Protests in the university town of Göttingen induced the Hanoverian government in 1833 to introduce a moderately liberal constitution, which gave
a greater role to the territorial estates *(Landstände)* in the formation of legislation. Four years, later, however, King Ernst August suspended the new
constitution. Jacob and Wilhelm Grimm joined five other professors in a
protest against this arbitrary act of royal power and, as a result, were sum-
marily dismissed from their positions. Jacob Grimm was hardly a radical: his
politics inclined more to the moderate liberalism of fellow protester Friedrich Christoph Dahlmann than the Rhenish left liberalism of Karl Rotteck
and Karl Welcker's "deeply irritating" *Staatslexikon*.[173] But his support for a
politics grounded in "national" traditions, including the *Landstände* and
Germanic law, had brought him into opposition against both the Metternichian system and his own king.

Grimm's political views reinforced his growing antipathy to Catholicism.
Already in the 1820s, he had proclaimed his sympathy for theological ra-
tionalism against what he called the "wide cloud" of Catholic mysticism.[174]
Then in 1837 the Prussian government arrested and briefly imprisoned the
Catholic archbishop of Cologne because of his opposition to mixed mar-
riages, a move that gave rise to vigorous protests among Rhineland Catholics.
But Grimm felt that the Prussian government had not acted harshly enough.
"It has often occurred to me that there is only one measure that will cut off
the dispute once and for all and is required for all Protestants if they still have
pride and self-esteem: retaliation against the arrogance of the Catholics."[175]
In practical terms, Grimm was prepared to envision a complete segregation
of Protestants from Catholics, which he believed would only strengthen the
"Protestant people *[Volk]*" in their beliefs. Given Grimm's newly gained status as political martyr, his utter lack of sympathy for the Catholic minority
in Prussia was telling. Yet these attitudes help to explain the dichotomies
that characterize his *Deutsche Mythologie*.

The structure of Grimm's *Deutsche Mythologie*, in which an original
Germanic faith and an indigenous law foreshadowed the eventual arrival of
(Protestant) Christianity, has led Wolf-Daniel Hartwich to term it an "Old
Testament" of German mythology.[176] Indeed, in Grimm's scheme the myths
and legends of the ancient Germans took over the role once assigned to the
stories of the Hebrew Bible. Yet the material for Grimm's national mythology was not simply "invented," as Hartwich suggests, but was instead drawn
from local religious practices, Catholic legends of Mary and the saints, fairy
tales, and popular folklore. In doing so, Grimm created the illusion that religious and geographical divisions within Germany masked an underlying
unity that only the historian could see. To paraphrase Susan Crane, Grimm's

"mythical gaze" transfigured the image of everyday life, giving it a kind of religious resonance.[177] In the *Deutsche Mythologie,* what was most local and
quaint became that which was most national, and—just as Hegel had once
hoped—the landscape suddenly seemed to be the repository of a noble religion rather than base superstition.

HEINRICH HEINE AND NATIONAL MYTHOLOGY

By the 1830s, the basic elements of a German "national mythology" had
fallen into place. An epic literary tradition had been uncovered, the folktales
were widely read, and the outlines of a Germanic pantheon had been reconstructed. Artists had begun to produce paintings, songs, and stories based on
the *Kaiser* legends, the oak tree, and the *Nibelungenlied.* Moreover, the elements of this mythology had been connected to the geography of Germany:
the Rhine River, the Teutoburg Forest, and the North Sea. In 1842, the Bavarian king Ludwig would complete construction of the Walhalla, an enormous
shrine to Germany's heroes that overlooked the Danube River near Regensburg. Of course, these images had achieved far more popularity among the
educated classes than in other sectors of Germany society. In this sense, what
was emerging was a literary tradition or canon rather than what Romantic
theorists or later anthropologists would have identified as a mythology. Yet
the power of the discourse on myth was such that writers were prepared to
speak of an established set of national "myths," which formed the literary-
religious patrimony of the German nation. As the great age of discovery came
to an end, what emerged was a process of commentary and criticism, which
was carried forth in large part by writers outside the universities.

One of the most knowledgeable commentators on the emerging national
mythology was the poet Heinrich Heine (1797–1856). Although typically
viewed as a critic of *Deutschtümlei,* Heine retained a fascination for the politics and imagery of nationalism long after he had become uncomfortable
with its more extreme exponents. Further, while Heine came to see many nationalists as advancing hatred in the guise of patriotism, the years directly
after 1815 witnessed his greatest enthusiasm for the old Germanic past.[178] As
a student in Bonn in 1819, he attended the lectures of A. W. Schlegel on the
history of the German language, of Johann Gottlieb Radloff on ancient German history, and of Arndt on Tacitus's *Germania,* where he learned of the
cult of Hertha.[179] Looking back several years later, Heine wrote:

> At the time, the legend of old Hertha probably interested me more than now.
> I didn't let her reside on Rügen but moved her to an East Frisian island. A

young scholar likes to have his private hypothesis. But in no case would
I have believed at that time that I would one day walk along the North
Sea beach without thinking about the old goddess with patriotic enthusiasm. But that turns out not to be the case. I am here now thinking about
other, younger goddesses.[180]

Indeed, Heine eventually championed the "young" Greek goddesses and
gods as an alternative to what he saw as a morbid and politically dangerous
cult of the German *Vorzeit*. The murder of Kotzebue in 1819 made a deep impression on Heine, as he recognized the homicidal potential of the cause he
had once supported. In a letter, Heine fantasized about being attacked by a
crazed elderly German patriot, whom he would force into supplication with
a handy copy of the *Nibelungenlied*. "O sancta Chrimhilda, Brunhilda &
Uta, ora pro nobis!" the imagined assailant would cry.[181] Paranoid delusions
of grandeur perhaps, but Sand spent the days before his execution muttering
about the mythical identity of Hermann and Siegfried.[182]

In the context of the 1820s, in which many Romantic intellectuals declared their opposition to liberalism, Heine came to see the fascination
for the German *Vorzeit* as a deception designed to lure the public into the
ranks of what he called the "servile" party.[183] "While we wrap ourselves dis-
gruntledly in the purple coat of German heroes' blood, some political scoun-
drel comes along and puts a dunce cap on our head."[184] Heine was especially
repulsed by the "marriage" that took place in the 1820s between conservative Romantics like Friedrich Schlegel and Joseph Görres and the "Catholic"
parties in Vienna and Munich. These developments only reinforced his belief
that the Romantics had been nothing more than shock troops for a Catholic
reaction. Such sentiments were widespread among the writers and poets of
Young Germany, who came of age during the late Romantic period but who
emerged during the *Vormärz* as outspoken critics of monarchism, religious
orthodoxy, sexual puritanism, and mystical nationalism.

Nonetheless, Heine nourished a passion for the old German myths, and
he reserved special praise for the scholarship of the Grimms. "In the study of
old German, Jacob Grimm towers sublimely over [A. W. Schlegel]. With his
Deutsche Grammatik he has freed us from that superficiality with which,
following the Schlegels' example, old German literary artifacts were previously explained."[185] This was not just a scholarly opinion but also an aesthetic and political judgment. Heine had been baptized as a Protestant in
1825 primarily out of practical considerations, but during the early 1830s his
religious sentiments verged toward Saint-Simonianism and its doctrine of
the rehabilitation of the flesh. In his writings, he contrasted the healthy sen-

sualism of the Greeks and the Romans with the morbid spiritualism of Judaism and Christianity, identifying the former with freedom and republicanism and the latter with repressive tyranny.[186] Given these views, Jacob Grimm's Protestant-Germanic religion was far more appealing to Heine than the Catholic medieval mythologies of A. W. Schlegel, Görres, or Fouqué. Yet whereas Grimm identified the original Germanic faith with a monotheistic worship of Wotan, Heine maintained that it was a pantheistic natural religion.

Thus, when he sat down to paint a portrait of the German people for the French, Heine included a work on German mythology. *Elementargeister* (1835) is the least read of the trio of works that includes *Die Romantische Schule* (1833) and *Zur Geschichte der Religion und Philosophie in Deutschland* (1834) and that appeared together in French as *De l'Allemagne* (1835).[187] "In Westphalia, the former Saxony, not all that is buried is dead," Heine begins. "When one wanders through the old oak groves, one hears the voices of the *Vorzeit*. There one still hears the echo of pensive incantations, in which more life flows than in the entire literature of the Mark Brandenburg."[188] Borrowing wholesale from the Grimm brothers, Heine found traces of a lost German mythology in popular beliefs about ghosts, fairies, and witches. He linked these myths to a supposed old Germanic belief in pantheism, whose return, he maintained, was imminent. Like Barbarossa, not all that lay buried was dead.

The title *Elementargeister* was derived from the fifteenth-century alchemist Paracelsus, who coined the term to refer to the spirits of the four elements. In his book, Heine delineated what he called a "Germanic cultus" based on stones, trees, rivers, and fire, which corresponded to the elements earth, air, water, and fire. Each element had a mythical being: elves lived in trees, water genies swam in rivers, stones were often unlucky dwarves, and the fire spirit was the devil. Whereas the elves were rather Celtic—a view seemingly confirmed by the English fascination with fairies—the Germans harbored a special love for all manner of water beings.[189] Heine was an admirer of Fouqué's *Undine* and readily explained the lore surrounding water genies. "There is something so mysterious in the ways of water nymphs. A person can imagine under the surface of the water so much that is sweet and so much that is terrible."[190] And also much that was absurd: Heine cited early modern theological speculations about whether the undersea world of nymphs and water kings also had water bishops. "Perhaps the majority of the water creations are Christians, at least as good Christians as the majority of the French."[191]

The dwarves played a special role in Heine's loose system. The Grimms' *Deutsche Sagen* was filled with tales of helpful dwarves who lived largely unseen in the world of humans, and Heine retold some of these stories. At night while peasants slept, the dwarves would come out of their holes in the mountains and finish the work of harvesting or cherry picking that remained to be done. The humans usually repaid the dwarves by making fun of them, and sometimes they demanded a share of the dwarves' ample supplies of gold and diamonds before they would allow them to leave the land.[192] According to Jacob Grimm, the dwarves would retaliate with fraud or thievery, sometimes making off with human children. In his view, the legends of dwarves and elves reflected the memory of an abandoned paganism, which now appeared in the form of a marginalized or suppressed race.[193] Heine, however, compared the dwarves to Jews, who served the needs of the broader population but were frequently mistreated by them. Thus, he likened the dwarves begging humans for mercy to Jewish pleas before King Ferdinand before their expulsion from Spain in 1492.[194] When Richard Wagner developed the connection between Jews and dwarves in the *Ring*, he would be following a tradition established by Heine rather than the Grimm brothers.[195]

Jacob Grimm argued in *Deutsche Mythologie* that most stories about the devil could be traced to myths of German gods whom Christian priests had jealously transformed into demons. Thus, the opposition between God and the devil reflected a deeper conflict between Christianity and paganism.[196] In *Elementargeister*, Heine used these themes to highlight the opposition between "sensualism" and "spiritualism" in European culture. Thus, the devil appears as a sensualist, individualist, and logician, while Jesus Christ represents asceticism, spiritualism, and faith. Most important, "the devil does not believe. He does not rely blindly on foreign authorities. To the contrary, he puts more trust in his own thoughts, and he uses reason! This is admittedly something terrible, and the Roman Catholic apostolic church has quite rightly condemned self-thinking as the work of the devil."[197] This was less scholarship than a parody of scholarship, used by Heine to ridicule the resurgent theological conservatism of his day.

Throughout *Elementargeister*, Heine excoriated the efforts of the Catholic Church to uproot the pagan faith, sighing at the "war of destruction" that felled the holy trees and forced Wittekind to convert. The Christians built their churches near the once holy springs of the pagans or at the spots of fallen holy trees, hoping to exploit their magical powers. Those trees that resisted the Christians' axes were slandered as sites of devil worship and witchcraft. "But the oak remained the favorite tree of the German people. The oak

is still today the symbol of German nationality."[198] Like Jacob Grimm, Heine
exploited the themes of occupation and imperialism and pointed to Martin
Luther as the man who had restored German religion to its roots. But while
Grimm's chief enemies were French culture and Roman Catholicism, Heine
was most incensed by the recent exploitation of national themes by Romantic conservatives (both Catholic and Protestant), who hoped to use the public's natural affinity for mythology to perpetuate the policies of monarchical
absolutism, literary censorship, and religious restoration. Such efforts could
only be partly successful, however. As paganism had lived on under the shell
of medieval Christianity, the liberating force of German patriotism would
resist the Christian axe and rise one day from underneath the mountain.

Viewed in the context of the *De l'Allemagne* trilogy, the purpose of *Elementargeister* becomes clear: to document the contention that pantheism
constituted the "national belief" of the German people. Writing at the peak
of his involvement with Saint-Simonianism, Heine maintained that in advo-
cating pantheism the young Schelling and his followers had stumbled upon
a potentially revolutionary doctrine. They had awakened gods that had long
slept peacefully but who would now inspire the terrible lust for battle that
had animated the Germanic race before it was softened by the promises of the
cross. "That talisman is rotten, and the day will come when it collapses
pitifully. The old stone gods will rise up out of the lost ruins and rub the
thousand-year-old dust from their eyes. Thor with his giant hammer will
jump up high and smash the Gothic cathedrals."[199] Whether he meant more
with this dream of a "German revolution" than a release from the bonds of
Christian morality is unclear, but even at his most enthusiastic an element
of caution ran through Heine's work. Beware the Germans, he told his French
readers. The goddess who carries a spear and always wears helmet and armor
is the goddess of wisdom.[200]

The year Heine published *Elementargeister,* his works and those of the
other Young German writers were censored or banned throughout Germany
by an act of the Federal Diet in Frankfurt. An increasingly conservative
Prussian state led the charge against Heine, and there was no change in
Hohenzollern policy after the accession in 1840 of Friedrich Wilhelm IV, who
was viewed initially as a liberal but was in fact steeped in the cultures of the
Neo-Pietist Awakening and late Romantic historicism. Beginning in 1844,
Heine was subject to arrest whenever he stepped on Prussian soil.[201] In
Deutschland: Ein Wintermärchen (1844), he imagined such a homecoming,
starting on the border at the Rhine and traveling to Aachen, Cologne, Hagen,
Münster, Paderborn, and Minden and ending in Hamburg.[202] On the way the
narrator confronts the topography of "German mythology" as it had been es-

tablished in the works of the Grimms and others. As in *Elementargeister*, Heine juxtaposes gods, heroes, and other mythical beings with the modern world, often inverting their usual meanings in the process.

One of the first stops is Cologne. Only two years earlier a *Domverein* (cathedral society) had been founded to complete the city's thirteenth-century cathedral. This project became an important symbol not only of medievalist nationalism but of cooperation between the confessions. After his accession in 1840, the new Prussian king Friedrich Wilhelm IV granted his approval to the cathedral project. In doing so, he hoped to make amends for the Cologne Affair, while taking advantage of a brief upsurge in nationalist sentiment occasioned by a diplomatic dispute with France.[203] Heine, by contrast, labeled the cathedral a "Bastille of the Spirit," deriding a project that threatened not only to buttress nationalism but also to bring about a rapprochement of the confessions on conservative terms. "It never was finished—and that is good. / Its very unfinished condition / Makes it a landmark of Germany's strength / And of the Protestant mission."[204] Here, as elsewhere, Heine adopted the rhetoric of Reformation in order to push for a theological position beyond not only Catholicism but also orthodox and even enlightened forms of Protestantism.

The narrator wanders over to the Rhine River where it flows through Cologne. In popular representation and in the political poetry of the 1840s, the Rhine had been presented as a virgin girl, in danger of being violated by rapacious Frenchmen.[205] Here the Rhine is a lascivious old man, complaining about the poor poetry being written on his behalf and lusting for the return of the French. "For if the French come back again, / My cheeks will blush and burn, / I who so often prayed to heaven / That they might soon return."[206] Later the narrator passes the Teutoburg Forest, the scene of Hermann's famous defeat of the Roman legate Publius Quintilius Varus. Heine wistfully imagines what Germany might have looked like had Varus won and Berlin become another Rome. But Hermann's victory had rendered such a scenario impossible, and now Heine waxed sarcastic. "O Hermann, we give you thanks for this! / And, to honor you and your tribe, / In Detmold they're building a monument. / I was one of the first to subscribe."[207]

The high point of *Deutschland* is the narrator's imagined meeting with Friedrich Barbarossa. In an evident parody of Görres's *Die teutschen Volksbücher*, Heine's narrator falls asleep only to awaken deep inside Barbarossa's magical mountain. There the old emperor leads the narrator through the rooms of his cave, tiptoeing past his sleeping army, and shows off his weapons, treasures, and flags like the curator of an antiquities museum. The emperor reveals that he is in no hurry to redeem Germany and is instead much more concerned about the state of his horse collection. "Who comes not now, comes later on; / Oaks don't grow in a day; / And *chi va piano, va sano,* my friend; / That's what in the Roman Empire they say."[208] When the narrator tells Barbarossa about the French Revolution, implicitly threatening him with the guillotine, the kaiser reacts like a typical absolutist, accusing his guest of lèse-majesté. "'Sir Barbarossa!' I cried out loud— / 'You're a mythical creation. / Go, get some sleep! Without your help / We'll work out our salvation.'"[209]

This rejection of the "mythical" emperor appears at first glance to be a call for republican revolution. But upon waking the narrator notices a grove of oak trees shaking their branches in disapproval. He repents and then slips into a mood of dejection and apathy. He says that he would gladly have the Middle Ages back: *Reich,* the estates, injustice, and all. He asks only that the modern enthusiasts of medieval Germany shut up. "Chase away the pack of clowns / And close up the theater stages / Where they imitate the lost old ages / Come soon, come soon, O Emperor!"[210] Heine's republican commitment is as much a dream as Barbarossa himself. On awakening, he slips back into the everyday realm of artistic squabbles and bad taste.

Heine's sarcastic play on old German myths and legends in *Deutschland: Ein Wintermärchen* constituted neither a negation nor a debunking of this discourse. Heine took a similar approach to the *Nibelungenlied,* invoking the warrior Siegfried in 1840 to call for German unification and citing the fallen Siegfried in 1849 to lament a shattered revolution. Hans Blumenberg has described such inversions as "work on myth," the reshaping of a myth to fit new situations and new ends.[211] Yet such "work" only became possible in the 1830s and 1840s, due to the efforts of earlier scholars to construct a national mythology out of the scattered fragments of the *Vorzeit.* Borrowing a religious narrative that in Grimm's *Deutsche Mythologie* emphasized nostalgia for a lost paganism, Heine argued for the emergence of a pantheist faith as the logical outcome of both Germanic mythology and the Protestant Reformation. In this way, he rebelled against Protestant and Catholic theological orthodoxies, as well as against a Romanticism that in his eyes had grown stagnant and conservative.

The attempt to "recover" a national mythology in Germany paralleled European-wide trends. In England, fairies and elves were seen enchanting the countryside, while legends of King Arthur and Celtic bards enjoyed wide circulation.[212] The French rediscovered Celtic mythology and the legends surrounding Joan of Arc, and the Russians resurrected the medieval *Song of Igor.*[213] What distinguished the German effort, however, was its attachment

Caspar David Friedrich, *Cromlech in Autumn* (ca. 1820). Cromlechs *(Hünengräber)*
were among the sole relics of Germany's pre-Christian past.
Source: Galerie Neve Meister, Staatliche Kunstsammlungen Dresden.
By permission.

to a self-conscious discourse of myth and its close linkage with a theological
and aesthetic critique of the Bible. The key spokesmen for the emerging "national mythology"—A. W. Schlegel, Joseph Görres, and the Grimm brothers—shared the early Romantics' dissatisfaction with the Bible as a source of
religious revelation and their impatience with a market-driven civil society's
inability to produce a culture of "publicness" similar to that found in ancient
Greece. In epics like the *Nibelungenlied* or in the Nordic pantheon of the
*Edda*s, they saw not just German counterparts to the *Iliad* or the *Theogony*
but the potential mythical substrate for a reconfigured religious identity.

Within the discourse of national mythology, a range of theological and political positions was possible. Jakob Fries and W. M. L. de Wette, inspired by
the writings of Arndt and Jahn, envisioned a new epic poetry, which would
provide the foundation for a political and religious life based on the ideals of
freedom, community, and Protestant Christian piety. But most scholars,
wary of revolution at home or abroad, envisioned the national mythology in

terms of a past tradition, which could be recovered only through a process of research, investigation, and public education. Even among scholars, however, there was a fundamental split between those, such as A. W. Schlegel, Görres, and Franz Mone, who viewed the "national mythology" as consistent with Catholic Christianity and those who viewed the national mythology as the basis for an individualistic Protestantism (Jacob Grimm) or a Protestant paganism (Heine). Thus, while all of these writers rejected the restrictive conception of revelation offered by Catholic and Protestant orthodoxy, there was room for considerable political and theological divergences within the discourse of myth.

In the end, it was the vision of "Germanic" mythology advocated by the Grimm brothers that won over the academic community and the literary public. Unlike his predecessors, Jacob Grimm anchored the national mythology not just in Eddic lays or medieval poems but in the customs and practices of everyday life. In his scheme, harvest festivals, common sayings, and old wives' tales, all elements of popular culture that seemed threatened by the process of modernization and secularization, became evidence for a lost Germanic religion. Likewise, the existing cycle of Christian holidays, rituals, and legends was co-opted by Grimm on behalf of a forgotten pagan pantheon. Thus, the construction of a national mythology involved less an outright process of "invention" than viewing the existing landscape with new, "mythopoetic" eyes.

The result of Grimm's efforts was not so much a pro-pagan rejection of Christianity as a reconfigured Christian narrative, in which the Protestant Reformation appeared as the logical and necessary outcome of German religious history and the Catholic Church was treated as an imperial interloper on German soil. This postcolonial moment in Grimm's *Deutsche Mythologie* appealed not only to Germans frustrated with the conditions and consequences of the Napoleonic invasions but also to those like Heinrich Heine who saw in it a means of articulating their frustration with the religious and political situation in *Vormärz* Germany. At the same time, however, Grimm's defiant narrative offered a challenge to those disciplines that still dictated the parameters of German education and culture: classical philology and theology. In the next two chapters, the impact of the new mythical discourse will be examined in these contexts.

CHAPTER THREE

Olympus under Siege: Creuzer's *Symbolik* and the Politics of the Restoration

Laßt die Klage uns erneuern!
Rufet zu geheimen Feyern,
Die Adonis heilig nennen,
Seine Gottheit anerkennen,
Die die Weihen sich erworben,
Denen auch der Gott gestorben.

Karoline von Günderode[1]

Suche nicht verborgne Weihe! Unterm Schleier laß das Starre!
Willst du leben, guter Narre, Sieh nur hinter dich ins Freie.

Goethe[2]

In the town of Marburg, nestled along the river Lahn, stands the fourteenth-century Elisabethkirche. Its patron saint, Elisabeth (1207–31), dedicated the last years of her life to an ascetic regimen of prayer and fasting and to charitable works in Marburg. Within the Elisabethkirche, her remains are preserved in a spectacular shrine decorated with golden figurines of the Twelve Apostles and the Madonna and child. Up through the nineteenth century, these treasures remained hidden except on certain Catholic holy days, when they were revealed to the laity. On these days, a young Protestant named George Friedrich Creuzer came to gaze at the statues, enchanted by their medieval marriage of art and religion. "My inborn seed of mysticism could only grow happily in such soil. Who knows whether the Lutheranism into which I was born had already suffered a slight blow."[3]

Creuzer published this anecdote in 1822.[4] The Heidelberg philologist evidently hoped to show that since childhood he had possessed an inborn genius for the interpretation of myth. But some read in his affinity for Catholic imagery a secret allegiance to Rome, none more so than his colleague Johann

Heinrich Voss. "Our *Symboliker* confesses in his autobiography that already as a boy, before 1782, he had turned from preached Christianity to the priestly ceremonies of the old-papal liturgy."[5] Creuzer was a crypto-Catholic, Voss claimed, channeling gullible Protestants into the clutches of the Vatican, not least by means of his *Symbolik und Mythologie der alten Völker*. For that reason, he should be rooted out of the field of classical philology and his influence destroyed.

Though little known in the English-speaking world, Creuzer's *Symbolik und Mythologie der alten Völker* (1810–12) exercised a powerful influence in its day. Friedrich Schlegel maintained that Creuzer had "newly founded" the science of myth, "or, more accurately, he restored it to its old dignity with his sweeping intellect."[6] A generation before Bachofen, Creuzer's survey of ancient religion presented the dark side of ancient Greece, uncovering orgies and other cult practices and tracing them back to the Orient.[7] His notion of the symbol, with roots both in archaeology and idealist philosophy, decisively shaped Hegel's lectures on aesthetics, while his exposition of the Dionysian and Eleusinian mysteries provided the framework for Schelling's later philosophy of mythology. Gustave Flaubert read a French translation of Creuzer's masterwork while researching *La tentation de Saint Antoine* (1849).[8] Indeed, the influence of *Symbolik und Mythologie* would extend into the twentieth century, providing a powerful, if controversial, alternative to the neohumanist image of antiquity.[9]

The dispute over *Symbolik und Mythologie* between Creuzer and his critics Voss, Gottfried Hermann, August Lobeck, and Karl Otfried Müller was nasty and unpleasant even by the standards of its day. Over the years it attracted the commentary and participation of Schelling, Hegel, Goethe, and others.[10] Although it revolved around ancient Greek mythology, the *Symbolik* dispute drew its intensity from a mixture of personal antipathy, confessional prejudice, professional dogma, and political ideology. As the publicist Wolfgang Menzel noted at the time, the dispute was "not only important with regard to scholarship but also as a historical fact. . . . In a word, this controversy reaches into the soul of scholarship and is also a highly characteristic sign of the times."[11] This chapter examines the *Symbolik* affair in some detail, focusing on the situation of classical philology in the early nineteenth century as it sought to defend its hegemonic position against the internal challenge of Creuzer's mythography and the external threats of both Restoration theology and the new philologies of medieval Germany and the Orient. In this dispute classical philology would win a Pyrrhic victory, purging itself of romanticizing and orientalizing influences but making itself less relevant to the theological and political debates at the center of German public life.

ROMANTIC PHILOLOGIST

Whatever his inborn genius, the life of George Friedrich Creuzer (1771–1852) began in thoroughly mundane surroundings. His father was a bookbinder and tax collector in Marburg. In 1789, when Creuzer enrolled at the local university, he paid the standard *Bürger*'s tax, while his contemporaries training for the priesthood received government subsidies. Throughout these years, Creuzer fought a nagging sense of inferiority. "Through extraordinary industry, I hoped to make up for my lack of genius. I had almost no confidence in my natural abilities," he later wrote.[12] Creuzer's physical attributes could not have helped his self-confidence. "As ugly as he was, it was inconceivable that he could ever interest a woman," sniped Bettina von Arnim.[13]

At Marburg, Creuzer trained as a historian and a philologist, absorbing the theories of Heyne and Wolf. Outside his regular study, Creuzer benefited from the intellectual flowering in Marburg during the 1790s. The jurist Friedrich Karl von Savigny befriended Creuzer and imbued in the young philologist the same reverence for antiquity that animated his work in legal history. "Everything was arranged by him," wrote Creuzer of Savigny. "He encouraged me to take up an academic career."[14] These arrangements included a stipend that sustained Creuzer for two years.[15] Through Savigny, Creuzer met the Grimm brothers, who were then studying law. In addition, Creuzer came into the circle of the preacher Johann Heinrich Jung-Stilling, whose mystical pietism anticipated the religious revival of the 1800s.

Inspired by Savigny and Jung-Stilling, Creuzer read himself into the Romantic movement, then simply known as the "new school." He digested the works of Schleiermacher, Schelling, and Friedrich Schlegel as they appeared, and with some effort he completed Fichte's *Neue Darstellung der Wissenschaftslehre* (1797). Like the Romantics, Creuzer interpreted idealist philosophy as an esoteric doctrine available only to the elite (he rather tentatively included himself in this group).[16] Among other writings, he took particular interest in the studies of Greek art and literature by August Wilhelm Schlegel and Friedrich Schlegel. "What a new world we will discover with the Schlegels in the ancient world!" he exclaimed in 1799.[17] In this spirit, Creuzer began investigating the Greek historians, publishing *Herodot und Thucydides* (1798) and *Die historische Kunst der Griechen* (1803).[18] On the basis of these books and a recommendation from the theologian Carl Daub, Creuzer received a call in 1804 to a professor's chair in Heidelberg.

In 1804, an appointment to Heidelberg carried little prestige. Heidelberg was the kind of place where shepherds led their flocks straight through the middle of town. While nearby Mannheim housed a national theater, the citizens of Heidelberg had forbidden drama.[19] The small Catholic university was undistinguished, like many that disappeared during the Napoleonic wars. After the reorganization of the Reich in 1803, Heidelberg had acceded to the Grand Duchy of Baden. Newly enlarged and suddenly powerful, Baden sought legitimacy and status among the other German states, and the Protestant grand duke Karl Friedrich set out to transform the university in Heidelberg from a Jesuit backwater into a model university.[20] As one of the first intellectual lights to arrive in Heidelberg, Creuzer exercised considerable influence on these reforms. Meanwhile, he envisioned a retooling of his own discipline of philology, which he hoped to reorient toward the Romantic idealism of the "new school."

During these years, the key text for aspiring idealists was Schelling's *Method of Academic Study* (1803). The *Method* outstripped in influence most of Schelling's previous works and anything written by Fichte because it concisely demonstrated the political, religious, and pedagogical implications of idealist philosophy. Convinced of the unity of all science, Schelling endorsed the idea of a research university. As he put it, "whoever lives in his science as if on a foreign possession, whoever does not personally own it . . . is an unworthy [teacher]."[21] Schelling grounded his scholarly ideal in the principles of his identity philosophy. The identity of the real, empirical world with the theoretical realm of ideas should underpin all scholarly inquiry, he argued, freeing science from utilitarian demands and outworn models. Professors in the faculty of medicine, for example, could set aside their textbooks and investigate the hidden unity of spirit and nature. Those in the faculty of law would turn away from the external regulations of government and instead investigate the means for harmonizing public and private life within an ideal state.[22]

Schelling's philosophy appealed deeply to Creuzer, who had long been uncomfortable with the dominant trends of classical scholarship. He had written of Friedrich August Wolf's *Prolegomena ad Homerum* that "no single book had more influence on my studies," but he remained ambivalent about its implications for philology. In particular, he rejected the view of some Wolfians "that a young philologist isn't worth anything until he has declared the work of some first-rate author to be falsely attributed."[23] Creuzer agreed with Wolf that no single author had composed the Homeric epics, but he had little interest in engaging in further acts of historical debunking. Schelling had written that "[h]istory only attains consummation for reason when the empirical causes that satisfy the understanding are viewed as tools and means for the appearance of a higher necessity. In such a presentation, history cannot fail to have the effect of the greatest and most astounding drama, which could be composed only in an infinite mind."[24] On this basis he had argued that theologians should neither criticize the Bible nor preach morality but instead foster a higher, supraconfessional view of the history of religion. Creuzer now sought to apply Schelling's dictum to his own discipline, as he investigated not merely Homer's poetry but the totality of ancient Greek religious life.

Creuzer laid out his understanding of classical philology in "Das Studium des Alterthums, als Vorbereitung zur Philosophie" (1805).[25] Here he argued that philology should be grounded in the identity of the real and ideal worlds. Evoking Schelling's descriptions of the Greek mysteries in *Philosophie und Religion*, Creuzer suggested that exoteric instruction in the historical world of philology precede esoteric instruction in the philosophical Absolute. The means for this exoteric instruction lay in the realm of myth. For even though myth was widely despised by enlightened scholars as the language of "the childhood of man" or the product of a "barbarous race," Socrates and Plato had long ago recognized the usefulness of symbols and allegories for initiating their students into higher philosophical truths.[26] In Creuzer's scheme, philology would thus serve as a kind of lesser mystery before the initiate reached the greater mystery of (idealist) philosophy. At that stage, the student would experience the same religious intoxication and loss of individuality that had produced Greek poetry.[27]

Yet Creuzer's hopes for a circle of students schooled in his ideas were soon frustrated. Karl Friedrich and his minister Sigismund von Reitzenstein were more interested in attracting established scholars than in promoting philosophical uniformity. Among their hires was the Aufklärer Johann Heinrich Voss, who was meant to serve as a "signpost" for the university.[28] Upon his arrival, Voss took steps to curtail Creuzer's influence, complaining to Reitzenstein about the new spirit of Romantic classicism. "We have been flooded with the unconditional . . . , with idealism, esoteric wisdom, poetic philosophy, and mystical religion, with a higher standpoint above the basely empirical or real facts," he wrote.[29] A year later, conflicts with Voss over *Des Knabens Wunderhorn* would help drive Görres, Arnim, and Brentano away from Heidelberg, leaving Creuzer isolated and unhappy. In 1808, he accepted a post at the University of Leiden but returned almost as soon as he left, complaining of Holland's cold, its wetness, and its drab intellectual life.[30] Arnim teased him, "Christus ist zum Leiden geboren und Sie sind auch dort gewesen" (Christ was born for suffering *[Leiden]* and you were also there).[31]

Creuzer's personal life only added to his misery. He had married Sophie

Friedrich Creuzer. "As ugly as he was, it was inconceivable that he could ever
interest a woman," wrote Bettina von Arnim.
Source: Richard Wilhelm, *Die Günderrode: Dichtung und Schicksal* (Frankfurt:
Societäts-Verlag, 1938).

Leske in 1798, although she was more than ten years his senior. When in 1804
he encountered the twenty-four-year-old poet Karoline von Günderode,
Creuzer fell in love. An aristocrat of the house Alt-Limpurg, Günderode had
achieved fame through poems such as "Mohammed's Dream" and "Bona-
parte in Egypt." The pair met on the balcony of the Heidelberg castle, and
within a month Creuzer was scheming to disengage himself from his wife.
But Sophie Leske's resistance and Creuzer's concerns about money and
his own mental health ultimately led him to cut off the relationship with
Günderode in 1806. Günderode's response, to stab herself to death on the
banks of the Rhine, has given the affair a legendary quality. Nonetheless, her
obsessions—with the infinite, with the Orient, and with self-destruction—
left a deep mark on Creuzer's psyche and on his scholarship.[32]

THE DOCTRINE OF THE *SYMBOLIK*

Remarkably, in the midst of this turmoil Creuzer began to pull together the strands of his *Symbolik und Mythologie*. In 1805, Creuzer had promised Günderode "to apply the best fruit of my manly intellectual power to a work that, insofar as it strives to reveal the center of pious, holy antiquity, would not be unworthy to be brought as a sacrifice to poetry."[33] The result was the four-volume *Symbolik und Mythologie der alten Völker* (1810–12).[34] In this work, Creuzer argued that an esoteric symbolism *(Symbolik)* had provided the basis for religious life throughout the ancient world. Thus, while Homer entertained the masses, the Eleusinian mysteries contained the Greeks' true religious doctrine.[35] Through its myths and dogmas, this religion had anticipated essential aspects of the Christian faith, including the belief that God had become man, suffered death, and risen to new life.

The origins of this *Symbolik* lay among the priestly castes of ancient India. Based on their observations of the heavens the Brahmanic clerics had created an esoteric cosmology, which they expressed by means of religious symbols.[36] But in their attempt to explain this theology to the people, the priests were forced to transform these symbols into narratives, thus giving rise to mythology.[37] Eventually the ancient prelates spread their wisdom beyond India, traveling to Asia Minor, Egypt, and even Israel. Here they encountered primitive hunters and shepherds, whose religion consisted of a crude fetishism. The priests taught the natives religion, as well as the elements of agriculture and statecraft. From Egypt, the clerics crossed the Mediterranean, colonizing the Pelagian people of Samothrace and establishing the Cabiri mysteries. The island of Samothrace would become the great "dividing line" between Asia and Europe, as the ancient *Symbolik* spread into Greece and Italy.[38]

These were bold claims. To justify them, Creuzer relied especially on the writings of Herodotus. In his *Histories* (ca. 425 B.C.), Herodotus had identified the homeland of the Greek gods as Egypt, where he claimed to have found worshipers of Dionysus. Herodotus's theory of the Egyptian origins of classical myth had been relatively popular during the eighteenth century, since it fit in well with enlightened notions of an esoteric truth passed down through the ages by a small elite. Over the years, a variety of Masons, including Cagliostro, Guillaume de Sainte-Croix, and Johann August Starck, had claimed access to the "secret wisdom" of ancient Egypt. When classical philologists discussed the Homeric myths, however, they tended to emphasize the unique linguistic, geographic, or political features of ancient Hellas

Title page of Friedrich Creuzer, *Symbolik und Mythologie der alten Völker,*
2nd ed., vol. 1.

while downplaying the Greeks' borrowings from other cultures.[39] Friedrich
Creuzer challenged his fellow philologists to take Herodotus seriously. "Did
the nations of the past only deliver elephant teeth, gold, and slaves to one
another? And not also knowledge, religious practices, and gods? . . . One
should not close one's eyes when even trustworthy Greek guides point to the
foreign homeland and foreign origin of a doctrine."[40] Creuzer accepted

Herodotus's claim that the Greek deities had been brought from ancient Egypt via the island of Samothrace. At the same time, he identified other routes by which the *Symbolik* had passed into Greece, including the eastern region of Thrace, the northern region of Scythia, and the trade routes of the Phoenicians.[41]

Although Creuzer emphasized the ties between Greece and Egypt, he departed from his eighteenth-century predecessors in tracing the origin of ancient religion to India.[42] "When dealing with almost all major myths, . . . we must, so to speak, first orient ourselves toward the Orient," Creuzer wrote.[43] *Symbolik und Mythologie* was just one example of a new enthusiasm for the Orient, which had been sparked in the 1780s by the work of the British jurist and imperial official William "Oriental" Jones. Jones had demonstrated the common relationship between Sanskrit, Latin, and Greek, and argued for the Indian roots of classical mythology.[44] The fascination with oriental religion was stimulated further by translations of the Persian *Zend-Avesta* and the Hindu *Upanishads* by Abraham Anquetil-Duperron.[45] Many scholars saw these texts as the oldest records of religious belief in the ancient world, predating Homer and even the Hebrew Bible. By the first decade of the nineteenth century, Joseph Görres, Friedrich Schlegel, Johann Arnold Kanne, and Joseph Hammer von Purgstall had published works tracing the origin of ancient religion and mythology to India or the Caucasus.[46] Explaining the fascination with the Orient, Charles de Villers wrote, "We love the distant, the unknown, where we can transport ourselves and realize somehow the most beautiful, the most holy, and the most ideal that our imagination has to offer."[47] For Creuzer, the Orient seemed the homeland of genuine religious feeling, an alternative to classical Western traditions of aesthetics, rationality, and morality.

The key to Creuzer's historical approach was his theory of the symbol.[48] In his view, the ancients had expressed their beliefs not in discursive language but in signs.[49] So rather than concentrate on the etymology or narrative structure of ancient myths, he investigated the images inscribed on coins, vases, reliefs, and other physical artifacts, in many cases exploiting the findings generated by Napoleon's invasion of Egypt in 1798.[50] Like most Europeans at this time, Creuzer assumed that Egyptian hieroglyphs encoded not a phonetic but a symbolic language, which could easily be transferred from one culture to another.[51] By comparing evidence from Greece, Egypt, and Asia Minor, Creuzer attempted to show the universality in the ancient world of a few key symbols. For example, a slaughtered steer betokened not only animal sacrifice but the death of Dionysus-Zagreus, who was often associated with the bull. The discovery of this image on artifacts from both Greece and

Siava-Mahadeva-Iswara next to Parvati-Bhavani-Isani, receiving the deities of the
Indian pantheon.
Source: Friedrich Creuzer, *Symbolik und Mythologie der alten Völker*, 3rd ed.
(Leipzig and Darmstadt: Leske, 1840), vol. 1, pt. 3, pl. 3.

Egypt seemed to prove that these cultures had possessed a common deity,
known variously as Dionysus or Osiris.[52]

For Creuzer, the power of the symbol resided in its ability to sum up an
entire theology in one potent image. Through a process of "combination"
(implicit in the Greek word σύμβολον) the symbol dramatized the various elements of ancient religion in "a moment that claims our entire essence, a look

into an infinite distance, from which our spirit returns enriched."[53] Like Schelling and Moritz, Creuzer viewed the symbol as a union of the infinite with the finite, the "idea embodied."[54] Unlike Schelling, however, Creuzer insisted that the symbol overwhelmed the limits of classical aesthetics, shattering the perfect forms that Schiller and Winckelmann had praised in their accounts of Greek art. In the true symbol, there was an "incongruence of essence with form" and an "overflow of the content in comparison with its expression."[55] Such a symbol could not be invented in the imagination of a poet or derived through discursive logic. It could be known only by plunging into the mysterious depths of the universe. In this way, an individual would receive "momentary intuition" into the hidden bonds between the ideal and the real, God and nature.[56]

To illustrate his theory of the symbol, Creuzer turned to the Cabiris, a mysterious group of deities whose worship, according to Herodotus, had been transplanted from Egypt to the island of Samothrace at the dawn of Greek history. "Who were they?" Creuzer asked at one point. "There is almost no doubt that the Egyptians thought [the Cabiris] were the planets."[57] Yet the ancient *Symbolik* was based not only on astronomical observation but on a deeper cosmological vision. In their deeper sense, the Cabiri deities were "potences" in the creation of the world. The first Cabiri, Axieros, was the undifferentiated chaos at the beginning of creation, the man-woman. This deity was followed by Axiokersos, the procreating male potence, who was followed in turn by Axiokersa, the begetting female potence. The last potence, Kasmilos, was the "serving potence," who healed the split in nature between its male and female polarities.[58]

This dialectic of sexual differentiation and unification underlay the ancient religious cultus, which featured cross-dressing, enlarged phalluses, ritual intercourse, and orgies. "In the natural world, nothing was too secret to be drawn into the light and presented to the eyes in image and shape," Creuzer argued. "What the civilized person modestly and carefully hides in social life was viewed as religious in name and likeness by the sensibility of the natural man and consecrated to the public liturgy."[59] The ancients had taken the private realm of sexuality and put it at the center of their religion. For these reasons, the ancient theogony could not be equated with the movements of sun and the planets, as some eighteenth-century rationalists had argued. The rising and setting of the sun were instead metaphors for the more fundamental experiences of lust, procreation, impotence, and death.

Creuzer's belief in a gender dynamic running through all mythology reflected the influence not only of Schelling but of his colleague Joseph Görres. Görres's Heidelberg years coincided with the most creative years of Creuzer's life, and scholars have long argued who influenced whom. In *Glauben und Wissen* (1805), *Wachstum der Historie* (1808), and the monumental *Mythengeschichte der asiatischen Welt* (1810), Görres narrated the history of religion from its beginnings in the Caucasus to the Nordic myths of the *Edda*s. Like Creuzer, Görres highlighted the orgiastic, Bacchantic nature of Asian mythology, while evoking a sense of pagan religious frenzy with his exuberant prose style. He believed that discoveries in the field of *Naturphilosophie* had revealed the doctrine at the heart of paganism: the opposition between male and female polarities in nature.[60] He used these principles to explain the course of world history, the origins of the races, and the rise and fall of various forms of the state.

Creuzer never fully endorsed Görres's theory that primal sexual urges among ancient peoples had brought forth their gods. Instead, he preferred to see the *Symbolik* as the creation of a small elite, who had combined philosophical speculation, scientific inquiry, and religious doctrine when forming their mythological doctrines. This was in line with the early Romantic theories of Friedrich Schlegel and Schelling, who had taken as their starting point the emergence of an idealist doctrine that was understood by only a narrow group of intellectuals. But despite the differences between Creuzer and Görres, contemporaries were most struck by their similarities: both emphasized the "oriental" origin of ancient Greek mythology, and both argued that the pagans had deified desires that modern bourgeois society preferred to keep under wraps.

To demonstrate the influence of early *Naturphilosophie* on Greek religion, Creuzer provided an extensive analysis of the mystery cults of Demeter and Dionysus. According to Creuzer, the symbolic system embodied in the Cabiri theology had spread into Greece, where it formed the basis for the Eleusinian mysteries. These secret rites, held during the harvest season each year in the city of Eleusis, commemorated the story of Demeter and her daughter, Persephone.[61] As related in the Homeric hymn to Demeter, Hades kidnapped Persephone and carried her off to hell. After Hades tricked her into tasting the pomegranate seed, Persephone was forced to spend half of the year in the underworld with her captor and the other half above ground with her mother. In the Homeric account, Demeter's alternating moods of joy and suffering explained the cycle of the seasons. For Creuzer, however, the characters in the Eleusinian mysteries were extensions of the Cabiri deities. Axieros was Demeter, Axiokersa was Persephone, and Axiokersos was Hades. The last deity of the Cabiri mysteries, Kasmilos, reappeared as Iakchos, a child version of Dionysus who was conceived by the virgin Persephone.[62]

Like the servant god of the Cabiri doctrine, Iakchos arrived to bring comfort and reconciliation to the mourning Demeter.

Creuzer's interpretation of the Eleusinian mysteries was based in part on a comparison with the Near Eastern cults of Mithras and of Cybele, the great mother goddess. According to Creuzer, the Eleusinian mysteries exalted Demeter far above the status of a goddess of agriculture. In the mysteries she became like the goddess Gaia, a symbol of the totality of nature, the "all-begetting mother earth."[63] Indeed, Demeter, Persephone, and the other female deities were all aspects of a single goddess, whose worship constituted a "monotellurism," or worship of the earth.[64] At the same time, however, Creuzer's portrayal of Demeter-Persephone evoked the Catholic cult of the Virgin Mary—precisely at a time when Marian devotion was becoming ever more central to popular Catholicism and Ultramontanist theology.

Dionysus was the other key deity in Creuzer's system. This god showed two faces to the Greek public. For most Greeks, he existed as a national deity, an exuberant wine god who rode a donkey and inspired tragic drama.[65] But in the mystery cults Dionysus appeared as the *Weltseele*, the demiurge who oversaw the creation of the material world and yet became intertwined with its suffering. This latter aspect of Dionysus was symbolized in the figure of Zagreus, who was torn into pieces by the Titans. Apollo then collected these pieces and restored him whole. "Dionysus . . . is multiplicity," Creuzer explained. "In other words, he is the universe that presents itself in many forms: in air, water, earth, plants, and animals. . . . Apollo . . . is unity, which presides over nature in its development to protect it from complete disintegration and to secure it again unharmed to the One."[66] For Creuzer, the tension between Dionysus and Apollo formed a key dualism in Greek culture, although by no means the only one.[67]

The mysteries of Dionysus and Demeter not only dramatized the origin of the world, they prepared the soul for the process of metempsychosis. "All souls must first be purified through cleansing in order to return to the blissful dwellings from which they came."[68] Initiates to the mysteries underwent symbolic purifications by fire, air, and water, at each stage achieving a higher level of being. According to the doctrine of the mysteries, only Dionysus could heal the split between the female and male principles in nature and return the soul back to the moment before all creation. Here the suffering Dionysus was transformed into the redeeming Dionysus, a compassionate and merciful god who, as the child Iakchos, appeared in the arms of Demeter-Persephone.[69] This doctrine of incarnation, suffering, and redemption would eventually return to form the central teaching of Christianity.[70]

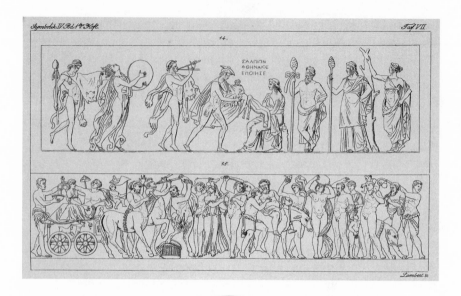

Top: Marble relief of the baby Dionysus being handed to his nurse. *Bottom:* Relief of
a triumphal march of Dionysus, with Ariadne in the wagon.
Source: Friedrich Creuzer, *Symbolik und Mythologie der alten Völker,* 3rd ed.
(Leipzig and Darmstadt: Leske, 1840), vol. 4, pt. 1, pl. 7.

Given Creuzer's fascination with the esoteric and the universal in paganism, those elements of Greek mythology that reflected the purely national
character of the Greeks occupied a fairly low position in his hierarchy of values. He described the epic, for example, as a product of the practical needs of
the emerging polis. "Sanctified by lawgivers and the constitution, the popular cult demanded and required an abundance of legends, because the folk
had to know the history of those before whom it kneeled."[71] The epics eventually took the form of tragedy, which reflected the interests of priests and
magistrates. "The works of piety merged with the demands of the state, and
the institution of holy dances and dramatic plays became at the same time
the duty of the citizen. . . . So in Greece the religion of the people, along with
its poetry and art, became plastic and political."[72]

As the myths were joined to historical events to form epics, they gradually lost their religious meaning for the people. In a moment of literary
pathos, Creuzer described the transition from theology to epic:

> After the extinction of many older races, when powerful northern tribes had
> gained a foothold throughout Greece and into the Peloponnesos, the strong
> tastes of the robust crowd became more and more the master in all things.

Custom and constitution, thought and poetry, turned more and more from
the deep-thinking Orient and became more understandable, lighter, tougher,
but naturally also emptier.[73]

With citizens and nobles in charge of civic life, "popular" singers and poets
arose to entertain them. Echoing A. W. Schlegel, Creuzer described how the
Greeks constructed a "knightly poetry" that emphasized deeds and actions
at the expense of religious doctrine. In the *Iliad*, "the life of the gods is the
glorified life of Greek knights; Olympus . . . is set up exactly like the palace
of a Greek king."[74] The formerly theological myths became transformed into
stories about merely human needs and passions, the glorious accomplish-
ments of a nation and its people. The poets then collected these legends
together and, in a jealous pique, assigned their authorship to a fiction
they named "Homer." Meanwhile, the esoteric religion persisted underground, awaiting the arrival of a god who could fulfill Dionysus's promise of
redemption.

In detailing this story over four lengthy and often repetitive volumes,
Creuzer created an imposing narrative of the history of religion. In contrast
to Schelling's *Philosophy of Art*, Creuzer's *Symbolik und Mythologie* downplayed the difference between paganism and Christianity, as well as that between Greece and the Orient. Christianity was presented as the necessary
and logical outcome of the ancient *Symbolik*, with the liturgy and hierarchy
of the church offering a more ethical version of rituals already established in
paganism. As Gerhart von Graevenitz has shown, the comparison of the pagan mysteries with Christianity had a long history, beginning in the patristic
era, dropping off during the Middle Ages, and then reviving once more in the
work of Renaissance scholars like Giordano Bruno.[75] In the context of the
Metternichian Restoration, however, Creuzer's argument served to buttress
a Christianity whose revelation was under attack from critics both inside and
outside German faculties of theology, while blunting the potential challenge
of neohumanism to both the existing confessions and the old regime as a
whole. These factors would ensure a massive controversy in the years ahead.

THE *SYMBOLIK* CONTROVERSY:
PHILOLOGY, POLITICS, AND GREEK AUTOCHTHONY

Creuzer's *Symbolik und Mythologie* was a bold challenge to the profession
of classical philology. Winckelmann, Schiller, and their neohumanist disciples had viewed ancient Greek society as guided by the republican virtues of
freedom and individuality, which were celebrated in the Homeric epics and

portrayed in the beautiful forms of sculpture. Creuzer, by contrast, emphasized the primacy of the priesthood and a religious symbolism that featured
such unbeautiful images as slaughtered steers and enlarged phalluses. In his
scheme, the republican era was a period of relative decline, as the demands of
popular taste distorted and obscured the original religious revelation.
Creuzer also departed from the methodological norms of his discipline. Since
the ascent of Heyne at Göttingen and Wolf at Halle, philology had emerged
as the model science for the research university: critical, inquisitive, and
grounded in an expert command of the Greek language.[76] But Creuzer seemed
to replace this critical approach with a cult of the exegete that eschewed
texts in favor of mystical symbols. Further, his emphasis on the oriental
antecedents to classical mythology threatened the individuality of Greek
culture, the very premise on which neohumanism was founded. To be sure,
Friedrich Schlegel, Görres, and others had proffered similar arguments, but
none occupied a chair of philology. In this respect, Creuzer posed a unique
threat to his profession.

Creuzer's readers, surprisingly numerous considering the arcane, obscure, and sometimes frustrating nature of this work, responded to *Symbolik und Mythologie* in large part according to their attitudes toward classical
philology. An early critic was the Leipzig philologist Gottfried Hermann
(1772–1848). Although Hermann never produced a definitive work, his elo-
quence and personal charisma made him one of the most influential philologists in Germany.[77] During the 1820s, he engaged in a major debate with the
Berlin scholar August Boeckh over the future of philology, championing a
research program that emphasized the analysis of literary texts over an approach that attempted to reconstruct the concrete reality of ancient Greek
life. In his approach to Greek mythology, Hermann followed the theory of his
teacher Heyne but interpreted it through the lens of Kantian philosophy.
Thus, he viewed the *sermo mythicus* not just as a primitive reaction to the
world but as an ordered, quasi-philosophical natural science, which could
best be recovered by an analysis of its language.[78]

Hermann and Creuzer carried out their dispute in a series of letters,
which were published as *Briefe über Homer und Hesiodus, vorzüglich über
die Theogonie* (1818). Hermann agreed with Creuzer that the poetry of
Homer and Hesiod had evolved from an earlier philosophical cosmogony,
which he described as "the most admirable masterpiece of antiquity."[79] But
Hermann maintained that this cosmogony was encoded not in symbols but
in the names of the elements, and that the Greek gods had emerged when
these names were confused with real existing personages. "Personification is
the only true characteristic of that mythology," he wrote. "Therefore, all the

names and nicknames of the gods belong to them alone, and the etymological interpretation is the only one that is needed to understand them."[80] This involved tracing the linguistic origins of a myth in order to reconstruct its underlying "philosopheme." Thus, Hermann rejected Creuzer's attempt to reduce mythology to a series of translinguistic symbols and argued that in the *Symbolik* there were "no longer any borders" and the uniquely Hellenic aspects of Greek myth were erased.[81]

Hermann also bemoaned Creuzer's insistence on the dogmatic nature of Greek mythology. "[R]eligious faith as such, as dogma, does not belong to mythology, but only to the philosopheme that forms the basis of that dogma."[82] Hermann differentiated three periods in Greek mythology: the era of the original philosophemes; a period of misunderstanding, which gave rise to the epic poetry of Homer and Hesiod; and the theologizing era of the Orphic and Dionysian cults. Creuzer, by contrast, insisted on a single theology, as permanent and unchanging as the "Orient" from which it had arisen. "[T]hrough all the changes in Greek poetry, there was never such change or such a longing for innovation in the theological and priestly doctrines of the Greeks as modern skepticism would like us to think," Creuzer argued.[83] When the original symbolic first emerged, there were no philosophers, only "priests, priestly wisdom, and priestly dogmas."[84]

The dispute between Creuzer and Hermann raised the eyebrows of many contemporaries, among them Goethe. Goethe had met Creuzer in Heidelberg in 1815, and the two had exchanged ideas on oriental literature and the nature of myth.[85] But when the *Symbolik* dispute became public two years later, Goethe took the side of Hermann. "We gladly assume an ancient popular faith," Goethe wrote Creuzer. "But for us, purely characteristic personification, without allegory or anything else, is worth everything. We can ignore what the priests later did in the dark or the philosophers did in the light. So reads our confession of faith!"[86] In private, Goethe was much harsher, describing Creuzer's theory as a "dark-poetic-philosophical-priestly labyrinth" that should be avoided at all costs.[87] Hermann's theory, while not entirely satisfactory, more closely approximated Goethe's ideas about the purpose of poetry and the centrality of the Greeks. "To me it is all the same whether the hypothesis is philosophically or critically defensible. It suffices that it is critical, Hellenic, and patriotic, and that from its development there is such an infinite amount to learn."[88]

"Critical, Hellenic, and patriotic." The conjunction of these words offers a clue to the reactions of Goethe and many of his generation to *Symbolik und Mythologie*. In their eyes, Creuzer had violated the rules of textual criticism as they had been set down in Göttingen and Halle. Rather than breaking

down the wholes into their component parts, he seemed interested in reconstructing a historical totality that would encompass not just Greece but all
of antiquity, bringing the ancient world into a typological relationship with
Christianity. In doing so, however, Creuzer threatened to undermine the
critical force of Greek myth and drag its gods into a morass of Christian-
inspired mysticism. For Goethe, the argument of *Symbolik und Mythologie*
was a particular affront. He was not averse to the nonclassical world—the
Persian imagery of his *West-östlicher Divan* (1819) and the Christian motifs
in *Faust: Part Two* (1832) were proof of that. But he did insist that art strive
for a humanistic form of beauty, an aesthetic doctrine neatly summarized in
his image of Faust pursuing Helen of Troy.[89] For the philologists, however, the
danger was more fundamental. In their view, Creuzer threatened to reassim-
ilate their discipline into an intellectual framework dictated by Christian
theology.

In the eyes of his detractors, Creuzer's shift of focus from Greece to the
Orient and from aesthetics to piety found an obvious parallel in the Romantics' love affair with the Middle Ages. In *Der Symbolik Triumph* (1825), the
philologist Wilhelm Adolf Becker complained that "Teutonomania, which
has spread its influence into everyday life, . . . now attacks the serious sciences, which were already infected with the plague of mysticism and the secondary symptoms of Indomania."[90] Creuzer's supporters echoed this view.
The nationalist publicist Wolfgang Menzel lamented how classical philologists held onto "their old prejudice for classical antiquity and against
Germanic barbarism. They smile disparagingly at the fools who value the
Nibelungenlied and the minnesinger next to Homer and Horace. They are
embittered against the Orientalists, who threaten to tear away their mon-
opoly on judging antiquity."[91] Creuzer himself seemed to endorse the new
appreciation for medieval and Germanic mythology. In the second edition of
his *Symbolik und Mythologie,* he appended two volumes devoted to Nordic
mythology by his colleague Franz Mone.[92] In sum, the *Symbolik* controversy
was seen as part of a larger conflict over the value of ancient myth in German
culture, which posed the neohumanists against anyone who might challenge
their dominance.

The wider implications of the *Symbolik* controversy were addressed
most forcefully by Johann Heinrich Voss. Born in 1751, Voss embodied the
type of eighteenth-century "patriotism" described by Goethe. He first gained
renown as a member of the Göttingen Grove, a clique of poets that formed in
the 1770s in honor of Klopstock. Politically enlightened in an age before liberalism, Voss, Ludwig Hölty, and the brothers Friedrich and Christian Graf

zu Stolberg rebelled against the neoclassicism of Racine, Corneille, and Christoph Martin Wieland, and emphasized instead the bardic poetry of Ossian and Homer. Voss had published his translation of the *Odyssey* in 1781, in the hope that it would become a German epic. Then in 1793 he had issued a translation of the *Iliad*, along with a completely revised *Odyssey*. Hegel later wrote to Voss, "Luther made the Bible speak German, and you have done the same for Homer—the greatest gift that can be bestowed on a people."[93] Indeed, Voss defined his German identity largely in terms of Luther, although he had in mind Luther the German fighter rather than Luther the devout theologian. Through his translation of the Bible, Voss believed, Luther had freed German literature from the dominance of the Latin language. Through the Reformation, he had freed the German nation from the Catholic Church.

These aesthetic and religious commitments left Voss ill-disposed to appreciate the new scholarship of the 1790s and 1800s. Already skeptical of Heyne's theory of myth, he emphatically rejected the "many-headed Homer" of Friedrich August Wolf.[94] But Voss reserved his greatest contempt for the writers and artists of the Romantic school. In the early 1800s he quarreled with August Wilhelm Schlegel over how to translate Homer, and in Heidelberg he fought a pitched battle with Arnim and Brentano, accusing them of academic fraud in their edition of *Des Knaben Wunderhorn* (1806). Meanwhile, he became associated with a "liberal" party in Heidelberg that included such anti-Romantics as H. E. G. Paulus, Christian F. Winter, and Jakob Fries and that stood close to both the *Burschenschaften* and the opposition delegates in the Badenese parliament.[95] Despite Voss's reputation as a fighter, his vitriolic attacks on Creuzer shocked many observers. Heine would later describe Voss as "a lower Saxon peasant like Luther. He lacked all chivalry, all courtesy, all graciousness. He belongs to that tough, manly tribe to which Christianity had to be preached with fire and sword, . . . that in its material and spiritual struggles showed itself as bold and stubborn as its old gods."[96] In the *Antisymbolik* (1824–26), Voss dismantled Creuzer's scholarship, defaming the character of its author and his associates in the process.[97] As Creuzer knew so well, "when Voss hates once, he hates irreconcilably."[98]

In targeting *Symbolik und Mythologie*, Voss hoped to reverse what he saw as a trend in recent scholarship to devalue Greek art and poetry. "As the sun incubates vermin from the Nile's slime," he wrote, "so the insect of the Creuzerian *Symbolik* grew out of Heyne and Hermann's decaying *Symbolik* in the sun of India, a lovely swarm. Everything from rot."[99] Voss took partic-

ular offense at the emphasis in Heyne and Creuzer on the nonanthropomor-
phic qualities of early Greek myth. To collapse the naked, beautiful bodies of
Homer into the animals or half-animals worshiped by the Egyptians and the
Indians was to corrupt the essentially humanistic qualities of Greek mythology. "Listen to this old Homer! Your chaste Pallas Athena is the Indian *Bha-
vani*, a hideous man-woman! Out of the triangle of her female *yoni* arises a
male *lingam* of creation, which in Indian also means *phallus*. From this secret *phallus* she got the name *Pallas*, which can be used as male or female."[100]
The racist overtones in Voss's prose were unmistakable. But Voss viewed the
denigration of Indian and Egyptian culture as necessary in order to promote
the cause of individual freedom, which for him was symbolized in the perfect
(white) human forms of the Greek gods.[101] He thus insisted that the weird
beings depicted in *Symbolik und Mythologie* could only be of foreign origin
or deformations of an originally anthropomorphic deity.

Voss's own ideas about the origins of Greek mythology were rather vague.
Scattered comments indicated that he saw the gods arising from stories
about revered elders or guardians of hunting and fishing. For example, he de-
scribed Dionysus as a deified hero, the son of a woman named Semele.[102]
Voss's chief concern, however, was to rehabilitate Homer as the real author of
the *Iliad* and the *Odyssey*. "Let us imagine a feast of the hero Odysseus in
Ithaca . . . ," he wrote. "Homer, already famous because of the emerging
Iliad, pleases the gathering with a short odyssey, to the praise of the celebrated sea hero Odysseus. To please other sea lands he gradually adds
Odysseus's friendship with the king of the seafaring Cretans, [etc.] . . . You
smile, friend? Ask Klopstock or Goethe!"[103] Neither the imprimatur of revelation nor the mysteries of natural science explained the origin of myth,
according to Voss. Myth required nothing more—and nothing less—than a
society in which the dignity of the individual human poet was appreciated.

While these were plausible, if somewhat outdated, arguments, they were
overshadowed by Voss's denunciation of *Symbolik und Mythologie* as the
weapon of a papal conspiracy that sought to eliminate all Protestant free-
doms and return Germany to the Middle Ages.[104] As parties to this conspiracy, Voss indicted the Schlegels, Schelling, Brentano, Sulpiz Boisserée, and
Görres. In his view, Creuzer's graphic descriptions of orgiastic rites were
designed to lead young men astray by destroying their aesthetic sense.
"[W]hat is more tasteless than all this Indian myth hubbub? And one must
make youth tasteless before one dares to make them popish. So away with
ancient Greek clarity of thought."[105] Like Goethe and Schiller, Voss believed
that good taste guaranteed personal freedom in both politics and religion.
When the former collapsed, the latter was sure to follow.

The *Antisymbolik* often echoed the anti-Catholic rhetoric of Friedrich Nicolai in his campaign against the Jena Romantics, but it was aggravated considerably by personal experience. During the 1790s, Voss's close friend Friedrich von Stolberg had come into contact with the circle of pious Catholics around Princess Amalie Gallitzin in Münster. After several years of deliberation, Stolberg declared his allegiance to the Roman Church in 1800.[106] This conversion, involving one of Germany's most prominent poets, shook the Protestant world. Goethe, Jacobi, and others viewed it like a death in the family. "As I love God and his truth," wrote Jacobi, "so do I hate, despise the papacy."[107] The archaeologists Winckelmann and Georg Zoega had converted to Catholicism, but they had done so in a transparent bid to gain access to Vatican collections. What made Stolberg's conversion so disturbing was its evident sincerity. Voss broke all personal ties with his one-time friend but remained silent about the affair for two decades. Then in 1819 he published *Wie ward Friz Stolberg ein Unfreier?* which mercilessly attacked Stolberg's character, beliefs, and personal life.[108] Stolberg died that year, unreconciled with Voss. By that time, Voss had come to see any openness toward Catholicism on the part of Protestants as a sign of intellectual and confessional treason.

In this regard, Creuzer was more than suspect. He had been close to Görres during their time together in Heidelberg and had served as godfather at the (Catholic) baptism of his daughter Marie.[109] Görres dedicated his *Mythengeschichte der asiatischen Welt* (1810) to Creuzer, while the frontispiece of *Symbolik und Mythologie* was adorned with a quote from Görres. In the *Antisymbolik*, Voss spared no opportunity to rail against the unholy influence of "godfather" Görres. This man had taught Creuzer and others to proclaim that all faiths originated in the Caucasus and led, eventually, to the Church in Rome. As if to confirm Voss's suspicions, Görres began publishing a journal called *Der Katholik* (1821–24), and in 1824 he announced his return to the Catholic Church. But where Görres's biographers have seen enormous shifts, Voss saw a pernicious consistency. "Thus the rootless fanatic . . . always the same! He wanted to dredge up slime, first democratic then theocratic."[110] Such rabble-rousing was a natural product of the Creuzerian-Görresian *Symbolik*.

Creuzer's other associations aroused suspicion as well. He had cultivated contacts with Stolberg before his death and had kind words for his *Geschichte der Religion Jesu Christi* (1806–16). Further, Creuzer's fascination for the religion and language of India was shared by Friedrich Schlegel, who had announced his conversion to Roman Catholicism in 1808. Each of these authors seemed to agree that an original universal religion (whether conceived as Hindu or as biblical) had spread out from Asia to provide the religious foundations for the rest of the world.[111] This vision of human history also echoed the views of the French traditionalist writers Louis de Bonald and Joseph de Maistre, who insisted on the divine origins of all human institutions and called for a papal theocracy in Europe.[112] Indeed, in his emphasis on sacrifice, his attacks on humanism, and his fascination with the religions of late antiquity, de Maistre's corpus offered a striking parallel to Creuzer's *Symbolik*.

This was more than enough evidence to convince Voss that the Romantics had formed a cabal dedicated to overturning the Enlightenment and delivering Germany into the hands of the foulest despotism. Praise for the Middle Ages and the *Nibelungenlied* went hand in hand with the denigration of Homer and the exaltation of gruesome, immoral rituals performed by an oriental priesthood. "Certainly already in the year 1804 Creuzer belonged to a secret alliance of Romantics, whose goal, the revival of the Middle Ages, was . . . thoughtlessly given away by the vain Wilhelm Schlegel. Friedrich Schlegel and several of his acquaintances publicly proclaimed their loyalty to the pope. Wilhelm believes, like Creuzer, that he is still a Protestant."[113] A. W. Schlegel would take issue with Voss's claims, drawing a distinction between praise for medieval piety and actual endorsement of Catholicism.[114] But such declarations made little impression on Voss. In his eyes the entire tendency of Romanticism had aided and abetted religious and political reaction.

Voss's *Antisymbolik* could be taken as the raving of an aged fanatic. Yet a measure of paranoia among enlightened liberals was understandable in the dark days of the 1820s. The announcement in 1815 of the Holy Alliance had signaled the onset of an explicitly Christian politics of restoration, and the imposition of the Carlsbad Decrees four years later sharply limited intellectual freedom throughout the German Confederation. Voss witnessed as the *Burschenschaften* were banned and their leaders arrested or forced into exile.[115] Meanwhile, a new confessionalism, hostile to the Aufklärung and its vision of civil society, had emerged among both Protestants and Catholics. Many of Germany's rulers were eager to accommodate the religious revival, in some cases reversing decades of enlightened church policy in favor of a new conservative ecumenicism. Baden, which had one of the few functioning parliaments in Germany, was spared the worst of this reaction. Yet it was not immune to the *Zeitgeist*. Grand Duke Ludwig (r. 1818–30) was more conservative than his predecessor Karl Friedrich, and he worked to improve relations with the Vatican, negotiating the framework of a concordat in 1818–19 in the face of considerable opposition from Protestant liberals.[116]

In this context of political and religious restoration, the outbreak of the Greek War of Independence in 1821 had given Philhellenism a renewed political relevance. Unlike other revolutionary struggles at this time, the Greeks' struggle against the Ottoman Turks had the tacit support of Europe's rulers, who felt sympathy with the Greeks on religious and, no doubt, racial grounds. Within Germany, a series of associations *(Vereine)* were established to provide moral and financial aid to the Greek cause. These associations were as much political as they were charitable, and for many in the middle classes, the passionate embrace of Philhellenism became a relatively safe way to criticize the "oriental" or Ottoman cast of Metternichian Europe.[117] Wolfgang Menzel—a critic of the Philhellenists—noted that support for the modern Greeks often became a vehicle for promoting a "French-style" liberalism based on popular sovereignty and individual rights.[118] Indeed, Voss was an active supporter of Greek independence and warmly received several Greek students and scholars in Heidelberg.[119]

So if few accepted Voss's accusations of conspiracy, many liberals did believe that Creuzerian "mystery-mongering" had strengthened the forces of reaction. A reviewer in *Le globe* noted that Creuzer seemed "to accord the clergy a wisdom infinitely superior to that of the vulgar and a sort of Roman infallibility."[120] The Erlangen pastor Karl Gös criticized the attempts by Schelling and Creuzer to revive the ancient mysteries, pointing out the immorality of the pagan cultus and its structural similarity to Catholic monasticism.[121] Such concerns also inspired the Königsberg philologist Christian August Lobeck to publish a two-volume study of the Greek mysteries, *Aglaophamus; sive, De theologiae mysticae Graecorum* (1829). The book took its name from an initiate to the Orphic mysteries who supposedly reveals that behind them stood "nothing but trickery and superstition."[122] Far from preceding the Homeric era, Lobeck maintained, these mysteries had been late imports into Greek culture.

Creuzer was even criticized by his former ally Jacob Grimm. In 1820, during the controversy between Stolberg and Voss, Grimm had informed Savigny that he found much to praise in Voss's polemics, including the notion—surely disquieting to his noble patron—that an easygoing friendship between *Bürger* and *Adel* was as much an impossibility as one between Protestant and Catholic. "An undeniable, genuine feeling bristles up against intimate intercourse with someone who is of another nation or another faith; similar embarrassing situations arise [here]." Like Voss, Grimm gravitated toward an enlightened faith that would be better represented in a pagan like Aristotle than a Christian "blind believer."[123] He judged that Voss's review of Creuzer, while certainly vulgar in tone, would ultimately be helpful to the study of mythology insofar as it undermined the tendency to derive everything from "foreign" sources.[124] In this respect, Grimm found himself moving away from the ecumenical "wild philology" of his earlier mythography to the more "national" and "Protestant" stance of the *Deutsche Mythologie.*

Support for Creuzer came from intellectuals in south German cities like Heidelberg, Freiburg, and especially Munich, where Romantic aesthetic ideas were promoted enthusiastically by the young Crown Prince Ludwig. In 1816, Ludwig had begun construction on an antiquities museum intended to house his extensive collection of Egyptian, Greek, Roman, and modern sculpture. The "Glyptothek" was designed by the architect and recent Catholic convert Leo von Klenze, who proposed a monumental building that resembled a Greek temple but was not linked definitively to any particular epoch or style.[125] The layout of the museum, which was opened to the public in 1830, betrayed the influence of Creuzer's *Symbolik und Mythologie.* In order to represent the Egyptian origins of art, the entrance to the first room contained a relief depicting the discovery by Isis of her lover Osiris's body in a mummy's coffin.[126] In their guide to the museum, Klenze and Ludwig Schorn noted that the Egyptians had passed on their culture to the Greeks by colonizing the Pelagian peoples. An "Incunabula Room" was dedicated to those works "that belong to the time when Greek sculpture still more or less imitated the old images of the gods that the colonists had brought"—in other words, those that seemed more "Egyptian" than "Greek."[127] Indeed, the museum's most valuable single holding, the sculptures and fragments dug up near the Aphaia temple in Aegina, fell well short of the Winckelmannian ideal. Their rough forms and somewhat abstract facial features were described as representing a missing link between Egyptian and Greek art.[128] The parallels between the Glyptothek and Creuzer's *Symbolik und Mythologie* were not accidental: Ludwig Schorn, who wrote the museum catalog, was a one-time collaborator with Creuzer, for which he was vigorously attacked in the *Antisymbolik.*[129]

Among Creuzer's staunchest defenders was Schelling, who from 1806 to 1816 was director of the Academy of Fine Arts in Munich and who had since removed to the university at Erlangen. In *Ueber die Gottheiten von Samothrace* (1815) Schelling had attempted to derive a proto-idealist philosophy from the Cabiri system described by Creuzer. This essay eventually became part of a broader project to rethink the history of mythology in light of the Christian revelation. In his unpublished lectures titled "Philosophie der Mythologie," which he first held in Erlangen in 1830, Schelling praised Creuzer's scholarship, and he took it as a sign of weakness that his enemies were forced to rely on "certain customary accusations" (i.e., crypto-Catholicism) to defame the "higher" view of myth "among the less educated and thoughtful part of the public."[130]

As the *Symbolik* controversy began to die down, the future belonged to neither Voss nor Creuzer, but rather to scholars like Karl Otfried Müller (1797–1840), who were able to integrate the new interest in religion into the existing framework of philological scholarship. Müller was born the son of a Silesian pastor and grew up in a household infused with Pietism.[131] During his youth he cultivated a certain Romantic temperament, viewing nature as a manifestation of the divine and even attempting a few lines of poetry.[132] As a student in Berlin, he was repelled by Friedrich August Wolf's arrogant personality and gravitated instead toward August Boeckh, who pioneered the comprehensive approach to antiquity known as *Altertumswissenschaft.* After writing a dissertation on the culture of the Aeginetans, Müller took over Heyne's former chair at Göttingen in 1819. As he began to study Greek mythology in more depth, Müller found himself drawn to Creuzer's *Symbolik und Mythologie,* in particular its emphasis on the religious aspects of myth. In this respect he departed from his more rationalist colleagues in Göttingen, who were implacably hostile to Romantic trends in scholarship.[133]

Despite his sympathy for Creuzer, Müller's scholarship on Greek mythology departed significantly from *Symbolik und Mythologie.* In the three-volume *Geschichten hellenischer Stämme und Städte* (1820–24), Müller traced the origins of Greek mythology to the national characteristics of the Greek race rather than to a coherent philosophical doctrine.[134] "[A]ll religion is in its essence traditional and positive," he wrote, and its origin lay in a time when "not only the nation but also its individual tribes existed in clearly marked particularity."[135] Müller especially emphasized the role of the Doric tribes, who migrated from the north into Greece during earliest antiquity as part of an early migration of peoples from the Caucasus. There they conquered the agrarian Pelagians, whose nature religion was characterized by orgiastic practices and ecstatic states. The Dorians suppressed this cult in favor of a national religion centered on the manly god Apollo. But the old faith persisted in the form of mysteries, such as those dedicated to the Cabiris in Samothrace or to Demeter in Eleusis.

Müller's insistence on the autochthony of Greek religion flew in the face of those ancient and modern historians who emphasized the contributions of colonists from across the Mediterranean. Müller took special aim at Herodotus, whom he accused of an "unrestrained admiration for the Orient" and a "mania for derivation," as well as contemporary admirers like Creuzer, who sought to derive everything that was great in ancient Greek culture from the East.[136] In his eyes, the most recent scholars were repeating the mistakes of earlier Christian theologians. "[A]fter earlier scholars' practice of connecting everything directly to the scripture of the Old Testament and turning paganism into nothing but a torn and distorted Judaism has been abandoned, a few very learned spirits, just like those old ones, turn their eyes steadily toward Egypt, Phoenicia, and the farthest Orient. And these scholars strive especially to force the Hellenic as far as possible out of the Hellenic race [Art] and through the confused fabric of mythical ideas lead it toward an Indian original wisdom or Asia Minor's and Egypt's opaque and somber religions."[137] In the Geschichten, Müller debunked many of Herodotus's bolder claims of massive borrowings by the Greeks from foreign cultures, arguing that in fact influences were flowing in the other direction by the time of the Histories.[138] Meanwhile, he emphasized the intimate connections between the legends of the Greeks and the particular details of their history and geography.

In order to defend his thesis of Greek autochthony, Müller at times relied on an anticolonial logic similar to that employed by Herder and Jacob Grimm. Referring to the argument that the Greeks had been deeply influenced by the Egyptians, he wrote, "I will grant that there were contacts but I would not grant an influence. Would the Germans, without partially being conquered by the Romans, have accepted Roman customs and practices, myths, and religious ideas? Does Wotan become more similar to Mercury because Tacitus calls him this? Such an influence could happen only to a nation that was still unindependent or in a state of decline, because all its powers would set it in opposition against the foreign."[139] Champollion's discovery in 1821 that the hieroglyphs represented a phonetic, rather than a symbolic, language seemed to confirm this view, since it ruled out any easy diffusion of Egyptian religion into Greece.[140] But Müller also noted the racial differences between Egyptian and Greek artworks, while making it clear which he thought was the superior culture: "[I]n every higher spiritual activity the weak and cowardly Egyptians stood below the young nation of Hellenes, as a nobler race [Race] consistently defeats the less noble race."[141]

In his Prolegomena zu einer wissenschaftlichen Mythologie (1825), Müller attempted to explain the approach to mythology that had guided his earlier studies.[142] He rejected those theories that emphasized the role of either poets or priests in the creation or transmission of myth. In earliest antiquity there was no separate class of poets; the priests did not stand apart from the people nor did they possess special training or discipline.[143] While Heyne and Creuzer had cited the allegorical myths of the *Theogony* or the Orphic cosmogonies in order to demonstrate the philosophical nature of Greek mythology, Müller pointed out that such narratives constituted only a small portion of Greek myth.[144] It was thus pointless to try to reduce Greek mythology to an original system of philosophy or theology. Instead, myth was the result of a certain "mood of the soul" in which the inward life was represented through the actions of personalities. The farther one went back in history, he argued, the more tightly the "ideal" and "real" elements of myth were bound together, and the more the Olympic pantheon dissolved into a plurality of local deities and legends. Indeed, even pan-Hellenic myths and deities were often shaped to fit particular cultic practices or to explain features of nearby geography.

The importance of such local factors was demonstrated in the myth of Apollo and Marsyas.[145] According to the received narrative, Marsyas was a Phrygian satyr, a virtuoso of the double flute (also the instrument of Dionysus). Foolishly he challenges Apollo, a master of the lyre, to a musical contest. Apollo prevails, and as his prize he chooses to flay Marsyas alive. The satyr's skin is hung upon a tree, and his blood flows into the river Marsyas. According to Müller, this myth grew out of the Greeks' belief in their inherent superiority over the Phrygians. In their eyes, any contest involving the Hellenic national deity Apollo had to end in the defeat of his opponent. But this national prejudice combined with details of local geography to produce the story of Marsyas's flaying: in Celaenae in Phrygia, at a spot where the river Marsyas flowed out of a grotto, there hung an animal skin, which was called the "skin of Marsyas." In order to explain the origin of this skin, the ancient Greeks had deduced (rather than simply concocted) the story of Marsyas's grisly fate.

Not only did the Apollo-Marsyas story confirm the dictum that "all mythology is local," but it also revealed the intimate connections between art and religion in early Greece. According to Müller, much of Greek art and music developed in the context of religious worship, which pervaded all aspects of early Greek life. Religion had also helped to order political life, which among the Dorians was characterized by a striving for order and unity. Müller especially idealized the Spartans, whose freedom contrasted strongly with what "in the modern era is conventionally called freedom."[146] This praise for Sparta was a sharp departure from the Athens-centered Philhellenism of Winckelmann, Schiller, and Voss. Instead, Müller's emphasis on piety, manliness, order, and nationality evoked aspects of the *Burschen-*

schafts' political program while at the same time anticipating the moderate liberal nationalism that would become widespread among the Protestant German professoriate in the second half of the nineteenth century.

In the midst of the controversy surrounding *Symbolik und Mythologie,* Creuzer remained mostly mute. This was probably a wise decision. His one attempt at a response, the pamphlet *Vossiana* (1821), was a weak effort whose publication he soon rued.[147] One wonders if the Günderode scandal, seventeen years earlier, had sapped Creuzer of the will to fight or robbed him of the moral certitude that guided his opponents. In any event, Creuzer restricted his polemics to private letters. "Yes, we would have to be burned along with all those that see something in the Orient, in Moses, Zoroaster, Buddha, or whatever the swindlers are named. In a word: we should teach in the name of the devil and hold Voss's *Mythologische Briefe* for the book of books."[148] Creuzer became convinced that the *Antisymbolik* was symptomatic of a "theological-philosophical-political chilling process," which was also manifested in the rise of political and theological liberalism.[149] The Baden state authorities took a dim view of the *Symbolik* affair, as well, and initiated proceedings to censure Voss for the tone and contents of his *Antisymbolik.* Mercifully for all concerned, Voss died in 1826, bringing the most heated phase of the controversy to an end.

Nonetheless the damage to Creuzer's reputation had been done. By the 1830s, he found himself increasingly on the margins of the philological profession, as well as of his own university. An 1838 review of the third edition of *Symbolik und Mythologie* reads like an obituary, whose subject is treated with ironic detachment.[150] Indeed, while Creuzer still had adherents in Ludwig Schorn and Eduard Gerhard, the curator of the Altes Museum in Berlin, they were not philologists but archaeologists, who were attracted to his theory of the symbol as a means of interpreting ancient art. But for most philologists, the notion of a transhistorical *Symbolik,* passed down unchanged from one culture to another, seemed unacceptable on both scholarly and political grounds.

In the end, it was Karl Otfried Müller who won over the philological discipline. In his theories, he was able to integrate the Romantic interest in religion into a historicist framework that preserved the autochthony of Greek culture and the ethos of Protestant scholarship, all while avoiding the overt political and religious polemics that had characterized the writings of Voss and Creuzer. On such questions, he preferred a studied neutrality, even when circumstances seemed to dictate a principled response—for example, in 1837, when he refused to join the protest of the Göttingen Seven, signing his

name instead to the much narrower "Nachprotest."[151] In this affair, Müller's
primary concern was not the Hanoverian constitution but the reputation of
his university. But future students and colleagues, increasingly wary of political engagement, would be willing to forgive such lapses. Instead, they
would commemorate the skill and erudition of his scholarship, while creating a narrative of Byronic martyrdom based on his death in 1840 during an
archaeological expedition to Greece.

The significance of the *Symbolik* affair extended well beyond classical
philology, however. "One felt in this question that it was a matter of more
than merely mythology," Schelling wrote.[152] Indeed, this conflict tapped into
a broader debate in Restoration era Germany concerning the nature of religion and its relationship to art, politics, and scholarship. Creuzer was just
one of a number of scholars in these years who emphasized the Christian
qualities of ancient paganism while tracing paganism's doctrines to the Orient. Further, like Bonald, de Maistre, and Stolberg, Creuzer stressed the primacy of priestly authority against the deductive logic of the philosophers or
the inductive logic of the natural scientists. According to his autobiography,
the purpose of *Symbolik und Mythologie* was to show "how all moral and political edification of the human race was passed on and improved only
through priestly institutions."[153] This position marked a considerable departure from the *Frühromantik*, which had affirmed the necessity of progress in
matters of religion and sought a delicate balance between art, scholarship,
and religion.

Thus, for all his excesses, Voss was essentially correct to label *Symbolik
und Mythologie* as a document of reaction. The Restoration, sponsored by
Vienna and embraced with increasing fervor by Romantic intellectuals in
Munich and Heidelberg, sought to demonstrate the value of positive institutions, such as the church, the monarchy, and the estates. Part of this movement involved rediscovering the oriental heritage of Christianity in the Old
Testament and elsewhere. By tracing the roots of Christianity to oriental
despotism, by de-emphasizing the importance of Protestant "freedom" versus Catholic "authority," and by undercutting the humanist image of ancient
Greece by emphasizing an unbeautiful, even antihumanist, *Symbolik*,
Creuzer's scholarship supported this restoration. The fact that Voss resorted
to the language of crypto-Catholicism to make his point did nothing to help
interconfessional relations in Germany, but it reflected the legitimate fears
among the Protestant educated classes of a resurgent Ultramontanism and
an increasingly conservative political climate.

The political and theological conflicts of the Restoration era, fought out
around Creuzer's *Symbolik und Mythologie*, also offer a context in which to

understand the transition from the theory that Greece was dependent on Egypt for its myths to the view that Greek culture was more or less autochthonous. According to Martin Bernal, this shift occurred in the decades after 1800 because of an upsurge in racism and a new emphasis on religiosity. This is only partly true, however. For while race undoubtedly played a role in the thinking of Voss and Müller, it must be seen as part of a broader complex of motives. In terms of religion, for example, it was the theological conservatives who sought to emphasize the Egyptian connection, while liberals insisted on Greek autochthony. Moreover, the defenders of Greek culture did not draw a sharp distinction between Egypt and India; instead, both were seen as part of an Orient that was corrupt, effeminate, and unfree. The debunking of *Symbolik und Mythologie* allowed philologists like Karl Otfried Müller to highlight the national dimensions of Greek culture, pointing out the role of history, geography, and ordinary people in the fashioning of Greek myth.

The defense of Greek autonomy from Egypt and the Bible, though accomplished with the poisonous rhetoric of confessional hatred, preserved ancient Athens and Sparta as a rallying point for the critique of the Christian monarchy. The collapse of Greece onto Asia would have conceded the primacy of the Orient, while reconstituting the traditional biblical narrative on a wider geographical and historical basis. With Greece autonomous, radical critics were free to hold up its mythology and religion as an alternative to Christianity. In the face of stiff censorship and political repression, however, such critics were mostly old Aufklärer, more intent on preserving the intellectual gains of the eighteenth century than in involving Germany in democratic experiments. Classical philologists, by contrast, sought to avoid the liberal, pagan, and potentially anti-Christian implications of Philhellenism, retreating instead into the safety of an increasingly specialized and apolitical *Wissenschaft*. As we shall see, only in the 1840s did a new group of writers emerge who were prepared to join Philhellenism, radical politics, and the longing for myth.

CHAPTER FOUR

From Scriptural Revelation to Messianic Myth:
The Bible in *Vormärz*

> Paganism ends as soon as the gods are rehabilitated by the
> philosophers as myths. Christianity has reached the same point.
> Strauss is the Porphyry of our era.
>
> Heine, "Bruchstücke zu 'Elementargeister,'"

In *Das Leben Jesu, kritisch bearbeitet* (1835), the Tübingen theologian David Friedrich Strauss dismantled the central dogma of the Christian religion, the belief that Jesus Christ was God incarnate. Using the concept of myth as a critical knife, Strauss peeled away the life history of Jesus. In its stead he left a hollow Christology, consigned to a brief "dissertation" that interpreted Jesus as a symbol of the progress of the human race. Just as Romantic and Neo-Pietist theologies were emphasizing the individual personalities of God, the king, and the artistic genius, Strauss reduced Jesus to an abstract idea. Moreover, this attack on the referentiality of the biblical text came at a time when rising literacy and newly founded Bible societies had made the Scriptures widely available to Protestant households. The key to Strauss's argument in *Das Leben Jesu* was an innovative and decidedly anti-Romantic use of the term "myth." For whereas Schelling, Creuzer, and the Grimms had used this term to denote a symbol or narrative that transcended the limits of logical reflection, Strauss treated myth as an error or illusion that should be replaced with a philosophical concept.

Most of Strauss's critics denied the existence of myth in the New Testament, arguing that the Gospels related actual historical events. A few critics did concede that the gospel history contained myths but maintained that Strauss had interpreted them incorrectly. In place of his "negative" mythography, they offered their own "positive" readings of biblical myth. This hermeneutical opposition between negative and positive schools of mythography built on earlier philological disputes, notably the controversy over Friedrich Creuzer's *Symbolik und Mythologie*. In addition, however, the debate over the life of Jesus reflected ongoing conflicts in *Vormärz* Germany concerning the sources of religious, cultural, and political authority. To understand the multilayered debates that swirled around Strauss's *Leben Jesu*, it will be necessary first to examine the uses of myth in biblical theology over the previous three decades, beginning with the work of W. M. L. de Wette.

W. M. L. DE WETTE AND THE CRITIQUE OF MOSAIC HISTORY

Protestant Old Testament scholarship had long served two masters.[1] Since the Reformation, its purpose had been to establish the figural and typological links between the Old and New Testaments. Proof of such connections would demonstrate the unity of the biblical canon while affirming the centrality of the Hebrew Scriptures for the gospel message (a key claim of Luther against the Catholics). But during the eighteenth century, enlightened scholars sought increasingly to distance the "rational" religion of Jesus from its "primitive" Jewish roots. Using contemporary travel accounts from the Middle East, "Orientalists" like Johann David Michaelis advanced rather unflattering ethnologies of the Jewish people, comparing them to the neighboring Canaanites, Persians, Egyptians, and Babylonians. The historian Christoph Meiners took this type of argument to an extreme, attempting to show that the ancient Hebrews had engaged in human sacrifice and idol worship and disavowing any connection between the (proto-Christian) religion of the prophets and that of the Jewish people as a whole.[2] Other critics, such as Reimarus, simply denied the historicity of the Bible altogether and suggested that many stories in the Old Testament were the product of deceit or fraud.

The rise of the "mythical school" in the 1790s muted some of the more extreme attacks on the Old Testament. Johann Eichhorn and Johann Philip Gabler interpreted the more fantastic stories of the Old Testament, such as the Garden of Eden or the Tower of Babel, as philosophical myths, the products of an early stage of human development. According to Gabler, a "philosophical myth emerged either from mere speculation about the origins of things in the world or other moral issues, after which this philosopheme was clothed in the garb of history, or it emerged when a true story was retold by a wise man for his own purposes and thereby imbued with the ideas and opinions of that age's way of thinking."[3] Eichhorn and Gabler believed that the first five books of the Bible, in particular, contained an amalgamation of both myths and authentic history, which was later compiled by Moses into the literary form of the Pentateuch. For Eichhorn and Gabler, as well as for Herder, the term "myth" could be applied to individual episodes of Genesis or Exodus but not to the Old Testament books as a whole.

The major challenge to the mythical school came from the theologian Wilhelm Martin Leberecht de Wette (1780–1849).[4] A pastor's son, he enrolled at the University of Jena in 1799, where he studied theology under Gabler and the rationalist H. E. G. Paulus. During these years he also acquired some familiarity with the philosophy and aesthetics of Jena Romanticism. While it is doubtful if de Wette attended Schelling's lectures on the philosophy of art, he was certainly familiar with his *Method of Academic Study* (1803).[5] In addition, he likely encountered the aesthetic ideas of Friedrich Schlegel, who taught at Jena between 1799 and 1801. Based on his thinly veiled autobiographical novel, *Theodor, oder des Zweiflers Weihe* (1822), it would appear that de Wette's time in Jena was marked by doubt and frustration as he moved from one philosophy to the next.[6] He would eventually settle on the philosophy of Johann Jakob Fries, though not before he had published several pathbreaking works of Old Testament criticism.[7]

De Wette's most important innovation in biblical studies was his application of a concept of myth derived from early Romanticism to the Pentateuch. Like Herder and Schelling, he viewed art as a revelation of the divine and saw mythology in particular as a form of religious poetry. In his first major work, *Beiträge zur Einleitung in das Alte Testament* (1806–7), de Wette claimed that not just certain passages of Genesis or Exodus but the entire Pentateuch was based on myth.[8] The five books of Moses formed "an authentic Hebrew national epic, of true nationalism, completely in the spirit of Hebraism."[9] This epic was the "product of the patriotic [vaterländisch] religious poetry of the Israelite people. It reflects their spirit, their manner of thinking, their patriotism, their philosophy, and their religion."[10] De Wette declared the Pentateuch useless as a chronology of events and ridiculed those who attempted to distill a historical substrate from its narratives. Instead, these books were to be interpreted as a national poetry that mirrored the spirit and mentality of Hebrew theocracy.

De Wette based this argument on discrepancies between the two books of Chronicles and the books of Samuel and Kings. Samuel and Kings, which portrayed the reigns of David and Solomon, contained references to neither the Pentateuch nor most of the religious and legal practices that the Pentateuch prescribed.[11] Chronicles, however, related the same events while including such references, which led de Wette to conclude that these books were the product of a later era. He next turned to the Pentateuch itself, which appeared to explain or presage many traditional Jewish beliefs and practices.

God's day of rest after the creation of the world, for example, explained the origin of the Hebrew Sabbath, Noah's curse of Ham and his offspring Canaan justified the occupation of the Promised Land, and Abraham's obedience to God explained the idea of the Israelites as the chosen people, as well as their practice of circumcision. In a similar manner, the Book of Exodus justified the existence of hundreds of laws and rituals by ascribing them to divine commands received by Moses. On this basis, de Wette concluded that the Pentateuch was not history but rather an "epic of Hebrew theocracy," written hundreds of years after the events it purported to describe in order to legitimate religious practices that had emerged only after the Babylonian captivity.[12]

De Wette described the Hebrew national mythology with an unmistakable tone of condescension, declaring it useless as history while slighting its aesthetic and religious content. This attitude would sharpen over the years. In *Ueber Religion und Theologie* (1815), de Wette postulated a simple, original Hebrew religion, whose conception of God as spirit raised it high above pagan mythologies. Moses "lifted the mythological veil that hid the idea of the highest holy God and released the bonds that had chained men to nature," wrote de Wette.[13] Since the years of captivity, however, Judaism had fallen into decline, succumbing to the influence of Persian pneumatology and legalistic pedantry. The Jewish religion of the Torah and subsequent rabbinic practice had distorted the archaic religion of the Hebrews. The priestly class then attempted to give their liturgies, laws, and customs the sheen of venerability by tracing them back to the national hero Moses. Thus, while Gabler and Eichhorn distinguished between tradition, poetry, and history in the biblical text, de Wette viewed the entire Pentateuch as a product of the collective imagination of the postexilic Hebrew priesthood.[14]

Upon completion of the *Beiträge*, de Wette took up a post as professor of exegesis in Heidelberg, where he cemented his friendship with Jakob Fries and with Johann Heinrich Voss. In 1810, he accepted an appointment at the newly founded university in Berlin. An ardent nationalist, de Wette flourished in the Prussia of Stein, Hardenberg, and the anti-Napoleonic War of Liberation. Meanwhile he extended his theological project, applying the mythical approach to Christian dogma and the New Testament in the *Lehrbuch der christlichen Dogmatik* (1813) and *Ueber Religion und Theologie* (1815). Of the New Testament, de Wette wrote that "the miraculous narratives of the Gospels must be seen from the standpoint of the reporters, that is, as symbols of ideas that already existed in the history of early Christianity."[15] This would foreshadow the argument of *Das Leben Jesu*.

De Wette put forth his theology in the spirit of pious moralism that characterized the radical wing of the *Burschenschaft* movement. Close to Fries in his political and religious sentiments, he equated Protestantism with obedience to conscience and the defense of individual and national autonomy. As was shown in chapter 2, de Wette believed that this required distancing the Protestant churches from the myths of Judaism and Roman Catholicism and establishing an "ecclesiastical aesthetic" that would serve as the basis for a new "symbolic cultus." After the murder of Kotzebue in 1819, both Fries and de Wette fell under suspicion for their radical views.[16] The police eventually uncovered a letter from de Wette to Karl Sand's mother that condemned the crime but appeared to excuse the spirit in which it was committed. Suspended with pay from his teaching position, de Wette resigned and was eventually replaced by a young conservative theologian, Ernst von Hengstenberg. De Wette moved first to Weimar before eventually accepting a position in Basel.[17] For the next twenty years, those who favorably cited de Wette ran the risk of being branded radicals, democrats, and demagogues. No theologian would be willing to follow de Wette and declare significant portions of the Bible to be myth—until Strauss.

HERMENEUTICAL DYNAMITE: *Das Leben Jesu*

David Friedrich Strauss (1808–74) emerged from the same cradle of Swabian Pietism that had produced Schelling, Hegel, and Hölderlin.[18] Born to a merchant family in the town of Ludwigsburg, he enrolled at the University of Tübingen in 1827 with the intention of becoming a pastor. There Strauss made fast friends with the future theologians Gustav Binder and Christian Märklin, the poet Eduard Mörike, and the future aestheticist Friedrich Vischer. All were members of a generation for whom the French Revolution was merely history and the Metternichian Restoration their primary experience. Like other young men of their age and social background, they were caught up in the wave of Romantic sentiment that swept across Germany after 1815. They indulged in the popular mysticism of Swabia, associating with the poet Justinus Kerner and paying visits to Frederike Hauffe, the so-called Oracle of Prevorst, who claimed to communicate with the spirits of the dead. Eventually they turned to philosophy: first to Schelling, then Schleiermacher, and finally Hegel.

By the 1820s, Hegel had replaced Schelling as the most influential philosopher in Protestant Germany.[19] Hegel had borrowed much from Schelling, including the notion of the Absolute as a "concrete, dynamic totality" that revealed itself in nature, history, and religion.[20] But with the publication of the *Phenomenology of Spirit* (1807) Hegel distanced himself from Schel-

ling and the Romantics by insisting that philosophy could provide a fully scientific explication of the Absolute. The Hegelian Absolute was revealed by
means of dialectical logic rather than through mystical leaps of intuition. For
that reason, Hegel's system promised to overcome the gap between philosophy and the public that the Schellingian doctrine of intellectual intuition
seemed to encourage. This system first began to gain adherents in the 1810s,
while Hegel was teaching in Heidelberg alongside Creuzer and Voss. In 1818,
he was called to the chair of philosophy in Berlin. There he set out to extend
the principles of his philosophy into the fields of law, history, aesthetics, and
religion. In doing so, he made sure to differentiate his position from Lutheran
orthodoxy, the historicist Romanticism of Görres, Savigny, and the Grimms,
and what he termed the subjectivist "Romanticism" of Fries and de Wette,
all the while maintaining good relations with reform-oriented officials in the
Prussian government.[21]

Hegel's conception of history has been aptly described as a "celebration
of Christianity's surpassing of Greek polytheism tempered by a nostalgia for
the classic."[22] In his lectures on aesthetics and on the philosophy of religion,
Hegel praised the Greek "religion of beauty," which had made the divinity of
humanity visible in its anthropomorphic gods. Greek polytheism represented an advance over the "symbolic" stage of culture, whose geographical
locus was Egypt and India and which had represented the gods as animals or
as wild multiarmed beings. Yet Hegel saw himself as a Christian philosopher,
and he maintained that the Christian revelation had demonstrated the
divinity of not only the human form but the human spirit. In its Protestant
form, this religion had provided the foundation of the modern world, including its notions of freedom, law, and the state. The philosophical concept offered a higher understanding of this revelation, Hegel argued, but its content
was not substantially different from that of Protestant theology.

Within Hegel's system, the concept of "myth" played a relatively subordinate role. Instead, symbol, myth, dogma, and historical narrative were
grouped under the rubric of "representation" (Vorstellung) and treated as
necessary stages of consciousness leading up to the philosophical Absolute.[23]
In his lecture series Philosophy of Religion (1821–27), Hegel wrote that pagan myths, which included the classical "narratives of Jupiter and other
deities" and such biblical myths as the story of the serpent in the Garden of
Eden, possessed an inward meaning separate from their outward representa-
tional form. "We are directly conscious that they are only images, but that
they [also] have a significance distinct from that which the image as such
primitively expresses—that the image is something symbolic or allegorical

and that we have before us something twofold, first the immediate and then what is meant by it, its inner meaning."[24] Myth, to summarize Hegel, was the aesthetic representation of the Absolute in the form of narrative. The narrative shell of myth was ultimately separable from its true meaning and possessed no significance in itself.

The story of Christ was not a myth, according to Hegel, because it was true both as history and as a revelation of the Absolute.[25] But many other church doctrines, including those concerning the Trinity, the Creation, and the Last Judgment, were best interpreted as forms of "representation." While Hegel did not reject these doctrines outright, he saw them as true only to the degree that they produced a consciousness of the Absolute in history. In his account of the "consummate religion" in the *Philosophy of Religion*, Hegel argued that the Christian community attained a true religious consciousness only after Jesus had departed the scene. Thus, it was the disciples' spiritual comprehension of Christ—rather than his physical presence—that gave rise to the Christian religion.

Because both history and myth were forms of representation in Hegel's system, no clear criteria existed by which to distinguish between them: both were valid, not in themselves, but as expressions of a particular stage of consciousness. Thus, Hegel maintained a posture of equanimity in the face of challenges to the historicity of the gospel narratives. The truth of Christianity was spiritual: "it does not lie in the sensible, and cannot be accomplished in an immediate, sensible fashion. (Accordingly, objections can always be raised against the sensible facts.)"[26] Hegel did not want to abandon Christian doctrine, but he was not interested in making it dependent on the veracity of a certain set of "sensible facts." Thus, he affirmed the "orthodoxy" of his Christian philosophy—a shrewd move given the increasingly conservative political climate in Prussia—while avoiding the task of refuting historical critics like de Wette. This position was problematic in two respects, however: first, the distinction between philosophy and religion tended in practice to reinforce the very division between esoteric and exoteric modes of knowledge that Hegel had hoped to overcome; second, neither his followers nor his critics were willing to elide the ever more paramount question of the Bible's historical truth.

Since the 1820s, a number of theologians seeking a more "objective" or "scientific" basis for the restoration of Christian dogma had turned to Hegel.[27] Creuzer's friend and colleague Carl Daub, the theologian Philipp Marheineke, and the Berlin theologian Karl Göschel had all refused to accept the ambiguity of Hegel's position. They insisted instead that speculative philosophy confirmed not only Christianity's broad truths but its specific historical and dogmatic content. Toward the end of his life, Hegel gave tacit approval to the efforts of these "right" Hegelians to reconcile his philosophy with a conservative Lutheran theology. The prominent positions of Marheineke and Göschel on the theological faculty in Berlin seemed to guarantee the dominance of right-Hegelian orthodoxy in Prussia after Hegel's death in 1831.

This shift to the right within Hegelianism reflected the intellectual and institutional pressure exerted by an increasingly ascendant Lutheran confessionalism.[28] The announcement of a Prussian church union in 1817 had brought dogmatic issues to the forefront of public discussion, as theologians attempted to arrive at a common catechism and a common liturgy for the combined Protestant Church. At the same time, a religious awakening among the Junker aristocracy began to shift the balance of power away from the liberal clergy and their bureaucratic allies and toward a group of conservative theologians associated with Crown Prince Friedrich Wilhelm and the Berlin theologian Ernst von Hengstenberg (1802–69), editor of the *Evangelische Kirchenzeitung*. Convinced of the primacy of a personal conversion experience and the inerrancy of Scripture, the Neo-Pietists of the Erweckungsbewegung (Awakening movement) had first gathered together in small devotional circles during the Napoleonic era in order to study the Bible. In the years after 1815, they formed themselves into a kind of party, using the *Evangelische Kirchenzeitung* and their extensive contacts in the bureaucracy and the royal court to launch an assault on political and theological liberalism and to defend the doctrinal authority of the Lutheran Church and the social authority of the Prussian aristocracy.[29] A special target of Neo-Pietist criticism was the privileged position enjoyed by Hegel's disciples in Berlin. The Neo-Pietists forced the Hegelians to defend themselves against charges that they were promoting pantheism, atheism, and revolution.

During the 1830s, Strauss became unhappy with Hegel's system as well, but for different reasons. As a young pastor, he struggled with the seeming contradiction of preaching to his congregation (those of "ordinary consciousness") in the language of "representation" while thinking in the language of the Hegelian Absolute.[30] For one year he tried to convince himself and others that he could lead his congregation to a speculative standpoint in this way. But in the end he gave up his ministry, resolving to study theology full-time under Hegel. His stated reason, to be "initiated in the mysteries of science," suggests that even if Hegel had moved beyond the Romantics' esoteric language of "intellectual intuition," he had not really bridged the divide between the philosopher and the public. Indeed, if Hegelianism offered an escape from the "Romantic labyrinth," as John Toews argues, it did so only by replacing one set of boundaries with another.[31]

Strauss arrived in Berlin in 1831, just a few weeks before Hegel's death, to find a philosophical faculty tilting ever more toward theological orthodoxy and political conservatism. But he had already absorbed too much biblical criticism to accept this interpretation of Hegel's philosophy. At Tübingen he had studied with Ferdinand Christian Baur, who maintained that the dogmas and scriptures of the Christian Church had to be subjected to historical criticism before they could be taken as valid. Whereas the Berlin Hegelians envisioned an unproblematic transition from representation to the concept, Strauss felt that theologians must deal with the messy positive material of the biblical testimony before engaging in confident abstractions about the Absolute. "Whoever by a kind of intellectual intuition wants to see immediately the absolute truth in the gospel history as such denies the *Phenomenology* in the realm of theology," he later wrote.[32] For Strauss, Hegel's claim that the historical truth of the biblical narrative was derived from the concept of absolute religion did not render the results of criticism moot. Instead, the concept of religion could only be established once the task of historical criticism was complete.[33] *Das Leben Jesu*, though conceived as part of a larger work on dogmatic theology, would also serve as a vindication of the rights of historical criticism against a priori philosophical speculation.

Strauss recognized that his commitment to historical criticism represented a break not just from the right Hegelians but also, in many respects, from the master himself. Although he insisted that *Das Leben Jesu* was consistent with the letter of Hegel's philosophy, he would admit several years later that it might have violated its spirit. "When [the Hegelians] appeal to Hegel himself and protest that he would not have recognized my book as an expression of his own feelings, I agree. Hegel was personally no friend of historical criticism. It annoyed him, as it annoyed Goethe, [to] see the heroic figures of antiquity, to which their higher feeling clung lovingly, gnawed at by critical doubt. If, occasionally, these figures were puffs of mist which they took to be pieces of rock, they did not want to know; they did not want to be disturbed in the illusion by which they felt exalted."[34] There was an element in Hegel's philosophy (a residue of Schelling, Strauss claimed) that was "more positive and accepting of the status quo—the system of restoration versus the system of revolution."[35] Strauss came to see himself as the recoverer of the critical, "Fichtean" element in Hegel's philosophy against those who would pull it back toward the mystical realm that he associated with Schelling. The irony, of course, was that as a seminarian Schelling had uttered similar complaints, venting against those supernaturalist theologians who misused Kant's practical philosophy in order to cut the "Gordian knot" of biblical criticism.

The life of Jesus had become a subject of serious theological controversy only recently.[36] During the 1820s, Schleiermacher held a series of lectures, based heavily on the Gospel of John, which presented Jesus as a model *(Urbild)* of humanity while eliding the evident contradictions between historical criticism and Christian dogma. The rationalist theologian H. E. G. Paulus then published his own *Leben Jesu* (1828), which followed the text of the Gospels closely but explained away supernatural elements as the product of "oriental" modes of perception.[37] These rationalistic lives of Jesus were opposed by supernaturalists, who argued for the literal truth of Jesus' birth narratives, his miracles, and the Resurrection. That the Christian religion should be rendered as a life narrative testifies to the incipient growth of biography as a literary genre, as well as the penetration of the Romantic categories of "genius" and "individuality" into the broader intellectual culture.[38] Despite these precedents, however, Strauss broke radically from previous efforts in biography, whether secular or sacred. Indeed, *Das Leben Jesu* was more antibiography than biography.

As an 1832 letter to Christian Märklin attests, Strauss believed that the problem of biography drove straight to the heart of Hegel's claim that the Christian representation differed from all other forms of religious representation. Describing plans for a lecture on the life of Jesus, Strauss wrote that he would investigate "what it means when in a religion the intuition of the divine appears as a life story. Then the life stories of an Adonis, an Osiris, or Hercules must be compared with the Christian according to their essential difference."[39] In what sense was the Jesus narrative only a higher version of the lives of Hercules, Osiris, or Adonis (all of them pagan gods who had suffered)? Was it legitimate to treat one as true and the others as false without any justification other than belief in a philosophical Absolute? Strauss's interest in the comparative truth of different religious representations—left unstated in the text of *Das Leben Jesu*—opened the possibility of the mythical solution. His distaste for Berlin Hegelianism guaranteed it.

In *Das Leben Jesu* (1835–36), Strauss introduced the concept of myth as a means of resolving the long-standing conflict between rationalist and supernaturalist approaches to the Bible.[40] Despite their differences, both rationalists and supernaturalists shared the belief that the Bible related true events. Strauss attacked precisely this assumption. For some time, scholars had been willing to accept that the New Testament contained elements of mythology, especially in the birth narratives and the ascension story. In

David Friedrich Strauss, at one point the most hated man in Germany.
Source: David Friedrich Strauss, *Ausgewählte Briefe*, ed. Eduard Zeller (Bonn: Emil
Strauss, 1895), frontispiece.

Strauss's hands, the mythical mode of explanation, "instead of trying to split
hairs about details, takes the whole not for true history but for a sacred legend."[41] In a single stroke, he had jettisoned the minutiae over which theologians had wrangled for decades. According to Strauss, the details of the life of
Jesus formed a single myth, which gave historical expression to the religious
idea that animated the early Christian community.

In his preface, Strauss strove to show that "whoever applies the mythical
approach to the evangelical history is not following a momentary fancy but
rather the centuries-long course of the subject."[42] He traced the history of
New Testament scholarship through the eighteenth and early nineteenth
centuries, citing the works of Heyne, Gabler, Eichhorn, and the young Schelling. These footnotes have led contemporary critics and some recent commentators to claim that Strauss's methodology can be traced straight back to
the mythical school.[43] But while Strauss owed much to his predecessors, his
view of myth was not simply an extension of the mythical school's.[44] For
while Eichhorn and Gabler sought to discover individual philosophemes in

Old Testament narratives, Strauss viewed myth as the expression of the spirit of a community or a nation.[45]

This understanding of myth was derived from Herder and, especially, de Wette.[46] Like de Wette, Strauss made the Romantic leap from history to myth: he now treated the sacred text as a whole, whose unity was derived not from the coherence of events but from the religious consciousness of a nation. At the same time, however, he reversed de Wette's hermeneutic. For while de Wette saw the Pentateuch as a projection of postexilic customs and traditions onto the distant Hebrew past, Strauss described the origin of the gospel narratives as a thrusting of Old Testament messianic hopes onto a contemporary figure named Jesus. The Gospels grew out of the "individual characteristics of an already-existing expectation of the Messiah among the Jewish people, which was independent from Jesus."[47] This expectation of the Messiah shaped the legends surrounding the person of Jesus and explained how such a complex myth could arise in the short years between the death of Jesus and the composition of the Gospels. "[M]any of the legends about Jesus were not newly invented but only transferred from the image of the Messiah that lived in popular hope and that came largely from the Old Testament, though with frequent distortions, onto the person of Jesus."[48] These existing legends combined with the personal impression of Jesus to form the gospel narrative.

In practice, Strauss ascribed almost all myth-forming power to the traditional messianic expectations of the Jews and granted little importance to either Jesus or the new Christian "idea." Jesus the person remained in the background, vague and undefined. Miracles, the element of the Gospels most heavily contested between rationalists and supernaturalists, were treated as secondary elaborations of the messianic idea. The cure of the lepers, for example, was derived from Old Testament narratives concerning the healing powers of Moses and Aaron. Likewise, Jesus' "transfiguration" in the company of Moses and Elijah reflected the desire by early Christians to connect the Messiah to his Old Testament forerunners as well as an oriental predilection for imagery involving light.[49] Over two volumes of ironic, often biting prose, Strauss subjected the entire gospel narrative to the same relentless criticism.[50] The result was a work that not only challenged the divinity of Jesus but also exposed the synthetic quality of the traditional Christian biblical narrative.

Successive editions of *Das Leben Jesu* reflected Strauss's evolving understanding of his own critical methodology. In the third edition (1838), Strauss expanded the preface to answer the objections raised to his mythical approach.[51] For help he turned to the work of Karl Otfried Müller, who explained Greek myth by referring to the conditions of its origin, including the local history, customs, and geography of the various tribes and races of Greece. In particular, Strauss cited Müller's discussion of the myth of Apollo and Marsyas, which he interpreted as an expression of long-standing prejudices and beliefs within the Greek psyche.[52] Just as Apollo's flaying of Marsyas reflected his status as a Greek national deity, so the life of Jesus was a secondary elaboration on a previous set of Jewish beliefs and myths about the coming Messiah. Although Strauss did not read Müller's *Prolegomena* until after he had written the first edition of *Das Leben Jesu*, his comments in the preface to the third edition suggested the numerous connections between philological debates over Greek mythology and the theological problem of the life of Jesus.

Despite such parallels, however, it was extraordinarily bold to claim that the biblical Jesus—not only the founder of Christianity but also the man whose life narrative constituted the chief content of the Gospels—was nothing but a mythical projection. Defenders of the Bible had traditionally cited a moral difference between the ennobling stories of the Bible and the scandalous legends of the Greeks and Romans, a difference Strauss saw as more apparent than real. "Divine commands, such as that the Israelites should embezzle golden jugs during their exodus from Egypt, are hardly less offensive for a refined ethical feeling than the thievery of the Greek Hermes," he wrote.[53] This was only one of many instances in which immoral behavior was apparently sanctified within the Bible.

Another traditional objection to describing the narratives of the Bible as myths was that they seemed intrinsically more realistic than pagan stories, with God residing in heaven rather than intermingling in the day-to-day affairs of men and women. "We . . . take offense at the idea that the gods themselves have a history: that they are born, grow up, marry, have children, carry out deeds, endure struggles and difficulties, conquer and are conquered. Since it is irreconcilable with our idea of the Absolute to suppose it subjected to time and change, to opposition and suffering, we recognize a narrative in which these characteristics are attributed to a divine being as unhistorical, mythical."[54] Yet this point obtained only to a limited extent. In the Hebrew Bible, to be sure, God had no history and the hero of the Old Testament was the Hebrew people themselves.[55] In the New Testament, however, the Old Testament notion of God was transferred to God the Father, while his Son was recognized as a divine being who suffered death and was buried. In this sense, "the New Testament has more of a mythical character than the Old."[56] But the Old Testament was not entirely free of myth. The narratives of Genesis and Exodus in which God spoke to Abraham, gave Moses the Ten Com-

mandments, and otherwise intervened in the lives of the ancient Hebrews
were myths, even if they lacked the beauty and grace of Homeric epic.[57]
"[T]he mythical element can be lacking only under or above the real standpoint of religion," Strauss maintained. "Inside the real religious sphere, it is
necessarily and essentially present."[58]

Although he reduced much of the Gospels to myth, Strauss maintained
that the life of Jesus possessed a religious meaning. In the so-called positive
section of his work (spanning a mere fifteen pages), Strauss offered his Christology. Abandoning Hegel's mediating position, he interpreted the Incarnation as a sign of the merger of God with humanity over the course of history.
"If reality is to be ascribed to the idea of the unity of divine and human nature, does this mean that it must become real at one time and in one individual, and before and after not again? That is hardly the way in which the
idea realizes itself, to pour out its contents into one example and to be stingy
to all others."[59] Beneath the ironic surface of Strauss's prose lay a powerful argument: that God manifested himself in the totality of humanity and not just
in a single individual. "Humanity is the union of both natures, the incarnate
God: the infinite manifesting itself as finitude and the finite spirit remem-
bering its infinitude. It is the child of the visible mother and the invisible
father: of spirit and nature. It is the miracle worker: insofar as in the course
of human history spirit takes possession of nature ever more completely, so
that nature is reduced to the material of spirit's activity. It is without sin: insofar as the course of its development is blameless, and impurity increasingly
attaches only to the individual but is sublated in the species and its history."[60]
The divine rested not in one soul but in the union of all souls across history.

This argument was not without political significance. By denying the per-
sonhood of Jesus Christ and identifying the Incarnation with all of humanity,
Strauss implicitly denied the mystical role assigned to the monarch as the individual embodiment of the state.[61] This line of reasoning seemed to lend
support to the left-liberal opposition, whose message of popular sovereignty
and democratic reform had gained momentum since the July Revolution.[62]
Indeed, the left-Hegelian Arnold Ruge initially greeted the author of *Das
Leben Jesu* as an apostle of democracy, even though Strauss's own politics
tended toward a very moderate brand of liberalism.[63] Fewer commentators,
however, have noticed that *Das Leben Jesu* undermined a third component
of Restoration philosophy: the referentiality of the historical text. Once the
concept of myth was introduced, it tended to gobble up author and event and
replace them with a vaguely defined "spirit of the *Volk*." The Straussian concept of myth dissolved the evangelists into the faceless mass of the Hebrew

people and replaced an experience of the "real" Jesus with a merely ideal union of finite and infinite, human and divine.

All this placed the individual pastor in a difficult quandary, which Strauss termed the "last dilemma." For if the gospel narrative had only a speculative significance, how was a preacher to deal with a congregation who took these stories for true history? "Insofar as an insurmountable divide becomes attached to the common affair of religion, speculative theology threatens us with an opposition between an esoteric and an exoteric doctrine, which is hardly appropriate to Jesus' saying that 'all should be taught of God.'"[64] This "last dilemma" recalled Strauss's own experience as a pastor four years earlier, when he had tried to negotiate between his Hegelian understanding of Christianity and the beliefs of his congregation. In addition, it echoed the young Schelling's complaint that a discredited notion of revelation was being retained solely in order to secure the clergy's authority over the people.[65] Schelling, it will be recalled, demanded an end to this hypocrisy and the creation of a public sphere defined by a new mythology. Strauss viewed the options rather differently. Of course, one could lie to the congregation or leave the clergy altogether, but neither alternative addressed the widening gap between the minister and the laity. The best solution was therefore to remain with one's congregation and gradually lead it up to the speculative standpoint, hoping that the people would eventually follow. Still a theologian, Strauss insisted that his thesis did not entail the end of the Christian Church. Unsurprisingly, his enemies would see things otherwise.

THE POSITIVE MYTHOGRAPHY OF CHRIST:
WEISSE AND SCHELLING

The reaction to *Das Leben Jesu* was immediate and furious. Strauss was fired from his position at Tübingen, and he never again held an academic position. Meanwhile, his book incited a flood of polemic, scholarship, and popular interest in the problem of the historical Jesus. A year later, after the first wave of the storm had passed, Strauss divided the responses to his book into three categories. First, there were those "screams for help" that were "mere expressions of surprise, terror, disgust, without going into details, as women scream when a shot goes off."[66] The screamers included those clergymen who labeled Strauss the Antichrist, the minister who discovered that the Hebrew letters of Strauss's name added up to 666, and the pastors who paid personal visits to his home in Tübingen in order to save him from perdition.[67] One satirist wrote an imaginary history from the year 2838, which used the historical-critical method to demonstrate that the life of Luther was a myth.[68] Then there was a second group of responses, which criticized details of Strauss's presentation while ignoring the substance of his argument. The final group of critics countenanced the application of the concept of myth to the gospel narratives but objected to *Das Leben Jesu* on other grounds, such as the book's ironic tone.[69]

What was striking in these responses was their concern to preserve the validity of the gospel history. In the controversy over Fichte's philosophy, irreligion had been defined primarily in terms of "atheism," but now it centered on violating the biblical text. The changing terms of debate reflected a broader shift in the content and practice of Protestant religiosity. With the introduction of mandatory primary education and the consequent spread of literacy, Bible societies *(Bibelgesellschaften)* had been founded throughout Germany to deliver inexpensive copies of the Scriptures to the laity. During the 1810s and 1820s, such societies sprang up in numerous communities, including Erlangen, where Schelling himself served as honorary chairman.[70] Many of these societies were associated with the Neo-Pietist Awakening; indeed, the strident literalism of theologians like Hengstenberg reflected the new centrality of the biblical text in the religious lives of ordinary Protestants. But the emphasis on the biblical text was shared by other, more moderate opponents of *Das Leben Jesu.*

Among Strauss's critics, the Leipzig philosopher Christian Hermann Weisse (1801–66) stands out as one of the most sophisticated. Weisse was one of a group of "speculative theists" who gathered around Immanuel Hubert Fichte (son of Johann) and the *Zeitschrift für Philosophie und spekulative Theologie* during the 1830s.[71] A native of Leipzig, the nephew of an operetta composer, and a connoisseur of contemporary art, music, and literature, Weisse had adhered to Hegelianism during his youth before rejecting its purely scientific definition of the Absolute. Whereas Hegel treated the Christian notion of "God" as a pictorial representation of the philosophical Absolute, Weisse identified the personal God with the Absolute itself. Thus, the idea of the Absolute was religious, not scientific.[72] As Warren Breckman has shown, Weisse's philosophical evolution was part of a general shift on the part of idealist philosophers like Schelling and Friedrich Schlegel away from the implicit pantheism of early Romanticism toward a philosophy oriented toward the concept of "personality." In the "political theology of restoration," the personality of God was linked directly with the personality of the monarch, both to be defended against the logical pantheism of the Hegelian system.[73] Weisse was more a political centrist than a Restoration conservative and he never downplayed the importance of scholarship *(Wissenschaft)* for religious life. Nonetheless, he upheld the value of the Christian revelation and the monarchy, which he defined in terms of a philosophy of personality. These commitments placed him at odds with Strauss's theology.

Weisse set forth his view of the Gospels in *Die evangelische Geschichte, kritisch und philosophisch bearbeitet* (1838).[74] Albert Schweitzer has called Weisse's discussion of the life of Jesus, "both from the religious and from the historical point of view, the most satisfying treatment of it with which we are acquainted."[75] For Schweitzer, Weisse's chief importance lay in his formulation of the so-called Marcan hypothesis: that Mark was the first synoptic Gospel written and that it had formed the basis for Matthew and Luke. Until that time, many biblical theologians (including Strauss) had viewed Matthew as the oldest and, consequently, the most accurate of the synoptic Gospels. A number of others, including Schleiermacher, favored the Gospel of John, since it seemed to stand closest to Christian doctrine. While the Marcan hypothesis eventually won the day in the field of New Testament theology, it grew out of an attempt by Weisse to account for both the historical and the mythical elements in the gospel narratives.

Unlike many of Strauss's rationalist or orthodox critics, Weisse accepted the existence of myths in the New Testament. What he rejected was Strauss's purely "negative" approach to these myths. Taking his cue from Romantics like Schelling and Creuzer, Weisse proposed a "positive" interpretation of myth, which would elucidate the religious ideas at the heart of these narratives. But while he conceded some ground to the mythical approach, Weisse maintained nonetheless that most of the Gospels were grounded in a substrate of real history. He dismissed Strauss's argument that the bulk of the gospel narratives could be derived from Jewish messianic expectations or early Christian polemical motives. Instead, he stressed the existence of a real historical Jesus, whose religious significance could be reduced to neither a philosophical concept nor a theological dogma but instead had to be intuited directly from the text of the Gospels.

Weisse saw a clear connection between debates in classical philology and the controversy over the life of Jesus. He linked Strauss's critical approach to the Gospels to a "tradition hypothesis" first articulated by Friedrich August Wolf, according to which the Homeric epics had emerged from a tradition of oral poetry. In an earlier work, *Ueber das Studium des Homer und seine Bedeutung für unser Zeitalter* (1826), Weisse had challenged this theory, taking on both Wolf and the man he saw as Wolf's key disciple, Karl Otfried Müller.[76] Against both scholars, Weisse maintained that a single artistic genius had composed the bulk of the *Iliad* and the *Odyssey*.[77] Since writing was the foundation of all literature, it was likely that these epics were written down shortly after their initial composition.[78]

In Weisse's view, every mythology was founded on a religious idea.[79] The mythology of the Greeks reflected the rise of an ideal of individuality in Western culture as it broke away from the moral slackness, sexual uncertainty, and racial mixing of the Orient. That transition had left its imprint in Hesiod's account of the conflict between the Olympians and the Titans and in Homer's description of the Trojan War. Homer, in particular, represented the supreme manifestation of the Greek religious spirit. "Just as the highest divine revelation of the world spirit can be completed only in one man, or just as the moral order of human cohabitation—the state—achieves completion of existence and reality only in the gathering together of its rays in a single person—the prince: in the same way, a life-encompassing original art *[Urkunst]* must emerge fresh and complete . . . from of the spirit of a single man."[80] In the end, Weisse concluded, a recognition of the reverence due Homer was the only bulwark against a rising tide of "historical pantheism," which threatened to swallow up individuals into the "mass of the people *[Volkes]*."[81]

Weisse was hardly the only scholar to criticize Wolf's *Prolegomena* in these years.[82] By the 1820s, a credible alternative to the "tradition hypothesis" had been put forth by the philologists Johann P. Kreuser and Gregor W. Nitzsch.[83] Kreuser and Nitzsch challenged Wolf's most fundamental assumption: that the Greeks had not possessed a written language when the Homeric epics were composed. The decipherment of the hieroglyphs in 1821 by Jean-François Champollion had shown that the ancient Egyptians possessed a phonetic, and not merely a symbolic, language.[84] Since hieroglyphs were in use as early as the third millennium B.C., it seemed likely that written language had spread to the Greeks (probably via the Phoenicians) well before the composition of the *Iliad* in the eighth century B.C. The earlier date for the beginning of writing also undermined Wolf's thesis that rhapsodes had composed a series of independent "Homeric" poems, which were stitched together only centuries later. Nitzsch found it far more plausible that a single poet had composed the *Iliad* and the *Odyssey*, and that they had been preserved not through oral tradition but as written texts.[85] For Wolf's critics, therefore, it seemed high time that the legend of the "blind Homer" be replaced with the notion of Homer, the literate and quite real artist.

Taking his cue from the critics of Wolf, Weisse attempted in *Die evangelische Geschichte* to reassert the primacy of written scripture over oral tradition in the formation of the New Testament. This applied even to those sections of the Bible that he conceded were myths, namely the birth narratives in Matthew and Luke. Because these stories could be linked to a real person, Weisse argued, they should be classified as legends or historical myths.[86] In this respect, they paralleled the tales surrounding such historical figures as Alexander the Great.[87] In Weisse's scheme, the legends of Jesus emerged in the years between the writing of Mark's "eyewitness" account and the composition of the more mythical Gospels of Matthew and Luke. The Gospel of John, favored by Schleiermacher, had the least connection to the historical Jesus.

Weisse identified two strains of myth in the New Testament, one the product of what he termed "Jewish Christianity" (Judenchristenthum) and the other the product of "pagan Christianity" (Heidenchristenthum). The former included the genealogies connecting Jesus to King David, which Matthew and Luke had used to preface their Gospels. Such genealogies could be found in other traditions, and they formed a core element of all mythologies, including Hesiod's Theogony. Still, Weisse maintained like Strauss that the genealogy in Matthew was designed to satisfy the Old Testament prophecy that the Messiah would be descended from the House of David.[88]

The other key group of myths, Heidenchristenthum, was designed to connect Christianity to the pagan traditions of Greece and the Orient.[89] In Weisse's view, this was the source of the narrative of the Immaculate Conception. Strauss had traced this story to the prophecy in Isaiah (7:14), "Behold, a virgin shall conceive, and bear a son."[90] But according to Weisse, a virgin birth was not part of Jewish messianic expectations and clashed with arguments for Jesus' royal patrimony. By contrast, the Eleusinian mysteries had depicted the birth of a future god Dionysus to the virgin Persephone. "[T]o the Jews, the Hellenic-Christian interpretation of this supposedly messianic prophecy was in no way familiar. On the contrary, it must have been foreign to them."[91]

The legends of the Magi and the Star of Bethlehem were another sign of Christianity's pagan heritage. Strauss had derived these narratives from the Moabite prophecy of Balaam, "a star shall come out of Jacob" (Numbers 24:17).[92] But Weisse maintained that the Magi, guided by their astrological studies, represented the "complete content of that nature symbolism which . . . lay at the basis of the religious ideas of paganism. . . . That this symbolism, that the entire religious core of paganism—conceived spiritually and in its truth—pointed toward Christianity, and that it taught [the pagans] to search for Christ and recognize him when found: this and nothing else is the clear meaning of this bold and yet sublime image of wonder [Wunderbild]."[93] This argument echoed Creuzer's Symbolik, but now it was applied directly to the text of the New Testament. For Weisse, the Gospels' two cycles of myth, Judenchristenthum and Heidenchristenthum, were not empty husks that could be explained away in a rationalistic fashion. Both expressed significant religious ideas in their own right and were thus an essential part of the Christian revelation.

This pointed to what Weisse saw as the crux of his dispute with Strauss: the latter's shallow and unscientific concept of myth.[94] In his view, Strauss had turned to myth as a last resort once the inviability of the gospel narrative had been demonstrated. "When it appears in the work of this critic, the 'mythical view' has the importance only of a hypothesis brought in to aid negative criticism, . . . not of a positive and meaningful historical-idealistic view."[95] Noting Strauss's praise of Karl Otfried Müller in the third edition of *Das Leben Jesu*, Weisse concluded (mistakenly) that Strauss had derived his theory of myth from Müller's *Prolegomena zu einer wissenschaftlichen Mythologie*. For that reason, Weisse devoted several pages to showing how Müller had eviscerated the religious "idea" of the Greek gods by reducing their meaning to the outward circumstances of their origin.[96]

Weisse detected other reverberations from the *Symbolik* controversy in Strauss's *Leben Jesu*. "The Straussian task was to demonstrate myth in the evangelical history; the Müllerian task (which formed itself in unmistakable opposition to the mythological system of Creuzer) was to demonstrate history [*Historie*] in Greek myth."[97] While Weisse was careful to distinguish the views of Müller and Strauss from those of a rationalist like Johann Heinrich Voss, he maintained that ultimately they, like the poet, were unable to comprehend how a myth could be anything other than a poetic fable.[98] But even Weisse's allusion to the Müller-Creuzer controversy was a bit unfair, since the crux of that dispute was not whether Greek mythology was "religious"— both writers agreed that it was—but the degree to which it was derived from the Orient. Weisse, however, was engaged in a polemic. He hoped to show that both the mythical narratives of Greece and the gospel narratives possessed an ineffable religious content, which could not be explained away by historical criticism.

Weisse's suspicions about the connections between Strauss and Müller were shared by more conservative commentators as well. In *Die Authentie des Pentateuches* (1836), Ernst von Hengstenberg traced Strauss's lineage to Wilhelm de Wette and Karl Otfried Müller, who together embodied the modern era's disrespectful attitude toward the past. "This general position of the era toward history cannot be ignored when one is researching the causes of the present-day attitude to the holy books," Hengstenberg wrote.[99] Just as de Wette had undermined the believability of the Old Testament, Müller applied the theory of myth to undermine the belief in Homer. "Since every particular rests on a universal, the attacks against Homer . . . grew out of the same soil as the attacks against the Holy Scriptures."[100] While Karl Otfried Müller seemed to be an "excellent" man otherwise, he was possessed by "the corrosive historical skepticism that has thrust such deep roots into our age."[101] Hengstenberg hoped that the type of historical "pantheism" advocated by Müller and manifest in Strauss would eventually be overturned by Nitzsch, Kreuser, and other anti-Wolfian philologists.[102] As Hengstenberg realized, the further back one dated the invention of writing, the more plausible claims became for an ancient and inerrant biblical scripture.

Hengstenberg's attacks on the critical traditions within classical philology demonstrate once again how disputes over ancient mythology tended to skip over formal disciplinary boundaries when broader theological issues were at stake. For while the editor of the *Evangelische Kirchenzeitung* directed his main fire at Hegelian philosophy, he was also aware of the threat posed by Wolfian philology to his program of Lutheran orthodoxy and biblical literalism. Wolf had been dead since 1824, but his legacy lived on in Berlin, Göttingen, and elsewhere in the tradition of *Altertumswissenschaft*. This philology threatened to dissolve the holy texts of ancient Greece into the details of local geography, replacing a single, divinely inspired author with the faceless mass of the *Volk*. It was in opposition to this argument, and its implications for biblical theology, that the archconservative Hengstenberg joined the centrist Weisse in opposing Karl Otfried Müller.

Before resuming the discussion of Weisse, it will be useful to say a few words about Schelling's approach to Christology in his later lectures on the "philosophy of mythology."[103] Schelling first delivered these lectures in 1830 in Erlangen, revising and expanding them during the 1830s in Munich and during the 1840s in Berlin in conjunction with his lectures on the "philosophy of revelation." Like Weisse, he developed his later philosophy as a critique of the Hegelian philosophy, albeit one far more radical than that of the speculative theists. Starting from the premises of a personalist monotheism, Schelling argued that the freedom of God demanded that he remain beyond logical proof or demonstration. Thus, although purely logical or "negative" philosophy (and here Hegelianism was meant) could deduce the necessary parameters of God's existence, it was the task of "positive philosophy" to describe God's actual revelation of himself. Unlike orthodox theologians, however, Schelling viewed revelation as an eminently historical process, which roughly paralleled the history of human religion from its beginnings to the birth of Christ. This history unfolded as an interplay of three "potences," which together constituted the reality of both divine and human freedom but in separation led to incomplete or merely mythological revelations of God.

Schelling's theory of the potences helped him to avoid what he saw as a major shortcoming of Creuzer's *Symbolik und Mythologie:* the dependence of his history on the random wanderings of priests across Asia and Europe. But he was even more dismissive of Karl Otfried Müller's approach, which bound the origin of myth to details of local cultic practice or geography. Instead, Schelling envisioned the history of mythology as unfolding entirely within the human psyche, so that a given configuration of potences would be constitutive of a nation's political, economic, and religious life. In this sense, the meaning of the gods was the gods themselves—an interpretation that he carried over from his earlier philosophy of art. Indeed, Schelling went even further in this regard, viewing the physical characteristics of a given people as dependent on where they stood within the unfolding of the potences. For example, Africans, who were left out of the theogonic process, had dark skin and thus an abundance of "race," whereas the Greeks, who stood at a fairly high level in the mythological hierarchy, were seen as without "race."[104]

Over the course of his lectures, Schelling explained the history of mythology in copious detail starting with the "Fall" and progressing to the ancient Greeks. In his view, the Fall was a real event, which was represented both in the Garden of Eden narrative and in the myth of the rape of Persephone. This "spiritual" catastrophe had broken the perfection of God's creation, setting the potences into conflict with each other. It also destroyed the early unity of humanity, giving rise to the varied peoples, languages, and religions of the earth. The earliest phase of religion was dominated by the first potence and was characterized by a primitive, "exclusive" monotheism, such as was found in the worship of the Phrygian "Great Mother" or in more popular forms of Judaism. The arrival of the second potence marked the beginning of polytheism proper, which could be found in Egypt, India, and Greece. Schelling distinguished this historical scheme from those of "Indomaniacs" like Creuzer and especially Friedrich Schlegel (thirty years had done nothing to diminish their rivalry), and at various points he criticized the Brahmanic religion while praising that of Egypt. But he identified the highest mythology as that of the Greeks, whose comprehension of the theogonic process was evidenced in Hesiod's *Theogony* and in their conception of Dionysus. According to Schelling, Dionysus took three forms: Zagreus (who corresponded to the first potence and who was torn to pieces by the Titans), Dionysus proper (the prevailing deity of polytheism and the public, boisterous face of the god), and Dionysus Iakchos (the third potence). Iakchos appeared in the Eleusinian mysteries as a child in the arms of Demeter, consoling her for the loss of Persephone.

The prophecy of a third Dionysus found its fulfillment in the person of Christ, whom Schelling took as a historical person. The Dionysian origins of Christology were attested in the biblical story of Jesus' transforming water into wine at Cana. Indeed, Schelling viewed Christ as having appeared more for the pagans than the Jews, and so he placed little significance on those elements of *Judenchristenthum* that Weisse had highlighted. "The Jews were . . . only something as bearers of the future, and the medium became useless as the husk was blown away from the kernel."[105] Schelling maintained that this Christology was far preferable to that of Strauss, who possessed "a trivial, eminently philistine mind."[106] It also provided the launching point for his conception of church history, which he divided into a Petrine Age (dominated by Catholicism), a Pauline Age (the era of Protestantism), and a coming Johannine Age. This last stage would be achieved when the existing churches joined with scholarship to form a "philosophical religion" that would affirm the doctrines of freedom and personality at the heart of Christianity. The Johannine Age would mark the final phase of religion and the outcome of the theogonic process that had begun with the Fall.

Schelling's lectures on the philosophy of mythology, it should be noted, were never published in his lifetime. After writing so rapidly and confidently in his youth, he seems to have lost his nerve in middle age, endlessly revising his treatises and at one point withdrawing a book from the press just before it was to go to the printer. If he harbored plans to resume publishing after his arrival in Berlin in 1841, they were soon quashed in the face of the largely negative reaction he received from students, scholars, and the press, who (rightly) viewed his appointment to the chair of philosophy as an effort by Friedrich Wilhelm IV to combat the influence of Hegelianism and promote the cause of Christian monarchy. Schelling's lectures would first appear posthumously in the 1850s as part of an edition of his collected works, and even then they were received with skepticism and indifference. Nonetheless, they would exercise a kind of underground influence on nineteenth-century myth scholarship, shaping the views of Friedrich Max Müller, Eduard von Hartmann, and Friedrich Nietzsche.

THE CULT OF GENIUS: FROM SCHILLER TO JESUS

Like Schelling, Weisse was highly critical of Strauss's theory of myth, a weakness he attributed to Hegel's failure to offer a real aesthetic of myth. Hegel had treated myth as little more than a fable and had misleadingly labeled Hellenic religion an art religion, thereby obscuring its serious religious content.[107] Myth, Weisse believed, expressed the essence of religion through the aesthetic faculty of imagination *(Phantasie)*. "[W]hat we call myth is nothing other than the inadequate expression, the *caput mortuum,* of a living activity of imagination on the part of the myth-forming peoples, which is filled with spirit and namely with religious spirit."[108] The task of a science of mythology was not to discover the outward circumstances of mythopoeisis but to highlight its underlying religious ideas.[109] For only a religious nature could breathe life into the images of poetry.

Hegel's inability to understand the religious dimension of aesthetic experience, Weisse argued, had fundamentally distorted his Christology. In his lectures on the philosophy of religion, Hegel dismissed the details of Christ's sensible appearance as irrelevant compared to the consciousness of the early Christian community. But in Weisse's view, these outward details expressed a meaning that transcended the abstractions of the Hegelian concept. The recognition of the divinity of Christ contained a "concrete, irrational" moment, which could not be replaced by philosophical speculation.[110] This helped to explain the importance of miracles. The miracles did not contradict nature, nor were they simply testimonies to the power of faith. Instead, they were the acts of a spiritual genius. In Weisse's view, Jesus' "gift of miracles" was best understood as "an inborn talent, a specifically determined corporeal apparatus, which belongs essentially to every true spiritual vocation, in that it formed the aspect of his immediate, external existence, the basis or fundament of his organic presence in external reality."[111] For Weisse, the phenomenon of "animal magnetism"—the paranormal healing process known in France as Mesmerism—offered a useful analogue to Jesus' ability to cure the sick.[112] Jesus, of course, was no typical mesmerist but a genius among mesmerists. His "power of miracle relates to the natural healing power [of a mesmerist] as perhaps the artistic genius of Mozart relates to the . . . talent of the ordinary virtuoso."[113]

Weisse's notion of genius, while rooted in Romantic and idealist aesthetics, also reflected the emergence of a "cult of genius" surrounding the bourgeois culture heroes Beethoven, Goethe, and especially Schiller.[114] Schiller's early death in 1805 had contributed to the rapid canonization of his works, as did the perception that he had contributed through his manly ethos to the cause of political freedom.[115] Although the study of modern German literature was not a regular part of the curriculum, knowledge of Schiller's work became a central component of middle-class *Bildung*, so that a ten-year-old Theodor Fontane was required by his father to memorize "Das eleusische Fest" even though neither really understood the poem. In *Die deutsche Lit-*

eratur (1828), Wolfgang Menzel identified Schiller with the impending triumph of middle-class liberalism over aristocratic and plebeian "servilism"
and the victory of the Protestant spirit of freedom over church authority.[116]
Goethe was a more problematic figure for Menzel and for others because of
his "feminine" appeal and "immoral" sensibility, but he benefited from his
association with Schiller. By the mid-1830s the notion of a "classical" German literature had become widely accepted among literary critics and in
the pages of their increasingly influential journals. In this sense, the late-
eighteenth-century hopes for a "German Homer" had been fulfilled.[117]

The literary canonization of Schiller was accompanied by public initiatives to commemorate his life and achievements. In 1838, a Schiller festival
was held in Stuttgart, where a statue of the poet was unveiled before the gathered public. The event was something of a media sensation, as it attracted the
enthusiastic support of nationalist writers like Menzel, as well as opposition
from the local clergy, who objected to the ringing of church bells during the
ceremony. Gustav Schwab, who had written adoring biographies of Goethe
and Schiller (and who was an ardent defender of the "single Homer" hypothesis), read the opening address. There he headed off charges that publicly
honoring the author of "Die Götter Griechenlands" amounted to paganism.
"We are not celebrating a form of idol worship when out of the love and veneration of nations we set up this statue as a pilgrimage image, when we who
are present greet the herald of grace and dignity, the creator of so much [that
is] beautiful and sublime, with our hats in our hands. . . . Indeed, nothing pre-
pares us for more devotion, for prayer to the living God, than the appearance
and incarnation of genius on earth."[118] Schiller's talent was a gift from on high
to all of humanity and thus an appropriate object of veneration.

Schwab's admonitions notwithstanding, many observers questioned
whether such a ceremony was consistent with the Christian faith.[119] It did
not help matters that Strauss, perhaps the most reviled man in Germany at
this time, had described the "cultus of genius" as an implicitly post-
Christian phenomenon. "A new paganism, or perhaps just as well said, a new
Catholicism, has arrived over Protestant Germany. One incarnation of God
is now not sufficient, and there has arisen a desire for a series of ever more
complete avatars such as are found in Indian religion. Around Jesus, who
used to stand alone, the people want to put a garland of other holy persons.
. . . This is a mark of the time, to venerate the Spirit of God in all the spirits
who have affected humanity in a vital and creative way."[120] This notion of
genius was not without influence on Strauss's theology. In the third edition
of his *Leben Jesu* (1838), he tried to demonstrate that Christ, too, was a kind

of virtuoso, who had perfected the spiritual faculties available to humanity. Strauss's apparent retreat from the pantheist humanism of the first edition did not win him any new friends, while it engendered hostile criticism from left-Hegelian skeptics of the new cult of genius.[121]

Compared to Strauss, Weisse was far more thoroughgoing in integrating the notion of aesthetic genius into his Christology. In the *Evangelische Geschichte*, he argued that Jesus was not simply the subject of the Gospels but also, to a certain degree, their author. According to Weisse, the relationship of Jesus to his disciples resembled the secret tie that bound initiates to the pagan mysteries. So it was entirely possible that the images Jesus used to explain his parables to his disciples had found their way into the text of the Gospels. "Perhaps much else in the form and expression of our narrative and its symbolic details . . . is drawn from the metaphorical explanations of the Lord, and in this manner the Lord himself gave the disciples occasion to clothe the entire event in the symbolic form in which it stands before us today."[122] The story of the transfiguration, for example, was an instance in which the esoteric explication of a parable could have been converted into a gospel narrative.

Weisse's description of Jesus as the secret author of the Gospels reflected his conviction that the personality of the Savior was indispensable to the Christian faith. True Christianity, he insisted, depended not only on the consciousness of the post-Resurrection Christian community but also on a sensible experience of Christ's person. This face-to-face encounter transcended allegory, history, or abstraction—like Creuzer's symbol it overflowed the boundaries of logic or form. Further, the preservation of Christ's personality was the only way to avoid what Strauss had called the "final dilemma," that is, the permanent division of the Christian revelation into esoteric meaning and exoteric representation.[123] But for latter-day pilgrims, Christ the person could be experienced only through the biblical text. "Only through [the written record] could the image of the divine personality of the Savior be preserved in such a way that for all time forward the possibility remains open to every individual to bring the image within his spirit to that living intuition from which alone . . . a true insight into faith can be generated."[124] Dismissing the written text of the Bible as a Jewish myth or replacing it with an abstract philosophical concept would only ensure the demise of Christianity.

Weisse's defense of the biblical text provided a convincing account of the limits of Strauss's "mythical view" in evaluating the history of religion. The problem, as he saw it, was not that Strauss had identified certain narratives as myths, but rather that he had adopted a wholly negative approach to these myths and to the gospel history as a whole. Rather than discerning the meaning of individual myths or sifting out history from legend, Strauss had reduced the life of Jesus to a single causal factor: the messianic expectations of the Jewish people. In place of a meaningful Christology, he offered a paean to progress. Weisse was well aware of the antimonarchist implications of this sort of argument—he had articulated them earlier in his study of Homer. Yet his chief concern was with the religious and cultural content of *Das Leben Jesu*. For without a notion of Christ as an individual, Christianity would become a bare philosophical formula, with little ethical or religious staying power. The encounter with Christ had to take place at the concrete level of personality, and this was only available in the historical and narrative details of the gospel texts.[125] Weisse did not intend to reproduce the Neo-Pietists' language of verbal inspiration or conversion. Instead, he envisioned a heightened form of the aesthetic or mythological experience described by Schelling and Creuzer. Both the Old Testament prophetic history and the pagan mythological history found their end point in Christ, Weisse believed. The recognition of this fact, he hoped, would form the basis for a "philosophical faith" that would not be abandoned at the first sign of difficulty.

In the wake of the controversy over *Das Leben Jesu*, many conservatives presumed that Strauss had demonstrated the folly of all speculative approaches to religion and that this would inspire a gradual return to true Christianity. Baron Christian Josias Bunsen, a diplomat in the court of Friedrich Wilhelm IV, wrote, "The historical faith has long since become very weak . . . and the Hegelian philosophy has spread such a systematic indifference to facts and history . . . that Strauss's attack was a necessary phenomenon."[126] In fact, Strauss's *Leben Jesu* marked only the first blow in a protracted struggle in Protestant Germany between left-Hegelian critics of Christianity and the defenders of the biblical revelation. Observing this conflict, Heinrich Heine identified Strauss as the Porphyry of his age. Just as the appearance of Porphyry's Neoplatonist mythography in the third century A.D. had marked the end of paganism, so the emergence of Strauss's Hegelian mythography signaled the end of the Christian religion.

The publication of *Das Leben Jesu* not only marked a watershed in Christian theology but also illustrated the destructive potential of the discourse on myth. In interpreting the gospel narratives as the product of the collective messianic expectations of the Jewish people, Strauss had relied on the earlier theories of Herder, Schelling, and de Wette, all of which viewed myth as a necessary expression of the spirit of a nation. But while these earlier writers sought to derive a positive religious content from myth, Strauss viewed myth primarily as an illusion, which should be replaced by reason, history, and a generalized notion of human progress. Moreover, he made these claims at a time when Neo-Pietist Lutheranism was maintaining a defensive doctrine of scriptural authenticity and the reading of the Bible was becoming increasingly central to Protestant religiosity. It is impossible to know how many people lost their Christian faith as a direct consequence of reading this book, but the number is considerable. Further, once Strauss's ironic notion of myth had been applied to the person of Christ, a figure with no apparent connection to pre-Christian paganism, scholars and writers felt much less inhibited in labeling other sacred truths, be they religious or scientific, with the epithet "myth." In this sense, *Das Leben Jesu* set the stage for Nietzsche's far more extensive project of unmasking and demythologizing.

There were other dangers in Strauss's approach, however. In particular, Strauss failed in *Das Leben Jesu* to explain the connection between the Jewish *Volksgeist*, whose messianic expectations brought forth the gospel narratives, and the universal religious community that he had defined as the true meaning of Christianity. The traditional biblical narrative, which had assumed a figural link between the Old and New Testaments, was effectively sundered. Conservative Neo-Pietists like Hengstenberg responded to this crisis by attempting to restore the old typological interpretation. The alternative was to establish a "mythological" narrative, in which pre-Christian paganism anticipated the central truths of the Christian religion. In his *Evangelische Geschichte*, Weisse supplemented the *Judenchristenthum* of the Old Testament with a *Heidenchristenthum* derived from Creuzer's *Symbolik und Mythologie*. Meanwhile, Schelling would opt for an even more radical approach in his philosophy of mythology, treating Christianity as the natural culmination of pagan history and Jesus as the secret of the Eleusinian mysteries. This type of approach had the advantage of pushing back the roots of Christianity beyond the history of one nomadic tribe to encompass the entire history of civilization. The problem was that it now became possible to deny the Jews any role in the salvation history of the West.

In 1835 such considerations did not cross the minds of Strauss's more devout readers. For them *Das Leben Jesu* could only appear as a shock and an affront, a mockery of religion by a young man who was paid by the state of Württemberg to preserve the doctrines of Christianity. Strauss's protestations that he was simply building on the legacy of earlier theologians were beside the point. Not only were the works of the Aufklärer far more restrained, they were written in an era when biblical literalism was far less central to the self-conception of Lutheran orthodoxy. Thus, Strauss succeeded in offending many, and most cheered at his subsequent professional struggles, as one academic position after another was denied to him. August Wilhelm

Schlegel, known to have played fast and loose with religion in the past, praised the people of Zurich, who in 1839 ousted a city council that was about to hire Strauss. "You hear that Strauss teaches to split hairs about the gospel, and you come, well armed with clubs, to fight for the old faith."[127] Few could have expected that this man would return thirty years later to dominate religious debate in Germany once again.

CHAPTER FIVE

Richard Wagner and Revolutionary Humanism

All my subsequent feelings about the ugliness of our present-day
world come from looking at illustrations in Moritz's mythology.
Perseus with his fine helmet, but otherwise naked. . . .

Wagner

More than any other individual, Richard Wagner brought the gods and
heroes of the German "national mythology" to life for a European
public. Whatever their literary or historical provenance, it was the Wagnerian
versions of Wotan, Siegfried, Brünnhilde, and Parsifal that determined the
image of the pagan and medieval *Vorzeit* in the second half of the nineteenth
century. The immense and unprecedented nature of this success has sometimes obscured the untimeliness of Wagner's initial turn to myth. During the
1840s, Romanticism appeared to be a fading movement, associated by its critics with the Metternichian Restoration, Holy Alliance, and the project of a
"Christian state." "Myth," in particular, was a discredited category in Protestant circles, rejected by liberal and young Hegelian critics in favor of the
real world of contemporary politics and society, but equally problematic for
conservatives worried about its democratic and pantheist implications. Intellectuals instead affirmed the canonical status of Goethe and Schiller,
while enlisting these (now safely dead) writers in the service of their own cultural and political projects.

In such a context, Wagner's project of a "new myth" that would be "justified by . . . history" appeared extremely precarious. On the one hand, it could
be seen as a last Romantic-medieval attack on the spirit of the Enlightenment. Indeed, Wagner's free appropriation of the images of both Protestantism and Catholicism and his emphasis on the need for "redemption"
seemed to confirm this view. But insofar as the music drama revitalized those

dimensions of "myth" that conservatives (as well as many moderates) had disparaged—rootedness in the *Volk*, historical and theological pantheism, affirmation of sensual life—it could be seen as revolutionary as well. Ultimately, Wagner saw the music drama not merely as an aesthetic phenomenon but as the vehicle of a religious experience, a conviction that was shared by his admirers. "It is *not* music that Wagner used to conquer the young people, it is the 'idea,'" Nietzsche wrote.[1] Here Wagner's theoretical writings were of paramount importance, for they not only articulated the nature of this "idea" but also presented it as the logical culmination of two thousand years of European history.

Wagner's aesthetic thought has been the subject of a considerable literature, which has emphasized its importance for the development of German nationalism, the spread of anti-Semitism, and the evolution of attitudes toward the public sphere in the nineteenth century.[2] While these contexts are crucial to understanding Wagnerism as a historical phenomenon, the emphasis in this chapter is on the role of *Vormärz* theological debates in defining Wagner's aesthetic-religious project. In his study of left Hegelianism, Warren Breckman identifies Ludwig Feuerbach's critique of "Christian civil society" as a crucial prerequisite for the emergence of Marxian social theory.[3] Yet in many respects, it was Wagner who was the more faithful disciple of Feuerbach and his vision of a "political economy of love." In works like *Das Kunstwerk der Zukunft* and *Oper und Drama*, Wagner drew on the language of Feuerbachian humanism to describe a "new myth" that would be "justified by history" and grounded in an anthropology of "longing." This new myth, conceived by Wagner as both an alternative to and a completion of Christian modernity, would provide the content of the emerging music drama and the basis for the "social religion of the future."

Musical Idealism

Richard Wagner first turned to myth while he was living in Paris. Since the July Revolution, the French capital had become a haven for exiles, misfits, and fortune-seekers from all over Europe. Wagner arrived in 1839, an obscure traveling conductor and composer of operas, but the conquest of the grand opera by another German expatriate, Giacomo Meyerbeer, buoyed his hopes for success in Paris. Answering the public's demand for spectacle, Meyerbeer had filled his operas with rambunctious music and historical adventure.[4] Wagner wrote *Rienzi* (1838–39), about the rise and fall of a fourteenth-century Roman tribune, with this Paris audience in mind, but he had little success negotiating the maze of professional and personal connections that determined the staging of new operas. Faced with failure, he denied that he had ever sought popularity and condemned those who desired it.[5] "*Renom-mée* is everything in Paris, the happiness and the corruption of the artist."[6]

Wagner's professional disappointment coincided with a surge of patriotism among the exile community in Paris, occasioned by a diplomatic row between France and the German Confederation. Beginning in 1840, Wagner wrote a series of articles for the *Gazette musicale,* in which he turned his back on Meyerbeer's tradition of "grand opera" and declared his allegiance to German Romantic opera, exemplified by the works of E. T. A. Hoffmann, Heinrich Marschner, and Carl Maria von Weber.[7] The key to this tradition, Wagner argued, was its rootedness in the folk songs and mythology of the German people. In Weber's *Freischütz* (1821), for example, a hunter makes a Faustian bargain with a shadowy figure in order to win a shooting test and a bride and manages to escape with his soul and his marriage intact. The chthonic world of nature sprites, demons, and ghosts portrayed in this opera exercised a peculiar attraction on the German imagination, Wagner argued. "[B]y glorifying the old folk saga of his home the artist was ensuring himself an unparalleled success. . . . The most opposite directions of political life met here together at a common point. From one end of Germany to the other, *Der Freischütz* was heard, sung, and danced."[8]

Although Wagner revered Weber, he had no intention of using *Der Freis-chütz* as a model. Germany's musical genius, he maintained, lay not in opera but in its tradition of instrumental music, exemplified by the classical composers Haydn, Mozart, and Beethoven.[9] Unlike the French, the Germans had cultivated a devotion to the cause of "pure" music, which was centered on home and hearth. "Among these simple, homely souls, where it is not a matter of entertaining a large, mixed public, art naturally removes every coquettish and showy covering and appears in its proper charm of purity and truth."[10] This experience of pure or "absolute" music could be shared only among a small (homogeneous) group of friends and would be corrupted if extended outside that circle. The grand opera, by contrast, was forced to draw on the machinery of Baroque Catholicism in order to satisfy the French crowd's lust for outward display.

Wagner's "musical idealism" reflected a stance that had become widespread among critics and cognoscenti after 1810. It had found early expression in the works of the Romantic writer, critic, and composer E. T A. Hoffmann before being taken up by the music journals, which emerged as important arbiters of public taste in the 1830s. The notion of a "pure" form of music proved particularly enticing to critics dismayed by the growing commercialization of the music world, which was driven by the public's taste for virtuoso display and for easy melodies that could be published as sheet music. Like their literary counterparts, the music critics of the *Vormärz* tended to condemn the contemporary music scene while they idealized the "classical" works of the late eighteenth century.[11] Meanwhile, the growth of singing associations and music festivals helped extend the *Vormärz* cult of genius to composers like Bach, Mozart, and Beethoven.[12] In his Paris essays, Wagner played on these ideas, while rooting them in a rather artificial metaphysic of national and confessional differences. According to Wagner, the French were bound to "convention," which he associated with critics, journals, and fickle audiences, while the Germans cultivated a musical "pietism" rooted in the domestic sphere and in Protestantism's simple liturgy. Any future German opera would have to build on this tradition, abandoning conventional forms like the aria and the duet in favor of a purely "musical" work.[13]

In 1843, having acknowledged the failure of his Paris sojourn, Wagner took a position as orchestra director of the Royal Saxon Theater in Dresden. According to Heine, Wagner had finally heard "the voice of reason and of his stomach," but the Dresden position was not without some prestige, having been held previously by Weber.[14] Wagner won the appointment on the strength of *Rienzi*, which premiered in Dresden in 1842 to a thunderous ovation and received similar praise in Hamburg, Berlin, and other European cities. According to one observer, "seldom has a young German genius succeeded in winning such quick and universal recognition in his German fatherland as Richard Wagner."[15] Yet by this time Wagner had already turned away from the historical drama in order to compose operas based on the emerging canon of German mythology. These included his "Romantic" operas: *The Flying Dutchman* (1841), *Tannhäuser und der Sängerkrieg auf Wartburg* (1842), and *Lohengrin* (1847).

The legend of Tannhäuser, wrote one correspondent to the Leipzig *Illustrirte Zeitung*, had found more response in Germany than any other legend.[16] It was not hard to see why: the tale combined sexual adventure, pious chastity, and (for non-Catholics) a slap at the pope. For models, Wagner could draw on adaptations by Tieck, Hoffmann, and the Grimms, as well as Heine's *Elementargeister*.[17] In Wagner's version of the story, Heinrich von Tannhäuser has spent years in the mountain of Venus, tortured by a life of eternal pleasure. The seductions of the goddess are enticing but insincere, suggesting the outward spectacle characteristic of Paris and the world of "convention." Tannhäuser returns to Germany, where he falls in love with the chaste and pure Elisabeth (the same Elisabeth whose shrine inspired Friedrich Creuzer). Tannhäuser is about to win Elisabeth's hand when he embarrasses her with a song praising the sensual pleasures of love. Chastened, he undertakes a pilgrimage to Rome, but the pope denies him absolution for his sins. But while Heine returns his Tannhäuser to Venus, Wagner has Elisabeth intervene before God on Tannhäuser's behalf. Death brings sainthood to Elisabeth and redemption to Tannhäuser. If Heine's poem suggested a certain anti-Catholic paganism, *Tannhäuser* retained the framework of Romantic medievalism associated with A. W. Schlegel or Friedrich de la Motte Fouqué.

Given the success of *Rienzi*, Wagner's plunge into the world of medieval legend baffled his acquaintances. "If that is not pure medieval Catholicism, I don't understand the piece at all," commented Alfred Meissner. "If one came to the material with a somewhat modern spirit, one would think of Tannhäuser as a man who would want to emancipate himself from the medieval Christian perspective. But everything was conceived in the sense of a monasticism that represents the ancient gods as a degraded pack of ghosts and sees in the enthusiast for the ancient world only a man with lewd morals."[18] The architect Gottfried Semper accused Wagner of polemicizing for the Catholic king Friedrich August II and was only mollified when assured that the composer's true interest lay in the "pagan territory."[19]

This reaction to *Tannhäuser* testifies to the deep suspicion toward Romanticism that prevailed in liberal and radical circles at this time, especially among the writers associated with Young Germany.[20] Liberals in matters of religion, politics, and sexuality, they found themselves subjected to strict censorship in the German Confederation beginning in 1835. Wagner's friend Heinrich Laube and his colleague Karl Gutzkow served time in prison, while Heine and Ludwig Börne spent much of their lives in exile. Despite numerous differences among them, the Young German writers shared a common critique of contemporary social conditions, a suspicion of traditional religion, and a consequent aversion to the Romanticism of Fouqué, Schelling, and Friedrich Schlegel, who by now were firmly aligned with political and theological conservatism. In *Die Romantische Schule* (1835), Heine expressed some sympathy for early Romantic pantheism but condemned its later manifestations as a revival of Catholicism—"that religion that both through its doctrine of the abomination of all earthly goods and its enforced canine submissiveness and angelic patience has become the most reliable support of despotism."[21] As far as Heine was concerned, Voss had been fully justified in labeling the Romantic movement a crypto-Catholic conspiracy.

The hostility toward Romanticism was equally as intense among the left Hegelians. In "Der Protestantismus und die Romantik" (1839), Theodor Echtermeyer and Arnold Ruge explicated the connections between Romanticism and Catholicism at a more sophisticated (but no less polemical) level than Heine.[22] In their view, Romanticism was not simply a revival of medieval Catholicism but rather a rejection by Protestant intellectuals of the Reformation's principles of freedom and subjectivity. Luther had transformed Christianity's outward dualism of heaven and earth into an inner dualism of faith and doubt, providing the foundation for an eventual resolution of this contradiction in the realm of "thought" (i.e., Hegel's philosophy). The Romantics had started from the dualism inherent in Protestantism, but rather than moving on to "thought" they remained locked in their own subjectivity, adopting an attitude of irony, paradox, and longing toward the world. This type of egoism had led them into a (peculiarly female) spiritual sickness, which they healed by abandoning their critical faculties and falling back into Catholicism. This "self-created Catholicism is only the product of a Protestant development," Echtermeyer and Ruge argued, "that puts the confessor in the place of a false king . . . while replacing philosophy with intuition."[23] Romantics like Schlegel, Novalis, and Tieck had embraced Catholicism not on its own terms but instead as a bulwark of authority against an excess of freedom. Rejecting Romanticism, Echtermeyer and Ruge emphasized the emancipatory potential of a politics that took its inspiration from Protestantism and a reforming Prussian state.

They would not retain this confidence in Prussia for long, however. After acceding to the throne in 1840, Friedrich Wilhelm IV announced his intention of transforming Prussia into a "Christian state."[24] He drew this idea from the Erlangen jurist Friedrich Julius Stahl, who advocated an alliance of throne and altar as the strongest bulwark against the rising tide of liberalism and democratic radicalism in Germany. In the first years of his reign, Friedrich Wilhelm IV worked to implement reforms that would free the churches from the control of the Prussian bureaucracy and, in a spirit of conservative ecumenicism, granted more autonomy to the Protestant and especially Catholic Churches in his kingdom. Meanwhile, he appointed a series of Romantic intellectuals to key academic positions, including Schelling, the Grimm brothers, and Stahl himself. These appointments helped to make Berlin an influential center of Romantic historicism, even as they dismayed followers of Kant, Schleiermacher, and Hegel.

Friedrich Wilhelm IV's ecumenical initiatives were in many respects a response to the embittered state of confessional relations in Germany. Since 1835, Ultramontanism had gained increasing influence among Catholic clergy and laity, most notably in the Rhineland regions of Prussia. In their essay "Der Protestantismus und die Romantik," Echtermeyer and Ruge noted the connections between the Stolberg circle and Clemens August von Droste-Vischering, the intransigent archbishop of Cologne whose detention in 1837 by Prussian authorities had sparked the "Cologne confusions." In 1844, as a sign of piety and a demonstration of strength, the bishop of Trier initiated a pilgrimage of Catholics to view the "Holy Coat" of Trier, which had reportedly belonged to Christ. The Holy Coat would attract around half a million viewers, including peasants, workers, and members of the upper classes. Joseph Görres, who by this time had completed the circuit from Romantic nationalist to Ultramontanist activist, described this as a "pilgrimage of the peoples of the Rhine."[25] For Görres, this mobilization of believers from all walks of life demonstrated the theological and social unity of the Catholic Church and stood as a powerful rebuke to its Protestant critics.

But Catholic liberals were appalled by what they viewed as a celebration of medieval superstition and political reaction. Later that year a group of radical clergy and politicians, led by the Silesian priest Johannes Ronge, formed the "German Catholic" movement.[26] The German Catholics called for a more humanist form of Christianity, which would abandon outmoded beliefs and dogmas, adopt a more positive view of women and sexuality, work to overcome confessional divisions, and, ultimately, secede from the church in Rome. While most German Catholics subscribed to an enlightened form of rationalism, a significant number advocated a religion of humanity in the spirit of Strauss, Feuerbach, or the Saint-Simonians. For these radicals, the growing social crisis in Germany called into question the premises of not only laissez-faire liberalism but all individualistic theologies. Without abandoning Christianity, they shifted the focus from "God" to the "essence of humanity" and called for a dissolution of the self into a broader "kingdom of love." As a consequence, the German Catholic movement won the support of left-leaning Protestants who rejected the "Christian state" but who, since the 1840s, had become disillusioned with liberal "egotism."[27]

In Saxony, the birthplace of the movement, the German Catholics constituted an important and politically influential minority.[28] In August 1845, a protest in Leipzig against the Saxon crown prince by several pro-Ronge Catholics resulted in a small massacre when jittery soldiers fired into the crowd. As Martin Gregor-Dellin notes, the Dresden premiere of *Tannhäuser* occurred just two months later, and Wagner was immediately forced to explain why his opera should not be seen as Catholic royalist propaganda.[29] In fact, the opposite was the case: Wagner had come into contact on numerous occasions with prominent German Catholics and appears to have sympathized with their demands. Still, it is dangerous to identify Wagner too closely with any particular religious (or political) movement. While German Catholicism shaped his views, he was primarily interested in reconstituting the Romantic mythological inheritance so as to vindicate his own artistic vision of redemptive sacrifice.

This was evident in Wagner's next opera, *Lohengrin* (1847). The myth of Lohengrin had entered the canon of German mythology thanks to the work of Romantic scholars and artists. Joseph Görres, in particular, had published an edition of the epic in which he linked it to a broader cycle of poetry concerning the Holy Grail.[30] Wagner would later claim that he had rejected this "Catholic" version of the myth as unauthentic. "The medieval poem conveyed Lohengrin to me in a mystical twilight shape, which filled me with mistrust and a certain ill will that we feel at the sight of the carved and painted saints on the highways and in the churches of Catholic states." Only when the outward medieval trappings had been forgotten did the true shape of the Lohengrin myth as a "poem of the people *[Volk]*" appear.[31] Wagner certainly removed the more obviously Catholic trappings of the legend when he reworked it as an opera, but in the end *Lohengrin* affirmed not a pre-Christian paganism so much as an aestheticized and humanized form of Christianity.[32]

On one level, *Lohengrin* relates the psychology of love, fear, and doubt through the figure of Elsa, whose curiosity about her husband Lohengrin's secret leads to misfortune. At another level, this story revolves around the conflict between Lohengrin and the polytheistic, God-hating Ortrud, a character entirely the invention of Wagner. As Wolf-Daniel Hartwich notes, Ortrud represents the tribal, narrowly national ground of Germanic paganism, which had been overcome through the creation of the Holy Roman Empire.[33] In the face of Ortrud's challenges, Elsa is unable to preserve her faith in her husband. Lohengrin, purveyor of a new religion, retreats from the world to the sanctuary of the Holy Grail. But at that moment Elsa's long-missing brother, Gottfried, reappears, transformed from a swan back into a man. Ortrud sinks to the ground, defeated, while Gottfried takes over the kingship of his people. With this story, *Lohengrin* recalled the Romantic mythographies of Schelling and Creuzer, defining Christianity as an esoteric revelation within the body of ancient paganism. According to Wagner, however, "nature—in this case human nature—is bound to take her revenge and destroy the revelation." Contact between "human nature" and a "metaphysical phenomenon" could not be sustained, and ultimately a purely humanistic religion would have to emerge.[34]

While he developed new ideas for operas, Wagner read intensively in contemporary philological scholarship. In his autobiography, he described how a search for "expressive and meaningful symbols" led him to Jacob Grimm's

Deutsche Mythologie. Out of the abundant but fragmentary information in this book, "[t]here rose up in my soul a whole world of figures. . . . The effect they produced upon my innermost being I can only describe as a complete rebirth."[35] Grimm's scholarly reputation and his argument that the poetry and mythology of the Middle Ages were rooted in an earlier pagan *Götterlehre* had a definite appeal. But whereas Grimm focused on reconstructing a strictly "Germanic" mythology, Wagner was interested in linking the legends and stories of the Middle Ages to a wider circle of Nordic and classical myths. This standpoint became more pronounced in the late 1840s, as he abandoned the Protestant nationalism of his Paris essays in favor of a vaguely socialist form of internationalism.

The shift in Wagner's thinking led him to the historical theories of Franz Josef Mone.[36] A disciple of Creuzer, Mone had argued in *Geschichte des Heidenthums im nördlichen Europa* (1822) that all ancient myths were derived from an oriental sun cult that celebrated the death and rebirth of an archetypical sun hero over the calendar year. The introduction of this religion into northern Europe had given rise to the Nordic deities Wotan and Thor and the hero Siegfried. Whether Wagner was familiar with this work is unclear, but he did read Mone's studies of the *Nibelungenlied.* In *Untersuchungen zur Geschichte der teutschen Heldensage* (1836), Mone argued that medieval epics like the *Nibelungenlied* fused a timeless substrate of myth to the accidental events of history. "One could say that the body of the heroic legend is history and its spirit is myth. The animating power lies in the spirit, and thus the historical events have attached themselves to the myth and given up their own coherence."[37] Thus, the outlines of the German epic first emerged when a race of Frankish kings, the Nibelungen, attached their own heroes to the ancient solar myth. As the old pagan faith receded ever deeper into the past, new historical names and personages joined themselves to the Nibelungen story, but its underlying myth remained the same.

In Mone's scheme, myth determined history far more than history determined myth, and the conflict described in the Nibelungen myth could be seen as underlying many of the fundamental polarities of German history.[38] In a study of the sources of the *Nibelungenlied,* Mone traced the Ghibellines of the Holy Roman Empire to the Nibelungen kings while linking the papalist Guelphs to the medieval Wolfingen. The Nibelungen had since spread throughout Europe, and their descendants could be detected in such family names as Neveling, Nibelungus, and, in Italy, Napoleon.[39] On this reading, even the Reformation was an expression of a fundamental conflict between the Nibelungen and their Welf opponents that went back to the earliest days of German history. While Jacob Grimm had seen Martin Luther as leading

Germany back to the ancient grounds of its faith, the Catholic Mone treated the Reformation as only one episode in a longer-running conflict, which would be resolved only when the schism between the confessions had been repaired.

Many of Mone's arguments would reappear in Wagner's essay "Die Wibelungen: Weltgeschichte aus der Sage" (1848). More than one historian has described this piece as an embarrassment, but that speaks less to Wagner's "lack of scholarly control" than to the rather speculative nature of myth scholarship in Germany.[40] In "Die Wibelungen," Wagner reiterated Mone's theory of the relationship between myth and history, arguing that the *Nibelungenlied* originated among a ruling race of Franks who had invaded the agrarian, nature-worshiping Germans. Wagner took pains to emphasize that the Siegfried myth predated the imposition of the "Roman Church" and had reinforced belief in a god who died and rose again. Even Wagner's suggestion—left unpublished—that Napoleon was the last Nibelungen king, come to conquer the papal Guelphs, stemmed from Mone.[41] Under the tutelage of Mone, Wagner came to see history as subordinate to a timeless and unchanging mythical substrate, with the Protestant Reformation playing a relatively insignificant role.

Yet Wagner also transformed Mone's historical scheme in important respects. First, he highlighted the alleged racial origins of the German nation, which he traced to central Asia. Wagner used the concept of race variously to denote the royal bloodlines of the Frankish kings and the broader ethnicity of the German nation. He maintained that the Nibelungen myth was intimately bound up with the history of the Franks as a race: once their line began to falter, the myth lost its influence. Second, Wagner stressed the economic dimensions of the story. Like Mone, he saw the "Nibelungen hoard" as originally a symbol for the "heroic-human" system of deeds and rewards that had been the foundation of the early medieval economy. But as land became hereditary and guaranteed by contract, the hoard was replaced by a system of purely "material" private property. Its "ideal" element, represented in the Christian image of a grail, disappeared into the depths of the Orient. Meanwhile, the kingship of the emperor became open to the highest bidders, who used the throne to expand their personal dominions. The true meaning of the hoard was preserved only among the common people, who spoke of a king and a treasure buried in a mountain, waiting for "better times."[42]

The speculative arguments of "Die Wibelungen" offer a useful insight into Wagner's frame of mind on the eve of 1848–49. He remained attached to a pagan version of Christianity, which revolved around the life and death of a god and depended on neither the biblical revelation nor church doctrine.

Likewise, he gravitated toward a notion of kingship founded in racial blood-lines, as found in *Lohengrin*, which would provide an alternative to a legal order based on private property and individual rights. Yet within a few months, Wagner would abandon this historical narrative and the political theory that it supported, locating the source of decline not in the Middle Ages but in Greek antiquity, where the collapse of a pagan-heroic worldview had created the conditions for the modern state and the Christian religion. This scheme would reflect a new understanding of his aesthetic project as an expression not of nationalist Romanticism but of European-wide revolution.

FEUERBACH AND REVOLUTIONARY HUMANISM

By the end of the 1840s, political challenges to the Metternichian state system, combined with a rapidly growing population, strains in the guild system, an acute agrarian crisis, and a stagnant economy had created the conditions in Germany for rebellion. News of the July Monarchy's collapse in February 1848 spread rapidly across the Rhine, and the ensuing demonstrations forced monarchs throughout the German Confederation to announce constitutional reforms and pledge cooperation with liberals. In Saxony, King Friedrich August brought opposition leaders into his cabinet, announced the suspension of censorship, promulgated a new electoral law, and proclaimed parity in church relations.[43] Within weeks a series of political associations and newspapers, reflecting every hue of the political spectrum, had sprung into existence. Meanwhile, elections were held for a national parliament in Frankfurt that would draw up a constitution for a future united Germany.

For Richard Wagner, this revolution was a godsend. Over the previous five years he had grown deeply dissatisfied with his situation at the Dresden state theater. As he lost interest in his professional responsibilities, he fell increasingly out of favor with the *intendants* who oversaw his work. To compound his misery, he dug himself into a deep financial hole, securing loan after loan against promised profits that never materialized.[44] These personal difficulties helped radicalize Wagner's economic and political views, and by 1847 he was praying for a revolution that would overturn the existing order.[45] With the outbreak of rebellion in 1848, Wagner threw himself into political activities. He joined the radical Vaterlandsverein and called publicly for a "republican monarchy" based on the abolition of capitalism and the creation of a loving union of king and people.[46] Meanwhile, he proposed that the Dresden theater be transformed into a "German National Theater for the Kingdom of Saxony" with himself as director (the proposal was rejected).[47] Both projects testified to Wagner's distrust of the market-oriented public sphere and the legal structures of representative democracy. Instead, he maintained that political, economic, and cultural relations could be based on a higher principle of "love," guaranteed by a charismatic ruler or man of genius.

As prospects for an immediate transformation of Saxony's cultural and political institutions began to fade, however, Wagner began to lose interest in political events. By 1849, debates about the future of Germany, its constitution, and its borders seemed formalistic and superficial to him. "[F]or the first time I clearly perceived . . . that a real revolution will never come from above, from the standpoint of the learned intelligentsia, but only from below, from the craving of human need."[48] For Wagner, science, culture, politics, and law were all obstacles to "need" *(Not)*, a term that implied both necessity born of deprivation and a sensualist form of longing. He expressed these sentiments in a manifesto entitled "Die Revolution" (1849). "Now I know only one god. The name of that god is—need."[49] Wagner envisioned a cataclysm that would destroy the "paper world order" and create the condition for a "gospel of happiness" that would free the human race.

These dark fantasies were inspired by Wagner's brief association in Dresden with the Russian anarchist Mikhail Bakunin, as well as by the course of the revolution itself. In April 1849, Friedrich Wilhelm IV rejected the Frankfurt Parliament's offer of a German imperial crown and implemented measures to restore order. In a desperate attempt to defend the Frankfurt constitution, workers and middle-class radicals took to the streets of Dresden, erecting barricades and setting fire to government buildings (including the opera house). Wagner played an active, if minor, role in this uprising, encouraging the royal militia to desert and serving as a lookout during the actual fighting. But within a few days Prussian troops had crushed the rebellion. Aware of the danger to his safety, Wagner slipped out of Dresden and made his way first to Paris and then Zurich. There, in a series of aesthetic treatises, he would rework his revolutionary experience into a distinctive form of "Wagnerian" humanism.

Wagner's postrevolutionary aesthetic was based on a fundamental contrast between the "human," which was expressed in myth, and "convention," which was expressed in history. Already in the "Wibelungen" essay, he had described the origin of German legend as a fusion of history and myth, so that Siegfried, Hermann, Charlemagne, Friedrich Barbarossa, and other heroes could be seen as incarnations of a single solar deity. After the revolution, Wagner argued for a strict dichotomy between myth and history, describing the former as the pure and timeless expression of the human and the latter as its insubstantial shell. This dualism reflected Wagner's increasingly hos-

Richard Wagner in Zurich (1853). Tempera by Clementine Stockar-Escher.
Source: Herbert Barth, Dietrich Mack, and Egon Voss, eds., *Wagner: A Documentary Study* (New York: Oxford University Press, 1975).

tile stance to Christianity, which he came to view as an expression of the political, social, and sexual alienation caused by the collapse of pagan mythology. The music drama, by embodying authentic human "need," would provide the basis for a "new mythos," which would escape the realm of convention and yet be "justified by history."

Wagner's idea of the human was deeply indebted to the philosophy of Ludwig Feuerbach.[50] He had first become acquainted with Feuerbach during the revolution, thanks to a recommendation by the German Catholic priest Carl Metzdorff. Wagner was immediately impressed by Feuerbach's lyrical style, his vigorous attacks on Christian doctrine, and his insistence on "healthy" sensuality. "Feuerbach became for me the proponent of the ruthlessly radical liberation of the individual from the bondage of conceptions associated with the belief in traditional authority," Wagner wrote.[51] He dedicated a treatise to Feuerbach, recommended his works to friends, and invited the philosopher to join him in Zurich (Feuerbach declined).[52]

In *Das Wesen des Christenthums* (1841), Feuerbach had argued that the essence of human nature lay in material activity *(Handlung)* rather than an abstract concept. Thus, the God of Christianity was simply an alienated representation of this core human essence. This argument struck at contemporary justifications of the monarchy, including the late Romantic argument that the king was God's counterpart on earth, but it also undermined the modern apotheosis of the ego in bourgeois capitalism. In its place, Feuerbach developed what Warren Breckman has described as a "political economy of love."[53] This notion of love applied at three levels: the sexual love between a man and a woman, the friendship between individuals, and the love that bound the human race together. "Love is the universal law of intelligence and nature;—it is nothing else than the realization of the unity of the species through the medium of moral sentiment."[54] This was not just a materialism of economic need but also a materialism of psychological and physiological "need" *(Not)*—the "one god" of Wagner's revolutionary manifesto.

Feuerbach traced the origin of religion to a displacement of need from social relations onto the realm of the imagination. "God springs out of a feeling of a want; what man is in need of, whether this be a definite and therefore conscious, or an unconscious need,—that is God."[55] Yet it was not enough that God exist as a distant object in heaven: feeling demanded that he also love us. Thus, God had taken the form of a real human being, who suffered and bled for the sins of the world. In Feuerbach's view, Jesus Christ was the goal of all religious "longing" *(Sehnsucht)*, since he combined masculine and feminine principles in a single person. In Christianity, what appeared as necessary for individual feeling immediately became real for the imagination, even if this meant the sensual self was sacrificed to an immaterial idol. This reversal of predicates from human subject to divine object constituted the essence of religion.

For Feuerbach, Christianity marked an obvious decline from the polytheism of ancient Greece. The Greeks had insisted on the connection, even subordination, of humans to nature and of the individual to the community, a standpoint that encouraged the development of art and philosophy in ancient Athens. "[S]cience, like art, arises only out of polytheism, for polytheism is the frank, open, unenvying sense of all that is beautiful and good without distinction, the sense of the world, of the universe."[56] Judaism, by contrast, represented mere national egotism transformed into the guise of religion. Jehovah was nothing more than the "personified selfishness of the

Israelitish people, to the exclusion of all other nations,—absolute intolerance, the secret essence of monotheism."[57] Christianity took this selfishness
a step further, however, transferring it from the nation to the individual. In
Feuerbach's view, both Judaism and Christianity were "essentially oriental,"
since they required the destruction of a healthy pantheism and the creation
of monotheistic despotisms.[58]

Yet in the figure of the loving Christ, the new religion had also incorporated "the principle of humanity contained in Greek culture."[59] This hybrid
quality of Christianity (particularly Catholic Christianity) meant that its
images embodied the higher human qualities of love, suffering, and solidar-
ity, even as they remained attached to an imaginary entity. Protestantism represented a further step in the direction of freedom, because it reintroduced
material love into the sphere of morality and rejected such ascetic practices
as celibacy and monasticism. Yet Feuerbach did not share the general enthusiasm among enlightened or Hegelian theologians for Luther's Reformation,
which he saw as a halfway revolution at best. For while Protestantism had
freed material existence from the life-denying demands of the Catholic
Church, it was still grounded in an essentially subjective spiritual relationship between the individual and an unseen God.[60] In this respect, it provided
the religious analog to the liberal doctrines of laissez-faire economics and political individualism.

Within Saint-Simonian circles, Protestantism had come under attack on
just these grounds, as the conservative critique of the Reformation developed
by Bonald and de Maistre "crossed over" to the radical left. During the 1840s,
left Hegelians like Moses Hess, August Cieszkowski, and Arnold Ruge gravitated toward Saint-Simonianism and its "associative" model of economic
organization, in many cases absorbing its critique of Protestantism.[61] This
line of argumentation appears also to have influenced Feuerbach, but he still
presented Protestantism as more advanced than Catholicism. In his view,
what was crucial was that any divine entity (whether conceived as God or as
the Hegelian Absolute) be abandoned and its predicates transferred back to
humanity as a whole. In this way, the space would be created for a community in which human "needs" were fulfilled at the level of real social relations. In such a community, the sacraments of water, bread, and wine would
be considered sacred for their real material qualities rather than their allegorical significance, and "life, as such," would have "a religious import."[62]

Like many of his contemporaries, Richard Wagner initially attempted to
mediate Feuerbach's ideas through the symbols of traditional Christianity.[63]
In the winter of 1848–49, he sketched out an opera based on the life of "Jesus
of Nazareth," in which Jesus appears as an opponent of capitalism and the ad-

vocate of a new political order. Echoing Feuerbach, Jesus argues that love is based on a renunciation of the individual self. The highest act of love, therefore, is death, "the last and most definite sublation of egoism."[64] In the projected drama, Christ's sacrificial death would serve as a model of loving sacrifice for all of humanity. But Wagner soon dropped the "Jesus" sketch in favor of an opera based on the life of Achilles. In this plan, which never went beyond a few notes, Achilles waives the immortality offered by his mother, the demigod Thetis. Mortal man, Wagner explained, represented a higher stage of being than the gods, who were only the pale reflection of the being of the human species.[65] In the end, he would settle on the figure of Siegfried, a hero who was fully human but whose death acquired sublime religious meaning in the Nibelungen myth.

Feuerbach's significance for Wagner went beyond concerns with love, suffering, or death, however. *The Essence of Christianity* had led philosophy away from Hegelian rationalism—not toward the Christian "God" but rather to the divine soil of nature itself. In this respect, it offered the basis for a humanistic and socially radical version of Romanticism, which could break from the individualistic philosophies of liberalism and Hegelianism.[66] Further, in describing the origin of Christian imagery as the result of a longing for "God," Feuerbach's philosophy provided Wagner with the language for articulating his own longing for "myth." He would undertake that task in his Zurich writings, *Die Kunst und die Revolution* (1849), *Das Kunstwerk der Zukunft* (1849), and *Oper und Drama* (1851).

OPER UND DRAMA: ANTIQUITY, MODERNITY, AND THE ART OF THE FUTURE

The discourse on "myth" in Germany was an outgrowth of eighteenth-century Philhellenism and its idealization of Greek art, literature, and religion. Winckelmann, Schiller, and Schelling had suggested that classical paganism, whatever its shortcomings, offered a surer basis for aesthetic culture and public life than Christianity, with its metaphysics of transcendence and its doctrines of sin and redemption. This was no less the case for Wagner.[67] In his Zurich writings, Wagner drew on his extensive reading in Greek literature and classical philology to formulate his vision of an artwork grounded in myth. Before the revolution, he had managed to work through the dramas of Sophocles, Aeschylus, and Aristophanes, the commentaries on Greek tragedy by Johann Gustav Droysen and August Wilhelm Schlegel, and Karl Otfried Müller's history of the Dorians.[68] That hardly amounted to a systematic education in classical philology. Yet in some respects it was precisely his lack of formal training that enabled Wagner to endorse the ideals of Romantic Philhellenism. Had he studied at a university during the 1830s or 1840s, he would have found these ideals compromised by critical historical theories, a heightened emphasis on comparative linguistics, and an increasingly conservative professoriate.

Instead, Wagner viewed the ancient Greeks in the spirit of Winckelmann, Schiller, and Moritz: as an aesthetic and a sexual ideal. Years later he told Cosima, "All my subsequent feelings about the ugliness of our present-day world come from looking at illustrations in Moritz's mythology [*Götterlehre*]. Perseus with his fine helmet, but otherwise naked."[69] According to Wagner, however, this ideal of human form was the basis not only of Greek mythology but also of Germanic mythology. Describing his prerevolutionary readings, he wrote:

> My studies took me through the poetry of the Middle Ages back to the foundation of the old Germanic myth. I was able to remove one garment after another, which later poetry had distortedly wrapped around it, until finally I could view it in its chaste beauty. What I now saw was no longer the historical, conventional figure, in which the garment interests us more than the true shape, but rather the real, naked human [*Mensch*], on whom I could recognize every pulse of blood, every twitch of powerful muscles in unrestricted, freest movement. All in all, the true man.[70]

For Wagner, myth revealed human nature in its naked essence, before it had been corrupted by succeeding layers of religion, history, and convention. This stance was reflected in his use of the singular term "Mythos" as opposed to the plural "Mythologie." For whereas the early Romantics envisioned Greek mythology as a plurality of gods emanating from a single ineffable Idea (or "God"), Wagner insisted that Greek myth was centered on a singular image of the "human."

In *Oper und Drama*, Wagner traced the origins of myth to the need of a people to make sense of its natural environment. The world confronted primeval humans with a seemingly infinite variety of phenomena. Seeking an underlying cause behind these phenomena, they imagined beings not unlike themselves—gods. Since all knowledge came about through love, it was natural that these entities would be given a human form. Following Feuerbach, Wagner viewed the creation of myth as an attempt by the *Volk* to recognize itself in "an admired or beloved object of representation."[71] While many of the ancient gods depicted the workings of nature, the emotions, or fate, the god Apollo embodied the Greek nation. "The Greek spirit . . . found its corresponding expression in Apollo, the real national god of the Hellenic races. . . . Apollo was the fulfiller of Zeus's will on the Greek earth. He was the Greek people."[72] In certain respects this description of Apollo as the Greek national god paralleled Feuerbach's account of Jehovah, but Wagner insisted that the Greek god was not an image of "national egoism" but rather an expression of communal identity.

Wagner's account of Greek mythology was derived in large part from Karl Otfried Müller, whose two-volume *Die Dorier* (1824) found its way into the composer's Dresden library.[73] Müller had argued that Apollo was the national deity of the heroic and active Dorians, a northern race that invaded Greece during the archaic era. While the indigenous agricultural tribes worshiped the elemental deities of nature, the Dorians, as a warrior race, worshiped a national god.[74] Their religion demonstrated "a thoroughly idealistic direction of the spirit, which conceived the deity less in relation to the life of nature than in terms of free human activity. . . . Therefore, everything mystical was pushed into the background, which in religious feeling is based on a knowledge of absolute difference and therefore predominates in nature cults. To the contrary, the deity was thought of as more human, more heroic, although not so much as in the epic poetry."[75] In general, Wagner accepted Müller's account of the tribal roots of Greek culture and shared his sympathy for the Spartans versus the more corruptible and egoistic Athenians.[76] In particular, he was attracted to the ideal of a seamlessly unified, male-oriented community.

Yet Wagner granted Apollo a centrality beyond anything found in *Die Dorier*. Whereas Müller had traced the roots of Greek tragedy to the cult of Dionysus, Wagner maintained that tragedy had evolved out of religious festivals in honor of Apollo. "The Greek work of art was Apollo transformed into real, living art. That was the Greek people in its highest truth and beauty."[77] By representing the *Volksmythos* as human activity *(Handlung)*, tragedy fulfilled the human longing for self-representation and brought myth to its artistic completion.[78] In Wagner's eyes, the Greek festival-tragedy was a complete and perfect social experience, a moment of transparent human presence that the modern theater could not duplicate. That is perhaps why he chose to link tragedy to Apollo rather than Dionysus, whose "Greekness" was uncertain and who was not known as particularly chaste.

Although he idealized Greek tragedy, Wagner broke sharply from eighteenth-century Philhellenism in his assessment of sculpture. Winckelmann had associated Greek statuary with the superiority of the Greek political system, describing these artworks as representative of a republic of free individuals. Likewise, Schelling had called Greek sculpture the "perfected informing of the infinite into the finite" and an example of "consummate beauty."[79] But for Wagner, the development of sculpture was the objective corollary to individual lust and the breakdown of communal values. The Spartans had enjoyed a refined form of homosexuality (*Männerliebe*), based on both a physical and a spiritual enjoyment of the human form.[80] Lyric and dance, of which no traces remained, were the artistic expression of this love. In Athens, however, an egoistic spirit had led artists to produce individual works of art for rulers and rich philanthropists. The rise of sculpture therefore represented the victory of the enlightened individual over the artistic community and the degeneration of the Spartans' spiritual homosexuality into a lascivious perversity. What the Athenian sculptor depicted was not so much beauty per se as the memory of vanishing beauty. It was "as if in holding onto a lost communality, [sculpture] wanted to preserve it for monumental enjoyment."[81] When beauty departed from real life, as in the modern world, it could only be memorialized in a cold monument, a "mummy of Hellenism."[82]

Wagner's attack on sculpture signaled the radicalism of his critique of modern civil society, which had given itself up to the idols of property and impotent lust. Departing from traditional Philhellenism, he adopted an ambiguous stance toward the polis itself.[83] For Wagner, the transformation of the Doric tribal community into an "arbitrarily constructed political state" and the consequent shift from customary law to written law entailed an oppression of the individual "life instinct."[84] The creation of this state resulted in a conflict between what was recognized collectively as "good" (the law) and the desire of the individual for personal happiness. In the state, the individual became a stranger to himself and began to seek redemption outside life itself. This fundamental political shift, which Wagner placed at a relatively early stage of Greek history, helped to explain the origins of the Christian "mythos."

At the heart of the Christian myth was the image of the individual transfigured by a martyr's death at the hands of the state. Wagner traced the source of this myth not to Jewish messianism but to the political situation of fifth-century Greece, portrayed by Sophocles in the conflict between Antigone and Creon. The conflict was exacerbated in ancient Rome, where private property formed the basis of the legal system and religion was increasingly used to sanctify an unequal social and political order. This political context formed the true basis for Christianity, which had first gained a following among the ignorant and suffering masses of the Roman Empire.[85] The new religion promised an escape from the world into the heavenly bliss of the hereafter. Thus, "death, and the longing for it, are the only true content of art based on the Christian myth: it expresses itself as horror, loathing, and flight from true life and as a demand for death."[86] Ultimately, this myth only reinforced the power of the state, while destroying the somatic image that formed the basis of Greek paganism.

The spread of Christianity had led to the death of not only the Greek gods but also the central myth of the Germanic peoples. Like Greek myth, Germanic myth was derived from the observation of nature, especially the rising and setting of the sun. Yet in the figure of Siegfried it had advanced beyond the merely divine standpoint to take a fully human form, which was reflected in the legends and stories of the *Heldensage*. Christianity had undermined all of this, not by attacking the "branches and leaves of the Germanic folktree," but by uprooting it from the soil in which it had grown.[87] The German heroic legend split into a thousand fragments, which were attached in their dying form to the new faith. These remnants then formed the basis for the literature of the Christian era, which Wagner characterized under the broad rubric of "romance" *(Roman)*. Unlike Grimm and Heine, Wagner did not argue that Protestantism had somehow recaptured the spirit of ancient Germanic religion: in his view, the rebirth of German myth would require a more thorough overcoming of Christianity and its legacies.

Wagner's account of the history of literature was oriented around a dictum of A. W. Schlegel from his *Lectures on Dramatic Art and Literature* (1809–11): "the poetry of the ancients was that of possession, ours is that of longing: the former stands on the soil of the present, the latter hovers between memory and anticipation."[88] Like Schlegel, Wagner saw a natural progression from the knightly romances of the Middle Ages to the historical dramas of Shakespeare and, finally, to the dramatic efforts of Schiller and Goethe. Likewise, he described the progressive but ultimately unsuccessful attempt by these writers to condense the material of history into a suitably dramatic form. Yet Wagner took a far dimmer view of Christian modernity than had Schlegel, blaming it for the social problems of his own day: the expansion of the modern state, the rise of industrial society, the deep divisions among the classes, and the continuing dominance of priestly dogma. Christian modernity, in his view, had fundamentally disfigured the human form, such that it was tolerable only if the artist covered it up in the cloak of history. "If we removed this garment, we would see to our horror a shriveled, horrifying shape that [resembled the human only] in the painful suffering glance of the dying sick—this glance from which Christianity drew its fanatical enthusiasm."[89] Indeed, the tendency of recent novels *(Romane)* had been to depart from the great events of history and instead depict the reality of contemporary society in ever starker terms. But as literature grew closer to reality, it lost its unity and collapsed into myriad pieces. Art became politics, propaganda, or journalism, leading Wagner to lament that "no one can be poetic without being political," because "politics is the secret of our history and the present situation."[90]

According to Wagner, therefore, the modern world stood in the thrall of a religious imagery whose essence consisted of a rejection of life and a vain search for transcendence. This situation was the end result of the development of the legal state in ancient Greece. With the rise of law, humans no longer conceived of themselves in their full individuality, but only as citizens (or criminals) who belonged to a certain "class." Faced with this situation, Wagner demanded nothing less than the destruction of politics. With the state removed and private property abolished, artificial barriers of class and geography would disappear. The instinct of love would be liberated from the tyranny of convention, and women and men would draw together in a truly human society. "In the free self-determination of individuality lies the basis for the social religion of the future."[91]

What made such a religion possible was the long development over history of "science," or what Wagner preferred to call "experience." A scientific worldview had only become possible once the mythical tie that bound humanity to nature was destroyed. Nonetheless, Wagner viewed it as a "necessary error" that—like Christianity itself—had allowed the human species to expand its horizons beyond the old limits of tribal or national life in order to view the the world as it really was.[92] This development eventually turned against Christianity, as the spread of enlightenment led to a rejection of the miracles of the Bible. But as science penetrated ever deeper into the mysteries of the world, it also came to understand that nature was an "everbecoming" organism that "contains within itself both the procreating and parturient as male and female."[93] Here Wagner may have been alluding to Romantic *Naturphilosophie,* the Saint-Simonian ideal of androgyny, or the appropriation of those ideas by Feuerbach. In any case, the bond between the male and the female—love—would provide the basis for a reconciliation of nature and humanity. This knowledge also made it possible to conceive of an aesthetic "miracle" that would compress the knowledge of the world into a form comprehensible to human feeling—in a word, "myth."[94]

No mere "word-poetry" could adequately express the secret realm of "need," however. Spoken language remained mute to feelings; like sculpture, it was a monument, a deferral of feelings into an abstract realm of signs and conventions. The solution to this dilemma was to be found instead in "absolute music," whose development paralleled the history of religion. The simple melody based in a single key emerged within the context of ancient paganism, while multiple tonalities only became possible with the rise of

Christianity. "Christianity announced the unity of the human race in prophetic rapture: the art that is responsible to Christianity for its peculiar development, music, took this gospel in itself and shaped it as modern tonal language into a delightfully ravishing proclamation to sensual feeling."[95] In particular, absolute music was able to express precisely those qualities of longing—memory of the past, anticipation of the future—that A. W. Schlegel (and, later, E. T. A. Hoffmann) had identified as distinctive of modern art. Among modern composers, Beethoven had brought music to the logical limit of its expressive powers. The entry of the chorus in the final movement of the Ninth Symphony prefigured the end of music as an individual art form and its necessary merger with drama. Now music had to sacrifice its individual existence and become part of a "total work of art."

To illustrate this argument, Wagner pointed to the history of world exploration. The Greeks had always sailed close to the coastline, never letting it fade from sight. The Christian, driven by greed and lust, had wandered out into the ocean and become lost in its boundless expanse. But Columbus had shown that at the end of even the widest sea, solid land awaits the sailor. Beethoven, Wagner contended, was the Columbus of music. In his attempt to discover a new expressive language, Beethoven had burst the bounds of formal music. He had sailed the sea of absolute music until he reached a distant coast, which would be the foundation of the art of the future.[96] But neither Beethoven nor his successors recognized this fact. "Beethoven's error was that of Columbus, who only wanted to find a new route to familiar old India, but in the process discovered a new world."[97] This linking of Christianity and imperialism effectively inverted the postcolonial rhetoric of Jacob Grimm: whereas Grimm looked back with nostalgia to the religion that was lost, Wagner saw Christian musical idealism as pointing the way to a new world, which he alone had recognized.

Wagner envisioned the final union of poetry and music in the music drama as a joining of male "understanding" and female "feeling." Science, or experience, had demonstrated that nature was composed of male and female elements, but this knowledge could be made actual only in the realm of art. With the rise of absolute music, feeling was now accessible to the "aims" of poetic understanding.[98] Music, the "female mother-element," would receive the "longing" of male poetry as a "fertilizing seed" and would "nourish and shape this seed through its own necessary essence so that it gives birth to it in the form of a materializing and redemptive expression of feeling."[99] In turn, music's "eternal female" would draw poetry out of the egoism of the understanding and into contact with the purely human through the union of male and female potences. From the homosexual society of Sparta to the

division of the sexes in Christian modernity, the history of art would culminate in this moment of aesthetic androgyny.

Thus, the key to Wagner's mythical thought in the Zurich writings was
not a return to the purely national soil of the German *Heldensage* or a re-
trieval of Greek paganism. Instead, like the early Romantics, he envisioned a
new myth arising from processes internal to Christian modernity: science
and music. In Wagner's view, this would be a myth that was "justified by history" and that would provide an "understandable image of life" and serve as
the basis for a new, rejuvenated drama.[100] Unlike the early Romantics, however, Wagner saw this new myth as arriving, not from the unconscious soil
of the nation or race, but instead from the work of a single genius who
would redeem German culture more perfectly than even Schiller, Goethe,
or Beethoven. "Where the statesman despairs, the politician drops his hands,
and the socialist plagues himself with fruitless systems, and even the
philosopher can only hint at but not predict, . . . there it is the artist who with
clear eyes can see shapes that reveal themselves to a longing that demands
the one true thing—the human."[101] While Feuerbach sought to undermine
the egoistic principle at the heart of modern culture, Wagner used his philosophical language to articulate an image of the individual artist as the culmination of world history.

Since the artist of the future was already present (in the form of Wagner),
the main obstacle to realizing this vision was the operagoing public. Wagner
complained that modern theater audiences felt no need for art. Instead of
forming a whole, they scattered into clusters before the stage and were always ready to turn their backs on anything that challenged their already low
expectations. The chief reason for this appalling state of affairs, according
to Wagner, was that artistic life had passed from the hands of the aristocracy into the hands of the bourgeois philistine, "the most heartless and cowardly creation of our civilization."[102] The philistine controlled contemporary
taste not through patronage but through money, rejecting what was truly
"human" in favor of the base and the petty. These preferences were reinforced
by critics and journalists, who praised the familiar and the expected while rejecting the possibility of anything new. If this situation were to change, modern audiences would have to be replaced by a community that felt a common
"need" for a truly "human" work of art.[103] This community, or *Volk*, would
transcend national and linguistic boundaries to encompass the entire world.

Wagner's notion of a "universal *Volk*" reflected his gravitation to socialist modes of thinking. For that reason, he can be seen as transcending a narrower form of nationalism based on geographical or political borders in favor
of what he sometimes referred to as a "communism" that would encompass

all of Europe.[104] But while Wagner's *Volk* was not necessarily *"völkisch,"* it was not as all-inclusive as some commentators would have it.[105] Instead, as he made clear on several occasions, Wagner envisioned the "nation" as incorporating only "Christian" Europe. Indeed, for all of his criticisms of Christianity, Wagner still saw this religion as a "necessary error," which had created the conditions for modern "understanding" and for "absolute music." Those who were not part of its circle presumably would be unable to respond to the artwork of the future.

This leads to the issue of Wagner's anti-Semitism. For although Wagner never discusses Judaism in any length in *Oper und Drama*, his description of the philistine parallels his portrayal of the "Jew" in *Judentum in der Musik* (1850). Here the main object of attack is not Judaism as a religion but rather those educated, middle-class Jews who had benefited from the small steps taken toward legal emancipation since 1812 and whom Wagner had encountered on his travels to Paris and Berlin. Wagner assailed these "modern" Jews on several grounds: their alleged association with money and capitalism; their physical appearance; a supposed inability to master European languages without a noticeable "jargon"; and a lack of "passion" or "longing." This last deficit had supposedly resulted in a lack of aesthetic productivity among composers like Mendelssohn and Meyerbeer, whom Wagner described as latecomers to a musical form that Beethoven had already perfected.[106]

The savagery of Wagner's attacks on Judaism has long puzzled scholars of his musical oeuvre.[107] Several historians have sought explanations in his biography, citing artistic competition or simply a sadistic mentality, whereas others have linked his views to a revolutionary tradition of anti-Semitism that combined hatred of Judaism with hostility to capitalism.[108] Yet a focus on personal factors cannot fully account for the appeal of this sort of anti-Semitism, while an emphasis on continuities can miss the clear discursive shift underlying Wagner's views. To be sure, the project of a new mythology had always been predicated at least partly on a rejection of the biblical revelation or the "Jewish" aspects of Christianity. Schelling and Friedrich Schlegel viewed Judaism as a necessary but insufficient substrate for Christian modernity, which required a set of images that would more clearly reflect the historical experiences and expectations of modern Europeans (especially Germans). In their view, Judaism was a relic of the past with no essential connection to modernity.

Wagner, however, traced the origins of Christian modernity to the confrontation of the individual with the state, which resulted in an alienation of human essence into an imaginary afterlife. The Christian move toward the "ideal" had brought forth absolute music and scientific understanding, which had created the conditions for the artist of the future to create a "new myth." Yet this artist confronted an absolutist state, an egoistic civil society, a fragmented public sphere, and an indifferent public, which Wagner blamed less on Judaism as a religion than on the modern "Jew," who stood outside the universal *Volk* that would be the audience of the future and who competed for its affections and its money. As Wagner came to envision the artist not just as a genius but as the fulfillment of human history, he began to equate his own success—envisioned as a kind of self-sacrifice—with the overcoming of this modern Jew. In a sense, anti-Semitism became more modern, more physiological, and ultimately more personal for Wagner than it had ever been for his early Romantic predecessors. This was the conception of religious history that underlay *Der Ring des Nibelungen.*

GRASPING THE *RING*

Oper und Drama was written as a justification for Wagner's most ambitious project, a four-opera cycle based on the *Nibelungenlied*. Given the tenor of the times, this was a logical subject for an opera. A. W. Schlegel, August Zeune, and the Grimms had all identified the *Nibelungenlied* as the quintessential national epic. Moreover, this story had few Catholic or even Christian overtones, which meant that it could be linked without much difficulty to the gods of Nordic mythology. Fouqué had published *Sigurd, der Schlangentödter* in 1808, which was the first of over twenty different dramatizations of the epic. But the idea of an *opera* based on the *Nibelungenlied* had been proposed in 1844 by the Hegelian aestheticist Friedrich Theodor Vischer. Strauss rejected this idea with the comment "I would not recognize a singing Kriemhild."[109] Nonetheless, Vischer's suggestion was taken up by a series of different writers over the course of the 1840s, including Heinrich Dorn, Friedrich Dräseke, and the early feminist Louise Otto Peters.[110]

Wagner, however, came to this material only indirectly. Up through the fall of 1848, he had considered writing an opera based on the life of Friedrich Barbarossa, only to reject that figure in favor of Jesus of Nazareth and then Achilles. But as the revolution's prospects for success began to dim, Wagner decided to focus on the more mythical *Nibelungenlied*. "I returned to Siegfried at the same time as, disgusted with the empty formalistic tendency of the doings of our political parties, I withdrew from contact with our public life—and now with a full consciousness of the unsuitability of pure history for art," he wrote later.[111] In October 1848, Wagner wrote a preliminary sketch of the opera, *Der Nibelungen-Mythus,* which contained the first outlines of what would become the *Ring* cycle.[112] Wagner was uniquely successful in linking the medieval epic to the pantheon of Nordic deities, creating a seamless and coherent narrative of gods and heroes.

At the heart of Wagner's narrative was the original theft of the Rhine gold. Although commentators had long stressed the centrality of this incident, Wagner was the first to use the theft as the basis for an indictment of the entire legal and economic order of modern Europe. To make this point, he transformed the Nibelungen from a race of warriors into a race of dwarves. In Wagner's drama, the dwarves Alberich and Mime serve as symbols of capitalism, swearing off all human love and dedicating themselves to purely material lust, which they satisfy by stealing the Rhine gold and oppressing hordes of worker dwarves underground. The gods, by contrast, signify an aristocratic political class, whose folly and desire for glory lead to their eventual demise. Siegfried, of course, is the emblem of humanity, whose strength and lack of fear allow him to defeat the dragon and win control of the treasure. In the 1848 draft of the *Nibelungen*, Siegfried's death leads to the overthrow of the dwarves and the return of the Rhine gold to its rightful owners. The gods are redeemed, and Walhalla is preserved.[113] In the final version of the *Ring*, however, the realm of the gods collapses alongside that of the dwarves.

Wagner's reworking of the *Nibelungenlied* created a mythical narrative of sin and redemption that paralleled the viewpoint of his Zurich writings. As in *Oper und Drama*, Wagner identified the end of the mythical golden age with the beginnings of private property. But while he traced this development in his aesthetic theory to a universal tendency toward greed and self-aggrandizement, the *Ring* identified a specific villain: the dwarf Alberich. Like the serpent of Genesis 3, the dwarves were meant to be physically repulsive, an antithesis to the healthy human body. Likewise, in rejecting love Alberich denies what both Feuerbach and Wagner had identified as the most fundamental human "need."[114] Given his earlier description of modern Jews as lacking "passion" or "longing," Wagner's more knowledgeable readers did not have to work hard to draw the necessary comparisons. Whether his entire audience would have understood these associations is doubtful—there was room for a wide variety of interpretations of the *Ring*.

The meaning of the gods is also open to interpretation. Wotan, the father of the gods, is responsible for the onset of the tragedy, since it is his quest for glory that leads him to make a contract with the giants for the building of Walhalla. Thus, for Wagner, the onset of the legal order coincided with the attempt to construct a heavenly home for the gods, which destroyed the connection between nature and the divine. In this sense, Wotan is responsible for the modern legal order and the foundation of a supernaturalistic religion (Christianity). To redeem himself, Wotan must sacrifice Siegfried, the em-

Scenes from Wagner's *Rheingold:* the dwarf Alberich stealing the Rhine gold; Fasolt
and Fafner attempting to carry away Freia in return for building Walhalla; Wotan and
Loki among the dwarves. Drawing by Theodor Pixis.
From the Leipzig *Illustrirte Zeitung,* Oct. 23, 1869, p. 333. Photo courtesy of
Newberry Library, Chicago.

bodiment of the pagan hero. Yet there are severe limitations to Siegfried as a character: strong but cruel, ignorant of the ways of the world, his death at the hands of Hagen does not bring the story to an end. Instead, it is the Valkyrie Brünnhilde, the only character fully aware of the cosmic drama being played out—the only character "justified" by the knowledge and experience of history—who dies the redeemer's death by throwing herself on Siegfried's funeral pyre.[115] The Rhine River rises up and sweeps away the ring, while Walhalla bursts into flame. The end of the gods clears the ground for the creation of a new humanity and a universal religion of love. Yet this ending could also be read in a different manner, as the long-desired end of the world and its suffering. Wagner would come to adopt this interpretation in the wake of his encounter with Schopenhauer.

Wagner read Arthur Schopenhauer's *Die Welt als Wille und Vorstellung* (1819) for the first time in 1854 and would read it again on three separate occasions.[116] While Kant had divided the world into phenomenal appearance and the "thing-in-itself," Schopenhauer described it as the product of a universal "will" and its projected illusion ("representation"). This "will" drove all creation forward in a meaningless cycle of birth, procreation, and death, from which there was no escape. Because of the fundamental unity of all existence, Schopenhauer based his ethics on a sense, not of duty, but rather of compassion *(Mitleid)*, that is, a recognition of one's own suffering in the suffering of another. But ultimately there could be no relief from the will—especially not through optimistic notions of "progress." One could only hope to quiet the will by listening to music, which Schopenhauer described as "the likeness of the will itself."[117] Poetry, by contrast, was a decidedly lesser art in his scheme. Thus, while Schopenhauer flattered Wagner the musician, his evaluation of the branches of art overturned the delicate balance between poetry and music established in *Oper und Drama.*

The encounter with Schopenhauer required Wagner to rethink his views on religion as well. The philosopher's deep and abiding anti-Semitism, which was expressed most emphatically in *Parerga und Paralipomena* (1851), only reinforced Wagner's existing prejudices. According to Schopenhauer, the "Jewish" doctrines of creation ex nihilo and Last Judgment had obscured the true nature of the world, leading to an endorsement of cruelty to animals, among other sins.[118] Arguing that Jews formed a kind of foreign nation in the body of Europe, he rejected the idea of granting them full political rights.[119] But Schopenhauer was almost equally dismissive of Greek paganism, describing the efforts of scholars like Friedrich Creuzer to find a meaningful doctrine in this mythology as a waste of time.[120] This religion was "without any true moral tendency and sacred writings, so that it hardly merited the name of religion, but was rather a mere play of the imagination, a product of the poets from popular fairy-tales, and for the most part an obvious personification of the powers of nature. We can hardly believe that grown men ever took this childish religion seriously."[121] In Schopenhauer's view, the Greeks and Romans lived like "big children" until the arrival of Christianity.[122]

The Christian religion was treated in the *Parerga* as a hybrid of Jewish "optimism" and Buddhist "pessimism," which gave it a rather incoherent character. Schopenhauer largely endorsed Strauss's description of the life of Jesus as a Jewish myth, yet he saw a core of Indian teaching in the Christian doctrines of suffering, pity, and the "avatar." How this doctrine came to Palestine remained unclear, although Schopenhauer suggested half jokingly that Jesus learned his religion during Mary and Joseph's flight to Egypt. In any case, he viewed the grafting of the New Testament onto the Old Testament simply as an act of expediency: "As ivy needs support and something to hold on to, it twines around a rough-hewn post. . . . In the same way, Christ's teaching that has sprung from Indian wisdom has covered the old and quite different trunk of crude Judaism and what had to be retained of the original form is changed by that teaching into something quite different, true and alive."[123] Interpreted literally, Christianity with its doctrines of heaven and hell was a moral monstrosity, but interpreted allegorically it yielded the sublimest pessimistic doctrine.[124]

These arguments exercised an immense influence on Wagner, not only because they confirmed his instincts about the metaphysical significance of music, but also because they opened a path back to the Christian religion and the monarchical state that he had reviled in the Zurich writings. As a consequence, he would gradually abandon the goal of creating a new, post-Christian "myth." This move in Wagner's thought is already evident in the essay "Zukunftsmusik" (1860), where he recapitulates the arguments of *Oper und Drama* but passes over the section dealing with poetry and myth in embarrassed haste: "I believed [at the time] . . . that I had to identify the ideal material of the poet as "myth," this originally nameless poetry of the *Volk.*" He now argued that myth was valuable not as an expression of the "human" but rather because it encouraged the "dreamlike state" required to perceive the true nature of the world.[125] Meanwhile, Wagner quietly rehabilitated the concept of "revelation" *(Offenbarung)*, which came to mean an insight into the reality that existed beyond the phenomenal world of appearances. In "Staat und Religion" (1864) he maintained that "revelation," available to most Christians only in the allegorical form of dogma, constituted the true content of his operas.[126] This revelation, he insisted, was also the indispensable foundation of both religion and the monarchical state. As a result, by the time Nietzsche met Wagner, the composer had largely abandoned the mythical discourse that had dominated his Zurich writings.

More than any single individual, Richard Wagner popularized the images and stories of "German mythology" for the nineteenth-century public. In composing his operas, he relied on the previous half century of myth scholarship, which had created a consensus among educated Germans that the ancient Teutons had indeed possessed a pantheon of gods. This scholarship in German philology provided him with a set of canonical themes and motifs, which formed the poetic basis of his music dramas. Nietzsche would later say of Wagner that "all scholars worked only for him; now, after the work of resurrecting the German myth is complete, that species of scholar has become superfluous."[127] Yet Wagner did not want to simply revive Germanic mythology—that would do no more than to reaffirm a principle of nationality that was associated with a political liberalism that he rejected. Instead, he was determined to build an essentially *new* myth that would emerge from the characteristic features of Christian modernity, science and music.

By the time Wagner revived this early Romantic project, the configuration of political, religious, and cultural forces had shifted significantly in Germany. Rationalist and Hegelian forms of Protestantism were on the defensive, while Neo-Pietist and late Romantic theologies affirmed an inherent connection between throne and altar in the "Christian state." Meanwhile, however, the advance of the "social question" in Europe had encouraged the spread of Saint-Simonian, German Catholic, and left-Hegelian critiques of economic, political, and theological liberalism. Such critiques reinforced Wagner's growing disdain for a public culture that had abandoned aristocratic patronage and was now dictated by the tastes of journalists and philistines. Following Feuerbach, he linked the egoism of modern society to Christianity and in *Oper und Drama* called for a new religion grounded in human "need." But whereas Feuerbach believed that "need" could be fulfilled strictly through human social relations, Wagner insisted on the necessity of a "new myth," which would be manifested in the work of a singular genius. The result would be a religion in which the artist—who was inhabited by an unquenchable "longing"—occupied the role of redeemer.

Wagner, of course, felt no compunction about abandoning the aesthetic philosophy he had developed in his Zurich writings. If in *Oper und Drama* he advocated a new myth grounded in Feuerbachian sensualism, his later writings would promote the pessimistic "revelation" supposedly at the heart of Christianity. Wherever his thought fell along this axis, however, Wagner maintained consistently that his aesthetic project stood independent of a biblical revelation associated with both Judaism and ecclesiastical power and, further, that it represented both the solution to Christian modernity and the authentic religion of the *Volk*—whether this was defined as the German nation, the Christian-European population, or simply the audience of the future. This straddling of the pagan-Christian divide was typical of the German discourse on myth and, as we have seen, a major source of its appeal; now, however, it would serve an aesthetic project intended to reshape the nature of German culture and become the foundation of a new, post-Christian religion.

CHAPTER SIX

Myth and Monotheism in the Unification Era, 1850–1880

The path to origins leads everywhere to barbarism.

Nietzsche

The 1848–49 revolution signaled a watershed not only in German politics but also in German intellectual history. The failure of the Frankfurt Parliament to create a unified nation-state helped discredit the *Vormärz* brand of liberalism, with its roots in Romanticism and idealist philosophy. But what succeeded it was not so much conservatism as a more practical and materialistic form of liberalism. Supported by middle-class notables in local governments and associations, this new postrevolutionary, or *Nachmärz*, liberalism survived the brief reaction of the early 1850s to acquire a predominant influence in bourgeois cultural and political life. Massive celebrations of Schiller's and Fichte's birthdays stoked enthusiasm for Protestant "national" culture, unprecedented economic growth appeared to validate liberal economic doctrines, and the onset of the "New Era" in Prussia seemed to promise the emergence of a liberal monarchy.[1]

The new orientation in liberal culture was reflected in scholarship. In philosophy, the Promethean era of system-building gave way to a period of relative skepticism, as scholars scaled back the claims of metaphysics and placed new value on empirical experience.[2] New scholarship in ethnology, folklore, and culture history *(Kulturgeschichte)* reoriented the study of culture away from art and religion and toward the artifacts of work, home, and technology.[3] Like liberalism, therefore, academic scholarship emerged from the 1848–49 revolution more practical, more materialistic, and, in some respects, less ambitious. The French linguist and historian Ernest Renan blamed this on the early 1850s reaction, when a number of politically suspect professors lost their positions: "The golden age in Germany, at least with respect to the external conditions of intellectual life, has passed."[4] Yet scholars were not forced to adopt the new *Nachmärz* standpoint. Instead, as Woodruff Smith argues, many intellectuals believed that evolutionary and empirical approaches offered a better grounding for economic liberalism and national unification than Romantic or Hegelian concepts of the nation.[5] Given the failure of the working classes to support middle-class demands during 1848–49, a less idealized notion of the *Volk* and its culture seemed prudent.

In this new climate of scholarship and opinion, "myth" lost much of its former cachet.[6] To be sure, individual scholars continued to work in this field. Eduard Gerhard and Friedrich Welcker published voluminous, if not necessarily pathbreaking, studies of Greek mythology in the Romantic mode.[7] Schelling's lectures on the philosophy of mythology and revelation appeared posthumously, although most scholars dismissed them as irrelevant.[8] In general, this was an era of empirical accumulation rather than theoretical speculation, a phenomenon sometimes characterized as "Romantic positivism."[9] For Jacob Grimm or Friedrich Creuzer, every fragment, however insignificant in itself, represented a piece in a larger puzzle; the goal of their efforts was to reconstruct the ancient mythological revelation in its totality. After 1850, the Romantic paradigm continued to justify the collection of anecdotes and fragments, but hopes for final synthesis were quietly abandoned. Meanwhile, the Romantics' categories of analysis ("nation," "language," "spirit") were adopted to fit a new postidealist epistemology.

This process can be seen in the new approaches to myth that came to the fore between 1850 and 1880. "Comparative mythology," founded by Adalbert Kuhn and Friedrich Max Müller, was an attempt to ground the study of myth in the new discipline of comparative philology. Kuhn and Müller emphasized the Indo-Germanic ("Aryan") roots of both Germanic and Greek mythology, challenging the philological partisans of Greek autochthony, who had emerged seemingly victorious from the *Symbolik* controversy. But whereas Creuzer saw mythology as a divine revelation, Müller and especially Kuhn emphasized its accidental, even mundane, origins.

In a similar manner, the founders of "folk psychology" *(Völkerpsychologie)*, Moritz Lazarus and Heymann Steinthal, attempted to explain the intellectual life of nations according to epistemological principles derived from the psychologist Johann Friedrich Herbart. Lazarus and Steinthal devoted particular attention to mythology, which they saw as an authentic expression of the national spirit, and they welcomed the work of the comparative mythologists. At the same time, however, they were all too aware of the dangers inherent in an uncritical reverence for the *Volk* and its myths. Steinthal, in particular, would become involved in a bitter dispute concerning the origins and merits of Hebrew ("Semitic") monotheism as compared to "Aryan" polytheism.[10] In the course of that debate, he contested the Romantic veneration of mythology by insisting that true religion involved an elevation beyond myth, toward the ideal realm of the good, the true, and the beautiful.

Adalbert Kuhn, Max Müller, and Comparative Mythology

From the 1850s until the 1870s, the study of myth in Germany followed the lead of a man whose life and writings have been largely forgotten. Even in his own lifetime, the official recognition accorded Adalbert Kuhn (1812–81) was quite meager. Despite his editorship of two learned journals and his status as Germany's leading mythographer, Kuhn spent his entire career at the Köllnisches Gymnasium in Berlin. Although he was eventually named to the Prussian Academy of Sciences, his failure to acquire a university position offers stark testimony to the relatively marginal status of myth research in the two decades preceding German unification.

Born in Königsberg, Kuhn achieved competence in Sanskrit as a gymnasium student.[11] He went to Berlin to earn his doctorate, where he worked under the linguist Franz Bopp and became life-long friends with the novelist and historian Gustav Freytag.[12] After completing his studies, Kuhn embarked on field research of the type inspired by (but rarely practiced by) the Grimm brothers. Traveling through Brandenburg and Westphalia, he collected folktales, sayings, and customs from local peasants.[13] Based on his observations, Kuhn concluded that the Grimms had erred when they described folktales and customs as remnants of an original *Götterlehre*. Present-day peasants, he discovered, had a capacity for spontaneous mythopoeisis when confronted with the forces of nature. There was thus no need to posit a "golden age" or an original revelation when explaining the origin of myth, because mythical thinking was a feature of all primitive, undeveloped cultures.

This discovery shaped Kuhn's approach to the study of ancient myth. Since the publication of the first volume of Bopp's *Vergleichende Grammatik* (1833), it had become widely accepted that the ancient Aryans had spoken the root language of the Indo-Germanic peoples. In the succeeding decade, practitioners of "comparative philology" began to explore the structural and etymological connections among the various Indo-European languages. This discipline first emerged within German faculties of philology, but it soon spread to France and Great Britain. Convinced of the Indian origins of the European languages, philologists turned to the "root mythology"

Adalbert Kuhn. Nach einer Photographie von Schwarh u. Co. in Berlin.

The comparative mythologist Adalbert Kuhn.
From the Leipzig *Illustrirte Zeitung*, Oct. 22, 1864, p. 280. Photo courtesy of
Newberry Library, Chicago.

of the *Rig Veda*, which began to appear in print during the 1830s. Hundreds
of years older than the Brahmanic texts on which Creuzer and Schlegel relied, the *Rig Veda* contained over a thousand hymns to nature deities, many
with unmistakable likenesses to Greek and Germanic gods. Unlike the epic
poetry of Homer or the *Eddas*, however, the Vedic hymns were linked to religious rituals and practices that seemed to reflect an early stage of cultural
evolution. Beginning in the 1840s, Kuhn published a series of studies in
which he compared the Vedic hymns with Germanic myths, relying especially on etymological analysis. He did not attain real notoriety, however,
until the appearance of *Die Herabkunft des Feuers und des Göttertranks*
(1859), in which he traced the Greek myth of Prometheus to Aryan conceptions of fire.[14]

The central myth of the *Rig Veda*, according to Kuhn, was the theft of

Agni (the ritual fire) from the sky. "Mâtariçvan, a divine or half-divine being, about whose origin and nature we learn little from the songs, took the Agni back from the gods, because it had disappeared from the earth and had hidden itself in a hole. He gave it to the Bhrgus, one of the oldest races of priests, or to Manu, humanity itself or the first human."[15] This story bore a striking resemblance to the Prometheus story. In both narratives, a being one step removed from divinity preserved the element of fire for humankind, and in both myths this act of disobedience was linked to the creation of the human race.

Unlike the Greek myth, however, the Vedic hymns to Agni were shot through with references to the practical details of fire making. The ancient Aryans had produced fire by rubbing a stick in a hole bored out of a block of wood. The Sanskrit name for that stick was *pramantha*, close enough to the Greek "Prometheus" to suggest an etymological connection. In addition, the Sanskrit verb for "rubbing" was *mathnâmi*, which evoked the Vedic hero Mâtariçvan. Thus, Kuhn established a link between the myth and the actual acquisition of fire. Before Prometheus was a fire-robber *(Feuerrauber)*, he was a fire-rubber *(Feuerreiber)*.[16] Kuhn then linked the story of Mâtariçvan to a further complex of myths concerning the *soma*, a sacred drink with life-giving powers. The verb *mathnâmi*, used to describe rubbing, was also used to describe the churning action involved in making butter and soma. The Vedas reported that the gods often fought over the soma, and that at one point it had been stolen from the heavens by the god Indra.

But the chain of connections went further. Because of an undeveloped sense of causality, the primitive Aryans linked the rubbing action involved in starting fire or churning butter to another kind of rubbing action that produced a liquid residue. "To the simple natural man, the procedure for producing fire . . . must have easily recalled the act of procreation. That this was in fact the case can be seen from a song of the *Rig Veda* . . . : 'that is the turn-stick, the procreator (penis) is ready. Bring the mistress of the tribe here. Let us churn Agni according to the old practice.'"[17] In this way the origin of fire became indelibly associated with the origin of humanity. The medium for that association was the *pramantha*, a useful tool but also—and this remained unspoken—the Freudian fetish.[18] Eventually the primitive Aryans would trace the origins of fire, soma, and the human race back to the heavens. After all, fire had first come to earth by means of lightning. Thinking that the same process that created earthly fire must have created the heavenly fire, the primitive Aryans interpreted lightning as a kind of *pramantha* and the clouds as trees that were rubbed by the *pramantha* to create sparks.

According to Kuhn, the Vedic myths of Agni and soma reflected a primitive intuition of the world from which the major myths of Greek culture had evolved. Its traces were to be found especially in the beliefs and practices surrounding Dionysus, the god of wine. For example, the myth of Dionysus's birth, in which Zeus seduces Persephone, could be traced to the perception of lightning in storm clouds, which was influenced in turn by the experiences of fire making and soma churning.[19] Echoes of the *pramantha* were apparently found in the Bacchic staff, the thyrsus, used by Dionysus to extract wine from rocks, as well as in the wood, ivy, and phallic practices associated with his cult.[20] Thus, while Creuzer and Schelling viewed Dionysus as a "divine child" and a predecessor to Christ, Kuhn saw in this deity a combination of rain and soma.

The Vedas also offered clues to the origins of old German folk practices. In the *Deutsche Mythologie*, Jacob Grimm had described how on Saint John's Day (Johannistag), German villagers carried a wooden wheel to the top of a hill, set it on fire, and let it roll down the hill, through the village, and into the river.[21] According to Kuhn, the descent of this "fire-wheel" evoked not only Prometheus's theft of fire from the sky but also the old practice of rubbing to produce fire.[22] Likewise, the drinking of the yearly Johannisbier echoed the drinking of the soma. In other words, the Vedic texts, with their emphasis on ritual, provided the evidence that connected German folklife to some of the earliest systems of mythology. The parallels between modern folk practices and ancient rituals showed "with what tenacity the lower classes of highly developed peoples hold on to their old traditions and how suited these are for enlightening us about the myths of even the most distant times. One would hardly exaggerate when one ascribed to this practice an age of three to four thousand years."[23]

Unlike Grimm, Kuhn refrained from ascribing to these myths any deep religious meaning. He believed that they simply sprang from the day-to-day activities of the earliest Indo-Germans. "It is natural that among such a people we cannot look for that oft-dreamt-of ancient wisdom, which has supposedly left only scanty crumbs for us later generations. Instead, the myths of the [Indo-Germans] revolved around a center that by all reckoning corresponded to that form of life."[24] The newly emerging discipline of cultural history had begun to stress the importance of material and technological factors in the evolution of culture, and even philologists were beginning to accept the importance of such concrete realities for the evolution of classical culture. Now Kuhn was applying these notions to Greek myth. One scholar noted crassly, "Fifty years ago, who would not have sworn till he was blue in the face that there was nothing to be found in Prometheus besides the personification of philosophical and religious ideas? Now Kuhn has proved beyond a doubt in his epochal work that these heaven-storming ideas have their beginnings in the wretched business of preparing butter and fire."[25] The Romantic approach to mythology, which traced myth to a religious intuition, seemed to have been overturned at last.

The term "comparative mythology" dates from an essay published in 1856 by the German ex-patriot Friedrich Max Müller (1823–1900), then deputy professor of modern languages and literatures at All Souls College, Oxford.[26] Müller was born in Dessau and was the son of the poet Wilhelm Müller (most famous for the words to Schubert's "Die Winterreise"). He attended university in Leipzig, where he studied philosophy under Christian Hermann Weisse, philology under Gottfried Hermann, and Sanskrit under Hermann Brockhaus before moving to Berlin in order to study under Schelling. On arrival he made the acquaintance of the aging philosopher and paid a considerable sum to hear his private lectures on the philosophy of revelation.[27] Over the next year, he worked with Franz Bopp and a slew of other Orientalists, including Kuhn.[28] Müller also made the acquaintance of Baron Christian Josias Bunsen, a biblical scholar, Egyptologist, and Prussian diplomat who sponsored his trip to England in 1846.[29] Three years later he received the appointment to Oxford University, where he would spend the remaining years of his career, most of them as professor of comparative philology.

Although he relied on the same sources and came to many of the same conclusions about the nature of Aryan myth as Kuhn, Müller's methodology and intellectual style could not have been more different. While Kuhn traced the origin of myth to copulation and butter churning, Müller spoke of a Schleiermacherian feeling for the divinity that inspired the primitive Aryans to burst out in song at the sight of the dawn. Like his friend Bunsen, Müller viewed his own efforts in the field of mythology as part of a general effort to establish a "science of religion."[30] Müller identified himself as a Protestant believer throughout his life, although he had given up the notion of biblical revelation at a young age and viewed the ecclesiastical and liturgical disputes of his Oxford colleagues with ironic distance.[31] He was confident that his research into mythology would contribute to a renewal of religious consciousness in the world and help bring about an end to religious conflict.

Müller brought language to the very heart of mythology. Prior to the separation of peoples and languages, he argued, the primitive Aryans had been inspired to verse by the rising and setting of the sun. Their language as yet lacked abstraction, and so every word embodied a metaphor. "Where we speak of the sun following the dawn, the ancient poets could only speak and think of the sun loving and embracing the dawn," Müller wrote. "What is with us a sunset, was to them the Sun growing old, decaying, or dying."[32] The Aryans were a race of poets or, more specifically, a race of Wordsworths, and Müller often quoted the old Romantic as a worthy successor to his ancestors.

Language as unconscious metaphor was a beautiful thing in Müller's eyes. He warmly praised the natural theology of the *Rig Veda*, in which the original solar mythology still lay close to the surface. Problems began, however, when the words that had been used to describe the heavenly bodies began to break loose and take on a life of their own. "[E]very name, as it ceased to be understood, became, like a decaying seed, the germ of an abundant growth of myth and legend," Müller wrote.[33] By the time of Homer or Hesiod, these myths had lost their original associations, often mixing with real historical figures and events.[34] The myths had become "spurious coins in the hands of the many," which required the historian and linguist to recover their original associations.[35] Müller went on to cite dozens of myths, from the story of Orpheus and Eurydike to the death of Siegfried. Each story, he argued, could be traced back to an ancient metaphor that celebrated the interplay between sun, dawn, dew, and night.

Ultimately, Müller's distinction between language as beautiful metaphor and mythology as corrupt metaphor rested on an aesthetic judgment, which was influenced no doubt by his father's vocation. While myth echoed the confusion and unbelief of a decadent society, poetry had sprung from the "healthy and strong feelings of a youthful race of men, free to follow the call of their hearts,—unfettered by the rules and prejudices of a refined society, and controlled only by those laws which nature and the graces have engraved on every human heart."[36] The rediscovery of the original poetry brought modern people back in contact with the purer religious sentiments of their ancestors, while offering a promise of that religious unity toward which, Müller believed, history inevitably led.[37]

The theories of Kuhn and Müller, when combined with the work of a number of other scholars, would achieve a dominant position in German myth scholarship from the mid-1850s through the mid-1870s. What accounted for the quick acceptance of comparative mythology? In their search for an original religion in India, Kuhn and Müller seemed to reiterate the conclusions of their Romantic predecessors, Creuzer, Kanne, and Görres, who had been roundly condemned by two generations of philologists. But Müller and Kuhn were linguists and thus had at their disposal the residual prestige of their mentor Bopp and his predecessor Wilhelm von Humboldt. Unlike Creuzer's *Symbolik und Mythologie*, comparative philology seemed to offer a reliable method for demonstrating the connection of one culture to another. While the classical philologists may have looked askance at the results of comparative mythology, they lacked the linguistic skills in Sanskrit or Old German to refute them. Linguistics had opened up the field of mythology once again.

The results of comparative mythology, especially as presented by Kuhn, were particularly attractive to liberal and left-leaning scholars in the post-1848 decades.[38] Kuhn's thesis that the earliest myths were the result of primitive ideas about butter churning and lighting fires reinforced the new orientation of scholarship toward a more material conception of "culture" and the implementation of evolutionary (if non-Darwinist) models of history.[39] Instead of romanticizing folklife or seeing in it a hidden revelation, Kuhn traced its origins to the primitive mental apparatus of ancients unable to fathom the most basic notions of causality. Further, while the Oxford-based Max Müller promoted a theologically liberal but politically conservative agenda, Kuhn and most other German exponents of comparative mythology did not. They adhered instead to an evolutionary and progressive notion of culture that reflected the new "practical" orientation of political liberalism and university scholarship in the decades of the 1850s and 1860s.

Heymann Steinthal: Monotheism and Mythology

For these reasons it is not surprising that two of the leading Jewish intellectuals of the era of unification, the folk psychologists Heymann Steinthal (1823–99) and Moritz Lazarus (1824–1903), seized on Kuhn's results with alacrity.[40] Steinthal was the son of a linen salesman from the town of Gröbzig in Anhalt, where he attended Hebrew school before enrolling in a nearby gymnasium. Lazarus was the son of a rabbinical scholar from Posen. The two met as students in Berlin during the winter of 1848–49, where they were studying linguistics.[41] They would remain close friends throughout their lives, with Steinthal eventually marrying Lazarus's sister Jeannette. Both went on to teach linguistics at the University of Berlin: Steinthal beginning in 1856, Lazarus beginning in 1873. But neither became a full professor, and neither was accepted into the Prussian Academy of Sciences. Such distinctions were forbidden to Jews at this time.[42]

Lazarus and Steinthal's chief legacy was the *Zeitschrift für Völkerpsychologie und Sprachwissenschaft*, which began in 1860 as an attempt to found a "psychological ethnology."[43] The *Zeitschrift's* contributors included

Hermann Cohen, Wilhelm Windelband, and Wilhelm Dilthey, but Lazarus and Steinthal dominated the proceedings. Both scholars were guided by the assumption that the *Volk* formed the most important category for the study of human history, culture, and belief. Persians of differing classes, they argued, had more in common with one another than Persians and Greeks of the same class.[44] Among European nations, the Germanic peoples had historically played the leading role, and they would continue to do so in the future.[45] These views mirrored Lazarus and Steinthal's *kleindeutsch* political stance, which favored Protestant Prussia against the Catholic states of the south.[46] Throughout their careers the two friends would remain moderate liberals, insisting on individual freedom and religious tolerance but never calling the authority of the state or the values of the *Bildungsbürgertum* into question.

As defined by Lazarus and Steinthal, the goal of folk psychology *(Völkerpsychologie)* was to investigate the elements that constituted the unity and individuality of the national spirit *(Volksgeist)*. Language, for example, was one such component: Steinthal wrote that "every language is a national metaphysic and national logic."[47] The other key artifact for folk psychology was mythology. "Next to language, myth forms the innermost core of the folk spirit, from which its entire theoretical and practical life flows."[48] Other elements of the national spirit included religion, liturgy, poetry, ethics, and law.[49] Yet despite their use of Romantic concepts, Steinthal and Lazarus conceived of the nation as a historical-empirical phenomenon rather than an ontological ideal. They were deeply suspicious of attempts to mystify the nation or, worse, treat it as some sort of biological entity. The *Volk*, in their view, was essentially a mental phenomenon. "A nation is a group of people which sees itself as one nation, which counts itself as part of one nation."[50] As such, it could only be understood psychologically.

Of *Völkerpsychologie*'s two founding fathers, Steinthal took the more active role in contemporary controversies concerning the nature of mythology. While he accepted myth as a central category of human experience, he was determined to disengage the study of myth from its roots in idealist philosophy and inject it with the new values of empiricist psychology and ethical individualism. In this manner, Steinthal saw himself carrying on the work of Hegel, Wilhelm von Humboldt, and the Grimms, while placing their legacy on a more secure epistemological foundation. Steinthal's prominent position within the Berlin Jewish community provided added incentive to take on the assumptions of Romantic mythography. In 1872, he helped to found the Hochschule für die Wissenschaft des Judenthums, an institution devoted to a largely secular scholarship of Judaism. There he lectured on ethics, philosophy of religion, and biblical theology.[51] By that time, Steinthal had established himself as a defender of the Jewish cultural heritage (including the ancient Hebrew "mythology") against attacks by gentile scholars from Germany, France, and Great Britain.

Lazarus and Steinthal greeted the comparative mythology of Adalbert Kuhn with open arms, and in the opening essay of the *Zeitschrift* they offered lavish praise for *Die Herabkunft des Feuers*. Whereas earlier efforts at comparison (notably Creuzer's) "had erred not only often but widely," Kuhn offered "the substantiated proof of the original identity of various gods."[52] This was a decisive rebuff to those philologists who still insisted on the autochthony of Greek culture.[53] Steinthal, in particular, rejected the claims of the Philhellenists. Reviewing an edition of Wilhelm von Humboldt's correspondence, he cited a letter in which Humboldt rejected any commingling of Greek mythology with German legends and tales. Steinthal was indignant: "I recommend this passage to anyone who wants to write a work about the power of prejudices."[54] In his eyes, Humboldt's devotion to the Greeks constituted a kind of religious belief, which was similar in its delusions to Schelling's claim that the gods were real. The bitterness of Steinthal's comments points to the fact that whereas in the *Vormärz* Philhellenism was still linked to liberalism, by the 1860s many liberals saw it as simply a thin veil for institutional privilege, academic closed-mindedness, and hostility to progress.

Despite Steinthal's enthusiasm for the new comparative mythology, he remained concerned about Kuhn's lack of a clear methodology.[55] Kuhn had certainly displayed a gift for linguistic combination, but he had not explained how one word or representation became associated with another in the minds of the ancient Indo-Germans. How exactly did the *Urmensch* (primitive human) come to join lightning, the butter churn, the *pramantha*, and the phallus into one set of myths? To answer this question, Steinthal turned to the thought of Johann Friedrich Herbart (1776–1841). In the early nineteenth century, Herbart had emerged as a critic of neohumanism and the advocate of a pragmatic pedagogy.[56] In addition, he had challenged Hegelian-Schellingian idealism with a mechanistic psychology grounded in mathematics and empiricism. For Herbart, the representations of thought were not the product of logic but rather physical activities within the brain.[57] Through the process of "apperception," new representations became assimilated to an older mass of representations, thereby generating knowledge. Within any combination of representations, however, one or two tended to be dominant while the others were largely repressed.

As far as Steinthal was concerned, Herbart's theory had the advantage of steering a path between idealism and the hard-core materialism of writers like Ludwig Büchner and Karl Vogt.[58] In addition, it suggested how a childlike mind could link the disparate realms of fire making, procreation, and weather into a single mass of representations. In the *Zeitschrift für Völkerpsychologie*, Steinthal applied Herbart's theory of apperception to explain the formation of myth among the ancient Aryans. According to Steinthal, the myth of Prometheus originated, not from some protoscientific curiosity about the origin of fire, but rather from the inability of the *Urmensch* to differentiate between types of representations. "When the primitive man visualizes the act of procreation, it is the representation group of fire rubbing that comes to consciousness because of its similarity in movement."[59] Since only one representation could be dominant within a given mass of representations, the act of procreation was subsumed under the act of making a fire.

The act of fire making also determined how the *Urmensch* viewed lightning and storms (the "heavenly fire"). The earthly experiences of fire were "clearer, more numerous, more definite, and more certain, because the human is nearer the earthly fire and works with it, and because work is a rich source of knowledge."[60] Once these representations had fused together, the *Urmensch* confused cause and effect and came to assign primacy to the heavenly fire. This gave rise to the myth of fire descending from heaven. Steinthal's last point was crucial, for with this evaluation he refuted not only the Romantics but also Max Müller's theory of the poetic origins of myth.

In his own work on linguistics, Steinthal sought to reinforce this distinction between mythmaking and poetry. In *Einleitung in die Psychologie und Sprachwissenschaft* (1871), Steinthal described how language had gradually accumulated a collection of useful word-symbols, each an apperception of a given content onto a given sign in a useful system of knowledge. Not all language was functional, however. Poets, for example, used similes and metaphors in order to compare two different objects. A myth, however, was based on an illusion, because it collapsed the distinction between different objects, simply attaching them to one another. "That is the difference between poetry and illusion. In illusion a perception 'y' is immediately apperceived via a perception 'a.' It is just like this in myth. The dawn 'y' is itself the newborn god-child 'a': the dusk is itself the bleeding hero."[61] Thus, the origin of myth did not lie in a poetic celebration of the dawn, as Max Müller had argued, but rather in a mistaken perception of reality.

Steinthal's application of Herbartian psychology to the study of ancient myth initiated a broader trend toward the historicization of Kant's epistemological categories, which was carried forward by Windelband and found its most famous exponent in Ernst Cassirer.[62] In the context of the 1860s, Steinthal's emphasis on the shortcomings of mythical perception reaffirmed the

Nachmärz values of progress, science, and materialism. As he was well aware, this antimythical stance distanced him from the glorification of Greek, Germanic, and other pagan religions found in much of Romantic culture. "I basically agree with the judgment of the naïve mind, which saw nothing but delusion and superstition in paganism," he affirmed.[63] Yet Steinthal's antipaganism was motivated not only by his political and scholarly convictions but also by his desire to defend the legacy of the Hebrew Bible and Jewish monotheism against a series of harsh critiques that appeared during the 1850s and 1860s. In particular, Steinthal was concerned to refute the charge that the Jews had never had a mythology.

The charge that the Jews had no mythology marked a reversal in academic attitudes toward ancient Judaism. Christian theologians had traditionally drawn a sharp contrast between the true history of the Old Testament and the untrue myths of the pagans. But between 1780 and 1835, enlightened and liberal scholars had relentlessly exposed various residues of myth in the Old Testament. Eichhorn and Gabler pointed out the philosophemes within Genesis, placing them on a par with the mythologies of Greece and Egypt. Later, Wilhelm de Wette interpreted the entire Pentateuch as a Hebrew national mythology, designed to justify the rituals and practices of the postexilic priestly class. More recently, the theologian Wilhelm Vatke had pointed out numerous parallels between the Old Testament and the myths and rituals of neighboring peoples, such as the Babylonians and Canaanites. But beginning in the 1850s, scholars began to shift the focus of their critique, arguing that the Jews had lacked a genuine (i.e., polytheistic) mythology because they were instinctually monotheistic. Although this newest charge seemed to contradict fifty years of scholarship, it paralleled a shift in attitudes toward Jews and in the nature of anti-Semitism in Europe. Before the 1840s, Jews were associated largely with a premodern, unenlightened stage of civilization; thus, their religious practice was backward, superstitious, and mythical. After 1848, and especially in light of the reform movements within Judaism and a gradual move toward acculturation, they were identified by critics with the urban, commercial, secular, and (hence) antimythical culture of modernity. These associations were already evident in Wagner's *Judentum in der Musik* (1850), but they would become a staple of anti-Semitic discourse in subsequent decades.

The chief critic of Hebrew monotheism in these years was the French linguist Ernest Renan (1823–92).[64] In his *L'histoire générale et système comparé des langues sémitiques* (1855), Renan argued that the Semitic peoples (who included the Arabs, the Egyptians, and the Hebrews) had a natural "instinct" for monotheism. Even such seemingly polytheistic peoples as the ancient Canaanites and Babylonians were, on closer inspection, worshipers of a single god.[65] But where earlier writers had seen monotheism as a triumph over paganism, Renan characterized it as a deficit of religion, which reflected the Semites' intolerant and exclusive nature. Compared to the Aryans, the Semites lacked scientific or artistic originality, had created no national epic or mythology, showed no ability to think abstractly, and had proven incapable of organizing large governments or military campaigns.

Renan was a devotee of German scholarship, and early in his career he evinced the desire to do "for the Semitic languages what Professor Bopp did for the Indo-European languages."[66] Language, he believed, explained the nature of the various races and was the key to the origins of Semitic monotheism. Unlike Aryan words, Semitic words did not inflect; instead, their radicals remained stable and unchanging. Thus, they did not generate the metaphors that were characteristic of the Aryan languages and the source of their polytheism. Instead, the Semites were forced to settle for what Renan described condescendingly as a "minimum of religion."[67] This viewpoint affected his understanding of the Gospels. In an 1849 essay, Renan critiqued the Straussian position that the life of Jesus was composed of myths grounded in Jewish messianic expectations. He maintained instead that the gospel narratives were "legends" based on an actual historical fact, which had outstripped anything in prior Jewish tradition.[68] In his *Vie de Jésus* (1863), Renan would go on to argue that, despite Jesus' origins among the Jews, Christianity was a product of the Aryan race.[69]

Renan helped to spark a broader, Europe-wide discussion of the nature and value of monotheism. In his essay "Semitic Monotheism" (1859), Friedrich Max Müller challenged Renan's assumption that monotheism was a characteristic trait of the Jewish people.[70] If this was so, he asked, why had the ancient Hebrews relapsed back into polytheism so often? In its earlier phases, Müller argued, Jewish monotheism was neither true monotheism nor polytheism but a kind of "henotheism," that is, the worship of a single god that did not exclude the possibility that other gods existed. Thus, Joshua could say to the Hebrews, "Choose ye this day, whom you will serve; whether the gods which your fathers served, . . . or the gods of the Amorites, in whose land ye dwell." (Josh. 24:2).[71] True monotheism was revealed to only one man, Abraham, and he alone was responsible for its spread throughout the world.[72] This historical scheme, it should be noted, was patently derived from Schelling's later lectures on the philosophy of mythology. Like Schelling, Müller used the concept of "narrow monotheism" or henotheism to affirm the uniqueness of Christian monotheism, while disengaging it from its roots in ancient Hebrew beliefs and practices.

The criticisms of Jewish monotheism by Renan and Müller presented a formidable challenge for Steinthal. For years, he noted, Christian writers had insisted on an original monotheism, seeing the fall into polytheism as a source of evil. Now modern writers presented the move to polytheism as a source of progress, while denigrating the monotheism of the Jews. According to Steinthal, both views were wrong. The Jews, he argued, had at one time possessed a polytheistic mythology. "[N]ot only is all of Genesis full of transformed polytheism," Steinthal noted, but "heathen legends are entwined even in the life history of Moses, of the judges, of David . . . : does that not prove an original polytheism among the Semites?"[73] At the same time, though, Steinthal maintained that the transition among the Hebrews from the stage of polytheism to the stage of monotheism had been an advance to a higher form of religion and a higher form of culture.

To demonstrate the existence of an ancient Hebrew polytheism, Steinthal launched an investigation of the legend of Samson.[74] In Steinthal's view, Samson had originally been a solar deity or hero of the type generally associated with Aryan mythology.[75] His long hair, the source of his power in the Old Testament narrative, represented the abundant growth of nature or the rays of the sun. Like Hercules or his Phoenician counterpart Melkarth, Samson was a friendly god, who protected the people from the harmful, destructive aspect of the sun. Thus, Samson's slaughter of the long-maned lion could be taken as a victory over harsh sun gods like Typhon or Moloch, while paralleling the struggles of Indo-Germanic heroes like Siegfried or Apollo with dragons and other beasts. The cutting of Samson's hair by Delilah, the loss of his physical strength, and his eventual demise all testified to the existence of an earlier solar myth, which was inspired originally by the setting of the sun during the winter solstice.

Samson's personality seemed typical of a pagan hero. Throughout his life, he showed an indifference to the destruction caused by his violent rages and his penchant for trickery. Samson "is precisely an old pagan god and like all idols is therefore unethical. Because these [gods] are nothing but the personified powers and events in nature."[76] In this respect, Samson strongly resembled Siegfried, who stole the Nibelungen treasure and fooled Brünhild without any qualms of conscience. Given these parallels, it seemed reasonable to conclude that the Indo-Germanic and Semitic mythologies had at one time been identical. Contrary to Renan's claims, there was no essential difference between Semites and Aryans in terms of their "instinct" for myth. Indeed, it seemed likely that the Greeks had borrowed from the Semitic myths rather than the other way around.

Having demonstrated the existence of a Hebrew mythology, Steinthal went on to show how the Hebrews advanced beyond paganism to embrace monotheism. In his view, monotheism was not the product of instinct but the result of a long struggle in which the "delusion and superstition" of paganism were defeated. Monotheism was more than the worship of a single god. Instead, it reflected a distinct ethical vision. "Monotheism does not mean that Jehovah is like Indra and Vrita, that He does by Himself what the other gods divide among themselves. Instead, He does something completely different from these [other gods]. In the storm he does not fight a dragon. Instead, He announces from the midst of thunder and lightning the ten words that are the eternal pillars of every human ethical community."[77] The Jews did not possess a higher intelligence than other peoples, Steinthal argued. Nor were they the beneficiaries of a special revelation. Monotheism was rather the product of "another direction of the spirit," a direction that eventually led the Hebrews beyond the Greeks.[78]

The victory of monotheism was the triumph of one god over an older one in the consciousness of the Jewish people.[79] Traces of this struggle, monuments to a forgotten polytheism, were scattered throughout the Bible. For just as the medieval Germans incorporated pagan practices into their Christian rituals, so the Hebrews assimilated the pagan gods into their history. By the time the Book of Judges was written, Samson had ceased to be a deity and instead was a Nazirite, an individual specially devoted to God who could neither drink wine nor cut his hair. "And so out of the god that could not last next to Yahweh came a man who accomplished superhuman deeds with Yahweh's power."[80]

Monotheism, Steinthal believed, had given the biblical mythology a character that set it apart from the polytheistic mythologies. In the Greek myth of Hercules the jealousy of Hera leads to the hero's death, but in the end Hercules is accepted into the pantheon as a god. As Steinthal knew, scholars from Creuzer to Bunsen had cited this myth to show that the Greeks possessed a presentiment of Jesus' death and resurrection. But in the Hebrew Bible, Steinthal noted, Samson's death was final, because God tolerated no competition. "The pagan god is dead, and he takes his world with him into oblivion. His struggles were a shadow dance. Yahweh lives. . . . He lives as the Lord of the World, the King of the Earth, and His hero is Israel."[81]

The contrast between monotheism and paganism could also be seen in a comparison of the myths of Prometheus and Moses. Both were heroes who delivered their peoples from enslavement. Likewise, both myths reflected earlier Vedic practices: just as the Aryans used a stick to create fire, so Moses smashed his staff against a rock to create water. Despite these similarities, however, their differing fates pointed to two very different types of religious orientation. "[I]n Prometheus . . . the entire essence of paganism is summarized: the deification of man and of nature. To this most characteristic figure of the mode of perception that created gods in the image of men, the opposite mode of perception, which has man created in the likeness of one god and demands that he imitate him in life, presents a different figure: Moses."[82] The story of Moses reflected the Hebrews' transition from paganism to monotheism. "[I]nsofar as Moses uses his staff to strike water from the stone, he is a pagan god, a Mâtariçvan, a Pramantha. He thus stands in conflict with the one, true God and therefore must die. Insofar as he gives man the word of God, he is a prophet without equal."[83] But ultimately Moses was no half-divine creature, only a man. He did not incite rebellion against the heavens but delivered God's word in the form of the law. In this way, the story of Moses helped usher in an ethical consciousness not available to pagan polytheism.[84]

Steinthal's account of monotheistic mythology challenged not only Renan but an entire tradition of Romantic mythography and theology. Since the late eighteenth century, Schelling, Hölderlin, Görres, Creuzer, Weisse, and Wagner had sought antecedents to the Christian revelation in pagan mythology. In particular, they had found in the stories of suffering gods or heroes (Prometheus, Hercules, Dionysus, Siegfried) an anticipation of Christ's suffering and redemption. Now Steinthal rejected the possibility of a genuine ethical consciousness in any religion that deified the human, without denying the Romantics' linking of Christ and the pagan gods. What remained, therefore, was an implicit critique of Christianity and its conception of ethics, which Steinthal saw as rooted in a pagan worldview.[85]

Steinthal's belief in a fundamental distinction between paganism and Judaism also led him to rebuff those who would credit other, "Aryan" peoples with the invention of monotheism. In 1862, the philosopher Eduard Zeller, a veteran of the Tübingen school and friend of David Strauss, published a lecture entitled "Die Entwicklung des Monotheismus bei den Griechen."[86] Zeller rejected the theory, recently put forth by Friedrich Welcker, that the ancient Greeks had originally been monotheistic worshipers of Zeus.[87] He emphasized that monotheism was achieved only after long years of reflection and progress. The greatest Greek monotheists had not been the primitive worshipers of Zeus but rather the philosophers, especially Plato.

So both Zeller and Steinthal saw the achievement of monotheism as the product of a long evolution and not as a gift from on high. But Steinthal in-

Heymann Steinthal in 1884.
Source: Ingrid Belke, ed., *Moritz Lazarus und Heymann Steinthal: Die Begründer
der Völkerpsychologie in ihren Briefen* (Tübingen: Mohr, 1983), vol. 2, pt. 1, after
p. 176.

sisted that the only true monotheism was that of the Hebrews. In a review of
Zeller's essay, Steinthal argued that the speculative monotheism of the ancient Greek philosophers had lacked an ethical dimension and for that reason had failed to capture the imagination of the Greek populace. "Because
the monotheism of the Greeks was a philosophical thought, the creation of
self-conscious, logical reflection, it never penetrated into the people," Steinthal wrote.[88] For this reason, Greek monotheism exercised no influence on
the origin of Christianity. Whether monotheist or not, the Greek philosophers had been vehement opponents of Christianity, and the new faith had
taken root instead among the lowest ranks of pagan society. This suggested
that the roots of Christian monotheism lay in Judaism alone.

Steinthal's defense of Judaism against paganism and his insistence on the singularity of Jewish monotheism placed him in the company of more conservative Christian theologians. The Bonn theologian Ludwig Diestel, for example, had insisted on the uniqueness of Jewish monotheism, contrasting it with the Semitic monotheisms cited by Renan.[89] The cult of a local god like Baal, Diestel argued, was vastly different from the conception of a single, all-powerful Creator and giver of laws. But while Steinthal linked monotheism to the national spirit of the ancient Hebrews, Diestel traced it to a divine revelation. Still, both writers found themselves pressed to show against the claims of Renan that it was mistaken to equate religion with mythology or to view a poverty of gods as a poverty of religion.

Steinthal summed up these views in the popular lecture "Mythos und Religion" (1869).[90] Here he argued once again for a strict differentiation between the notions of "myth" and "religion," chiding those philologists who equated a culture's religion with its myths. Mythology was a form of perception characteristic of the earliest stage of human development. Lacking the logical categories necessary to explain the sense phenomena, the *Urmensch* relied on myth. For the *Urmensch*, "[e]very event is seen as an action of a being, who is normally dreamed up at the beginning of the event."[91] In the grip of the seasons and the elements, the *Urmensch* could not understand the natural world except by means of myth. "He thinks *mythically*, and thus every thought becomes a myth, every intuition a symbol."[92]

Religion, Steinthal believed, began when humans started to distance themselves from the finite world. "Because what is religion? Nothing other and nothing further than the feeling of elevation, which is awakened first by ideals and later by all real things insofar as and in the measure to which they realize the ideal."[93] Whereas myth belonged only to a particular stage of human development, every culture had religion. The more a people cultivated the feeling for the sublime in art, religion, and science, the more religious it became. But this first required discarding the remnants of mythical thinking that clung to religion, including such dogmas as the Messiah, the Last Judgment, and the chosen people. Steinthal called instead for an abstract, imageless religion to replace the mythical religions. "Religion is eternal, it is a universal holiness of man," Steinthal wrote. "Myth, on the other hand, is a finite form. To destroy this form so that the content shines through so much the purer and brighter: that is a necessary deed, that is the task of our day."[94] The destruction of myth in philosophy, religion, and culture became a central aim of Steinthal's philosophy of religion in the years before German unification.[95]

THE BIBLE AND THE CANON

Steinthal's defense of Jewish monotheism essentially inverted the arguments of Schiller and the Romantics, who had defended pagan mythology against both orthodox and enlightened critics. While Schelling and Wagner saw a mythology as the necessary condition of aesthetic culture, Steinthal argued that modern literary culture was predicated on a break from mythology. Myth and poetry, he averred, were as different as myth and science.[96] For while myth remained mired in a primitive view of the world, poetry pointed the reader to a higher ethical and spiritual plane. Like many liberal, middle-class Jews, Steinthal was a devotee of Schiller, Beethoven, and the other icons of German bourgeois culture. "A symphony by Beethoven is holier than much church music," he asserted.[97] He predicted that the growing availability of art in museums, statues, public concerts, and photographs would have a morally uplifting effect on modern German society.[98] Ultimately these might even take the place of existing religious ceremonies and rituals.

In Steinthal's view, the roots of modern literary culture lay not in Greek mythology but in the poetry of the Bible. For it was in the verses of the Psalms that human culture first broke from the tyranny of metaphor and, with the addition of the word "as," moved toward simile and a clearer distinction between God and his predicates.[99] "A poem like the 104th Psalm . . . is impossible in all of paganism. It alone can refute the still persistent superstition that a poetic view of nature is impossible without a polytheistic mythology. It alone can show that only nature conceived monotheistically, nature as the wise creation of the good God, can appear as both reasonable and beautiful."[100] Steinthal suggested that a time might come when the Bible would "claim its rightful place as a work of literary art, which a free interpretation in literature grants it."[101] His purpose was clear: to raise the Hebrew Bible to the status of Dante or Shakespeare, so that it might take its place in the modern literary canon.

Steinthal's effort to "canonize" the Bible led him to exalt it as a prose epic every bit the equal and, in some respects, the superior of the *Iliad* or the *Nibelungenlied*.[102] Reversing Romantic standards of taste, Steinthal praised the simplicity and artlessness of the biblical narrative. While Homer relied on metaphors, epithets, and other linguistic ornaments, the Bible spoke directly from the human spirit. While the Indo-Germanic epics tarried in describing circumstances and surroundings, "the Hebrew seems on the contrary only to hurry straight to its goal."[103] In addition, Steinthal was concerned to show that the Bible, no less than Homer, had left its mark on what was already identified as German "classical" literature. The conversation between God and the devil in the prologue to Job had found its echo in Goethe's *Faust*. Likewise, Jacob's lament about the loss of Joseph reappeared in *Die Räuber*. Notwithstanding Schiller's laments, it was the richness of human situations and characters of the Bible rather than the "gods of Greece" that anticipated the best qualities of modern German literature.

Steinthal's efforts on behalf of the Bible constitute a kind of *Kulturjudentum*. For just as liberal Protestants attempted to link modern secular culture to the historical legacy of Protestantism (in *Kulturprotestantismus*), Steinthal seemed determined to trace modern culture to the religion and outlook of the Hebrew Bible. Essentially an atheist, Heymann Steinthal did not participate in the efforts by Abraham Geiger and others to reform the religious rituals and practices of Judaism. In his view, faith in this sort of religion was dead among ordinary citizens. "The people—the poor and the poorer, the oppressed and the depressed, the favorites of the socialists, as well as the happily employed, the materially blessed—no longer believe."[104] Instead, he took his orientation from modern German culture and the modern German state, which had removed all legal restrictions against the Jews in 1870. Steinthal's "assimilationist" stance has drawn criticism from numerous twentieth-century writers, who have seen in it an acquiescence to the dominant culture and a dissolution of the Jewish religion.[105] But Steinthal was far from passive in his assimilation of German culture: on the one hand, he emphasized its roots in the literary heritage of the Hebrew Bible; on the other hand, he attempted to demonstrate the distance between this modern culture and the delusions of the Christian-pagan worldview.[106]

In the decades after unification, Steinthal became increasingly outspoken in his defense of the Bible. He was spurred in part by the rapid growth of anti-Semitism in Berlin after 1878, which was encouraged by the onset of the "Great Depression" and by Bismarck's turn against liberalism. Beginning in 1878–79, Jews found themselves the object of vehement public attacks in the press, in Parliament, and from the pulpit, including by such highly placed individuals as the court preacher Adolf Stoecker and the historian Heinrich von Treitschke.[107] The growth of political anti-Semitism in these years coincided with a gradual reawakening of interest in aspects of Romanticism, including its concept of myth. By the 1890s, Steinthal had begun to soften his own hostility to myth. "Is a myth a lie? Or perhaps an imagined fairy tale formed in a playful imagination? No, it is also a law. It has the content of a law, but in the form of an image. It is an ideal, holy archetype *[Urbild]*." In a lecture at the Hochschule für die Wissenschaft des Judenthums, Steinthal recommended to his audience that they preserve these myths as markers of their ethnic identity: "preserve in yourselves and in your children the sublime

myths of the Bible. . . . Let us not forget the meaning of our name Israel: fighters for God. Let us educate our children for the struggle for God, that is, the
struggle for freedom of the spirit."[108]

The scholarship of Heymann Steinthal and Adalbert Kuhn shows that alternatives to Wagnerism existed in German thought on myth. Steinthal, especially, recognized the importance of "myth" while maintaining a dedication
to Herbartian empiricism and evolutionary models of society. Like many of
his contemporaries in the liberal *Bildungsbürgertum*, he was also a committed cultural nationalist, although he tended to take his cue from modern literature and music rather than from Norse myths or medieval epics. Steinthal
repeatedly insisted that true poetry required a move beyond the primitive
level of myth, and he contrasted the feeling of elevation that he called "religion" with the distortions and delusions of the mythical mode of thought.

The antimythical moment constituted only one aspect of Steinthal's
thought, however. Faced with the attacks by Müller and Renan against
ancient Hebrew monotheism, Steinthal felt compelled to demonstrate
the prior existence of a Hebrew polytheist mythology. In his articles for the
Zeitschrift für Völkerpsychologie, he pointed out the similarity and common roots of Aryan and Semitic polytheism, just as he sought in his linguistics to stress the common roots of the Aryan and Semitic language families.[109] At the same time, he showed how the rise of monotheism among the
ancient Hebrews had transformed the old pagan myths into the sublime, ethical, and religious narratives of the Bible. Thus, while Steinthal distanced
himself from Romantic mythophilia, he also sought to defend the narratives
of the Bible, and while he sought to identify the Bible as a product of Hebrew
national spirit, he also insisted on its relevance for modern German culture.

In the end, Steinthal's ambivalence reflected not only his awkward position, straddling Jewish and gentile cultures in Germany, but also an ambivalence within the discourse on myth. By describing not only Samson and
Moses but also such central religious doctrines as God and immortality as
myths, Steinthal distanced himself from the Bible as a source of timeless and
eternal truth. In this sense, he contributed to the secularization or "spiritualization" of Judaism. However, by labeling key stories within the Bible as
myths, he identified them as narratives that possessed a special force and attraction—not only for the Israelites but for all peoples. In the peculiar context of "comparative mythology," identifying the Bible as myth, rather than
history, constituted a defense of the Bible and of Judaism.

Heymann Steinthal sensed that in an era of rising anti-Semitism, the
Bible—rather than Kabbalah or some other form of mysticism—constituted

a key cultural battleground for Jews in Germany. If the Hebrew Bible could be viewed somehow as both a document of one religious community and yet a document for all peoples, it might provide a template for the existence of Jews and Judaism in postemancipation Germany. Paul's saying that there was "neither Jew nor Gentile, Greek nor Barbarian," offered an insufficient basis for Jewish life in Germany, Steinthal argued.[110] Instead, he cited Isaiah's prophecy that one day the Egyptians, Assyrians, and Jews would live together peacefully. "He, like all subsequent prophets, had no inkling of a world in which all nationality should be destroyed. But he foresaw a future in which all nations would live next to each other and interact with each other in ethical peacefulness."[111] Steinthal's multinational, posthistoricist model of culture, rooted in the stories of the Bible, would remain a distant ideal in his lifetime and the generations to come.

CHAPTER SEVEN

Nietzsche's *Kulturkampf*

The idea of Dionysus . . . goes beyond Dionysus himself, and only
then does the idea appear in all its magnificence.

Schelling

In the fall of 1870, the combined forces of Prussia and its south German allies had just defeated the French troops of Napoleon III, and Otto von Bismarck stood in the midst of negotiations that would culminate a few months
later in the proclamation of the Kaiserreich. But looking on these events
from his outpost in Switzerland, young Friedrich Nietzsche worried for Germany's future. "[W]e must be philosophers enough to remain sober in the
universal ecstasy," he wrote a friend, "so that the thief does not come and
steal or diminish something to which—for me—all the greatest military
deeds, even all national uprisings, cannot compare. For the coming period of
culture, fighters *[Kämpfer]* will be needed. We must save ourselves for this."[1]
This higher purpose, to which Nietzsche now pledged his services, involved
a transformation of German culture on the basis of Schopenhauerian philosophy and Wagnerian mythology.

Nietzsche's expectations of a coming cultural struggle in Germany were
shared by a wide range of Protestant intellectuals. Liberal nationalists, in particular, hoped that the process of political unification might lead to greater
spiritual and cultural unity in Germany.[2] But while Bismarck's wars had expanded Germany's frontiers and had given it a new constitution, the new
Kaiserreich remained deeply divided along political, regional, and confessional lines. Both Junker conservatives and working-class socialists questioned the legitimacy of the new state and its liberal economic regime. Likewise, regional loyalties in Hanover, Alsace, and the south German states
challenged the hegemony of Prussia in the Reich. But in the short term, it

was the confessional split between Catholics and Protestants that proved the most immediate threat to the new Germany. Even before unification, Protestant publicists had begun to call for restrictions on the political activity of the Catholic Church. After 1871, this conflict escalated into the *Kulturkampf*, a decades-long conflict between the Catholic Church and the Protestant-dominated state. From the beginning, this conflict was conducted on several fronts, as liberal Protestants fought not only Catholics but their more conservative coreligionists in order to define the cultural and religious landscape of Germany. In this way, the *Kulturkampf* would become (as Nietzsche predicted) a comprehensive "struggle for culture."

There are obvious objections to using the figure of Friedrich Nietzsche (1844–1900) to approach this particular phase of German intellectual history. His thought, after all, was atypical not only of his generation but even of the small circle of intellectuals who shared his passions for Greece, Schopenhauer, and Wagner. From 1869 through 1889, the productive years of his career, he lived only intermittently in Germany, spending his time between various haunts in Switzerland and Italy and declaring himself *"Heimatlos"* (homeless).[3] During this period, he acquired no substantial following; indeed, the circle of his acquaintances grew smaller rather than larger. Then there is the problem of Nietzsche's style: ironic, parodic, and contradictory, it resists any attempt to be reduced to a coherent doctrine or political program.[4]

Despite Nietzsche's atypicality as a thinker and writer, however, he remains indispensable for understanding the development of German thought on myth in the later nineteenth century. In an era when the prestige of science and positivism had reached a peak, Nietzsche was one of a handful of Germans who interpreted the Wagner phenomenon within the context of Romantic scholarship on myth. Even after his break from Wagner, however, Nietzsche continued to engage and, at the same time, subvert the categories of Romanticism, while articulating a new sacred narrative for himself and those he called "higher men." By the time of his death in 1900, Nietzsche's thought on myth would be appropriated and misappropriated by increasing numbers of German-speaking intellectuals, with consequences that continue to be debated by philosophers and historians.[5]

Even in his own lifetime, however, Nietzsche's thought intersected and interacted with the intellectual currents of his day far more than is usually assumed.[6] Not only Wagnerism, but new scholarship in comparative mythology, anthropology, and psychology provided him with interpretive tools that are now seen as characteristic of his "mature" thought. These were deployed in the service of a "struggle for culture" that drew much of its energy from the confessional conflict of the 1870s and the polemical literature that it gen-

erated among Protestant intellectuals. Indeed, although he became the most
vociferous of anti-Christians, Nietzsche identified closely with the traditions and culture of German Protestantism. Not only *The Birth of Tragedy*
but later writings up through and including *Thus Spake Zarathustra* demonstrate a continuing engagement with the rhetoric and assumptions of contemporary Protestant theology, including its "secular" manifestations in art,
scholarship, and politics.[7] In the process, he would rework, extend, and ultimately dismantle the Romantic discourse on myth as it had developed from
the eighteenth century onward.

THE BIRTH OF TRAGEDY (1): THE DIONYSIAN SYMBOLISM OF INSTINCT AND THE REVIVAL OF ROMANTIC PHILOLOGY

To be hired at age twenty-four to the rank of professor, having written neither
dissertation nor habilitation, would have surpassed the hopes of most aspiring philologists. But in 1869, on the strength of several published articles, his
inspired leadership of the Leipzig Philological Society, and a sparkling letter
from his mentor, Nietzsche leapfrogged over the competition into the chair
of philology at Basel.[8] Arriving in April, he quickly acclimated himself to his
new surroundings. He held lectures at 7:00 in the morning, ate lunch at a
restaurant near the train station, and paid visits to his colleagues and Basel's
"aristocratic philistines."[9] He could be charming and witty, and he generally
made a good impression. Yet Nietzsche experienced his appointment as more
of a crisis than a triumph.

He was, first of all, ambivalent about his future in a profession increasingly oriented toward the commentary and codification of Greek and Latin
texts and ever more forgetful of its links to grand theory.[10] After graduating
from the Pforta School in Saxony, Nietzsche had begun his studies in Bonn
with the intention of becoming a theologian. But he soon abandoned these
plans and instead took up the study of classical philology under two of Germany's most distinguished scholars, Friedrich Ritschl and Otto Jahn.[11] While
Ritschl was known as a scrupulous editor of Plautus's plays and Jahn ranged
into the fields of archaeology and musicology, both were interested primarily
in Roman antiquity and in the detailed interpretation of individual works.[12]
During Nietzsche's time in Bonn, the two scholars fell out with each other,
sparking a controversy that had little to do with philology and much to do
with outside political rivalries.[13] Nietzsche, though a devotee of Jahn, followed Ritschl to Leipzig in 1865, submitting himself to the rigors of the latter's textual-critical method. Over the next four years he produced a series of
studies based on individual figures, including Theognis of Megara, Diogenes

Laertius, and the atomist philosopher Democritus, while drawing up plans for more ambitious and wide-ranging projects.[14]

Despite his success as a student of philology, Nietzsche was painfully aware of his discipline's relative isolation from broader developments in German culture. In Leipzig, he formed a circle of admirers of Arthur Schopenhauer, then still a secret pleasure among those finely tuned spirits who rankled against the era's striving for progress and profit. Among his friends, Nietzsche promoted the philosophy of pessimism with apostolic zeal, speaking reverently of "father" Schopenhauer as "our master."[15] Before the majesty of such ideas, the day-to-day work of philology seemed mechanical, no better than working in a screw factory. Even the greatest philologists could only hope to be servants of a philosophical "demigod" like Schopenhauer.[16] Nietzsche did not embrace pessimism blindly (he was well versed in the skeptical philosophy of Friedrich Albert Lange), and his exorbitant praise of Schopenhauer sometimes rings a bit hollow.[17] Ritschl would later remark that Nietzsche possessed two souls, one controlled by "the strictest method of schooled scientific research" and the other "imaginary-exuberant overspiritual incomprehensible."[18] Yet Nietzsche hoped that he might somehow unite them into a single whole, joining the historical-critical methods of philology to a broader program of aesthetic-religious reform.

For Nietzsche, the move from Leipzig to Basel also meant loss of a certain familial bliss. His father, a Lutheran pastor in the Saxon town of Röcken, had died when he was just four, and Nietzsche had grown up under the care of his mother, his grandmother, and his sister. Much of his youth was taken up by a thinly veiled search for a father figure, which he seemed to have found in Ritschl in Leipzig. As professor in Basel, however, he again found himself alone and without guidance. "The unhappy thing is that I have no model, and I am in danger of playing the fool at my own expense," he wrote Erwin Rohde in 1870. "[T]he charming ignorance at the hand of teachers and traditions was so happy and safe."[19] Uncomfortable in his new surroundings and unsure of his scholarly vocation, Nietzsche was drawn into a new orbit, whose center was Richard Wagner.

We left Wagner in 1851, as he began work on his most ambitious project, *Der Ring des Nibelungen*. Since that time he had experienced a series of stunning successes and shattering defeats. After abortive attempts to establish a following in Vienna and Paris, Wagner had issued a general plea for financial assistance in 1863. To his surprise and delight, the Bavarian crown prince and soon to be king Ludwig II chose to intervene on his behalf. The composer immediately moved his operation to Munich and began work on *Die Meistersinger* (1867). The Munich idyll was short-lived, however. Wagner's imprudent political suggestions and his affair with Cosima von Bülow, the daughter of Franz Liszt and wife of orchestra conductor Hans von Bülow, provided the excuse that Ludwig's opponents needed to create a scandal. Wagner was forced to leave Germany for the Swiss hamlet of Tribschen. There, with Cosima, Bülow's two daughters, and Wagner's illegitimate children, Eva, Isolde, and (later) Siegfried, he maintained his typically extravagant standard of living, composing the music for the *Ring* and planning his final assault on the German public. On May 15, 1869, responding to an invitation he had received from Wagner in Leipzig, Friedrich Nietzsche arrived at his door.

Socially, the encounter between Nietzsche and Wagner was a meeting of opposites.[20] While Nietzsche had grown up secure in his father's good reputation as a local pastor, Wagner had been born into a family of semireputable bohemian artists. While Nietzsche enjoyed the prestige and security of a professorship, Wagner was a known philanderer and was still considered an outlaw in parts of Germany. To be sure, the two shared an abiding interest in Schopenhauer and an obsession with music, and that served for a time to bridge the social divide. But given their enormous differences in background and temperament, it was perhaps inevitable that they would attach different meanings to their relationship. For Wagner, Nietzsche was one in a series of gifted young men whom the composer invited to share his family circle, to entertain him, and later to be forgotten. The friendship with Nietzsche provided a useful alliance with respectability, sincerity, and enthusiasm. For Nietzsche, a devotee of Wagner's music and ideas since 1868, this was the experience of a lifetime. "I have the incalculable happiness to possess as a friend the true spiritual brother of Schopenhauer, who is related to him as Schiller was to Kant," he gushed. "He is a genius who has suffered the terribly sublime fate of coming a century before he could be understood."[21] Fascinated by Wagner's ambition, his lifestyle, and his wife, the young professor became a regular at Tribschen.

The encounter with Wagner not only provided Nietzsche with a personal orientation but also cast the world of antiquity in a new light. "I . . . am aware of how my philosophical, moral, and scholarly efforts push toward *one* goal, and that I—perhaps the first of all philologists—am becoming whole. How wonderfully new and transformed history looks to me, especially the Greek world!"[22] Suddenly it seemed as if the rift between Nietzsche's philology and his aesthetic enthusiasms had been overcome. In classroom lectures and public presentations, he developed a view of the Greek past that complemented and explained Wagner's efforts to bring German national myth onto the stage.[23] These scholarly efforts culminated in January 1872 with the publication of *The Birth of Tragedy out of the Spirit of Music*. Dedicated to Wagner, it marked a radical departure from Ritschlian philology and a return to the seemingly abandoned terrain of myth. Nietzsche would attempt in this book to overcome the divide between antiquity and present, a venture with uncertain consequences for both.

The stated purpose of *The Birth of Tragedy* was to set forth the "secret doctrines" of Greek aesthetics.[24] Greek culture, Nietzsche argued, originated from the interaction of two antagonistic forces, represented by the deities Apollo and Dionysus.[25] Apollo was the power that created the images of dreams and fantasy. The beautiful forms of Greek sculpture, the coherence of the individual psyche, even the ordered veneer of the phenomenal world were all products of Apollonian illusion. Dionysus, by contrast, was the formless abyss of suffering that coursed underneath these tranquil surfaces. The Dionysian reached its perfect expression in music, an art form without images. According to Nietzsche's scheme, the cultural flowering of Greece depended on the continual tension between Apollo and Dionysus, just as procreation depended on a dualism of the sexes, "with continuous strife and only periodic reconciliation."[26]

It was the Apollonian impulse that had given rise to the bright Homeric deities, whose serene images had led Winckelmann and Schiller to praise the blessedness and naïveté of Greek life. But now, Nietzsche contended, "the Olympic magic mountain opens up for us and shows us its roots."[27] For the Apollonian images did not reflect Greek happiness but rather compensated for a darkly pessimistic (and recognizably Schopenhauerian) worldview. From time to time this world of appearances would fall away, as the hard-won individuality of the Greeks collapsed in a torrent of Dionysian ecstasy. On such occasions social distinctions were overturned, "the slave became a free man," and neighbor was reconciled with neighbor in an ecstatic celebration of unity. "Man is no longer an artist, he has become a work of art. The aesthetic power of all nature, to the highest satisfaction of the primordial unity, reveals itself here in the tremblings of intoxication."[28]

In articulating this vision of ancient Greece, Nietzsche drew heavily from the traditions of Romantic philology, which he encountered in Basel in the person of Johann Jakob Bachofen, author of *Mutterrecht* (1861), but even more decisively through his own readings of Friedrich Creuzer and Karl Otfried Müller.[29] Like Friedrich Creuzer, he treated the Dionysian as a nearly universal phenomenon in the ancient world that had entered Greece from Asia Minor.[30] The "barbarian" festivals of Dionysus centered on an "excessive sexual licentiousness, whose waves overwhelmed family life and its

Title page of Friedrich Nietzsche, *Die Geburt der Tragödie*.
Source: Herbert Barth, Dietrich Mack, and Egon Voss, eds., *Wagner: A Documentary Study* (New York: Oxford University Press, 1975).

venerable precepts. The wildest beasts of nature were unleashed, including that repulsive mixture of sensuality and cruelty which has always seemed to me as the real 'witches brew.'"[31] As in *Symbolik und Mythologie*, the rituals of paganism appeared as the very inversion of bourgeois society, which now inspired Nietzsche to mock exclamations of horror.

Yet Nietzsche stressed that there was an enormous gap between the "Dionysian Greek" and "the Dionysian barbarian."[32] Following Karl Otfried Müller, Nietzsche cited the role of the Doric national god Apollo, who resisted the influence of foreign cults while suppressing the remnants of an indigenous nature worship. This confrontation was most apparent at the level of music. "The music of Apollo was Doric architectonic in tones but only in suggestive tones as is peculiar to the kithara." By contrast, the followers of

Dionysus played the flute, an instrument that revealed a "disturbing violence of tone" and that had originated in Asia Minor and Phrygia.[33] But whereas Müller emphasized the Dorians' ritual suppression of foreign elements (symbolized by Apollo's flaying of Marsyas), Nietzsche spoke of an eventual "peace accord" that allowed the Dionysian to be expressed in "festivals of redemption and transfiguration."[34]

The Greeks' confrontation with the Dionysian was deeply unsettling, for it soon dawned on them that its expressions of suffering and self-abandonment were not so foreign after all but reflected a long-repressed folk wisdom. "The Greek knew and felt the terror and horror of existence. In order to live at all, he had to interpose between himself and life the radiant dream birth of the Olympians."[35] The anthropomorphic deities of the *Iliad* and the *Odyssey* had been created out of a powerful will to live. Rather than succumb to pessimism, the Greeks "justified" existence as an aesthetic phenomenon, such that heroes like Achilles and Hector could lament their parting from the world. Homer, in other words, was not the product of a "naïve" first stage of civilization. "Only an age that could conceive of the artist in terms of Rousseau's *Émile* . . . could believe this."[36] Rather than signifying a single poetic personality, "Homer" was a monument to the triumph of Apollonian illusion over the folk philosophy of the wood god Silenus.[37]

Once ensconced on Greek soil, the cult of Dionysus eventually gave rise to Attic tragedy.[38] In the Dionysian dithyramb, the singing and dancing celebrants threw off the "finery" of culture and imagined themselves as satyrs of nature. These festivals evolved gradually into a singing chorus, which provided the eventual basis for tragic drama. According to Nietzsche, the music of the chorus generated a system of tonal symbols, which were rooted in the instincts of the Schopenhauerian will. Out of these tonal symbols a series of dramatic actions hypostatized, which together constituted the tragic myths, the narratives bearing the Dionysian knowledge of the universe.[39] The dramatic figures, be they gods, Titans, or humans, were only masks of singing—and suffering—Dionysus.

A paradigmatic instance of the reincarnation of Dionysus in the form of the tragic hero was Aeschylus's *Prometheus*. Nietzsche described the Prometheus myth as "an original possession of the entire Aryan community of peoples and evidence of their gift for the profoundly tragic."[40] In addition, it suggested a worthy alternative to the supposedly "Semitic" myth of the Fall in Genesis. Since the perpetrator of the original outrage was a man, not a woman, the Aryans avoided the Augustinian and—to Nietzsche's mind—Semitic conflation of sin and sexuality.[41] In the Schopenhauerian scheme, succumbing to sexual urges could hardly be seen as an act of liberation, since the entire apparatus of male-female attraction was built on illusion. Prometheus's act of self-definition had the advantage that it was freed from any link to sexuality whatsoever.

Nietzsche's theory of the "Aryan" reflected his familiarity with recent literature in comparative mythography, including the works of Adalbert Kuhn and Max Müller. In his "Encyclopedia of Classical Philology" lectures, he noted that "the interest of comparative myth research is the tracing of ethical ideas to sensible intuitions. We cast a view into a totally raw prehistory, which transfers its economic household to all natural appearances."[42] Despite his acquaintance with this scholarship, Nietzsche concluded, "In the long run this kind of examination is somewhat boring."[43] At another point he was even more emphatic, attacking

> those who are not satisfied until they have reduced the profound and magnif-
> icent mythology of the Greeks to physical trivialities, to the sun, lightning,
> weather, and fog of its original beginnings, and who fancy that they have
> found in the limited worship of a celestial body by the upright Indo-Germans
> a purer form of religion than the polytheism of the Greeks. The path to ori-
> gins leads everywhere to barbarism.[44]

The significance of a given mythology could not be reduced to its linguistic or material origins, Nietzsche insisted. Instead, it resided in its aesthetic and ethical meaning.

This was certainly the case with the myth of Prometheus. To be sure, this story depended to some degree on the preeminent value assigned to fire by primitive cultures. But because of the difficulty of creating fire, its free possession was seen by the ancients as a sin. Here arose the first moral dilemma, "like a boulder at the gate of culture."[45] The Greeks resolved this problem by adopting a pessimistic worldview, in which self-definition and individuation led inevitably to suffering. They saw Prometheus's torments not as the wages of sin but rather as a source of dignity, so that his bold defiance of the gods as well as his subsequent torments were "justified." At the same time, Aeschylus's drama pointed to a higher sense of justice, embodied in the Fates, that transcended even the Olympians and would eventually bring about a "twilight of the gods."[46] As performed in Athens, the Prometheus tragedy reconciled the Apollonian instinct for order with the Dionysian impulse to sacrilege.

In Nietzsche's view, the religious significance of Attic drama was articulated most fully in the Eleusinian mysteries. Creuzer had described how these rituals commemorated the dismemberment of Dionysus Zagreus. The death of the god symbolized the moment in creation when the one god divided into many and the elements of the world—earth, air, fire, water—came into being. In *The Birth of Tragedy*, this Neoplatonic emanation narrative was transformed into a Schopenhauerian parable about the sufferings of individuation. Yet Nietzsche's pessimism allowed room for hope. As Schelling had noted, the mysteries also portrayed the arrival of a "third Dionysus," the child of Demeter. This "coming god" symbolized the promise of an escape from individuation and a return to primordial unity.[47] For Nietzsche, the symbol of the smiling Demeter transcended the world of Greek mythology and offered a timeless reminder of the redemptive power of art.

By emphasizing the Dionysian and specifically cultic qualities of Greek tragedy, Nietzsche distanced himself from commentators like A. W. Schlegel or the British classicist George Grote, who had linked Greek drama to republican politics.[48] Nietzsche insisted instead that the roots of tragedy lay in religion, a region where "absolutely every political-social sphere is excluded."[49] Thus, he dismissed the "edifying liberal notion" that the chorus represented the Athenian citizenry, who were empowered to judge and comment on the actions of the nobility.[50] In the dithyrambic chorus, Nietzsche argued, every trace of class or civic distinction was forgotten in the service to the god. In a metapolitical sense, tragedy reversed the process of individuation symbolized in the mysteries and reinforced by civil society, replacing it with an "overpowering feeling of unity" that led back to the "heart of nature."[51]

This feeling of unity did not overturn the foundations of ancient Greek society, however. Instead, it sustained a social and political system that was inherently unequal. For the most part, Schiller and the early Romantics had ignored the problem of slavery, so that they could portray ancient Greece as a kind of idealized civil society. Nietzsche, by contrast, brought this issue to the fore.[52] In his 1872 essay "The Greek State," Nietzsche contended that Greek artistic genius depended on the continued suffering of slaves and the lower classes, which evoked sympathy among poets and dramatists.[53] Elsewhere, he noted that such suffering was also present in modern society, as could be seen from the agitations of the socialist internationals. In both cases, he argued, it was dangerous and useless to attempt to overturn the social order: in the end, the Greek idea of "humanity" had nothing to do with democracy or "human rights" *(Grundrechte)*.[54] With this brusque rejection of political equality, Nietzsche departed sharply from the republican ideals of eighteenth-century Philhellenism. Yet his views—and even his rather brutal manner of articulating them—were typical of quite a few unification-era intellectuals, who sought to excuse the all-too-apparent inequalities of late-nineteenth-century industrial society in the face of challenges from the working classes and the political left.[55]

For all its splendor, Nietzsche saw the pinnacle of Greek art as short-lived, coinciding more or less with the career of Aeschylus. Sophocles' insistence that his characters be individuals and not simply masks of the Dionysian began to undermine the delicate balance between music and dramatic action. But it was Euripides who delivered the fatal blow. He eliminated the chorus and transformed tragedy into a "chesslike" comedy of everyday "bourgeois mediocrity."[56] Euripides, Nietzsche argued, was himself only a mask—of Socrates! The dialectical philosopher (only fourteen when Euripides performed his first play) introduced an aesthetic based on the notion that "everything must be understandable in order to be beautiful."[57] This "murderous principle" chased the Dionysian out of Greek art, where it took refuge in the mysteries.[58] With Dionysus gone, Apollo left, too. In place of these gods, the Socratic ideal of rational improvement took hold of Greek culture, condemning successive centuries to a barren, abstract, "mythless existence."[59]

In this situation, only a hero who could restore the primacy of music to drama would bring about a new mythical society. Fortunately, Nietzsche proclaimed, such a hero was at hand. Richard Wagner, a musician, would accomplish what the poets Schiller and Goethe could not: the spiritualization and idealization of myth. Alluding again to the *Ring,* Nietzsche counseled, "Let no one believe that the German spirit has lost its mythical homeland forever when it still clearly understands the voice of the bird that speaks of that homeland. One day it will awake in the morning freshness from a deep sleep. Then it will kill the dragon, destroy the malicious dwarf, and awaken Brünnhilde—and even Wotan's spear will not block its path!"[60] Throwing caution to the wind, Nietzsche declared the Wagnerian music drama to be the reincarnation of Greek tragic myth. Instead of a work of philology, he seemed to have penned a piece of propaganda.

Many of Nietzsche's comments in *The Birth of Tragedy* seemed expressly designed to alienate his colleagues in the philological profession. Instead of citing Ritschl, he quoted Goethe and Wagner. He described the decline of Greek culture as concurrent with the rise of "Alexandrian" man, a disparaging reference to the traditional birthplace of philology.[61] While claiming to offer the "secret doctrine" of Greek aesthetics, he insisted that it seemed "as if our proudly strutting classical-Hellenic scholarship has up until now mainly known how to subsist on only shadow plays and superficialities."[62] Worst of all, perhaps, he singled out Otto Jahn as a man of dubious character—not on account of his scholarship but because he had dared criticize Wagner. Nietzsche apparently intended to stir up a controversy and thereby achieve a profile in his discipline and in Germany at large. Instead, his colleagues answered him with silence.[63]

The one exception was the young nobleman Ulrich von Wilamowitz-Moellendorff, whose highly critical *Zukunftsphilologie!* (1872) served as both a defense of his mentor Jahn and a blood initiation into the philological guild.[64] Among his many objections to *The Birth of Tragedy*, Wilamowitz disagreed most vehemently with Nietzsche's interpretation of the Dionysian. Correctly he smelled the influence of Creuzer. "[I] would have thought that the time was long behind us when in the archaeological interpretation [we] would be spooked with nunnish creatures. . . . Whoever is serious about our science must find it 'disgraceful and laughable' that today people speak in the Saint-Croix–Creuzer manner about the 'wonderful myths in the mysteries.'"[65] Nietzsche was repeating the errors of Creuzer, Wilamowitz implied, resurrecting the "nunnish creatures" that had animated his *Symbolik und Mythologie*. It was clear, Wilamowitz complained, that "the *Aglaophamus* [of August Lobeck] stands on the Index of the Dionysian Curia."[66]

Wilamowitz insisted that the Dionysian was essentially a Greek, rather than an oriental, myth and that later commentators had overstated its importance. He cited the arguments of Gottfried Hermann, Karl Lachmann, and August Lobeck—each more or less hostile to Creuzer—in order to defend the autochthony of Greek culture. Certainly, there had been an important Dionysian element in Greek culture, but "one really should not bring into the Dionysian of such an early era all the nonsensical mystical fog and crude syncretism that it later accumulated."[67] In the last analysis, Wilamowitz implied, the contention that the Greeks had built their mythology on the foundation of barbarian mythology gave comfort and support to those who would encourage the influence of outside forces ("the Dionysian Curia") in Germany's religious and scholarly affairs. Here Wilamowitz echoed the polemics of Johann Heinrich Voss fifty years earlier, as Nietzsche, like the Romantics, found himself linked to crypto-Catholic mystery-mongers. Given the religio-political situation of the 1870s, such accusations were potentially harmful to the standing of a Protestant academic, although in this case they were probably less damaging than the style and argumentation of *The Birth of Tragedy* itself. Subsequent attempts by Nietzsche's allies to restore his scholarly reputation would prove ineffective. The damage had been done.

The Birth of Tragedy (2): Theological Politics
and Protestant Hero Worship

At several points, *The Birth of Tragedy* reads strikingly like an account of
contemporary German religious history. In one section, Nietzsche writes,

> this is the way in which religions are wont to die off: namely, when the
> mythical suppositions of a religion become systematized under the strict,
> rationalistic eyes of an orthodox dogmatism into a finished sum of historical
> events, and one begins to fearfully defend the believability of the myth while
> striving against a continuation of its natural growth or life; when, therefore,
> the feel for the myth dies away and in its place steps the claim of religion to a
> historical basis.[68]

This passage, about the decline of belief among the ancient Greeks, seemed
also to describe recent developments in Protestant theology. As the gospel
narratives came under criticism, theologians had attempted to render them
plausible as history. But in doing so, they had ceded the high ground to a new
breed of scholar: the historical critic.[69] De Wette, David Friedrich Strauss,
and their successors had gradually chipped away at the foundations of the
Christian religion, leaving it weak and exposed.

In Nietzsche's day, liberal theologians continued to seek paths out of the
dilemma posed by historical criticism. Beginning in the 1840s, Ferdinand
Christian Baur and his successors in the Tübingen school had reconstructed
the early history of the Christian Church using concepts derived from
Hegelian philosophy. Others, such as Karl Heinz Weizsäcker, Heinrich
Holtzmann, and Daniel Schenkel, attempted to capture the historical Jesus
by presenting him as the founder of an ethical community—an effort
Schweitzer derided as "drawing a bourgeois Messiah."[70] Nietzsche, however,
believed that attempts to reconstruct religion and its myths via academic
history or philosophical speculation were doomed to failure.[71] As he wrote
later, "recent theology appears to have gotten itself involved with history
purely out of innocence and still does not want to notice that in doing so,
probably very much against its will, it stands in the service of the Voltairean
écrasez."[72]

Nietzsche saw liberal theology as symptomatic of a "historical-critical"
trend in modern intellectual culture that had robbed Europe of its myths.
Contemporary education had disintegrated the individual, while the overweening drive toward specialization in the sciences had atomized even
philology, a discipline charged with preserving the integrity of classical cul-

ture. As a result, modern society had foregone myth, stripping the individual of a reference point and depriving the state of a powerful fundament of unwritten law. Now came the "mythless man, eternally hungry, who seeks digging and burrowing for roots among all pasts, even when he must dig in the most distant pasts. What explains the huge historical need of our unsatisfied modern culture, the collection of numerous other cultures, the all-consuming desire for knowledge, if not the loss of a mythical homeland, the mythical mother's womb?"[73] The passion for history, which drove German scholars to all corners of the globe, built museums, and filled them with artifacts, was a pathetic attempt by Europeans to compensate for the loss of their mythological "horizon."[74] Only by drawing a tight boundary around the world would the disparate imaginative powers of European culture unite at a common point.

Nietzsche's critique of contemporary theology had an institutional target as well. Since 1865, the flag-bearer of liberal Protestantism in Germany had been the Protestantenverein (Protestant Association). Founded to promote ecclesiastical and theological freedom, the Protestant Association's supporters included many of the leading lights of liberal theology: Richard Rothe, Daniel Schenkel, and Carl Schwarz.[75] Despite their many theological differences, these individuals rejected both Lutheran orthodoxy and what they saw as the antimodernism of the Catholic Church. Many in the association viewed the development of Protestantism as synonymous with the emergence of modern civilization, scholarship, and progress. Indeed, Rothe maintained that if the church were not to become a mere "peasant religion" it would have to fuse with the ethical and moral institutions of the emerging *Kulturstaat*.[76] Nietzsche, however, identified this group with the growing influence of historicism on Christian theology, which threatened to replace myth with a Hegelian-Socratic "spirit of optimism."[77]

Much of the immediate work of the Protestant Association involved resisting attempts by state churches to dictate dogma or impose elaborate liturgies on individual congregations. Over the course of the 1860s, however, the association became ever more involved in anti-Catholic polemics. In Baden and Württemberg, Protestant liberals attacked the traditional role of the church in elementary education and supported efforts by reformist state governments to take control of the primary schools. The Heidelberg theologian Schenkel predicted that "the great principles of Catholicism and Protestantism must . . . compete once more in a struggle that will shake the life of the nation to its deepest foundations."[78] Pope Pius IX's publication of the Syllabus of Errors in 1864 and the Vatican Council of 1870 further exacerbated the confessional conflict, leaving Catholics divided on the question of papal infallibility and Protestants deeply apprehensive about Vatican influence in a future united Germany.

Bismarck shared these fears, and with the founding of the Empire he resolved to wipe out Catholicism as a political force in Germany. Between 1871 and 1875, he and his allies in the National Liberal party passed a series of anti-Catholic measures, which banned the Jesuit order, limited clerical influence in education, mandated government approval of all appointments to church office, and outlawed statements from the pulpit that threatened a vaguely defined "public peace." Not until 1873 did Rudolf Virchow christen this conflict the *"Kulturkampf."*[79] By that time Bismarck had succeeded in mobilizing the liberal parties and intellectuals in a crusade for the "unity" of German culture. The Protestant Association, in particular, campaigned against the supposedly all-powerful Jesuit order while cynically inviting Catholics to join them in a future "national church" *(Volkskirche).*[80]

In the context of the emerging *Kulturkampf, The Birth of Tragedy* reflected the ambivalence of Nietzsche toward his Protestant inheritance. Like his Romantic predecessors, Nietzsche derived his image of a society guided and informed by myth in part from his understanding of Catholicism. In his notebook of 1869 he wrote, "The ancient music drama has an analogy in the Catholic liturgy: only the action is still presented symbolically or even only narratively."[81] Indeed, distinctions between Greece and Catholic Christianity seemed fluid. "Even in the German Middle Ages crowds convulsed from the same Dionysian power, singing and dancing from place to place: in these Saint John's and Saint Vitus's dances we recognize again the Bacchic choruses of the Greeks."[82] Reciting what was by now a well-known historical trope, Nietzsche presented the practices and customs of medieval Catholicism as holdovers from an earlier, pagan era.

Such fascination for medieval religiosity was offset by frequent expressions of hostility toward the Catholic Church. For example, Nietzsche blamed the historical-critical spirit on an unhealthy "Roman" hunger for knowledge.[83] This animosity toward Rome overlapped with nationalist hostility toward French culture. The external battle against Roman culture may have been won at Sedan, he noted, "but [the German] may never believe that he can fight similar struggles without his household gods, without his mythical homeland, without a 'restoration' of all things German!"[84] Like Heine, Nietzsche embraced the revolutionary power of a subterranean, Protestant paganism, which would find its expression in music:

> Out of this abyss grew the German Reformation: the future of German
> music first rang in its chorale. So deep, brave, and soulful, so exuberantly

good and sweet sounded this chorale of Luther's. It was the first Dionysian
mating call of the approaching spring that issued from the overgrown bush.
It was answered by the competing echo of the solemnly jubilant procession
of Dionysian enthusiasts, whom we thank for German music—and whom
we will thank for the *rebirth of the German myth!*[85]

Nietzsche had indicated how the Dionysian tonal symbolism of the instincts
had generated the myths of Greek tragedy. Now German music, born from
the spirit of Protestantism, would be the basis for a new German "myth"
(Mythus).

The celebration of German music as particularly Protestant had been a
recurrent theme in nationalist discourse since the early nineteenth century.
The heroes of German literature, Schiller and Goethe, had long been celebrated not only for their class background but for their roots in Protestant
culture. In the case of the Catholics Mozart and Beethoven such connections
were somewhat less obvious. Nonetheless, Wagner claimed that although
Beethoven was "[b]aptized and raised a Catholic, through his [personal] convictions the whole spirit of German Protestantism lived in him."[86] Nietzsche
had taken part in the Beethoven festivals that dominated mid-nineteenth-
century bourgeois culture and was very much a product of the midcentury
"cult of genius."[87] In *The Birth of Tragedy*, he sought to trace the roots of German Protestantism to the spirit of Greek Dionysianism, now reborn in a German tradition of absolute music that promised to overturn the optimistic
foundations of modern culture and give rise to a "new" cult of genius.

The conception of music as the bearer of a Protestant-Dionysian "longing" was crucial to the scheme of *The Birth of Tragedy*, which at many points
echoed the argument of *Oper und Drama*. Starting from Schopenhauer's
description of music as an "immediate language of the will," Nietzsche
claimed that music could objectify itself in the realm of images and, in effect,
"give birth to myth."[88] This trajectory was paralleled by science, which
Socrates launched on a Faustian-Columbian quest for knowledge but which
had now reached the "boundary points" where "logic coils up . . . and finally
bites itself in the tail" (a reference perhaps to the Kantian and Schopenhauerian critiques of reason). At that point, the optimistic spirit suffered
"shipwreck," to be replaced by a "tragic insight that merely to be endured
needs art as a protection and remedy."[89] The conjunction of these two phenomena—absolute music and idealist philosophy—would allow German
culture to pass through the stages of Hellenic civilization in reverse order, so
that the current "Alexandrian" age would be succeeded by a rebirth of tragic
myth.

Nietzsche's vision of a rebirth of myth out of the spirit of modernity complicated what is usually viewed as his general condemnation of Christianity as an "optimistic" religion. In the notebooks of 1869–72, he reiterated some of the familiar nationalist and anti-Semitic attacks on Christianity, complaining of the "artificially inoculated religion" that dominated Germany: "Either we will die from this religion or it will die from us. I believe in the old Germanic saying: all gods must die."[90] It was necessary for Germany to discover its own deities, so that it would not remain in the service of the Jewish "national god."[91] Wagner, it should be noted, had just published a second edition of *Judentum in der Musik* (1869), and this had proved no obstacle to Nietzsche's affections.

Yet Nietzsche also entertained the notion of a Hellenic or "Johannine" religion that would be imbued with the spirit of Dionysus rather than that of Judea.[92] One fragment reads "the Gospel of John born from the Greek atmosphere, from the soil of the Dionysian: its influence on Christianity, in opposition to the Jewish."[93] Elsewhere, Nietzsche described the Gospel of John as the "most beautiful fruit" of Christianity.[94] Like Schopenhauer, he suggested that the doctrine of "pity" *(Mitleid)* had formed the basis of an early, esoteric Christianity. Only later had Christianity been "Judaized" and democratized, and thus perverted into an optimistic religion that promised an end to suffering.[95] One scheme for *The Birth of Tragedy* (admittedly one of many) began with the "birth of tragic thought" and ended with the Gospel of John. Indeed, while Nietzsche's published text made no explicit mention of the Johannine, his discussion of Dionysus as the suffering god often evoked the language and terminology of orthodox Lutheran Christology. At one point, he described the Dionysian hero as having taken the burden of suffering "on his back," thereby bringing about a form of atonement.[96] With the rise of Socratism, however, Dionysus had fled into "the depths of the sea, namely, the mystical flood of a secret cult that gradually covered the entire world."[97]

The Birth of Tragedy provided not only a challenge to classical philology but also a theological alternative to the liberalism of the Protestant Association. Nietzsche suggested that the future of Protestant culture did not lie in historical investigations of the life of Jesus (which led inevitably to the foreign terrain of Judaism) or the mediating abstractions of Hegel or Schleiermacher, but instead in a rebirth of the German "myth" *(Mythus)*. Yet Nietzsche also made it clear that this Protestant myth would be reborn only in the domain of the aesthetic. Here the terminology was crucial: Nietzsche did not call for a "mythology" in the sense of a full system of narratives, symbols, and rituals; nor did he refer to "mythos" *(Mythos)* as a timeless basis of the human. Instead, he spoke simply of "myth" *(Mythus)*, which suggested a

mere veil or veneer of appearance that would make the tragic insight of pessimism bearable.

In this sense, Nietzsche's idea of myth was both more artificial and more
aesthetic than that of either Schelling or Wagner, a difference that reflected
his skepticism toward idealist metaphysics.[98] Just as importantly, the Nietzschean "new myth" was divorced from these earlier writers' hopes for a free
civil society or a revitalized public sphere. Instead, it was used to justify social hierarchy and inequality at a moment when liberalism and democracy
appeared triumphant in Europe. Yet however tenuous its ties to the metaphysical or political assumptions of early Romanticism, Nietzsche's concept
of a "new myth" still relied on the same historical scheme that had structured Schelling's philosophy of art. Much of his work in the next decade
would involve dismantling the assumptions about paganism, Christianity,
and modernity that had guided the thinking of his Romantic forebears.

Just as Nietzsche was raising the cry for a new German myth, the great myth-
destroyer spoke. Since the 1850s, David Friedrich Strauss had taken significant strides toward rehabilitating his public image. Frustrated by theology, he
had turned to history, publishing popular and successful biographies of such
figures as the Protestant reformer Ulrich von Hutten. By 1869 his reputation
had grown to the point that he was invited by Princess Alice of Hesse (sister
of Crown Princess Victoria) to deliver a series of six lectures on the life of
Voltaire.[99] In the meantime he had returned to theology, publishing *Das
Leben Jesu für das deutsche Volk* (1864).[100] Unrepentant after thirty years,
Strauss reiterated his earlier conclusion that the gospel narrative was a tissue
of myths. But he showed little interest in engaging his critics and dismissed
the objections of Weisse and the liberal theologians out of hand. Of the Marcan hypothesis, Strauss wrote, "the whole theory appears to me a temporary
aberration, like the 'music of the future' or the anti-vaccination movement."[101] Differences did exist between this *Leben Jesu* and the first edition:
there was now more of an effort to flesh out the personality of Jesus, granting
him a unique spiritual mission independent of Jewish messianism. But such
concessions did little to appease Strauss's critics in Germany or abroad.

A year earlier, Ernest Renan had published the fabulously successful *Vie
de Jésus* (1863), which emphasized the influence of the geography and the
natural environment of Palestine in the formation of Jesus' character.
Though he disagreed with this approach, Strauss was restrained in his criticisms, writing off Renan's idiosyncrasies to the differing tastes of German
and French scholars. This issue of national differences would come to the
fore in 1870, as the two scholars debated the causes and merits of the Franco-

Prussian War. The Prussophile Renan sought out Strauss in an attempt to conduct a public discussion about the war on the plane of philosophy rather than propaganda. But Strauss would have none of it, glorifying Germany as Europe's spiritual "leader," celebrating the Prussian military victory, and rejecting any thought of a compromise peace.[102] The exchange brought Strauss to new heights of fame and made him, contrary to all expectations, an icon of bourgeois culture.

With Germany unified, Strauss addressed the future of religion in the Kaiserreich. In his final work, *Der alte und der neue Glaube* (1872), he announced his break from Christianity. All liberal and mediating theologies, he now declared, were half-measures in the face of Christianity's imminent intellectual bankruptcy. "If we don't want to twist and split hairs, if we want to leave behind 'yes and no'—in a word, if we want to speak as honorable and honest people, then we must confess: we are no longer Christians."[103] Strauss rejected God, he rejected Jesus, and he rejected the immortality of the soul. Nor was he more charitable to the non-Christian religions: he described paganism as the product of primitive fears and desires, and he derived Jewish monotheism from a Hebrew prejudice for a single national deity.[104] For Strauss, the religions of the past offered no guide to the future.

While Strauss did not advocate the abolition of Christianity, he felt it important to suggest a "new faith" for the growing minority of Germans who could no longer accept traditional religion (he numbered this group in the thousands). This new creed would be based on a "feeling of absolute dependence" on the universe. Rejecting Schopenhauerian pessimism, he described the world as an arena for rational action and thus deserving of respect, even reverence. "We demand the same piety toward the universe that the old-fashioned pious man demands for his God." Whether this was a religion or not, he would not say: "yes or no, however one wants to understand it."[105]

Strauss maintained that his view of the universe was rooted in Darwin's theory of evolution, although he ignored the potential difficulties of Darwinism for his own deep-seated optimism.[106] Indeed, while he rejected the belief in Providence, Strauss could not imagine a better world than the one natural selection had produced or a better state than the Kaiserreich. As proof, he cited the recent victory of "the good German people" over the "restless and arrogant" French.[107] Never a political radical, Strauss now aligned himself with the Prussian monarchy, arguing that this political *mysterium* would hold the new nation together. The government had only to counter the dual threat of the socialist and Ultramontanist internationals and a golden future would be assured.

Once again, Strauss had struck a chord in the *Zeitgeist. Der alte und der neue Glaube* ran through eleven editions in nine years and unleashed a fury of pamphlet literature.[108] Although the conservative response was predictably negative, a surprising number of Strauss's readers were willing to entertain the idea of a post-Christian religion. As one reviewer noted, "for a long time this question hung in the air: Strauss has brought it into public discussion."[109] Indeed, since the 1860s the growing interest in scientific materialism, Darwinian evolution, and Schopenhauerian pessimism had led many intellectuals to question not only the biblical revelation but the philosophical premises of monotheism.[110] Some Protestants had gravitated toward "Free Religious Communities," which based their worship and doctrine entirely on natural science.[111] But many more decided not to attend church at all, a trend that now included not just the urban middle classes but also the urban working classes and many rural populations as well. Between 1862 and 1880, annual religious communions per hundred Protestants fell from 72 to 49 in the Kingdom of Saxony, from 52 to 42 in Prussia, and from a paltry 17 to 13 in Berlin.[112] With Prussia victorious and a *Kulturkampf* under way, theological radicals hoped that the fury unleashed against Catholicism might be used to bypass the churches altogether and clear the ground for a new, philosophical religion.

Strauss certainly understood the *Kulturkampf* in this way. Although skeptical of liberal Protestantism, he endorsed Bismarck's "strong hand" in Catholic affairs and hoped out loud that these actions would weaken not only the Ultramontanists but the established Protestant churches.[113] But he was skeptical of attempts by the Free Religious Communities and like-minded groups to form new modes of religious "worship." In Strauss's view, church and cultus were neither necessary nor desirable for the "new faith." The Christian liturgy, after all, was centered on the cannibalistic acts of drinking blood and eating flesh, an ugly survival from an (alleged) Semitic era of human sacrifice.[114] Strauss even found the word *Gottesdienst* (service to God) objectionable, since it implied prostration before an imagined power.[115] Instead of going to church, adherents of the "new faith" could enjoy the benefits of German literary culture. Lessing and Goethe would replace the Bible, while Beethoven and Mozart supplanted the hymns.[116] In this sense, the existing bourgeois cult of genius would replace the worship service of the church. The new faith was simply the old faith.

While many readers were sympathetic or at least interested in Strauss's project, most found his "new faith" too materialist, too smug, or too shallow. Richard and Cosima Wagner read the book but judged Strauss's style and arguments distasteful and wondered whether he was actually a Jew.[117] Liberal theologians, meanwhile, fought a rear-guard action to preserve at least mini-

mal ideas of God, freedom, and immortality against the rising tide of materialist skepticism.[118] The Catholic philosopher Jacob Frohschammer contended that the future lay not with Strauss's "new faith" but in the "Christianity of Christ," free of "papal hierarchy and . . . confessional orthodoxy."[119]
Others endorsed the idea of a scientific "religion of spirit" but rejected specific tenets of Strauss's program.[120] In the midst of this hubbub, Heymann
Steinthal noted that these questions of God, the soul, and the future of religion "perhaps have never been discussed so heatedly as today."[121]

Nietzsche's engagement with Strauss dated back to his student days.
While at Bonn he had read *Das Leben Jesu für das deutsche Volk*, which contributed to his loss of faith and eventual abandonment of theology.[122] At the
time, he had tortured his still-faithful sister with discourses on its contents,
and for a while he was unwilling to brook challenges to its main conclusions
by liberal or "mediating" theologians.[123] Since then, however, Nietzsche had
aligned himself with Wagner, whose enmity to Strauss dated back to their
time together in Munich. It was thus in service to Wagner, as well as to his
own "struggle for culture," that Nietzsche penned the first of his "untimely
meditations," *David Strauss: Der Schriftsteller und der Bekenner* (1873).[124]

This essay is a rather peculiar affair. It practically ignores the theology of
the "new faith" and focuses instead on the aesthetic and cultural issues
raised by Strauss's book. As an advocate of the "music of the future," Nietzsche rejected Strauss's static concept of German culture. In his view, Goethe
and Schiller did not create a world literature so that it could sit on someone's
bookshelf or so that a cultural philistine could wax eloquent. To maintain
this was to profane the "mystery of our Germanness."[125] As if to illustrate
this point, Nietzsche mocked and derided Strauss's written style and the
rather amateurish attempts at literary and music criticism that made up the
last section of *Der alte und der neue Glaube*. Explaining the vehemence of
this attack several years later, Nietzsche would cite the theologian's status as
a literary icon. "[T]he general admiration of Strauss was the monument that
was set at the lowest ebb of the current of German culture: a freethinking,
aging theologian became the herald of public comfort."[126] Nietzsche, by contrast, sought to destroy the complacency of the German public in order to
create the conditions for a tragic culture grounded in philosophical and religious pessimism. Yet many found the essay mean-spirited, and it seems to
have done little to advance his cause.

Among the more substantial responses to Strauss's book, three are deserving of special comment. In *Ueber das Verhältnis des deutschen Staates
zu Theologie, Kirche und Religion* (1873), the Orientalist Paul Lagarde proposed a German faith based on the historical study of religion.[127] Lagarde was

deeply critical of Catholicism, claiming that the post-Tridentine church effectively constituted a new religion, and he was vehemently hostile to Judaism, which he felt had corrupted the essential message of the Christian gospel through the teachings of Paul. But Lagarde's most bitter attacks were reserved for Protestantism, which he accused of offering only a half-hearted protest against the Roman Church, propping itself up against the biblical canon (itself a Catholic institution) while embracing dogmas (such as justification by faith) with no basis in the Gospels. The solution to Germany's religious future was not a new *Kulturkampf*, Lagarde argued, but the transformation of theology from a confessional practice to the historical study of *all* religions insofar as they anticipated the truth of the original gospel message.

Nietzsche's friend and housemate, the theologian Franz Overbeck, offered a violent rebuke both to liberal theology and to the alternatives proposed by Strauss and Lagarde in *Ueber die Christlichkeit unserer heutigen Theologie* (1873).[128] Overbeck, a New Testament specialist and like Nietzsche a former student at Leipzig, had been appointed at Basel to serve as a representative of theological liberalism. But as Lionel Gossman notes, his first book was an assault on precisely this school of thought.[129] Because it had lost its fundament in myth, liberal theology was simply a "religion of thought," Overbeck argued. "A religion can be indifferent to its myths only so long as its myth-forming power still lives, that is, so long as the power of miracle that created its myths still operates."[130] This power had long since been extinguished in Christianity, and theology had no capacity to offer a substitute for the myths it had destroyed.

Overbeck's critique also applied to post-Christian attempts to set up a new faith. He dismissed David Strauss's "new faith" as a "middle-class" religion centered on egoism and a typically "Roman" worship of the state, which was guaranteed to transform Germany into a "cage."[131] While open to Lagarde's ideas, Overbeck felt that the academic's "underestimation of the mythical forms and overestimation of the historical basis of religion" did little to address the practical needs of a congregation for myths.[132] Revisiting Strauss's "last dilemma," Overbeck argued that in the wake of historical criticism there was no alternative but to divide the Christian Church into an esoteric community of doubters and an exoteric congregation of believers. Deprived of the Christian myth, the elite would presumably find satisfaction from other sources, such as Wagner's operas. Indeed, Overbeck's manifesto could be seen as the theological complement to Nietzsche's aesthetic dismantling of Strauss in the first "untimely meditation."

A third response to Strauss came from the pen of Eduard von Hartmann, a former Prussian army officer who had emerged as a popularizer of Schopenhauer's philosophy. Crippled by a riding accident, the largely self-taught Hartmann achieved striking success in his twenties with *Die Philosophie des Unbewußten* (1869), a work that combined philosophical pessimism with the eschatological vision of Schelling's later philosophy.[133] Like Schopenhauer, Hartmann believed that many of the great truths of pessimism could be traced back from Christian mysticism, through "Johannine" Christianity, to Pythagoras, and, before that, to the Indian mystics. The task of the present age was to transform the "negative" knowledge of pessimism into "positive" collective action. Because life led inevitably to suffering, the only redemption for humanity and the universe lay in a collective negation of the will, which would involve all the inhabitants of the earth and would take place at some specific time. As bizarre as this doctrine might sound, Hartmann's book became something of a philosophical bestseller, proving that even during the economic boom of the unification era, there was still a market for pessimism.

Five years later, Hartmann directed his attention to religion in *Die Selbstzersetzung des Christenthums und die Religion der Zukunft* (1874).[134] Citing the debate surrounding Strauss's "new faith," he noted with some accuracy that "[s]eldom has there been a more irreligious era than ours, yet religious questions have rarely agitated an era more profoundly than right now."[135] Declaring the rise of liberal theology a sign of Protestantism's imminent demise, Hartmann proposed a new reformation through which monistic pantheism would become the new world religion. To highlight the sense of urgency, he invoked the Catholic menace, claiming that "[o]nly German metaphysics is in a position to offer something positive to overcome Ultramontanism."[136] The other great menace, however, was Judaism, whose monotheistic doctrine had emerged in opposition to the Brahmanic pantheism of antiquity. The subsequent history of religion had consisted of a battle between "Aryan" and "Semitic" philosophies.

Hartmann maintained that Schopenhauer's discovery of the Vedas had incorporated the original Aryan theories into the heart of German metaphysics. Since then pantheism had become the hidden religion of Germany, just as Heine had predicted some thirty years earlier. Indeed, if such statements were possible from "Semitic Jewry," "we certainly cannot give up hope that in the true Aryan Germany pantheism can go from a hidden religion of esoteric philosophy to a universal worldview, first of the educated then of the whole people *[Volk]*, which can form the basis of a new religious life."[137] Despite his hostility to Strauss's "new faith," Hartmann acknowledged that as a young man Strauss had rendered a useful service by showing that Jesus Christ was "a Jew from head to toe."[138] The subsequent attempts by liberal Protestants to discover the historical Jesus were fundamentally misguided, he maintained, since Jesus had never intended to found a new religion. It was high time for German metaphysics to abandon the Old Testament altogether and take up the legacy of the Hellenistic Johannine religion. But whereas Schelling had envisioned this religion as an ideal synthesis of the Christian confessions, Hartmann saw it instead as a victory of "Protestantism" over Catholicism. It was the Protestant principle, he maintained, that would lead Germany beyond Christianity to the pessimistic religion of the future.

Following on the heels of Strauss's "new faith," Hartmann's vicious little tract managed to spark a controversy in its own right.[139] Indeed, the consideration given to both books testifies once again to the volatile religious situation of the early 1870s. Not surprisingly, Catholic observers saw these proposals as proof that liberal Protestantism intended to establish atheism as the German national philosophy. In a series of speeches, the Catholic bishop Wilhelm von Ketteler singled out Strauss and Hartmann as exposing the true face of Protestantism, in particular liberal Protestantism. Praising their honesty, he concluded that these "open enemies show us the essence of modern culture and the meaning of the emergent *Kulturkampf.*"[140]

Over the next few years, Nietzsche observed the religious conflict in Germany with growing distaste. In early 1874 he noted, "The struggle against the Catholic Church is an act of the Enlightenment, nothing higher, and strengthens it disproportionately, which is hardly desirable. Of course, it is right, in general. If only the state and church wanted to consume each other!"[141] While hardly a friend of the papacy, Nietzsche distrusted the Protestants' claim that the *Kulturkampf* was being fought on behalf of German culture. One day, he predicted, music, tragedy, and philosophy would also be declared *"reichsfeindlich"* (hostile to the empire).[142] In Nietzsche's eyes, the essence of liberal Protestantism consisted of nothing more than worship of the state. In *Schopenhauer als Erzieher* (1874) he launched a diatribe against neo-Kantian "state philosophy," which applied as much to the theological exponents of the *Kulturstaat* as it did to the National Liberals in the Reichstag. At the same time, Nietzsche evinced deep skepticism toward the attempts by Hartmann and others to popularize Schopenhauer. Such a pessimistic philosophy could find little understanding in a country still preoccupied with the ideas of "progress," "national," and *"Kulturkampf."*[143]

What was needed, Nietzsche concluded, was not a political campaign on behalf of existing Protestant civilization but rather a struggle for a *new* culture—a "reformation."[144] Up through 1875 Nietzsche continued to identify this reformation with the spirit of "Protestantism" broadly drawn. When his housemate and protégé Heinrich Romundt announced that he was joining

the Catholic priesthood, Nietzsche was devastated. "I have never felt my inner dependence on the spirit of Luther more strongly than now," he wrote.[145]
Yet this "inner dependence" proved fleeting. By the end of 1875, isolated
comments in notebooks and letters show Nietzsche rethinking his relationship to Protestantism.[146] He now claimed as his hero Empedokles, the pre-
Socratic philosopher who espoused a doctrine of transmigration of souls and
who had been viewed by the early Romantics (especially Hölderlin) as the exponent of a "new mythology."[147] Nietzsche at one point formulated the great
opposition of the age as Empedokles versus Strauss and envisioned a reformation carried out in the spirit of ancient Greece.[148] Nietzsche had begun to
move away from the rhetorical Protestantism of *The Birth of Tragedy* and
toward a standpoint beyond—and against—both confessions.[149]

So as Germany wrenched itself apart in the *Kulturkampf*, Nietzsche was
deeply engaged in his own "struggle for culture." During these years of religious crisis it seemed possible that the Catholic and Protestant Churches
were on the verge of succumbing to the forces of revolution, to be replaced by
either a post-Christian religion or a secular culture masquerading as religion.
This situation was analogous in many respects to the turn of the nineteenth
century, which was perhaps one reason why Nietzsche expressed his opposition in the language of Romantic myth discourse. Yet many of the assumptions that had underlain the *Frühromantik* notion of a "new mythology," including a confidence in the imminent triumph of idealism in the arts and
sciences and the vision of a revitalized public life as the center of the modern
state, had evaporated by the time Nietzsche published *The Birth of Tragedy*.
In this book he did not abandon the link between Dionysus and Christ—
indeed, his reliance on the language of justification heightened the distinctly
Lutheran dimensions of his narrative—and he reiterated the vision of a rebirth of tragic myth out of the spirit of German Protestant music. Nonetheless, whereas Schelling and the Schlegels felt they were riding the crest of
European history, Nietzsche's hopes rested on the fortunes of a single "genius," Richard Wagner. As a result, there was something tenuous, even artificial, in this version of the new mythology. As he came to abandon Wagnerism, he would quickly turn against Romanticism, its understanding of
religion, and its vision of the future.

NIETZSCHE'S ENCOUNTER WITH THE CHTHONIC

With the publication of *The Birth of Tragedy*, Nietzsche's work as a philologist and university teacher became much more difficult. The book had proved
to be a fiasco, and Nietzsche now found himself shunned by students and col-

leagues alike. He was forced to cancel one of his classes when no one signed up for it, and enrollment in his lectures generally remained meager. Nietzsche concluded that a philological *"Vehme"* (secret tribunal) was at work against him, and he began to lose contact with the academic community in Leipzig.[150] For these reasons, scholars have viewed these years primarily in terms of his relationship to Richard Wagner.

Yet this friendship was becoming increasingly difficult as well. The two men were agreed that Nietzsche should sacrifice his career to Wagner. But while Nietzsche stylized himself as the scholarly apostle of the new musical genius, Wagner hoped he might simply become his son Siegfried's tutor.[151] After Wagner's move from Tribschen to Bayreuth, a series of indiscretions and small offenses led to a growing estrangement between the two men. Wagner would not tolerate any sign of intellectual independence in the young professor; Nietzsche, plagued by chronic ill health, took to avoiding Bayreuth, which provoked further rebukes from Wagner. In his notebooks of 1874, Nietzsche began to describe the composer as a charlatan and a tyrant, a man who believed not in God but only in himself. "No one is more honorable to himself than someone who believes only in himself. Wagner gets rid of all his weaknesses by imputing them to his era or his enemies."[152] By the time Nietzsche attended the first Bayreuth Festival in 1876, his relationship with Wagner had become deeply unsettled.

Throughout these years, Nietzsche continued to lecture and teach in Basel. But rather than remaining rooted in either the textual critical philology of Ritschl or the Romantic mythographies of Schelling, Creuzer, or Bachofen, Nietzsche began to investigate and absorb new scholarship in art history, anthropology, and cultural history *(Kulturgeschichte)*. His voracious reading in these fields soon transformed his understanding of ancient mythology and religion. As Andrea Orsucci notes, Nietzsche "renovated his conceptual apparatus from the ground up and directed his attention to new motives, to which he would repeatedly return in the years ahead."[153] Nietzsche would use this "conceptual apparatus" not only to challenge the accepted view of antiquity but to analyze and criticize the contemporary world.

Nietzsche encountered much of this literature in preparation for his 1875–76 lectures, "The Worship Service of the Greeks." Familiar since 1873 with the work of Edward Tylor, he now read books by the historian Karl Müllenhof, the mythographer Wilhelm Mannhardt, the art historian Karl Boetticher, and other contemporary scholars on the margins or outside of classical philology. Their research confirmed his view, still controversial within the philological guild, that Greek culture was the product of both foreign and autochthonous elements. To prove this case, these scholars had shifted at-

Friedrich Nietzsche as a professor in Basel, ca. 1876.
Photo: Stiftung Weimar Klassik. GSA 101/17. Source: David Farrell Krell and
Donald L. Bates, *The Good European: Nietzsche's Work Sites in Word and Image*
(Chicago: University of Chicago Press, 1997), 104.

tention away from Olympian deities like Zeus and Apollo to the primordial realm of "chthonic mythology," those lower deities who lived among
the common people in the realm of "superstition."[154] Creuzer, Müller, and
Bachofen had already pointed to the subterranean forces in Greek religion,
especially as manifested in the Dionysian mysteries. What the newer scholarship suggested, however, was a view of mythology that downplayed the role
of individual symbols and intuitions, stressing instead the practical, impro-
vised, and syncretistic nature of ancient religion.

Among the pioneers in this view of Greek religion was the art historian
Karl Boetticher. Boetticher (1806–89), a professor at the Berlin Bauakademie
(School of Architecture), was led by his study of Greek temple architecture to
an investigation of the ancient cultus. In *Der Baumkultus der Hellenen*
(1856), he concluded that the earliest Greeks had worshiped under trees,

The holy olive tree of Athena, with attributes of the goddess: helmet, spear, and
snake, as well as a lamb about to be sacrificed. Drawing by Karl Boetticher.
Source: Karl Boetticher, *Der Baumkultus der Hellenen* (Berlin: Weidmann, 1856),
fig. 34.

where they believed their deities to reside.[155] They adorned the trees with
masks and clothing and sometimes carved images into their trunks and
branches. Only much later were the sacred groves with their graven images
replaced by freestanding temples of stone and marble. The continued use of
ivy crowns and olive branches in worship services up through the Hellenistic era testified to the forgotten origins of the Greek cultus.

While Boetticher traced the roots of all religion to an original monotheism, others argued that belief in chthonic deities had actually preceded monotheism and polytheism. During the 1840s, Wilhelm Schwartz traveled throughout the German countryside with his brother-in-law Adalbert Kuhn, collecting legends and myths. During these tours he was impressed by the ability of peasants to invent myths spontaneously. Once during a storm, a farmer saw a bolt of lightning and exclaimed, "What a splendid snake that was!"[156] Inspired by this incident, Schwartz devoted an entire study to the role of snakes in ancient mythology. Believing that lightning and snakes were identical, the earliest Europeans had placed snakes at the center of their cultus, which eventually evolved into the anthropomorphic mythologies of Homer and the *Eddas*. Like Kuhn, Schwarz identified the root cause of myth as a mistaken perception, which only later acquired the veneer and function of religion. "[T]he further one goes back in mythological production, the less one can expect what is usually called a system, an error that until now has spoiled much research."[157]

Schwartz's understanding of chthonic mythology corresponded to the broader shift in German historical scholarship since midcentury away from the Romantic model of "diremption and return" and toward a model of evolutionary progress. Like his contemporaries Kuhn and Steinthal, Schwartz assumed that the earliest humans were neither divine nor uniquely gifted. Instead, they were primitive, prereligious, largely unethical beings caught in a web of custom and superstition, just like modern "Botocudo, Bushmen, Kamchatkans, and Papuan Negroes."[158] As this quotation suggests, these scholars derived their conception of ancient religion less from European textual sources than from the travel literature on Africa, Siberia, and the South Pacific. But while the racism and condescension of European mythographers ran deep, many still had difficulty believing that anyone—even a "primitive"—could confuse lightning with a snake. By the 1870s, they had begun to turn to the theories of religion emerging from ethnology.

The English anthropologist Edward B. Tylor stood in the first rank of contemporary ethnologists, in large part due to his theory of animism.[159] In *Primitive Culture* (1871), Tylor combined data collected in Australia, New Zealand, and Africa with recent archaeological findings concerning the progression of ancient European civilization from the Stone Age to the Iron Age. Based on this evidence, he argued that aboriginal peoples saw rocks, trees, and other natural objects as possessing an independent will or soul.[160] This belief was not a result of mistaken apperception, as Schwartz had suggested, but of the experience of dreams. To the primitives, dreams seemed literally to remove the sleeper from his or her body, a misconception that gave rise to belief in the transmigration of souls. As a result, they attributed souls to such inanimate objects as "sticks and stones." As evidence of prehistoric stone worship, Tylor cited the menhirs, dolmens, and cromlechs that still dotted the European landscape; only gradually had the various races advanced to "higher" stages of idolatry.[161]

The theory of animism offered a seemingly plausible account of the origin of ancient nature worship, and it had the further advantage of decoupling the history of religion from the science of linguistics. Tylor disparaged the attempts by comparative mythologists to link myths to each other on the basis of etymology, and he was especially critical of the thesis that mythology could be traced to an original system of metaphors.[162] "For myself, I am disposed to think (differing here in some measure from Professor Max Müller's view of the subject) that the mythology of the lower races rests especially on a basis of real and sensible analogy, and that the great expansion of verbal metaphors into myth belongs to more advanced periods of civilization."[163] The origin of myth lay in a prelinguistic process in which the primitive mind ascribed its own will to the phenomena of nature. Once nature seemed alive, all manner of tales about water fairies, elves, and the like could spring forth.

Tylor's theory of animism made a deep impression on the librarian and amateur mythographer Wilhelm Mannhardt.[164] In the 1850s, Mannhardt had been one of the most fervent enthusiasts of Kuhn's style of comparative mythology, and in works like *Germanische Mythen* (1858) he had tirelessly traced various Nordic myths to their supposed roots in Indo-Germanic cloud worship.[165] By the 1870s, however, he had begun to rethink this approach in light of Tylor's theses and the work of Boetticher. He began to gather data on central European planting and harvesting practices, using written records, interviews with French prisoners of war, and an innovative series of surveys that he mailed throughout Germany. Like Jacob Grimm before him, Mannhardt discovered striking parallels between contemporary customs and ancient religious beliefs.

In *Wald- und Feldkulte* (1875–77), Mannhardt argued that at an early stage of culture the ancients had believed in a basic continuity between human and plant life (especially trees).[166] The plant was seen as a shell for the soul after the death of the body, and so trees and other vegetation were treated with veneration and assigned a central role in religious practices.[167] Mannhardt linked celebrations around the Maypole, Christmas tree decorations, and even the use of the crucifix to a belief in the spiritual personality of trees and plants.[168] Like Jacob Grimm and Adalbert Kuhn, Mannhardt described the "sun-wheels" that some German peasants burned on Saint John's Day, but he derived these practices not from primitive fire making but rather

from a primitive reverence for the sun and its crop-growing powers.[169] In
Mannhardt's view, this ancient tree worship explained numerous features of
Germanic mythology, including the world-tree Yggdrasil, the cult of the
Earth Mother Nerthus, and the Irminsul that Charlemagne had so assidu-
ously destroyed. Yet he refused to ascribe the origin of this cult to either a lost
Germanic *Götterlehre* or an Aryan linguistic heritage. The fact that such
practices could be found throughout the world suggested that they were
instead the product of a universal stage of cultural evolution.

The influence of Boetticher, Tylor, and Mannhardt on Nietzsche can be
detected in his lectures on the Greek cultus, which were held in the winter
semester, 1875–76.[170] Nietzsche began the course by listing the cultural factors that had first led to a belief in magic: inexact observation, a false concept
of causality, a taste for the bizarre, a tendency to link similar things together,
and natural laziness. Gone was any reference to musical symbolism or to the
Schopenhauerian will. Instead, Nietzsche revealed his new affinity for evolutionary thought. "One discovers the same way of thinking everywhere one
still finds peoples at a low stage of culture and likewise everywhere among
the lower, poorly educated classes of people in civilized nations."[171] In light
of both contemporary ethnology and the all-too-evident social divisions
within modern industrial society, a strictly historicist notion of culture no
longer seemed viable.[172]

Based on of this, Nietzsche concluded that Greek religion was a result of
multiple levels of synthesis. First, the Doric races had conquered the original
inhabitants of Greece. These earliest inhabitants had practiced a nature religion that consisted of tree, snake, and stone worship.[173] In their eyes, "the tree
and the seed from which it grew seem to prove that they are only incarnations
of a single spirit. A stone that suddenly rolls is the body in which a spirit acts.
If a huge block lies in a lonesome heath, it must have moved there by itself,
hiding a spirit."[174] After the Dorian invasion, this primitive animism merged
with the invaders' Indo-Germanic sky worship. For this reason, Greek mythology often incorporated two different layers of religion. A well-known myth
related how the goddess Athena carried the snake-shaped Erichthonios and
the first olive tree to the top of a mountain in Athens and placed him there to
watch over the tree and the city. But in fact tree and snake cults were indigenous to this mountain. The narrative was probably invented in order to link
Athena, an Indo-Germanic moon goddess, to these original nature cults.[175]

Nietzsche described other phases of synthesis as well. After the Hellenic
nomads had assimilated their deities to the indigenous cults of Greece, they
absorbed the Dionysian cults from Thrace. Further, some of the Semitic
deities brought in by the Phoenicians found their way into Greek mythology.

Thus, Greek culture was a synthesis of indigenous, Hellenic, oriental, Semitic, and Egyptian elements, but carried to a higher level. As we have seen, Nietzsche was already deeply skeptical of claims by philologists for Greek autochthony.[176] But whereas *The Birth of Tragedy* emphasized a struggle between the indigenous Apollonian and the foreign Dionysian impulses, Nietzsche now described the Greeks as "happy dilettantes," perfectly willing to collect and appropriate useful practices and ideas, no matter what their origin.[177] After decades of "postcolonial" resistance, Nietzsche appeared to reinstate diffusionism back into the narrative of Greek cultural history.

The lectures on the Greek worship service also revealed Nietzsche's new understanding of the origins of religious practice. At the stage of primitive animism, he argued, the natural world seemed inhabited by independent spirits. The ancients thus saw nature not as bound by natural laws but rather as a realm of freedom and caprice. Indeed, it was humans who hoped to impose some degree of law or regularity on nature, especially by means of the liturgy. The ancient cultus usually revolved around an object that was linked to a spirit—a stone, a piece of wood, anything that might be a guarantee (σύμβολον) of the spirit's cooperation. By applying prayers, flattery, bribery, and even physical force to the religious cult object, the ancients sought to bend the spirit to their will.[178] Nietzsche maintained that it was these practices, rather than philosophical doctrines or symbolic intuitions, that characterized the earliest stage of religious life. "There was no forced belief, no forced attendance at temples, no orthodoxy. All variety of opinions about the gods were tolerated. But one could not attack the *cultus*. That is ancient religiosity."[179] At such a level of culture, concepts like "faith" or "belief" were largely irrelevant.[180]

The historical perspective on ancient religion developed in the "Greek Worship Service" was applied to a critique of the modern world in Nietzsche's later works, notably *Human, All Too Human* (1878–80).[181] Rejecting the notion of a timeless *Volksgeist*, he compared cultures according to a fixed evolutionary scale. "What are seen as national differences are in fact—far more than has yet been recognized—only the differences of various *culture levels* and only in the smallest bit something permanent."[182] Religion was thus the product of a low level of civilization, in which a lack of logic and an inability to distinguish dreams from reality led primitive humans to imagine unseen beings and to create bizarre rites and practices.[183]

Yet Nietzsche did differentiate among the various religious cults. While the Greeks bargained with their gods as if with equals, the Jewish-Christian God demanded a complete sacrifice. Christian believers were required to grovel in the mud, confess their sins, and beg forgiveness from the almighty deity. While Greek religiosity inspired public festivals and joyous celebrations, Christianity generated a private spectacle of self-torment and self-abasement within the conscience of the individual believer. For this reason, Christianity was "in its deepest sense barbaric, Asiatic, unrefined, un-Greek."[184] The free and almost irreverent relationship that a poet like Homer enjoyed vis-à-vis the gods represented a stage of culture unimaginable to the Christian or, for that matter, most philologists.[185]

Nietzsche's critique of Christianity as "barbaric" and "Asiatic" eventually became the launching point for an attack on all metaphysical and scientific systems of truth, which he saw as shot through with religious delusion and fantasy. Kant's thing-in-itself, he argued, was a modern survival of the animist belief in the souls of things.[186] Schopenhauer's philosophy was a similar relic, a resurrection of "the whole medieval Christian worldview."[187] In *Human, All Too Human*, Nietzsche rejected the notion that philosophy should serve as a substitute for religion. The "religious needs" postulated by Kant, Schelling, and Schopenhauer did not need to be satisfied; rather, they could be set aside and, ultimately, destroyed. True philosophy had nothing at all to do with religion. Between them was "neither kinship nor friendship nor even enmity. They live on different stars."[188]

The aphorisms of *Human, All Too Human*, taken together, sketched the outlines of a negative cultural theology, in which the idols of the day—religion, science, the state—were subjected to relentless criticism. In this critique, Nietzsche applied a new set of conceptual tools, which he had acquired through his reading in 1875–76 of scholarship in the fields of ethnology, history, and archaeology. In particular, his interest in the chthonic deities and their worship led him to direct new attention to ritual—rather than intuition—as the basis of ancient and modern religious life. The Romantic valorization of myth, so central to his earlier works, gave way now to an enlightened conception of myth as an illusion or mistake, and Christianity, viewed formerly as a logical outgrowth of the Dionysian worldview, was now treated as a regression to primitive barbarism.[189] Nietzsche had entered new territory, far removed from *The Birth of Tragedy* or the worldview of Richard Wagner.

THE WAGNERIAN CULTUS: NIETZSCHE AND *PARSIFAL*

At the end of his career, Nietzsche spun a story of how he sent two copies of *Human, All Too Human* to Bayreuth. "Through a miracle of meaningful coincidence, a beautiful copy of the Parsifal text arrived, inscribed with Wagner's dedication, 'to his dear friend, Friedrich Nietzsche, Richard Wagner,

Church councilor.'—This crossing of two books—to me it was as if I heard an ominous sound at the same time. Did it not sound like swords crossing?"[190] The historical inaccuracy of this account is well documented, but like every good fable it has its moral.[191] During the 1880s, as he mulled over the collapse of his relationship with Wagner, Nietzsche constantly returned to *Parsifal*. It was an insult, an apostasy. In 1888, he still maintained that he could not "forgive" Wagner for this opera.[192]

Nietzsche could not have been surprised that Wagner would choose the legend of Parsifal as the subject of an opera. Wolfram von Eschenbach's thirteenth-century text was one of the most widely discussed works of medieval literature in the nineteenth century. Wagner read the poem in 1845 and immediately began to consider the possibility of using it as the basis for an opera.[193] By 1865, he had written a sketch of *Parsifal*, which he read to Nietzsche in Tribschen in 1869.[194] But the final libretto was not put together until the spring of 1877. Bearing the title *Parsifal: Ein Bühnenweihfestpiel*, a copy reached Basel in January 1878.

Wagner's opera, like Eschenbach's poem, revolved around the legend of the Holy Grail. The grail has the capacity to convert wine into the blood of Christ, a Eucharist in reverse that grants life-sustaining powers to all who partake of it. Rescued from the Holy Lands during the Crusades, the grail is guarded in a Spanish mountain by King Amfortas and his secret order of knights, who also have charge over the magic lance—the very weapon that pierced Christ's side at Golgotha. Amfortas is opposed by the evil magician Klingsor, who has created his own fantastic kingdom across the mountains. As the opera begins, we learn that Amfortas has been mortally wounded in an assault on Klingsor's realm. During the attack he was seduced by Kundry, a beautiful woman cursed to wander the ages and seduce souls because of her laughter at the crucifixion. Klingsor has used this moment of weakness to steal the magic spear from Amfortas and wound him with it. Amfortas now longs for an end to his suffering, but he can only be healed by a touch of the holy lance. In the meantime, he places his hopes on the prophecy of a coming savior: "Knowing through pity [*Mitleid*], the pure fool; to be awaited, he whom I chose."

The hero of the opera, Parsifal, appears as an ignorant boy, who desecrates the Grail kingdom by killing a swan. But he is eventually transformed into a conquering knight, capable of penetrating deep into Klingsor's realm. There he encounters Kundry, who with a seductive kiss unintentionally conveys to him a knowledge of his destiny. Suddenly Parsifal feels infinite pity for Amfortas's suffering and can think of no other goal than relieving it. Pushing aside Kundry, he wrests the spear from Klingsor, shattering his magic

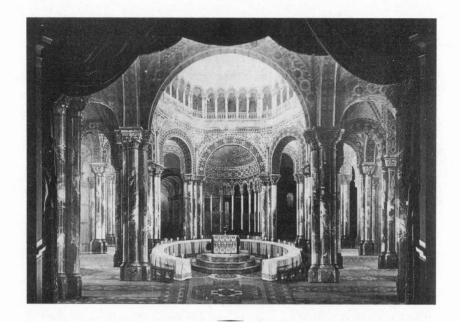

Paul von Joukowsky's stage design for the Temple of the Grail, from the Bayreuth
production of *Parsifal* (1882).
Source: Frederic Spotts, *Bayreuth: A History of the Wagner Festival* (New Haven:
Yale University Press, 1994), 82.

kingdom. With the lance in hand, Parsifal returns to the Grail shrine, heals
Amfortas, and fulfills the prophecy. Amfortas, saved from perpetual suffering, hands over his office to Parsifal. Kundry, released from her curse and redeemed back into humanity, sinks lifeless to the ground.

Parsifal represented a shift from the more "pagan" *Ring* cycle.[195] Relying
heavily on Christian-Catholic imagery, it conveyed a Schopenhauerian message of pity and renunciation of the will. Rather than bringing the world of
the gods to an end, it featured prayers to God. Yet there were also important
continuities between the *Ring* and *Parsifal*. Both operas turn on the education of ruthless, amoral, and none-too-intelligent male characters (Siegfried
and Parsifal), who through their actions bring about death and redemption to
a compromised father figure (Wotan and Amfortas). Further, in both operas
the hero achieves understanding through the mediation of a woman
(Brünnhilde and Kundry), who has become an outcast through her rebellion
against divine authority. In their different ways, therefore, both operas offered
a Christian-idealist narrative of alienation and reconciliation. What differentiated *Parsifal* from the *Ring* was its stance toward sexuality, which was ex-

pressed through an opposition between Christian asceticism and Semitic licentiousness. Thus, whereas Brünnhilde's illicit love for Siegfried serves as the vehicle for humanity's redemption, Kundry is made to play the role of Wandering Jew, condemned through her sinful laughter to wander the ages knowing neither love nor peace. Indeed, even at the moment of her death, she is excluded from the eucharistic feast.

Wagner made his religious ambitions surrounding this opera explicit in the manifesto *Religion und Kunst* (1880). "One could say that when religion becomes artificial, it is the task of art to save the core of religion. It grasps the mythical symbols, which religion would have believed as literally true, according to their symbolic value, in order through an ideal representation of them to reveal their hidden, deep truth."[196] The core truth of religion was of the "decrepitude" of the world and the necessity of a "regeneration" of the human race. The great challenge for religious figures from the Hindus to Jesus was to create mythical allegories by which the people could be led to these insights. In the present era, however, Germans found themselves caught between a corrupt church establishment, an ever-rising tide of atheism, and the quotidian preoccupations defined by the popular press (modern journalism remained a *bête noir* for Wagner). Only music could take the central truths of religion and translate them into a form that would be accepted by the great mass of the people.

A striking feature of Wagner's writings from this period, as well as *Parsifal* itself, was his openness to Roman Catholic ideas and imagery. During these years he read the works of Joseph Görres on medieval mythology and Christian mysticism with newfound appreciation.[197] He attempted to rehabilitate such arch-Catholic doctrines as the Virgin Birth on the basis of Schopenhauerian philosophy (only because the Will was broken *before* his birth could Christ live a sinless life).[198] In addition, he applauded the medieval ban on reading the Bible and lamented that Luther had based his Reformation on such a faulty text. This new fascination with Catholicism was in certain respects a reaction to liberalism and the *Kulturkampf*. To be sure, Wagner, like most Protestants, was deeply suspicious of the Catholic clergy, in particular the Jesuits, whom he attacked repeatedly as manufacturers of artifice and falsehood.[199] To this end, he endorsed Bismarck's struggle against the Ultramontanists. But Wagner rejected the "optimism" of the liberals and their version of the Protestant *Kulturstaat*. Instead, he took an interest in the Old Catholic movement, supporting leaders like Ignaz Döllinger in their struggle against the pope and entertaining an eventual union of the confessions.[200]

While Wagner expressed a degree of ambivalence toward Catholicism, his attitude toward Judaism remained one of hostility mixed with condescension. Like a proud but stern father, Wagner surveyed the rise of organized anti-Semitism since unification, reproving it for its materialistic tendencies and pushing it toward his own "idealistic" doctrine of regeneration.[201] The Jews, Wagner maintained, had infiltrated all aspects of German life. On the one hand, they were masters of the contemporary cult of credit, the sole faith for many in an atheistic era. On the other hand, they were responsible for the inherently contradictory nature of Christianity, which attempted to connect Jesus' sublime doctrine of "pity" to the legalistic, state religion of the Old Testament. In Wagner's view, there was no need to connect Christ to the prophecies of Abraham and Isaiah, since it was doubtful whether he was a Jew at all.[202] The image of the "suffering god" on the cross was essentially Greco-Roman, and the roots of Christian truth were Aryan in origin.

Here Wagner tapped into the increasingly influential racial ideologies of his day, while at the same time "idealizing" them through his peculiar theology of blood.[203] In "Heldenthum und Christenthum" (1881), he attributed the decrepitude of the world to the corruption of Aryan white blood, which was brought about by meat eating and the intermixing of the white race with "inferior" races, notably the Jews. The sign of pure blood, he argued, was the "capacity for conscious suffering," which allowed the mind to overcome the sensual strivings of the Will.[204] This explained the connection between the passion of Christ and the drinking of his blood during the eucharistic meal. By partaking of Christ's blood, not only the Aryans but other—"inferior"—races might raise themselves up to the level of the gods. In this way, individuals Jews—if not Judaism itself—could be redeemed.

Parsifal was first performed at the Bayreuth Festival in 1882, a year before Wagner's death. To the composer's disappointment, the festival had never become a truly popular event, attracting instead a collection of the rich, the powerful, and the curious from all over Europe.[205] Even the most hostile of them were impressed by Wagner's achievement, but very few took it for the life-transforming experience that he had originally envisioned. Still, a scattering of disaffected intellectuals did begin to congregate in Bayreuth, treating Wagner's home Wahnfried as a kind of pilgrimage site. In the pages of the *Bayreuther Blätter*, they would systematize Wagner's scattered theories into a formal doctrine, putting particular emphasis on the Aryan-Christianity of *Parsifal*. For thirty years after Wagner's death, performances of this opera were permitted only in the Bayreuth Festspielhaus.

Parsifal became for Nietzsche the symbol and, retrospectively, the occasion for his break with Wagner. Indeed, it would not be much of an exaggeration to describe his entire later philosophy—or at least the works from *Daybreak* to *Zarathustra*—as a repudiation of this one music drama. The abundance of Christian imagery, Wagner's seeming advocacy of chastity, and his emphasis on the redemptive power of death seemed to mark a break from his earlier, "healthier" operas. "I took his slow, crawling return back to Christianity and to the church as a personal insult," Nietzsche wrote in an 1883 letter. This, he maintained, was the "mortal insult" that had divided them since 1877. Yet there are reasons to be skeptical of this account. Nietzsche had long known of Wagner's plans for a *Parsifal* opera, and he had listened with enthusiasm to a first draft of the libretto. Moreover, as has been shown, Nietzsche incorporated numerous Christianizing elements into his portrayal of Greek paganism in *The Birth of Tragedy*. So if "Christianity" was not the "mortal insult," what was? A number of scholars now maintain that this phrase referred instead to Wagner's correspondence with Nietzsche's physician, Otto Eiser, in which the composer hinted that Nietzsche's health problems were due to the effects of masturbation.[206] Nietzsche's discovery of this indiscretion would end a relationship that had been fraying at the edges for several years.

All of this has consequences for the interpretation of Nietzsche's late philosophy, for it suggests, first, that his adamant anti-Wagnerism was as much the cause as the consequence of his hostility to Christianity and, second, that there was something rather performative in his condemnations of *Parsifal*, just as there had been in his earlier praise of the *Ring*. Indeed, Nietzsche often seemed more intent on inverting Wagner's worldview than in presenting an alternative to take its place, which gave his philosophy the "agonic" quality often cited by commentators. Whatever his motivations (and they were multiple), Nietzsche's criticism opened new perspectives onto the Wagnerian project, as well as the Romantic religiosity that inspired it.

Much of Nietzsche's anti-*Parsifal* polemic was directed at what he saw as the opera's glorification of the Christian cultus. "[N]o flesh and much too much blood (in particular, it was too bloody for me in the Eucharist)," he wrote on receipt of the libretto.[207] In later years Nietzsche would revisit a conversation that he had had with Wagner in which the composer allegedly spoke of the "delights" of the Eucharist. "That was the end of my patience," Nietzsche claimed.[208] Perhaps. In any case, Nietzsche came to see *Parsifal* as an attempt to recapture the dark, remorseful, and unhealthy religious moods associated with the Christian liturgy by means of architecture, music, and ritual. "Who would want to bring back such proceedings if the prerequisites for them are no longer believed?" he asked.[209] By reviving traditional Christian symbols in the context of a work of art, Wagner had given them a new—albeit temporary—lease on life.

Nietzsche also deployed the familiar anti-Romantic arguments of Nicolai, Voss, and Heine to condemn *Parsifal* as an accommodation to the Catholic Church—"[t]he spirit of the Counter-Reformation," he wrote in 1878.[210] Four years later, on reading the score, he declared that the spirit of Catholicism sang out even from the music. "On hearing this music one certainly puts aside Protestantism as a misunderstanding."[211] Nietzsche looked back mournfully at Wagner's plans to stage a drama based on Luther's wedding; that, he argued, would have meant a celebration of sensuality. Instead, Nietzsche wrote, Wagner had turned the son of nature, Parsifal, into a Catholic.[212] Perhaps Wagner meant to repent for the anti-Roman character of a hero like Siegfried. Perhaps he had sensed the political shift that would lead Bismarck in 1878 to abandon the *Kulturkampf* and seek accommodation with Pope Leo XIII.[213]

The problem for Nietzsche with this particular line of attack was his own growing hostility to Protestantism. Under the influence of Jacob Burckhardt, he came to see the Renaissance as an era of unparalleled cultural and scientific achievement, in which the power of the church was weakened and the individual human spirit set free. This had been destroyed by the Reformation, which was the product of backward Germans still caught up in the Middle Ages.[214] Martin Luther, he concluded, was a fanatical peasant, who stirred up the masses in resentment against a powerful, aristocratic clergy.[215] Here Nietzsche was influenced by a reading of Johannes Janssen's Ultramontanist *Geschichte des deutschen Volkes seit dem Ausgang des Mittelalter* (1878–94), whose unflattering portrayal of Luther had sparked indignation and outrage among Protestants.[216]

As he distanced himself from the rhetoric of Protestant identity, Nietzsche began to reevaluate those aspects of Roman Catholicism that contradicted both liberal theology and the Schopenhauerian-Wagnerian philosophy of pity. The Jesuit order, for example, now appeared to Nietzsche as a fine example of a moral and political elite, and the confession seemed a worthy sacrament.[217] Indeed, Nietzsche came to evince a grudging respect for what he saw as the ritualistic nature of the Catholic Church. Its conscious manufacture of illusion and its focus on the "deed" rather than "faith" made it in many respects a healthier form of religion than a Protestantism obsessed with inwardness and emotion. "Works, first and foremost! That means practice, practice, practice! The corresponding 'faith' will certainly kick in—you can be sure of that!" he wrote in *Daybreak* (1881).[218] Although Nietzsche detested the Eucharist and abhorred the papacy, the outward, custom-laden, and therefore "pagan" nature of Catholicism seemed an antidote to Wagnerian "idealism" and its cult of pity and suffering.

The conflict with Wagner also influenced Nietzsche's stance toward Judaism. In *Human, All Too Human* he denounced the upsurge in anti-Semitism as a "literary indecency" that was the by-product of artificial nationalism. "Every nation, every man, has unpleasant, indeed dangerous qualities: it is cruel to demand that the Jew should be an exception." Whatever their unpleasant qualities (and here Nietzsche cited the "youthful stock-exchange Jew"), it was the Jews who had preserved freethinking in the era of the Middle Ages. "If Christianity has done everything to orientalize the Occident, Judaism has provided vital help in occidentalizing it again: which in a certain sense means making Europe's mission and history a *continuation of the Greek.*"[219] In this analysis, Nietzsche inverted the Wagnerian equation of Christianity with the West and Judaism with the East, finding precisely those qualities that he associated with the Greeks, namely hardness and racial purity, recapitulated in modern, Diaspora Judaism.

Indeed, while Nietzsche was relentlessly hostile to Jewish monotheism, he evinced an admiration for its ancient moral code, suggesting in *Daybreak* that it was Paul's inability to fulfill this law that transformed Christianity from a Jewish sect into a new religion. Originally a fanatical defender of the law, Paul had tortured himself with the question of whether he would be able to live up to its demands. "The law was the cross on which he felt nailed: how he hated it!" So Paul decided to destroy it, giving himself up to an "epileptic" vision through which the law became fulfilled in Christ's death. "Now the law is dead. Now the carnality in which it lived is dead—or at least in continuous dying."[220] Freed from the law, Paul gave himself up to the intoxication of complete submission to God, as would Martin Luther fifteen centuries later. All that was left at that point was to claim that the new *Rausch* religion was the fulfillment of the law, and that the Christians were the true people of Israel. In this way the dubious enterprise known as "Old Testament theology" was born.[221]

Based on statements like these, it is sometimes argued that although Nietzsche was an anti-Semite in his youth he became an anti-anti-Semite after his break from Wagner.[222] This tells only part of the story, however, for even in his later writings Nietzsche still drew on a remarkable range of anti-Semitic tropes and metaphors. In some cases he turned them on their heads, applying them to Germans or to Protestants while praising Jews and other "non-Germans." At other times his prejudices seem more conventional, as the quotation about the "stock-exchange Jew" reveals. In other words, Nietzsche found it impossible and even undesirable to escape the maze of confessional and religious rhetoric in which he lived and worked. While he was capable of inverting the received dichotomies of antiquity and modernity,

Christian and Jew, Protestant and Catholic, he never envisioned a plane where such dualisms would become unnecessary or attacks based on them irrelevant.[223] Nietzsche was no multiculturalist, after all, but a man of the nineteenth century, driven to original positions and insights by his opposition to both the prevailing liberal culture and its nonliberal alternatives.

In this struggle, the chief target of Nietzsche's ire was less traditional religion than the Romantics' attempts to restore its symbols, myths, and emotional states. "Art raises its head where the religions are in decline," Nietzsche wrote in *Human, All Too Human.* "The growing Enlightenment undermined the dogmas of religion and instilled in them a basic mistrust; and so feeling, banished from the religious sphere by the Enlightenment, throws itself into art."[224] Romanticism, he argued, had breathed temporary life into the dying myths of Christianity not out of any sincere religious sentiment but purely for effect. In the end, the Romantic artist was not interested in establishing any religion outside the cult of his own "genius." Such hero worship could easily go to an artist's head, however, producing all sorts of irresponsibility and self-delusional behavior.[225]

In Richard Wagner, Romanticism had reached its apogee. He had participated in the Romantic "Catholicism of feeling" but linked it to the artificial Germanic mythology of the Grimm brothers.[226] "When the imagination of a nation declines," Nietzsche noted, "there arises in it the tendency to present its legends on the stage."[227] Indeed, Wagner was less interested in the "national" qualities of his art than in creating an audience for himself. Over his career, he moved from one intellectual movement to the next—French Romanticism, Feuerbach, revolution, Schopenhauer, Luther, the Kaiserreich—all according to the dictates of fashion and the needs of the moment.[228] In the end, Wagner believed in nothing but his own will to power. For that reason, he had welcomed the creation of a "Wagner cultus" in Bayreuth, which differed from previous such cults only in that its regnant deity was still alive.[229]

Given his current opposition to Wagnerism, Nietzsche was somewhat at a loss to explain his earlier enthusiasm for it. In 1878 he wrote, "I thought at the time that I had discovered in Wagner's art the path to a German paganism, or at least a bridge to a specifically un-Christian way of viewing the world and humans. 'The gods are evil and knowing, they deserve destruction. The human is good and dumb, he has a more beautiful future and will reach it only when the gods have finally gone into their twilight'—that is how I would have formulated my confession of faith at that time."[230] The statement strains credibility, given *The Birth of Tragedy*'s dependence on a Romantic discourse on myth that had close ties to Christian theology. It is true that this type of Romanticism squared only imperfectly with Nietzsche's philological

"Out of Modern Mythology: Wagner's Apotheosis in Bayreuth" (1876). From the
satirical magazine *Der Ulk* (1876).
Source: Herbert Barth, Dietrich Mack, and Egon Voss, eds., *Wagner: A Documentary
Study* (New York: Oxford University Press, 1975).

training, and it was a sign of his devotion to Wagner that he had adopted it in
the first place. Yet it is clear that he took the aesthetic-religious dimension
of this work seriously, presenting mythic appearance as the necessary condition for cultural life in any future Germany. Eventually his intellectual development, combined with a series of personal slights, would undo the alliance with Wagner. But Nietzsche would emerge not just as a critic of Wagner

but also as a rival, who sought to create a sacred narrative that would overcome that of Bayreuth. The result of that competition would be *Thus Spake
Zarathustra.*

POST-ROMANTIC EPIC: *THUS SPAKE ZARATHUSTRA*

For Nietzsche, it seemed obvious that the intelligent people of his generation
had abandoned Christianity and that the rest of the educated middle classes
possessed only a moderate, surrogate Christianity. This "simplified" Christianity did not consist, as the Aufklärer had predicted, in the rational postulates of God, freedom, and immortality, but rather in a "mild moralism" and
a generally "upright disposition."[231] Protestants, in particular, tended to
gravitate toward a stance that was neither friendly nor hostile, merely indifferent. "They are no enemies of religious practices: if participation in such
practices is required in certain cases, perhaps on the part of the state, they do
what is demanded, as one does so much else—with a patient and modest seriousness and without much curiosity or discomfort—they live too much
apart or outside to think it necessary to come to a definite for or against in
these things."[232] Yet such indifference could hardly be characterized as religious belief, Nietzsche argued. Rather, it represented the *"euthanasia* of
Christianity."[233]

Nietzsche expressed the same idea more lyrically in the famous passage
from *The Gay Science* (1882), in which a madman runs into a village square
declaring, "God is dead." "How do we console ourselves, the murderers of all
murderers? The holiest and most powerful thing that the world has hereto-
fore possessed has bled to death under our knives. With what water can we
clean ourselves? What ceremony of atonement, which holy games will we invent? Isn't the greatness of this deed too great for us? Must we not become
gods to appear worthy of it?"[234] A great historical event had occurred, but no
one seemed to have noticed. The purpose of philosophy, Nietzsche suggested,
was to explore the ramifications of this event—for ethics, for art, for "religion" itself—for those who understood it. He would attempt to do this in the
form of a philosophical epic, *Thus Spake Zarathustra: A Book for Everyone
and No One* (1883–85).

By the time he began writing *Zarathustra*, medical difficulties had forced
Nietzsche to give up teaching in Basel and adopt a peripatetic existence,
moving from town to town in Italy, Germany, and Switzerland. These circumstances may have drawn him to the Persian prophet Zarathustra, who reportedly withdrew to the solitude of a mountain before bringing his doctrine
down to the people. In the third edition of his *Symbolik und Mythologie,*

Creuzer had described Zarathustra's doctrine as the earliest religion of the Aryan world, while Schopenhauer identified him as the source of the Jewish system of morality.[235] In general, however, knowledge of Zarathustra was rather sketchy. He lived around 1000 B.C. and had taught a dualistic religion, described in the *Zend-Avesta*, in which the forces of good and evil were radically opposed. In this sense, he stood in the Mosaic tradition of "hard legislators" rather than in the Hindu/Buddhist tradition of introspective teachers. Indeed, the style Nietzsche adopts throughout *Zarathustra* is self-consciously biblical, parodying verses and settings from both the Old and the New Testaments. By returning to the beginning of civilization, he hoped to overturn the fundamental errors of religion. But his true target was Romanticized religion, particularly as embodied in the work and person of Richard Wagner.

The book begins with the prophet Zarathustra, aged forty (Nietzsche was thirty-nine when the book was published), coming down from the mountains to deliver his gift to humanity. Passing through a forest, he is astounded to hear a hermit speak of his love for God. "Could it be possible!" Zarathustra asks himself. "This old saint has not yet heard in his forest that *God is dead!*"[236] He eventually arrives at the market square of a town, where he proclaims his new doctrine. "I teach you the Superman. Man is something to be overcome."[237] Rejecting the comforts of transcendence or resignation, Zarathustra suggests a mode of being that entails a radical critique of the existing world and yet remains tied to immanent processes of historical evolution. "[R]emain true to the earth, and do not believe those who speak to you of superterrestrial hopes!"[238]

Zarathustra attempts to win disciples for his new teaching, but his success as a prophet is mixed. He constantly chides his followers for their false hopes and their misunderstandings. At the same time he is racked with doubts about his own mission, and by the end of the third book he has abandoned his disciples altogether. Through this narrative, Nietzsche undermines the idealist claim that philosophy requires intuiting reality in terms of an Absolute. Zarathustra is instead oriented toward practical decisions and actions, and creativity and self-overcoming are his highest values. His cautious stance toward the world ensures that he will not become either the object of a religious cult (like Schopenhauer or Wagner) or a martyr to its prejudices (like Jesus). Indeed, he most resembles Moses, who tried to deliver his people from slavery and give them new laws, but who did so only reluctantly and with incomplete success.

Zarathustra is most comfortable in nature, especially among his animals, the eagle and the serpent. Here Nietzsche tapped into Persian mythology, available from a reading of Creuzer's *Symbolik und Mythologie,* according to which the eagle symbolized the god of light, Ormuzd, and the serpent or dragon symbolized the god of darkness, Ahriman. Mortal enemies in Zoroastrian myth, the friendly relations between eagle and serpent in *Zarathustra* suggest a standpoint beyond good and evil.[239] The prominence given these animals can also be seen as a play on the "chthonic turn" in myth scholarship, while repeated references to the sun as a living being evoked the solar mythology of Max Müller.[240] But Nietzsche was not seeking to reproduce the results of contemporary scholarship. The purpose of the animals was to give the book a certain mythological resonance while amplifying qualities within Zarathustra himself.

Nietzsche's use of animal symbolism also had the effect of destabilizing a timeless ideal of the "human." Since Winckelmann, German Philhellenism had assumed that the essence of humanity had been embodied in the beautiful forms of Greek sculpture. This assumption had been incorporated by the Grimms and especially by Wagner in their theories of myth. But the rise of evolutionary thought in biology and in anthropology had undermined the notion of an "eternally human" to which culture might return. At the beginning of history, Nietzsche wrote in *Daybreak,* stood not a Greek god but an ape.[241] In *Zarathustra,* the idea of the superman serves to deconstruct humanism from the direction of the future rather than the past. "What is the ape to men? A laughing-stock or a painful embarrassment. And just so shall man be to the Superman."[242] The human species was becoming ever more comfortable, ever uglier, and ever smaller, culminating in the being called the "Last Man." The Superman, by contrast, pointed beyond the present bourgeois dispensation, out to new seas and new dangers. For the present, however, only Zarathustra's animals could understand this doctrine, not present-day men.

Despite Nietzsche's reliance on evolutionary tropes, he conceived the achievement of the superman more as a matter of values than of biology. Before this new morality could be taught, it was necessary to "break the tablets" of the old morality. Zarathustra would slay the great dragon of "thou shalt," associated in particular with Moses' Ten Commandments, and replace it with the spirit of "I will" or simply the "sun will."[243] The resignation and weariness that created fables about gods and that longed for "afterworlds" and "redeeming drops of blood" would be rejected in favor of health, honesty, and creativity.[244] "If there were gods, how could I endure not to be a god! *Therefore* there are no gods! . . . [My] will lured me away from Gods and gods; for what would there be to create if gods—existed!"[245] Zarathustra offers no theological grounds for breaking with religion but justifies his decision in terms of its practical possibilities for life in the world.

In describing the obstacles to Zarathustra's philosophy, Nietzsche leveled a bitter attack against the "new idol," the state. The state was the "coldest of all cold monsters," which claimed to embody the nation *(Volk)* but instead consumed it in an endless human sacrifice.[246] This critique applied not only to the state as a political or bureaucratic entity but also to the entirety of modern urban society. Full of "superfluous" people, its life revolved around money, markets, newspapers, and the monarchy. It lacked any culture of its own but sought to hide this fact by stealing from the historical cultures of different ages and nations. Such criticisms echoed the younger Wagner, who had linked the bureaucratic state to an egotistic bourgeois society. In the meantime, however, most European states, including the Kaiserreich, had adopted universal suffrage, political parties, and other elements of mass democracy. "Once Spirit was God, then it became man, and now it is even becoming a mob," Zarathustra complains.[247] Nietzsche rejected any appeal to the *Volk* in either politics or aesthetics. "Free from the happiness of serfs, redeemed from gods and worship, fearless and fearful, great and solitary, that is how the will of the genuine man is."[248] For Zarathustra, true freedom entails not only a freedom from oppression but a freedom from events writ large.

The opposite of authentic existence is life in the marketplace, the home of "great actors" who seek glory and popularity. Though he goes unnamed in *Zarathustra*, the quintessential actor is Wagner, who feigned great passions but believed in nothing except his own will to power. "The actor possesses spirit but little conscience of the spirit. He always believes in that with which he most powerfully produces belief—produces belief in *himself!* Tomorrow he will have a new faith and the day after tomorrow a newer one. He has a quick perception, as the people have, and a capricious temperament. To overthrow—to him that means: to prove. To drive frantic—to him that means: to convince. And blood is to him the best of all arguments."[249] Far from escaping the market, Wagner had catered to it all too successfully. So instead of the grandiose spectacles like Bayreuth, Zarathustra proposes new, more intimate festivals: a festival of the friend, a festival of death.

The book reaches a climax as Zarathustra ascends a high mountain harassed by the "Spirit of Gravity," which takes the form of a dwarf rather similar to Siegfried's nemesis, Mime. On the path, Zarathustra has a vision of a new metaphysical doctrine: "eternal recurrence." Since the universe is infinitely old and infinitely young, all of its possibilities have already been played out and must play themselves out again an infinite number of times. Thus, everything recurs eternally. "This life, as you now live and have lived, you will have to live again and again an infinite number of times. There will be nothing new in it. Instead, every pain and every joy and every thought and sigh and every thing in your life, no matter how large or how small, must come to you again, and everything in the exact same sequence and succession."[250] Zarathustra is oppressed by this dark and gloomy "knowledge," which is symbolized by a snake that offers no apples but crawls inside the mouth of a man and bites his throat. The only way to free oneself is to bite off the snake's head. In this way, Zarathustra affirms eternal recurrence while overcoming his emotions of disgust and resignation with an affirmative "Yes!"

Having acquired this insight, Zarathustra returns to civilization and seeks to gather a group of men who will be his "chosen people [Volk]."[251] Inverting the language of Romantic nationalism, Zarathustra calls for "new origins" and "new nations." Those who long for the Superman will gather together in a nation, which will be based not on a "contract" but on an "experiment." They will look not toward the past of their fathers but toward the future of their children. "Come on, you old seaman-hearts! What of fatherland! Our helm wants to fare *away*, out to where our *children's land [Kinder-Land]* is! Out, away, more stormy than the sea, storms our great longing!"[252] Like Columbus, they will sail westward until they have reached their new homeland.

With *Zarathustra*, Nietzsche created a post-Romantic epic, which was designed to be not just a book of philosophy but a work of art. Adopting the guise of an ancient Persian, he overturned the fundamental categories of Wagnerian Romantic thought, including "history," the "nation," and the "human." In their stead, he offered a philosophy premised on solitude and "longing," while denying the possibility of redemption, community, or "mythology." Throughout the book, Nietzsche used a style more reminiscent of the Bible than of classical antiquity. Yet he did so while thoroughly rejecting God, dogma, and faith. Even Zarathustra's animals, the eagle and serpent, were released from their traditional function in the ancient liturgy, so that they became not just attributes but friends. They would accompany him on a journey without any clear destination, but that led far away from the comfortable shores of the present.

Zarathustra did not mark the end of Nietzsche's engagement with mythical thought. While he generally avoided the term "myth" in the works of his "middle" period, it appeared again in the writings of 1886–89, now understood as an illusion that, while seemingly timeless, was actually infinitely mutable. Nietzsche used this concept to undermine such Kantian philosophical categories as freedom of the will, causality, and the thing-in-itself, characterizing each as a "mythology" that had been imputed to the nature of things.[253] But there were other fictions that Nietzsche saw as necessary and useful for creative activity in the present. In describing them, he eschewed the metaphysically and culturally loaded word "myth" in favor of "appearance" *(Schein)*, "image" or "parable" *(Gleichnis)*, or simply "lie" *(Lüge)*, all terms that conveyed a sense of self-conscious metaphor rather than unconscious symbolism.

Meanwhile, after a prolonged absence, the god Dionysus returned. In *Beyond Good and Evil* (1886) he was identified as the "tempter god" who bore a teaching that was "new, strange, wonderful, uncanny." Nietzsche described himself as "the last disciple and initiate of the god Dionysus," who had sacrificed his firstborn to his cult.[254] In the last years before his breakdown and collapse, Nietzsche's identification with this deity became nearly absolute. In *Ecce Homo* (1888), he ascribed the teachings of Zarathustra to Dionysus, and he composed a series of "Dionysus-Dithyrambs" that culminated in a duet between the god and his mortal lover Ariadne. But it was the relationship of Dionysus to the "Crucified" that was of paramount importance. In the end, Nietzsche's Dionysus acquired his power not simply as a symbol of antimodernist irrationalism but rather as a complement and foil to the suffering redeemer of Christian belief.

That relationship was already apparent in *The Birth of Tragedy*. In this work, Nietzsche deployed a Romantic concept of myth in opposition to historicist trends in liberal theology, classical philology, and German bourgeois culture as a whole. Railing against attempts to replace a mythical "horizon" with the results of historical-critical research, he pointed back to the ancient Greek festival-tragedy, in which social and political divisions were overcome in a brief but powerful moment of unity. Yet Nietzsche's interpretation of antiquity broke from many of the assumptions of the early Romantics or even Wagner. Rather than treating ancient Greece as organically unified on the basis of a common mythology, he posited a dualism within Greek culture and the Greek psyche, symbolized in the opposition of Apollo and Dionysus. On this view, the turning point from antiquity to modernity coincided with the rise of Socratism, which caused tragic drama to degenerate into an optimistic and purely popular spectacle. Paradoxically, this scheme actually allowed Nietzsche to emphasize the Christian, even Protestant, dimensions of the Dionysian. The current optimistic era would end only when philosophy returned to the pessimistic foundations of art, a development that was heralded by Schopenhauer's philosophy and the Wagnerian music drama.

The Birth of Tragedy was just one of a series of proposals in postunifica-tion Germany for a reform of aesthetic and religious culture along national-ist lines. In the context of the Franco-Prussian War and an emerging *Kul-turkampf*, Strauss, Lagarde, and Hartmann had all suggested "new faiths" that were designed to replace Christianity with a religion more "suitable" to modern German Protestant culture. Nietzsche, too, affirmed the "Protes-tant" nature of Wagnerian mythology, although this squared uneasily with the medieval subject matter of operas like *Tannhäuser* and *Lohengrin*. More-over, the Romanticism of *The Birth of Tragedy* ran contrary to the main cur-rents of literature and scholarship in Germany, not to mention his own philo-logical training. Just two years prior Rudolf Haym had noted that "what is called 'Romantic' enjoys no favor in contemporary consciousness."[255]

After the breakdown of his relationship with Richard Wagner, Nietz-sche's engagement with the scholarship of Tylor, Mannhardt, and Boetticher, as well as Darwin's theory of evolution, provided him with a set of concep-tual tools that he used to distance himself from the thought world of *The Birth of Tragedy*. While the proximate target of *Human, All Too Human*, *Daybreak*, and *The Gay Science* was Wagner, Nietzsche also managed in these works to arrive at a fundamentally new understanding of religion. Re-jecting the Romantic emphasis on interiority, belief, and emotion, he privi-leged the exterior, the ritual, and the practical, in the process inverting tradi-tional Protestant critiques of Catholicism and Judaism. He came to see in the transition from Judaism to Christianity, and from Catholicism to Protes-tantism, not Luther's "freedom of a Christian," but rather a denial of the body that enslaved the spirit. In this way, Nietzsche undermined the historical nar-ratives that had provided the foundation for not only the Protestantenverein but also the post-Christian variants of Protestantism offered by Strauss, Hartmann, and Wagner.

The emphasis here on the religious and, indeed, specifically Christian contexts of Nietzsche's thought challenges both modern and postmodern in-terpretations that treat him primarily as a proponent of secularization, un-masking, or the "hermeneutics of suspicion." To be sure, Nietzsche was a fierce critic of religion, and he sought to carry forth the Straussian project of demythologization into the seemingly secular realms of art, science, and phi-losophy. Yet he was also discomfited by the spread of religious "indifference" among the educated classes of his generation, especially insofar as religious faith was simply replaced by a narrow concern with profit and pleasure. His critique of Wagner and the Romantics therefore focused not on their reli-giosity per se but rather on what he saw as their cynical attempt to revive the decaying images of religion purely for aesthetic effect. Nietzsche's polemic fell well short as a historical explanation of Romanticism, for it ignored the degree to which these intellectuals saw themselves not simply as encroaching on but also advancing Christianity or, at the very least, Protestantism through their art and scholarship. But this critique does point to a key facet of Nietzsche's thought: his determination to generate an entirely new set of images, which would not simply fulfill existing religious "instincts" but would in fact fundamentally transform those instincts, giving rise to a new kind of human life.

These efforts culminated in *Zarathustra*, which was intended as both critique of and competition for *Parsifal*. Here Nietzsche sought to invert the basic categories of Romanticism, including "history," the "nation," "language," and the "human." As Foucault and other commentators have noted, these were also some of the basic categories of the human sciences as they had emerged at the end of the eighteenth century. In this respect, Nietzsche's "death of God" could be seen as signifying the "death of man."[256] But this interpretation understates the degree to which for Nietzsche the destruction of God was not merely preparatory but in many respects constitutive of humanism's demise. Schelling, Hegel, Strauss, and the younger Wagner had identified Christianity, in particular, with the idea of "Providence," that is, history as a meaningful process that contained within it the means for its own resolution (whether through idealist philosophy or absolute music). The loss of any concept of "incarnation," whether in the form of the individual, the nation, or the human race, meant that there was no longer any connection between "man" and a universal "idea" or "God."

The simultaneous demise of these intellectual categories in the text of Nietzsche's later philosophy points to the degree to which narratives of national liberation, historicism, humanism, and Christianity had become intertwined over the course of the nineteenth century. For many intellectuals, the foundation of the Kaiserreich in 1871 demonstrated the triumph of these ideals, while dissidents like Wagner viewed the new state as a betrayal and sought to cultivate an "alternative" Germany. In Nietzsche's case, however, alienation from both Berlin and Bayreuth confirmed his suspicion that the Romantic ideals themselves were oppressive. In his view, liberation could be accomplished only once they were cast aside or exposed as illusions. Nonetheless, he retained important aspects of Romanticism even in his later thought: the belief in the heroic individual; the necessity of aesthetic appearance as the basis for human life; and, finally, a notion of longing as the fundamental condition of existence. In this respect, Nietzsche was not just the Romantics' harshest critic but also their most devoted disciple.

EPILOGUE

Whither does this mighty longing draw us? This longing that is
worth more to us than any pleasure? Why just in this direction,
thither where all the suns of humanity have hitherto *gone down?*
Will it perhaps be said of us one day that we, too, *steering westward*,
hoped to reach an India—but that it was our fate to be wrecked
against infinity? Or, my brothers? Or?

Nietzsche, Daybreak

By any standard, the two decades after 1890 were a period of religious
ferment in Germany, especially among Protestants.[1] Dozens of new religious organizations, representing the widest variety of beliefs and philosophies, came into being during these years, each catering to what contemporaries perceived as a "spiritual crisis."[2] Church attendance among the Protestant urban middle classes and working classes continued to decline (although at a slower rate than in the period 1850–80), a trend that was all the more striking given the relatively high rates of participation among Catholics.[3] But after two decades of liberal and anticlerical *Kulturkampf*, religion possessed considerable appeal for those educated elites who were alienated from a liberalism that seemed exhausted but who were wary of the scientism and apparent atheism of the Social Democrats.[4] Instead of returning to their old churches, however, these individuals flocked to a series of new religious associations, organizations, and movements.

These groups ranged across the theological and political spectrum. The "Free Religious Communities" continued to promote a religion that was based solely in natural science, while encouraging their members to formally leave the established churches. Branching away from this movement, Ernst Haeckel founded his own "Monist League" in 1906, which was dedicated to a pantheist worldview based in evolutionary biology.[5] Theosophy, which promised communication with the spirits of dead Indian mystics, was brought to Germany by followers of Madame Blavatsky and transformed by Rudolf Steiner into the new movement of Anthroposophy. But while these associations grounded their religiosity in science or the occult, the revival of a specifically "Germanic" religiosity formed the basis for many of the groups attached to the *völkische Bewegung* (folkish movement).

The *völkisch* movement arose between 1890 and 1920 as a loose collection of some one hundred different organizations, all of which were inspired by a mystical-racial notion of the German *Volk.*[6] It was part of a broader movement of *Lebensreform*, which sought alternatives to the seeming materialism of modern life by promoting vegetarianism, natural healing, antivivisectionism, and nudism. The *völkisch* movement combined these impulses with a profound anti-Semitism, which was drawn from foreign sources like the Austrian pan-Germanist Georg von Schönerer and home-grown thinkers like Richard Wagner and Paul Lagarde. The Jews were blamed for the ills of modern society, including both industrialization and socialism. The only way out of this situation, *völkisch* writers argued, was through a "regeneration" of the German nation.

One of the most influential statements of the *völkisch* ideology was put forth by the Englishman-turned-German Houston Stewart Chamberlain, who drew heavily on early-nineteenth-century conceptions of myth even as he bent them to his own ends. Chamberlain was a fanatical disciple of Richard Wagner, enough so that he married Wagner's daughter Eva, but he sought to place Wagner's racial theory more in line with eugenics and contemporary social Darwinism.[7] In his *Grundlagen des neunzehnten Jahrhunderts* (1899), Chamberlain presented the entire progress of civilization as the work of the Aryan race, which was in eternal struggle with the "non-German" races, especially the Semites. Taking his cue from Ernest Renan, Chamberlain described the Semitic races as incapable of grasping the mystery at the heart of true religion, which explained why they had no mythology, only historical chronicles.[8] The Aryans, by contrast, expressed their religious beliefs in myth and thereby anticipated many of the key doctrines of the Christian religion, including the Virgin Birth and the Trinity. The Christian religion was an uncertain amalgamation of these two traditions, but there was little doubt in Chamberlain's mind that Jesus was a blond-haired, blue-eyed Aryan. Jesus' doctrine of "redemption," when purified of all Jewish and Roman influences and molded into a principle of action, would be the basis for a new "Aryan" Christianity.

The decades after 1890 witnessed the emergence of literally dozens of organizations dedicated to the creation of an authentic "German" religion.[9] These took a variety of names, many of which evoked the world of Nordic paganism (Werdandi-Bund, Wodanbund, Urda-Bund), and they engaged in endless internecine squabbles, which led to frequent splintering along grounds of ideology and personality. In general, however, these groups can be divided into two broad types: those that sought to maintain a connection to Christianity and those that demanded outright paganism. The former group included those who took their inspiration from the later Wagner, Chamberlain, and other exponents of a Germanized Christianity. In general, they insisted on a heroic Aryan Christ and a heroic Aryan Luther, while they denied any connection between the Old Testament and "authentic" Christianity. By 1903, the core of what would emerge in the Third Reich as the Deutsche Christen (German Christians) had begun to hold religious services at the Hermann monument in the Teutoburg Forest.[10]

Another set of *völkisch* groups demanded a religion based entirely on "Germanic" sources, such as the *Eddas*. In works like Josef Weber's *Allvater (Wodan) oder Jehova?* (1906) and Otto Reuter's *Sigfried oder Christus?* (1911), the neopagans established a stark opposition between a heroic Germanic religion and a weak-willed Christianity. "The Nazarener wants us to win victory through suffering and patience, through peace," Reuter wrote. "OUR Religion is that of the active warrior of light, through victory to peace. That is the word of Sigfried."[11] Interestingly, very few of the neopagans advocated worship of the Nordic gods themselves, professing allegiance instead to a "spirit of nature" or a "Nordic soul." The sentiments that united them were a fundamental hostility to Christianity and the demand for a more "manly" worldview.

In the search for a "manly" religion, many fin de siècle writers turned to the work of Nietzsche. As Steven Aschheim has shown, these included not only neopagans but also Protestants who sought a revitalized form of Christianity.[12] Albert Kalthoff, pastor of a "free-religious" congregation in Bremen, delivered a series of sermons, the *Zarathustra Sermons* (1904), in which he sought to replace Jesus with Nietzsche as the prophet of a true, that is, Marxist Christianity. Ernst Bertram, an associate of the poet Stefan George, fashioned Nietzsche into a prophet of "Nordic Christianity," whose key texts included the *Eddas*, *Zarathustra*, and the works of Martin Luther and the German Romantics. As in the case of Schiller and Goethe, Nietzsche's posthumous prestige was such that he became a reference point for the most varied and contradictory impulses.

As the reception of Nietzsche demonstrates, the new religiosity of the fin de siècle period was not exclusively the province of the right. Expressionist artists like Vassily Kandinsky and Franz Marc described their paintings using the language of religion or symbolism, and the poet Hugo von Hofmannsthal attempted to revive the mystery play tradition with his *Jedermann* (1911).[13] The so-called Neue Gemeinschaft, founded in 1900, united a number of writers, many of Jewish origin, who eventually became active in anarchist or socialist causes. These included Martin Buber, Gustav Landauer, and Erich Mühsam. The avowed goal of the Neue Gemeinschaft was the discovery of a "new religion."[14] Members wandered out into the forest to celebrate "festivals of consecration" and Dionysian mysteries, and they associated with artists and writers from the *völkisch* movement, suggesting the free flow between the political "left" and "right" in these groups. Within the Neue Gemeinschaft, Landauer was especially interested in the idea of a new mythology, which he saw as crucial to the project of creating a nation based on socialist principles. "A new era is awakening out of decadence and restful privation: it is there that myth emerges, *and only where myth emerges will a new Volk come into being.*"[15] This close connection between myth and the *Volk* recalled the early "humanist" Wagner, and Landauer indeed revered the composer as the quintessential embodiment of Romantic "longing."

Given the short-lived and constantly shifting nature of these groups, it is difficult to speak of them as "religions." Max Weber, commenting from his university chair in Heidelberg, proclaimed, "No matter how much the appearance of a widespread religious interest may be stimulated, no religion has ever resulted from the needs of intellectuals or their chatter. The whirligig of fashion will presently remove this subject of conversation and journalism, which fashion has made popular."[16] But Weber was only half right, for although it is true that these groups expressed more "religiosity" than religion, they represented far more than a passing fad.[17] Like the early Romantics, these organizations expressed a felt need for a new religious feeling and imagery, which would overcome the fragmentation of the contemporary world while superseding existing ecclesiastical traditions. Unlike the Romantics or even Wagner, few fin de siècle intellectuals saw this religion as arising from within Christian modernity, a factor that led many of them toward outright paganism as opposed to a Christian-Germanic hybrid.

In another contrast with their Romantic forebears, most members of these new religious associations shared a distinct distrust of academia, which they associated with dry-as-dust scholarship and seemingly useless knowledge. Heinrich Schliemann's claim in 1874 to have discovered the Homeric city of Troy had fascinated the public but was greeted with skepticism by philologists reluctant to see Wolf's *Prolegomena* turned on its head.[18] By 1890, in fact, classical philology had come under intense pressure to make itself more relevant to the modern German nation.[19] But scholars like Wilamowitz, by now chair of classical philology at the University of Berlin, shied away from the "darker," Dionysian side of antiquity that so fascinated Gustav Landauer and the poet Stefan George. Instead, most philologists remained tied to the themes and methods of the mid–nineteenth century.

The dominance of classical philology in German academic and cultural life was increasingly challenged by other disciplines. German *Vorgeschichte* (prehistory), long an academic stepchild, began to acquire a certain degree of scholarly prestige during these years.[20] The leading researcher in this field was Gustav Kossina, who rallied the local *Altertumsvereine* to his cause from his chair in Berlin. But Kossina, like many in this field, carried a large chip on his shoulder, which was reflected in his claim that the German race had originated from the north. That thesis contradicted the Aryan theory favored by linguists and comparative mythologists (but with no apparent gain in judiciousness or sanity).[21] In contrast to *Vorgeschichte,* the field of Old Testament studies was eminently respectable; yet here, too, an anti-Jewish strain was evident. Already in the 1880s, Julius Wellhausen had argued (much like de Wette) that the earliest Hebrews had practiced a simple form of monotheism, and that the law and the priesthood emerged in the post-exilic era.[22] By the 1890s, the expansion of German archaeology deep into the Ottoman Empire had opened up the worlds of ancient Babylonia and Mesopotamia for researchers. In his 1902 lecture "Babel und die Bibel," the theologian Franz Delitzsch used these findings to argue for the Babylonian origins of such quintessentially Old Testament concepts as "God," "sin," "Sabbath," and "paradise."[23] The scholarly content of Delitzsch's lecture was less problematic than the evident *Schadenfreude* it evoked in Kaiser Wilhelm II and in those *völkisch* writers who sought to discredit the Hebrew Bible.

The outbreak of World War I led to a coarsening and hardening of intellectual life, as German writers ridiculed the "shopkeeper" mentality of the British, and Western writers blamed the war on the philosophies of Wagner and, especially, Nietzsche. It was true that some soldiers went off to war with *Zarathustra* in their knapsacks, although this was no more than a tiny minority of university students—recruits were far more likely to bring the Bible. In his *Betrachtungen eines Unpolitischen* (1918) Thomas Mann took special pains to defend the legacies of Nietzsche and Wagner from the attacks of the British and French. Strikingly, however, Mann had little to say about their mythological doctrines, preferring to see them as exponents of a kind of aesthetic conservatism. Thus, even as he defended Romantic culture from outside attacks, Mann sought to remove it from the grasp of neopagan nationalists.

This, as it turned out, would be only the first in a long series of conflicts between Mann and various ideologues of *völkisch* nationalism. Germany's defeat in World War I (blamed by the General Staff on a Nibelungen-style "stab in the back"), combined with the threat of Communist revolution, a harsh peace at Versailles, and general economic chaos, prepared the ground for a surge of right-wing nationalism in the 1920s. During these years, Mann engaged in a notable dispute with Alfred Baeumler, one of the most articulate spokesmen of the new nationalism, over the exact nature of the Romantic mythological heritage.[24] In a masterful introduction to Bachofen's works, Baeumler had surveyed the history of mythological thought in Germany from Winckelmann to Nietzsche.[25] Baeumler maintained that the authentic "Romantic" view of *Mythos* reflected a sense of the "deep" *(Tiefe)*, the "primitive" *(Urzeit)*, the "religious," and what he called the "deepest foundations of the human soil," all of which were intimately tied to notions of blood and tradition.[26] As a result, Baeumler dismissed the early Romantics as too enlightened and instead championed Joseph Görres and, of course, Bachofen. With Baeumler it is possible at last to speak of a genuine irrationalism, in which myth became the opposite of reason, progress, and individuality.[27]

In his numerous responses to Baeumler, Thomas Mann promoted Nietzsche's notion of myth as an aesthetic illusion that masked the pessimism and despair of existence. In these debates Mann developed the argument, referred to at the outset of this book, that German culture had a natural proclivity for myth that distanced it from the English and French traditions of social realism. This was a polemical position, of course, since it ignored a long tradition of German social novels (including those by his brother Heinrich), as well as the degree to which the discourse on myth had begun to influence non-German literature and scholarship. But Mann felt that a vital tradition of nineteenth-century German culture was at stake in his debate with Baeumler, and he refused to simply cede the ground of "myth" to the irrationalists.[28] In the short run, however, the course of this argument would be dictated not by rhetoric or logic but by the onset of economic depression and by Adolf Hitler's talent for exploiting the fears and resentments of the German populace.

Aside from an affirmation of the "Führer" principle and a pathological anti-Semitism, there was no single National Socialist policy toward issues of religion, art, or mythology. But some insight into how the Nazis exploited earlier traditions of mythological thought can be gained through an examination of Alfred Rosenberg's *Der Mythus des zwanzigsten Jahrhunderts* (1930).[29] Rosenberg was born in Estonia and studied architecture in Moscow at the height of the Russian Revolution. After the war, he came to Munich, where he quickly became active in *völkisch* causes. He was an early member of the Nazi party, and his ideas about the connections between Judaism and Bolshevism exercised a considerable influence on Hitler's *Mein Kampf* (1925). In *Der Mythus des zwanzigsten Jahrhunderts*, Rosenberg attempted a comprehensive statement of the Nazi worldview, which would serve as a twentieth-century update of Chamberlain's *Grundlagen des neunzehnten Jahrhunderts*. But while Rosenberg borrowed many themes from the *Grundlagen*, including its portrayal of world history as a conflict between the Nordic and the Semitic races, his thinking was both more pagan and more political than Chamberlain's.

The great tragedy of the current generation, Rosenberg asserted, was that it lived in a "mythless" time. In deepest antiquity, the Nordic peoples had been animated by the myths of Ahura-Mazda, Zeus, and Odin, which were all manifestations of the Nordic (i.e., Aryan) "race-soul" and its heroic will. From the beginning, however, the Nordic myth was opposed by the Jewish myth of the "Chosen," which led the Jews to deny the greatness of the Nordic race through their own parasitical striving for world dominion. For Rosenberg all of history consisted of a conflict between these two opposing forces. In this way, Manfred Frank notes, Rosenberg overturned nineteenth-century conceptions of progress and replaced them with an image of perpetual struggle.[30] With his emphasis on the force of the will, Rosenberg clearly borrowed from Nietzsche's notion of the "will to power." But Nietzsche had envisioned struggle as involving one individual against multiple antagonists, not a duel between nations or races.

What was required, Rosenberg argued, was a "new myth" *(Mythus)* that would be at the same time the "old myth" stripped of its ancient trappings. This new myth would consist of the values of honor, will, and discipline, and its victory would propel the German people toward a new era of heroic "activity." Here Rosenberg abandoned the terrain of the Romantics, who strove to intuit an unseen Absolute, or even Baeumler, who had emphasized the dark, chthonic aspects of myth *(Mythos)*. Instead, he embraced a Sorelian or classically fascist concept of myth, whose purpose was simply to inspire political action. But Rosenberg still wanted to see his Nordic myth housed in a church. "The longing to give the Nordic race soul its form as a German church under the sign of the *Volksmythos*, that is for me the greatest task of our century."[31] As Rosenberg envisioned it, this church would maintain the outward trappings of Christianity, with more tradition-minded congregants celebrating those elements of the liturgy that were of "Germanic" origin. The true believers, however, would maintain a purely racial religion. Indeed, Rosenberg would be active throughout the 1920s and the 1930s in the German Faith movement, which sought to establish just such a post-Christian paganism in Germany.

Contrary to Rosenberg's expectations, the Nazi seizure of power in 1933 did not lead to the introduction of a state-sanctified paganism. Instead, Hitler supported the efforts of the Deutsche Christen to take over the Protestant churches, although even here he backed off in the face of criticism by mainstream pastors.[32] The Catholic Church was allowed to continue its religious operations, while the Nazis took over its social associations and charities. The fortunes of Rosenberg's German Faith movement rose and fell according to the politics of the moment, but in general this group remained at the extreme margins of German society. There were some officials, notably SS-Chief Heinrich Himmler, who were fascinated by Germanic antiquity and who sought to promote research into Ariosophy, runes, *Hunengräber*, and the like. Hitler, however, had little but contempt for such enterprises, declaring in 1938 that "the infiltration of mythically inclined researchers of the occult hereafter into the party cannot . . . be tolerated."[33]

Hitler, of course, was a devotee of Wagner. Indeed, during the early 1920s he had become a regular visitor to the Wagner family home in Bayreuth, now occupied by Wagner's son Siegfried and his wife, Winifred, who—like Houston Stewart Chamberlain—had arrived from England to take up the role of right-wing German nationalist. In scenes bizarrely reminiscent of Nietzsche's visits to Tribschen, Hitler became a friend of the Wagner children, tucking them in at night and allowing them to call him by his nickname "Wolf."[34] After his accession to power, Hitler tried to impose his taste for Wagner on the party rank and file, who squirmed and fidgeted their way through performances of *Lohengrin* and *Die Meistersinger von Nürnberg.* But despite Hitler's enthusiastic support for Bayreuth, neither Wagner nor Wagnerism ever became an official state ideology.[35] There were other efforts to create a national cult through art, the most ambitious being the *Thing-Spiele*—massive dramas designed for thousands of participants and spectators that were meant to evoke the tribal gatherings of pagan Germany. A typical production portrayed an allegorical "Germany" oppressed by its enemies before achieving final victory.[36] The *Thing-Spiele* attracted considerable excitement at the beginning of the Third Reich, but after a few years this movement faded into well-deserved oblivion. Finally, of course, there were the numerous party rallies, the remembrances of war dead, the "national moments," the Hitler salute, and the omnipresent swastika, which once upon a time had been an Indian symbol of life.

Surveying these varied movements—many in fundamental conflict with each other—it becomes difficult to speak of a "political religion" of National

Socialism, as some historians have tried to do.[37] On the other hand, if we borrow from Ian Kershaw's functionalist model of the Third Reich, it is possible to see each of these groups as "working toward the Führer" or, in this case, toward a vision of German religiosity that Hitler's dictatorship seemed to demand.[38] There was little question that any form of Nazi religiosity would include among its fundamental premises a veneration of the Aryan race and a pathological hostility to Jews, Communists, and the racially and morally "unfit." Within the nineteenth-century mythological tradition, the Nazis found a number of tropes and images that were particularly advantageous for expressing this racial ideology. These included the premise that all art and religion should be "national," the affirmation (particularly strong in Wagner) of strength, honor, and decisiveness as the most important qualities of a hero, and a close link between religion, aesthetics, and race or "blood." When deployed in combination with older forms of Christian anti-Semitism, appeals to defend the German Fatherland, and the scientific language of contemporary eugenics, these images served to reinforce the notion of a "racial community" and to promote acquiescence and even participation in the murderous plans of the Nazi elites. Mythological thought, it must be emphasized, did not create National Socialism or anti-Semitism, nor did it ensure their victory in 1933—here the factors of war, economic blight, and fear of Bolshevism played the dominant role—but in its Wagnerian or *völkisch* guise myth offered a way of thinking about art, religion, and the nation that was particularly suited to the political fantasies of Hitler and the racist policies of the Nazi state.

The Third Reich did not close the era of mythical thought, however. In fact, a vigorous debate raged throughout the war, if not in Germany itself, then among German-speaking exiles. In particular, Max Horkheimer and Theodor Adorno insisted in *Dialectic of Enlightenment* (1944) on what they saw as the "mutual implication of myth and enlightenment."[39] Rather than treating archaic Greece as purely naïve, Horkheimer and Adorno argued that the formation of Homer's Olympian gods launched a process of abstracting from nature that would become characteristic of "bourgeois science." "Mythology itself set off the unending process of enlightenment in which ever and again, with the inevitability of necessity, every specific theoretic view succumbs to the destructive criticism that it is only a belief—until even the very notions of spirit, of truth and, indeed, enlightenment itself, have become animistic magic."[40] By linking myth and enlightenment in this way, Horkheimer and Adorno hoped to show how the rationalistic society of the nineteenth century had produced the "nihilism" and anti-Semitism of the twentieth century. In doing so, they helped lay the groundwork for a wide-ranging discussion in postwar Germany about the role and function of myth, a debate whose ramifications are still felt today.[41]

Horkheimer and Adorno's engagement with a version of the "Homer question" is one more indication that the roots of myth discourse lie in the problems and assumptions of eighteenth-century neohumanism. The belief that ancient Greece represented a universal norm for European culture and that its art and philosophy were uniquely in touch with the fundamental qualities that defined the "human" was so widely accepted among the intellectual classes in Germany that scholars have only recently begun to treat it as a contingent, historically conditioned phenomenon. There were, to be sure, competing humanist traditions in France, Italy, Great Britain, and the Netherlands, but none of them focused so single-mindedly on the ancient Greeks or acquired such influence over the institutions of education and scholarship as German Philhellenism. Classical philology, with its devotion to language, literature, and the aesthetic and its historicist assumptions about the unity and integrity of ancient Greek culture, established a model for the historical understanding of cultures that would be taken up within other disciplines, including Germanic philology, comparative mythology, and folk psychology. In Germany, therefore, *Mythos* was not simply a Greek word but also implied a distinctly Greek melding of art, religion, and public life, which was notably absent from Christian modernity.

The neohumanists' unfavorable juxtaposition of Christianity to Greek antiquity reflected the significance of the discourse on myth as a religious, indeed *theological* phenomenon. The early Philhellenists, including Winckelmann, Goethe, and Moritz, were largely satisfied to cultivate a form of humanist aestheticism within the confines of literature or scholarship. They did not demand an immediate reckoning with Christianity and sought instead to preserve a space for artistic and moral autonomy free of the demands of civil society, the churches, and the absolutist state. In the wake of the French Revolution, however, the early Romantics Schelling and Friedrich Schlegel envisioned a new mythology that would supersede not only the classical gods but also the existing institutions of Christian modernity. By defining religion in terms of intuition, as opposed to dogma or ethics, they claimed religion for art (or an aesthetically inclined philosophy). From their perspective, the symbols and images of a new mythology offered the prospect of a rejuvenated and reunified public life, which would overcome the fragmentation and dislocation of a market-based civil society and provide the basis for a republican political life in a new "Germany" or "Europe."

While the call for a new mythology reflected the cultural ambitions of the early Romantics, its significance cannot be reduced to an expression of material interest or political ideology. For Schelling, in particular, the new mythology offered a radical solution to problems of revelation and positivity that had haunted Protestant theology since the early Aufklärung. As the impetus for the creation of a "new race" *(Geschlecht)*, the new symbolism would replace a biblical revelation that had little connection with the language, culture, and experience of modern Europeans and that relied on the authority of the established churches and the ignorance of the masses for its continued influence. But despite their rhetoric of a "new religion," the early Romantics insisted that any future aesthetic-religious system build on conceptions of freedom, reflection, and metaphysical idealism that had emerged within Christian modernity. Indeed, if there was a "legitimation crisis" on the eve of the nineteenth century, as Manfred Frank and others have suggested, then it was a crisis of both Enlightenment philosophy *and* Christian theology.[42] For this reason, the early Romantic project of a new mythology can be seen as "post-Christian" only insofar as this term implies a continuing engagement with the rhetoric, narratives, and categories of Christian thought. As articulated by Schelling, this cultural vision relied on a modification of the earlier Protestant biblical narrative, in which the figural connection between Old and New Testaments gave way to a quasi-historical scheme emphasizing the revolutionary nature of the shift from pagan antiquity to Christian modernity. But underlying both schemes was the assumption that Christianity had superseded all earlier religious cultures, even if Schelling lamented Christianity's "oriental" affinity for the infinite and called for a return of the divine to the soil of nature.

The argument developed in this book points to an important but often underappreciated feature of nineteenth-century intellectual history: the persistence of religious modes of thinking and perception within the allegedly secular institutions of art, literature, and scholarship. In recent years, historians have demonstrated the continued influence of confessional life and confessional conflict in modern Germany at the level of political and social history. It is now abundantly clear that the gradual decline in church or synagogue attendance after 1750 did not entail the disappearance of Protestant, Catholic, or Jewish identities. Instead, religious sentiment of various kinds continued to be expressed in newspapers, in associations, in political parties, and in large-scale pilgrimages. Yet this shift in perspective is only beginning to have an impact on the study of German intellectual history.[43] In particular, the search for normative forms of political liberalism or Marxism (or their

perceived opposites) has often obscured the degree to which German thought
continued to be shaped by the rhetoric, assumptions, and narratives of not
just "religion" but specifically Christian and/or Jewish theologies.

This was particularly the case among the Protestant educated middle
classes, where anticlericalism of the type found in France was weak and
where confessional identity required at least a token nod to Martin Luther
and his "German" Bible. Many Protestant intellectuals sought to maintain
the legitimacy of the Reformation even as they attempted to establish an
overarching religious identity for Germany, a stance that had the effect of ex-
acerbating confessional conflict between Protestants and Catholics and between Christians and Jews. Yet Protestant theological traditions were not
simply preserved but also transformed in the confrontation with nineteenth-
century modernity, as the history of mythical thought amply demonstrates.
Not only did scholars and artists grant theological significance to the study
of Greek, Germanic, and oriental cultures, but in many cases they called into
question the traditional Protestant claims to superiority over Catholicism.
Neither Schelling nor Creuzer (nor, for that matter, Novalis) denied the historical necessity of the Reformation, but it played such a minor role in their
religious schemes that they were able to form alliances with Catholics in
south Germany who shared their dissatisfaction with Enlightenment traditions of theology and politics. Unhappiness with this type of conservative
ecumenicism would inspire a reaction among liberal intellectuals like Heine
and the Grimms, who adopted a strident Protestantism in their writings of
the 1830s. Nor was the discipline of theology unaffected by this new discourse on myth. Strauss, of course, used a critical concept of myth to unravel
the gospel life of Jesus, but Weisse used a Romantic notion of myth to reconstruct this evangelical history, describing Christ as a higher-order genius and,
as the author of the parables, the creator of his own mythology. Nietzsche's
and Overbeck's combined efforts thirty years later to denounce Strauss's
"new faith" would demonstrate once again the close links between Roman-
ticist aesthetics and Protestant theology in the nineteenth century.

In the end, however, the understanding of religion in terms of "myth" created severe problems for the Christian religion in Germany. It is sometimes
forgotten that this formation was the result of a confluence of at least three
historical cultures: German, Greek, and Hebrew. Thus, it could retain its coherence only so long as these were seen to constitute a single viable tradition,
such as that offered in the traditional Christian biblical narrative. But as assumptions about national integrity began to harden, it became difficult for
the more extreme nationalists to imagine the biblical revelation, in particular, as anything but the product of a foreign culture. Moreover, the existence

of a viable Jewish intellectual culture in Germany further challenged the
ability of educated Protestant intellectuals to identify reflexively with the
patriarchs and prophets of the Old Testament or the fate of ancient Israel in
the same manner as their more conservative coreligionists, as well as their
counterparts in countries with smaller Jewish populations, such as Great
Britain or the United States.

One result of this state of affairs was a "postcolonial" reaction in the
writings of Herder, the Grimms, Heine, and many of their contemporaries.
The neohumanist image of the "mythical age" had been shaped in no small
part by European colonial counters with indigenous peoples in Africa and the
New World. Now the Christian Church was imagined as a colonizing power,
which had destroyed an indigenous Germanic paganism and replaced it with
a religion that was essentially "oriental" or "Roman." Jacob Grimm, in particular, cultivated a nostalgia for the lost pagan religion and nurtured a sense
of grievance against Roman Catholicism for having co-opted the authentic
religion and practices of the "folk." Such impulses were not confined to
the field of Germanic philology, however. Grimm's Göttingen colleague Karl
Otfried Müller criticized Creuzer's *Symbolik und Mythologie* precisely because it appeared to deny an indigenous religious tradition to the ancient
Greeks and, by implication, contemporary Germans. The key point here,
however, is that the "reverse supersessionism" (paganism to Christianity)
implied in Grimm's *Deutsche Mythologie* ensured that anti-Catholicism
and, increasingly, anti-Semitism were not matters simply of individual prejudice or hatred (although these factors also played a role) but instead structural features of the discourse on Germanic mythology. In the absence of an
obvious oppressor nation and with unity defined in terms of religion or culture, it became easier to blame such "internal" forces for the fragmentation
of German political and cultural life.[44]

The alternative to recovering the "lost" Germanic mythology was to envision an entirely new one, a project contemplated with varying degrees of
seriousness by the early Romantics, Wagner, and the early Nietzsche. Although highly critical of Christianity, these writers saw that religion as having given rise to a form of idealism (whether philosophical or musical) that
had created the conditions for a truly universal symbolism. The international dimensions of this project have led some commentators to treat it as a
useful antidote to a narrow nationalism, although the hoped-for European
communities often implied their own sets of boundaries and restrictions,
particularly in the case of Wagner. Indeed, differences of "nationalism" and
"cosmopolitanism" were rather less consequential in this context than has
often been argued, just as the dichotomy liberal/illiberal does little to capture

the essentially religious polarities at work in the thought of Grimm, Wagner, and Nietzsche.

Despite a number of continuities across the nineteenth century, there were also considerable differences in context and content between the early Romantics' call for a "new mythology" and subsequent phases of myth discourse. The *Frühromantik* project was conceived at the outset of bourgeois civil society, at a time when it was still possible to attach utopian hopes to an emerging nonecclesiastical public sphere. By the 1830s, however, a bourgeois public culture had emerged that was characterized, on the one hand, by a cult of past geniuses like Schiller and Beethoven and, on the other hand, by a journalistic devotion to the realities of contemporary social and political life. Richard Wagner envisioned a radical break from this public culture, which he identified with the monarchist state, a market economy, and "history" itself, and plunged instead into the supposedly subterranean world of German folklife. In doing so, however, he relied on a well-established canon of German mythological themes, while he proclaimed himself, in the language of his day, a "genius."

A third major turning point was the creation of the Kaiserreich itself. Hopes for cultural unity, which Nietzsche expressed in *The Birth of Tragedy*, quickly foundered on the reality of *Kulturkampf*, social strife, and power politics. While Wagner attempted to establish Bayreuth as an alternative capital of German culture, Nietzsche began to dismantle the Romantics' assumptions that the historical process was inherently meaningful and that cultures could be, or ever had been, integrated along national, religious, or racial lines. For all his criticism of Romanticism, however, Nietzsche shared its assumption that the problems and possibilities of modernity were rooted in its religious beliefs and practices, and that the task of the individual was creative self-overcoming and the production of beautiful, if ephemeral, images. In this sense, Nietzsche embodied both the critical and the creative potential of the Romantic discourse on myth, just as his *Zarathustra* was both commentary on and competition with the Wagnerian project of a national mythology.

The longing for myth was not an expression of political impotence or compensation for something not achieved in the realm of government or legislation. Instead, it reflected a concrete experience of a German society fragmented along confessional, social, and territorial lines, lacking a common national or religious tradition, and facing dislocation and disorientation brought on by the experience of political upheaval, economic transformation, and the rapid expansion of a market-driven culture. For intellectuals immersed in Philhellenist neohumanism the solution to this crisis seemed to lie in the creation of an aesthetic-religious imagery that would unite modern society just as Greek mythology had supposedly once united the polis. This vision of a society infused with myth was problematic not because it was apolitical or impotent—Bayreuth is sufficient testimony to its influence—but because it tended to harden already existing divisions of class, religion, and ethnicity. In doing so, the discourse on myth ignored not only the potential for human communities that crossed such lines but the very possibility of meaningful cultural transfer or translation from one epoch, nation, or "race" to another.[45] Heymann Steinthal's fruitless efforts to have the Hebrew Bible accepted into the canon of German bourgeois culture after the collapse of the Christian biblical narrative demonstrate precisely this problem. With precious few exceptions, the mythophiles of the nineteenth century denied the possibility of a cultural artifact that was both their own and not their own, that was both foreign and indigenous, and whose ethical immediacy resisted assimilation to a purely aesthetic intuition. Instead, they longed for "myth," swaying between memory of a past that never was and anticipation of a future that would never be.

⚜

NOTES

INTRODUCTION

1. Thomas Mann, *Pro and contra Wagner*, trans. Allan Blunden (London and Boston: Faber and Faber, 1985), 201.

2. Friedrich Schelling, *System of Transcendental Idealism (1800)*, trans. Peter Heath (Charlottesville: University of Virginia Press, 1978), 232–33.

3. Immanuel Kant, *Anthropology*, cited in Bernard Yack, *The Longing for Total Revolution: Philosophic Sources of Social Discontent from Rousseau to Marx to Nietzsche* (Princeton: Princeton University Press, 1986), 5.

4. On the idea of longing, see Susan Stewart, *On Longing: Narratives of the Miniature, the Gigantic, the Souvenir, the Collection* (Durham, N.C.: Duke University Press, 1993); Charles Maier, "The End of Longing? (Notes toward a History of Postwar German National Longing)," in *The Postwar Transformation of Germany: Democracy, Prosperity, and Nationhood*, ed. John S. Brady, Beverly Crawford, and Sarah Elise Wiliarty (Ann Arbor: University of Michigan Press, 1999), 271–85. In conjunction with "nostalgia," see Svetlana Boym, *The Future of Nostalgia* (New York: Basic Books, 2001); Peter Fritzsche, "Specters of History: On Nostalgia, Exile, and Modernity," *American Historical Review* 106 (2001): 1587–1618.

5. The English phrase "longing for myth" was used by George Mosse in *The Nationalization of the Masses: Political Symbolism and Mass Movements from the Napoleonic Wars through the Third Reich* (New York: Howard Fertig, 1975), 6.

6. See the positivist work of Fritz Strich, *Die Mythologie in der deutschen Literatur von Klopstock bis Wagner*, 2 vols. (Halle: Niemeyer, 1910), still unmatched as a reference work on this topic; also Alfred Baeumler, "Bachofen der Mythologe der Romantik," introduction to Johann Jakob Bachofen, *Der Mythus von Orient und Occident: Eine Metaphysik der alten Welt aus den Werken von J. J. Bachofen*, 2nd ed., ed. Manfred Schröter (Munich: Beck, 1926), xxiii–ccxciv, an erudite study by an extreme nationalist philosopher. For general studies, see Otto Gruppe, *Geschichte der Klassischen Mythologie und Religionsgeschichte während des Mittelalters im Abendland und während der Neuzeit* (Leipzig: Teubner, 1921); Richard Chase, *Quest for Myth* (Baton Rouge: Louisiana State University Press, 1949); Burton Feldman and

Robert D. Richardson, Jr., *The Rise of Modern Mythology, 1680–1860* (Bloomington: Indiana University Press, 1972); Axel Horstmann, "Der Mythosbegriff vom frühen Christentum bis zur Gegenwart," *Archiv für Begriffsgeschichte* 23 (1979): 7–54, 197–245; Christoph Jamme, *Einführung in die Philosophie des Mythos*, vol. 2, *Neuzeit und Gegenwart* (Darmstadt: Wissenschaftliche Buchgesellschaft, 1991).

7. Peter Viereck, *Metapolitics: From the Romantics to Hitler* (New York: Knopf, 1941); Georg Lukács, *The Destruction of Reason*, trans. Peter Palmer (Atlantic Highlands, N.J.: Humanities Press, 1981). While Viereck and Lukács say little about mythology per se, their heavy-handed criticism of Romanticism (esp. Schelling) set the tone for later studies. See, e.g., Martin Vogel, *Apollinisch und Dionysisch: Geschichte eines genialen Irrtums* (Regensburg: Gustav Bosse, 1966); and Mosse, *Nationalization*. A more nuanced approach focusing on key literary figures is offered by Henry Hatfield, *Aesthetic Paganism in German Literature from Winckelmann to the Death of Goethe* (Cambridge: Harvard University Press, 1964); Henry Hatfield, *Clashing Myths in German Literature from Heine to Rilke* (Cambridge: Harvard University Press, 1974).

8. Hans Blumenberg, *Work on Myth*, trans. Robert Wallace (Cambridge: MIT Press, 1985); Karl Heinz Bohrer, ed., *Mythos und Moderne: Begriff und Bild einer Rekonstruktion* (Frankfurt a.M.: Suhrkamp, 1983); Kurt Hübner, *Die Wahrheit des Mythos* (Munich: Beck, 1985). For a thoughtful survey of these debates, see Christoph Jamme, *"Gott an hat ein Gewand": Grenzen und Perspektiven philosophischer Mythos-Theorien der Gegenwart* (Frankfurt a.M.: Suhrkamp, 1991).

9. Manfred Frank, *Vorlesungen über die neue Mythologie*, vol. 1, *Der kommende Gott* (Frankfurt a.M.: Suhrkamp, 1982), vol. 2, *Gott im Exil* (Frankfurt a.M.: Suhrkamp, 1988).

10. See, e.g., Jochen Fried, *Die Symbolik des Realen: Über alte und neue Mythologie in der Frühromantik* (Munich: Fink, 1985); Andrew Bowie, *Aesthetics and Subjectivity: From Kant to Nietzsche* (Manchester: Manchester University Press, 1990); Markus Winkler, *Mythisches Denken zwischen Romantik und Realismus: Zur Erfahrung kultureller Fremdheit im Werk Heinrich Heines* (Tübingen: Niemeyer, 1995). See also in this vein, Maike Oergel, *The Return of King Arthur and the Nibelungen: National Myth in Nineteenth-Century English and German Literature* (Berlin: de Gruyter, 1998). Although it rightly links the rise of national mythology to developments in biblical criticism, Oergel's study is structured according to rather teleological categories and maintains (incorrectly, in my view) that the cultures of myth in Germany and England were roughly equivalent.

11. This is not true for the literature on Wagner, however. See esp. Marc Weiner, *Richard Wagner and the Anti-Semitic Imagination* (Lincoln: University of Nebraska Press, 1995); and esp. Wolf-Daniel Hartwich, *Deutsche Mythologie: Die Erfindung einer Kunstreligion* (Berlin: Piper, 2000), whose orientation is similar in many respects to mine.

12. A partial exception is Gerhart von Graevenitz's *Mythos: Geschichte einer Denkgewohnheit* (Stuttgart and Weimar: Metzler, 1987), a work inspired by Michel Foucault's type of "archaeology." Replying to Manfred Frank, Graevenitz attempts to show the deep roots of Romantic mythography in a patristic *Bildtheologie* (image theology). For Graevenitz, the Romantics were never interested in "myth" per se but

rather in a kind of idealized intuition that would counter the disorienting effects of modern journalism. Graevenitz's skepticism vis-à-vis the Romantic notion of myth is well founded. However, in focusing on a two-thousand-year-old episteme, Graevenitz tends to overlook the connections between the Romantics' mythical thought and specific political, theological, and scholarly developments of their day.

13. Here the phrase "discourse on myth" refers to a set of literary and scholarly practices that converged around the term "myth" and that transcended the boundaries of any single philosophical system or academic discipline.

14. *NKSA*, 8:531: "Poetic invention can become myth if it finds widespread belief: how fluctuating is the use and abuse of a word." Unless indicated otherwise in the notes, all translations are mine.

15. Mosse, *Nationalization*; Jürgen Link and Wulf Wülffing, eds., *Nationale Mythen und Symbole in der zweiten Hälfte des 19. Jahrhunderts* (Stuttgart: Klett-Cotta, 1991); Rudolf Speth, *Nation und Revolution: Politische Mythen im 19. Jahrhundert* (Opladen: Leske und Budrich, 2000).

16. Ivan Strenski, *Four Theories of Myth in Twentieth-Century History: Cassirer, Eliade, Lévi-Strauss, and Malinowski* (Iowa City: University of Iowa Press, 1987); Daniel Dubuisson, *Mythologies du XXe siècle* (Lille: Presses Universitaires de Lille, 1993); Robert Ellwood, *The Politics of Myth: A Study of C. G. Jung, Mircea Eliade, and Joseph Campbell* (Albany: State University of New York Press, 1999); Robert A. Segal, *Theorizing about Myth* (Amherst: University of Massachusetts Press, 1999); Bruce Lincoln, *Theorizing Myth: Narrative, Ideology, and Scholarship* (Chicago: University of Chicago Press, 1999); Andrew Von Hendy, *The Modern Construction of Myth* (Bloomington: Indiana University Press, 2002).

17. Strenski, *Four Theories of Myth*, 1–2.

18. Lincoln, *Theorizing Myth*, back cover.

19. See Edgar Quinet, "The State of Christianity in Germany," trans. in A[lexander] McCaul, *Thoughts on Rationalism, Revelation, and the Divine Authority of the Old Testament* (London: Seeleys, 1850), 75.

20. Marcel Detienne, *The Creation of Mythology*, trans. Margaret Cook (Chicago: University of Chicago Press, 1986); Lincoln, *Theorizing Myth*, 1–43.

21. Suzanne Marchand, *Down from Olympus: Archaeology and Philhellenism in Germany, 1750–1970* (Princeton: Princeton University Press, 1996), 7–16.

22. On this, see Hans Gerth, *Bürgerliche Intelligenz um 1800: Zur Soziologie des deutschen Frühliberalismus*, 2nd ed., Ulrich Hermann (Göttingen: Vandenhoeck und Ruprecht, 1976); Anthony La Vopa, *Grace, Talent, and Merit: Poor Students, Clerical Careers, and Professional Ideology in Eighteenth-Century Germany* (Cambridge: Cambridge University Press, 1988).

23. Hans-Ulrich Wehler, *Deutsche Gesellschaftsgeschichte*, 4 vols. (Munich: Beck, 1987 –), 1:210.

24. On these themes, see esp. Reinhart Koselleck, *Futures Past: On the Semantics of Historical Time*, trans. Keith Tribe (Cambridge: MIT Press, 1985).

25. See esp. the discussion in Heinz Gockel, *Mythos und Poesie: Zum Mythosbegriff in Aufklärung und Frühromantik* (Frankfurt a.M.: Klostermann, 1981), 58–87; also Frank Manuel, *The Eighteenth Century Confronts the Gods* (Cambridge:

Harvard University Press, 1959); Feldman and Richardson, *Rise of Modern Mythology;* Jamme, *Einführung,* 7–25.

26. In addition to Marchand, *Down from Olympus,* see also Josef Chytry's *The Aesthetic State: A Quest in Modern German Thought* (Berkeley and Los Angeles: University of California Press, 1989); and David S. Ferris, *Silent Urns: Romanticism, Hellenism, Modernity* (Stanford: Stanford University Press, 2000). None of these authors ignores the issue of religion entirely, but the connections to Christianity (and Judaism) remain largely peripheral to their concerns.

27. See esp. Hartmut Lehmann, ed., *Säkularisierung, Dechristianisierung, Rechristianisierung im neuzeitlichen Europa: Bilanz und Perspektiven der Forschung* (Göttingen: Vandenhoeck und Ruprecht, 1997); Hugh McLeod, *Secularisation in Western Europe, 1848–1914* (New York: St. Martin's, 2000).

28. Steve Bruce, ed., *Religion and Modernization: Sociologists and Historians Debate the Secularization Thesis* (New York: Oxford University Press, 1992); William H. Swatos, Jr., and Daniel V. A. Olson, eds., *The Secularization Debate* (Lanham, Md.: Rowman and Littlefield, 2000).

29. See esp. the essays in Helmut Walser Smith, ed., *Protestants, Catholics, and Jews in Germany, 1800–1914* (Oxford: Berg, 2001).

30. Anthony La Vopa, *Fichte: The Self and the Calling of Philosophy, 1762–1799* (Cambridge: Cambridge University Press, 2001), 13. See also the astute comment of Hans Erich Bödeker regarding the German Enlightenment: "The greatest challenge to the churches and the greatest danger for them lay in the fact that the Aufklärung, far from turning itself from religion, instead took up its questions and attempted to answer them itself in order achieve a new foundation for religion. This is the true problem of secularization"; "Die Religiosität der Gebildeten," in *Religionskritik und Religiosität in der deutschen Aufklärung,* ed. Karlfried Gründer and Karl Heinrich Rengstorf (Heidelberg: Lambert Schneider, 1989), 148.

31. Hans Frei, *The Eclipse of Biblical Narrative: A Study in Eighteenth and Nineteenth Century Hermeneutics* (New Haven: Yale University Press, 1974); on Frei, see John David Dawson, *Christian Figural Reading and the Fashioning of Identity* (Berkeley and Los Angeles: University of California Press, 2002), 141–85.

32. Frei, *Eclipse,* 224; cf. Karl Marx, "Contribution to the Critique of Hegel's Philosophy of Right," in *The Marx-Engels Reader,* 2nd ed., ed. Robert Tucker (New York: Norton, 1978), 53.

33. This identification was formative for American national identity. See Sacvan Bercovich, *The Puritan Origins of the American Self* (New Haven: Yale University Press, 1975).

34. In a fascinating study, Jeffrey S. Librett has also emphasized the importance of this figural interpretation for German intellectual history, but I depart in this book from what I see as his overly schematic (and successionist) notion of a "rhetorical wheel of German-Jewish misfortune." See *The Rhetoric of Cultural Dialogue: Jews and Germans from Moses Mendelssohn to Richard Wagner and Beyond* (Stanford: Stanford University Press, 2000).

35. Jürgen Habermas, *The Structural Transformation of the Public Sphere,* trans. Thomas Bürger with Frederick Lawrence (Cambridge: MIT Press, 1989); Lucian

Hölscher, *Öffentlichkeit und Geheimnis: Eine begriffsgeschichtliche Unter-*
suchung zur Entstehung der Öffentlichkeit in der frühen Neuzeit (Stuttgart: Klett-
Cotta, 1979); and Craig Calhoun, ed., *Habermas and the Public Sphere* (Cambridge:
MIT Press, 1992) are fundamental; see also Peter Uwe Hohendahl, *Building a*
National Literature: The Case of Germany, 1830–1870, trans. Renate Bacon Fran-
ciscono (Ithaca: Cornell University Press, 1989); and now Peter Uwe Hohendahl, ed.,
Öffentlichkeit: Geschichte eines kritischen Begriffs (Stuttgart: Metzler, 2000).

36. On the contrast between Humboldtian and Romantic notions of individuality, see Gerald N. Izenberg, *Impossible Individuality: Romanticism, Revolution, and*
the Origins of Modern Selfhood, 1787–1802 (Princeton: Princeton University Press,
1992), 18–53.

37. In their different ways, both Habermas, *Structural Transformation*, and
Mosse, *Nationalization*, treat liturgy as an atavism, inherently opposed to a genuine
"public sphere." For the "modernity" of ritual and liturgy, see Rudy Koshar, *From*
Monuments to Traces: Artifacts of German Memory, 1870–1990 (Berkeley and Los
Angeles: University of California Press, 2000).

38. There are useful comments on liturgy in Fried, *Symbolik des Realen*,
Hartwich, *Deutsche Mythologie*, and Renate Schlesier, *Kulte, Mythen, und*
Gelehrte: Anthropologie der Antike seit 1800 (Frankfurt a.M.: Fischer, 1994), but
these works do not examine the topic in connection with parallel concerns in Christian (or Jewish) culture during these years.

39. Edward Said, *Orientalism* (New York: Vintage, 1979).

40. Susannah Heschel, *Abraham Geiger and the Jewish Jesus* (Chicago: Univer-
sity of Chicago Press, 1998); Jonathan M. Hess, "Johann David Michaelis and the
Colonial Imaginary: Orientalism and the Emergence of Racial Antisemitism in
Eighteenth-Century Germany," *Jewish Social Studies* 6 (2000): 56–101; and now
Jonathan M. Hess, *Germans, Jews, and the Claims of Modernity* (New Haven: Yale
University Press, 2002).

41. Martin Bernal, *Black Athena: The Afroasiatic Roots of Classical Civiliza-*
tion, vol. 1, *The Fabrication of Ancient Greece, 1785–1985* (New Brunswick: Rutgers
University Press, 1987); see also the responses to this book in Mary R. Lefkowitz and
Guy MacLean Rogers, eds., *Black Athena Revisited* (Chapel Hill: University of
North Carolina Press, 1996); and most recently Martin Bernal, *Black Athena Writes*
Back: Martin Bernal Responds to His Critics, ed. David Chioni Moore (Durham,
N.C.: Duke University Press, 2001).

42. For recent research on the confessional division and its impact on cultural
history, see esp. Smith, *Protestants, Catholics, and Jews*; also Uriel Tal, *Christians*
and Jews in Germany: Religion, Politics, and Ideology in the Second Reich, 1870–
1914, trans. Noah Jacobs (Ithaca: Cornell University Press, 1975); Wolfgang Altgeld,
Katholizismus, Protestantismus, Judentum: Über religiös begründete Gegensätze
und nationalreligiöse Ideen in der Geschichte des deutschen Nationalismus (Mainz:
Matthias Grünewald, 1992); Helmut Walser Smith, *German Nationalism and Reli-*
gious Conflict: Culture, Ideology, Politics, 1870–1914 (Princeton: Princeton University Press, 1995). In emphasizing confessional "ambivalence" rather than simply
conflict, my interpretation departs in some respects from those of Tal, Altgeld, and
Smith.

43. The term "political religion" derives from Eric Voegelin's 1938 work *Political Religions*, trans. T. J. Di Napoli and E. S. Easterly III (Lewiston, N.Y.: E. Mellen Press, 1986), and has been taken up by a number of historians of modern Germany, most recently Michael Burleigh, *The Third Reich: A New History* (London: Hill and Wang, 2000).

44. For a strong critique of the notion of "political religion," see Altgeld, *Katholizismus, Protestantismus, Judentum*, 9–24; see also the comments of Friedrich Wilhelm Graf, "Die Nation—von Gott 'erfunden'? Kritische Randnotizen zum Theologiebedarf der historischen Nationalismusforschung," in *"Gott mit uns": Nation, Religion, und Gewalt im 19. und frühen 20. Jahrhundert*, ed. Gerd Krumeich and Hartmut Lehmann (Göttingen: Vandenhoeck und Ruprecht, 2000), 285–317.

45. For recent work on the nineteenth century, see esp. Alon Confino, *The Nation as a Local Metaphor: Württemberg, Imperial Germany, and National Memory, 1871–1918* (Chapel Hill: University of North Carolina Press, 1997); Rudy Koshar, *From Monuments to Traces*; Susan Crane, *Collecting and Historical Consciousness in Early Nineteenth-Century Germany* (Ithaca: Cornell University Press, 2000); Alon Confino and Peter Fritzsche, eds., *The Work of Memory: New Directions in the Study of German Society and Culture* (Urbana: University of Illinois Press, 2002).

46. Koshar, *From Monuments to Traces*, 8–10; Crane, *Collecting and Historical Consciousness*, 28–29. These arguments are directed especially at Eric Hobsbawm and Terence Ranger, eds., *The Invention of Tradition* (Cambridge: Cambridge University Press, 1983).

47. Many different books could have been written on this subject. Indeed, some readers may find that literary figures and issues, such as Hölderlin, Goethe, or Wagner's librettos, receive short shrift in this study. The emphasis here, however, is on how a discourse on myth encouraged the fusion of aesthetic, religious, and national categories in the theoretical and scholarly writings of the Romantics, their disciples, and their critics.

48. See esp. D. G. Charlton, *Secular Religions in France, 1815–1870* (London: Oxford University Press, 1963); Frank M. Turner, *Between Science and Religion: The Reaction to Scientific Naturalism in Late Victorian England* (New Haven: Yale University Press, 1974).

49. On this process, see Von Hendy, *Modern Construction of Myth*; also Steven M. Wasserstrom, *Religion after Religion: Gershom Scholem, Mircea Eliade, and Henry Corbin at Eranos* (Princeton: Princeton University Press, 1999).

50. The term is from Karl Kerényi and dates from the immediate post–World War II era; see *Mythology and Humanism: The Correspondence of Thomas Mann and Karl Kerényi*, trans. Alexander Gelley (Ithaca: Cornell University Press, 1975), 15.

CHAPTER ONE

1. Schelling to Hegel (Jan. 1796), Plitt, 1:91–92.

2. Schelling to parents (Apr. 3, 1796), Plitt, 1:99.

3. Ibid., 102–3.

4. On the educated middle classes, see Werner Conze and Jürgen Kocka, eds.,

Bildungsbürgertum im 19. Jahrhundert, 4 vols. (Stuttgart: Klett-Cotta, 1985–92). Somewhat dated but still intriguing is Hans Gerth, *Bürgerliche Intelligenz um 1800: Zur Soziologie des deutschen Frühliberalismus,* 2nd ed., ed. Ulrich Hermann (Göttingen: Vandenhoeck und Ruprecht, 1976). On the situation of seminary students and tutors in particular, see Gerth, *Bürgerliche Intelligenz,* 51–60, and Anthony La Vopa, *Grace, Talent, and Merit: Poor Students, Clerical Careers, and Professional Ideology in Eighteenth-Century Germany* (Cambridge: Cambridge University Press, 1988).

5. Schelling to parents (Feb. 4, 1797), Plitt, 1:189.

6. Schelling to parents (Apr. 3, 1796), Plitt, 1:108. Henri Brunschwig, *Enlightenment and Romanticism in Eighteenth-Century Prussia,* trans. Frank Jellinek (Chicago: University of Chicago Press, 1974), 147–63, argues that Romanticism can be traced in part to the awkward confrontation of young bourgeois academics with the customs of polite society. The existence of a Romantic salon culture undercuts this claim somewhat, but the young Schelling, whom Friedrich Schlegel described as "very raw," doubtless felt uncomfortable in most aristocratic settings. See Friedrich Schlegel to Caroline Schlegel (Apr. 1799), *SBD,* 1:158 n.

7. Schelling to parents (Apr. 3, 1796), Plitt, 1:97. On the context of this remark, see La Vopa, *Grace, Talent, and Merit,* 111–33.

8. Schelling to parents (Apr. 29, 1796), Plitt, 1:115–16. For the original comments, see Friedrich Nicolai, *Beschreibung einer Reise durch Deutschland und die Schweiz im Jahre 1781* (Berlin and Stettin, 1796), 11:117–29, 206, 288–94.

9. Schelling to parents (Apr. 3, 1796), Plitt, 1:106–7.

10. Ludwig Trauzettel, "Die Wörlitzer Anlagen—Geschichte und Gegenwart," in *Der Englische Garten zu Wörlitz,* ed. Staatlich Schlösser und Gärten Wörlitz, Oranienbaum, Luisium (Berlin: Verlag für Bauwesen, 1987), 165–211; Frank-Andreas Bechtoldt and Thomas Weiss, eds., *Weltbild Wörlitz: Entwurf einer Kulturlandschaft* (Stuttgart: Hatje, 1996).

11. Schelling to parents (July 1, 1796), Plitt, 1:124.

12. Ibid., 126–27; cf. Karl Philipp Moritz's comments on "night" in *Götterlehre oder Mythologische Dichtungen der Alten* (1791), ed. Horst Günther (Frankfurt a.M.: Insel, 1999), 36–40. See also Novalis's comments in *Novalis Schriften,* 3rd ed., ed. Paul Kluckhohn and Richard Samuel, 5 vols. (Stuttgart: Kohlhammer, 1977–88), 4:6.

13. Schelling to parents (July 1, 1796), Plitt, 1:127.

14. For an overview of the critical literature, see Gerthart Hoffmeister, "Forschungsgeschichte," in *Romantik-Handbuch,* ed. Helmut Schanze (Tübingen: Kröner, 1994), 177–206.

15. Brunschwig, *Enlightenment and Romanticism;* Jerome McGann, *The Romantic Ideology: A Critical Investigation* (Chicago: University of Chicago Press, 1983); Jürgen Schulte-Sasse, "The Concept of Literary Criticism in German Romanticism," in *A History of German Literary Criticism,* ed. Peter Uwe Hohendahl (Lincoln: University of Nebraska Press, 1988), 99–177. On the market origins of the literary "sacred," see Pierre Bourdieu, *The Rules of Art: Genesis and Structure of the Literary Field,* trans. Susan Emanuel (Stanford: Stanford University Press, 1996).

16. See, e.g., Hermann Timm, *Die heilige Revolution, das religiöse Totalitäts-*

konzept der Frühromantik: Schleiermacher—Novalis—Friedrich Schlegel (Frankfurt a.M.: Syndikat, 1978); Manfred Frank, *Vorlesungen über die neue Mythologie,* vol. 1, *Der kommende Gott* (Frankfurt a.M.: Suhrkamp, 1982); also Andrew Bowie, *Aesthetics and Subjectivity: From Kant to Nietzsche* (Manchester: Manchester University Press, 1990).

17. Philippe Lacoue-Labarthe and Jean-Luc Nancy, *The Literary Absolute: The Theory of Literature in German Romanticism,* trans. Philip Barnard and Cheryl Lester (Albany: State University of New York Press, 1988); Ernst Behler, *Frühromantik* (Berlin: de Gruyter, 1992); Azade Seyhan, *Representation and Its Discontents: The Critical Legacy of German Romanticism* (Berkeley and Los Angeles: University of California Press, 1992). Influenced by postmodernism but emphasizing the genuine contradictions in the views of Schleiermacher and Schlegel is Gerald Izenberg, *Impossible Individuality: Romanticism, Revolution, and the Origins of Modern Selfhood, 1787–1802* (Princeton: Princeton University Press, 1992).

18. Hans Frei, *The Eclipse of Biblical Narrative: A Study in Eighteenth and Nineteenth Century Hermeneutics* (New Haven: Yale University Press, 1974). On Frei, see esp. John David Dawson, *Christian Figural Reading and the Fashioning of Identity* (Berkeley and Los Angeles: University of California Press, 2002).

19. For recent overviews of the Christian churches in Old Regime Germany, see Michael Maurer, *Kirche, Staat und Gesellschaft im 17. und 18. Jahrhundert* (Munich: Oldenbourg, 1999); W. R. Ward, *Christianity under the Ancien Régime, 1648–1789* (Cambridge: Cambridge University Press, 1999). For Protestant theology, see Emanuel Hirsch, *Geschichte der neueren evangelischen Theologie im Zusammenhang mit den allgemeinen Bewegungen des europäischen Denkens,* 5 vols. (repr., Münster: Stenderhoff, 1984), vol. 4, pt. 1, 1–119.

20. Maurer, *Kirche, Staat und Gesellschaft,* 6; Ward, *Christianity,* 102.

21. Maurer, *Kirche, Staat und Gesellschaft,* 17.

22. On Pietism in an international context, see W. R. Ward, *The Protestant Evangelical Awakening* (Cambridge: Cambridge University Press, 1992); also the accounts in Ward, *Christianity,* 71–130; Maurer, *Kirche, Staat und Gesellschaft,* 24–32.

23. Hartmut Lehmann, *Pietismus und weltliche Ordnung in Württemberg vom 17. bis zum 20. Jahrhundert* (Stuttgart: Kohlhammer, 1969); Laurence Dickey, *Hegel: Religion, Economics, and the Politics of Spirit, 1770–1807* (Cambridge: Cambridge University Press, 1987), 40–76.

24. Lehmann, *Pietismus und weltliche Ordnung,* 135–51.

25. On this, see Friedrich Wilhelm Graf, "Protestantische Theologie und die Formierung der bürgerlichen Gesellschaft," in *Profile des neuzeitlichen Protestantismus,* vol. 1, *Aufklärung, Idealismus, Vormärz,* ed. Friedrich Wilhelm Graf (Gütersloh: Gerd Mohn, 1990), 11–54, here 35.

26. Anthony La Vopa, *Fichte: The Self and the Calling of Philosophy, 1762–1799* (Cambridge: Cambridge University Press, 2001), 62–64.

27. J. S. Semler, *Theologische Briefe* (1781), cited by Gottfried Hornig, *Johann Salomo Semler: Studien zu Leben und Werk des Hallenser Aufklärungstheologen* (Tübingen: Niemeyer, 1996), 170 n. On the individualization of Christianity, see esp. Hans Erich Bödeker, "Die Religiosität der Gebildeten," in *Religionskritik und Reli-*

giosität in der deutschen Aufklärung, ed. Karlfried Gründer and Karl Heinrich Rengstorf (Heidelberg: Lambert Schneider, 1989), 145–95.

28. Gottfried Hornig, "Die Freiheit der christlichen Privatreligion: Semlers Begründung des religiösen Individualismus in der protestantischen Aufklärungstheologie," *Neue Zeitschrift für systematische Theologie und Religionsphilosophie* 21 (1979): 198–211, here 209.

29. For an excellent brief description of these overlapping processes, see David Sorkin, *The Berlin Haskalah and German Religious Thought: Orphans of Knowledge* (London: Vallentine Mitchell, 2000).

30. See Michael A. Meyer, ed., *German-Jewish History in Modern Times,* 4 vols. (New York: Columbia University Press, 1996), 1:144–64, 2:7–18.

31. See Leonard Swidler, *Aufklärung Catholicism, 1780–1850: Liturgical and Other Reforms in the Catholic Aufklärung* (Missoula: Scholars Press, 1978); Harm Klueting, with Norbert Hinske and Karl Hengst, eds., *Katholische Aufklärung: Aufklärung im katholischen Deutschland* (Hamburg: Meiner, 1993).

32. "Absicht und Einrichtung dieser periodischen Schrift," *Beyträge zur Verbesserung des äussern Gottesdienstes in der katholischen Kirche* 1, no. 1 (1789): 26.

33. Swidler, *Aufklärung Catholicism,* 15; cf. Friedrich Schelling, *On University Studies,* trans. E. S. Morgan, ed. and with an introduction by Norbert Guterman (Athens: Ohio University Press, 1966), 101. On the problem of clergymen as civil servants, see esp. La Vopa, *Grace, Talent, and Merit.*

34. On liturgical reform in the eighteenth century, see Swidler, *Aufklärung Catholicism;* also Anton L. Mayer, *Die Liturgie in der europäischen Geistesgeschichte: Gesammelte Aufsätze,* ed. Emmanuel von Severus, O.S.B. (Darmstadt: Wissenschaftliche Buchgesellschaft, 1978); Waldemar Trapp, *Vorgeschichte und Ursprung der liturgischen Bewegung, vorwiegend in Hinsicht auf das deutsche Sprachgebiet* (Würzburg: Richard Mayr, 1939).

35. See Hugh McLeod, "Weibliche Frömmigkeit—männlicher Unglaube? Religion und Kirchen im bürgerlichen 19. Jahrhundert," in *Bürgerinnen und Bürger: Geschlechterverhältnisse im 19. Jahrhundert,* ed. Ute Frevert (Göttingen: Vandenhoeck und Ruprecht, 1988), 134–56.

36. Lucian Hölscher, "Die Religion des Bürgers: Bürgerliche Frömmigkeit und Protestantische Kirche im 19. Jahrhundert," *Historische Zeitschrift* 250 (1990): 595–630, here 628–29.

37. "Ob das Christenthum ohne den äußern Cultus wol bestehen könne?" *Neue Monatsschrift von und für Mecklenburg* 8 (1799): 1–10, here 7.

38. La Vopa, *Grace, Talent, and Merit,* 326–41.

39. Erich Förster, *Die Entstehung der preußischen Landeskirche unter der Regierung König Friedrich Wilhelms des Dritten: Ein Beitrag zur Geschichte der Kirchenbildung im deutschen Protestantismus,* 2 vols. (Tübingen: Mohr, 1905–7), 1:67–70.

40. On the broad lines of this debate, see esp. Frei, *Eclipse;* also Hans-Joachim Kraus, *Geschichte der historisch-kritischen Erforschung des Alten Testaments von der Reformation bis zur Gegenwart* (Neukirchen: Buchhandlung des Erziehungsvereins, 1956); Peter G. Bietenholz, *Historia and Fabula: Myths and Legends in Historical*

Thought from Antiquity to the Modern Age (Leiden: Brill, 1994), 220–69; Edward Breuer, *The Limits of Enlightenment: Jews, Germans, and the Eighteenth-Century Study of Scripture* (Cambridge: Harvard University Center for Jewish Studies, 1996), 77–107.

41. Benedict de Spinoza, *"A Theological-Political Treatise" and "A Political Treatise,"* trans. R. M. H. Elwes (New York: Dover, 1951), 82. On Spinoza's significance, see J. Samuel Preus, *Spinoza and the Irrelevance of Biblical Authority* (Cambridge: Cambridge University Press, 2001).

42. See Peter Hanns Reill, *The German Enlightenment and the Rise of Historicism* (Berkeley and Los Angeles: University of California Press, 1975), 82.

43. On Michaelis, see Frank Manuel, *The Broken Staff: Judaism through Christian Eyes* (Cambridge: Harvard University Press, 1992), 252–62; Jonathan M. Hess, "Johann David Michaelis and the Colonial Imaginary: Orientalism and the Emergence of Racial Antisemitism in Eighteenth-Century Germany," *Jewish Social Studies* 6 (2000): 56–101.

44. Hermann Samuel Reimarus, *Fragments*, ed. Charles H. Talbert, trans. Ralph S. Fraser (Philadelphia: Fortress, 1970), 239–69.

45. Frei, *Eclipse*, 113–16.

46. Kant, *Religion within the Limits of Mere Reason*, in *Religion and Rational Theology*, trans. and ed. Allen W. Wood and George di Giovanni (Cambridge: Cambridge University Press, 1996), 140.

47. Ibid., 154.

48. See La Vopa's comments in *Fichte*, 131–49.

49. Axel Horstmann, "Der Mythosbegriff vom frühen Christenthum bis zur Gegenwart," *Archiv für Begriffsgeschichte* 23 (1979): 7–54, esp. 7–11.

50. Frank Manuel, *The Eighteenth Century Confronts the Gods* (Cambridge: Harvard University Press, 1959).

51. See Axel Horstmann, "Mythologie und Altertumswissenschaft: Der Mythosbegriff bei Christian Gottlob Heyne," *Archiv für Begriffsgeschichte* 16 (1972): 60–85; Burton Feldman and Robert D. Richardson, Jr., *The Rise of Modern Mythology, 1680–1860* (Bloomington: Indiana University Press, 1975), 215–23; Christian Hartlich and Walter Sachs, *Der Ursprung des Mythosbegriffes in der modernen Bibelwissenschaft* (Tübingen: Mohr, 1952).

52. Christian Gottlob Heyne, "Inquiry into the Causes of Fables or the Physics of Ancient Myths" (1764), trans. in Feldman and Richardson, *Rise of Modern Mythology*, 219.

53. See the discussion in Hartlich and Sachs, *Ursprung des Mythosbegriffes*, 20–38; also Maike Oergel, *The Return of King Arthur and the Nibelungen: National Myth in Nineteenth Century English and German Literature* (Berlin: de Gruyter, 1998), 13–33.

54. Eichhorn, *Einleitung in das Alte Testament* (1780–83), cited in Hartlich and Sachs, *Ursprung des Mythosbegriffes*, 25.

55. On Herder and the Old Testament, see Feldman and Richardson, *Rise of Modern Mythology*, 224–40; Oergel, *Return of King Arthur*, 18–33; Strich, *Mythologie in der deutschen Literatur*, 1:41–71, 106–82; Frei, *Eclipse*, 183–201.

56. Herder, *Vom Geist der ebräischen Poesie, HSW,* 12:6.

57. On Herder's unsystematic use of "myth," Hartlich and Sachs, *Ursprung des Mythosbegriffes,* 47–53.

58. See Herder's rejection of these theories in *Aelteste Urkunde des Menschengeschlechts, HSW,* 6:330–35; see also Fritz Strich, *Die Mythologie in der deutschen Literatur von Klopstock bis Wagner,* 2 vols. (Halle: Niemeyer, 1910), 1:117.

59. Reinhart Koselleck, *Futures Past: On the Semantics of Historical Time* (Cambridge: MIT Press, 1985), 3–38.

60. The problems arising from identifying the Bible (especially the Old Testament) as a primarily "Jewish" narrative, while crucial to the present study, have been ignored by most previous commentators on this topic, including Frei, Hartlich and Sachs, and Oergel.

61. On Herder and the pantheist controversy, see Frederick C. Beiser, *The Fate of Reason: German Philosophy from Kant to Fichte* (Cambridge: Harvard University Press, 1987), esp. 163.

62. On their competing conceptions of anthropology, see John H. Zammito, *Kant, Herder, and the Birth of Anthropology* (Chicago: University of Chicago Press, 2002).

63. On this topic, Suzanne Marchand, *Down from Olympus: Archaeology and Philhellenism in Germany, 1750–1970* (Princeton: Princeton University Press, 1996), is now the standard work; see also E. M. Butler, *The Tyranny of Greece over Germany* (Cambridge: Cambridge University Press, 1935); Walter Rehm, *Griechentum und Goethezeit: Geschichte eines Glaubens* (Leipzig: Dieterich, 1936); Henry Hatfield, *Aesthetic Paganism in German Literature from Winckelmann to the Death of Goethe* (Cambridge: Harvard University Press, 1964); Anthony Grafton, "Polyhistory into *Philolog:* Notes on the Transformation of German Classical Scholarship, 1780–1850," *History of Universities* 3 (1983), 159–92; Josef Chytry, *The Aesthetic State: A Quest in Modern German Thought* (Berkeley and Los Angeles: University of California Press, 1989); Anthony La Vopa, "Specialists against Specialization: Hellenism as Professional Ideology in German Classical Studies," in *German Professions, 1800–1950,* ed. Geoffrey Cocks and Konrad H. Jarausch (Oxford: Oxford University Press, 1990), 27–45.

64. On Winckelmann, see Chytry, *Aesthetic State,* 11–37; Alex Potts, *Flesh and the Ideal: Winckelmann and the Origins of Art History* (New Haven: Yale University Press, 1994).

65. Johann Joachim Winckelmann, *History of Ancient Art,* trans. Alexander Gode, 4 vols. (New York: Ungar, 1968), 3:191.

66. Hatfield, *Aesthetic Paganism,* 1–22.

67. Grafton, "Polyhistory into *Philolog,*" 182.

68. On Göttingen, see Friedrich Paulsen, *Geschichte des gelehrten Unterrichts auf den deutschen Schulen und Universitäten vom Ausgang des Mittelalters bis zur Gegenwart,* 2nd ed., 2 vols. (Leipzig: Veit, 1896–97), 2:9–45; Charles McClelland, *State, Society, and University in Germany, 1700–1914* (Cambridge: Cambridge University Press, 1980), 34–98; Carl Joachim Classen, ed., *Die klassische Altertums-*

wissenschaft an der Georg-August-Universität Göttingen (Göttingen: Vandenhoeck und Ruprecht, 1989).

69. For the broad lines of this development, see Gerth, *Bürgerliche Intelligenz*, 43–44.

70. The entire verse deserves to be cited: "Alle jene Blüthen sind gefallen / von des Nordes winterlichem Wehen. / *Einen* zu bereichern, unter allen, / mußte diese Götterwelt vergehn. / Traurig such ich an dem Sternenbogen, / dich, Selene, find ich dort nicht mehr; / Durch die Wälder ruf ich, durch die Wogen, / ach! sie wiederhallen leer!" (Friedrich Schiller, "Die Götter Griechenlands" [1788], in *Schillers Werke: Nationalausgabe*, ed. Julius Petersen and Gerhard Fricke, 39 vols. to date [Weimar: Hermann Böhlaus Nachfolger, 1943–], 1:194).

71. Friedrich Stolberg, "Gedanken über Herrn Schillers Gedicht: 'Die Götter Griechenlandes,'" *Deutsches Museum* 2, no. 4 (1788): 97–105, here 103.

72. For a summary of the controversy, see Strich, *Mythologie in der deutschen Literatur*, 1:271–88; also Heinz Gockel, *Mythos und Poesie: Zum Mythosbegriff in Aufklärung und Frühromantik* (Frankfurt a.M.: Klostermann, 1981), 190–203.

73. On Goethe's paganism and Schiller's "semblance of paganism," see Hatfield, *Aesthetic Paganism*, 119–141.

74. Moritz, *Götterlehre*, 24.

75. For a discussion of Moritz and Goethe in this context, see esp. Tzvetan Todorov, *Theories of the Symbol*, trans. Catherine Porter (Oxford: Blackwell, 1982), 147–64. Many of the texts in which Goethe articulated his theory of the symbol remained unpublished in his lifetime.

76. Moritz, *Götterlehre*, 133.

77. On aesthetic autonomy, see Wolfgang Wittkowski, ed., *Revolution und Autonomie: Deutsche Autonomieästhetik im Zeitalter der Französischen Revolution* (Tübingen: Niemeyer, 1990); John H. Zammito, *The Genesis of Kant's "Critique of Judgment"* (Chicago: University of Chicago Press, 1992); Jonathan M. Hess, *Reconstituting the Body Politic: Enlightenment, Public Culture, and the Invention of Aesthetic Autonomy* (Detroit: Wayne State University Press, 1999).

78. Paulsen, *Geschichte des gelehrten Unterrichts*, 2:189–244, 276–312; Gerth, *Bürgerliche Intelligenz*, 43–45; La Vopa, *Grace, Talent, and Merit*, 264–78; Marchand, *Down from Olympus*, 24–35.

79. La Vopa, "Specialists"; Marchand, *Down from Olympus*, xx and passim; also Grafton, "Polyhistory into *Philolog*," 162–71, 182–83.

80. Horst Fuhrmans, editorial notes, *SBD*, 1:14.

81. See Wilhelm G. Jacobs, *Zwischen Revolution und Orthodoxie? Schelling und seine Freunde im Stift und an der Universität Tübingen: Texte und Untersuchungen* (Stuttgart: Frommann-Holzboog, 1989), 21–24. On the broader context of this issue, see La Vopa, *Grace, Talent, and Merit*, esp. 19–57.

82. The scholarship on Hegel has explored the significance of this context in detail. See esp. John Toews, *Hegelianism: The Path toward Dialectical Humanism, 1805–1841* (Cambridge: Cambridge University Press, 1980), 13–29; Dickey, *Hegel*.

83. See Jacobs, *Zwischen Revolution und Orthodoxie?* 33–45, which offers a

useful corrective to Pierre Berteaux, *Hölderlin und die französische Revolution* (Frankfurt a.M.: Suhrkamp, 1969).

84. See esp. Schelling's later comments to Hegel (July 21, 1795), *SBD*, 2:69; Berteaux, *Hölderlin*, 85–113.

85. Karl-Heinz Hinfurtner, "Biblischer Supranaturalismus: Gottlob Christian Storr (1746–1805)," in *Profile*, ed. Graf, 1:113–27, here 116; also Martin Brecht, "Die Anfänge der idealistischen Philosophie und die Rezeption Kants in Tübingen (1785–1795)," in *500 Jahre Eberhard-Karls-Universität Tübingen: Beiträge zur Geschichte der Universität Tübingen, 1477–1977*, ed. Hansmartin Decker-Hauff, Gerhard Fichtner, and Klaus Schreiner (Tübingen: Attempto, 1977), 381–428; Dieter Henrich, "Dominant Philosophical-Theological Problems in the Tübingen *Stift* during the Student Years of Hegel, Hölderlin, and Schelling," in *The Course of Remembrance and Other Essays on Hölderlin*, ed. Eckart Förster (Stanford: Stanford University Press, 1997), 31–54.

86. Schelling, "Ueber Offenbarung und Volksunterricht" (1798), *SSW*, 1:476; cf. Schelling's letter to Hegel (Jan. 6, 1795), *SBD*, 2:56–57: "All possible dogmas are already stamped postulates of practical reason and, where theoretical-historical proofs are nowhere sufficient, there practical (Tübingen) reason cuts the knot."

87. Schelling, "Entwurf der Vorrede zu den historisch-kritischen Abhandlungen der Jahre 1793–1794," Plitt, 1:41–42; cf. Schelling, "Vom Ich als Prinzip der Philosophie," *SSW*, 1:151–52.

88. "Entwurf der Vorrede," Plitt, 1:45.

89. See Schelling, "Antiquissimi de prima malorum humanorum origine philosophematis Genes. III explicandi tentamen criticum et philosophicum" (1792), *SSW*, 1:1–40; trans. Reinhold Mokrosch under the title "Ein kritischer und philosophischer Auslegungsversuch des ältesten Philosophems von Genesis III über den ersten Ursprung der menschlichen Bosheit," in Schelling, *Historisch-kritische Ausgabe*, ed. Hans Michael Baumgartner et al. (Stuttgart: Frommann-Holzboog, 1976–), 1:101–81; Schelling, "Ueber Mythen, historische Sagen und Philosopheme der ältesten Welt" (1793), *SSW*, 1:41–83; also the fragment of Schelling's "Proben eines Kommentars über die früheste Geschichte Jesu nach Lukas und Matthäus," in Plitt, 1:46–50.

90. "Hymne an den Genius Griechenlands," in Friedrich Hölderlin, *Werke in einem Band*, ed. Hans Jürgen Balmes (Munich: Hanser, 1990), 19–20.

91. "Ueber Mythen," *SSW*, 1:63; Hartlich and Sachs, *Ursprung des Mythosbegriffes*, 56–58, and most other commentators ignore the degree to which Schelling in this essay departs from the Heynean conception of myth if not in theory then in attitude.

92. "Ueber Mythen," *SSW*, 1:67.

93. Ibid., 45.

94. Ibid., 74.

95. Ibid., 81.

96. On the early Fichte, see La Vopa's authoritative *Fichte*.

97. Johann Gottlieb Fichte, *Attempt at a Critique of All Revelation* (1792),

trans. and with an introduction by Garrett Green (Cambridge: Cambridge University Press, 1978), 73, cited in La Vopa, *Fichte*, 98.

98. La Vopa, *Fichte*, 98–99.

99. Manfred Frank and Gerhard Kurz, eds., *Materialien zu Schellings philosophischen Anfängen* (Frankfurt a.M.: Suhrkamp, 1975), 473.

100. Johann Gottlieb Fichte, *Ueber den Begriff der Wissenschaftslehre* (1794) and *Grundlage der gesammten Wissenschaftslehre* (1794–95). On Fichte's changing conception of the *Wissenschaftslehre*, see Frederick Neuhouser, *Fichte's Theory of Subjectivity* (Cambridge: Cambridge University Press, 1989); also Frederick C. Beiser, *Enlightenment, Revolution, Romanticism: The Genesis of Modern German Political Thought, 1790–1800* (Cambridge: Harvard University Press, 1992), 60–68; La Vopa, *Fichte*, 183–230.

101. La Vopa, *Fichte*, 200–202.

102. Beiser, *Enlightenment*, 63.

103. Schelling to Hegel (Jan. 6, 1795), *SBD*, 2:57.

104. Schelling, "Über die Möglichkeit einer Form der Philosophie" (1794); "Vom Ich als Prinzip der Philosophie oder über das Unbedingte im menschlichen Wissen" (1795); "Philosophische Briefe über Dogmatismus und Kritizismus" (1795). See the translations by Fritz Marti in *The Unconditional in Human Knowledge: Four Early Essays (1794–1796)* (Lewisburg, Pa.: Bucknell University Press; London: Associated University Presses, 1980). On Schelling's early philosophical development, see Manfred Frank, *Eine Einführung in Schellings Philosophie* (Frankfurt a.M.: Suhrkamp, 1985), 49–52; Andrew Bowie, *Schelling and Modern European Philosophy: An Introduction* (London and New York: Routledge, 1993), 15–90.

105. "Vom Ich als Prinzip der Philosophie" (1795), *SSW*, 1:167. Manfred Frank, *Eine Einführung in Schellings Philosophie*, 61–70, argues that Schelling's reformulation of the Fichtean absolute reflected the influence of Hölderlin. On this transition, see also Bowie, *Schelling and Modern European Philosophy*, 25–29.

106. Schelling to Hegel (Feb. 2, 1795), *SBD*, 2:65–66.

107. On Schelling's *Naturphilosophie*, see Joseph Esposito, *Schelling's Idealism and Philosophy of Nature* (Lewisburg, Pa.: Bucknell University Press; London: Associated University Presses, 1977).

108. Esposito, *Schelling's Idealism*, 88–89.

109. Frederick Gregory, "Kant, Schelling, and the Administration of Science in the Romantic Era," in *Science in Germany: The Intersection of Institutional and Intellectual Issues*, ed. Kathryn Olesko (Philadelphia: University of Pennsylvania Press, 1989), 37–56; Thomas Broman, "University Reform in Medical Thought at the End of the 18th Century," in *Science in Germany*, ed. Olesko, 13–36.

110. Schelling, *Ideas for a Philosophy of Nature*, trans. Errol E. Harris and Peter Heath (Cambridge: Cambridge University Press, 1988), 11, 35.

111. Goethe to Voigt (May 5, 1798), cited in *SBD*, 1:132 n.

112. Schelling to parents (Sept. 4, 1797), Plitt, 1:208.

113. On Schlegel's life, see Ernst Behler, *Friedrich Schlegel in Selbstzeugnissen*

und Bilddokumenten (Reinbek bei Hamburg: Rowohlt, 1966); also Izenberg, *Impossible Individuality*, 54–138.

114. Schelling to parents (June 28, 1797), Plitt, 1:202; cf. his attacks on H. E. G. Paulus as "der Jude Shylock," in Schelling to parents (Mar. 13, 1806), *SBD*, 1:347.

115. Friedrich Schlegel to Caroline Schlegel (Apr. 1799), *SBD*, 1:158 n.

116. Schelling to father (Dec. 7, 1796), Plitt, 1:185; Schelling to parents (May 19, 1798), Plitt, 1:222.

117. Izenberg, *Impossible Individuality*, 101–38.

118. Schelling's earlier political ideas were sketched out (in rather abstract form) in "Neue Deduction des Naturrechts" (1796/97), in *Historisch-kritische Ausgabe*, 3:113–75. Compare the rather anarchist standpoint developed here with the positive reevaluation of the state in his *Vorlesungen über die Methode des akademischen Studiums* (1803), trans. Morgan as *On University Studies*, 109–14.

119. *Briefe über die ästhetische Erziehung des Menschen* (1795), trans. Elizabeth M. Wilkinson and L. A. Willoughby as *Letters on the Aesthetic Education of Man*, in Friedrich Schiller, *Essays*, ed. Walter Hinderer and Daniel O. Dahlstrom (New York: Continuum, 1995), 96.

120. *Aesthetic Education of Man*, in Schiller, *Essays*, 98.

121. Ibid., 163.

122. Ibid., 99.

123. Ibid., 90. Most previous commentators have overlooked the theological implications of Schiller's arguments.

124. *Aesthetic Education of Mankind*, in Schiller, *Essays*, 178.

125. Schelling to Obereit (Mar. 12, 1796), *SBD*, 2:86.

126. Jochen Schulte-Sasse, *Die Kritik an der Trivialliteratur seit der Aufklärung: Studien zur Geschichte des modernen Kitschbegriffs* (Munich: W. Fink, 1971), 46.

127. Given this, it seems inaccurate to claim, as Manfred Frank does in *Der kommende Gott*, 195–98 and passim, that the early Romantics were interested in constituting a previously nonexistent public sphere. A public sphere did exist by this time; it just did not possess the qualities of "publicness" that Schelling in particular believed it should have.

128. See La Vopa, *Fichte*, 269–97.

129. F. Schlegel to Novalis (Dec. 2, 1798), *KFSA*, 24:205–6.

130. See esp. the discussion in Klaus Epstein, *The Genesis of German Conservatism* (Princeton: Princeton University Press, 1966), 84–111; also Brunschwig, *Enlightenment and Romanticism*, 184–190; Wolfgang Hardtwig, *Genossenschaft, Sekte, Verein in Deutschland*, vol. 1, *Vom Spätmittelalter bis zur Französischen Revolution* (Munich: Beck, 1997).

131. Michelle Vovelle, *The Revolution against the Church: From Reason to the Supreme Being*, trans. Alan José (Columbus: Ohio State University Press, 1991); Nigel Ashton, *Religion and Revolution in France, 1780–1804* (Washington, D.C.: Catholic University of America Press, 2000); on Germany, see T. C. W. Blanning, *The*

French Revolution in Germany: Occupation and Resistance in the Rhineland, 1792–1802 (Oxford: Clarendon, 1983), 207–54.

132. For the background to this discussion, see esp. Friedrich Wilhelm Graf, "'Dechristianisierung': Zur Problemgeschichte eines kulturpolitischen Topos," in *Säkularisierung, Dechristianisierung, Rechristianisierung im neuzeitlichen Europa: Bilanz und Perspektiven der Forschung*, ed. Hartmut Lehmann (Göttingen: Vandenhoeck und Ruprecht, 1997), 32–66.

133. Joachim Christian Gaß, *Ueber den christlichen Cultus* (1815), cited in Graf, "'Dechristianisierung,'" 44.

134. On the Atheism Controversy, see the discussion in La Vopa, *Fichte*, 368–424.

135. Kant, *The Conflict of the Faculties*, in *Religion and Rational Theology*, 269–93.

136. "Ueber Offenbarung und Volksunterricht" (1798), *SSW*, 1:479–80; cf. the critique of Kant's use of the Bible in *On University Studies*, 95–96. For further evidence of Schelling's desire for a new, more popular mode of expressing philosophical ideas, see "Neue Deduktion des Naturrechts" (1796), in *Historisch-kritische Ausgabe*, 3:175.

137. F. Schlegel, "Ideen," *KFSA*, 2:262 (§60), 2:259 (§32), 2:264–65 (§92).

138. Friedrich Schleiermacher, *On Religion: Speeches to Its Cultured Despisers*, trans. and with an introduction by Richard Crouter (Cambridge: Cambridge University Press, 1988), 83.

139. On the Romantics' gravitation to the language of mystery religions, see Dirk von Petersdorff, *Mysterienrede: Zum Selbstverständnis romantischer Intellektueller* (Tübingen: Niemeyer, 1996).

140. Novalis, "Pollen" (1798), in *The Early Political Writings of the German Romantics*, ed. and trans. Frederick Beiser (Cambridge: Cambridge University Press, 1996), 22–23 (§74).

141. Schleiermacher, *On Religion*, 109 and passim.

142. "Ideen," *KFSA*, 2:263 (§81).

143. This interpretation differs considerably from that of Lacoue-Labarthe and Nancy, *Literary Absolute*, 76, whose *Frühromantik* religion is described as "not religion, and especially not Christianity" or even something analogous to Christianity.

144. Novalis, "Christianity or Europa?" in *Early Political Writings of the German Romantics*, ed. and trans. Beiser, 59–79.

145. Herder, "Iduna, oder der Apfel der Verjüngung," *HSW*, 18:483–502. The significance of this essay is discussed in Frank, *Der kommende Gott*, 143–51; Gockel, *Mythos und Poesie*, 330–33.

146. "Ideen," *KFSA*, 2:269–70 (§135).

147. Novalis, "Christianity or Europa?" *Early Political Writings of the German Romantics*, ed. and trans. Beiser, 66; Schleiermacher, *On Religion*, 134–35, also 164.

148. "Die Erziehung des Menschengeschlechts," in *Lessings Werke*, ed. Georg Witkowski (Leipzig and Vienna: Bibliographisches Institut, 1911), 7:448.

149. F. Schlegel to Novalis (Oct. 20, 1798), *KFSA*, 24:183. As a preview of this no-

tion, see the "Athenäum Fragmente" (1798), *KFSA*, 2:167 (§12): "It has been said of many a monarch that he would have been a lovable private man but he was unsuited to be king. Is this perhaps also so with the Bible? Is it also merely a lovable private book, which should not be the Bible?"

150. "Ideen," *KFSA*, 2:265 (§95).

151. F. Schlegel to Schleiermacher (Nov. 1799), in Friedrich Schleiermacher, *Aus Schleiermachers Leben*, ed. Ludwig Jonas and Wilhelm Dilthey, 4 vols. (Berlin: Reimer, 1861), 3:134.

152. Schelling, "Epikurisch Glaubensbekenntnis Heinz Widerporstens," in *Materialien*, ed. Frank and Kurz, 145–53, here 147.

153. Ibid., 151: "Reden von Religion als einer Frauen, / Die man nur dürft' durch Schleier schauen / Um nicht zu empfinden sinnlich Brunst, / Machen darum viel Wörterdunst." Cf. "Ideen," *KFSA*, 2:256 (§1): "There is talk already of even religion. It is time to tear away the veil of Isis and to reveal the secret. Whoever cannot endure the gaze of the goddess, let him flee or perish."

154. Plitt, 1:246.

155. Schelling, "Das sogenannte 'Aelteste Systemprogramm,'" in *Materialien*, ed. Frank and Kurz, 110–12, here 110–11.

156. Ibid., 112.

157. On Hegel as the author, see H. S. Harris, *Hegel's Development: Towards the Sunlight, 1770–1801* (Oxford: Clarendon, 1972), 249–57; Otto Pöggeler, "Hegel, der Verfasser des ältesten Systemprogramms des deutschen Idealismus," in *Mythologie der Vernunft: Hegels "älteste Systemprogramm" des deutschen Idealismus*, ed. Christoph Jamme and Helmut Schneider (Frankfurt a.M.: Suhrkamp, 1984), 126–43. For a review of the literature, see the works cited in *Mythologie der Vernunft*; and Frank-Peter Hansen, *"Das älteste Systemprogramm des deutschen Idealismus": Rezeptionsgeschichte und Interpretation* (Berlin: de Gruyter, 1989). Frank, *Der kommende Gott*, 153–87, proceeds under the assumption that Schelling was, if not the formal author, then at least the guiding spirit behind the System Program; Chytry, *Aesthetic State*, 123–31, assigns authorship to Hölderlin.

158. F. Schlegel, "Gespräch über die Poesie," *KFSA*, 2:312.

159. Ibid.

160. Cf. Peter Gay, *The Naked Heart* (New York: Norton, 1995), 37–102.

161. "Gespräch über die Poesie," *KFSA*, 2:322.

162. F. Schlegel to Schleiermacher (Jan. 1800), *Aus Schleiermachers Leben*, 3:151–52.

163. Dorothea Veit to Schleiermacher (Feb. 14, 1800), *Aus Schleiermachers Leben*, 3:156. Schleiermacher's reply (if there was one) has been lost.

164. Friedrich Schelling, *System of Transcendental Idealism*, trans. Peter Heath (Charlottesville: University of Virginia Press, 1978), 230.

165. Kant had actually suggested the role of art in bridging the gaps between freedom and necessity in his *Kritik der Urteilskraft* (1790) (see above). See Manfred Frank, *Einführung in die frühromantische Aesthetik* (Frankfurt a.M.: Suhrkamp, 1989); also Hans Freier, *Die Rückkehr der Götter, von der ästhetischen Über-*

schreitung der Wissensgrenze zur Mythologie der Moderne: Eine Untersuchung zur systematischen Rolle der Kunst in der Philosophie Kants und Schellings (Stuttgart and Weimar: Metzler, 1976).

166. Schelling, *System of Transcendental Idealism*, 232–33.

167. "Race" is used here in the sense of a new "people" or "generation," not in the sense of a new biological race.

168. Schelling, *Philosophie der Kunst* (1802–3), *SSW*, 5:353–737; citations are from the English edition, *Philosophy of Art*, ed. and trans. with an introduction by Douglas W. Stott (Minneapolis: University of Minnesota Press, 1989).

169. See, e.g., Schelling to A. W. Schlegel (Oct. 21, 1802), Plitt, 1:425–28. On A. W. Schlegel in this context, see esp. Claudia Becker, *"Naturgeschichte der Kunst": August Wilhelm Schlegels ästhetischer Ansatz im Schnittpunkt zwischen Aufklärung, Klassik und Frühromantik* (Munich: Fink, 1998).

170. Schelling, *Philosophy of Art*, 14–15.

171. Ibid., 41.

172. Ibid., 37 (trans. modified); cf. Schiller, "Letters on the Aesthetic Education of Man," in Schiller, *Essays*, 163.

173. Schelling, *Philosophy of Art*, 43.

174. Schelling derived his notion of the symbol in large part from Goethe and Karl Philipp Moritz. On this see Todorov, 207–12; also Bernhard Barth, *Schellings Philosophie der Kunst: Göttliche Imagination und ästhetische Einbildungskraft* (Munich: Karl Alber, 1991), 106–14, 162–76.

175. Johann Heinrich Voss, *Mythologische Briefe*, 2 vols. (Königsberg: Nicolovius, 1794). See Conrad Bursian, *Geschichte der classischen Philologie in Deutschland*, 2 vols. (Munich and Leipzig: Oldenbourg, 1883), 1:559–62.

176. Voss, *Mythologische Briefe*, cited in Wilhelm Herbst, *Johann Heinrich Voß*, 2 vols. in 3 (Leipzig: Teubner, 1872–76), 2:1, 202.

177. Schelling, *Philosophy of Art*, 47; cf. Schelling to A. W. Schlegel (May 20, 1803), *SBD*, 2:505.

178. Friedrich August Wolf, *Prolegomena to Homer, 1795*, trans. with an introduction by Anthony Grafton, Glenn W. Most, and James E. G. Zetzel (Princeton: Princeton University Press, 1985). On Wolf, see Anthony Grafton, "Prolegomena to Friedrich August Wolf," in his *Defenders of the Text: The Traditions of Scholarship in an Age of Science, 1450–1800* (Cambridge: Harvard University Press, 1991), 214–43; also Ulrich von Wilamowitz-Moellendorff, *History of Classical Scholarship*, trans. Alan Harris, ed. and with an introduction by Hugh Lloyd-Jones (London: Duckworth, 1982), 108.

179. Wolf borrowed his method of interpreting the scholia from Johann Gottfried Eichhorn's use of the Masoretic commentaries to the Hebrew Bible. See Grafton, "Prolegomena to Friedrich August Wolf," 234–41.

180. On the reception, see Richard von Volkmann, *Geschichte und Kritik der Wolfschen "Prolegomena zu Homer": Ein Beitrag zur Geschichte der Homerischen Frage* (Leipzig: Teubner, 1874).

181. Schelling, *Philosophy of Art*, 51.

182. Ibid., 52.

183. Schelling, *On University Studies*, 151 (trans. modified).

184. Schelling, *Philosophy of Art*, 66 (trans. modified).

185. F. Schlegel, *Geschichte der Poesie der Griechen und Römer, KFSA*, 1:412–13.

186. Schelling, *Philosophy of Art*, 56; this was typical of the fundamental divergence between Friedrich Schlegel and Schelling on the "classical" quality of ancient Greece. Schlegel was willing to grant more scope to the infinite and the indeterminate in ancient Greek life, whereas Schelling saw the infinite as fundamentally foreign to Greek culture.

187. Ibid., 61–62.

188. Schelling, *On University Studies*, 83 and 85 (this translation follows that of Stott, *Philosophy of Art*, 62–63).

189. Schelling, *Philosophy of Art*, 59–60.

190. The language of Schelling and A. W. Schlegel is nearly identical on this point. Cf. Schelling, "System der Gesammten Philosophie" (1804), *SSW*, 6:564: "The modern world did not come out of the ancient world through steady progress but through a complete overturning *[gänzliche Umkehrung]*"; and A. W. Schlegel, *Vorlesungen über schöne Literatur und Kunst*, pt. 1, "Die Kunstlehre," in *Kritische Ausgabe der Vorlesungen*, ed. Ernst Behler and Frank Jolles (Paderborn: Schöningh, 1989), 1:455: "What resulted was a complete overturning *[gänzliche Umkehrung]* of all ideas, the most remarkable revolution of the human spirit."

191. Schelling, *Philosophy of Art*, 64.

192. For a discussion of this image, see esp. Frank, *Der kommende Gott*, 285–359.

193. Schelling, *On University Studies*, 85 (trans. modified).

194. Ibid., 110–12.

195. *SSW*, 6:572–73.

196. See Schelling, *Philosophy of Art*, 210–11; also ibid., 65: "The predominating factor in antiquity is the sublime, the masculine, that of modernity the beautiful and hence the feminine"; cf. A. W. Schlegel, "Kunstlehre," in *Kritische Ausgabe der Vorlesungen*, 1:457: "Worship of love under the image of the purest femininity. In paganism the masculine character dominant."

197. Schelling, *Philosophy of Art*, 58.

198. David Strauss recognized that his argument had been foreshadowed by Schelling. See Strauss's *In Defense of My "Life of Jesus" against the Hegelians*, trans., ed., and with an introduction by Marilyn Chapin Massey (Hamden, Conn.: Archon Books, 1983), 12.

199. Schelling, *Philosophy of Art*, 59 (trans. modified). Schelling is reported to have declared one evening to his dinner guests that the snake was a much higher personality than Jesus. See Ernst Behler, "Schellings Aesthetik in der Ueberlieferung von Henry Crabb Robinson," *Philosophisches Jahrbuch* 83 (1976): 143.

200. Schelling, *Philosophy of Art*, 59.

201. On attitudes to Catholicism in German literature, see Jutta Osinski,

Katholizismus und deutsche Literatur im 19. Jahrhundert (Paderborn: Schöningh, 1993). For a more cynical view, see Siegmar V. Hellerich, *Religionizing, Romanizing Romantics: The Catholico-Christian Camouflage of the Early German Romantics, Wackenroder, Tieck, Novalis, Friedrich and August Wilhelm Schlegel* (New York and Frankfurt a.M.: Peter Lang, 1995).

202. A. W. Schlegel, "Die Kunstlehre," in *Kritische Ausgabe der Vorlesungen,* 1:458. This position was an implicit criticism of Moritz, who had treated the symbol as essentially timeless. Indeed, Schlegel believed that Moritz's purely aesthetic concept of the symbol had to give way to a more cultural and cultic concept of the symbol.

203. Schelling, *Philosophy of Art,* 65; see also Behler, "Schellings Aesthetik," 178: "Christianity, since in it the finite is taken up into the infinite, is necessarily church and Catholicism. All finite appearances in it are parts of a great drama, and in it all take part in the mysteries."

204. Schelling, *Philosophy of Art,* 67.

205. Schelling, *On University Studies,* 100.

206. Ibid., 97.

207. Schelling was often rumored to have converted to Catholicism, and Henry Crabb Robinson was surprised (and pleased) to learn that he had not when he visited him in Munich in 1829 (Behler, "Schellings Aesthetik," 144).

208. Schelling, *On University Studies,* 97–98.

209. Schelling, *Philosophy of Art,* 72 (trans. modified).

210. Ibid., 71.

211. Ibid., 72.

212. A. W. Schlegel, "Die Kunstlehre," in *Kritische Ausgabe der Vorlesungen,* 1:356.

213. Schelling, *Philosophy of Art,* 240 (trans. modified). The original was published as "Ueber Dante in philosophischer Beziehung," *SSW,* 5:152–63, here 153–54; cf. *Philosophy of Art,* 74: "[W]e can assert that until that time in the yet undetermined and distant future when the world spirit itself has completed the great poem upon which it now reflects, and when the succession of the modern world has transformed itself into a *simultaneity*—until that point, every great poet is called to structure from this evolving (mythological) world, a world of which his *own age* can reveal to him only a part. I repeat: from this world he is to structure into a whole that particular part revealed to him, and to create from the content and substance of that world *his* mythology."

214. Schelling, *Philosophy of Art,* 271.

215. Ibid., 277.

216. *SSW,* 6:571–72.

217. Schelling, *Philosophy of Art,* 76 (trans. modified).

218. At an early stage (ca. 1799–1800), Schelling appears to have envisioned composing the new mythology himself. See Friedrich Schlegel to Schleiermacher (Sept. 16, 1799): "He is very serious . . . about poetry, and I will faithfully help him with it"; in *Aus Schleiermachers Leben,* 3:121.

219. Schelling, *Philosophy of Art,* 76; cf. Behler, "Schellings Aesthetik," 165.

220. Schelling, *On University Studies*, 107.

221. *SSW*, 6:573.

222. Schelling, *On University Studies*, 112–13.

223. On the Bavarian context, see Philipp Funk, *Von der Aufklärung zur Romantik: Studien zur Vorgeschichte der Münchener Romantik* (Munich: Josef Kösel and Friedrich Pustet, 1925), esp. 1–62; Werner K. Blessing, *Staat und Kirche in der Gesellschaft: Institutionelle Autorität und mentaler Wandel in Bayern während des 19. Jahrhunderts* (Göttingen: Vandenhoeck und Ruprecht, 1982). On the Protestant–Catholic, north–south dimensions of this conflict, see Wolfgang Altgeld, "'Akademische Nordlichter': Ein Streit um Religion, Aufklärung und Nation nach der Neueröffnung der Bayerischen Akademie der Wissenschaft im Jahre 1807," *Archiv für Kulturgeschichte* 67 (1985): 339–88.

224. These accusations are summarized in *SBD*, 1:324–25 n.

225. Ernst Behler, *Unendliche Perfektibilität: Europäische Romantik und Französische Revolution* (Paderborn: Schöningh, 1989).

CHAPTER TWO

1. G. W. F. Hegel, "The Positivity of the Christian Religion," in *Early Theological Writings*, trans. T. M. Knox and Richard Kroner (Philadelphia: University of Pennsylvania Press, 1948), 146–47.

2. Ibid., 149.

3. Ibid. (trans. modified).

4. For the purposes of this book, the term "Germanic" is used to denote the broad group of peoples, languages, and cultures whose linguistic history Jacob Grimm charted in *Deutsche Grammatik* (1819) and *Geschichte der Deutschen Sprache* (1848) and whose religion he described in *Deutsche Mythologie* (1835). On this, see Hans Friede Nielsen, "Jacob Grimm and the 'German Dialects,'" in *The Grimm Brothers and the Germanic Past*, ed. Elmer H. Antonsen (Amsterdam: Benjamins, 1990), 25–32.

5. On the importance of theology for German nationalism, see Wolfgang Altgeld, *Katholizismus, Protestantismus, Judentum: Über religiös begründete Gegensätze und nationalreligiöse Ideen in der Geschichte des deutschen Nationalismus* (Mainz: Matthias Grünewald, 1992); also Friedrich Wilhelm Graf, "Die Nation—von Gott 'erfunden'? Kritische Randnotizen zum Theologiebedarf der historischen Nationalismusforschung," in *"Gott mit uns": Nation, Religion, und Gewalt im 19. und frühen 20. Jahrhundert*, ed. Gerd Krumeich and Hartmut Lehmann (Göttingen: Vandenhoeck und Ruprecht, 2000), 285–317. For an earlier approach, see Gerhard Kaiser, *Pietismus und Patriotismus im literarischen Deutschland: Ein Beitrag zum Problem der Säkularisation*, 2nd ed. (Frankfurt: Athenäum, 1973).

6. On the history of *Germanistik* in this period, see Jürgen Fohrmann and Wilhelm Voßkamp, eds., *Wissenschaft und Nation: Studien zur Entstehungsgeschichte der deutschen Literaturwissenschaft* (Munich: Wilhelm Fink, 1991); Jürgen Fohrmann and Wilhelm Voßkamp, eds., *Wissenschaftsgeschichte der Germanistik im 19. Jahrhundert* (Stuttgart and Weimar: Metzler, 1994); Andreas Michael Schaffry, *An der Schwelle zur Wissenschaft: Ideologische Funktionen und gesellschaftliche*

Relevanz bei der Organisierung des Diskurses "Altdeutsche Literatur" zwischen 1790 und 1815 (Munich: Iudicium, 1995); and esp. Lothar Bluhm, *Die Brüder Grimm und der Beginn der Deutschen Philologie: Eine Studie zu Kommunikation und Wissenschaftsbildung im frühen 19. Jahrhundert* (Hildesheim: Weidmann, 1997); also useful is Jost Hermand, *Geschichte der Germanistik* (Hamburg: Rowohlt, 1994).

7. Kurt Böhner, "Altertumssammlungen des 18. und 19. Jahrhunderts im Rheinland," in *Das Kunst- und Kulturgeschichtliche Museum im 19. Jahrhundert*, ed. Bernhard Deneke and Rainer Kahnsitz (Munich: Prestel, 1977), 59–76.

8. On the emerging Protestant nationalism of the eighteenth century, see esp. Hans Peter Hermann, Hans-Martin Blitz, and Susanna Moßmann, *Machtphantasie Deutschland: Nationalismus, Männlichkeit und Fremdenhaß im Vaterlandsdiskurs deutscher Schriftsteller des 18. Jahrhunderts* (Frankfurt a.M.: Suhrkamp, 1996).

9. On Herder, see Friedrich Meinecke, *Historism: The Rise of a New Historical Outlook* (New York: Herder and Herder, 1972), 295–372; Isaiah Berlin, *Vico and Herder* (1960), repr. in *Three Critics of Enlightenment: Vico, Hamann, Herder*, ed. Henry Hardy (Princeton: Princeton University Press, 2000).

10. Herder, *Alte Volkslieder*, pt. 1, preface, *HSW*, 25:9, cited in Schaffry, *An der Schwelle zur Wissenschaft*, 50.

11. See, e.g., Herder, *Ideen zur Philosophie der Geschichte der Menschheit* (1784–87), *HSW*, 14:390–416.

12. Ibid., 383.

13. Recent research has emphasized the roots of nationalism (and not simply "patriotism") in the eighteenth century and earlier. See, e.g., Wolfgang Hardtwig, *Nationalismus und Bürgerkultur in Deutschland, 1500–1914: Ausgewählte Aufsätze* (Göttingen: Vandenhoeck und Ruprecht, 1994); Wolfgang Burgdorf, *Reichskonstitution und Nation: Verfassungsreformprojekte für das Heilige Römische Reich Deutscher Nation im politischen Schrifttum von 1648 bis 1806* (Mainz: Philipp Zabern, 1998); Hans-Martin Blitz, *Aus Liebe zum Vaterland: Die Deutsche Nation im 18. Jahrhundert* (Hamburg: Hamburger Edition, 2000). Nonetheless, for Protestant intellectuals, especially those of a Kantian or Romantic stripe, the decisive shift to a nationalist mode of argumentation occurred in the years 1796–1806, to some degree confirming Thomas Nipperdey's dictum that "in the beginning there was Napoleon," *Deutsche Geschichte, 1800–1866* (Munich: Beck, 1983), 11.

14. *Bragur* 1 (1791): 2; on Gräter, see Bluhm, *Die Brüder Grimm*, 251–75; also Schaffry, *An der Schwelle zur Wissenschaft*, 58–100.

15. F. D. Gräter, "Briefe über den Geist der Nordischen Dichtkunst und Mythologie," *Bragur* 7, no. 2 (1802): 15.

16. Ulrich Hunger, "Die altdeutsche Literatur und das Verlangen nach Wissenschaft: Schöpfungsakt und Fortschrittsglaube in der Frühgermanistik," in *Wissenschaftsgeschichte der Germanistik*, ed. Fohrmann and Voßkamp, 238. For a broader discussion of national-historical collecting in this era, see Susan A. Crane, *Collecting and Historical Consciousness in Early Nineteenth-Century Germany* (Ithaca: Cornell University Press, 2000).

17. Hunger, "Die altdeutsche Literatur und das Verlangen nach Wissenschaft," 243–45.

18. Johann Andreas Schmeller, *"Lauter gemähte Wiesen für die Reaktion": Die erste Hälfte des 19. Jahrhunderts in den Tagebüchern Johann Andreas Schmellers*, ed. Reinhard Bauer and Ursula Münchhoff (Munich: Piper, 1990), 59.

19. Crane, *Collecting and Historical Consciousness*, 161–66.

20. On nostalgia in this era, see Peter Fritzsche, "Specters of History: On Nostalgia, Exile, and Modernity," *American Historical Review* 106 (2001): 1587–1618; also Svetlana Boym, *The Future of Nostalgia* (New York: Basic Books, 2001).

21. For a good summary of A. W. Schlegel's views on national myth, see Markus Winkler, *Mythisches Denken zwischen Romantik und Realismus: Zur Erfahrung kultureller Fremdheit im Werk Heinrich Heines* (Tübingen: Niemeyer, 1995), 51–60.

22. A. W. Schlegel, "Ueber das Mittelalter: Eine Vorlesung, gehalten 1803," *Deutsches Museum* 2 (1812): 432–62, here 434.

23. Ibid., 443.

24. Ibid., 446.

25. This view of the ancient Germans as giants or at least exceptionally tall humans dated from Tacitus and was shared by such eighteenth-century anthropologists as Christoph Meiners and Johann Friedrich Blumenbach. On this, see Susanne Zantop, *Colonial Fantasies: Conquest, Family, and Nation in Precolonial Germany, 1770–1870* (Durham, N.C.: Duke University Press, 1997), 81–97.

26. A. W. Schlegel, "Ueber das Lied der Nibelungen," *Deutsches Museum* 1 (1812): 34.

27. Ernst Behler, *Friedrich Schlegel in Selbstzeugnissen und Bilddokumenten* (Reinbek bei Hamburg: Rowohlt, 1966), 86–88.

28. On Görres, see Jon Vanden Heuvel, *A German Life in the Age of Revolution: Joseph Görres, 1776–1848* (Washington, D.C.: Catholic University of America Press, 2001); also Johann Nepomuk Sepp, *Görres und seine Zeitgenossen, 1776–1848* (Nördlingen: Beck, 1877); Ernst Rudolf Huber, "Joseph Görres und die Anfänge des katholischen Integralismus in Deutschland," in *Nationalstaat und Verfassungsstaat: Studien zur Geschichte der modernen Staatsidee* (Stuttgart: Kohlhammer, 1965), 107–26; Heribert Raab, *Joseph Görres: Ein Leben für Freiheit und Recht* (Paderborn: Schöningh, 1978).

29. Joseph von Eichendorff, "Halle und Heidelberg" (1866), cited by Max Koch, "Einleitung," in *Deutsche National-Litteratur: Historisch kritische Ausgabe*, ed. Joseph Kürschner, vol. 146, div. 1, *Arnim, Klemens und Bettina Brentano, J. Görres*, 2 pts. (Stuttgart: Union Deutsche Verlagsgesellschaft, 1884–93), 1:lvi; see Alfred Baeumler's comment, "Bachofen der Mythologe der Romantik," in Johann Jakob Bachofen, *Der Mythus von Orient und Occident: Eine Metaphysik der alten Welt aus den Werken von J. J. Bachofen*, 2d ed., ed. Manfred Schröter (Munich: Beck, 1926), clxxvii: "Earth, folk, nature, past, *night*—only Görres could feel that all as one. This feeling made him the leader of the Romantic movement in Heidelberg."

30. Görres, *Die teutschen Volksbücher: Nähere Würdigung der schönen Historien-, Wetter- und Arzneybüchlein, welche theils innerer Werth, theils Zufalls, Jahrhunderte hindurch bis auf unsere Zeit erhalten hat* (1807), GGS, 3:171.

31. Ibid., 173.

32. Ibid., 277.

33. This development is discussed in chapter 3.

34. *Die teutschen Volksbücher, GGS*, 3:283.

35. Ibid., 286.

36. Ibid., 282.

37. Ibid., 289.

38. On this point, see Görres, "Ueber den Fall Teutschlands und die Bedingungen seiner Wiedergeburt" (1810), *GGS*, 4:227–29.

39. Review of *Des Knaben Wunderhorn* (1809), *GGS*, 4:28–29; cf. *Die teutschen Volksbücher, GGS*, 3:290.

40. *Die teutschen Volksbücher, GGS*, 3:292.

41. The literature on the Grimms is vast, but given the unfolding state of the Grimm *Nachlass* and the still incomplete edition of Jacob Grimm's collected works, it is fair to say that the definitive scholarship on Jacob Grimm still remains to be done. In addition to the literature already cited, see Murray B. Peppard, *Paths through the Forest: A Biography of the Brothers Grimm* (New York: Holt, Rinehart, and Winston, 1971); Roland Feldmann, *Jacob Grimm und die Politik* (Kassel: Bärenreiter, 1970); Ulrich Wyss, *Die wilde Philologie: Jacob Grimm und der Historismus* (Munich: Beck, 1979); Jack Zipes, *The Brothers Grimm: From Enchanted Forests to the Modern World* (New York and London: Routledge, 1988); Klaus von See, *Die Göttinger Sieben: Kritik einer Legende* (Heidelberg: Winter, 1997).

42. Bluhm, *Die Brüder Grimm*, 141–44.

43. J. Grimm to Savigny (Dec. 26, 1811), in *Briefe der Brüder Grimm an Savigny*, ed. Wilhelm Schoof (Berlin: E. Schmidt, 1953), 127. These comments were made in partial criticism of Barthold G. Niebuhr's *Römische Geschichte* (1811), which Grimm had just read.

44. Cited in Otfrid Ehrisman, "Philologie der Natur—die Grimms, Schelling, die Nibelungen," *Brüder-Grimm-Gedenken* 5 (1985): 35–59, here 45. Ehrisman's evidence for a wide-ranging influence by Schelling on the Grimms seems rather circumstantial at times. Nonetheless, he is able to demonstrate that the Grimms were interested in Schelling's project and sympathized with its basic conclusions.

45. Wyss, *Die wilde Philologie*, 212–16, argues for the influence here of Johann Arnold Kanne, but see the critique by Ehrisman, "Philologie der Natur," 36.

46. Jacob Grimm, "Gedanken über Mythos, Epos und Geschichte," *Deutsches Museum* 1 (1812): 56.

47. Ibid., 72.

48. On the Grimms' criticism of the work of others, see Bluhm, *Die Brüder Grimm*, 158–64.

49. Despite two centuries of scholarship, certain basic questions about the origins of the *Nibelungenlied* (such as its author, its proper genre, and the relationship of the extant manuscripts to each other) remain unresolved. For good introductions to these issues, see Joachim Heinzle, *Das Nibelungenlied: Eine Einführung* (Munich and Zurich: Artemis, 1987); and Otfrid Ehrisman, *Nibelungenlied: Epoche, Werk, Wirkung* (Munich: Beck, 1987).

50. Goethe noted "no trace of a ruling deity." "Das *Nibelungenlied*," in *Goethe's Sämmtliche Werke*, 30 vols. (Stuttgart: Cotta, 1851), 26:194.

51. A. T. Hatto, trans., *The Nibelungenlied* (New York: Penguin, 1969), 17.

52. On the reception of the *Nibelungenlied* in the nineteenth century, the literature is vast and growing: Joseph Körner, *Nibelungenforschungen der deutschen Romantik* (Leipzig: Haessel, 1911); Otfrid Ehrisman, *Das Nibelungenlied in Deutschland: Studien zur Rezeption des Nibelungenlieds von der Mitte des 18. Jahrhunderts bis zum Ersten Weltkrieg* (Munich: Fink, 1975); Ehrisman, *Nibelungenlied: Epoche, Werke, Wirkung*; Lerke von Saalfeld, "Die ideologische Funktion des Nibelungenlieds in der preußisch-deutschen Geschichte von seiner Wiederentdeckung bis zum Nationalsozialismus" (Ph.D. diss., Freie Universität, Berlin, 1977); Werner Wunderlich, *Der Schatz des Drachentödters: Materialen zur Wirkungsgeschichte des Nibelungenliedes* (Stuttgart: Klett-Cotta, 1977); Ulrich Schulte-Wülwer, *Das Nibelungenlied in der deutschen Kunst des 19. und 20. Jahrhunderts* (Gießen: Anabas Verlag Kampf, 1980); Herfried Münkler, *Siegfrieden: Politik mit einem deutschen Mythos* (Berlin: Rotbuch, 1981); Wolfgang Frühwald, "Wandlungen eines Nationalmythos: Der Weg der Nibelungen ins 19. Jahrhundert," in *Wege des Mythos in der Moderne: Richard Wagner "Der Ring des Nibelungen,"* ed. Dieter Borchmeyer (Munich: Deutscher Taschenbuch Verlag, 1987), 17–40; Joachim Heinzle and Anneliese Waldschmidt, eds., *Die Nibelungen, Ein deutscher Wahn, ein deutscher Alptraum: Studien und Dokumente zur Rezeption des Nibelungenstoffs im 19. und 20. Jahrhundert* (Frankfurt a.M.: Suhrkamp, 1991); most recently, Maike Oergel, *The Return of King Arthur and the Nibelungen: National Myth in Nineteenth-Century English and German Literature* (Berlin: de Gruyter, 1998).

53. Ehrisman, *Nibelungenlied: Epoche, Werk, Wirkung*, 248–50.

54. August Wilhelm Schlegel, "Mythologie des Mittelalters," in *Kritische Schriften und Briefe*, vol. 4, *Geschichte der romantischen Literatur*, ed. Edgar Lohner (Stuttgart: Kohlhammer, 1965), 102–14.

55. Ibid., 108–9.

56. Ibid., 113.

57. Ibid., 114.

58. A. W. Schlegel, "Ueber das Lied der Nibelungen," 20–21.

59. See Saalfeld, "Die ideologische Funktion des Nibelungenlieds," 56–68, 79–91; Körner, *Nibelungenforschungen der deutschen Romantik*, 166, 182–83.

60. These developments are discussed in Schaffry, *An der Schwelle zur Wissenschaft*, 175–200.

61. A. W. Schlegel, "Ueber das Lied der Nibelungen," 18; see also ibid., 21: "In our day there has been much idle quibbling about education. The Greeks knew better: they let all freeborn learn to read with Homer."

62. Cf. Saalfeld, "Die ideologische Funktion des Nibelungenlieds," 87–89.

63. Cited by Koch, "Einleitung," in *Fouqué und Eichendorff*, 1:xxix.

64. Koch (ibid., xxxv) notes Fouqué's interest in Aeschylus beginning in 1801.

65. Friedrich de la Motte Fouqué, *Sigurd, der Schlangentödter: Ein Heldenspiel* (1808), in *Fouqué und Eichendorff*, 1:44 (lines 1038–42).

66. Ibid., 49 (line 1155).

67. A. W. Schlegel, *Kritische Schriften und Briefe*, 4:113.

68. Sigurd says, "Verpfändet meine Lieb', mein Wort gebrochen, / Nun hält mich Treue hier, reißt dort mich hin. / Ich bin verloren!—"; Fouqué, *Sigurd*, 65 (lines 2615–17).

69. On some of the reactions to Fouqué, see Fritz Strich, *Die Mythologie in der deutschen Literatur von Klopstock bis Wagner*, 2 vols. (Halle: Niemeyer, 1910), 2:261–65; Koch, "Einleitung," in *Fouqué and Eichendorff*, 1:xxxv–xxxvii.

70. Wilhelm to Jacob Grimm (Oct. 3, 1809), *Briefwechsel zwischen Jacob und Wilhelm Grimm aus der Jugendzeit*, 2nd ed., ed. Herman Grimm, Gustav Hinrichs, and Wilhelm Schoof (Weimar: Hermann Böhlaus Nachfolger, 1963), 165; Wilhelm Grimm, review of *Sigurd, der Schlangentödter*, in *Kleinere Schriften*, ed. Gustav Hinrichs, 8 vols. (Berlin: Dümmler, 1881–87), 1:237–44.

71. Brentano to Görres (Jan. 1810), cited in Koch, "Einleitung," in *Fouqué and Eichendorff*, 1:xxxvi.

72. Jacob to Wilhelm Grimm (Oct. 18, 1809), *Briefwechsel aus der Jugendzeit*, 167–68.

73. Ibid., 168.

74. On these critiques, see Körner, *Nibelungenforschungen der deutschen Romantik*, 71–188.

75. Jacob to Wilhelm Grimm (May 17, 1809), *Briefwechsel aus der Jugendzeit*, 101.

76. A. W. Schlegel, *Kritische Schriften und Briefe*, 4:108. As Otfrid Ehrisman points out, this marked a subtle break from Wolf, who had seen the epic as evolving across several different ages and not just one. In this respect, Grimm was a truer disciple of Wolf than Schlegel was, although he added a mystical element to the interpretation of myth. See Ehrisman, *Nibelungenlied in Deutschland*, 62.

77. A. W. Schlegel, "Ueber das Nibelungen-Lied," *Deutsches Museum* 2 (1812): 1–23; for an excellent analysis of Schlegel's Ofterdingen hypothesis with respect to philological questions, see Körner, *Nibelungenforschungen der deutschen Romantik*, 144–65; also Ehrisman, *Nibelungenlied in Deutschland*, 100–102.

78. A. W. Schlegel's critique forced Jacob Grimm to direct closer attention to the historical development of language and grammar, which resulted in the pathbreaking *Deutsche Grammatik* (1819–37). On this, see Konrad Koerner, "Jacob Grimm's Position in the Development of Linguistics as a Science," in *The Grimm Brothers and the Germanic Past*, ed. Antonsen, 7–24.

79. Jacob Grimm, "Ueber die Nibelungen," *Altdeutsche Wälder* 2 (1815): 152–53.

80. J. Grimm to Savigny (Dec. 26, 1811), *Briefe der Brüder Grimm an Savigny*, ed. Schoof, 127.

81. On Lachmann's theory, see Ehrisman, *Nibelungenlied in Deutschland*, 119–23; Körner, *Nibelungenforschungen der deutschen Romantik*, 191–202.

82. Karl Lachmann, *Ueber die ursprüngliche Gestalt des Gedichts von der*

Nibelungen Noth (Berlin, 1816), in *Kleinere Schriften*, ed. Karl Müllenhof (Berlin: Reimer, 1876), 1–80, here 63–64.

83. On these points, see Bluhm, *Die Brüder Grimm*, 130–34, 214–50.

84. Saalfeld, "Die ideologische Funktion des Nibelungenlieds," 93–94.

85. Saul Ascher, *Die Germanomanie* (1815), in *Vier politische Flugschriften: Eisenmenger der Zweite, Napoleon, die Germanomanie, die Wartburgfeier* (Berlin: Aufbau Verlag, 1991), 216.

86. G. W. F. Hegel, *Vorlesungen über die Aesthetik*, vol. 3, in *Werke* (Frankfurt: Suhrkamp, 1970), 15:406.

87. Friedrich von der Hagen, *Die Nibelungen: Ihre Bedeutung für die Gegenwart und für immer* (Breslau: Josef Max, 1819), 214.

88. Ibid., 207.

89. Ibid., 146.

90. Saalfeld, "Die ideologische Funktion des Nibelungenlieds," iii–iv.

91. On these reforms, see Erich Foerster, *Die Entstehung der preußischen Landeskirche unter der Regierung König Friedrich Wilhelms des Dritten: Ein Beitrag zur Geschichte der Kirchenbildung im deutschen Protestantismus*, 2 vols. (Tübingen: Mohr, 1905–7).

92. On Schleiermacher's view of liturgy, see Christoph Albrecht, *Schleiermachers Liturgik: Theorie und Praxis des Gottesdienstes bei Schleiermacher und ihre geistegeschichtlichen Zusammenhänge* (Göttingen: Vandenhoeck und Ruprecht, 1963); Albrecht Geck, *Schleiermacher als Kirchenpolitiker: Die Auseinandersetzungen um die Reform der Kirchenverfassung in Preußen (1799–1823)* (Bielefeld: Luther Verlag, 1997).

93. Friedrich Schleiermacher, *On Religion: Speeches to Its Cultured Despisers*, trans. and with an introduction by Richard Crouter (Cambridge: Cambridge University Press, 1988), 170–88.

94. Friedrich Schleiermacher, "Der Werth des öffentlichen Gottesdienstes" (1801), in *Kleine Schriften und Predigten, 1800–1820*, ed. Hayo Gerdes and Emanuel Hirsch, 3 vols. (Berlin: de Gruyter, 1969–70), 1:208–22.

95. Friedrich Schleiermacher, "Uber die Mittel, dem Verfall der Religion vorzubeugen" (1804), in *Kleine Schriften und Predigten*, 2:71–95.

96. On nationalism in Prussia during these years, see Otto Johnston, *The Myth of a Nation: Literature and Politics under Napoleon* (Columbia, S.C.: Camden House, 1989); Jörg Echternkamp, *Der Aufstieg des deutschen Nationalismus (1770–1840)* (Frankfurt a.M.: Campus, 1998), 216–90; Matthew Bernard Levinger, *Enlightened Nationalism: The Transformation of Prussian Political Culture, 1806–1848* (Oxford: Oxford University Press, 2000).

97. Friedrich Ludwig Jahn, *Deutsches Volkstum* (1810) (Berlin: Aufbau, 1991), 102–3.

98. Ibid., 231–32; on Jahn's views of festivals, see Dieter Düding, *Organisierter Gesellschaftlicher Nationalismus in Deutschland (1808–1847): Bedeutung und Funktion der Turner- und Sängervereine für die deutsche Nationalbewegung*

(Munich: Oldenbourg, 1984), 111–20; also George Mosse, *The Nationalization of the Masses: Political Symbolism and Mass Movements in Germany from the Napoleonic Wars through the Third Reich* (New York: Howard Fertig, 1975), 73–79 and passim.

99. Jahn, *Deutsches Volkstum*, 241.

100. Ernst Moritz Arndt, "Entwurf einer deutschen Gesellschaft" (1814), in *Ausgewählte Werke in sechzehn Bänden*, ed. Heinrich Meisner and Robert Geerds (Leipzig: Max Hesses Verlag, 1908), 13:250–67, here 261. I am indebted to Wolfgang Hardtwig for this reference.

101. Ibid., 264–65. On Arndt, the cross, and the role of religion in Prussia during the War of Liberation, see Gerhard Graf, *Gottesbild und Politik: Eine Studie zur Frömmigkeit in Preußen während der Befreiungskriege, 1813–1815* (Göttingen: Vandenhoeck und Ruprecht, 1993).

102. Fichte developed a plan for a national cultus in his unpublished "Die Republik der Deutschen" (1807); see *J. G. Fichte — Gesamtausgabe*, ed. Reinhard Lauth, Hans Jacob, and Hans Gliwitzky (Stuttgart and Bad Cannstatt: Frommann-Holzboog, 1994), pt. 2, 10:373–423.

103. On Fries, see the excellent study of Gerald Hubmann, *Ethische Überzeugung und politisches Handeln: Jakob Friedrich Fries und die deutsche Tradition der Gesinnungsethik* (Heidelberg: Winter, 1997).

104. Jakob Friedrich Fries, *Neue oder anthropologische Kritik der Vernunft*, 2nd ed., 3 vols. (Heidelberg: Winter, 1828–31), 3:367–80.

105. Jakob Friedrich Fries, *Dialogues on Morality and Religion*, trans. David Walford (Oxford: Basil Blackwell, 1982), 122.

106. On the attraction of Fries's philosophy to nationalist students, see Hubmann, *Ethische Ueberzeugung und politisches Handeln*, 151–234.

107. On de Wette, see chap. 4.

108. W. M. L. de Wette, *Ueber Religion und Theologie: Erläuterungen zu seinem Lehrbuche der Dogmatik* (Berlin: Realschulbuchhandlung, 1815), 240.

109. Ibid., 106, 99.

110. Ibid., 116.

111. Ibid., 233.

112. Ibid., 247.

113. Ibid., 244.

114. Cf. Jakob Fries, *Ueber die Gefährdung des Wohlstandes und Charakters der Deutschen durch die Juden* (Heidelberg: Mohr and Winter, 1816).

115. On this, see my essay "What Killed August von Kotzebue? The Temptations of Virtue and the Political Theology of German Nationalism, 1789–1819," *Journal of Modern History* 72 (2000): 890–943.

116. Foerster, *Entstehung der preußischen Landeskirche*, 55–69.

117. Mosse, *Nationalization of the Masses*; also Bernhard Giesen, *Intellectuals and the Nation: Collective Identity in a German Axial Age* (Cambridge: Cambridge University, 1998), 80–102.

118. On this point, see Altgeld, *Katholizismus, Protestantismus, Judentum*, 125–37.

119. See the insightful discussion by Wolf-Daniel Hartwich, *Deutsche Mythologie: Die Erfindung einer Kunstreligion* (Berlin: Piper, 2000), 24–35.

120. For histories of research, see P. D. Chantepie de la Saussaye, *The Religion of the Teutons*, trans. Bert J. Vos (Boston: Ginn, 1902), 7–48; Horst Seipp, *Entwicklungszüge der germanischen Religionswissenschaft (von Jacob Grimm zu Georges Dumézil)* (Berlin: Ernst-Reuter Gesellschaft, 1968); see also Wolfgang Emmerich, *Germanistische Volkstumsideologie: Genese und Kritik der Volksforschung im Dritten Reich* (Tübingen: Vereinigung für Volkskunde, 1968). The invented nature of "German mythology" is emphasized by Hartwich, *Deutsche Mythologie*, 9–15.

121. But from the perspective of modern scholars they were deeply flawed. For a devastating critique of Jacob Grimm's methodology, see Beate Kellner, *Grimms Mythen: Studien zum Mythosbegriff und seiner Anwendung in Jacob Grimms "Deutscher Mythologie"* (Frankfurt a.M.: Peter Lang, 1994).

122. Herder, "Iduna, oder der Apfel der Verjüngung" (1796), *HSW*, 18:493.

123. Joseph Görres, "Hunibalds Chronik," *Deutsches Museum* 3 (1813): 505.

124. Friedrich Rühs's works included *Geschichte der Religion, Staatsverfassung und Cultur der alten Skandinavier* (Göttingen: Röwer, 1801); and *Die Edda: Nebst einer Einleitung über nordische Poesie* (Berlin: Realschulbuchhandlung, 1812). Rühs's first anti-Semitic writings dealt with the question of Jewish emancipation: *Ueber die Ansprüche der Juden an das deutsche Bürgerrecht* (Berlin: Realschulbuchhandlung, 1816).

125. Friedrich Rühs, *Ueber den Ursprung der isländischen Poesie aus der angelsächsischen* (Berlin: Reimer, 1813).

126. Ibid., 31.

127. Peter Erasmus Müller, *Ueber die Aechtheit der Asahlehre und den Werth der Snorrischen Edda*, trans. L. C. Sander (Copenhagen: Brummer, 1811); review by Wilhelm Grimm, repr. in Wilhelm Grimm, *Kleinere Schriften*, ed. Gustav Hinrichs, 8 vols. (Berlin Dümmler, 1881), 2:14–32; on Rühs and P. E. Müller, see Seipp, *Entwicklungszüge der germanischen Religionswissenschaft*, 12–15.

128. W. Grimm, review of Rühs, *Ueber den Ursprung der islandischen Poesie* (1813), repr. in *Kleinere Schriften*, 2:137–54.

129. Jacob Grimm, *Deutsche Mythologie*, 4th ed., ed. Elard Hugo Meyer, 3 vols. (Basel: Schwabe, 1953), 1:v.

130. For an account of a masked ball based on characters from the *Prose Edda*, see "Großer Charakteristischer Maskenball in Leipzig am 26. Februar 1816," *Journal für Literatur, Kunst, Luxus und Mode* (Mar. 1816): 186–99.

131. Rühs, *Die Edda*; Friedrich Heinrich von der Hagen, *Lieder der älteren oder Sämundischen Edda* (Berlin: Haude und Spener, 1812); Jacob and Wilhelm Grimm, *Lieder der alten Edda* (Berlin: Realschulbuchhandlung, 1815).

132. Cited in Karl Adolf Menzel, *Ueber die Undeutschheit des neuen Deutschtums* (Breslau: Graß, Barth, 1818), 117–18.

133. Hegel, *Vorlesungen über die Aesthetik*, vol. 3, in *Werke*, 15:404.

134. Karl Rosenkranz, *Das Heldenbuch und die Nibelungen* (Halle: Eduard Anton, 1829), 14–15.

135. Franz Josef Mone, *Geschichte des Heidenthums im nördlichen Europa*, 2 vols. (Leipzig and Darmstadt: Leske, 1822–23).

136. See the detailed discussion of Creuzer in chapter 3.

137. Mone, *Geschichte des Heidenthums*, 2:273–80.

138. Karl Göttling, *Nibelungen und Gibelinen* (Rudolstadt: Hof-, Buch- und Kunsthandlung, 1816); reviewed by Wilhelm Grimm, repr. in *Kleinere Schriften*, 2:161–75; Franz Josef Mone, *Einleitung in das Nibelungenlied zum Schul- und Selbstgebrauch* (Heidelberg: August Oswald, 1818).

139. Mone, *Einleitung*, 66; see also Franz Josef Mone, *Untersuchungen zur Geschichte der teutschen Heldensage* (Quedlinburg and Leipzig: Gottfried Basse, 1836).

140. Mone, *Geschichte des Heidenthums*, 2:324.

141. Ibid., 1:xiv–xvii.

142. Jacob Grimm, *Kleinere Schriften*, 8 vols. (Berlin: Dümmler, 1864–90), 8:171.

143. J. Grimm, *Deutsche Mythologie*, 1:xxi (the citation is from Grimm's preface to the 1844 2nd ed.).

144. J. Grimm, *Kleinere Schriften*, 8:169.

145. This is particularly evident in Grimm's reaction to the Creuzer controversy. See chapter 3.

146. J. Grimm, *Deutsche Mythologie*, 1:ix.

147. This view contradicted Heinrich Leo, *Ueber Odins Verehrung in Deutschland: Ein Beitrag zur deutschen Alterthumskunde* (Erlangen: C. Heyder, 1822). Leo, who would become a leading Prussian conservative in the 1830s, wrote this piece as a youthful *Burschenschaftler*. In accordance with Rühs, Arndt, and Hans Ferdinand Maßmann, he argued that the earliest Germans had not worshiped Odin but had practiced a form of nature worship similar in its outlines to a rationalist Christianity. Odin worship had been brought into Germany by the Saxons, Goths, Langobards, and other conquering races from the east. These invaders also imposed the estate system on the Germans. In Leo's view, Odin was simply a deified king and not the representative of a higher metaphysical power as described by Jacob Grimm (see below).

148. J. Grimm, *Deutsche Mythologie*, 1:136.

149. Cf. J. Grimm to Savigny (Feb. 24, 1826), *Briefe der Brüder Grimm an Savigny*, ed. Schoof, 341: "That I am inclined to be antiliturgical, you can imagine for yourself."

150. J. Grimm, *Deutsche Mythologie*, 1:74.

151. Ibid., 97.

152. Cf. Grimm's earlier essay, *Irmenstrasze und Irmensäule: Eine mythologische Abhandlung* (Vienna: Mayer, 1815), repr. in *Kleinere Schriften*, 8:471–503. Many of this essay's more speculative claims were not repeated in the *Deutsche Mythologie*.

153. J. Grimm, *Deutsche Mythologie*, 1:127.

154. Ibid., 130.

155. Ibid., 132.

156. Cornelius Tacitus, *The Complete Works*, trans. Alfred John Church and William Jackson Brodribb (New York: Modern Library, 1942), 728–29 (trans. modified).

157. The same could be said about contemporary revivals of the "Goddess." The archaeologist Marija Gimbutas has argued that an "Earth Goddess" was universally worshiped in prehistoric Europe before being replaced by a male sky deity. See, e.g., Marija Gimbutas, *The Language of the Goddess: Unearthing the Hidden Symbols of Western Civilization* (San Francisco: Harper and Row, 1989); and Marija Gimbutas, *The Civilization of the Goddess: The World of Old Europe* (San Francisco: HarperCollins, 1991). For a time, Gimbutas's work inspired a significant "Goddess" movement among feminist scholars and laypeople in Europe and North America. For one critique, see Cynthia Eller, *The Myth of Matriarchal Prehistory: Why an Invented Past Won't Give Women a Future* (Boston: Beacon Press, 2000).

158. See, e.g., Joseph Lauer, "Hertha: Deutsche Mythe," *Deutsches Museum* 4 (1813): 376–84; Christian Karl Barth, *Die altteutsche Religion: Hertha und über die Religion der Weltmutter im alten Teutschland* (Leipzig: Friedrich Fleischer, 1835); Wilhelm Müller, *Geschichte und System der altdeutschen Religion* (Göttingen: Vandenhoeck und Ruprecht, 1844).

159. For a sampling of opinion, see Rosegarten, "Der Hain und See der Göttin Hertha," *Bragur* 5 (1797): 191–93; [Curt Wilhelm] Bose, "Über die Herthainsel; eine Erklärung der Stelle des Tacitus in seiner 'Germania,'" *Bericht vom Jahre 1834 an die Mitglieder der Deutschen Gesellschaft zu Erforschung vaterländischer Sprache und Alterthümer in Leipzig*, 1834, 20–28.

160. J. Grimm, *Deutsche Mythologie*, 1:210–11.

161. Ibid., 409.

162. Ibid., 2:711.

163. Jacob Grimm and Wilhelm Grimm, *The German Legends*, trans. Donald Ward, 2 vols. (Philadelphia: Institute for the Study of Human Issues, 1981), 1:33.

164. J. Grimm, *Deutsche Mythologie*, 2:798–99.

165. Arno Borst, "Barbarossas Erwachen—Zur Geschichte der deutschen Identität," in *Identität*, ed. Odo Marquard and Karlheinz Stierle (Munich: Wilhelm Fink, 1979), 17–60.

166. J. Grimm, *Deutsche Mythologie*, 2:802.

167. Ibid., 666–67.

168. Ibid., 1:3.

169. Zantop, *Colonial Fantasies*, 94–95. Zantop does not explore the theological implications of this analogy, however.

170. Herder, *Briefe zu Beförderung der Humanität* (1793–97), *HSW*, 18:222.

171. J. Grimm, *Deutsche Mythologie*, 1:xxxvii–xxxviii.

172. Ibid., xxxviii.

173. J. Grimm to Savigny (Dec. 28, 1836), in *Briefe der Brüder Grimm an Savigny*, ed. Schoof, 384. Klaus von See, *Die Göttinger Sieben*, is highly critical of Grimm and attempts to debunk the legends of Grimm the "democrat," Grimm the innovative scholar, and Grimm the man of integrity. But he fails to explain Grimm's

motivation for participating in the Göttingen Seven protest and, in the process, jeapardizing his career.

174. J. Grimm to Savigny (Feb. 24, 1826), in *Briefe der Brüder Grimm an Savigny*, ed. Schoof, 341.

175. J. Grimm to Savigny (Oct. 15, 1838), in ibid., 401–2.

176. Hartwich, *Deutsche Mythologie*, 58–65.

177. Crane, *Collecting and Historical Consciousness*, 18–19.

178. Heinrich Heine, "Ludwig Börne," in *Werke und Briefe in zehn Bänden*, ed. Hans Kaufmann (Berlin: Aufbau, 1961), 6:170.

179. Heine, "Die Nordsee. 1826. Dritte Abteilung," in *Werke*, 3:105.

180. Ibid.

181. Heine to Christiani (Mar. 7, 1824), in ibid., 8:142; cf. Heine, "Ludwig Börne," in *Werke*, 6:170.

182. Wunderlich, *Schatz*, 31.

183. Heine, review of Wolfgang Menzel, *Die deutsche Literatur* (1828), in *Werke*, 4:241.

184. Heine, "Die Nordsee. 1826. Dritte Abteilung," 3:118.

185. Heine, *Die romantische Schule*, in *Werke*, 5:67. See also *Elementargeister*, in ibid., 312: "[Grimm's] *Deutsche Grammatik* is a colossal work, a Gothic cathedral, in which all Germanic peoples raise their voices like giant choirs, each in its own dialect. Perhaps Jacob Grimm sold his soul to the devil, so that he would deliver the materials and serve him as handyman during this huge work of linguistic reconstruction." On Heine's attitude to A. W. Schlegel and the Grimms, see esp. Winkler, *Mythisches Denken zwischen Romantik und Realismus*.

186. On Heine and Saint-Simonianism, see E. M. Butler, *The Saint-Simonian Religion in Germany: A Study of the Young German Movement* (1926; repr., New York: Howard Fertig, 1968), 88–169.

187. Dates given are for the first French editions. On the complicated publication history, see Jeffrey Sammons, *Heinrich Heine: A Modern Biography* (Princeton: Princeton University Press, 1979), 189–90, 216–17.

188. Heine, *Elementargeister*, in *Werke*, 5:311.

189. Ibid., 318.

190. Ibid., 324.

191. Ibid., 327.

192. Ibid., 316–17; cf. "The Departure of the Dwarf Nation over the Bridge," no. 153 in J. Grimm and W. Grimm, *German Legends*, 1:146–47.

193. J. Grimm, *Deutsche Mythologie*, 1:380. I am indebted to Brian Vick for this reference.

194. Heine, *Elementargeister*, 317.

195. Grimm harbored his own anti-Semitic prejudices, which were expressed obliquely in his choice of fairy tales ("The Jew in the Thorn Bush") and more directly in his private correspondence with Wilhelm (see the letters regarding the hiring of Friedrich Murhard instead of Wilhelm Grimm to be editor of the *Kasseler Zeitung*,

cited in Feldmann, *Jacob Grimm und die Politik*, 90–93). But Grimm did not thematize Jews or Judaism directly in the *Deutsche Sagen* or the *Deutsche Mythologie*.

196. J. Grimm, *Deutsche Mythologie*, 2:822–60.

197. Heine, *Elementargeister*, 346.

198. Ibid., 341.

199. Heine, *Zur Geschichte der Religion und Philosophie in Deutschland*, in *Werke*, 5:306.

200. Ibid., 308.

201. Jeffrey Sammons, *Heinrich Heine: A Modern Biography* (Princeton: Princeton University Press, 1979), 252.

202. Ibid., 267.

203. W. D. Robson-Scott, *The Literary Background of the Gothic Revival in Germany: A Chapter in the History of Taste* (Oxford: Clarendon, 1965), 292.

204. Heinrich Heine, "Germany: A Winter's Tale," trans. Aaron Kramer, in *Poetry and Prose*, ed. Jost Hermand and Robert C. Holub (New York: Continuum, 1982), 239.

205. In *Elementargeister*, 326, Heine associated the Rhine with the legend of Lohengrin: "How often, when I rode down the Rhine and came by the Swan Tower of Kleves, did I think of the mysterious knight, who preserved his incognito with such sad strictness and who could be driven from the arms of love by the mere question about his origin."

206. Heine, "Germany: A Winter's Tale," 242 (trans. modified).

207. Ibid., 256.

208. Ibid., 266 (trans. modified).

209. Ibid., 269.

210. Ibid., 271 (trans. modified).

211. Hans Blumenberg, *Work on Myth*, trans. Robert M. Wallace (Cambridge: MIT Press, 1985); this theme has been developed in more detail (and with close reference to Heine's theological views) in Markus Küppers, *Heinrich Heines Arbeit am Mythos* (Münster: Waxmann, 1994).

212. For the British context, see Oergel, *Return of King Arthur*; also Sam Smiles, *The Image of Antiquity: Ancient Britain and the Romantic Imagination* (New Haven: Yale University Press, 1994); Carole G. Silver, *Strange and Secret Peoples: Fairies and Victorian Consciousness* (Oxford: Oxford University Press, 1999).

213. Ludolf Müller, ed. and trans., *Das Lied von der Heerfahrt Igor's* (Munich: Erich Wewel, 1989); Gerd Krumeich, *Jeanne d'Arc in der Geschichte: Historiographie, Politik, Kultur* (Sigmaringen: Thorbecke, 1989).

CHAPTER THREE

1. "Let the lamentation renew us! Call to secret ceremonies those who call Adonis holy, who recognize his divinity, who have earned the consecrations, for whom the god died." "Adonis Todtenfeyer," in Karoline von Günderode, *Der Schatten eines Traumes: Gedichte, Prosa, Briefe, Zeugnisse von Zeitgenossen*, ed. with an essay by Christa Wolf (Berlin: Luchterhand, 1979), 105.

2. "Seek not secret consecrations! Don't stare under the veil! If you want to live, my good fool, look back behind you into the open." J. W. Goethe, "Dem Symboliker," cited in Reinhold Herbig, "Die Beziehungen zu Friedrich Creuzer in Heidelberg," *Goethe und Heidelberg*, ed. Richard Benz (Heidelberg: F. H. Kerle, 1949), 267–74, here 273.

3. Friedrich Creuzer, "Aus dem Leben eines alten Professors," in his *Deutsche Schriften* (Leipzig and Darmstadt: Leske, 1837–56), pt. 5, vol. 1, 12. Years later Creuzer published a book on the art of the Elisabethkirche, entitled *Zur Gemmenkunde: Antike geschnittene Steine vom Grabmal der Heiligen Elisabeth in der nach ihr genannten Kirche zu Marburg in Kurhessen* (Darmstadt: Leske, 1834).

4. Creuzer published his anecdote in *Zeitgenossen: Biographen und Charakteristiken*, n.s., 2, no. 6 (Leipzig: Brockhaus, 1822).

5. Johann Heinrich Voss, *Antisymbolik*, 2 vols. (Stuttgart: Metzler, 1824–26), 1:344.

6. Schlegel, *KFSA*, 1:569.

7. The lands of the "Orient" in early-nineteenth-century Germany included Egypt, the Ottoman Empire, Persia, and India. Edward Said's *Orientalism* (New York: Vintage, 1979) has demonstrated the links between the term "Orient" and the field of "Orientalism" to the history of colonialism and racism. This terminology is retained in the present study for purposes of historical accuracy and because it was precisely the ambiguity of the concept "Orient" that made it alternately threatening and appealing to European intellectuals in this period.

8. Werner Paul Sohnle, *Georg Friedrich Creuzer's "Symbolik und Mythologie" in Frankreich: Eine Untersuchung ihres Einflusses auf Victor Cousin, Edgar Quinet, Jules Michelet und Gustave Flaubert* (Göppingen: Kümmerle, 1972); on this topic, see also Raymond Schwab, *The Oriental Renaissance: Europe's Rediscovery of India and the East, 1680–1880*, trans. Gene Patterson-Black and Victor Reinking (New York: Columbia University Press, 1984).

9. Carl Jung read the entire *Symbolik und Mythologie* in preparation for his *Wandlungen und Symbole der Libido* (1912); see Christoph Jamme, *Einführung in die Philosophie des Mythos*, vol. 2, *Neuzeit und Gegenwart* (Darmstadt: Wissenschaftliche Buchgesellschaft, 1991), 108.

10. The controversy over Creuzer's *Symbolik und Mythologie* has been the occasional subject of scholarly study. For an early account, see P. F. Stuhr, "Allgemeiner Ueberblick über die Geschichte der Behandlung der Mythen seit dem Mittelalter," in *Zeitschrift für spekulative Theologie* 1, no. 1 (1836): 88–124; 1, no. 2 (1836): 404–34; see also Ernst Howald, *Der Kampf um Creuzers Symbolik: Eine Auswahl von Dokumenten* (Tübingen: Mohr, 1926); Marc-Mathieu Münch, *La "Symbolique" de Friedrich Creuzer* (Paris: Ophrys, 1976); also the essays in Friedrich Strack, ed., *Heidelberg im säkularen Umbruch: Traditionsbewußtsein und Kulturpolitik um 1800* (Stuttgart: Klett-Cotta, 1987). Recent scholarship has shed a valuable light on the Creuzer controversy, in particular Josine Blok's "Quest for a Scientific Mythology: F. Creuzer and K. O. Müller on History and Myth," in *Proof and Persuasion in History*, ed. Anthony Grafton and Suzanne L. Marchand, *History and Theory* Theme Issue 33 (1994): 26–52; also Éva Kocziszky, "Samothrake: Ein Streit um Creuzers Symbolik und das Wesen der Mythologie," *Antike und Abendland* 43 (1997): 174–89. See also

Marchand's acute observations in her *Down from Olympus: Archaeology and Phil-hellenism in Germany, 1750–1970* (Princeton: Princeton University Press, 1996), 43–48. None of these studies has offered a detailed examination of the political and religious issues at stake in the *Symbolik* controversy.

11. Wolfgang Menzel, *Voß und die Symbolik* (Stuttgart: Franckh, 1825), 8–9.

12. Creuzer, "Aus dem Leben," 21.

13. Cited in Karl Preisendanz, ed., *Die Liebe der Günderode: Friedrich Creuzers Briefe an Caroline von Günderode* (Munich: Piper, 1912), p. v. Bettina von Arnim and Creuzer despised each other, so her opinion may be skewed.

14. Creuzer, "Aus dem Leben," 27.

15. Erwin Rohde, editorial notes to Friedrich Creuzer and Karoline von Günderode, *Briefe und Dichtungen* (Heidelberg: Carl Winter, 1896), 106.

16. Creuzer to Savigny (Nov. 16, 1799), in *Briefe Friedrich Creuzers an Savigny*, ed. H. Dahlmann (Berlin: Eric Schmidt Verlag, 1972), 67–68.

17. Creuzer to Savigny (Sept. 16, 1799), in ibid., 61. Creuzer admitted, "I owe many of my clearest insights into Greek antiquity to [Friedrich Schlegel's] works, es-pecially his history of Greek and Roman poetry"; Creuzer to Savigny (Dec. 15, 1799), in ibid., 73.

18. G. F. Creuzer, *Herodot und Thucydides: Versuch einer näheren Würdigung einiger ihrer historischen Grundsätze* (Leipzig: Müller, 1798); G. F. Creuzer, *Die his-torische Kunst der Griechen in ihrer Entstehung und Fortbildung* (Leipzig: Göschen, 1803). Contrary to the claims of Ludwig Preller, "Friedrich Creuzer, charakterisirt nach seinen Werken," *Hallische Jahrbücher für deutsche Wissenschaft und Kunst* 101 (Apr. 27, 1838): 802, there was no huge break between the earlier and later Creuzer.

19. Herbert Levin, *Die Heidelberger Romantik* (Munich: Paarcus, 1922), 20.

20. Franz Schneider, *Geschichte der Universität Heidelberg im ersten Jahr-zehnt nach der Reorganisation durch Karl Friedrich (1803–1813)* (Heidelberg: Winter, 1913).

21. Citations are from the English translation by E. S. Morgan under the title *On University Studies* (Athens: Ohio University Press, 1966), here 26–27 (trans. modified).

22. Ibid., 110–14, 134–42. On these issues see Frederick Gregory, "Kant, Schel-ling and the Administration of Science in the Romantic Era," in *Science in Germany: The Intersection of Institutional and Intellectual Issues*, ed. Kathryn Olesko (Philadelphia: University of Pennsylvania Press, 1989), 17–35; see also Thomas Bro-man, "University Reform in Medical Thought at the End of the Eighteenth Century," in *Science in Germany*, 36–53.

23. Creuzer, "Aus dem Leben," 31, also 119–21.

24. Schelling, *On University Studies*, 107 (trans. modified).

25. Friedrich Creuzer, "Das Studium des Alterthums, als Vorbereitung zur Philosophie," *Studien* 1 (1805): 1–28; see also Friedrich Creuzer, *Das akademische Studium des Alterthums* (Heidelberg: Mohr und Zimmer, 1807).

26. Creuzer, "Studium des Alterthums," 19–20.

27. These ideas paralleled the proposals for a new mystery religion by Schelling in *Philosophie und Religion* (1804), a work Creuzer read upon its appearance. See the summary of Creuzer's letter to his brother Leonard (Nov. 18, 1804), in *Briefe und Dichtungen*, 19.

28. Schneider, *Geschichte der Universität Heidelberg*, 129. See also Hartmut Fröschle, *Der Spätaufklärer Johann Heinrich Voß als Kritiker der deutschen Romantik* (Stuttgart: Heinz, 1985); Günter Häntzschel, "Johann Heinrich Voß in Heidelberg: Kontroversen und Mißverständnisse," in *Heidelberg im säkularen Umbruch*, ed. Strack, 301–21; Frank Baudach and Günter Hantzschel, eds., *Johann Heinrich Voß (1751–1826)* (Eutin: Struve, 1997), esp. the essays by Adrian Hummel and Helmut J. Schneider.

29. Johann Heinrich Voss, "Ueber klassische Bildung" (1807), published posthumously in his *Kritische Blätter nebst Geografischen Abhandlungen*, 2 vols. (Stuttgart: Metzler, 1828), 2:69–70; cf. Häntzschel, "Johann Heinrich Voß in Heidelberg," 310–11.

30. See Schneider, *Geschichte der Universität Heidelberg*, 284–97.

31. Arnim to Creuzer (Nov. 25, 1809), in Reinhold Steig, "Zeugnisse zur Pflege der deutschen Literatur in den Heidelberger Jahrbüchern," *Neue Heidelberger Jahrbücher* 11 (1902): 231.

32. On the Creuzer-Günderode affair, see Rohde, introduction to Creuzer and Günderode, *Briefe und Dichtungen*; Preisendanz, *Die Liebe der Günderode*; Wolf, introduction to Günderode, *Der Schatten eines Traumes*, 5–65.

33. Creuzer to Günderode (Dec. 7, 1805), in *Briefe und Dichtungen*, 79–80.

34. Friedrich Creuzer, *Symbolik und Mythologie der alten Völker, besonders der Griechen*, 4 vols. (Leipzig and Darmstadt: Heyer and Leske, 1810–12). Creuzer published a substantially enlarged 2nd ed. (Leipzig and Darmstadt: Heyer and Leske, 1819–21) and a still larger 3rd ed. (Leipzig and Darmstadt: Leske, 1837–43). Citations are from the 2nd ed., which was the first complete version and the most influential of the three.

35. In German usage, a *Symbolik* is not only a system of symbolism but also a coherent doctrine of faith. The implications of this terminology were not lost on Creuzer or his readers.

36. Creuzer's insistence on the astronomical origins of myth echoed the work of the French scholar Charles Dupuis, whose *Origine de tous les cultes ou la Religion universelle* (1795) traced the origins of religion to the zodiac. But while Dupuis's work was generally antireligious in tone and intent, Creuzer's *Symbolik und Mythologie* sought to venerate this process. On the significance of Dupuis, see Jonathan Z. Smith, *Drudgery Divine: On the Comparison of Early Christianities and the Religions of Late Antiquity* (Chicago: University of Chicago Press, 1990).

37. According to Creuzer, Homer's poetry was simply the "interpretation of a hieroglyph or a symbolic image"; *Symbolik und Mythologie*, 1:96.

38. Ibid., 2:302.

39. For this development, see the important but deeply flawed work of Martin Bernal, *Black Athena: The Afroasiatic Roots of Classical Civilization*, vol. 1, *The Fabrication of Ancient Greece, 1785–1985* (New Brunswick: Rutgers University

Press, 1987), esp. 212–15 and 281–316. It is true, as Bernal argues, that the period 1750–1850 saw an increased emphasis on Greek cultural autonomy and that this process was fraught with theological, political, and racial overtones. But Bernal's account of this history is one-sided and often misleading. First, Bernal cites an increased Christian religiosity as a result of the rise of Romanticism. In the context of the Restoration, however, this revival did not necessarily favor the Philhellenists (who were rather rationalist in their theology) but rather those conservatives who wanted to emphasize the dependence of Europe on oriental and, hence, biblical models of religion. Second, while Bernal makes much of the shift from Egypt to India as the seat of culture, most contemporaries saw both lands as part of a rather undifferentiated "Orient." The Philhellenists were no more eager to see Greek myths traced to India than they were to see them traced to Egypt. On the complex of issues raised by Bernal, see Mary R. Lefkowitz and Guy Maclean Rogers, eds., *Black Athena Revisited* (Chapel Hill: University of North Carolina Press, 1996), esp. the essays by Robert Palter, Robert E. Norton, and Richard Jenkyns; also Bernal's reply in *Black Athena Writes Back: Martin Bernal Responds to His Critics*, ed. David Chioni Moore (Durham, N.C.: Duke University Press, 2001), 165–97.

40. Creuzer, *Symbolik und Mythologie*, 1:xviii–xix.

41. Ibid., 2:293–98.

42. In 1808, Creuzer declared it a proven fact that India was the "motherland of ancient religion." See "Philologie und Mythologie in ihrem Stufengang und gegenseitigen Verhalten," *Heidelberger Jahrbücher der Literatur* 1 (1808): 4.

43. Creuzer, in Gottfried Hermann and Friedrich Creuzer, *Briefe über Homer und Hesiodus, vorzüglich über die Theogonie* (Heidelberg: Oswald, 1818), 142. In future references to this work, only the author of the cited passage will be named.

44. On Jones, see Garland Cannon, *The Life and Mind of Oriental Jones: Sir William Jones, the Father of Modern Linguistics* (Cambridge: Cambridge University Press, 1990); Bruce Lincoln, *Theorizing Myth: Narrative, Ideology, and Scholarship* (Chicago: University of Chicago Press, 1999), 76–100.

45. M. [Abraham] Anquetil-Duperron, *Zend-avesta, ouvrage de Zoroaster* (Paris: Tilliard, 1771); M. [Abraham] Anquetil-Duperron, *Opnek'hat* (Strasbourg: Levrault, 1801–2). Marie-Elisabeth Polier, ed., *Mythologie des Indous*, 2 vols. (Roudolstadt: Libraire de la Coeur; Paris: F. Schoell, 1809), was also influential for Creuzer's *Symbolik und Mythologie*.

46. These included Friedrich Schlegel, *Ueber die Sprache und Weisheit der Indier: Ein Beitrag zur Begründung der Alterthumskunde* (Heidelberg: Mohr und Zimmer, 1808); Joseph Görres, *Mythengeschichte der asiatischen Welt* (Heidelberg: Mohr und Zimmer, 1810), which was dedicated to "Professor Creuzer and my former hearers." On these developments, see René Girard, *L'orient dans la pensée romantique allemande* (Paris: M. Didier, 1963); A. Leslie Wilson, *A Mythical Image: The Ideal of India in German Romanticism* (Durham, N.C.: Duke University Press, 1964); Ernst Behler, "Das Indienbild der deutschen Romantik," *Germanisch-romanische Monatsschrift* 49, no. 1 (1968): 21–37; Jean Sedlar, *India in the Mind of Germany* (Washington, D.C.: University Press of America, 1982); Schwab, *Oriental Renaissance*, 203–21 and passim.

47. Charles de Villers, *Coup-d'oeuil sur l'état actuel de la littérature ancienne*

et de l'histoire en Allemagne (Amsterdam and Paris: Bureau des Arts et de la Littérature, 1809), 47.

48. On Creuzer's theory of the symbol, see Tzvetan Todorov, *Theories of the Symbol*, trans. Catherine Porter (Oxford: Blackwell, 1982), 216–19; for its influence on Hegel's notion of "symbolic art," see Johannes Hoffmeister, "Hegel und Creuzer," *Deutsche Vierteljahresschrift für Literaturwissenschaft und Geistesgeschichte* 8 (1930): 260–82.

49. See Creuzer, *Briefe über Homer und Hesiodus*, 29–32; Creuzer, *Symbolik und Mythologie*, 1:3–20.

50. See esp. E. F. Jomard, *Description de l'Egypte, ou Recueil des observations et des recherches qui ont été faites en Egypte pendant l'expédition de l'armée française* (Paris: Imprimerie Impériale, 1807); other key works included Antoine Isaac Silverstre de Saçy, *Lettre au citoyen Chaptal au sujet de l'inscription égyptienne du monument trouvé à Rosette* (Paris: Imprimerie de la République, 1802).

51. It was only in the 1820s, when Jean-François Champollion decoded the Rosetta Stone, that it became clear that the hieroglyphs formed a phonetic language. See Erik Iversen, *The Myth of Egypt and Its Hieroglyphs in European Tradition* (1961; repr., Princeton: Princeton University Press, 1994).

52. See, e.g., Creuzer, *Symbolik und Mythologie*, 4:120–35.

53. Ibid., 1:59, also 1:28–44 for the related meanings of σύμβολον.

54. Ibid., 70.

55. Ibid., 59.

56. Ibid., 45; also cf. 72–78; Creuzer, "Das Studium des Alterthums," 5–6.

57. Creuzer, *Symbolik und Mythologie*, 2:312.

58. Ibid., 316–22.

59. Ibid., 4:552.

60. For Görres's *Naturphilosophie*, see Reinhardt Habel, *Joseph Görres: Studien über den Zusammenhang von Natur, Geschichte und Mythos in seinen Schriften* (Wiesbaden: Franz Steiner, 1960).

61. See George E. Mylonas, *Eleusis and the Eleusinian Mysteries* (Princeton: Princeton University Press, 1961); Walter Burkert, *Ancient Mystery Cults* (Cambridge: Harvard University Press, 1987).

62. Cf. Creuzer, *Symbolik und Mythologie*, 3:335–49, 4:518–38.

63. Ibid., 2:420.

64. Ibid., 4:9. Here Creuzer anticipates Bachofen, as well as more recent theories of the "Goddess" (see the literature cited in chapter 2).

65. Ibid., 3:408.

66. Ibid., 385.

67. On the broader history of this opposition, see Martin Vogel, *Apollinisch und Dionysisch: Geschichte eines genialen Irrtums* (Regensburg: Gustav Bosse, 1966).

68. Creuzer, *Symbolik und Mythologie*, 3:446.

69. Ibid., 335–38.

70. Ibid., 4:551–59. The pagan "anticipations" of Christianity were also empha-

sized by the Heidelberg theologian Carl Ullmann in his brief study "Vergleichende Zusammenstellung des christlichen Festcyklus mit vorchristlichen Festen," in Creuzer, *Symbolik und Mythologie*, 4:577–614.

71. Creuzer, *Symbolik und Mythologie*, 1:201.

72. Ibid., 198–99.

73. Creuzer, *Briefe über Homer und Hesiodus*, 47.

74. Creuzer, *Symbolik und Mythologie*, 2:454, 462.

75. Gerhart von Graevenitz, *Mythos: Geschichte einer Denkgewohnheit* (Stuttgart and Weimar: Metzler, 1987), 1–120.

76. On philology as the model science, see Anthony La Vopa, "Specialists against Specialization: Hellenism as Professional Ideology in German Classical Studies," in *German Professions, 1800–1950*, ed. Geoffrey Cocks and Konrad Jarausch (Oxford: Oxford University Press, 1990), 27–45.

77. See Ulrich von Wilamowitz-Moellendorff's short appraisal, *A History of Classical Scholarship*, trans. Alan Harris, ed. Hugh Lloyd-Jones (London: Duckworth, 1982), 109–11.

78. See Gottfried Hermann, *Ueber das Wesen und die Behandlung der Mythologie, ein Brief an Herrn Hofrath Creuzer* (Leipzig: Gerhard Fleischer, 1818).

79. Hermann, *Briefe über Homer und Hesiodus*, 16.

80. Ibid., 15–16.

81. Ibid., 61.

82. Ibid., 69.

83. Creuzer, *Briefe über Homer und Hesiodus*, 39.

84. Ibid., 99.

85. Herbig, "Die Beziehungen zu Friedrich Creuzer in Heidelberg," 267–74.

86. Goethe to Creuzer (Oct. 1, 1817), cited in ibid., 270.

87. Goethe to Meyer (Aug. 25, 1819), cited in ibid., 272: "dunkel-poetisch-philosophisch-pfäffischen Irrgang."

88. Goethe to Sulpiz Boisserée (Jan. 16, 1818), cited in ibid., 271.

89. For a good brief discussion, see Henry Hatfield, *Aesthetic Paganism in German Literature: From Winckelmann to the Death of Goethe* (Cambridge: Harvard University Press, 1964), 212–38.

90. Wilhelm Adolph Becker, *Der Symbolik Triumph: Vier Briefe* (Zerbst: Kummer, 1825), 13.

91. Wolfgang Menzel, *Die deutsche Literatur*, 1st ed., 2 vols. (Stuttgart: Franckh, 1828), 1:195.

92. Franz Josef Mone, *Geschichte des Heidenthums im nördlichen Europa*, 2 vols. (Leipzig and Darmstadt: Leske, 1822–23).

93. Hegel to Voss (draft, Aug. 1805), in *Briefe von und an Hegel*, ed. Johannes Hoffmeister, 3 vols. (Hamburg: Meiner, 1952), 1:99–100.

94. The phrase is from Voss, *Antisymbolik*, 1:360.

95. Wilhelm Herbst, *Johann Heinrich Voß*, 2 vols. in 3 (Leipzig: Teubner, 1872–76), 2:2, 177–79.

96. Heinrich Heine, *Die romantische Schule,* in *Werke und Briefe in zehn Bänden,* ed. Hans Kaufmann (Berlin: Aufbau, 1961), 5:39.

97. Voss's polemic was carried forth posthumously in the later volumes of *Mythologische Briefe,* 2nd ed., ed. Heinrich Broska, 5 vols. (Stuttgart: Metzler, 1827).

98. Creuzer to Savigny (Mar. 9, 1807), in *Briefe Creuzers an Savigny,* 204.

99. Voss, *Antisymbolik,* 2:269.

100. Ibid., 1:44.

101. For a parallel, see Walter Benjamin's comparison of Baroque allegorism with classicist humanism in *The Origin of German Tragic Drama,* trans. John Osborne (London: Verso, 1985).

102. Voss, *Antisymbolik,* 1:36; cf. K. O. Müller's review of *Antisymbolik,* in his *Kleine deutsche Schriften,* ed. Eduard Müller, 2 vols. (Breslau: Josef Max, 1848), 2:26.

103. Voss, *Antisymbolik,* 2:236–37.

104. Ibid., 1:314–15 and passim. On the confessional dimensions of this polemic, see also Heribert Raab, "Görres and Voß: Zum Kampf zwischen 'Romantik' und 'Rationalismus' im ersten Drittel des 19. Jahrhunderts," in *Heidelberg im säkularen Umbruch,* ed. Strack, 322–36. Raab tends to see the dispute between Görres and Voss simply as a conflict between Catholicism and Protestantism, but as this chapter shows, a range of other scholarly, theological, and political factors also came into play.

105. Voss, *Antisymbolik,* 2:248.

106. See Detlev Schumann, "Aufnahme und Wirkung von Friedrich Leopold Stolbergs Uebertritt zur Katholischen Kirche," *Euphorion,* 3rd ser., 50 (1956): 271–306.

107. Ibid., 286.

108. Johann Heinrich Voss, *Wie ward Friz Stolberg ein Unfreier?* (Frankfurt a.M.: Wilmans, 1819); Johann Heinrich Voss, *Bestätigung der Stolbergischen Umtriebe* (Stuttgart: Metzler, 1820).

109. See Leo Just, "Görres in Heidelberg," *Historisches Jahrbuch* 74 (1955): 416–31, here 429.

110. Voss, *Antisymbolik,* 2:260.

111. Friedrich Leopold Graf zu Stolberg, *Geschichte der Religion Jesu Christi,* 12 vols. (Hamburg: Perthes, 1806–16). The *Geschichte* was continued after Stolberg's death and was completed in 1864 with a total of fifty-three volumes. For Creuzer's positive assessment, see his "Philologie und Mythologie in ihrem Stufengang und gegenseitigen Verhalten," 16. Creuzer believed that Judaism was an outgrowth of the oldest Indian religion.

112. On the French traditionalists, see David Klinck, *The French Counterrevolutionary Theorist Louis de Bonald (1754–1840)* (New York: Peter Lang, 1996); and esp. Owen Bradley, *A Modern Maistre: The Social and Political Thought of Joseph de Maistre* (Lincoln: University of Nebraska Press, 1999).

113. Voss, *Antisymbolik,* 2:315.

114. See A. W. Schlegel, "Beleuchtung der Beschuldigungen in der Anti-Symbolik von J. H. Voß," in his *Berechtigung einiger Mißdeutungen* (Berlin: Riemer, 1828), 21–89. This article was not published until after Voss's death.

115. Voss had approved of Jacob Fries's speech for the Wartburg festival in 1817. See Herbst, *Johann Heinrich Voß*, 2:2, 179.

116. See the account by Creuzer's student Franz Mone, *Die katholischen Zustände in Baden* (Regensburg: Manz, 1841), 35–44.

117. On Philhellenism, see Regine Quack-Eustathiades, *Der deutsche Philhellenismus während des griechischen Freiheitskampfes, 1821–1827* (Munich: Oldenbourg, 1984). Marchand, *Down from Olympus*, 32–35, notes the relative brevity of this political engagement, which reflected a general move among Philhellenist scholars toward apolitical academic asceticism.

118. Wolfgang Menzel, *Denkwürdigkeiten* (Bielefeld: Velhagen und Klasing, 1877), 194.

119. Herbst, *Johann Heinrich Voß*, 2:2, 203–5.

120. Review of *Religions de l'antiquité, considérées principalement dans leur formes symboliques et mythologiques*, by Friedrich Creuzer, trans. M. Guigniaut, in *Le globe* 2, no. 150 (Aug. 27, 1825): 776.

121. Karl Georg Friedrich Gös, "Die Mysterien der alten Völker, eignen sie sich nach dem Vorgeben einiger neuern Philosophen zu einer Propaganda des Christenthums?" *Kritisches Journal der neuesten theologischen Literatur* 13 (1821): 113–40, 225–57, 337–71.

122. Wilamowitz, *History of Classical Scholarship*, 111; cf. Christian A. Lobeck, *Aglaophamus; sive, De theologiae mysticae Graecorum causis libri III*, 2 vols. (Königsberg: Borntraeger, 1829); and K. O. Müller's review of this work in *Kleine deutsche Schriften*, 2:54–69.

123. J. Grimm to Savigny (Dec. 27, 1820), in *Briefe der Brüder Grimm an Savigny*, ed. Wilhelm Schoof (Berlin: Schmidt, 1953), 293.

124. J. Grimm to Savigny (July 24, 1821), in *Briefe der Brüder Grimm an Savigny*, ed. Schoof, 297; cf. Grimm to Savigny (Apr. 26, 1823), in ibid., 323–24.

125. On the design of the Glyptothek, see the essays in Klaus Vierneisel and Gottlieb Leinz, eds., *Glyptothek München, 1830–1980: Jubliäumsausstellung zur Entstehungs- und Baugeschichte* (Munich: Prestel, 1980); also Britta-R. Schwahn, *Die Glyptothek in München: Baugeschichte und Ikonologie* (Munich: Kommissionsverlag UNI-Druck, 1983).

126. Leo von Klenze and Ludwig Schorn, *Beschreibung der Glyptothek Seiner Majestät des Königs Ludwig I. von Bayern* (Munich: J. G. Cotta, 1842).

127. Ibid., 33. See, e.g., the description of the imperfections of form in an early Greek statue of Aphrodite that lacked hips, "a characteristic of female statues from the ancient Greek era which is still reminiscent of the Egyptian" (ibid., 46).

128. Johann Martin Wagner, *Bericht über die Aeginetischen Bildwerke in Besitz Seiner Königlichen Hoheit des Kronprinzen von Bayern, Mit kunstgeschichtlichen Anmerkungen von F. W. J. Schelling* (1817), *SSW*, 9:111–206. Hegel agreed with Wagner that the statues lacked "spiritual animation"; *Vorlesungen über die Aesthetik*, vol. 2, in *Werke* (Frankfurt a.M.: Suhrkamp, 1970), 14:456.

129. Voss, *Antisymbolik*, 1:236–68.

130. Schelling, "Historisch-kritische Einleitung in die Philosophie der

Mythologie" (1842), *SSW*, 11:226. For Schelling's later philosophy of mythology, see chapter 4.

131. On Müller, see esp. the essays in William Calder III and Renate Schlesier, with Susanne Gödde, eds., *Zwischen Rationalismus und Romantik: Karl Otfried Müller und die antike Kultur* (Hildesheim: Weidmann, 1998); also Blok, "Quest for a Scientific Mythology"; Josine Blok, "Proof and Persuasion in 'Black Athena': The Case of K. O. Müller," *Journal of the History of Ideas* 57 (1996): 705–24; Günther Pflug, "Methodik und Hermeneutik bei Karl Otfried Müller," in *Philologie und Hermeneutik im 19. Jahrhundert: Zur Geschichte und Methodologie der Geisteswissenschaften*, ed. Hellmut Flasher, Karlfried Gründer, and Axel Horstmann (Göttingen: Vandenhoeck und Ruprecht, 1979), 122–40; Klaus Nickau, "Karl Otfried Müller, Professor der Klassischen Philologie, 1819–40," in *Die klassische Altertumswissenschaft an der Georg-August-Universität Göttingen*, ed. Carl Joachim Classen (Göttingen: Vandenhoeck und Ruprecht, 1989), 27–50.

132. See esp. Josine Blok, "'Romantische Poesie, Naturphilosophie, Construktion der Geschichte': K. O. Müller's Understanding of History and Myth," in *Zwischen Rationalismus und Romantik*, ed. Calder and Schlesier, 60–64.

133. Ibid., 80–81; Blok, "Quest for a Scientific Mythology," 33. See also Müller's review of *Symbolik und Mythologie* in *Kleine deutsche Schriften*, 2:1–25.

134. Karl Otfried Müller, *Geschichten hellenischer Stämme und Städte*, pt. I, *Orchomenos und die Minyer* (Breslau: Josef Max, 1820), pt. II, *Die Dorier*, 2 vols. (Breslau: Josef Max, 1824). All citations are from the 2nd ed., ed. F. W. Schneidewin (Breslau: Josef Max, 1844).

135. Müller, *Dorier*, 1:x.

136. Müller, *Orchomenos*, 99.

137. Ibid., 2.

138. Bernal, *Black Athena*, 308–16, implies that Müller abandoned the theory of Egyptian influence primarily out of racial contempt and Philhellenist prejudice; but see Blok, "Quest for a Scientific Mythology," 34 n; Blok, "Proof and Persuasion"; and my comments below.

139. Karl Otfried Müller, "Ueber den angeblich ägyptischen Ursprung der griechischen Kunst" (1820), in *Kleine deutsche Schriften*, 2:523–37, here 526.

140. Iversen, *Myth of Egypt*, 124–46.

141. Müller, "Ueber den angeblich ägyptischen Ursprung," 536.

142. Karl Otfried Müller, *Prolegomena zu einer wissenschaftlichen Mythologie* (Göttingen: Vandenhoeck und Ruprecht, 1825).

143. Ibid., 249–50.

144. Ibid., 71–72.

145. Ibid., 113–15; cf. Müller, *Dorier*, 1:345–57.

146. Müller, *Dorier*, 2:2.

147. Friedrich Creuzer, *Vossiana mit Anmerkungen* (1821), reprinted at the end of Voss, *Antisymbolik*, 2:289–99. See also Creuzer to Hegel (Sept. 8, 1821), in *Briefe von und an Hegel*, 1:289.

148. Creuzer to Hammer-Purgstall (Dec. 3, 1821), in Joseph von Hammer-

Purgstall, *"Erinnerungen aus meinem Leben,"* *1774–1852,* ed. Reinhart Bachofen von Echt (Vienna: Holder-Pichler-Tempsky, 1940), 543.

149. Creuzer to the Boisserée brothers (July 5, 1824), in Oswald Dammann, "Friedrich Creuzer und die Brüder Boisserée: Unveröffentlichtes aus dem Boisserée-Nachlaß," *Zeitschrift für die Geschichte des Oberrheins* 90 (1938): 237–58, here 255. See also Creuzer's comments on Rotteck and Welcker: "the Freiburg heroes of the day are striving with power and commotion to North-Americanize our little land"; Creuzer to the Boisserée brothers (May 21, 1831), ibid., 257.

150. Ludwig Preller, "Friedrich Creuzer, charakterisirt nach seinen Werken," *Hallische Jahrbücher* 101–6 (Apr. 27–May 3, 1838).

151. The form of this protest was a letter to the *Casseler allgemeine Zeitung,* signed by Müller and five other professors, in which they disassociated themselves from the (relatively mild) published criticisms of the Göttingen Seven by the pro-rector of the university on the occasion of a visit by a deputation from the city and the university to the king of Hanover. For details, see Klaus von See, *Die Göttinger Sieben: Kritik einer Legende* (Heidelberg: Winter, 1997), 24–30; also Nickau, "Karl Otfried Müller," 47–48.

152. "Historisch-kritische Einleitung in die Philosophie der Mythologie," *SSW,* 11:226.

153. Creuzer, "Aus dem Leben," 56.

CHAPTER FOUR

1. On the history of that scholarship, see Hans-Joachim Kraus, *Geschichte der historisch-kritischen Erforschung des Alten Testaments von der Reformation bis zur Gegenwart* (Neukirchen: Buchhandlung des Erziehungsvereins, 1956); John Rogerson, *Myth in Old Testament Interpretation* (Berlin: de Gruyter, 1974); John Rogerson, *Old Testament Criticism in the Nineteenth Century: England and Germany,* 2nd ed. (Philadelphia: Fortress, 1985); Ulrich Kusche, *Die unterlegene Religion: Das Judentum im Urteil deutscher Alttestamentler, zur Kritik theologischer Geschichtsschreibung* (Berlin: Institut Kirche und Judentum, 1991).

2. See, e.g., Christoph Meiners, *Grundriß der Geschichte aller Religionen* (Lemgo: Meyer, 1785).

3. Gabler, *Urgeschichte,* 2:484, cited in Christian Hartlich and Walter Sachs, *Der Ursprung des Mythosbegriffes in der modernen Bibelwissenschaft* (Tübingen: Mohr, 1952), 32.

4. See John Rogerson, *W. M. L. de Wette, Founder of Modern Biblical Criticism: An Intellectual Biography* (Sheffield: Sheffield Academic Press, 1992); and Thomas Albert Howard, *Religion and the Rise of Historicism: W. M. L. de Wette, Jacob Burckhardt, and the Theological Origins of Nineteenth-Century Historical Consciousness* (Cambridge: Cambridge University Press, 2000).

5. Rogerson emphasizes the potential influence of Schelling's lectures on the philosophy of art (*De Wette,* 32–49); but Howard cites an 1841 letter by de Wette in which he denied attending these lectures (*Religion and the Rise of Historicism,* 182 n). In the end, de Wette followed Fries in granting myth a crucial but subordinate position within his conception of religion.

6. W. M. L. de Wette, *Theodor, oder des Zweiflers Weihe: Bildungsgeschichte eines evangelischen Geistlichen*, 2 vols. (Berlin: Reimer, 1822).

7. Hartlich and Sachs, *Ursprung des Mythosbegriffes*, 91–120, emphasize Fries's influence on de Wette; but Rogerson points out (*De Wette*, 51–60) that de Wette developed his mythical approach to the Old Testament before he was familiar with Fries's philosophy.

8. W. M. L. de Wette, *Beiträge zur Einleitung in das Alte Testament*, vol. 1, *Kritischer Versuch über die Glaubwürdigkeit der Bücher der Chronik mit Hinsicht auf die Geschichte der Mosaischen Bücher und Gesetzgebung* (Halle: Schimmelpfennig, 1806), vol. 2, *Kritik der israelitischen Geschichte, Erster Teil, Kritik der Mosaischen Geschichte* (Halle: Schimmelpfennig, 1807).

9. De Wette, *Kritik der israelitischen Geschichte*, 31.

10. Ibid., 398.

11. See Rogerson, *Old Testament Criticism*, 28–36.

12. De Wette, *Kritik der israelitischen Geschichte*, 31.

13. W. M. L. de Wette, *Ueber Religion und Theologie: Erläuterungen zu seinem Lehrbuch der Dogmatik* (Berlin: Realschulbuchhandlung, 1815), 85.

14. Hartlich and Sachs, *Ursprung des Mythosbegriffes*, 97–98, note this challenge but ignore its anti-Jewish implications.

15. De Wette, *Ueber Religion und Theologie*, 157.

16. See Rogerson, *De Wette*, 150–59.

17. On de Wette's career in Basel and his influence on Jacob Burckhardt, see Howard, *Religion and the Rise of Historicism*, 110–36.

18. On Strauss, see Theobald Ziegler, *David Friedrich Strauss*, 2 vols. (Berlin: Trübner, 1908); Horton Harris, *David Friedrich Strauss and His Theology* (Cambridge: Cambridge University Press, 1973); John Toews, *Hegelianism: The Path to Dialectical Humanism, 1805–1841* (Cambridge: Cambridge University Press, 1980), 165–75, 255–87, and passim; Jean-Marie Paul, *D. F. Strauss (1808–1874) et son époque* (Paris: Les Belles Lettres, 1982); Marilyn Chapin Massey, *Christ Unmasked: The Meaning of the "Life of Jesus" in German Politics* (Chapel Hill: University of North Carolina Press, 1983); Hans Frei, "David Friedrich Strauss," in *Nineteenth-Century Religious Thought in the West*, 3 vols., ed. Ninian Smart et al. (Cambridge: Cambridge University Press, 1985), 2:215–60.

19. On this, see esp. Toews, *Hegelianism*; John Toews, "Transformations of Hegelianism, 1805–1846," in *The Cambridge Companion to Hegel*, ed. Frederick C. Beiser (Cambridge: Cambridge University Press, 1993), 378–413. This process coincided with (and was partly spurred by) the increasing influence of Schelling's philosophy among conservative intellectuals (both Protestant and Catholic) in southern Germany.

20. Toews, "Transformations," 380.

21. Ibid., 378–87.

22. Robert Wicks, "Hegel's Aesthetics: An Overview," in *Cambridge Companion to Hegel*, ed. Beiser, 352.

23. On Hegel's philosophy of religion, see esp. Walter Jaeschke, *Reason in Religion: The Foundations of Hegel's Philosophy of Religion,* trans. J. Michael Stewart and Peter C. Hodgson (Berkeley and Los Angeles: University of California Press, 1990); also Laurence Dickey, "Hegel on Religion and Philosophy," in *Cambridge Companion to Hegel,* ed. Beiser, 301–47.

24. Georg Wilhelm Friedrich Hegel, *Lectures on the Philosophy of Religion, One-Volume Edition: The Lectures of 1827,* ed. Peter Hodgson, trans. R. F. Brown, P. C. Hodgson, and J. M. Stewart (Berkeley and Los Angeles: University of California Press, 1988), 145–46.

25. Ibid., 147.

26. Ibid., 472 (with text variation in note).

27. Toews, *Hegelianism,* 141–51; on the Hegelian school, see also Jürgen Gebhardt, *Politik und Eschatologie: Studien zur Geschichte der Hegelschen Schule in den Jahren 1830–1840* (Munich: Beck, 1963); Harold Mah, *The End of Philosophy, the Origin of "Ideology": Karl Marx and the Crisis of the Young Hegelians* (Berkeley and Los Angeles: University of California Press, 1987); Warren Breckman, *Marx, the Young Hegelians, and the Origins of Radical Social Theory: Dethroning the Self* (Cambridge: Cambridge University Press, 1999).

28. Robert M. Bigler, *The Politics of German Protestantism: The Rise of the Protestant Church Elite in Prussia, 1815–1848* (Berkeley and Los Angeles: University of California Press, 1972); Toews, *Hegelianism,* 243–54. For the social trends that encouraged the rise of conservatism in Prussia, see Robert M. Berdahl, *The Politics of the Prussian Nobility: The Development of a Conservative Ideology, 1770–1848* (Princeton: Princeton University Press, 1988).

29. On this, see esp. Friedrich Wilhelm Graf, "'Restaurationstheologie' oder neulutherische Modernisierung des Protestantismus? Erste Erwägungen zur Frühgeschichte des neulutherischen Konservatismus," in *Das deutsche Luthertum und die Unionsproblematik im 19. Jahrhundert,* ed. Wolf-Dieter Hauschild (Gütersloh: Mohn, 1991), 64–109.

30. Toews, *Hegelianism,* 170–71.

31. Ibid., 167.

32. David Friedrich Strauss, *In Defense of My "Life of Jesus" against the Hegelians* (1838), trans. with an introduction by Marilyn Chapin Massey (Hamden, Conn.: Archon Books, 1983), 11.

33. Toews, *Hegelianism,* 256.

34. Strauss, *In Defense of My "Life of Jesus,"* 8 (trans. modified).

35. Ibid.

36. On the history of the debate over the life of Jesus, see Albert Schweitzer, *The Quest of the Historical Jesus: A Critical Study of Its Progress from Reimarus to Wrede* (1906), trans. F. C. Burkitt, with an introduction by James Robinson (New York: Macmillan, 1968).

37. H. E. G. Paulus, *Das Leben Jesu als Grundlage einer reinen Geschichte des Urchristentums* (Heidelberg: Winter, 1828).

38. On the cult of genius, see the discussion below.

39. Strauss to Märklin (Feb. 6, 1832), *Ausgewählte Briefe*, ed. Eduard Zeller (Bonn: Emil Strauß, 1895), 12.

40. David Friedrich Strauss, *Das Leben Jesu, kritisch bearbeitet*, 1st ed., 2 vols. (Tübingen: Osiander, 1835–36).

41. Ibid., 1:37.

42. Ibid., 1:75.

43. See, e.g., Hartlich and Sachs, *Ursprung des Mythosbegriffes*, 5.

44. Hans Frei, in *Eclipse of Biblical Narrative: A Study in Eighteenth and Nineteenth Century Hermeneutics* (New Haven: Yale University Press, 1974), 243–44, and in "Strauss," 235, briefly notes the divergences between Strauss and the "mythical school," notably the former's notion of myth as the product of "cultural consciousness." But Frei does not trace this "Romantic" element to its real source: de Wette.

45. Strauss, *Leben Jesu*, 1:52.

46. See Strauss's citations in ibid., 32–34. This point is developed in detail by Howard, *Religion and the Rise of Historicism*, 78–109.

47. David Friedrich Strauss, *Das Leben Jesu, kritisch bearbeitet*, 4th ed., 2 vols. (Tübingen: Osiander, 1840), 1:97–98.

48. Ibid., 93.

49. Ibid., 1st ed, 2:269–74.

50. Massey, *Christ Unmasked*, has convincingly linked Strauss's ironic style to the literature of Young Germany, in particular Gutzkow and Heine.

51. This was carried over to the 4th ed. (1840), which is cited in the following section. See *Leben Jesu*, 4th ed., 87–89. On the various editions of *Das Leben Jesu*, see Peter Hodgson, "Strauss's Theological Development from 1825 to 1840," in *David Friedrich Strauss, "The Life of Jesus" Critically Examined*, trans. George Eliot (Philadelphia: Fortress Press, 1972), xv–l.

52. Strauss, *Leben Jesu*, 4th ed., 1:86–89; cf. Karl Otfried Müller, *Prolegomena zu einer wissenschaftlichen Mythologie* (Göttingen: Vandenhoeck und Ruprecht, 1825), 113–15.

53. Strauss, *Leben Jesu*, 4th ed., 1:75. This would become a favored trope of anti-Semites (see Arthur Schopenhauer, *Parerga und Paralipomena: Short Philosophical Essays*, trans. E. F. J. Payne, 2 vols. [Oxford: Clarendon, 1974], 2:357), although in Strauss's hands it was directed primarily against Protestant orthodoxy.

54. Strauss, *Leben Jesu*, 4th ed., 1:77.

55. Ibid., 79.

56. Ibid.

57. Ibid., 76–78.

58. Ibid., 85.

59. Ibid., 1st ed., 2:734.

60. Ibid., 735.

61. Massey, *Christ Unmasked*, 81–112; for the origins of this argument, see

Walter Jaeschke, "Urmenschheit und Monarchie: Eine politische Christologie des Hegelschen Rechts," *Hegel-Studien* 14 (1979): 73–107; and for a further elaboration, Breckman, *Marx, the Young Hegelians, and the Origins of Radical Social Theory.*

62. On this, see Thomas Nipperdey, *Deutsche Geschichte, 1800–1866: Bürgerwelt und starker Staat* (Munich: Beck, 1983), 366–77.

63. Massey, *Christ Unmasked,* 32. On Ruge, see esp. Breckman, *Marx, the Young Hegelians, and the Origins of Radical Social Theory,* 221–57.

64. Strauss, *Leben Jesu,* 1st ed., 2:739.

65. Schelling, "Ueber Offenbarung und Volksunterricht," *SSW,* 1:477–79.

66. Strauss to Rapp (Aug. 31, 1836), cited in Ziegler, *David Friedrich Strauss,* 1:202.

67. Harris, *Strauss and His Theology,* 67–68.

68. Anonymous, "Extracts from the Life of Luther, Mexico City 2838," trans. in J. R. Beard, *Voices of the Christian Church in Reply to Dr. Strauss* (London: Simpkin, Marshall, and Co., 1845), 324–44.

69. Ziegler, *David Friedrich Strauss,* 1:202.

70. Wilhelm Gundert, *Geschichte der deutschen Bibelgesellschaften im 19. Jahrhundert* (Bielefeld: Luther Verlag, 1997); cf. Schelling, "Ueber den Werth und die Bedeutung der Bibelgesellschaften (1821)," *SSW,* 9:247–52.

71. For biographical information, see Rudolf Seydel, *Christian Hermann Weisse: Nekrolog* (Leipzig: Breitkop und Härtel, 1866); also Albert Hartmann, *Der Spätidealismus und die Hegelsche Dialektik* (Berlin: Junker und Dünnhaupt, 1937); Volker Stümke, *Die positive Christologie Christian Hermann Weißes: Eine Untersuchung zur Hinwendung der Christologie zur Frage nach dem historischen Jesus als Antwort auf das "Leben Jesu" von David Friedrich Strauß* (Frankfurt a.M.: Peter Lang, 1992).

72. See Christian Hermann Weisse, *Die Idee der Gottheit: Eine philosophische Abhandlung, als wissenschaftliche Grundlegung zur Philosophie der Religion* (Dresden: Grimmer, 1833).

73. Breckman, *Marx, the Young Hegelians, and the Origins of Radical Social Theory,* 49–53.

74. Christian Hermann Weisse, *Die evangelische Geschichte, kritisch und philosophisch bearbeitet,* 2 vols. (Leipzig: Breitkopf und Hartel, 1838).

75. Schweitzer, *Quest of the Historical Jesus,* 131.

76. Christian Hermann Weisse, *Ueber das Studium des Homer und seine Bedeutung für unser Zeitalter* (Leipzig: Gerhard Fleischer, 1826).

77. Ibid., 78–96. Weisse offered a highly Creuzerian interpretation of the *Iliad,* which he saw as a parable describing the conflict between the "European" principles of freedom and purity and the "oriental" principles of sensual freedom, "people mixing," and despotism. He contended that the Greeks were in heavy contact with both the Egyptians and the other peoples of the Orient, and that these contacts had been retained in their collective memory in the figures of the Titans. See ibid., 168–78, 291–97.

78. Ibid., 115.

79. Ibid., 324–25.

80. Ibid., 105–6.

81. Ibid., 206.

82. For a thorough account of Wolfian debates in the nineteenth century, see the (anti-Wolfian) account of Richard von Volkmann, *Geschichte und Kritik der Wolfschen "Prolegomena zu Homer": Ein Beitrag zur Geschichte der Homerischen Frage* (Leipzig: Teubner, 1874).

83. [Johann P.] Kreuser, *Vorfragen über Homeros, seine Zeit und Gesänge*, pt. 1 (Frankfurt a.M.: Andreäische Buchhandlung, 1828); Gregor W. Nitzsch, *De historia Homeri: Maximeque de scriptorum carminum aetate meletemata*, 2 vols. (Hanover: Hahn, 1830–37).

84. See Weisse, *Studium des Homer*, 115–16 n.

85. Volkmann, *Geschichte und Kritik der Wolfschen "Prolegomena zu Homer,"* 276–315.

86. To differentiate his position from Strauss's, Weisse borrowed the theologian J. F. Georg's distinction between myth and legend. According to Georg, myth was a tradition that transformed an idea into the form of history, whereas a legend was a tradition that brought a true history into the realm of ideas. See J. F. Leopold Georg, *Mythus und Sage: Versuch einer wissenschaftlichen Entwicklung dieser Begriffe und ihres Verhältnisses zum christlichen Glauben* (Berlin: Schroeder, 1837); Christian Hermann Weisse, "Ueber den Begriff des Mythus und seine Anwendung auf die neutestamentliche Geschichte," *Zeitschrift für Philosophie und spekulative Theologie* 5 (1840): 128–29.

87. Weisse, *Evangelische Geschichte*, 1:154.

88. Ibid., 167–73; Strauss, *Leben Jesu*, 1st ed., 1:126–28.

89. Weisse, *Evangelische Geschichte*, 1:186.

90. Strauss, *Leben Jesu*, 1st ed., 1:173–80.

91. Weisse, *Evangelische Geschichte*, 1:177.

92. Strauss, *Leben Jesu*, 1st ed., 1:243–54.

93. Weisse, *Evangelische Geschichte*, 1:221.

94. Weisse, "Ueber den Begriff des Mythus und seine Anwendung auf die neutestamentliche Geschichte," *Zeitschrift für Philosophie und spekulative Theologie* 4 (1839): 74–102 (article 1), 211–54 (article 2); 5 (1840): 114–54 (article 3).

95. Weisse, "Begriff des Mythus" (article 1), 83.

96. Ibid., 86–90; see Müller, *Prolegomena*, 267.

97. Weisse, "Begriff des Mythus" (article 1), 93–94.

98. Ibid., 97–98.

99. Ernst Wilhelm von Henstgenberg, *Die Authentie des Pentateuches* (Berlin: Oehmigke, 1836), 1:xxi.

100. Ibid.

101. Ibid., 427.

102. Ibid., xlv–xlvi, 419–24.

103. On Schelling's later philosophy, see esp. Edward Allen Beach, *The Potencies*

of God(s): Schelling's Philosophy of Mythology (Albany: State University of New York Press, 1994); also Manfred Frank, *Der unendliche Mangel am Sein: Schellings Hegelkritik und die Anfänge der Marxschen Dialektik* (Frankfurt a.M.: Suhrkamp, 1975); Xavier Tilliette, *La mythologie comprise: L'interprétation schellingienne du paganisme* (Naples: Bibliopolis, 1984); Thomas Buchheim, *Eins von Allem: Die Selbstbescheidung des Idealismus in Schellings Spätphilosophie* (Hamburg: Meiner, 1992); J. E. Wilson, *Schellings Mythologie: Zur Auslegung der Philosophie der Mythologie und Offenbarung* (Stuttgart: Frommann-Holzboog, 1993).

104. Schelling, *Historisch-kritische Einleitung in die Philosophie der Mythologie* (1842), *SSW*, 11:95–100.

105. Friedrich Schelling, *Philosophie der Offenbarung 1841/2*, ed. Manfred Frank (Frankfurt a.M.: Suhrkamp, 1977), 285.

106. Cited by Friedrich Engels, in "Schelling and Revelation, Critique of the Latest Attempt of Reaction against the Free Philosophy," in *Marx-Engels Collected Works* (Moscow: Progress Publishers, 1975), 2:234.

107. Weisse, " Begriff des Mythus" (article 2), 215; Weisse, *Evangelische Geschichte*, 2:476. Hegel's lectures on aesthetics were being published while Weisse wrote his *Evangelische Geschichte;* see Georg Wilhelm Friedrich Hegel, *Vorlesungen über die Aesthetik*, ed. H. G. Hotho (Berlin: Duncker und Humblot, 1835–38).

108. Weisse, "Begriff des Mythus" (article 2), 219.

109. Weisse, *Evangelische Geschichte*, 2:477–78.

110. Ibid., 490.

111. Ibid., 1:336–37.

112. See Henri Ellenberger, *The Discovery of the Unconscious: The History and Evolution of Dynamic Psychiatry* (New York: Basic Books, 1970), 53–83. Paul shows that theologians had argued for a connection between magnetism and Jesus' miracles well before Strauss. See *D. F. Strauss (1808–1874) et son époque*, 135–40.

113. Weisse, *Evangelische Geschichte*, 1:352.

114. See Peter Uwe Hohendahl, *Building a National Literature: The Case of Germany, 1830–1870*, trans. Renate Bacon Franciscono (Ithaca: Cornell University Press, 1989).

115. The following two paragraphs are based largely Christian Grawe's fine article, "Das Beispiel Schiller: Zur Konstituierung eines Klassikers in der Öffentlichkeit des 19. Jahrhunderts," in *Wissenschaftsgeschichte der Germanistik im 19. Jahrhundert*, ed. Jürgen Fohrmann and Wilhelm Voßkamp (Stuttgart and Weimar: Metzler, 1994), 638–68, although I place greater emphasis on the theological dimensions of the Schiller cult.

116. Grawe, "Das Beispiel Schiller," 645, 652.

117. As Hohendahl makes clear, the institutional demand for such a "classical literature" very much created "Goethe and Schiller" as they would function in nineteenth-century German culture. See *Building a National Literature*, 140–73.

118. C. Reinhold, "Das Schillerfest in Stuttgart," in *Hallische Jahrbücher für deutsche Wissenschaft und Kunst* (1839): 1097–1140, here 1117.

119. Rudolf Binder, *Schiller im Verhältnis zum Christenthum*, vol. 1 (Stuttgart:

Metzler, 1839); C. Ullmann, "Der Cultus des Genius: Sendschreiben an Gustav
Schwab," *Theologische Studien und Kritiken* 13 (1840): 1–62; Gustav Schwab,
"Schiller und das Christenthum," *Theologische Studien und Kritiken* 13 (1840):
583–647.

120. David F. Strauss, "Ueber Vergängliches und Bleibendes in Christenthum,"
from *Zwei friedliche Blätter* (1839), cited in Massey, *Christ Unmasked*, 120. For an
interesting analysis of Strauss's connection to the 1830s "cult of genius," see Massey,
Christ Unmasked, 113–41.

121. Massey, *Christ Unmasked*, 137–41; also Friedrich Wilhelm Graf, "David
Friedrich Strauß und die Hallischen Jahrbücher: Ein Beitrag zur Positionalität der
theologischen Publizistik im 19. Jahrhundert," *Archiv für Kulturgeschichte* 60
(1978): 383–430.

122. Weisse, *Evangelische Geschichte*, 1:544.

123. Ibid., 2:441–42.

124. Ibid., 501.

125. Ibid. Weisse's complaint about the loss of a "realistic" biblical narrative
from Lessing to Strauss foreshadowed Hans Frei's critique of German biblical criticism in general; see *Eclipse*, 233–44.

126. Cited in Frances Bunsen, *A Memoir of Baron Bunsen*, 2 vols. (Philadelphia:
J. P. Lippincott, Longmans and Co., 1869), 1:427.

127. August Wilhelm Schlegel, "Der neueste Religionskrieg," in *Sämmtliche
Werke*, ed. Eduard Böcking (Leipzig: Weimann, 1846), 2:170: "Ihr hört, daß Doktor
Strauß gelehrt / Am Evangelium zu klauben, / Und kommt, mit Knüppeln stark
bewehrt, / Zu streiten für den alten Glauben."

CHAPTER FIVE

1. Nietzsche, "Der Fall Wagner," *NKSA*, 6:36.

2. On the aspects of Wagner and myth most relevant to the present study, see
Thomas Mann, *Pro and Contra Wagner*, trans. Allan Blunden (Chicago: University of
Chicago Press, 1985); Theodor Adorno, *In Search of Wagner*, trans. Rodney Living-
stone (London: Verso, 1984); Andrea Mork, *Richard Wagner als politischer Schrift-
steller: Weltanschauung und Wirkungsgeschichte* (Frankfurt: Campus, 1990); Dieter
Borchmeyer, *Richard Wagner: Theory and Theatre*, trans. Stewart Spencer (Oxford:
Clarendon Press, 1991); Jean-Jacques Nattiez, *Wagner Androgyne: A Study in Interpretation*, trans. Stewart Spencer (Princeton: Princeton University Press, 1993);
Petra-Hildegard Wilberg, *Richard Wagners mythische Welt: Versuche wider den Historismus* (Freiburg: Rombach, 1996); and Hannu Salmi, *Imagined Germany: Richard
Wagner's National Utopia* (New York: Peter Lang, 1999). Just as important are the
relevant sections of Gerhart von Graevenitz, *Mythos: Geschichte einer Denkgewohnheit* (Stuttgart and Weimar: Metzler, 1987), 261–89; Maike Oergel, *The Return
of King Arthur and the Nibelungen: National Myth in Nineteenth Century English
and German Literature* (Berlin: de Gruyter, 1998), 208–64; and Wolf-Daniel
Hartwich, *Deutsche Mythologie: Die Erfindung einer Kunstreligion* (Berlin: Piper,
2000), 139–59. While Oergel and Hartwich stress the religious dimensions of Wagner's operas, the focus here is on the theological dimensions of his aesthetic writings.

3. Warren Breckman, *Marx, the Young Hegelians, and the Origins of Radical Social Theory: Dethroning the Self* (Cambridge: Cambridge University Press, 1999).

4. Ernest Newman, *The Life of Richard Wagner*, 4 vols. (New York: Knopf, 1933), 1:256–324; Robert T. Laudon, *Sources of the Wagnerian Synthesis: A Study of the Franco-German Tradition in 19th-Century Opera* (Munich and Salzburg: Katzbichler, 1979).

5. Wagner, "Der Künstler und die Oeffentlichkeit" (1841), *RWGSD*, 1:223–30.

6. Wagner, "Autobiographische Skizze," *WSB*, 1:107.

7. On this tradition of opera, see Leon Plantinga, *Romantic Music: A History of Musical Style in Nineteenth-Century Europe* (New York and London: Norton, 1984), 150–65; John Warrack, *German Opera: From the Beginnings to Wagner* (Cambridge: Cambridge University Press, 2001), 265–337.

8. Wagner, "Der Freischütz: An das Pariser Publikum," *RWGSD*, 1:266.

9. Wagner, "Ueber deutsches Musikwesen," *RWGSD*, 1:194.

10. Ibid., 192.

11. See Carl Dahlhaus, *The Idea of Absolute Music*, trans. Robert Lustig (Chicago: University of Chicago Press, 1989); William Weber, "Wagner and Musical Idealism," in *Wagnerism in European Culture and Politics*, ed. David Clay Large, William Weber, and Anne Dzamba Sessa (Ithaca: Cornell University Press, 1984), 28–71. On Wagner in this context, see Borchmeyer, *Richard Wagner*, 3–76.

12. See, e.g., Elisabeth Eleonore Bauer, *Wie Beethoven auf den Sockel kam: Die Entstehung eines musikalischen Mythos* (Stuttgart: Metzler, 1992), 173–201.

13. Wagner, "Eine Pilgerfahrt zu Beethoven," *RWGSD*, 1:136.

14. Heinrich Heine, "Lutezia," in *Werke und Briefe in zehn Bänden*, ed. Hans Kaufmann (Berlin: Aufbau, 1961), 6:472–73.

15. *Illustrirte Zeitung* (Leipzig), Oct. 7, 1843, 233; on the reception of Rienzi, see *Wagner Handbook*, ed. Ulrich Müller and Peter Wapnewski, trans. John Deathridge (Cambridge: Harvard University Press, 1992), 12.

16. *Illustrirte Zeitung* (Leipzig), Jan. 3, 1846, cited in Helmut Kirchmeyer, ed., *Situationsgeschichte der Musikkritik und des musikalischen Pressewesens in Deutschland, dargestellt vom Ausgange des 18. bis zum Beginn des 20. Jahrhunderts,* pt. 4, *Das zeitgenössische Wagner-Bild*, 3 vols. (Regensburg: Bosse, 1967–72), 3:2.

17. On Wagner's sources for *Tannhäuser*, see Richard Wagner, *My Life*, trans. Andrew Gray, ed. Mary Whittall (New York: Da Capo, 1992), 212–13; Wagner, *Eine Mitteilung an meine Freunde* (1851), *RWGSD*, 4:331–32; Volker Mertens, "Wagner's Middle Ages," in *Wagner Handbook*, ed. Müller and Wapnewski, 238–41; Mary Cicora, *From History to Myth: Wagner's "Tannhäuser" and Its Literary Sources* (Bern and New York: Peter Lang, 1992). Wagner never mentions Heine's version in *Elementargeister*, although it was doubtless of influence. On Wagner's excision of Heine from his autobiography, see Karl Richter, "Absage und Verleugnung: Die Verdrängung Heinrich Heines aus Werk und Bewußtsein Richard Wagners," in *Richard Wagner: Wie antisemitisch darf ein Künstler sein?* Musik-Konzepte 5 (Munich: Text + Kritik, 1978), 5–15.

18. Alfred Meissner, *Ich traf auch Heine in Paris: Unter Künstlern und Revolu-*

tionären in den Metropolen Europas, ed. Rolf Weber (Berlin: Buchverlag der Morgen, 1973), 91.

19. Wagner, *My Life,* 313, 321.

20. Karl Heinz Bohrer, *Die Kritik der Romantik: Der Verdacht der Philosophie gegen die literarische Moderne* (Frankfurt a.M.: Suhrkamp, 1989), 97–137, 182–220.

21. Heinrich Heine, *Die romantische Schule,* in *Werke,* 5:15.

22. Theodor Echtermeyer and Arnold Ruge, "Der Protestantismus und die Romantik: Zur Verständigung über die Zeit und ihre Gegensätze, ein Manifest," *Hallische Jahrbücher für deutsche Wissenschaft und Kunst* (1839): 1953. On Ruge, see Breckman, *Marx, the Young Hegelians, and the Origins of Radical Social Theory,* 221–57, who locates his thought within the broader critique of theological and political personalism that emerged among the left-Hegelian writers between 1830 and 1848.

23. Echtermeyer and Ruge, "Protestantismus und die Romantik," 1987.

24. See Hans-Joachim Schoeps, *Das andere Preußen: Konservative Gestalten und Probleme im Zeitalter Friedrich Wilhelms IV,* 3rd ed. (Berlin: Haude und Spener, 1981); also David E. Barclay, *Frederick William IV and the Prussian Monarchy, 1840–1861* (Oxford: Clarendon, 1995), 75–98; Walter Bußmann, *Zwischen Preußen und Deutschland: Friedrich Wilhelm IV.: Eine Biographie* (Berlin: Siedler, 1990), 130–52 and passim.

25. Joseph Görres, *Die Wallfahrt von Trier* (1844), cited in Wolfgang Schieder, "Church and Revolution: Aspects of the Social History of the Trier Pilgrimage of 1844," trans. Richard Deveson, in *Conflict and Stability in Europe,* ed. Clive Emsley (London: Croom Helm, 1979), 65–95, here 69.

26. On German Catholicism, see Friedrich Wilhelm Graf, *Die Politisierung des religiösen Bewußtseins: Die bürgerlichen Religionsparteien im deutschen Vormärz: Das Beispiel des Deutschkatholizismus* (Stuttgart: Frommann-Holzboog, 1978); Dagmar Herzog, *Intimacy and Exclusion: Religious Politics in Pre-revolutionary Baden* (Princeton: Princeton University Press, 1996).

27. Graf, *Politisierung,* 67–95.

28. Günter Kolbe, "Demokratische Opposition in religiösem Gewande: Zur Geschichte der deutschkatholischen Bewegung in Sachsen am Vorabend der Revolution von 1848/49," *Zeitschrift für Geschichtswissenschaft* 20 (1972): 1102–12.

29. Martin Gregor-Dellin, *Richard Wagner: His Life, His Work, His Century,* trans. J. Maxwell Brownjohn (London: Collins, 1983), 131.

30. Joseph Görres, ed., *Lohengrin, ein altteutsches Gedicht, nach der Abschrift des Vaticanischen Manuscriptes von Ferdinand Gloekle* (Heidelberg: Mohr und Zimmer, 1813).

31. *Mitteilung an meine Freunde,* RWGSD, 4:353–54.

32. See, e.g., Wagner to Adolph Starr (May 31, 1851), in *Selected Letters of Richard Wagner,* trans. and ed. Stewart Spencer and Barry Millington (London and Melbourne: Dent, 1987), 224–25, where Wagner's notes the objections to his "Christian standpoint" in *Tannhäuser* and *Lohengrin* but justifies it on aesthetic grounds. Otherwise, "it would not be 'Tannhäuser' that I wrote."

33. Hartwich, *Deutsche Mythologie*, 97–113.

34. Wagner to Hermann Franck (May 30, 1846), in *Selected Letters*, 129–30.

35. Wagner, *My Life*, 260.

36. Ibid., 343. Graevenitz, *Mythos*, 275–80, argues that Wagner's *Ring* reflected the system of *Naturphilosophie* that Mone had described as the basis of Germanic mythology.

37. Franz Josef Mone, *Untersuchungen zur Geschichte der teutschen Heldensage* (Quedlinburg and Leipzig: Gottfried Basse, 1836), 2.

38. Franz Josef Mone, *Einleitung in das Nibelungenlied zum Schul- und Selbstgebrauch* (Heidelberg: August August Oswalds, 1818), 66.

39. Mone, *Untersuchungen*, 7–13; cf. Franz Josef Mone, *Quellen und Forschungen zur Geschichte der teutschen Literatur und Sprache* (Aachen and Leipzig: Jacob Anton Mayer, 1830), 27–30.

40. For this view, see George C. Windell, "Hegel, Feuerbach, and Wagner's *Ring*," *Central European History* 9 (1976): 43–44; Martin Gregor-Dellin, *Richard Wagner*, 155–56; also Bruce Lincoln, *Theorizing Myth: Narrative, Ideology, and Scholarship* (Chicago: University of Chicago Press, 1999), 60–61.

41. On this point, see Edward R. Haymes, "Richard Wagner and the *Altgermanisten: Die Wibelungen* and Franz Joseph Mone," in *Rereading Wagner*, ed. Reinhold Grimm and Jost Hermand (Madison: University of Wisconsin Press, 1993), 23–38; for a detailed examination, see Wilberg, *Richard Wagners mythische Welt*, 77–184.

42. Wagner, "Die Wibelungen," *RWGSD*, 2:199; cf. Mone, *Einleitung*, 151–91; and Hartwich, *Deutsche Mythologie*, 198–200.

43. Rolf Weber, *Die Revolution in Sachsen 1848/49: Entwicklung und Analyse ihrer Triebkräfte* (Berlin: Akademie-Verlag, 1970); on the broader context, see esp. Jonathan Sperber, *The European Revolutions, 1848–1851* (Cambridge: Cambridge University Press, 1984).

44. Newman, *Life of Wagner*, 1:411–12.

45. For Wagner's opportunistic hopes for revolution, see Wagner to Ernst Kossak (Nov. 23, 1847), *WSB*, 2:578; but see also Meissner's view of Wagner as a serious political revolutionary in *Ich traf auch Heine*, 89.

46. Wagner, "Wie verhalten sich republikanische Bestrebungen dem Königtume gegenüber?" (June 15, 1848), *RWGSB*, 12:7–17. According to Kolbe ("Demokratische Opposition," 1109), 65 of the 216 male members of Dresden's German-Catholic community were also members of the local Vaterlandsverein.

47. Wagner, "Entwurf zur Organisation eines deutschen National-Theathers für das Königreich Sachsen" (1849), *RWGSD*, 2:307–59; cf. Wagner to Martin Oberländer (May 16, 1848), *WSB*, 2:588–89.

48. *Mitteilung an meine Freunde*, *RWGSD*, 4:379.

49. Wagner, "Die Revolution," *RWGSB*, 12:39.

50. On Feuerbach's influence on Wagner, see esp. Windell, "Hegel, Feuerbach, and Wagner's *Ring*," 27–57; Sandra Corse, *Wagner and the New Consciousness: Language and Love in the "Ring"* (Rutherford, N.J.: Fairleigh Dickinson University Press, 1990); Nattiez, *Wagner Androgyne*, 122–27 and passim; Wilberg, *Richard*

Wagners mythische Welt, 235–54, 282–95. On Feuerbach's intellectual development between 1830 and 1848, see John Toews, *Hegelianism: The Path to Dialectical Humanism, 1805–1841* (Cambridge: Cambridge University Press, 1980), 175–202, 327–55; and Van Austin Harvey, *Feuerbach and the Interpretation of Religion* (Cambridge: Cambridge University Press, 1995).

51. Wagner, *My Life*, 407, 430; cf. Wagner to Karl Ritter (Nov. 21, 1849), *WSB*, 3:161.

52. Wagner to Feuerbach (Dec. 3, 1851), *WSB*, 4:205–6.

53. Breckman, *Marx, the Young Hegelians, and the Origins of Radical Social Theory*, 209.

54. Ludwig Feuerbach, *The Essence of Christianity*, trans. George Eliot (New York: Harper and Row, 1957), 266.

55. Ibid., 73.

56. Ibid., 114.

57. Ibid., 113–14.

58. Ibid., 58.

59. Ibid., 267.

60. On Feuerbach and Protestantism, see Breckman, *Marx, the Young Hegelians, and the Origins of Radical Social Theory*, 201–2 and passim. Breckman somewhat overstates Feuerbach's hostility to Protestant, as opposed to Catholic, Christianity. In almost every comparison of the two confessions in *The Essence of Christianity*, Protestantism is presented as the higher, more advanced religion. Moreover, both Christian confessions are treated as superior to Judaism.

61. On this point, see esp. Breckman, *Marx, the Young Hegelians, and the Origins of Radical Social Theory*, 151–64, 201–2, 252–53. On the crossover of the conservative critique, see Laurence Dickey, "Saint-Simonian Industrialism as the End of History: August Cieszkowski on the Teleology of Universal History," in *Apocalypse Theory and the Ends of the World*, ed. Malcolm Bull (Oxford: Blackwell, 1995), 159–99.

62. Feuerbach, *Essence of Christianity*, 278.

63. The German Catholic leader Johannes Ronge wrote that Feuerbach "has done more for the humanity of the century than all of the theologians and professors of our age put together": "Das Verhältniß der jungen Kirche zur sozialen Frage" (1848), cited in Graf, *Politisierung*, 252 n.

64. Wagner, "Jesus von Nazareth," *RWGSB*, 6:221.

65. Wagner, "Sketches and Fragments," in *Prose Works*, 8:367.

66. Modern studies (including Corse, *Wagner and the New Consciousness*; Nattiez, *Wagner Androgyne*; and James McGlathery, *Wagner's Operas and Desire* [New York: Peter Lang, 1998]) have largely overlooked the influence of the Feuerbachian concept of "need" for the formulation of Wagner's aesthetic ideology.

67. On Wagner and the Greeks, see Wolfgang Schadewaldt, "Wagner und die Griechen," in *Hellas und Hesperien*, 2nd ed., 2 vols. (Zurich and Stuttgart: Artemis, 1970), 2:341–405; Ulrich Müller, "Wagner and Antiquity," in *Wagner Handbook*, ed. Müller and Wapnewski, 227–35.

68. Wagner, *My Life*, 342–43; Schadewaldt, "Wagner und die Griechen," 347–50.

69. Cited in Cosima von Wagner, *Diaries*, trans. Geoffrey Skelton, ed. and annotated by Martin Gregor-Dellin and Dietrich Mack (New York: Harcourt Brace Jovanovich, 1978), 1:217 (May 4, 1870). The text in question was in fact Moritz's *Götterlehre*. Wagner's description of the picture is not entirely accurate (for the illustration see above, p. 39).

70. *Mitteilung an meine Freunde*, *RWGSD*, 4:380–81.

71. Wagner, *Oper und Drama*, *RWGSD*, 4:42.

72. Wagner, *Die Kunst und die Revolution*, *RWGSD*, 3:13.

73. Karl Otfried Müller, *Geschichten hellenischer Stämme und Städte*, pt. I, *Orchomenos und die Minyer* (Breslau: Josef Max, 1820), pt. II, *Die Dorier*, 2 vols. (Breslau: Josef Max, 1824). All citations are from the 2nd ed., ed. F. W. Schneidewin (Breslau: Josef Max, 1844). On Wagner's reading of Müller, see Curt von Westernhagen, *Richard Wagners Dresdener Bibliothek, 1842 bis 1849* (Wiesbaden: Brockhaus, 1966), 42–44. See also references to Müller in Cosima Wagner's *Diaries*, 2:499, 650.

74. Müller, *Dorier*, 1:200–370.

75. Ibid., 413.

76. Wagner, *Kunstwerk der Zukunft*, *RWGSD*, 3:159–60.

77. *Die Kunst und die Revolution*, *RWGSD*, 3:15; cf. Müller, *Dorier*, 2:359.

78. *Kunstwerk der Zukunft*, *RWGSD*, 3:125; *Oper und Drama*, *RWGSD*, 4:42–43.

79. Friedrich Schelling, *Philosophy of Art*, ed., trans., and introduced by Douglas W. Stott (Minneapolis: University of Minnesota Press, 1989), 192.

80. *Kunstwerk der Zukunft*, *RWGSD*, 3:159–60. Müller's account of *Knabenliebe* in *Die Dorier*, 2:286–93, probably provided the basis for Wagner's comments. On Müller's theory, see Michael S. Armstrong, "'Jene eigenthümliche Dorische Männerliebe': K. O. Müller's *Die Dorier* and Greek Homosexuality," in *Zwischen Rationalismus und Romantik: Karl Otfried Müller und die antike Kultur*, ed. William Calder III and Renate Schlesier, with Susanne Gödde (Hildesheim: Weidmann, 1998), 19–54.

81. *Kunstwerk der Zukunft*, *RWGSD*, 3:164; cf. "Das Künstlertum der Zukunft," *RWGSB*, 10:211.

82. *Kunstwerk der Zukunft*, *RWGSD*, 3:162.

83. Josef Chytry, *The Aesthetic State: A Quest in Modern German Thought* (Berkeley and Los Angeles: University of California Press, 1989), 287–90, presents Wagner as an unqualified admirer of the polis. But Wagner acknowledged the limitations of ancient Greek life, their reliance on slavery, and their oppression of subject races such as the Helots and Messenians; see "Künstlertum der Zukunft," *RWGSB*, 10:215–17.

84. *Oper und Drama*, *RWGSD*, 4:45.

85. "Künstlertum der Zukunft," *RWGSB*, 10:217.

86. *Oper und Drama*, *RWGSD*, 4:47.

87. Ibid., 50.

88. A. W. Schlegel, *Vorlesungen über dramatische Kunst und Literatur*, in *Sämmtliche Werke*, ed. Eduard Böcking, 12 vols. (Leipzig: Weidmann, 1846–47), 5:16. According to Borchmeyer, *Richard Wagner*, 50, Wagner had studied this work closely.

89. *Oper und Drama*, RWGSD, 4:64–65.

90. Ibid., 66–67.

91. Ibid., 91. In *Kunstwerk der Zukunft*, RWGSD, 3:159, Wagner referred to this society as "communist," but he had dropped this language by the time he wrote *Oper und Drama*.

92. *Oper und Drama*, RWGSD, 4:52–53. The linkage between *Erfahrung* and *Wissenschaft* is much less ambiguous in "Künstlertum der Zukunft," RWGSB, 10:206–7.

93. *Oper und Drama*, RWGSD, 4:106. Nattiez, *Wagner Androgyne*, provides an extensive analysis of Wagner's use of "male" and "female" principles in his aesthetic writings and the *Ring* cycle.

94. *Oper und Drama*, RWGSD, 4:109.

95. Ibid., 186.

96. *Kunstwerk der Zukunft*, RWGSD, 3:101–3.

97. *Oper und Drama*, RWGSD, 3:343.

98. Cf. Feuerbach, *Essence of Christianity*, 64: "The aim is the conscious, voluntary, essential impulse of life, the glance of genius, the focus of self-knowledge,—the unity of the material and spiritual in the individual man."

99. *Oper und Drama*, RWGSD, 4:126–27.

100. Ibid., 114.

101. Ibid., 282.

102. Ibid., 281.

103. *Kunstwerk der Zukunft*, RWGSD, 3:64–67.

104. "Künstlertum der Zukunft," RWGSB, 10:218.

105. Hartwich, *Deutsche Mythologie*, 147; see also Oergel, *Return of King Arthur*, 263–64.

106. Wagner, *Judentum in der Musik*, in RWGSD, 5:99–100, 103.

107. On Wagner and anti-Semitism, see Jacob Katz, *The Darker Side of Genius: Richard Wagner's Antisemitism* (Hanover, N.H.: Brandeis University Press, 1986). Among those who argue for a direct connection between Wagner and Nazism, see Paul Lawrence Rose, *Wagner: Race and Revolution* (London and Boston: Faber and Faber, 1992); and Hartmut Zelinsky, *Sieg oder Untergang, Sieg und Untergang: Kaiser Wilhelm II., die Werk-Idee Richard Wagners, und der "Weltkampf"* (Munich: Keyser, 1990). For a critique focusing on Wagner's conception of the Jewish body, see Marc A. Weiner, *Richard Wagner and the Antisemitic Imagination* (Lincoln: University of Nebraska Press, 1995). Among those who view Wagner's anti-Semitism as less central to his aesthetic project, see Dieter Borchmeyer, "The Question of Anti-Semitism," in *Wagner Handbook*, ed. Müller and Wapnewski, 166–85; also Oergel, *Return of King Arthur*, 231–32. For further debate, see Dieter Borchmeyer, Ami Maayani, and Susanne Vill, eds., *Wagner und die Juden* (Stuttgart: Metzler, 2000).

108. See Rose, *Wagner: Race and Revolution*, esp. 170–84.

109. Friedrich Theodor Vischer, "Vorschlag zu einer Oper," in *Kritische Gänge*, 2 vols. (Tübingen: Fues, 1844); Strauss to Vischer (Oct. 24, 1844), *Ausgewählte Briefe*, ed. Eduard Zeller (Bonn: Emil Strauß, 1895), 162–63.

110. See the (incomplete) list in Werner Wunderlich, *Der Schatz des Drachentödters: Materialien zur Wirkungsgeschichte des Nibelungenliedes* (Stuttgart: Klett-Cotta, 1977), 21–30.

111. *Mitteilung an meine Freunde*, RWGSD, 4:314.

112. From the enormous literature, see esp. Nancy Benvenga, *Kingdom on the Rhine: History, Myth, and Legend in Wagner's "Ring"* (Harwich: Anton, 1983); Robert Donington, *Wagner's "Ring" and Its Symbols: The Music and the Myth*, 3rd ed. (London and Boston: Faber and Faber, 1984); Dieter Borchmeyer, ed., *Wege des Mythos in der Moderne, Richard Wagner, "Der Ring des Nibelungen": Eine Münchner Ringvorlesung* (Munich: Deutscher Taschenbuch, 1987); Elizabeth Magee, *Richard Wagner and the Nibelungs* (Oxford: Clarendon, 1990); Udo Bermbach and Dieter Borchmeyer, eds., *Richard Wagner, "Der Ring des Nibelungen": Ansichten des Mythos* (Stuttgart: Metzler, 1995).

113. Cf. Windell, "Hegel, Feuerbach, and Wagner's *Ring*," 35.

114. Weiner, *Richard Wagner and the Antisemitic Imagination*, 261–306; on this see the comments of Alfred Rosenberg, *The Myth of the Twentieth Century: An Evaluation of the Spiritual-Intellectual Confrontations of Our Age*, trans. Vivian Bird (Torrance, Calif.: Noontide, 1982), 283: "We also know the dream of the black dwarf Alberich who cursed love for the sake of world domination. On Mount Zion a dream was cultivated for centuries, the dream of gold, of power, of lies and hatred. This dream drove the Jews around the entire world, a restless, strong dream. . . . Abandoning love, beauty, honor, the Jew dreamed only of the loveless, the ugly and the honorless."

115. In my interpretation of Brünnhilde, I have profited greatly from Hartwich, *Deutsche Mythologie*, 149–58.

116. Hartmut Reinhardt, "Wagner and Schopenhauer," in *Wagner Handbook*, ed. Müller and Wapnewski, 287.

117. Arthur Schopenhauer, *Die Welt als Wille und Vorstellung*, 3rd ed., 2 vols. (Leipzig: Brockhaus, 1859), 1:304.

118. Arthur Schopenhauer, *Parerga and Paralipomena: Short Philosophical Essays*, trans. E. F. J. Payne, 2 vols. (Oxford: Clarendon, 1974), 2:378–86. On Schopenhauer, Wagner, and anti-Semitism, see esp. Rose, *Wagner: Race and Revolution*, 89–101.

119. Schopenhauer, *Parerga*, 2:261–64.

120. Ibid., 409.

121. Ibid., 362.

122. Ibid., 349.

123. Ibid., 380.

124. Schopenhauer, *Welt als Wille und Vorstellung*, 2:719–21.

125. Wagner, "Zukunftsmusik," *RWGSD*, 7:143, 161–2.

126. Wagner, "Ueber Staat und Religion," *RWGSD*, 8:23.

127. *NKSA*, 8:212.

Chapter Six

1. On these developments, see esp. Peter Uwe Hohendahl, *Building a National Literature: The Case of Germany, 1830–1870*, trans. Renate Bacon Franciscono (Ithaca: Cornell University Press, 1989).

2. See esp. Klaus Christian Köhnke, *The Rise of Neo-Kantianism: German Academic Philosophy between Idealism and Positivism*, trans. R. J. Hollingdale (Cambridge: Cambridge University Press, 1991), who shows the roots of these developments in the 1830s and 1840s.

3. Woodruff D. Smith, *Politics and the Sciences of Culture in Germany, 1840–1920* (Oxford: Oxford University Press, 1991); Donald Kelley, "The Old Cultural History," *History of the Human Sciences* 9 (1996): 101–26.

4. Ernest Renan, "Les études savantes en Allemagne" (1857), in *Oeuvres complètes*, ed. Henriette Psichari, 10 vols. (Paris: Calmann-Lévy, 1955), 1:184–85.

5. Smith, *Politics and the Sciences of Culture*, 35–85.

6. Christoph Jamme, *Einführung in die Philosophie des Mythos*, vol. 2, *Neuzeit und Gegenwart* (Darmstadt: Wissenschaftliche Buchgesellschaft, 1991), 84; Jan De Vries, *Forschungsgeschichte der Mythologie* (Freiberg im Breisgau and Munich: Alber, 1961), 212–13.

7. Eduard Gerhard, *Griechische Mythologie*, 2 vols. (Berlin: Reimer, 1854–55); Friedrich Welcker, *Griechische Götterlehre*, 3 vols. (Göttingen: Dieterich, 1857–63).

8. For a contemporary reaction to Schelling's lectures, see Friedrich Max Müller, "Greek Mythology," in *Chips from a German Workshop*, 2nd ed. (London: Longmans, Green, and Co., 1868), 2:149: "his facts and theories defy all rules of sound scholarship, and . . . his language is so diffuse and vague, as to be unworthy of the century we live in."

9. Horst Seipp, *Entwicklungszüge der germanischen Religionswissenschaft (von Jacob Grimm zu Georges Dumézil)* (Berlin: Ernst Reuter Gesellschaft, 1968).

10. See the important discussion of the Aryan/Semitic distinction in Herder, Renan, F. Max Müller, and Ignác Goldziher in Maurice Olender, *The Languages of Paradise: Race, Religion, and Philology in the Nineteenth Century*, trans. Arthur Goldhammer (Cambridge: Harvard University Press, 1992); see also John Rogerson, *Myth in Old Testament Interpretation* (Berlin: de Gruyter, 1974), 33–44; Léon Poliakov, *The Aryan Myth: A History of Racist and Nationalist Ideas in Europe*, trans. Edmund Howard (New York: Basic Books, 1971); Ruth Römer, *Sprachwissenschaft und Rassenideologie in Deutschland* (Munich: Fink, 1985); Thomas R. Trautmann, *The Aryans in British India* (Berkeley and Los Angeles: University of California Press, 1997); Dorothy M. Figueira, *Aryans, Jews, Brahmins: Theorizing Authority through Myths of Identity* (Albany: State University of New York Press, 2002.

11. *Allgemeine deutsche Biographie*, 17:335.

12. "Adalbert Kuhn," *Illustrirte Zeitung* (Leipzig) 1112 (Oct. 22, 1864): 279. Frey-

tag shared Kuhn's interest in the German *Vorzeit*; see, e.g., *Bilder aus der deutschen Vergangenheit*, 4 vols. (Leipzig: Hirzel, 1859–67).

13. Adalbert Kuhn, ed., *Märkische Sagen und Märchen* (Berlin: Reimer, 1843); Adalbert Kuhn and Wilhelm Schwartz, eds., *Norddeutsche Sagen, Märchen und Gebräuche* (Leipzig: Brockhaus, 1848); Adalbert Kuhn, *Sagen, Gebräuche und Märchen aus Westfalen*, 2 vols. (Leipzig: Brockhaus, 1859).

14. Adalbert Kuhn, *Die Herabkunft des Feuers und des Göttertranks: Ein Beitrag zur vergleichenden Mythologie der Indogermanen* (Berlin: Ferdinand Dümmler, 1859).

15. Ibid., 5.

16. Ibid., 12–18. Modern scholars have rejected Kuhn's connection of Prometheus to the *pramantha*; see *The Encyclopedia of Religion*, ed. Mircea Eliade (New York: Macmillan, 1987), s.v. "Indo-European Religion—History of Study," by C. Scott Littleton.

17. Kuhn, *Herabkunft*, 70; cf. *Vedic Hymns*, trans. Hermann Oldenbourg, 2 vols. (Delhi: Motilal Banarsidass, 1897), 2:302: "This is the support on which the rubbing is performed; the creative organ has been prepared. Bring hither the housewife; let us produce Agni by rubbing in the old way. In the two firesticks dwells Gâtavedas, as the germ (lies) safe in pregnant women—Agni who should be magnified day by day by wakeful men who bring offerings. Place it skillfully into her who lies extended. Having conceived she has quickly given birth to the manly one. He whose summit is red—bright is his splendour—the son of Ilâ has been born in the (due) way."

18. Cf. Sigmund Freud, "Fetischismus," in *Gesammelte Werke* (Frankfurt a.M.: Fischer, 1968), 14:311–17.

19. Kuhn, *Herabkunft*, 166.

20. Ibid., 243–47. Here Kuhn relied on the work of the art historian Karl Boetticher, who had chronicled the role of trees in Greek religious life. See *Der Baumkultus der Hellenen, nach den gottesdienstlichen Gebräuchen und den überlieferten Bildwerken dargestellt* (Berlin: Weidmann, 1856).

21. Jacob Grimm, *Deutsche Mythologie*, 4th ed., ed. Elard Hugo Meyer, 3 vols. (Basel: Schwabe, 1953), 1:513–22.

22. Kuhn, *Herabkunft*, 95–100.

23. Ibid., 259.

24. Ibid., 1.

25. Berthold Delbrück, "Die Entstehung des Mythos bei den indogermanischen Völkern: Ein psychologischer Versuch," *ZfVp* 3 (1865): 296.

26. Friedrich Max Müller, "Comparative Mythology" (1856), in *Chips from a German Workshop*, 2:1–146. On Max Müller, see Frank M. Turner, *The Greek Heritage in Victorian Britain* (New Haven: Yale University Press, 1981), 104–15; Richard Dorson, "The Eclipse of Solar Mythology," in *Myth: A Symposium*, ed. Thomas Sebeok (Philadelphia: American Folklore Society, 1955), 15–38; Tomoko Masuzawa, *In Search of Dreamtime: The Quest for the Origin of Religion* (Chicago: University of Chicago Press, 1993), 58–75; Olender, *Languages of Paradise*, 82–92.

27. *The Life and Letters of the Right Honourable Friedrich Max Müller*, ed. Georgina Adelaide Müller (London and Bombay: Longmans, Green, and Co., 1902), 1:24–30.

28. Ibid., 25.

29. See Müller's appreciative essay, "Bunsen," in *Chips from a German Workshop*, 3:343–89.

30. Friedrich Max Müller, *Introduction to the Science of Religion* (London: Longmans, Green, and Co., 1873), 1–67. He also took issue with the British classicist George Grote's deprecation of myth as a "past which was never present." See "Comparative Mythology," 13. On Grote's theory of myth, see Turner, *Greek Heritage in Victorian Britain*, 83–104.

31. Friedrich Max Müller, *My Autobiography: A Fragment* (New York: Charles Scribner's Sons, 1901), 300–307.

32. Müller, "Comparative Mythology," 66.

33. Friedrich Max Müller, "Semitic Monotheism," in *Chips from a German Workshop*, 1:357.

34. Cf. Müller, "Comparative Mythology," 78: "The Veda is the real Theogony of the Aryan races, while that of Hesiod is a distorted caricature of the original image."

35. Ibid., 84.

36. Ibid., 132.

37. Ibid., 6.

38. See, e.g., the favorable (if not entirely uncritical) citation of Kuhn's views by Friedrich Engels in *Anti-Dühring* (1878), cited in Karl Marx and Friedrich Engels, *On Religion* (Moscow: Progress Publishers, 1975), 128.

39. On this distinction, see esp. J. W. Burrow, *Evolution and Society: A Study in Victorian Social Theory* (Cambridge: Cambridge University Press, 1966).

40. See Ingrid Belke's introduction to *Moritz Lazarus und Heymann Steinthal: Die Begründer der Völkerpsychologie in ihren Briefen*, 2 vols. (Tübingen: Mohr, 1971–86); Waltraud Bumann, *Die Sprachtheorie Heymann Steinthal, dargestellt im Zusammenhang mit seiner Theorie der Geisteswissenschaft* (Meinsenhaim am Glan: Hain, 1965); Georg Eckardt, ed., *Völkerpsychologie—Versuch einer Neuentdeckung: Texte von Lazarus, Steinthal und Wundt* (Weinheim: Psychologie Verlags Union, 1997).

41. Belke, *Moritz Lazarus und Heymann Steinthal*, 1:xc–xcii.

42. Ibid., xcix.

43. Moritz Lazarus and Heymann Steinthal, "Einleitende Gedanken über Völkerpsychologie, als Einladung zu einer Zeitschrift für Völkerpsychologie und Sprachwissenschaft," *ZfVp* 1 (1860): 13. Steinthal had spoken to Lazarus as early as 1852 about founding a journal for "psychische Ethnologie." See Steinthal to Lazarus (Apr. 6, 1852), in *Moritz Lazarus und Heymann Steinthal*, ed. Belke, 1:255.

44. Lazarus and Steinthal, "Einleitende Gedanken," 29.

45. Ibid., 7: "All creative powers of culture in the European Middle Ages are Germanic, not Celtic, not Iberian."

46. Cf. Moritz Lazarus, *Die sittliche Berechtigung Preußens in Deutschland* (Berlin: Schultze, 1850).

47. Heymann Steinthal, "Ueber den Idealismus in der Sprachwissenschaft," *ZfVp* 1 (1860): 305.

48. Heymann Steinthal, review of *Wilhelm von Humboldt's Briefe an F. G. Welcker*, *ZfVp* 1 (1860): 233.

49. Lazarus and Steinthal, "Einleitende Gedanken," 47–55.

50. Ibid., 35.

51. For a complete lecture plan, see *Bericht der Lehranstalt für die Wissenschaft des Judenthums in Berlin* (Berlin: Bernstein, 1885), 30–33. The original faculty roster included Steinthal, Abraham Geiger, Paulus Cassel (a Jewish convert to Lutheran Christianity), and Israel Lewy.

52. Lazarus and Steinthal, "Einleitende Gedanken," 46; Heymann Steinthal, "Die ursprüngliche Form der Sage von Prometheus," *ZfVp* 2 (1862): 2; see also Steinthal's review essay, "Neuere Arbeiten über vergleichende Mythenforschung," *Zeitschrift für die österreichischen Gymnasien* 16 (1865): 36–53.

53. Lazarus and Steinthal, "Einleitende Gedanken," 46.

54. Heymann Steinthal, review of *Wilhelm von Humboldt's Briefe an F. G. Welcker*, *ZfVp* 1 (1860): 238.

55. Steinthal, "Die ursprüngliche Form der Sage von Prometheus," 1–29.

56. Friedrich Paulsen, *Geschichte des gelehrten Unterrichts auf den deutschen Schulen und Universitäten vom Ausgang des Mittelalters bis zur Gegenwart*, 2nd ed., 2 vols. (Leipzig: Veit, 1896–97), 2:241–45.

57. Friedrich Ueberweg, *Grundriss der Geschichte der Philosophie*, vol. 4, *Die Deutsche Philosophie des Neunzehnten Jahrhundert und der Gegenwart*, ed. Traugott Oesterreich (Berlin: E. S. Mittler and Son, 1923), 156–75.

58. James Whitman, "From Philology to Anthropology in Mid-Nineteenth-Century Germany," in *Functionalism Historicized: Essays on British Social Anthropology*, ed. George W. Stocking, Jr. (Madison: University of Wisconsin Press, 1984), 214–29; Köhnke, *Rise of Neo-Kantianism*, 238–39.

59. Steinthal, "Die ursprüngliche Form der Sage von Prometheus," 25.

60. Ibid., 17. Steinthal's notions about the centrality of *Handlung* (action) for the perception of objects were given greater philosophical precision by Hermann Cohen. In "Mythologische Vorstellungen von Gott und Seele, psychologisch entwickelt," *ZfVp* 5 (1868): 396–434, Cohen used Kuhn's *Herabkunft* to explore the origin of such basic (Kantian) notions as causality, teleology, God, and the soul out of primitive psychology.

61. Heymann Steinthal, *Einleitung in die Psychologie und Sprachwissenschaft*, 2nd ed. (Berlin: Dümmler, 1881), 263.

62. Köhnke, *Rise of Neo-Kantianism*, 238–39; on Cassirer's thought, see esp. Ivan Strenski, *Four Theories of Myth in Twentieth-Century History: Cassirer, Eliade, Lévi-Strauss, and Malinowski* (Iowa City: University of Iowa Press, 1987), 13–41 (although Cassirer's debt to Steinthal is not discussed).

63. Heymann Steinthal, "Die Sage von Simson," *ZfVp* 2 (1862): 150. Delbrück, "Entstehung des Mythos bei den indogermanischen Völkern," 299, reinforced this opinion: "it is a frequently made mistake to seek out deep thoughts there where in truth only the colorful products of a disorderly and childlike soul are to be found."

64. On Renan, see Olender, *Languages of Paradise*, 51–81; Edward Said, *Orientalism* (New York: Vintage, 1979), 130–48; also H. W. Wardman, *Ernest Renan: A Critical Biography* (London: Athlone, 1964).

65. Ernest Renan, *L'histoire générale et système comparé des langues sémitiques* (1855), in *Oeuvres complètes*, 8:143–56; Ernest Renan, *Nouvelles considérations sur le caractère général des peuples sémitiques, et en particulier sur leur tendance au monothéisme*, Extrait du Journal Asiatique (Paris: Imprimerie impériale, 1859).

66. Cited in Olender, *Languages of Paradise*, 53.

67. Ernest Renan, "L'histoire des langues sémitiques," in *Oeuvres complètes*, 8:162; Renan, *Nouvelles considérations*, 40.

68. Ernest Renan, "Les historiens critiques de Jésus" (1849), in *Oeuvres complètes*, 7:116–67, here 144–49.

69. Olender, *Languages of Paradise*, 69–71.

70. Friedrich Max Müller, "Semitic Monotheism," in *Chips from a German Workshop*, 1:337–74.

71. Ibid., 360, 363.

72. Ibid., 367. Baron Bunsen had presented a similar view of Abraham in his *Gott in der Geschichte: oder, Der Fortschritt des Glaubens an eine sittliche Weltordnung*, 6 vols. (Leipzig: Brockhaus, 1857–58); see also *Aegyptens Stelle in der Weltgeschichte*, 5 vols. in 4 (Hamburg: Perthes, 1845–57), vol. 5, bk. 1:67. Translated by Susan Winkworth as *God in History; or, The Progress of Man's Faith in the Moral Order of the World*, 3 vols. (London: Longmans, Green, and Co., 1868–70). For Bunsen's views on the Old Testament, see Rogerson, *Myth in Old Testament Interpretation*, 124–27.

73. Heymann Steinthal, "Zur Charakteristik der semitischen Völker," *ZfVp* 1 (1860): 339.

74. Steinthal, "Die Sage von Simson," 129–78. As a linguist, Steinthal was certainly not restricted to the resources of the Hebrew language, as John Rogerson asserts in his *Myth in Old Testament Interpretation*, 37.

75. Steinthal, "Die Sage von Simson," 143. While Steinthal admitted many of the basic premises of comparative mythology, he criticized Bunsen and Müller's tendency to trace the beginnings of language to the creative act of an individual genius, whether Semitic or Aryan. See Heymann Steinthal, *Grammatik, Logik und Psychologie* (Berlin: Dümmler, 1855), xix–xxii. Steinthal also rejected the notion that language was the product of a religious or semireligious revelation.

76. Steinthal, "Die Sage von Simson," 150.

77. Steinthal, "Zur Charakteristik der semitischen Völker," 344. For a thorough critique of the notion of henotheism, see Heymann Steinthal, "Die Frage vom Ursprung des Monotheismus" (1891), in his *Zu Bibel und Religionsphilosophie: Vorträge und Abhandlungen*, 2 vols. (Berlin: Reimer, 1890–95), 2:25–34.

78. Steinthal, "Zur Charakteristik der semitischen Völker," 343; cf. Steinthal, "Die Sage von Simson," 176–77.

79. Steinthal's formulation of this "battle of the souls" *(Seelenkampf)* between two gods ("Die Sage von Simson," 168–76) parallels the late Schelling's account of the transition from "abstract" monotheism to polytheism to "true" monotheism. Schelling, however, did not conceive that the entire process could take place in a single people but believed that it progressed from one nation to the next.

80. Ibid., 177.

81. Ibid., 178.

82. Steinthal, "Die ursprüngliche Form der Sage von Prometheus," 28.

83. Ibid., 29.

84. Steinthal's work on Hebraic mythology set the stage for Ignác Goldziher's more extensive work, *Der Mythos bei den Hebräern und seine geschichtliche Entwicklung* (Leipzig: Brockhaus, 1876). On Goldziher, see esp. Olender, *Languages of Paradise*, 115–35.

85. Steinthal criticized Christianity even more directly in his personal correspondence. See, e.g., his rather Feuerbachian assessment of the Sermon on the Mount: Steinthal to Lazarus (Dec. 14, 1852), in *Moritz Lazarus und Heymann Steinthal*, ed. Belke, 1:270–71.

86. Eduard Zeller, "Die Entwicklung des Monotheismus bei den Griechen" (1862), in his *Vorträge und Abhandlungen geschichtlichen Inhalts* (Leipzig: Fues, 1865), 1–29.

87. Friedrich Welcker, *Griechische Götterlehre*, 3 vols. (Göttingen: Dieterich, 1857–63).

88. Heymann Steinthal, review of Eduard Zeller, *Die Entwicklung des Monotheismus bei den Griechen*, ZfVp 3 (1862): 383.

89. Ludwig Diestel, "Der Monotheismus des ältesten Heidenthums, vorzüglich bei den Semiten," *Jahrbücher für deutsche Theologie* 5 (1860): 669–760.

90. Heymann Steinthal, "Mythos und Religion," in *Sammlung gemeinverständlicher wissenschaftlicher Vorträge*, ed. Rudolf Virchow and Friedrich von Holtzendorff, 5th ser., 97 (Berlin: Luderitz, 1870), cited here according to the version in Steinthal, *Zu Bibel und Religionsphilosophie*, 1:127–50.

91. Steinthal, "Mythos und Religion," 134.

92. Ibid., 131.

93. Ibid., 141.

94. Ibid., 148.

95. See esp. Heymann Steinthal, "Zur Religionsphilosophie," ZfVp 8 (1875): 257–99.

96. Heymann Steinthal, "Poesie und Prosa," ZfVp 6 (1869): 310–13.

97. Steinthal, "Mythos und Religion," 149.

98. Steinthal, "Zur Religionsphilosophie," 296.

99. See, e.g., Steinthal, "Die Sage vom Simson," 176–77.

100. Heymann Steinthal, "Die Schöpfung der Welt, des Menschen und der

Sprache nach der Genesis" (1868), in *Zu Bibel und Religionsphilosophie,* 1:110. The target of criticism here was probably Max Müller.

101. Steinthal, "Zur Religionsphilosophie," 297.

102. Heymann Steinthal, "Der Semitismus," *ZfVp* 8 (1875): 349–50.

103. Steinthal, "Die Erzählkunst der Bibel," in *Zu Bibel und Religionsphiloso-phie,* 2:2–3.

104. Heymann Steinthal, "Zur Religionsphilosophie: Zweiter Artikel," *ZfVp* 9 (1877): 2.

105. See, e.g., Gershom Scholem, "The Science of Judaism—Then and Now" (1959), in his *The Messianic Idea in Judaism and Other Essays on Jewish Spiritual-ity* (New York: Schocken, 1971), 304–13; Gershom Scholem, "Reflections on Modern Jewish Studies" (1944), in *On the Possibility of Jewish Mysticism in Our Time and Other Essays,* ed. Avraham Shipira, trans. Jonathan Chipman (Philadelphia: Jewish Publication Society, 1997), 51–74.

106. The case of Steinthal offers an interesting contrast to that of Abraham Geiger, his colleague at the Hochschule für die Wissenschaft des Judenthums. While Geiger reclaimed Jesus for Judaism, Steinthal relegated Christ (and Christianity) to paganism. On Geiger's views, see Susannah Heschel, *Abraham Geiger and the Jew-ish Jesus* (Chicago: University of Chicago Press, 1998), esp. 127–61.

107. See esp. Uriel Tal, *Christians and Jews in Germany: Religion, Politics, and Ideology in the Second Reich, 1870–1914,* trans. Noah Jonathan Jacobs (Ithaca: Cornell University Press, 1975); Peter Pulzer, *The Rise of Political Antisemitism in Germany and Austria,* rev. ed. (Cambridge: Harvard University Press, 1988).

108. Heymann Steinthal, "Glaube und Kritik," in *Zu Bibel und Religion-sphilosophie,* 2:15–16.

109. Bumann, *Die Sprachtheorie Heymann Steinthal,* 103–15.

110. Renan had cited this Pauline dictum when he predicted a gradual disappear-ance of the races or, more accurately, the subsumption of the races of the world to Aryan thought and culture. See the quotation in Olender, *Languages of Paradise,* 59.

111. Heymann Steinthal, *Haman, Bileam und der jüdische Nabi* (Berlin: Bern-stein, 1885), 12.

Chapter Seven

1. Nietzsche to Gersdorff (Nov. 7, 1870), *NBW,* 2/1:156. References from Nietz-sche's works are to *NKSA* or to *NKGA.* I have also benefited from several English translations, which are noted at relevant points in the chapter.

2. For the implications of the liberal demand for a "unity of spirit" for Jews in the German Empire, see Uriel Tal, *Christians and Jews in Germany: Religion, Poli-tics, and Ideology in the Second Reich, 1870–1914,* trans. Noah Jonathan Jacobs (Ithaca: Cornell University Press, 1975), 31–80. Tal does not sufficiently consider the fact that this demand for "unity" resulted, first, in a conflict between Protestants and Catholics and then between liberal and conservative Christians. Further, anti-Semitism did not serve to integrate Catholics into the *Kaiserreich,* as Tal (95–96) im-plies. On this, see Helmut Walser Smith, *German Nationalism and Religious Con-*

flict: Culture, Ideology, Politics, 1870–1914 (Princeton: Princeton University Press, 1995); also Michael B. Gross, *"Kulturkampf* and Unification: German Liberalism and the War against the Jesuits," *Central European History* 30 (1997): 545–66.

3. *Morgenröte, NKSA,* 3:628 (§377).

4. Many of these concerns have been highlighted by Allan Megill, "Historicizing Nietzsche? Paradoxes and Lessons of a Hard Case," *Journal of Modern History* 68, no. 1 (Mar. 1996): 114–52.

5. For recent studies of Nietzsche's influence, see Steven E. Aschheim, *The Nietzsche Legacy in Germany, 1890–1990* (Berkeley and Los Angeles: University of California Press, 1992); Bernhard H. F. Taureck, *Nietzsche und der Fascismus: Ein Politikum* (Leipzig: Reclam, 2000); Jacob Golomb and Robert S. Wistrich, eds., *Nietzsche, Godfather of Fascism? On the Uses and Abuses of a Philosophy* (Princeton: Princeton University Press, 2002).

6. As noted by Megill and others, the attempt to link Nietzsche to his context has proved particularly difficult. Georg Lukács, in *The Destruction of Reason,* trans. Peter Palmer (Atlantic Highlands, N.J.: Humanities Press, 1981), interprets Nietzsche as a spokesman for the same conservative, irrationalist forces that gave rise to Nazism. Beginning in the 1950s, however, a reaction set in against this line of interpretation, due in large part to Walter Kaufmann, *Nietzsche: Philosopher, Psychologist, Antichrist* (Princeton: Princeton University Press, 1950), who presented Nietzsche as a protoexistentialist. During the 1970s and 1980s, a view of Nietzsche as a poststructualist, inspired by the works of Jacques Derrida, Gilles Deleuze, and Sarah Kofman, came to the fore. For samples of this type of interpretation, see David B. Allison, ed., *The New Nietzsche: Contemporary Styles of Interpretation* (New York: Dell, 1977). Meanwhile, however, continued work surrounding the critical edition of Nietzsche's works and letters, edited by Giorgio Colli and Mazzino Montinari, has revealed Nietzsche's debt to the scholarly and popular thought of his day.

7. The question of anti-Semitism (discussed below) has led in recent years to a broader reevaluation of Nietzsche as a specifically "religious" thinker. Among recent English-language works, see Tyler Roberts, *Contesting Spirit: Nietzsche, Affirmation, Religion* (Princeton: Princeton University Press, 1998); Tim Murphy, *Nietzsche, Metaphor, Religion* (Albany: State University of New York Press, 2001); Giles Fraser, *Redeeming Nietzsche: On the Piety of Unbelief* (London: Routledge, 2002). While these works note the broad significance of Protestantism for Nietzsche, only Murphy locates his thought in the *specific* context of late-nineteenth-century German Protestant culture, and this in reference to *The Antichrist* (1888).

8. For one example of the resentments Nietzsche's career path inspired, see William Calder III, "The Wilamowitz-Nietzsche Struggle: New Documents and a Reappraisal," *Nietzsche-Studien* 12 (1983): 214–54. Such appointments were not without precedent in Basel: Johann J. Bachofen received a professorial appointment in 1841 at the age of twenty-six. On this and for further background on the university, see Lionel Gossman, *Basel in the Age of Burckhardt: A Study in Unseasonable Ideas* (Chicago: University of Chicago Press, 2000), 122.

9. Nietzsche to Franziska and Elisabeth Nietzsche (Apr. 20, 1869), *NBW,* 2/1:4; Nietzsche to Friedrich Ritschl (May 10, 1869), *NBW,* 2/1:7.

10. On the mania for criticism and emendation, see Ulrich von Wilamowitz-Moellendorff, *History of Classical Scholarship*, trans. Alan Harris (London: Duckworth, 1982), 135–37: "Their only excuse is that the old belief in classical literature's absolute perfection was still unshaken, so that when they found much in it that they could no longer admire, they concluded that there was something wrong, which called for treatment—if necessary, by cauterisation and the knife."

11. On Ritschl, see Ernst Vogt, "Friedrich Ritschl," in *Classical Scholarship: A Biographical Encyclopedia*, ed. Ward W. Briggs and William Calder III (New York: Garland, 1990), 389–94; also Otto Ribbeck, *Friedrich Wilhelm Ritschl: Ein Beitrag zur Geschichte der Philologie (1879–1881)*, 2 vols. (repr., Osnabrück: Otto Zeller, 1969). On Jahn, see Carl Werner Müller, "Otto Jahn," in *Classical Scholarship*, ed. Briggs and Calder, 227–38; and William Calder III, Hubert Cancik, and Bernhard Kytzler, eds., *Otto Jahn (1813–68): Ein Geisteswissenschaftler zwischen Klassizismus und Historismus* (Stuttgart: Franz Steiner, 1991); on Jahn as mythologist, see Renate Schlesier, *Kulte, Mythen, und Gelehrte: Anthropologie der Antike seit 1800* (Frankfurt a.M.: Fischer, 1994), 33–64.

12. James Q. Whitman, "Nietzsche in the Magisterial Tradition of German Classical Philology," *Journal of the History of Ideas* 47 (1986): 453–68, notes Ritschl's (and hence Nietzsche's) roots in a dying intellectual tradition of *Altertumswissenschaft*, which stressed viewing antiquity as a whole. But in Ritschl's actual practice as a scholar, this hermeneutical approach seems to have remained largely in the background.

13. See the account in Carl Werner Müller, "Otto Jahn," 231–33; also Ribbeck, *Friedrich Wilhelm Ritschl*, 2:332–81.

14. On these early studies and their influence for Nietzsche's later thought, see James I. Porter, *Nietzsche and the Philology of the Future* (Stanford: Stanford University Press, 2000), which highlights the provocative nature of his "wayward conventional philology" (117).

15. Nietzsche to Gersdorff (Jan. 18, 1869), *NBW*, 1/2:363; Nietzsche to Rohda (Feb. 22 and 28, 1869), *NBW*, 1/2:378.

16. Nietzsche to Deussen (Sept. 1868), *NBW*, 1/2:316; see also Nietzsche to Deussen (June 2, 1868), *NBW*, 1/2:283, where Nietzsche complains of the "moral perversity" of most philologists.

17. On Nietzsche and Lange in this context, see esp. Porter, *Nietzsche and the Philology of the Future*, 32–81.

18. Friedrich Ritschl to Wilhelm Vischer (Feb. 2, 1873), *NKSA*, 15:46.

19. Nietzsche to Rohde (end of Jan. and Feb. 15, 1870), *NBW*, 2/1:94.

20. On the Wagner-Nietzsche encounter there is an enormous literature. Among the works most relevant for the present study, see Frederick Love, *Young Nietzsche and the Wagner Experience* (Chapel Hill: University of North Carolina Press, 1963); Dietrich Fischer-Dieskau, *Wagner and Nietzsche* (New York: Seabury, 1976); Roger Hollinrake, *Nietzsche, Wagner, and the Philosophy of Pessimism* (London: Allen and Unwin, 1982); Peter Wapnewski, "Nietzsche und Wagner: Stationen einer Beziehung," *Nietzsche-Studien* 18 (1989): 401–23; Dieter Borchmeyer and Jörg Salaquarda, eds., *Nietzsche und Wagner: Stationen einer epochalen Begegnung*, 2

vols. (Frankfurt a.M.: Insel, 1994); Marc A. Weiner, *Richard Wagner and the Anti-Semitic Imagination* (Lincoln: University of Nebraska Press, 1995), 307–47; Joachim Köhler: *Nietzsche and Wagner: A Lesson in Subjugation*, trans. Ronald Taylor (New Haven: Yale University Press, 1998); Manfred Eger, *Nietzsches Bayreuther Passion* (Freiburg im Breisgau: Rombach, 2001). Wapnewski, Borchmeyer, and Salaquarda present the key information but soft-pedal the scandals. Köhler relentlessly unearths unsavory details about the Nietzsche-Wagner relationship, but the book's mytho-poetic framework weakens its overall interpretive value. Eger offers a useful reevaluation of some of the key controversies from a pro-Wagner perspective.

21. Nietzsche to Deussen (Feb. 1870), *NBW*, 2/1:98.

22. Ibid.

23. See, e.g., Nietzsche, "Das griechische Musikdrama" (1870), *NKSA*, 1:515–32; "Socrates und die Tragödie" (1870), *NKSA*, 1:533–49. Among his courses, see esp. "Einleitung in die Tragödie des Sophocles" (1870), *NKGA*, 2/3:5–57.

24. *NKSA*, 1:25 (§1). Translations are my own, but I have benefited in many cases from Walter Kaufmann's edition of *"The Birth of Tragedy" and "The Case of Wagner"* (New York: Vintage, 1967).

25. On the Apollonian and Dionysian, and their roots in earlier traditions, there is a considerable literature. See esp. Alfred Baeumler, "Bachofen der Mythologe der Romantik," introduction to Johann Jakob Bachofen, *Der Mythus von Orient und Occident: Eine Metaphysik der alten Welt aus den Werken von J. J. Bachofen*, 2nd ed., ed. Manfred Schröter (Munich: Beck, 1926), ccvii–cclv; Martin Vogel, *Apollinisch und Dionysisch: Geschichte eines genialen Irrtums* (Regensburg: Gustav Bosse, 1966); Max L. Baeumer, "Nietzsche and the Tradition of the Dionysian," trans. Timothy Sellner, in *Studies in Nietzsche and the Classical Tradition*, 2nd ed., ed. James C. O'Flaherty, Timothy Sellner, and Robert M. Helm (Chapel Hill: University of North Carolina Press, 1979), 165–89; Ernst Behler, "Die Auffassung des Dionysischen durch die Brüder Schlegel und Friedrich Nietzsche," *Nietzsche-Studien* 12 (1983): 335–54; Manfred Frank, *Vorlesungen über die neue Mythologie*, vol. 2, *Gott im Exil* (Frankfurt a.M.: Suhrkamp, 1988), 9–71; Adrian DelCaro, "Dionysian Classicism, or Nietzsche's Appropriation of an Aesthetic Norm," *Journal of the History of Ideas* 50 (1989): 589–605; Barbara von Reibnitz, *Ein Kommentar zu Friedrich Nietzsche, "Die Geburt der Tragödie aus dem Geiste der Musik" (Kap. 1–12)* (Stuttgart and Weimar: Metzler, 1992); John Elbert Wilson, *Schelling und Nietzsche: Zur Auslegung der frühen Werke Friedrich Nietzsches* (Berlin: de Gruyter, 1996); James I. Porter, *The Invention of Dionysus: An Essay on "The Birth of Tragedy"* (Stanford: Stanford University Press, 2000).

26. *NKSA*, 1:25 (§1).

27. Ibid., 35 (§3).

28. Ibid., 30 (§1).

29. On Bachofen, see esp. Gossman, *Basel*, 149–70 and passim.

30. In June 1871, Nietzsche borrowed the relevant volume of *Symbolik und Mythologie* from the University of Basel library. See Luca Crescenzi, "Verzeichnis der von Nietzsche aus der Universitätsbibliothek in Basel entliehenen Bücher (1869–1879)," *Nietzsche-Studien* 23 (1994): 407. On Creuzer's influence on Nietzsche, see

Baeumler, "Bachofen der Mythologe der Romantik," ccxlii–ccxlv; and Frank, *Gott im Exil*, 29–34.

31. *NKSA*, 1:32 (§2).

32. Ibid., 31 (§2).

33. Ibid., 33 (§2); cf. Karl Otfried Müller, *Geschichten hellenischer Stämme und Städte*, pt. II, *Die Dorier*, 2nd ed., ed. F. W. Schneidewin, 2 vols. (Breslau: Josef Max, 1844), 1:345–49.

34. *NKSA*, 1:32 (§2). For Nietzsche's critique of the thesis of Greek autochthony, see also "Die vorplatonischen Philosophen," *NKGA*, 2/4:219. See also "Einleitung in die Tragödie des Sophocles," *NKGA* 2/3:12, where Nietzsche writes, "there is something Asiatic and oriental that the Greeks, with their enormous rhythmic and image-making power—in short, with their sense of beauty—overcame [in order to create] tragedy. As they also overcame the Egyptian style of temple." See also "Die Philosophie im tragischen Zeitalter der Griechen" (1873), *NKSA*, 1:806: "Nothing is more foolish than to credit the Greeks with an autochthonous culture *(Bildung)*. To the contrary, they soaked up all the living culture of other peoples. It was for just this reason that they came so far, because they knew to toss the spear farther on from where it had been left by another people."

35. *NKSA*, 1:35 (§3).

36. Ibid., 37 (§3).

37. Nietzsche developed his thoughts on Homer in his inaugural lecture to the Basel public, "Homer und die classische Philologie" (1869). There he departed from both the interpretation of Homer as an individual "personality" and the interpretation of Homer as an expression of the *"Volkseele."* Instead, the final form of the Homeric epics was the result of the work of a later, anonymous figure, who sacrificed his name. "We believe in one great poet of the Iliad and Odyssey, *but not in Homer as this poet,*" *NKGA*, 2/1:266. For illuminating comments on this piece, see Porter, *Nietzsche and the Philology of the Future*, 62–69.

38. On this origin, see also Nietzsche's lectures "Einleitung in die Tragödie des Sophocles," *NKGA* 2/3:10–17.

39. *NKSA*, 1:48–52 (§6); cf. the discussion in Nietzsche's notebooks, *NKSA*, 7:112–13.

40. Ibid., 1:68–69 (§9). Reibnitz, *Kommentar zu Friedrich Nietzsche*, 246, identifies as a potential source for this idea Kuhn's *Die Herabkunft des Feuers* (1859), which Nietzsche borrowed from the Basel library. Another likely source was Max Müller's essay "Semitic Monotheism," in *Chips from a German Workshop*, 2nd ed., 3 vols. (London: Longmans, Green, and Co., 1868).

41. *NKSA* 1:69–70 (§9). Hans Blumenberg, *Work on Myth*, trans. Robert Wallace (Cambridge: MIT Press, 1985), 613, in his discussion of the Prometheus myth in Nietzsche, consciously elides this point. Reibnitz, *Kommentar zu Friedrich Nietzsche*, 249, contends that Nietzsche argued "perhaps not according to a racial ideology of anti-Semitism but certainly doubtless in an anti-Judaic and that means above all anti-Christian interest." At this stage of his development, however, Nietzsche's anti-Semitism appears to have outweighed his hostility to Christianity.

42. *NKGA*, 2/3:412.

43. Ibid.

44. "Die Philosophie im tragischen Zeitalter der Griechen," *NKSA,* 1:806–7. In his notes, Nietzsche wrote of Max Müller that he was "to be pilloried as a German who has renounced [his] German character *[Wesen]* and succumbed to English superstitions," *NKSA,* 7:109.

45. Ibid., 1:69 (§9).

46. Ibid., 68–69 (§9); cf. Nietzsche, "Encyclopaedie der klassischen Philologie" (1871), *NKGA,* 2/3:414.

47. *NKSA,* 1:72 (§10). On the Schelling-Nietzsche parallel here, see esp. Frank, *Gott im Exil,* 57; and Wilson, *Schelling und Nietzsche,* 151–54.

48. On Nietzsche's relationship to earlier theories of tragedy, see Reibnitz, *Kommentar zu Friedrich Nietzsche,* 179–94; and M. S. Silk and J. P. Stern, *Nietzsche on Tragedy* (Cambridge: Cambridge University Press, 1981), 297–331.

49. *NKSA,* 1:52 (§7).

50. From the manuscript version, *NKSA,* 14:48.

51. Ibid., 1:56 (§7).

52. On the evolution of Nietzsche's political views in this period, see Peter Bergmann, *Nietzsche: The "Last Antipolitical German"* (Bloomington: Indiana University Press, 1987), 86–87; also Bernhard-Arnold Kruse, *Apollinisch-Dionysisch: Moderne Melancholia und Unio Mystica* (Frankfurt a.M.: Athenäum, 1987).

53. "Der Griechische Staat," *NKSA,* 1:764–77, esp. 776; on the political significance of this essay, see also Barbara von Reibnitz, "Nietzsches 'Griechischer Staat' und das deutsche Kaiserreich," in *Der altsprachliche Unterricht* 32 (1987): 76–89.

54. "Encyclopädie der klassischen Philologie," *NKGA,* 2/3:371.

55. See Heinrich von Treitschke's 1874 comment: "Millions have to plough the fields, forge and plane, so that thousands can research, paint, and rule. In vain does socialism try to use empty outcries of rage to eliminate this bitter knowledge from the world"; cited in Dieter Langewiesche, *Liberalism in Germany,* trans. Christiane Banerji (Princeton: Princeton University Press, 2000), 207.

56. *NKSA,* 1:77 (§11).

57. Ibid., 85 (§12); cf. Ulrich von Wilamowitz-Moellendorff, *Zukunftsphilologie! Eine Erwidrung auf Friedrich Nietzsches "Geburt der Tragödie"* (1872), repr. in *Der Streit um Nietzsches "Geburt der Tragödie,"* ed. Karlfried Gründer (Hildesheim: Georg Olms, 1989), 49.

58. *NKSA,* 1:87 (§12).

59. Ibid., 153 (§24).

60. Ibid., 154 (§24).

61. Ibid., 115 (§18).

62. Ibid., 104 (§16).

63. See Whitman, "Nietzsche in the Magisterial Tradition," 454–56. On Nietzsche's relation to the philological profession, see also Suzanne Marchand, *Down from Olympus: Archaeology and Philhellenism in Germany, 1750–1970* (Princeton: Princeton University Press, 1996), 124–33. Both Whitman and Marchand stress

Nietzsche's attempt to revive a vanishing tradition of grand theorizing in philology. It would seem, however, that his closest ties were not to Boeck and Ritschl but rather to the subterranean traditions of Schelling and Creuzer.

64. See esp. Calder, "Wilamowitz-Nietzsche Struggle"; Jaap Mansfeld, "The Wilamowitz-Nietzsche Struggle: Another Document and Some Further Comments," *Nietzsche-Studien* 15 (1986): 41–58. On Wilamowitz, see Manfred Landfester, "Ulrich von Wilamowitz-Moellendorff und die hermeneutische Tradition des 19. Jahrhunderts," *Philologie und Hermeneutik im 19. Jahrhundert: Zur Geschichte und Methodologie der Geisteswissenschaften*, ed. Hellmut Flashar, Karlfried Gründer, and Axel Horstmann (Göttingen: Vandenhoeck und Ruprecht, 1979), 156–80; William Calder III, Hellmut Flashar, and Theodor Lindken, eds., *Wilamowitz nach 50 Jahren* (Darmstadt: Wissenschaftliche Buchgesellschaft, 1985); also the comments in Marchand, *Down from Olympus*, 124–33; Reibnitz, *Kommentar zu Friedrich Nietzsche*, 64–65, 133–39, and passim; and Silk and Stern, *Nietzsche on Tragedy*, 90–106. None of these works interprets this dispute in the context of the Creuzer controversy or the religious politics of the 1870s.

65. Wilamowitz, *Zukunftsphilologie!* 42; see similar comments in *Zukunftsphilologie! Zweites Stück: Eine Erwidrung auf die Rettungsversuche für Fr. Nietzsches "Geburt der Tragödie"* (Berlin: Bornträger, 1873), 22, repr. in *Streit*, ed. Gründer, 133. Erwin Rohde made no reference to either Creuzer or Schelling in his defense of Nietzsche, *Afterphilologie* (Leipzig: E. W. Fritzsch, 1872), repr. in *Streit*, ed. Gründer, 65–111.

66. Wilamowitz, *Zukunftsphilologie!* 29 n. 2. Nietzsche had certainly read Lobeck, but he disagreed strongly with his interpretation. See *Götzendämmerung, NKSA*, 6:158, where Nietzsche writes, "one sees the almost laughable poverty of instinct of the German philologists when they come in the vicinity of the Dionysian. Especially the famous Lobeck, who, with the venerable sureness of a worm who has been dried out between books, crawled into this world of secret affairs and convinced himself that he was being scientific when he was being frivolous and childish to the point of nausea."

67. Wilamowitz, *Zukunftsphilologie!* 42.

68. *NKSA*, 1:74 (§10). On the connection of this passage to liberal theology in the context of Overbeck's development, see also Niklaus Peter, *Im Schatten der Modernität: Franz Overbecks Weg zur "Christlichkeit unserer heutigen Theologie"* (Stuttgart and Weimar: Metzler, 1992), 139.

69. Though described *in nucio*, Nietzsche's argument anticipates the position of Karl Barth and the account of theological history presented by Hans Frei in *The Eclipse of Biblical Narrative: A Study in Eighteenth and Nineteenth Century Hermeneutics* (New Haven: Yale University Press, 1974).

70. Albert Schweitzer, *The Quest of the Historical Jesus: A Critical Study of Its Progress from Reimarus to Wrede* (1906), trans. F. C. Burkitt, with an introduction by James Robinson (New York: Macmillan, 1968), 206.

71. *NKSA*, 1:145 (§23).

72. Nietzsche, *Vom Nutzen und Nachteil der Historie für das Leben, NKSA*, 1:296 (§7). Nietzsche was well informed on theological matters, especially due to his

friendship with Franz Overbeck. For a contemporary account, see Louis Kelterborn's report in *Begegnungen mit Nietzsche*, ed. Sander Gilman (Bonn: Bouvier, 1981), 219: "At the end of a second visit [with Nietzsche], he made important comments on . . . his own relationship to religion and Christianity in general and to mediating and reform theology in particular."

73. *NKSA*, 1:146 (§23); cf. *NKSA*, 7:308.

74. *NKSA*, 1:145 (§23).

75. On the Protestant Association, see Claudia Lepp, *Protestantisch-Liberaler Aufbruch in die Moderne: Der deutsche Protestantenverein in der Zeit der Reichsgründung und des Kulturkampfes* (Gütersloh: Christian Kaiser, 1996); also Josef Becker, *Liberaler Staat und Kirche in der Ära von Reichsgründung und Kulturkampf: Geschichte und Strukturen ihres Verhältnisses in Baden, 1860–1876* (Mainz: Matthias Grünewald, 1973). Christian Hermann Weisse, while sympathetic to the goals of the Protestant Association, was not a member.

76. Lepp, *Protestantisch-Liberaler Aufbruch in die Moderne*, 61.

77. *NKSA*, 1:117 (§18). See *Vom Nutzen und Nachteil*, 296 (§7): "Let no one suppose that there are any new, powerful instincts for construction behind [historical theology]. One would have to see the so-called Protestant Association as the mother's womb of a new religion." See also *NKSA*, 7:49: "Whoever no longer has the courage to experience miracles, run to the Protestant Association—*ultima ratio rationis.*"

78. Becker, *Liberaler Staat und Kirche*, 179.

79. On the *Kulturkampf*, see Margaret Lavinia Anderson, *Windthorst: A Political Biography* (Oxford: Oxford University Press, 1981); Margaret Lavinia Anderson, "The Kulturkampf and the Course of German History," *Central European History* 19 (1986): 82–115; Ronald Ross, *The Failure of Bismarck's Kulturkampf: Catholicism and State Power in Imperial Germany, 1871–1887* (Washington: Catholic University Press, 1998); for intellectual aspects, see esp. Tal, *Christians and Jews in Germany*, 81–120.

80. Lepp, *Protestantisch-Liberaler Aufbruch in die Moderne*, 319–60; on the *Volkskirche* see esp. 339 n.

81. *NKSA*, 7:22; cf. *NKSA*, 7:18 and 7:57.

82. *NKSA*, 1:29 (§1); cf. *NKSA*, 7:19.

83. *NKSA*, 1:148 (§23).

84. Ibid., 149 (§23).

85. Ibid., 147 (§23).

86. Wagner, "Beethoven" (1870), *RWGSD*, 9:116. For Nietzsche's linking of Beethoven to the Dionysian, see *NKSA*, 1:29 (§1), 50 (§6), 127 (§19); also "Einleitung in die Tragödie des Sophocles," *NKGA*, 2/3:17.

87. Bergmann, *Nietzsche*, 34–37, 59–107. On the "cult of genius" and its application to Wagner, see Nietzsche's letter to Rohde (Feb. 1–3, 1868), *NBW*, 1/2:249.

88. *NKSA*, 1:107 (§16).

89. Ibid., 101–2 (§15); cf. Kaufmann's translation, *Birth of Tragedy*, 97–98.

90. *NKSA*, 7:124–25.

91. Ibid., 100. This was also consistent with the young Nietzsche's anti-Semitism; see, e.g., Nietzsche to Richard Wagner (May 22, 1869), *NBW*, 2/1:9. On Nietzsche and anti-Semitism, see Hubert Cancik and Hildegard Cancik-Lindemaier, "Philhellénisme et antisémitisme en Allemagne, le cas Nietzsche: Philologie classique, philhellénisme, antisémitisme," in *De Sils-Maria à Jérusalem: Nietzsche et le Judaïsme, les intellectuels juifs et Nietzsche,* ed. Dominique Bourel and Jacques le Rider (Paris: Cerf, 1991), 21–46; Weaver Santaniello, *Nietzsche, God, and the Jews: His Critique of Judeo-Christianity in Relation to the Nazi Myth* (Albany: State University of New York Press, 1994); Sarah Kofman, *Le mépris des Juifs: Nietzsche, les Juifs, l'antisémitisme* (Paris: Galilée, 1994); Rudolf Kreis, *Nietzsche, Wagner und die Juden* (Würzburg: Königshausen und Neumann, 1995); Jacob Golumb, ed., *Nietzsche and Jewish Culture* (London: Routledge, 1997), 117–36; Christian Niemeyer, "Nietzsches Rhetorischer Antisemitismus," *Nietzsche-Studien* 26 (1997): 139–62; Yirmiyahu Yovel, *Dark Riddle: Hegel, Nietzsche, and the Jews* (University Park: Pennsylvania State University Press, 1998); Hubert Cancik and Hildegard Cancik-Lindemaier, *Philolog und Kultfigur: Friedrich Nietzsche und seine Antike in Deutschland* (Stuttgart: Metzler, 1999), 87–150.

92. J. E. Wilson, *Schelling und Nietzsche,* 154–58, has demonstrated Schelling's influence on Nietzsche here, but he does not investigate the nationalist and anti-Semitic twist given to Schelling's ideas by Nietzsche.

93. *NKSA*, 7:139. These comments reflected both Schopenhauer's notion of a "true," non-Jewish Christianity, as well as the historical work of Strauss, Baur, and the Tübingen school. The theologians had drawn a clear division between the synoptic Gospels and the Gospel of John, judging John inferior as a document of earliest Christianity or as a record of Jesus' life and sayings. This, however, is precisely what appears to have attracted Nietzsche, Eduard von Hartmann, and others to the Fourth Gospel.

94. *NKSA*, 7:340; see also ibid., 156.

95. Ibid., 45.

96. Ibid., 1:134 (§21).

97. Ibid., 88 (§12).

98. On this, see esp. Porter, *Invention of Dionysus,* 16–33. Porter offers a provocative and, in many respects, persuasive reading of *The Birth of Tragedy.* But by focusing on Nietzsche's engagement with "metaphysics," he overlooks the specifically Christian theological problematic of *The Birth of Tragedy.*

99. See the account in Theobald Ziegler, *David Friedrich Strauss,* 2 vols. (Strasbourg: Trübner, 1908), 2:652–57.

100. David F. Strauss, *Das Leben Jesu für das deutsche Volk* (Leipzig: Brockhaus, 1864).

101. Cited by Schweitzer, *Quest of the Historical Jesus,* 195.

102. David F. Strauss, "Krieg und Friede: Zwei Briefe an Ernst Renan nebst dessen Antwort auf den ersten," in *Kleine Schriften,* 3rd ed. (Bonn: Emil Strauss, 1898), 300; discussed in H. W. Wardman, *Ernest Renan: A Critical Biography* (London: Athlone, 1964), 117–27.

103. David Friedrich Strauss, *Der alte und der neue Glaube: Ein Bekenntniß,* 2nd ed. (Leipzig: Hirzel, 1872), 94.

104. Ibid., 97–100, 103–4.

105. Ibid., 146.

106. On Strauss's reception of Darwin, see Frederick Gregory, *Nature Lost? Natural Science and the German Theological Traditions of the Nineteenth Century* (Cambridge: Harvard University Press, 1992), 67–111.

107. Strauss, *Der alte und der neue Glaube,* 260.

108. For a survey of early responses to Strauss, see L. W. E. Rauwenhoff and F. Nippold, *D. Fr. Strauss' "Alter und neuer Glaube" und seine literarischen Ergebnisse: Zwei kritische Abhandlungen* (Leipzig: Richter und Harrassowitz; Leiden: von Doesburgh, 1873); also Peter Schrembs, "David Friedrich Strauss, *Der alte und der neue Glaube* in der zeitgenössischen Kritik" (Ph.D. diss., Universität Zurich, 1987).

109. W. Lang, *Preußische Jahrbücher* (Feb. 1873), cited in Rauwenhoff and Nippold, *Strauss' "Alter und neuer Glaube,"* 161.

110. In the novel *Kinder der Welt* (1875), Paul Heyse portrayed a generation wrestling with Schopenhauer-inspired atheism and searching for new sources of belief.

111. Frank Simon-Ritz, "Kulturelle Modernisierung und Krise des religiösen Bewußtseins: Freireligiöse, Freidenker und Monisten im Kaiserreich," in *Religion im Kaiserreich: Milieus—Mentalitäten—Krisen,* ed. Olaf Blaschke and Frank-Michael Kuhlemann (Gütersloh: Chr. Kaiser, 1996), 457–73.

112. Lucian Hölscher, *Weltgericht oder Revolution: Protestantische und sozialistische Zukunftsvorstellungen im deutschen Kaiserreich* (Stuttgart: Klett-Cotta, 1989), 135–98, esp. 143.

113. Strauss, *Der alte und der neue Glaube,* 294. The connection between Strauss and the *Kulturkampf* has often been overlooked, although it is noted by Wilhelm Lütgert, *Die Religion des deutschen Idealismus und ihr Ende* (Gütersloh: Gerd Mohn, 1930), 4:74–75; also Cancik and Cancik-Lindemaier, *Philolog und Kultfigur,* 53–55.

114. Strauss, *Der alte und der neue Glaube,* 91.

115. Ibid., 144.

116. Ibid., 299.

117. Cosima von Wagner, *Diaries,* trans. Geoffrey Skelton, ed. and annotated by Martin Gregor-Dellin and Dietrich Mack, 2 vols. (New York: Harcourt Brace Jovanovich, 1978), 1:593 (Feb. 7, 1873): "Dinner with the Wesendocks, dispute over Strauss's book *The Old Faith and the New,* which R. and I found terribly shallow, but which Frau W. admires." See also 1:612 (Mar. 3, 1873): "Strauss probably an Israelite."

118. Jürgen Bona Meyer, *Der alte und der neue Glaube: Betrachtungen über David Friedrich Strauss' Bekenntniß* (Bonn: Marcus, 1873).

119. Jacob Frohschammer, *Das neue Wissen und der neue Glaube* (Leipzig: Brockhaus, 1873), 201.

120. Gustav Adolph Wislicenus, *Gegenwart und Zukunft der Religion: Zu der*

von Strauss angeregten Frage über "Den alten und den neuen Glauben" (Leipzig: Ernst Keil, 1873).

121. Heymann Steinthal, "Zur Religionsphilosophie," *ZfVp* 8 (1875): 259.

122. See esp. the account by Paul Deussen in *Begegnungen mit Nietzsche*, ed. Gilman, 56.

123. See Elisabeth Nietzsche to Nietzsche (May 26, 1865), *NBW*, 1/3:45; Deussen to Nietzsche (June 29, 1866), *NBW*, 1/3:108–9. Nietzsche also read Strauss's polemic against Daniel Schenkel, *Die Halben und die Ganzen* (1865), Nietzsche to Mushacke (Sept. 20, 1865), *NBW*, 1/2:85.

124. Köhler, *Nietzsche and Wagner*, 94–96, overstates the extent to which Wagner forced Nietzsche to write an anti-Strauss book and the role of anti-Semitism in this particular episode. *David Strauss* followed quite naturally from positions adopted by Nietzsche even before his arrival in Basel.

125. *David Strauss*, NKSA, 1:228.

126. *NKSA*, 8:310. Nietzsche later spoke of the "degeneration of Strauss into the author of 'the old and the new faith,'" (*Entartung*), *NKSA*, 12:485.

127. Paul Lagarde, *Ueber das Verhältnis des deutschen Staates zu Theologie, Kirche und Religion: Ein Versuch Nicht-Theologen zu orientieren* (Göttingen: Dieterich, 1873). On Lagarde, see still Fritz Stern, *The Politics of Cultural Despair: A Study in the Rise of the German Ideology* (Berkeley and Los Angeles: University of California Press, 1961), esp. 35–52. On anti-Semitic religious thought in this period, see Tal, *Christians and Jews in Germany*, esp. 223–89.

128. Franz Overbeck, *Ueber die Christlichkeit unserer heutigen Theologie: Streit- und Friedensschrift* (Leipzig: E. W. Fritzsch, 1873). Citations are from Franz Overbeck, *Werke und Nachlaß*, vol. 1, *Schriften bis 1873*, ed. Ekkehard W. Stegemann and Niklaus Peter (Stuttgart and Weimar: Metzler, 1994), 167–256. On Overbeck's relationship to Nietzsche, Strauss, and Lagarde, see esp. Peter, *Im Schatten der Modernität*; Andreas Urs Sommer, *Der Geist der Historie und das Ende des Christenthums: Zur "Waffengenossenschaft" von Friedrich Nietzsche und Franz Overbeck* (Berlin: Akademie Verlag, 1997).

129. Gossman, *Basel*, 419–20.

130. Overbeck, *Ueber die Christlichkeit*, 179–80.

131. Ibid., 238, 234.

132. Ibid., 180–81.

133. Eduard von Hartmann, *Philosophie des Unbewußten: Versuch einer Weltanschauung* (Berlin: Duncker, 1869). Given Hartmann's importance as a historical figure, the literature on him is still meager. For a useful overview, see Dennis Darnoi, *The Unconscious and Eduard von Hartmann: A Historico-Critical Monograph* (The Hague: Nijhoff, 1967).

134. Eduard von Hartmann, *Die Selbstzersetzung des Christenthums und die Religion der Zukunft* (Berlin: Duncker, 1874). Hartmann had already published his views of Christianity under the pseudonym F. A. Müller, *Briefe über die christliche Religion* (Stuttgart: Kötzle, 1870).

135. Hartmann, *Selbstzersetzung*, 1.

136. Ibid., xv.

137. Ibid., 113.

138. Ibid., 43.

139. The book was translated into several foreign languages and inspired a number of counter-polemics. See, e.g., Carl Friedrich Heman, *Eduard von Harmann's Religion der Zukunft in ihrer Selbstzersetzung nachgewiesen* (Leipzig: J. C. Hinrichs, 1875).

140. Wilhelm Emmanuel Freiherr von Ketteler, "Der Culturkampf gegen die kathol. Kirche und die neuen Kirchengesetzentwürfe für Hessen" (1875), *Sämtliche Werke und Briefe*, pt. 1, vol. 4, *Schriften, Aufsätze und Reden, 1871–1877*, ed. Erwin Iserloh and Christopher Stoll (Mainz: v. Hase und Koehler, 1977), 383.

141. *NKSA*, 7:784.

142. Ibid., 815–16.

143. Nietzsche, *Schopenhauer als Erzieher, NKSA*, 1:407 (§7).

144. Ibid., 386 (§6).

145. Nietzsche to Rohde (Feb. 28, 1875), *NBW*, 2/5:27–28. Nietzsche went on to write, "[I]n the last instance it is I on whom the stain of this conversion will stay. God knows, I don't say this out of egoistic solicitude. But I also believe that I, too, represent something holy, and it would shame me deeply if I faced the suspicion that I had anything to do with this Catholic stuff that I hate so profoundly."

146. For a careful analysis of Nietzsche's view of Luther during these years, see Heinz Bluhm, "Nietzsche's Idea of Luther in *Human, All Too Human*," *PMLA* 65 (1950): 1053–68; Bluhm fails to connect Nietzsche's development to any external factors, notably the *Kulturkampf*.

147. See the discussion in Köhler, *Nietzsche and Wagner*, 68–71.

148. See *NKSA*, 8:281; also earlier comments, 8:105–10, 119. In *Richard Wagner in Bayreuth* (1876), Nietzsche would invoke Luther, along with Beethoven and Wagner, as an example of "German gaiety," *NKSA*, 1:480. Like much else in that essay, this statement seems insincere or at best ironic.

149. Elsewhere Nietzsche spoke of a "counter-reformation," which would replace the Protestant religion of transcendence with a new "Catholic" religion of beauty, art, and love. See *NKSA*, 7:774.

150. Nietzsche, *Chronik zu Nietzsches Leben, NKSA*, 15:44.

151. Köhler, *Nietzsche and Wagner*, 64–66.

152. *NKSA*, 7:765.

153. See Andrea Orsucci, *Orient–Okzident: Nietzsches Versuch einer Loslösung vom europäischen Weltbild* (Berlin: de Gruyter, 1996), 367.

154. Except for Tylor, these scholars remain relatively understudied. For relevant discussions, see Jan De Vries, *Forschungsgeschichte der Mythologie* (Freiburg im Breisgau and Munich: Alber, 1961), 212–25; Schlesier, *Kulte, Mythen und Gelehrte*, which focuses on developments from Jane Ellen Harrison into the twentieth century; and Frank Turner, *The Greek Heritage in Victorian Britain* (New Haven: Yale University Press, 1981), 115–34.

155. Karl Boetticher, *Der Baumkultus der Hellenen, nach den gottesdienst-*

lichen Gebräuchen und den überlieferten Bildwerken dargestellt (Berlin: Weidmann, 1856).

156. Wilhelm Schwartz, *Der Ursprung der Mythologie* (Berlin: Hertz, 1860), 26.

157. Wilhelm Schwartz, *Die altgriechischen Schlangengottheiten, ein Beispiel der Anlehnung altheidnischen Volksglaubens an die Natur* (1858; repr., Berlin: Hertz, 1897), 11.

158. Schwartz, *Ursprung,* xix–xx; Schwartz was one of the few Germans scholars to favorably cite the democratically inclined historian of Greece George Grote. See *Ursprung,* 14. On Grote's theory of myth, see Turner, *Greek Heritage in Victorian Britain,* 83–104.

159. Edward Tylor, *Primitive Culture,* 2 vols. (London: John Murray, 1871). Nietzsche checked out a German translation of this book from the Basel library in June 1875. See Max Oehler, *Nietzsches Bibliothek* (Weimar: Nietzsche Archiv, 1942), 54.

160. Tylor, *Primitive Culture,* 1:258.

161. Ibid., 2:152.

162. Ibid., 228–30.

163. Ibid., 1:271.

164. On Mannhardt, see De Vries, *Forschungsgeschichte der Mythologie,* 212–16; Karl Scheuermann, *Wilhelm Mannhardt: Seine Bedeutung für die vergleichende Religionsforschung* (Giessen: Meyer, 1933).

165. Wilhelm Mannhardt, *Germanische Mythen: Forschungen* (Berlin: Ferdinand Schneider, 1858).

166. Wilhelm Mannhardt, *Wald- und Feldkulte,* vol. 1, *Der Baumkultus der Germanen und ihrer Nachbarstämme,* vol. 2, *Antike Wald- und Feldkulte* (Berlin: Bornträger, 1875–77; repr., Darmstadt: Wissenschaftliche Buchgesellschaft, 1963). Nietzsche borrowed vol. 1 of this work from the Basel library in October 1875; see Oehler, *Nietzsches Bibliothek,* 54.

167. Mannhardt, *Wald- und Feldkulte,* 1:3.

168. On the Maypole, see ibid., 161–90; on the Christmas tree, ibid., 238–51; cf. ibid., 250: "And it may be a happy thought to us that our nation, in that it has made this symbol, in a certain sense, a sign of its nationality, declared the life-tree of pure humanity to be, as it should be, identical with its own life"; on the crucifix, ibid., 250–51.

169. Ibid., 186.

170. Friedrich Nietzsche, "Der Gottesdienst der Griechen: Alterthümer des religiösen Cultus der Griechen, dreistündig, Winter 1875–76," published in *Nietzsches Werke,* vol. 19 (pt. 3, vol. 3), *Unveröffentlichtes zur antiken Religion und Philosophie,* ed. Otto Crusius and Wilhelm Nestle (Leipzig: Alfred Kröner, 1913), 1–124. In their editorial notes, 393–98, Crusius and Nestle offer useful hints about the sources of Nietzsche's lectures, which have been investigated in detail by Orsucci, *Orient–Okzident,* 3–140 and passim.

171. "Gottesdienst," 4.

172. This evolutionary approach also characterized Nietzsche's essay "Ueber Wahrheit und Lüge im aussermoralischen Sinne" (1873), *NKSA*, 1:873–91.

173. See "Gottesdienst," 34–39, where Nietzsche cites both Mannhardt and Boetticher. As Orsucci shows, *Orient–Okzident*, 109–40, the historical conception of Nietzsche's "Gottesdienst" lectures was derived from the work of Heinrich Nissen, Karl Müllenhof, and Franz Movers.

174. "Gottesdienst," 8; cf. *Human, All Too Human*, *NKSA*, 2:114–15 (§111).

175. "Gottesdienst," 38; cf. Boetticher, *Baumkultus*, 204–7.

176. Orsucci, *Orient–Okzident*, 10, maintains that his 1875 readings pushed Nietzsche to abandon the theory of Greek autochthony. But given his reliance on Creuzer, Kuhn, and others in *The Birth of Tragedy*, it would seem that these readings served rather to confirm and refine his preexisting views.

177. Nietzsche, *NKSA*, 8:59. On this point, see esp. Orsucci, *Orient–Okzident*, 124–25.

178. Nietzsche drew at one point from Mannhardt's argument that burnt offerings were originally intended to chase away evil demons in the shape of animals or plants; "Gottesdienst," 13. For further textual references, see Orsucci, *Orient–Okzident*, 94–96.

179. "Gottesdienst," 50.

180. Here Nietzsche anticipated recent work in religious studies that critiques the tendency to define religion as essentially ideal or inward. See e.g., Talal Asad, *Genealogies of Religion: Discipline and Reasons of Power in Christianity and Islam* (Baltimore: Johns Hopkins University Press, 1993), 27–54.

181. Friedrich Nietzsche, *Menschliches, Allzumenschliches: Ein Buch für freie Geister* (Chemnitz: Schmeitzner, 1878). Citations are from *NKSA*, although I have also consulted the translation by R. J. Hollingdale (Cambridge: Cambridge University Press, 1996).

182. *Menschliches*, vol. 2, *NKSA*, 2:511 (§323); cf. *Morgenröte*, 3:52 (§44): "Mit der Einsicht in den Ursprung nimmt die Bedeutungslosigkeit des Ursprungs zu."

183. See, e.g., *Menschliches*, *NKSA*, 2:223–24 (§271).

184. See ibid., 118 (§114). See *NKSA*, 8:65 (notes from 1875): "With Christianity, a religion achieved preponderance that corresponded to a pre-Hellenic state of man: belief in magical occurrences in everything and everyone, bloody sacrifice, superstitious fear of demonic punishments, despair in oneself, ecstatic brooding and hallucination, man himself become an arena of good and evil spirits and their struggles."

185. *Menschliches*, *NKSA*, 2:121–22 (§125).

186. Ibid., 23–55 (§§1–34).

187. Ibid., 47 (§26).

188. Ibid., 111 (§110).

189. See, e.g., ibid., 384 (§9).

190. Nietzsche, *Ecce Homo*, *NKSA*, 6:327.

191. Nietzsche actually received his copy of *Parsifal* several months before mailing off the final manuscript of *Human, All Too Human*; see Dieter Borchmeyer,

"Wagner and Nietzsche," in *Wagner Handbook*, ed. Ulrich Müller and Peter Wapnewski, trans. John Deathridge (Cambridge: Harvard University Press, 1992), 338–39.

192. *NKSA*, 13:416.

193. Volker Mertens, "Wagner's Middle Ages," in *Wagner Handbook*, ed. Müller and Wapnewski, 262–66.

194. Borchmeyer, "Wagner and Nietzsche," 338–39; Köhler, *Nietzsche and Wagner*, 50–51.

195. For some of the polarized interpretations surrounding this opera, see Kreis, *Nietzsche, Wagner und die Juden*, 85–139; Daniel Schneller, *Richard Wagners "Parsifal" und die Erneuerung des Mysteriendramas in Bayreuth: Die Vision des Gesamtkunstwerks als Universalkultur der Zukunft* (Berne: Peter Lang, 1997); Wolf-Daniel Hartwich, *Deutsche Mythologie: Die Erfindung einer Kunstreligion* (Berlin: Piper, 2000), 187–210.

196. Wagner, "Religion und Kunst," *RWGSD*, 10:275.

197. Cosima Wagner, *Diaries*, 1:534–35 (Sept. 16–17, 1872); 1:849 (May 31–June 1, 1875).

198. "Religion und Kunst," *RWGSD*, 10:281.

199. E.g., "Beethoven," in *RWGSD*, 9:146. Cosima Wagner's diaries record that Wagner saw Klingsor as representing the "Jesuit"; see Kreis, *Nietzsche, Wagner und die Juden*, 102.

200. See Cosima Wagner, *Diaries*, 1:464, 505.

201. See esp. Wagner, "Erkenne dich selbst" (1881), in *RWGSD*, 10:338–50. On Wagner's critique of materialist anti-Semitism, see Wolfgang Altgeld, "Wagner, der 'Bayreuther Kreis' und die Entwicklung des völkischen Denkens," in *Richard Wagner, 1883–1983: Die Rezeption im 19. und 20. Jahrhundert*, ed. Ulrich Müller, Franz Hundsnorscher, and Cornelius Sommer (Stuttgart: Heinz, 1984), 35–64, esp. 50.

202. "Religion und Kunst," *RWGSD*, 10:299.

203. It is possible to interpret *Parsifal* as a symbolic representation of the racial theories put forth by Gobineau and Renan: Klingsor, the representative of the Arabic-Semitic spirit; the Jewish Kundry, allied to the Semites but also the vehicle for the Aryan-Christian doctrine of redemption manifested to Parsifal. (Cf. Weiner, *Richard Wagner and the Antisemitic Imagination*, 247–56, which interprets both Klingsor *and* Kundry as figures of Jews.) For a brief examination of Wagner's theories of race, see Léon Poliakov, *The Aryan Myth: A History of Racist and Nationalist Ideas in Europe*, trans. Edmund Howard (New York: Basic Books, 1971), 311–21, which usefully stresses the influence of Schopenhauer.

204. Wagner, "Heldenthum und Christenthum," *RWGSD*, 10:353; cf. Nietzsche, *Morgenröte, NKSA*, 3:30–32 (§18).

205. On Bayreuth, see Manfred Eger, "The Bayreuth Festival and the Wagner Family," in *Wagner Handbook*, ed. Müller and Wapnewski, 485–501; Frederic Spotts, *Bayreuth: A History of the Wagner Festival* (New Haven: Yale University Press, 1994). On Wagnerism, see Winfried Schüler, *Der Bayreuther Kreis von seiner Entstehung bis zum Ausgang der Wilhelminischen Ära: Wagnerkult und Kulturreform im Geiste völkischer Weltanschauung* (Münster: Aschendorff, 1971); David Clay Large,

William Weber, and Anne Dzamba Sessa, eds., *Wagnerism in European Culture and Politics* (Ithaca: Cornell University Press, 1984); Massimo Ferrari Zumbini, "Nietzsche in Bayreuth: Nietzsches Herausforderung, die Wagnerianer und die Gegenoffensive," *Nietzsche-Studien* 19 (1990): 246–91.

206. On the "mortal insult" as a reference to masturbation, see esp. Weiner, *Richard Wagner and the Antisemitic Imagination*, 335–47. Based on the 1883 letter, Peter Wapnewski, "Nietzsche und Wagner: Stationen einer Beziehung," *Nietzsche-Studien* 18 (1989): 418–19, interprets the "mortal insult" as Wagner's return to Christianity. But Manfred Eger calls this account into serious question, *Nietzsches Bayreuther Passion*, 207–33.

207. Nietzsche to von Seydlitz (Jan. 4, 1878), *NBW*, 2/5:300.

208. *NKSA*, 11:250.

209. *Menschliches, NKSA*, 2:123 (§130); cf. *Morgenröte, NKSA*, 3:30–32 (§18).

210. Nietzsche to Seydlitz (Jan. 4, 1878), *NBW*, 2/5:300; cf. Nietzsche, *Jenseits von Gut und Böse, NKSA*, 5:204 (§256): "what you hear is Rome,—Rome's faith without words."

211. *NKSA*, 12:199.

212. Nietzsche, *Genealogie der Moral, NKSA*, 5:340–43 (pt. 3, §§2–3).

213. *Jenseits von Gut und Böse, NKSA*, 5:204 (§256).

214. *Menschliches, NKSA*, 2:199–200 (§237).

215. See esp. *Genealogie, NKSA*, 5:394 (pt. 3, §22).

216. On the influence of Janssen, see Emanuel Hirsch, "Nietzsche und Luther" (1920), with an afterword by Jörg Salaquarda, *Nietzsche-Studien* 15 (1986): 398–439; Orsucci, *Orient–Okzident*, 351–64.

217. *NKSA*, 11:28, 39, 101.

218. *Morgenröte, NKSA*, 3:34 (§22).

219. *Menschliches, NKSA*, 2:309–11 (§475).

220. *Morgenröte, NKSA*, 3:66–68 (§68).

221. Ibid., 79–80 (§84).

222. This view dominates Santaniello, *Nietzsche, God, and the Jews*, as well as Kreis, *Nietzsche, Wagner und die Juden.*

223. On the "false dichotomies" that characterize Nietzsche's writings, see esp. Sander Gilman, *Inscribing the Other* (Lincoln: University of Nebraska Press, 1991), 99–142.

224. *Menschliches, NKSA*, 2:144 (§150); cf. *NKSA*, 8:206–7.

225. *Menschliches, NKSA*, 2:146–56 (§§155–66).

226. Ibid., 451 (vol. 2, §171).

227. *Morgenröte, NKSA*, 3:210 (§265).

228. *NKSA*, 11:250.

229. Ibid., 676–77; cf. *Chronik zu Nietzsches Leben, NKSA*, 15:85.

230. *NKSA*, 8:533–34.

231. *Morgenröte, NKSA*, 3:85–86 (§92).

232. *Jenseits von Gut und Böse, NKSA,* 5:76 (§58).

233. *Morgenröte, NKSA,* 3:86 (§92).

234. Nietzsche, *Die fröhliche Wissenschaft, NKSA,* 3:480–82 (§125).

235. Friedrich Creuzer, *Symbolik und Mythologie,* 3rd ed., 1:179–225; Arthur Schopenhauer, *Parerga und Paralipomena: Short Philosophical Essays,* trans. E. F. J. Payne, 2 vols. (Oxford: Clarendon, 1974), 2:378.

236. All citations are from *Thus Spake Zarathustra: A Book for Everyone and No One,* trans. R. J. Hollingdale (London: Penguin, 1961), 41.

237. Ibid.

238. Ibid., 42.

239. Cf. Creuzer, *Symbolik und Mythologie,* 3rd ed., 1:221–23. For this reference and others, see David Thatcher, "Eagle and Serpent in *Zarathustra,*" *Nietzsche-Studien* 6 (1977): 240–60.

240. In addition to Boetticher, Nietzsche's reading on the snake cult included Jacob Mähly, *Die Schlange im Mythus und Cultus der klassischen Völker* (Basel: Schultze, 1867); James Fergusson, *Tree and Serpent Worship* (London: W. H. Allen, 1868); on this, see the editorial comments of Crusius and Nestle to "Gottesdienst," 393–98.

241. *Morgenröte, NKSA,* 3:53–54 (§49): "Formerly, in order to get a feeling of the superiority of humans, their divine *origin* was mentioned; that has become a forbidden path, because at its door stands an ape . . . as if to say: no further in this direction!"

242. *Zarathusra,* 41–42. For another perspective on the critique of humanism, see Andrew Zimmerman, *Anthropology and Antihumanism in Imperial Germany* (Chicago: University of Chicago Press, 2001).

243. *Zarathustra,* 55, 193.

244. Ibid., 58–60. In part 4, Nietzsche stages a "last supper" that becomes, among other things, an elaborate parody of Wagner's *Parsifal.* On this, see Hollinrake, *Nietzsche, Wagner, and the Philosophy of Pessimism,* 136–71; Kreis, *Nietzsche, Wagner und die Juden,* 166–76.

245. *Zarathustra,* 110–11.

246. Ibid., 75.

247. Ibid., 67.

248. Ibid., 127.

249. Ibid., 78. On this, see also Eger, *Nietzsches Bayreuther Passion,* 213–16.

250. *Die fröhliche Wissenschaft, NKSA,* 3:570 (§341—labeled "The Greatest Weight"); *Zarathustra,* 178–79, 237–38.

251. *NKSA,* 11:359.

252. *Zarathustra,* 230–31.

253. *Jenseits von Gut und Böse, NKSA,* 5:36 (§21); cf. *Götzendämmerung, NKSA,* 6:80–81 ("How the 'real world' finally became fable").

254. *Jenseits von Gut und Böse, NKSA,* 5:238 (§295).

255. Rudolf Haym, *Die romantische Schule* (1870), cited in Gerhart Hoffmeister,

"Forschungsgeschichte," in *Romantik-Handbuch*, ed. Helmut Schanze (Tübingen: Kröner, 1994), 184.

256. Michel Foucault, *The Order of Things: An Archaeology of the Human Sciences* [1966], trans. by Unknown Translator (New York: Vintage, 1970), 367–87; Sarah Kofman, *Nietzsche and Metaphor*, trans. Duncan Large (Stanford: Stanford University Press, 1993).

Epilogue

1. For an excellent survey, originally published under the title *Religion im Umbruch* (1988), see Thomas Nipperdey, *Deutsche Geschichte, 1866–1918*, vol. 1, *Arbeitswelt und Bürgergeist* (Munich: Beck, 1990), 428–530, esp. 507–28; see also the collected essays in Olaf Blaschke and Frank-Michael Kuhlemann, eds., *Religion im Kaiserreich: Milieus — Mentalitäten — Krisen* (Gütersloh: Chr. Kaiser, 1996).

2. See Kurt Nowak, *Geschichte des Christenthums in Deutschland: Religion, Politik und Gesellschaft vom Ende der Aufklärung bis zur Mitte des 20. Jahrhunderts* (Munich: Beck, 1995), 163.

3. See the data in Hugh McLeod, *Secularisation in Western Europe, 1848–1914* (New York: St. Martin's, 2000), 171–215.

4. As Lucian Hölscher shows, this was in many respects a false perception, *Weltgericht oder Revolution: Protestantische und sozialistische Zukunftsvorstellungen im deutschen Kaiserreich* (Stuttgart: Klett-Cotta, 1989).

5. Frank Simon-Ritz, "Kulturelle Modernisierung und Krise des religiösen Bewußtseins: Freireligiöse, Freidenker und Monisten im Kaiserreich," in Blaschke and Kuhlemann, *Religion im Kaiserreich*, 457–73.

6. On the *völkische Bewegung*, see George Mosse, *The Crisis of German Ideology: Intellectual Origins of the Third Reich* (New York: Universal Library, 1964); Uwe Puschner, Walter Schmitz, and Justus H. Ulbricht, eds., *Handbuch zur "völkischen Bewegung," 1871–1918* (Munich: Saur, 1996); and Uwe Puschner, *Die völkische Bewegung im wilhelminischen Kaiserreich: Sprache — Rasse — Religion* (Darmstadt: Wissenschaftliche Buchgesellschaft, 2001).

7. Geoffrey G. Field, *Evangelist of Race: The Germanic Vision of Houston Stewart Chamberlain* (New York: Columbia University Press, 1981).

8. Houston Stewart Chamberlain, *Die Grundlagen des neunzehnten Jahrhunderts*, 2 vols. (Munich: Bruckmann, 1899), 1:391–422.

9. See Stefanie von Schnurbein, "Die Suche nach einer 'arteigenen' Religion in 'germanisch-' und 'deutschgläubigen' Gruppen," in *Handbuch zur "völkischen Bewegung,"* ed. Puschner, Schmitz, and Ulbricht, 172–85, here 172–73; Julia Zernack, "Germanische Restauration und Edda Frömmigkeit," in *Politische Religion, religiöse Politik*, ed. Richard Faber (Würzburg: Königshausen und Neumann, 1997), 143–60; Ekkehard Hieronimus, "Von der Germanen-Forschung zum Germanen-Glauben: Zur Religionsgeschichte des Präfaschismus," in *Die Restauration der Götter: Antike Religion und Neo-Paganismus*, ed. Richard Faber and Renate Schlesier (Würzburg: Königshausen und Neumann, 1986), 241–57.

10. Günter Hartung, "Völkische Ideologie," in *Handbuch zur "Völkischen Bewegung,"* ed. Puschner, Schmitz, and Ulbricht, 22–44, here 33.

11. Cited in Schnurbein, "Suche nach einer 'arteigenen' Religion," 181.

12. Steven E. Aschheim, "After the Death of God: Varieties of Nietzschean Religion," *Nietzsche-Studien* 17 (1988): 218–49; Steven E. Aschheim, *The Nietzsche Legacy in Germany, 1890–1990* (Berkeley and Los Angeles: University of California Press, 1992).

13. Nipperdey, *Deutsche Geschichte, 1866–1918*, 526.

14. In this context, see esp. the discussion of Rolf Kauffeldt, "Die Idee eines 'neuen Bundes' (Gustav Landauer)," in Manfred Frank's *Vorlesungen über die neue Mythologie*, vol. 2, *Gott im Exil* (Frankfurt a.M.: Suhrkamp, 1988), 131–79; also Eugene Lunn, *Prophet of Community: The Romantic Socialism of Gustav Landauer* (Berkeley and Los Angeles: University of California Press, 1973).

15. Frank, *Gott im Exil*, 175.

16. Max Weber, *The Sociology of Religion*, trans. Ephraim Fischoff (Boston: Beacon Press, 1963), 137.

17. Nipperdey, *Deutsche Geschichte, 1866–1918*, 521, speaks of a "'vagierende' Religiosität."

18. Suzanne Marchand, *Down from Olympus: Archaeology and Philhellenism in Germany, 1750–1970* (Princeton: Princeton University Press, 1996), 119–24.

19. Ibid., 133–38; on the background to this, see Fritz Ringer, *The Decline of the German Mandarins: The German Academic Community, 1890–1933* (Cambridge: Harvard University Press, 1969).

20. Ingo Wiwjorra, "Die deutsche Vorgeschichtsforschung und ihr Verhältnis zu Nationalismus und Rassismus," in *Handbuch zur "völkischen Bewegung,"* ed. Puschner, Schmitz, and Ulbricht, 186–207; Marchand, *Down from Olympus*, 154–82.

21. On early opposition to the Aryan theory, see the sources in Theobald Bieder, *Geschichte der Germanenforschung*, 3 vols. (Hildburghausen: Thüringische Verlagsanstalt, 1913–25).

22. Julius Wellhausen, *Prolegomena zur Geschichte Israels* (Berlin: Reimer, 1883); John Rogerson, *Old Testament Criticism in the Nineteenth Century: England and Germany*, 2nd ed. (Philadelphia: Fortress, 1985), 257–72.

23. Marchand, *Down from Olympus*, 223–26; see also Jürgen Ebach, "Babel und Bibel oder: 'Heidnische' im Alten Testament," in *Restauration der Götter*, ed. Faber and Schlesier, 26–44.

24. Herbert Brunträger, *Der Ironiker und der Ideologe: Die Beziehungen zwischen Thomas Mann und Alfred Baeumler* (Würzburg: Königshausen und Neumann, 1993); on the broader context of mythical thought in the 1920s, see esp. Theodore Ziolkowski, "Der Hunger nach dem Mythos: Zur seelischen Gastronomie der Deutschen in den Zwanziger Jahren," in *Die Sogenannten Zwanziger Jahre*, ed. Reinhold Grimm and Jost Hermand (Bad Homburg: Gehlen, 1970), 169–201.

25. Alfred Baeumler, "Bachofen der Mythologe der Romantik," in Johann Jakob Bachofen, *Der Mythus von Orient und Occident: Eine Metaphysik der alten Welt aus den Werken von J. J. Bachofen*, 2nd ed., ed. Manfred Schröter (Munich: Beck, 1926), xxiii–ccxciv.

26. Brunträger, *Der Ironiker und der Ideologe*, 91–92.

27. See Lukács's comments on Baeumler, in Georg Lukács, *The Destruction of Reason*, trans. Peter Palmer (Atlantic Highlands, N.J.: Humanities Press, 1981), 533–35.

28. The classicist Karl Kerenyi saw this notion of "'myth' as a specific force" as being of German provenance. "I was deeply saddened that the influence of myth in the false sense could make itself felt in Germany, or rather, that in Germany, and soon elsewhere too, people were ready to believe that a dynamic something called myth could exercise such an influence, irrespective of the direction it took"; *Mythology and Humanism: The Correspondence of Thomas Mann and Karl Kerényi*, trans. Alexander Gelley (Ithaca: Cornell University Press, 1975), 15–17.

29. Alfred Rosenberg, *The Myth of the Twentieth Century: An Evaluation of the Spiritual-Intellectual Confrontations of Our Age*, trans. Vivian Bird (Torrance, Calif.: Noontide Press, 1982).

30. Frank, *Gott im Exil*, 115–17, 127–28.

31. Rosenberg, *The Myth of the Twentieth Century*, 387.

32. See Doris L. Bergen, *Twisted Cross: The German Christian Movement in the Third Reich* (Chapel Hill: University of North Carolina Press, 1996).

33. Cited in Hieronimus, "Von der Germanen-Forschung zum Germanen-Glauben," 256.

34. Frederic Spotts, *Bayreuth: A History of the Wagner Festival* (New Haven: Yale University Press, 1994), 143.

35. On this, see Saul Friedländer and Jörn Rüsen, eds., *Richard Wagner im Dritten Reich: Ein Schloss Elmau-Symposion* (Munich: Beck, 2000).

36. See Sabine Behrenbeck, *Der Kult um die toten Helden: Nationalsozialistische Mythen, Riten und Symbole 1923 bis 1945* (Cologne: SH-Verlag, 1996); also Frank, *Gott im Exil*, 80–104.

37. See, e.g., Michael Burleigh, *The Third Reich: A New History* (London: Hill and Wang, 2000).

38. On this model, see Ian Kershaw, *Hitler* (London: Longmans, 1991).

39. Max Horkheimer and Theodor W. Adorno, *Dialectic of Enlightenment*, trans. John Cumming (New York: Continuum, 1972), 46.

40. Ibid., 11.

41. It has been possible here to provide only the barest outline of these developments. It is my intention to explore them in detail in a second volume, which will examine the history of mythical thought in Germany from 1890 to 1989.

42. Manfred Frank, *Vorlesungen über die neue Mythologie*, vol. 1, *Der kommende Gott* (Frankfurt a.M.: Suhrkamp, 1982), 165–70; Maike Oergel, *The Return of King Arthur and the Nibelungen: National Myth in Nineteenth-Century English and German Literature* (Berlin: de Gruyter, 1998), 216.

43. See now, e.g., Warren Breckman, *Marx, the Young Hegelians, and the Origins of Radical Social Theory: Dethroning the Self* (Cambridge: Cambridge University Press, 1999); Thomas Albert Howard, *Religion and the Rise of Historicism: W. M. L. de Wette, Jacob Burckhardt, and the Theological Origins of Nineteenth-Century Historical Consciousness* (Cambridge: Cambridge University Press, 2000); and Corinna

Treitel, "Avatars of the Soul: Cultures of Science, Medicine, and the Occult in Modern Germany" (Ph.D. diss., Harvard University, 1999).

44. See the perceptive point by Charles Maier, "The End of Longing (Notes toward a History of Postwar German National Longing)," in *The Postwar Transformation of Germany: Democracy, Prosperity, and Nationhood*, ed. John S. Brady, Beverly Crawford, and Sarah Elise Wiliarty (Ann Arbor: University of Michigan Press, 1999), 271-85, here 273.

45. On the problem of translation, see Antoine Berman, *The Experience of the Foreign: Culture and Translation in Romantic Germany*, trans. S. Heyvaert (Albany: State University of New York Press, 1992).

SELECTED BIBLIOGRAPHY

Only the works most central to the present study are cited here. Further references are located in the notes.

PRIMARY WORKS: BOOKS AND ARTICLES

Bachofen, Johann Jakob. *Das Mutterrecht: Eine Untersuchung über die Gynaikokratie der alten Welt nach ihrer religiösen und rechtlichen Natur.* Edited by Hans-Jürgen Heinrichs. Frankfurt a.M.: Suhrkamp, 1975.

Becker, Wilhelm Adolph. *Der Symbolik Triumph: Vier Briefe.* Zerbst: Kummer, 1825.

Beiser, Frederick, ed. and trans. *The Early Political Writings of the German Romantics.* Cambridge: Cambridge University Press, 1996.

Boetticher, Karl. *Der Baumkultus der Hellenen, nach den gottesdienstlichen Gebräuchen und den überlieferten Bildwerken dargestellt.* Berlin: Weidmann, 1856.

Bunsen, Christian Josias. *Aegyptens Stelle in der Weltgeschichte.* 5 vols. in 4. Hamburg: Perthes, 1845–57.

———. *God in History; or, The Progress of Man's Faith in the Moral Order of the World.* Translated by Susanna Winkworth. 3 vols. London: Longmans, Green, and Co., 1868–70.

Bunsen, Frances. *A Memoir of Baron Bunsen.* Philadelphia: J. P. Lippincott, Longmans and Co., 1869.

Chamberlain, Houston Stewart. *Die Grundlagen des neunzehnten Jahrhunderts.* 2 vols. Munich: Bruckmann, 1899.

Creuzer, Friedrich. *Das akademische Studium des Alterthums.* Heidelberg: Mohr und Zimmer, 1807.

———. *Briefe Friedrich Creuzers an Savigny.* Edited by H. Dahlmann. Berlin: Eric Schmidt Verlag, 1972.

———. *Deutsche Schriften.* 10 vols. Leipzig and Darmstadt: Leske, 1837–56.

———. "Philologie und Mythologie in ihrem Stufengang und gegenseitigen Verhalten." *Heidelberger Jahrbücher* 1 (1808): 3–24.

————. "Das Studium des Alterthums, als Vorbereitung zur Philosophie." *Studien* 1 (1805): 1–29.

————. *Symbolik und Mythologie der alten Völker, besonders der Griechen.* 1st ed. 4 vols. Leipzig and Darmstadt: Heyer and Leske, 1810–12.

————. *Symbolik und Mythologie der alten Völker, besonders der Griechen.* 2nd ed. 4 vols. Leipzig and Darmstadt: Heyer and Leske, 1819–21.

————. *Symbolik und Mythologie der alten Völker, besonders der Griechen.* 3rd ed. 4 vols. Leipzig and Darmstadt: Heyer and Leske, 1837–43.

Creuzer, Friedrich, and Karoline von Günderode. *Briefe und Dichtungen.* Edited with an introduction by Erwin Rohde. Heidelberg: Carl Winter, 1896.

Dahlmann, Hellfried, ed. *Briefe Friedrich Creuzers an Savigny (1799–1859).* Berlin: E. Schmidt, 1972.

de Wette, Wilhelm Martin Leberecht. *Beiträge zur Einleitung in das Alte Testament.* 2 vols. Halle: Schimmelpfennig, 1806–7.

————. *Theodor, oder des Zweiflers Weihe: Bildungsgeschichte eines evangelischen Geistlichen.* 2 vols. Berlin: Reimer, 1822.

————. *Ueber Religion und Theologie: Erläuterungen zu seinem Lehrbuch der Dogmatik.* Berlin: Realschulbuchhandlung, 1815.

Diestel, Ludwig. "Der Monotheismus des ältesten Heidenthums, vorzüglich bei den Semiten." *Jahrbücher für deutsche Theologie* 5 (1860): 669–760.

Feuerbach, Ludwig. *The Essence of Christianity.* Translated by George Eliot. With an introduction by Karl Barth. Foreword by H. Richard Niebuhr. New York: Harper and Row, 1957.

————. *Thoughts on Death and Immortality.* Translated by James A. Massey. Berkeley and Los Angeles: University of California Press, 1980.

Fouqué, Friedrich de la Motte. *Sigurd, der Schlangentödter: Ein Heldenspiel* (1808). In *Deutsche National-Litteratur: Historisch kritische Ausgabe,* edited by Joseph Kürschner, vol. 146, div. 2, *Friedrich de La Motte-Fouqué und Josef Freiherr von Eichendorff,* edited by Max Koch, 2 pts., 1:1–111. Stuttgart: Union Deutsche Verlagsgesellschaft, 1884–93.

Fries, Jakob Friedrich. *Dialogues on Morality and Religion.* Translated by David Walford. Oxford: Basil Blackwell, 1982.

————. *Neue oder anthropologische Kritik der Vernunft.* 2nd ed. 3 vols. Heidelberg: Mohr und Zimmer, 1828–31.

Görres, Joseph. *Gesammelte Schriften.* Edited by Wilhelm Schellberg. 16 vols. to date. Cologne: Gilde, 1926–.

————, ed. *Lohengrin, ein altteutsches Gedicht, nach der Abschrift des Vaticanischen Manuscriptes von Ferdinand Gloekle.* Heidelberg: Mohr und Zimmer, 1813.

————. *Mythengeschichte der asiatischen Welt.* Heidelberg: Mohr und Zimmer, 1810.

Götzen, Pfaffen und Christus: Eine Ansicht über das historische Christenthum und den historischen Christus. Aus den Papieren eines Theologen, herausgegeben von einem seiner Freunde. Darmstadt: Carl Wilhelm Leske, 1846.

Grimm, Hermann, Gustav Hinrichs, and Wilhelm Schoof, eds. *Briefwechsel zwi-*

schen Jacob und Wilhelm Grimm aus der Jugendzeit. 2nd ed. Weimar: Hermann Böhlaus Nachfolger, 1963.

Grimm, Jacob. *Deutsche Mythologie.* 4th ed. Edited by Elard Hugo Meyer. 3 vols. Basel: Schwabe, 1953.

———. *Kleinere Schriften.* 8 vols. Berlin: Dümmler, 1864–90.

Grimm, Jacob, and Wilhelm Grimm. *The German Legends.* Translated by Donald Ward. 2 vols. Philadelphia: Institute for the Study of Human Issues, 1981.

Grimm, Wilhelm. *Kleinere Schriften.* Edited by Gustav Hinrichs. 8 vols. Berlin: Dümmler, 1881.

Gründer, Karlfried, ed. *Der Streit um Nietzsches "Geburt der Tragödie."* Hildesheim, Zurich, and New York: Georg Olms Verlag, 1989.

Hagen, Friedrich von der. *Die Nibelungen: Ihre Bedeutung für die Gegenwart und für immer.* Breslau: Josef Max, 1819.

Hartmann, Eduard von [F. A. Müller, pseud.]. *Briefe über die christliche Religion.* Stuttgart: Kötzle, 1870.

———. *Philosophie des Unbewußten: Versuch einer Weltanschauung.* Berlin: Duncker, 1869.

———. *Die Selbstzersetzung des Christenthums und die Religion der Zukunft.* 2nd ed. Berlin: Duncker, 1874.

Hegel, Georg W. F. *Briefe von und an Hegel.* Edited by Johannes Hoffmeister. 3 vols. Hamburg: Meiner, 1952.

———. *Early Theological Writings.* Translated by T. M. Knox. With an introduction by Richard Kroner. Philadelphia: University of Pennsylvania Press, 1948.

———. *Lectures on the Philosophy of Religion, One-Volume Edition: The Lectures of 1827.* Edited by Peter C. Hodgson. Translated by R. F. Brown, P. C. Hodgson, and J. M. Stewart. Berkeley and Los Angeles: University of California Press, 1988.

———. *Werke.* 20 vols. Frankfurt a.M.: Suhrkamp, 1970.

Heine, Heinrich. *Historisch-kritische Gesamtausgabe der Werke.* Edited by Manfred Winfuhr. 22 vols. Hamburg: Hoffmann und Campe, 1973–.

———. *Poetry and Prose.* Edited by Jost Hermand and Robert C. Holub. New York: Continuum, 1982.

———. *Werke und Briefe in zehn Bänden.* Edited by Hans Kaufmann. 10 vols. Berlin: Aufbau Verlag, 1961–64.

Hengstenberg, Ernst Wilhelm von. *Die Authentie des Pentateuchs.* 2 vols. Berlin: Ludwig Oehmigke, 1836–39.

———. *Christology of the Old Testament.* Translated by Reuel Keith. Alexandria, Va.: William Morrison, 1836.

Herder, Johann Gottfried. *Sämmtliche Werke.* Edited by Bernhard Suphan. 33 vols. Berlin: Weidmann, 1877–1913.

Hermann, Gottfried. *Ueber das Wesen und die Behandlung der Mythologie, ein Brief an Herrn Hofrath Creuzer.* Leipzig: Gerhard Fleischer, 1818.

Hermann, Gotffried, and Friedrich Creuzer. *Briefe über Homer und Hesiodus, vorzüglich über die Theogonie.* Heidelberg: August Oswald, 1818.

Kant, Immanuel. *Religion and Rational Theology*. Translated and edited by Allen W. Wood and George di Giovanni. Cambridge: Cambridge University Press, 1996.

Klenze, Leo von, and Ludwig Schorn. *Beschreibung der Glyptothek Seiner Majestät des Königs Ludwig I. von Bayern*. Munich: J. G. Cotta, 1842.

Kreuser, [Johann P.]. *Vorfragen über Homeros, seine Zeit und Gesänge*. Pt. 1. Frankfurt a.M.: Andreäische Buchhandlung, 1828.

Kuhn, Adalbert. *Die Herabkunft des Feuers und des Göttertranks: Ein Beitrag zur vergleichenden Mythologie der Indogermanen*. Berlin: Ferdinand Dümmler, 1859.

———. *Sagen, Gebräuche und Märchen aus Westfalen*. 2 vols. Leipzig: Brockhaus, 1859.

———, ed. *Märkische Sagen und Märchen*. Berlin: Reimer, 1843.

Kuhn, Adalbert, and Wilhelm Schwarz, eds. *Norddeutsche Sagen, Märchen und Gebräuche*. Leipzig: Brockhaus, 1848.

Lagarde, Paul de. *Deutsche Schriften*. 4th ed. Göttingen: Horstmann, 1903.

Leo, Heinrich. *Ueber Odins Verehrung in Deutschland: Ein Beitrag zur deutschen Alterthumskunde*. Erlangen: C. Heyder, 1822.

Mannhardt, Wilhelm. *Germanische Mythen: Forschungen*. Berlin: Ferdinand Schneider, 1858.

———. *Wald- und Feldkulte*. 2 vols. Berlin: Bornträger, 1875–77. Reprint, Darmstadt: Wissenschaftliche Buchgesellschaft, 1963.

Menzel, Wolfgang. *Die deutsche Literatur*. 2 vols. Stuttgart: Franckh, 1828.

———. *Voß und die Symbolik*. Stuttgart: Franckh, 1825.

Meyer, Jürgen Bona. *Der alte und der neue Glaube: Betrachtungen über David Friedrich Strauss' Bekenntniß*. Bonn: Marcus, 1873.

Mone, Franz Josef. *Einleitung in das Nibelungenlied zum Schul- und Selbstgebrauch*. Heidelberg: Oswald, 1818.

———. *Geschichte des Heidenthums im nördlichen Europa*. 2 vols. Leipzig and Darmstadt: Leske, 1822–23.

———. *Quellen und Forschungen zur Geschichte der teutschen Literatur und Sprache*. Aachen and Leipzig: Jacob Anton Mayer, 1830.

———. *Untersuchungen zur Geschichte der teutschen Heldensage*. Quedlinburg and Leipzig: Gottfried Basse, 1836.

Moritz, Karl Philipp. *Götterlehre oder Mythologische Dichtungen der Alten*. 1791. Edited by Horst Günther. Frankfurt a.M.: Insel, 1999.

Müller, Friedrich Max. *Chips from a German Workshop*. 2nd ed. 3 vols. London: Longmans, Green, and Co., 1868.

———. *My Autobiography: A Fragment*. New York: Charles Scribner's Sons, 1901.

Müller, Karl Otfried. *Geschichten hellenischer Stämme und Städte*. Pt. I, *Orchomenos und die Minyer*. Pt. II, *Die Dorier*. 2 vols. 2nd ed. Edited by F. W. Schneidewin. Breslau: Josef Max, 1844.

———. *Kleine deutsche Schriften*. Edited by Eduard Müller. 2 vols. Breslau: Josef Max, 1848.

———. *Prolegomena zu einer wissenschaftlichen Mythologie.* Göttingen: Vandenhoeck und Ruprecht, 1825.

Nietzsche, Friedrich. *"The Birth of Tragedy" and "The Case of Wagner."* Translated by Walter Kaufmann. New York: Vintage, 1967.

———. *Briefwechsel: Kritische Gesamtausgabe.* Edited by Giorgio Colli and Mazzino Montinari. 10 vols. to date. Berlin: de Gruyter, 1978–.

———. *Daybreak.* Translated by R. J. Hollingdale. Edited by Maudemarie Clark and Brian Leiter. Cambridge: Cambridge University Press, 1997.

———. *Human, All Too Human.* Translated by R. J. Hollingdale. With an introduction by Richard Schacht. Cambridge: Cambridge University Press, 1996.

———. *Sämtliche Werke: Kritische Studienausgabe.* Edited by Giorgio Colli and Mazzino Montinari. 15 vols. Berlin: de Gruyter, 1988.

———. *Thus Spake Zarathustra: A Book for Everyone and No One.* Translated by R. J. Hollingdale. London: Penguin, 1961.

———. *Werke.* 20 vols. Leipzig: Alfred Kröner, 1910–26.

———. *Werke: Kritische Gesamtausgabe.* Edited by Giorgio Colli and Mazzino Montinari. 35 vols. to date. Berlin: de Gruyter, 1967–.

Novalis. *Novalis Schriften.* 3rd ed. Edited by Paul Kluckhohn and Richard Samuel. 5 vols. Stuttgart: Kohlhammer, 1975–88.

Overbeck, Franz. *Werke und Nachlaß.* Vol. 1, *Schriften bis 1873.* Edited by Ekkehard W. Stegemann and Niklaus Peter. Stuttgart and Weimar: Metzler, 1994.

Preisendanz, Karl, ed. *Die Liebe der Günderode: Friedrich Creuzers Briefe an Caroline von Günderode.* With an introduction by Karl Preisendanz. Munich: Piper, 1912.

Preller, Ludwig. "Friedrich Creuzer, charakterisirt nach seinen Werken." *Hallische Jahrbücher für deutsche Wissenschaft und Kunst* 101–6 (April 27–May 3, 1838).

Rauwenhoff, L. W. E., and F. Nippold. *D. Fr. Strauß' "Alter und neuer Glaube" und seine literarischen Ergebnisse: Zwei kritische Abhandlungen.* Leipzig: Richter und Harrassowitz; Leiden: von Doesburgh, 1873.

Renan, Ernest. *Nouvelles considérations sur le caractère général des peuples sémitiques, et en particulier sur leur tendance au monothéisme. Extrait du Journal Asiatique.* Paris: Imprimerie impériale, 1859.

———. *Oeuvres complètes.* Edited by Henriette Psichari. 10 vols. Paris: Calmann-Lévy, 1955.

Rosenberg, Alfred. *The Myth of the Twentieth Century: An Evaluation of the Spiritual-Intellectual Confrontations of Our Age.* Translated by Vivian Bird. Torrance, Calif.: Noontide Press, 1982.

Rosenkranz, Karl. *Das Heldenbuch und die Nibelungen.* Halle: Eduard Anton, 1829.

Rühs, Friedrich. *Ueber den Ursprung der isländischen Poesie aus der angelsächsischen.* Berlin: Reimer, 1813.

Schelling, Friedrich. *Aus Schellings Leben: In Briefen.* Edited by G. L. Plitt. 3 vols. Leipzig: Hirzel, 1869.

———. *Briefe und Dokumente.* Edited by Horst Fuhrmans. 3 vols. Bonn: Bouvier, 1962–75.

———. *Historisch-kritische Ausgabe.* Edited by Hans Michael Baumgartner et al. 7 vols. to date. Stuttgart: Frommann-Holzboog, 1976–.

———. *Ideas for a Philosophy of Nature.* Translated by Errol E. Harris and Peter Heath. With an introduction by Robert Stern. Cambridge: Cambridge University Press, 1988.

———. *On University Studies.* Translated by E. S. Morgan. Edited and with an introduction by Norbert Guterman. Athens: Ohio University Press, 1966.

———. *Philosophie der Offenbarung: 1841/42.* Edited and with an introduction by Manfred Frank. Frankfurt a.M.: Suhrkamp, 1977.

———. *Philosophy of Art.* Edited, translated, and introduced by Douglas W. Stott. With a foreword by David Simpson. Minneapolis: University of Minnesota Press, 1989.

———. *Sämmtliche Werke.* Edited by K. F. A. Schelling. 14 vols. Stuttgart and Augsburg: Cotta, 1856–61.

———. *Schelling's Treatise on "The Deities of Samothrace": A Translation and Interpretation.* Translated with an interpretative essay by Robert Brown. Missoula: Scholars Press, 1977.

———. *System of Transcendental Idealism (1800).* Translated by Peter Heath. With an introduction by Michael Vater. Charlottesville: University of Virginia Press, 1978.

———. *The Unconditional in Human Knowledge: Four Early Essays (1794–1796).* Translated and edited by Fritz Marti. Lewisburg, Pa.: Bucknell University Press; London: Associated University Presses, 1980.

Schiller, Friedrich. *Essays.* Edited by Walter Hinderer and Daniel O. Dahlstrom. New York: Continuum, 1995.

———. *Werke: Nationalausgabe.* Edited by Julius Petersen and Gerhard Fricke. 39 vols. to date. Weimar: Hermann Böhlaus Nachfolger, 1943–.

Schlegel, August Wilhelm. *Kritische Ausgabe der Vorlesungen.* Edited by Ernst Behler and Frank Jolles. 1 vol. to date. Paderborn: Schöningh, 1989–.

———. *Kritische Schriften und Briefe.* Edited by Edgar Lohner. 4 vols. Stuttgart: Kohlhammer, 1965.

———. *Sämmtliche Werke.* Edited by Eduard Böcking. 12 vols. Leipzig: Weidmann, 1846–47.

Schlegel, Friedrich. *Kritische Friedrich-Schlegel-Ausgabe.* Edited by Ernst Behler. 35 vols. to date. Paderborn: Schöningh, 1958–.

Schleiermacher, Friedrich. *Aus Schleiermachers Leben.* Edited by Ludwig Jonas and Wilhelm Dilthey. 4 vols. Berlin: Reimer, 1861.

———. *Kleine Schriften und Predigten, 1800–1820.* Edited by Hayo Gerdes and Emanuel Hirsch. 3 vols. Berlin: de Gruyter, 1969–70.

———. *On Religion: Speeches to Its Cultured Despisers.* Translated and with an introduction by Richard Crouter. Cambridge: Cambridge University Press, 1988.

Schoof, Wilhelm, ed. *Briefe der Brüder Grimm an Savigny.* Berlin: E. Schmidt, 1953.

Schopenhauer, Arthur. *Parerga und Paralipomena: Short Philosophical Essays.* Translated by E. F. J. Payne. 2 vols. Oxford: Clarendon, 1974.

———. *Die Welt als Wille und Vorstellung.* 3rd ed. 2 vols. Leipzig: Brockhaus, 1859.

Schwartz, Wilhelm. *Die altgriechischen Schlangengottheiten, ein Beispiel der Anlehnung altheidnischen Volksglaubens an die Natur.* 1858. Reprint, Berlin: Hertz, 1897.

———. *Der heutige Volksglaube und das alte Heidentum.* Berlin: Nauck, 1850.

———. *Der Ursprung der Mythologie.* Berlin: Hertz, 1860.

Steinthal, Heymann. *Einleitung in die Psychologie und Sprachwissenschaft.* 2nd ed. Berlin: Dümmler, 1881.

———. *Haman, Bileam und der jüdische Nabi.* Berlin: Bernstein, 1885.

———. "Mythos und Religion." In *Sammlung gemeinverständlicher wissenschaftlicher Vorträge,* edited by Rudolf Virchow and Friedrich von Holtzendorff, 5th ser., no. 97. Berlin: Luderitz, 1870.

———. *Zu Bibel und Religionsphilosophie: Vorträge und Abhandlungen.* 2 vols. Berlin: Reimer, 1890–95.

Stolberg, Friedrich Leopold Grafen zu. *Geschichte der Religion Jesu Christi.* 12 vols. Hamburg: Perthes, 1806–16.

Strauss, David Friedrich. *Der alte und der neue Glaube: Ein Bekenntniß.* 2nd ed. Leipzig: Hirzel, 1872.

———. *Ausgewählte Briefe.* Edited by Eduard Zeller. Bonn: Emil Strauß, 1895.

———. *In Defense of My "Life of Jesus" against the Hegelians.* Translated, edited, and with an introduction by Marilyn Chapin Massey. Hamden, Conn.: Archon Books, 1983.

———. *Kleine Schriften: Biographischen, literatur- und kunstgeschichtlichen Inhalts.* Leipzig: Brockhaus, 1862.

———. *Das Leben Jesu, kritisch bearbeitet.* 1st ed. 2 vols. Tübingen: Osiander, 1835–36. Reprint, Darmstadt: Wissenschaftliche Buchgesellschaft, 1969.

———. *Das Leben Jesu, kritisch bearbeitet.* 4th ed. 2 vols. Tübingen: Osiander, 1840.

———. *Das Leben Jesu für das deutsche Volk.* Leipzig: Brockhaus, 1864.

Stuhr, Peter F. *Das Verhältnis der christlichen Theologie zur Philosophie und Mythologie nach dem heutigen Standpuncte der Wissenschaft.* Berlin: Schroeder, 1842.

Tylor, Edward. *Primitive Culture.* 2 vols. London: John Murray, 1871.

Vatke, Wilhelm. *Die Religion des Alten Testaments nach den kanonischen Büchern entwickelt.* Berlin: Bethge, 1835.

Villers, Charles de. *Coup-d'oeil sur l'état actuel de la littérature ancienne et de l'histoire en Allemagne.* Amsterdam and Paris: Bureau des Arts et de la Litterature, 1809.

Vischer, Friedrich. *Kritische Gänge.* 2 vols. Tübingen: Fues, 1844.

Voss, Johann Heinrich. *Antisymbolik.* 2 vols. Stuttgart: Metzler, 1824–26.

———. *Kritische Blätter nebst Geografischer Abhandlungen.* 2 vols. Stuttgart: Metzler, 1828.

———. *Mythologische Briefe.* 2nd ed. Edited by Heinrich Broska. 5 vols. Stuttgart: Metzler, 1827.

———. *Wie ward Friz Stolberg ein Unfreier?* Frankfurt a.M.: Wilmans, 1819.

Wagner, Cosima von. *Diaries.* Translated with an introduction by Geoffrey Skelton. Edited and annotated by Martin Gregor-Dellin and Dietrich Mack. 2 vols. New York: Harcourt Brace Jovanovich, 1978.

Wagner, Richard. *Gesammelte Schriften und Briefe.* Edited by Julius Kapp. 14 vols. Leipzig: Hesse und Becker, 1914.

———. *Gesammelte Schriften und Dichtungen.* 10 vols. Leipzig: Fritzsch, 1871–83.

———. *My Life.* Translated by Andrew Gray. Edited by Mary Whittall. New York: Da Capo, 1992.

———. *Prose Works.* Translated by William Ashton Ellis. 8 vols. London: Paul, Trench, and Trubner, 1895–99.

———. *The Ring of the Nibelung.* Translated by Andrew Porter. New York: Norton, 1976.

———. *Sämtliche Briefe.* Edited by Gertrud Strobel and Werner Wolf. 12 vols. to date. Leipzig: Deutscher Verlag für Musik, 1967–.

———. *Selected Letters of Richard Wagner.* Translated and edited by Stewart Spencer and Barry Millington. London and Melbourne: Dent, 1987.

Weisse, Christian Hermann. *Die evangelische Geschichte, kritisch und philosophisch bearbeitet.* 2 vols. Leipzig: Breitkopf und Hartel, 1838.

———. *Ueber das Studium des Homer und seine Bedeutung für unser Zeitalter.* Leipzig: Gerhard Fleischer, 1826.

———. "Ueber den Begriff des Mythus und seine Anwendung auf die neutestamentliche Geschichte." *Zeitschrift für Philosophie und spekulative Theologie* 4 (1839): 74-102, 211-54; 5 (1840): 114-54.

Wilamowitz-Moellendorff, Ulrich von. *History of Classical Scholarship.* Translated by Alan Harris. Edited with an introduction by Hugh Lloyd-Jones. London: Duckworth, 1982.

Winckelmann, Johann Joachim. *History of Ancient Art.* Translated by G. Henry Lodge. 4 vols. in 2. New York: F. Ungar, 1968.

Wislicenus, Gustav Adolph. *Gegenwart und Zukunft der Religion: Zu der von Strauss angeregten Frage über "Den alten und den neuen Glaube."* Leipzig: Ernst Keil, 1873.

Wolf, Friedrich August. *Prolegomena to Homer.* Translated with an introduction by Anthony Grafton, Glenn W. Most, and James E. G. Zetzel. Princeton: Princeton University Press, 1985.

Zeller, Eduard. *Vorträge und Abhandlungen geschichtlichen Inhalts.* Leipzig: Fues, 1865.

PRIMARY SOURCES: PERIODICALS

Athenaeum. 1798–1800.

Bragur: Ein litterarisches Magazin der deutschen und nordischen Vorzeit. 1791–1812.

Deutsches Museum. 1812–13.

Zeitschrift für Völkerpsychologie und Sprachwissenschaft. 1860–90.

SECONDARY LITERATURE

Abrams, M. H. *Natural Supernaturalism: Tradition and Revolution in Romantic Literature.* New York: Norton, 1971.

Adorno, Theodor. *In Search of Wagner.* Translated by Rodney Livingstone. London: Verso, 1984.

Allison, David B., ed. *The New Nietzsche: Contemporary Styles of Interpretation.* New York: Dell, 1977.

Altgeld, Wolfgang. *Katholizismus, Protestantismus, Judentum: Über religiös begründete Gegensätze und nationalreligiöse Ideen in der Geschichte des deutschen Nationalismus.* Mainz: Matthias Grünewald, 1992.

Anderson, Benedict. *Imagined Communities: Reflections on the Origin and Spread of Nationalism.* Rev. ed. London and New York: Verso, 1991.

Asad, Talal. *Genealogies of Religion: Discipline and Reasons of Power in Christianity and Islam.* Baltimore: Johns Hopkins University Press, 1993.

Aschheim, Steven E. *The Nietzsche Legacy in Germany, 1890–1990.* Berkeley and Los Angeles: University of California Press, 1992.

Auerbach, Eric. *Mimesis: The Representation of Reality in Western Literature.* Translated by Willard Trask. Princeton: Princeton University Press, 1953.

Avni, Abraham. *The Bible and Romanticism.* The Hague and Paris: Mouton, 1969.

Baeumer, Max L. "Nietzsche and the Tradition of the Dionysian." Translated by Timothy Sellner. In *Studies in Nietzsche and the Classical Tradition,* 2nd ed., edited by James C. O'Flaherty, Timothy F. Sellner, and Robert M. Helm, 165–89. Chapel Hill: University of North Carolina Press, 1979.

Baeumler, Alfred. "Bachofen der Mythologe der Romantik." In Johann Jakob Bachofen, *Der Mythus von Orient und Occident: Eine Metaphysik der alten Welt aus den Werken von J. J. Bachofen,* 2d ed., edited by Manfred Schröter, xxiii–ccxciv. Munich: Beck, 1926.

Bausinger, Hermann. *Volkskunde.* Darmstadt: Habel, 1971.

Beach, Edward Allen. *The Potencies of God(s): Schelling's Philosophy of Mythology.* Albany: State University of New York Press, 1994.

Becker, Claudia. *"Naturgeschichte der Kunst": August Wilhelm Schlegels ästhetischer Ansatz im Schnittpunkt zwischen Aufklärung, Klassik und Frühromantik.* Munich: Fink, 1998.

Behler, Ernst. "Die Auffassung des Dionysischen durch die Brüder Schlegel und Friedrich Nietzsche." *Nietzsche-Studien* 12 (1983): 335–54.

————. *Friedrich Schlegel in Selbstzeugnissen und Bilddokumenten.* Reinbek bei Hamburg: Rowohlt, 1966.

————. "Friedrich Schlegels 'Rede über die Mythologie' in Hinblick auf Nietzsche." *Nietzsche-Studien* 8 (1979): 182–209.

————. *Frühromantik.* Berlin: de Gruyter, 1992.

————. "Nietzsche und die frühromantische Schule." *Nietzsche-Studien* 7 (1978): 59–87.

————. *Unendliche Perfektibilität: Europäische Romantik und Französische Revolution.* Paderborn: Schöningh, 1989.

Beiser, Frederick C. *Enlightenment, Revolution, Romanticism: The Genesis of Modern German Political Thought, 1790–1800.* Cambridge: Harvard University Press, 1992.

————. *The Fate of Reason: German Philosophy from Kant to Fichte.* Cambridge: Harvard University Press, 1987.

Belke, Ingrid, ed. *Moritz Lazarus und Heymann Steinthal: Die Begründer der Völkerpsychologie in ihren Briefen.* 2 vols. Tübingen: Mohr, 1971–86.

Benjamin, Walter. *Der Begriff der Kunstkritik in der deutschen Romantik.* Frankfurt a.M.: Suhrkamp, 1973.

————. *The Origin of German Tragic Drama.* Translated by John Osborne. With an introduction by George Steiner. London: Verso, 1985.

Benz, Richard, ed. *Goethe und Heidelberg.* Heidelberg: F. H. Kerle, 1949.

Bergen, Doris L. *Twisted Cross: The German Christian Movement in the Third Reich.* Chapel Hill: University of North Carolina Press, 1996.

Bergmann, Peter. *Nietzsche: The "Last Antipolitical German."* Bloomington: Indiana University Press, 1987.

Bernal, Martin. *Black Athena: The Afroasiatic Roots of Classical Civilization.* Vol. 1, *The Fabrication of Ancient Greece, 1785–1985.* New Brunswick: Rutgers University Press, 1987.

————. *Black Athena Writes Back: Martin Bernal Responds to His Critics.* Edited by David Chioni Moore. Durham, N.C.: Duke University Press, 2001.

Bieder, Theobald. *Geschichte der Germanenforschung.* 3 vols. Hildburghausen: Thüringische Verlagsanstalt, 1913–25.

Bietenholz, Peter G. *Historia and Fabula: Myths and Legends in Historical Thought from Antiquity to the Modern Age.* Leiden: Brill, 1994.

Bigler, Robert. *The Politics of German Protestantism: The Rise of the Protestant Church Elite in Prussia, 1815–1848.* Berkeley and Los Angeles: University of California Press, 1972.

Blaschke, Olaf, and Frank-Michael Kuhlemann. *Religion im Kaiserreich: Milieus, Mentalitäten, Krisen.* Gütersloh: Chr. Kaiser, 1996.

Blok, Josine. "Quest for a Scientific Mythology: F. Creuzer and K. O. Müller on History and Myth." In *Proof and Persuasion in History,* edited by Anthony Grafton and Suzanne L. Marchand. *History and Theory* Theme Issue 33 (1994): 26–52.

Bluhm, Lothar. *Die Brüder Grimm und der Beginn der Deutschen Philologie: Eine Studie zu Kommunikation und Wissenschaftsbildung im frühen 19. Jahrhundert.* Hildesheim: Weidmann, 1997.

Blumenberg, Hans. *Work on Myth.* Translated by Robert M. Wallace. Cambridge: MIT Press, 1985.

Bohrer, Karl Heinz, ed. *Mythos und Moderne: Begriff und Bild einer Rekonstruktion.* Frankfurt a.M.: Suhrkamp, 1983.

Borchmeyer, Dieter. *Richard Wagner: Theory and Theatre.* Translated by Stewart Spencer. Oxford: Clarendon Press, 1991.

Borchmeyer, Dieter, and Jörg Salaqarda, eds. *Nietzsche und Wagner: Stationen einer epochalen Begegnung.* 2 vols. Frankfurt a.M.: Insel, 1994.

Bourdieu, Pierre. *The Rules of Art: Genesis and Structure of the Literary Field.* Translated by Susan Emanuel. Stanford: Stanford University Press, 1996.

Bowie, Andrew. *Aesthetics and Subjectivity: From Kant to Nietzsche.* Manchester: Manchester University Press, 1990.

———. *Schelling and Modern European Philosophy.* London and New York: Routledge, 1993.

Breckman, Warren. *Marx, the Young Hegelians, and the Origins of Radical Social Theory: Dethroning the Self.* Cambridge: Cambridge University Press, 1999.

Briggs, Ward W., and William Calder III, eds. *Classical Scholarship: A Biographical Encyclopedia.* New York: Garland, 1990.

Bruce, Steve, ed. *Religion and Modernization: Sociologists and Historians Debate the Secularization Thesis.* Oxford: Oxford University Press, 1992.

Brunschwig, Henri. *Enlightenment and Romanticism in Eighteenth-Century Prussia.* Translated by Frank Jellinek. Chicago: University of Chicago Press, 1974.

Bursian, Conrad. *Geschichte der classischen Philologie in Deutschland.* 2 vols. Munich and Leipzig: Oldenbourg, 1883.

Butler, E. M. *The Saint-Simonian Religion in Germany: A Study of the Young German Movement.* New York: Howard Fertig, 1968.

———. *The Tyranny of Greece over Germany.* Cambridge: Cambridge University Press, 1935.

Calder, William, III, Hubert Cancik, and Bernhard Kytzler, eds. *Otto Jahn (1813–68): Ein Geisteswissenschaftler zwischen Klassizismus und Historismus.* Stuttgart: Franz Steiner, 1991.

Calder, William, III, Hellmut Flashar, and Theodor Lindken, eds. *Wilamowitz nach 50 Jahren.* Darmstadt: Wissenschaftliche Buchgesellschaft, 1985.

Calder, William, III, and Renate Schlesier, with Susanne Gödde, eds. *Zwischen Rationalismus und Romantik: Karl Otfried Müller und die antike Kultur.* Hildesheim: Weidmann, 1998.

Cancik, Hubert, and Hildegard Cancik-Lindemaier. *Philolog und Kultfigur: Friedrich Nietzsche und seine Antike in Deutschland.* Stuttgart: Metzler, 1999.

Chadwick, Owen. *The Secularization of the European Mind in the Nineteenth Century.* Cambridge: Cambridge University Press, 1977.

Charlton, D. G. *Secular Religions in France, 1815–1870.* London: Oxford University Press, 1963.

Chytry, Josef. *The Aesthetic State: A Quest in Modern German Thought.* Berkeley and Los Angeles: University of California Press, 1989.

Cicora, Mary. *From History to Myth: Wagner's "Tannhäuser" and Its Literary Sources.* Berne and New York: Peter Lang, 1992.

Classen, Carl Joachim, ed. *Die klassische Altertumswissenschaft an der Georg-August-Universität Göttingen.* Göttingen: Vandenhoeck und Ruprecht, 1989.

Conze, Werner, and Jürgen Kocka, eds. *Bildungsbürgertum im 19. Jahrhundert.* 4 vols. Stuttgart: Klett-Cotta, 1985–92.

Corse, Sandra. *Wagner and the New Consciousness: Language and Love in the "Ring."* Rutherford, N.J.: Fairleigh Dickinson University Press, 1990.

Crane, Susan A. *Collecting and Historical Consciousness in Early Nineteenth-Century Germany.* Ithaca: Cornell University Press, 2000.

Dahlhaus, Carl. *The Idea of Absolute Music.* Translated by Roger Lustig. Chicago: University of Chicago Press, 1989.

De Vries, Jan. *Forschungsgeschichte der Mythologie.* Freiburg im Breisgau: Alber, 1961.

Dickey, Laurence. *Hegel: Religion, Economics, and the Politics of Spirit, 1770–1807.* Cambridge: Cambridge University Press, 1987.

———. "Saint-Simonian Industrialism at the End of History: August Cieszkowski on the Teleology of Universal History." In *Apocalypse Theory and the Ends of the World,* 159-99. Oxford: Blackwell, 1995.

Echternkamp, Jörg. *Der Aufstieg des deutschen Nationalismus (1770–1840).* Frankfurt a.M.: Campus, 1998.

Eger, Manfred. *Nietzsches Bayreuther Passion.* Freiburg im Breisgau: Rombach, 2001.

Ehrisman, Otfrid. *Nibelungenlied: Epoche, Werke, Wirkung.* Munich: Beck, 1987.

———. *Das Nibelungenlied in Deutschland: Studien zur Rezeption des Nibelungenlieds von der Mitte des 18. Jahrhunderts bis zum Ersten Weltkrieg.* Munich: Fink, 1975.

Emmerich, Wolfgang. *Germanistische Volkstumideologie: Genese und Kritik der Volksforschung im Dritten Reich.* Tübingen: Vereinigung für Volkskunde, 1968.

Epstein, Klaus. *The Genesis of German Conservatism.* Princeton: Princeton University Press, 1966.

Esposito, Joseph. *Schelling's Idealism and Philosophy of Nature.* Lewisburg, Pa.: Bucknell University Press; London: Associated University Presses, 1977.

Faber, Richard, ed. *Politische Religion, religiöse Politik.* Würzburg: Königshausen und Neumann, 1997.

Faber, Richard, and Renate Schlesier, eds. *Die Restauration der Götter: Antike Religion und Neo-Paganismus.* Würzburg: Königshausen und Neumann, 1986.

Feldman, Burton, and Robert D. Richardson, Jr., eds. *The Rise of Modern Mythology, 1680–1860.* Bloomington: Indiana University Press, 1972.

Feldmann, Roland. *Jacob Grimm und die Politik*. Kassel: Bärenreiter, 1970.

Fischer-Dieskau, Dietrich. *Wagner and Nietzsche*. New York: Seabury, 1976.

Flashar, Hellmut, Karlfried Gründer, and Axel Horstmann, eds. *Philologie und Hermeneutik im 19. Jahrhundert: Zur Geschichte und Methodologie der Geisteswissenschaften*. Göttingen: Vandenhoeck und Ruprecht, 1979.

Fohrmann, Jürgen, and Wilhelm Voßkamp, eds. *Wissenschaftsgeschichte der Germanistik im 19. Jahrhundert*. Stuttgart and Weimar: Metzler, 1994.

Förster, Eric. *Die Entstehung der preußischen Landeskirche unter der Regierung König Friedrich Wilhelms des Dritten: Ein Beitrag zur Geschichte der Kirchenbildung im deutschen Protestantismus*. 2 vols. Tübingen: Mohr, 1905–7.

Foucault, Michel. *The Order of Things: An Archaeology of the Human Sciences*. Translated by Unknown Translator. New York: Vintage, 1970.

Frank, Manfred. *Einführung in die frühromantische Ästhetik*. Frankfurt a.M.: Suhrkamp, 1989.

———. *Eine Einführung in Schellings Philosophie*. Frankfurt a.M.: Suhrkamp, 1985.

———. *Vorlesungen über die neue Mythologie*. Vol. 1, *Der kommende Gott*. Frankfurt a.M.: Suhrkamp, 1982.

———. *Vorlesungen über die neue Mythologie*. Vol. 2, *Gott im Exil*. Frankfurt a.M.: Suhrkamp, 1988.

Frank, Manfred, and Gerhard Kurz, eds. *Materialien zu Schellings philosophischen Anfängen*. Frankfurt a.M.: Suhrkamp, 1975.

Fraser, Giles. *Redeeming Nietzsche: On the Piety of Unbelief*. London: Routledge, 2002.

Frei, Hans. *The Eclipse of Biblical Narrative: A Study in Eighteenth and Nineteenth Century Hermeneutics*. New Haven: Yale University Press, 1974.

Freier, Hans. *Die Rückkehr der Götter, von der ästhetischen Ueberschreitung der Wissensgrenze zur Mythologie der Moderne: Eine Untersuchung zur systematischen Rolle der Kunst in der Philosophie Kants und Schellings*. Stuttgart and Weimar: Metzler, 1976.

Fried, Jochen. *Die Symbolik des Realen: Über alte und neue Mythologie in der Frühromantik*. Munich: Fink, 1985.

Friedländer, Ludwig. *Die Homerische Kritik von Wolf bis Grote*. Berlin: Reimer, 1853.

Fritzsche, Peter. "Specters of History: On Nostalgia, Exile, and Modernity." *American Historical Review* 106 (2001): 1587–1618.

Fröschle, Hartmut. *Der Spätaufklärer Johann Heinrich Voß als Kritiker der deutschen Romantik*. Stuttgart: Heinz, 1985.

Fuhrmann, Manfred, ed. *Terror und Spiel: Probleme der Mythenrezeption*. Munich: Fink, 1971.

Gay, Peter. *The Bourgeois Experience from Victoria to Freud*. Vol. 4, *The Naked Heart*. New York: Norton, 1995.

———. *Freud, Jews, and Other Germans: Masters and Victims in Modernist Culture*. Oxford: Oxford University Press, 1978.

Gebhardt, Jürgen. *Politik und Eschatologie: Studien zur Geschichte der Hegelschen Schule in den Jahren 1830–1840.* Munich: Beck, 1963.

Gerth, Hans. *Bürgerliche Intelligenz um 1800: Zur Soziologie des deutschen Frühliberalismus.* 2nd ed. Edited by Ulrich Hermann. Göttingen: Vandenhoeck und Ruprecht, 1976.

Giesen, Bernhard. *Intellectuals and the Nation: Collective Identity in a German Axial Age.* Cambridge: Cambridge University Press, 1998.

Gilman, Sander. *Inscribing the Other.* Lincoln: University of Nebraska Press, 1991.

Gockel, Heinz. *Mythos und Poesie: Zum Mythosbegriff in Aufklärung und Frühromantik.* Frankfurt a.M.: Klostermann, 1981.

Gollwitzer, Heinz. "Zum politischen Germanismus des 19. Jahrhunderts." In *Festschrift für Hermann Heimpel zum 70. Geburtstag am 19. September 1971,* edited by the staff of the Max-Planck-Institut für Geschichte, vol. 1, 282–356. Göttingen: Vandenhoeck und Ruprecht, 1971.

Golomb, Jacob, ed. *Nietzsche and Jewish Culture.* London: Routledge, 1997.

Gossman, Lionel. "Basle, Bachofen and the Critique of Modernity in the Second Half of the Nineteenth Century." *Journal of the Warburg and Courtauld Institutes* 47 (1984): 136–85.

———. *Basel in the Age of Burckhardt: A Study in Unseasonable Ideas.* Chicago: University of Chicago Press, 2000.

Graevenitz, Gerhart von. *Mythos: Geschichte einer Denkgewohnheit.* Stuttgart and Weimar: Metzler, 1987.

Graf, Friedrich Wilhelm. *Die Politisierung des religiösen Bewußtseins: Die bürgerlichen Religionsparteien im deutschen Vormärz: Das Beispiel des Deutschkatholizismus.* Stuttgart: Frommann-Holzboog, 1978.

———, ed. *Profile des neuzeitlichen Protestantismus.* 2 vols. to date.Gütersloh: Gerd Mohn, 1990–.

Graf, Gerhard. *Gottesbild und Politik: Eine Studie zur Frömmigkeit in Preußen während der Befreiungskriege, 1813–1815.* Göttingen: Vandenhoeck und Ruprecht, 1993.

Grafton, Anthony. "Polyhistory into *Philolog:* Notes on the Transformation of German Classical Scholarship, 1780–1850." *History of Universities* 3 (1983): 159–92.

Gregor-Dellin, Martin. *Richard Wagner: His Life, His Work, His Century.* Translated by J. Maxwell Brownjohn. London: Collins, 1983.

Gregory, Frederick. *Nature Lost? Natural Science and the German Theological Traditions of the Nineteenth Century.* Cambridge: Harvard University Press, 1992.

Grimm, Reinhold, and Jost Hermand, eds. *Rereading Wagner.* Madison: University of Wisconsin Press, 1993.

Gründer, Karlfried, and Karl Heinrich Rengstorf, eds. *Religionskritik und Religiosität in der deutschen Aufklärung.* Heidelberg: Lambert Schneider, 1989.

Gruppe, Otto. *Geschichte der Klassischen Mythologie und Religionsgeschichte während des Mittelalters im Abendland und während der Neuzeit.* Leipzig: Teubner, 1921.

Habel, Reinhardt. *Joseph Görres: Studien über den Zusammenhang von Natur, Geschichte und Mythos in seinen Schriften.* Wiesbaden: Franz Steiner, 1960.

Habermas, Jürgen. *The Philosophical Discourse of Modernity: Twelve Lectures.* Translated by Frederick Lawrence. Cambridge: MIT Press, 1987.

———. *The Structural Transformation of the Public Sphere: An Inquiry into a Category of Bourgeois Society.* Translated by Thomas Bürger with Frederick Lawrence. Cambridge: MIT Press, 1989.

Hardtwig, Wolfgang. *Nationalismus und Bürgerkultur in Deutschland, 1500–1914: Ausgewählte Aufsätze.* Göttingen: Vandenhoeck und Ruprecht, 1994.

Harris, H. S. *Hegel's Development: Towards the Sunlight, 1770–1801.* Oxford: Clarendon, 1972.

Harris, Horton. *David Friedrich Strauss and His Theology.* Cambridge: Cambridge University Press, 1973.

Hartlich, Christian, and Walter Sachs. *Der Ursprung des Mythosbegriffes in der modernen Bibelwissenschaft.* Tübingen: Mohr, 1952.

Hartwich, Wolf-Daniel. *Deutsche Mythologie: Die Erfindung einer Kunstreligion.* Berlin: Piper, 2000.

Hatfield, Henry. *Aesthetic Paganism in German Literature from Winckelmann to the Death of Goethe.* Cambridge: Harvard University Press, 1964.

———. *Clashing Myths in German Literature from Heine to Rilke.* Cambridge: Harvard University Press, 1974.

Heinzle, Joachim, and Anneliese Waldschmidt, eds. *Die Nibelungen, ein deutscher Wahn, ein deutscher Alptraum: Studien und Dokumente zur Rezeption des Nibelungenstoffs im 19. und 20. Jahrhundert.* Frankfurt a.M.: Suhrkamp, 1991.

Hellerich, Siegmar V. *Religionizing, Romanizing Romantics: The Catholico-Christian Camouflage of the Early German Romantics, Wackenroder, Tieck, Novalis, Friedrich and August Wilhelm Schlegel.* New York and Frankfurt a.M.: Peter Lang, 1995.

Herbst, Wilhelm. *Johann Heinrich Voß.* 2 vols. in 3. Leipzig: Teubner, 1872–76.

Herzog, Dagmar. *Intimacy and Exclusion: Religious Politics in Pre-revolutionary Baden.* Princeton: Princeton University Press, 1996.

Heschel, Susannah. *Abraham Geiger and the Jewish Jesus.* Chicago: University of Chicago Press, 1998.

Hess, Jonathan M. "Johann David Michaelis and the Colonial Imaginary: Orientalism and the Emergence of Racial Antisemitism in Eighteenth-Century Germany." *Jewish Social Studies* 6, no. 2 (2000): 56–101.

———. *Reconstituting the Body Politic: Enlightenment, Public Culture, and the Invention of Aesthetic Autonomy.* Detroit: Wayne State University Press, 1999.

Hirsch, Emanuel. *Geschichte der neueren evangelischen Theologie im Zusammenhang mit den allgemeinen Bewegungen des europäischen Denkens.* 5 vols. Reprint, Münster: Stenderhoff, 1984.

Hodgson, Peter. "Strauss's Theological Development from 1825 to 1840." In *David Friedrich Strauss, "The Life of Jesus" Critically Examined,* translated by George Eliot, xv–l. Philadelphia: Fortress Press, 1972.

Hohendahl, Peter Uwe. *Building a National Literature: The Case of Germany, 1830–1870.* Translated by Renate Bacon Franciscono. Ithaca: Cornell University Press, 1989.

———, ed. *A History of German Literary Criticism, 1730–1980.* Lincoln: University of Nebraska Press, 1988.

Hollinrake, Roger. *Nietzsche, Wagner, and the Philosophy of Pessimism.* London: Allen and Unwin, 1982.

Hölscher, Lucian. "Die Religion des Bürgers: Bürgerliche Frömmigkeit und Protestantische Kirche im 19. Jahrhundert." *Historische Zeitschrift* 250 (1990): 595–630.

———. *Weltgericht oder Revolution: Protestantische und sozialistische Zukunfts-vorstellungen im deutschen Kaiserreich.* Stuttgart: Klett-Cotta, 1989.

Horstmann, Axel. "Der Mythosbegriff vom frühen Christentum bis zur Gegenwart." *Archiv für Begriffsgeschichte* 23, no. 2 (1979): 7–54, 197–245.

Howald, Ernst. *Der Kampf um Creuzers Symbolik: Eine Auswahl von Dokumenten.* Tübingen: Mohr, 1926.

Howard, Thomas Albert. *Religion and the Rise of Historicism: W. M. L. de Wette, Jacob Burckhardt, and the Theological Origins of Nineteenth-Century Historical Consciousness.* Cambridge: Cambridge University Press, 2000.

Iversen, Erik. *The Myth of Egypt and Its Hieroglyphs in European Tradition.* 1961. Reprint, Princeton: Princeton University Press, 1994.

Izenberg, Gerald N. *Impossible Individuality: Romanticism, Revolution, and the Origins of Modern Selfhood, 1787–1802.* Princeton: Princeton University Press, 1992.

Jacobs, Wilhelm G. *Zwischen Revolution und Orthodoxie? Schelling und seine Freunde im Stift und an der Universität Tübingen: Texte und Untersuchungen.* Stuttgart: Frommann-Holzboog, 1989.

Jaeschke, Walter. *Reason in Religion: The Foundations of Hegel's Philosophy of Religion.* Translated by J. Michael Stewart and Peter C. Hodgson. Berkeley and Los Angeles: University of California Press, 1990.

———. "Urmenschheit und Monarchie: Eine politische Christologie des Hegelschen Rechts." *Hegel-Studien* 14 (1979): 73–107.

Jamme, Christoph. *Einführung in die Philosophie des Mythos.* Vol. 2, *Neuzeit und Gegenwart.* Darmstadt: Wissenschaftliche Buchgesellschaft, 1991.

———. *"Gott an hat ein Gewand": Grenzen und Perspektiven philosophischer Mythos-Theorien der Gegenwart.* Frankfurt a.M.: Suhrkamp, 1991.

Jamme, Christoph, and Helmut Schneider, eds. *Mythologie der Vernunft: Hegels "Ältestes Systemprogramm" des deutschen Idealismus.* Frankfurt a.M.: Suhrkamp, 1984.

Janz, Curt Paul. *Friedrich Nietzsche: Biographie.* 3 vols. Munich: Hanser, 1978.

Johnston, Otto. *The Myth of a Nation: Literature and Politics under Napoleon.* Columbia, S.C.: Camden House, 1989.

Kaiser, Gerhard. *Pietismus und Patriotismus im literarischen Deutschland: Ein Beitrag zum Problem der Säkularisation.* 2nd ed. Frankfurt: Athenäum, 1973.

Katz, Jacob. *The Darker Side of Genius: Richard Wagner's Antisemitism.* Hanover, N.H.: Brandeis University Press, 1986.

Kaufmann, Walter. *Nietzsche: Philosopher, Psychologist, Antichrist.* 4th ed. Princeton: Princeton University Press, 1974.

Kellner, Beate. *Grimms Mythen: Studien zum Mythosbegriff und seiner Anwendung in Jacob Grimms "Deutscher Mythologie."* Frankfurt a.M.: Peter Lang, 1994.

Kofman, Sarah. *Nietzsche and Metaphor.* Translated by Duncan Large. Stanford: Stanford University Press, 1993.

Köhler, Joachim. *Nietzsche and Wagner: A Lesson in Subjugation.* Translated by Ronald Taylor. New Haven: Yale University Press, 1998.

Köhnke, Klaus Christian. *The Rise of Neo-Kantianism: German Academic Philosophy between Idealism and Positivism.* Translated by R. J. Hollingdale. Cambridge: Cambridge University Press, 1991.

Körner, Joseph. *Nibelungenforschungen der deutschen Romantik.* Leipzig: Haessel, 1911.

Koselleck, Reinhart. *Futures Past: On the Semantics of Historical Time.* Translated by Keith Tribe. Cambridge: MIT Press, 1985.

Koshar, Rudy. *From Monuments to Traces: Artifacts of German Memory, 1870–1990.* Berkeley and Los Angeles: University of California Press, 2000.

Kramer, Fritz. *Verkehrte Welten: Zur imaginären Ethnographie des 19. Jahrhunderts.* Frankfurt a.M.: Syndikat, 1977.

Kreis, Rudolf. *Nietzsche, Wagner und die Juden.* Würzburg: Königshausen und Neumann, 1995.

Krumeich, Gerd, and Hartmut Lehmann, eds. *"Gott mit uns": Nation, Religion, und Gewalt im 19. und frühen 20. Jahrhundert.* Göttingen: Vandenhoeck und Ruprecht, 2000.

Lacoue-Labarthe, Philippe, and Jean-Luc Nancy. *The Literary Absolute: The Theory of Literature in German Romanticism.* Translated by Philip Barnard and Cheryl Lester. Albany: State University of New York Press, 1988.

———. *Le mythe nazi.* Paris: Éditions de l'aube, 1991.

Large, David Clay, William Weber, and Anne Dzamba Sessa, eds. *Wagnerism in European Culture and Politics.* Ithaca: Cornell University Press, 1984.

La Vopa, Anthony. *Fichte: The Self and the Calling of Philosophy, 1762–1799.* Cambridge: Cambridge University Press, 2001.

———. *Grace, Talent, and Merit: Poor Students, Clerical Careers, and Professional Ideology in Eighteenth-Century Germany.* Cambridge: Cambridge University Press, 1988.

———. "Specialists against Specialization: Hellenism as Professional Ideology in German Classical Studies." In *German Professions, 1800–1950,* edited by Geoffrey Cocks and Konrad Jarausch, 27–45. Oxford: Oxford University Press, 1990.

Lefkowitz, Mary R., and Guy MacLean Rogers, eds. *Black Athena Revisited.* Chapel Hill: University of North Carolina Press, 1996.

Lehmann, Hartmut. *Pietismus und weltliche Ordnung in Württemberg vom 17. bis zum 20. Jahrhundert.* Stuttgart: Kohlhammer, 1969.

————, ed. *Säkularisierung, Dechristianisierung, Rechristianisierung im neuzeitlichen Europa: Bilanz und Perspektiven der Forschung.* Göttingen: Vandenhoeck und Ruprecht, 1997.

Lepp, Claudia. *Protestantisch-liberaler Aufbruch in die Moderne: Der deutsche Protestantenverein in der Zeit der Reichsgründung und des Kulturkampfes.* Gütersloh: Christian Kaiser, 1996.

Levin, Herbert. *Die Heidelberger Romantik.* Munich: Paarcus, 1922.

Librett, Jeffrey S. *The Rhetoric of Cultural Dialogue: Jews and Germans from Moses Mendelssohn to Richard Wagner and Beyond.* Stanford: Stanford University Press, 2000.

Lincoln, Bruce. *Theorizing Myth: Narrative, Ideology, and Scholarship.* Chicago: University of Chicago Press, 1999.

Link, Jürgen, and Wulf Wülffing, eds. *Nationale Mythen und Symbole in der zweiten Hälfte des 19. Jahrhunderts.* Stuttgart: Klett-Cotta, 1991.

Love, Frederick. *Young Nietzsche and the Wagner Experience.* Chapel Hill: University of North Carolina Press, 1963.

Lukács, Georg. *The Destruction of Reason.* Translated by Peter Palmer. Atlantic Highlands, N.J.: Humanities Press, 1981.

Magee, Elizabeth. *Richard Wagner and the Nibelungs.* Oxford: Clarendon, 1990.

Maier, Charles. "The End of Longing? (Notes toward a History of Postwar German National Longing)." In *The Postwar Transformation of Germany: Democracy, Prosperity, and Nationhood,* edited by John S. Brady, Beverly Crawford, and Sarah Elise Wiliarty, 271–85. Ann Arbor: University of Michigan Press, 1999.

Mann, Thomas. *Pro and contra Wagner.* Translated by Allan Blunden. London and Boston: Faber and Faber, 1985.

Manuel, Frank. *The Broken Staff: Judaism through Christian Eyes.* Cambridge: Harvard University Press, 1992.

————. *The Eighteenth Century Confronts the Gods.* Cambridge: Harvard University Press, 1959.

Marchand, Suzanne. *Down from Olympus: Archaeology and Philhellenism in Germany, 1750–1970.* Princeton: Princeton University Press, 1996.

Massey, Marilyn Chapin. *Christ Unmasked: The Meaning of the "Life of Jesus" in German Politics.* Chapel Hill: University of North Carolina Press, 1983.

McLeod, Hugh. *Secularisation in Western Europe, 1848–1914.* New York: St. Martin's, 2000.

Megill, Allan. "Historicizing Nietzsche? Paradoxes and Lessons of a Hard Case." *Journal of Modern History* 68, no. 1 (Mar. 1996): 114–52.

Meyer, Michael A., ed. *German-Jewish History in Modern Times.* 4 vols. New York: Columbia University Press, 1996.

Millington, Barry. *Wagner.* Rev. ed. Princeton: Princeton University Press, 1984.

Momigliano, Arnaldo. *New Paths of Classicism in the Nineteenth Century.* Middletown: Wesleyan University Press, 1982.

Mosse, George. *The Nationalization of the Masses: Political Symbolism and Mass*

Movements in Germany from the Napoleonic Wars through the Third Reich.
New York: Howard Fertig, 1975.

Müller, Ulrich, and Peter Wapnewski, eds. *Wagner Handbook.* Translated by John
Deathridge. Cambridge: Harvard University Press, 1992.

Nattiez, Jean-Jacques. *Wagner Androgyne: A Study in Interpretation.* Translated by
Stewart Spencer. Princeton: Princeton University Press, 1993.

Newman, Ernest. *The Life of Richard Wagner.* 4 vols. New York: Knopf, 1933.

Nipperdey, Thomas. *Deutsche Geschichte, 1800–1866: Bürgerwelt und starker Staat.*
Munich: Beck, 1983.

———. *Deutsche Geschichte, 1866–1918.* 2 vols. Munich: Beck, 1990–92.

Nowak, Kurt. *Geschichte des Christentums in Deutschland: Religion, Politik und
Gesellschaft vom Ende der Aufklärung bis zur Mitte des 20. Jahrhunderts.*
Munich: Beck, 1995.

O'Brien, W. Arctander. *Novalis: Signs of Revolution.* Durham, N.C.: Duke University
Press, 1995.

Oergel, Maike. *The Return of King Arthur and the Nibelungen: National Myth in
Nineteenth-Century English and German Literature.* Berlin: de Gruyter, 1998.

Olender, Maurice. *The Languages of Paradise: Race, Religion, and Philology in the
Nineteenth Century.* Translated by Arthur Goldhammer. Cambridge: Harvard
University Press, 1992.

O'Meara, Thomas. *Romantic Idealism and Roman Catholicism: Schelling and the
Theologians.* Notre Dame: University of Notre Dame, 1982.

Orsucci, Andrea. *Orient–Okzident: Nietzsches Versuch einer Loslösung vom europäischen Weltbild.* Berlin: de Gruyter, 1996.

Paul, Jean-Marie. *D. F. Strauss (1808–1874) et son époque.* Paris: Les Belles Lettres,
1982.

Paulsen, Friedrich. *Geschichte des gelehrten Unterrichts auf den deutschen Schulen
und Universitäten vom Ausgang des Mittelalters bis zur Gegenwart.* 2nd ed. 2
vols. Leipzig: Veit, 1896–97.

Peter, Niklaus. *Im Schatten der Modernität: Franz Overbecks Weg zur
"Christlichkeit unserer heutigen Theologie."* Stuttgart and Weimar: Metzler,
1992.

Petersdorff, Dirk von. *Mysterienrede: Zum Selbstverständnis romantischer Intellektueller.* Tübingen: Niemeyer, 1996.

Poliakov, Léon. *The Aryan Myth: A History of Racist and Nationalist Ideas in
Europe.* Translated by Edmund Howard. New York: Basic Books, 1971.

Porter, James I. *The Invention of Dionysus: An Essay on "The Birth of Tragedy."*
Stanford: Stanford University Press, 2000.

———. *Nietzsche and the Philology of the Future.* Stanford: Stanford University
Press, 2000.

Puschner, Uwe. *Die völkische Bewegung im wilhelminischen Kaiserreich:
Sprache — Rasse — Religion.* Darmstadt: Wissenschaftliche Buchgesellschaft,
2001.

Puschner, Uwe, Walter Schmitz, and Justus H. Ulbricht, eds. *Handbuch zur "völkischen Bewegung," 1871–1918*. Munich: Saur, 1996.

Quack-Eustathiades, Regine. *Der deutsche Philhellenismus während des griechischen Freiheitskampfes, 1821–1827*. Munich: Oldenbourg, 1984.

Rehm, Walter. *Griechentum und Goethezeit: Geschichte eines Glaubens*. Leipzig: Dieterich, 1952.

Reibnitz, Barbara von. *Ein Kommentar zu Friedrich Nietzsche, "Die Geburt der Tragödie aus dem Geiste der Musik" (Kap. 1–12)*. Stuttgart and Weimar: Metzler, 1992.

Roberts, Tyler. *Contesting Spirit: Nietzsche, Affirmation, Religion*. Princeton: Princeton University Press, 1998.

Robson-Scott, W. D. *The Literary Background of the Gothic Revival in Germany: A Chapter in the History of Taste*. Oxford: Clarendon, 1965.

Rogerson, John. *Myth in Old Testament Interpretation*. Berlin: de Gruyter, 1974.

———. *Old Testament Criticism in the Nineteenth Century: England and Germany*. 2nd ed. Philadelphia: Fortress, 1985.

———. *W. M. L. de Wette: Founder of Modern Biblical Criticism: An Intellectual Biography*. Sheffield: Sheffield Academic Press, 1992.

Römer, Ruth. *Sprachwissenschaft und Rassenideologie in Deutschland*. Munich: Fink, 1985.

Rose, Paul Lawrence. *German Question/Jewish Question: Revolutionary Anti-semitism from Kant to Wagner*. Princeton: Princeton University Press, 1990.

———. *Wagner: Race and Revolution*. London and Boston: Faber and Faber, 1992.

Rublack, Hans Christoph, ed. *Die lutherische Konfessionalisierung in Deutschland*. Gütersloh: Gerd Mohn, 1992.

Saalfeld, Lerke von. "Die ideologische Funktion des Nibelungenlieds in der preußisch-deutschen Geschichte von seiner Wiederentdeckung bis zum Nationalsozialismus." Ph.D. dissertation, Freie Universität, Berlin, 1977.

Said, Edward. *Orientalism*. New York: Vintage, 1979.

Salmi, Hannu. *Imagined Germany: Richard Wagner's National Utopia*. New York: Peter Lang, 1999.

Sammons, Jeffrey. *Heinrich Heine: A Modern Biography*. Princeton: Princeton University Press, 1979.

Sandys, John Edwin. *A History of Classical Scholarship*. 3 vols. New York: Hafner, 1958.

Schaffry, Andreas Michael. *An der Schwelle zur Wissenschaft: Ideologische Funktionen und gesellschaftliche Relevanz bei der Organisierung des Diskurses "Altdeutsche Literatur" zwischen 1790 und 1815*. Munich: Iudicium, 1995.

Schlesier, Renate. *Kulte, Mythen, und Gelehrte: Anthropologie der Antike seit 1800*. Frankfurt a.M.: Fischer, 1994.

Schrey, Dieter. *Mythos und Geschichte bei Johann Arnold Kanne und in der romantischen Mythologie*. Tübingen: Niemeyer, 1969.

Schüler, Winfried. *Der Bayreuther Kreis von seiner Entstehung bis zum Ausgang der*

Wilhelminischen Aera: Wagnerkult und Kulturreform im Geiste völkischer Weltanschauung. Münster: Aschendorff, 1971.

Schwab, Raymond. *The Oriental Renaissance: Europe's Rediscovery of India and the East, 1680–1880.* Translated by Gene Patterson-Black and Victor Reinking. New York: Columbia University Press, 1984.

Schweitzer, Albert. *The Quest of the Historical Jesus: A Critical Study of Its Progress from Reimarus to Wrede.* 1906. Translated by F. C. Burkitt. With an introduction by James Robinson. New York: Macmillan, 1968.

See, Klaus von. *Die Göttinger Sieben: Kritik einer Legende.* Heidelberg: Winter, 1997.

———. *Die Ideen von 1789 und die Ideen von 1914: Völkisches Denken in Deutschland zwischen Französischer Revolution und Erstem Weltkrieg.* Frankfurt: Athenaion, 1975.

Seipp, Horst. *Entwicklungszüge der germanischen Religionswissenschaft (von Jacob Grimm zu Georges Dumézil).* Berlin: Ernst Reuter Gesellschaft, 1968.

Seyhan, Azade. *Representation and Its Discontents: The Critical Legacy of German Romanticism.* Berkeley and Los Angeles: University of California Press, 1992.

Shaffer, E. S. *"Kubla Kahn" and "The Fall of Jerusalem": The Mythological School in Biblical Criticism and Secular Literature, 1770–1880.* Cambridge: Cambridge University Press, 1975.

Silk, M. S., and J. P. Stern. *Nietzsche on Tragedy.* Cambridge: Cambridge University Press, 1981.

Silver, Carole G. *Strange and Secret Peoples: Fairies and Victorian Consciousness.* Oxford: Oxford University Press, 1999.

Smart, Ninian, et al., eds. *Nineteenth-Century Religious Thought in the West.* 3 vols. Cambridge: Cambridge University Press, 1985.

Smiles, Sam. *The Image of Antiquity: Ancient Britain and the Romantic Imagination.* New Haven: Yale University Press, 1994.

Smith, Helmut Walser. *German Nationalism and Religious Conflict: Culture, Ideology, Politics, 1870–1914.* Princeton: Princeton University Press, 1995.

———, ed. *Protestants, Catholics, and Jews in Germany, 1800–1914.* Oxford: Berg, 2001.

Smith, Woodruff. *Politics and the Sciences of Culture in Germany (1840–1920).* Oxford: Oxford University Press, 1991.

Sorkin, David. *The Berlin Haskalah and German Religious Thought: Orphans of Knowledge.* London: Vallentine Mitchell, 2000.

Sperber, Jonathan. *Popular Catholicism in Nineteenth-Century Germany.* Princeton: Princeton University Press, 1984.

Speth, Rudolf. *Nation und Revolution: Politische Mythen im 19. Jahrhundert.* Opladen: Leske und Budrich, 2000.

Spotts, Frederic. *Bayreuth: A History of the Wagner Festival.* New Haven: Yale University Press, 1994.

Stern, Fritz. *The Politics of Cultural Despair: A Study in the Rise of the Germanic Ideology.* Berkeley and Los Angeles: University of California Press, 1961.

Stocking, George. *Victorian Anthropology.* New York: Free Press, 1987.

Strack, Friedrich, ed. *Heidelberg im säkularen Umbruch: Traditionsbewußtsein und Kulturpolitik um 1800.* Stuttgart: Klett-Cotta, 1987.

Strenski, Ivan. *Four Theories of Myth in Twentieth-Century History: Cassirer, Eliade, Lévi-Strauss, and Malinowski.* Iowa City: University of Iowa Press, 1987.

Strich, Fritz. *Die Mythologie in der deutschen Literatur von Klopstock bis Wagner.* 2 vols. Halle: Niemeyer, 1910.

Stümke, Volker. *Die positive Christologie Christian Hermann Weißes: Eine Untersuchung zur Hinwendung der Christologie zur Frage nach dem historischen Jesus als Antwort auf das "Leben Jesu" von David Friedrich Strauß.* Frankfurt a.M.: Peter Lang, 1992.

Swatos, William H., Jr., and Daniel V. A. Olson, eds. *The Secularization Debate.* Lanham, Md.: Rowman and Littlefield, 2000.

Tal, Uriel. *Christians and Jews in Germany: Religion, Politics, and Ideology in the Second Reich, 1870–1914.* Translated by Noah Jonathan Jacobs. Ithaca: Cornell University Press, 1975.

Timm, Hermann. *Die heilige Revolution, das religiöse Totalitätskonzept der Frühromantik: Schleiermacher—Novalis—Friedrich Schlegel.* Frankfurt a.M.: Syndikat, 1978.

Todorov, Tzvetan. *Theories of the Symbol.* Translated by Catherine Porter. Oxford: Blackwell, 1982.

Toews, John. *Hegelianism: The Path toward Dialectical Humanism, 1805–1841.* Cambridge: Cambridge University Press, 1980.

Turner, Frank M. *The Greek Heritage in Victorian Britain.* New Haven: Yale University Press, 1981.

Vick, Brian. *Defining Germany: The 1848 Frankfurt Parliamentarians and National Identity.* Cambridge: Harvard University Press, 2002.

Viereck, Peter. *Metapolitics: From the Romantics to Hitler.* New York: Knopf, 1941.

Vogel, Martin. *Apollinisch und Dionysisch: Geschichte eines genialen Irrtums.* Regensburg: Gustav Bosse, 1966.

Volkmann, Richard von. *Geschichte und Kritik der Wolfschen "Prolegomena zu Homer": Ein Beitrag zur Geschichte der Homerischen Frage.* Leipzig: Teubner, 1874.

Von Hendy, Andrew. *The Modern Construction of Myth.* Bloomington: Indiana University Press, 2002.

Wardman, H. W. *Ernest Renan: A Critical Biography.* London: Athlone, 1964.

Weiner, Marc A. *Richard Wagner and the Anti-Semitic Imagination.* Lincoln: University of Nebraska Press, 1995.

Welch, Claude. *Protestant Thought in the Nineteenth Century.* 2 vols. New Haven: Yale University Press, 1972.

Whitman, James Q. "From Philology to Anthropology in Mid-Nineteenth-Century Germany." In *Functionalism Historicized: Essays on British Social Anthropology,* edited by George W. Stocking, Sr., 214–29. Madison: University of Wisconsin Press, 1984.

————. "Nietzsche in the Magisterial Tradition of German Classical Philology." *Journal of the History of Ideas* 47 (1986): 453–68.

Wilberg, Petra-Hildegard. *Richard Wagners mythische Welt: Versuche wider den Historismus.* Freiburg: Rombach, 1996.

Williamson, George S. "What Killed August von Kotzebue? The Temptations of Virtue and the Political Theology of German Nationalism, 1789–1819." *Journal of Modern History* 72 (2000): 890–943.

Wilson, A. Leslie. *A Mythical Image: The Ideal of India in German Romanticism.* Durham, N.C.: Duke University Press, 1964.

Wilson, John Elbert. *Schelling und Nietzsche: Zur Auslegung der frühen Werke Friedrich Nietzsches.* Berlin: de Gruyter, 1996.

Windell, George C. "Hegel, Feuerbach, and Wagner's *Ring.*" *Central European History* 9 (1976): 27–57.

Winkler, Markus. *Mythisches Denken zwischen Romantik und Realismus: Zur Erfahrung kultureller Fremdheit im Werk Heinrich Heines.* Tübingen: Niemeyer, 1995.

Wunderlich, Werner. *Der Schatz des Drachentödters: Materialien zur Wirkungsgeschichte des Nibelungenliedes.* Stuttgart: Klett-Cotta, 1977.

Wyss, Ulrich. *Die wilde Philologie: Jacob Grimm und der Historismus.* Munich: Beck, 1979.

Yack, Bernard. *The Longing for Total Revolution: Philosophical Sources of Social Discontent from Rousseau to Marx to Nietzsche.* Princeton: Princeton University Press, 1986.

Yovel, Yirmiyahu. *Dark Riddle: Hegel, Nietzsche, and the Jews.* University Park: Pennsylvania State University Press, 1998.

Zantop, Susanne. *Colonial Fantasies: Conquest, Family, and Nation in Precolonial Germany, 1770–1870.* Durham, N.C.: Duke University Press, 1997.

Zelinsky, Hartmut. *Sieg oder Untergang, Sieg und Untergang: Kaiser Wilhelm II., die Werk-Idee Richard Wagners, und der "Weltkampf."* Munich: Keyser, 1990.

Ziegler, Theobald. *David Friedrich Strauss.* 2 vols. Berlin: Trübner, 1908.

Ziolkowski, Theodore. "Der Hunger nach dem Mythos: Zur seelischen Gastronomie der Deutschen in den Zwanziger Jahren." In *Die sogenannten Zwanziger Jahre,* edited by Reinhold Grimm and Jost Hermand, 169–201. Bad Homburg: Gehlen, 1970.

Zipes, Jack. *The Brothers Grimm: From Enchanted Forests to the Modern World.* New York: Routledge, 1988.

INDEX

Abraham, 154, 163, 224
Academy of Fine Arts (Munich), 144
Achilles, 195
Adelung, Johann Christoph, 100–102
Adorno, Theodor, 293–94
Aegina, 144
Aeschylus, 87, 195, 241, 244
Alexander the Great, 72
Alice of Hesse (Princess), 251
Anquetil-Duperron, Abraham, 129
Anthroposophy, 286
anti-Semitism
    as aspect of new mythical narratives,
      178
    Burschenschaften and, 97
    and folkish movement, 286
    Fries and, 97
    Grimm brothers and, 332n.195
    and National Socialism, 290, 293
    Nietzsche and, 250, 273–74, 368n.41
    Schelling and, 49
    Schopenhauer and, 207–8
    shift in focus ca. 1848, 223
    upsurge after 1878, 231
    Wagner and, 203–6
Apollo
    dualism with Dionysus, 133, 147, 239–44
    flaying of Marsyas, 147, 163, 241
    as Greek national god, 145, 147, 196–97
    Moritz on, 40
Apollo Belvedere, 35, 36
Aristophanes, 195
Aristotle, 26, 143
Arndt, Ernst Moritz, 94, 95, 97, 98, 112,
    119

Arnim, Archim von, 78, 81, 88, 104, 125,
    139
Arnim, Bettina von, 123
art
    as autonomous, 11, 40, 50
    as basis of early Romantic "religion,"
      54–55
    as organon of philosophy (Schelling),
      59–60
    as substitute for religion (Nietzsche), 274
    See also genius
Arthur, King, 78, 118
Aryan-Semite distinction, 2, 14, 212–33,
    241–42, 256, 270, 286
Ascher, Saul, 91
Athena, 264
Athens, 14, 35–36, 72, 197, 198
Attila, 84
Aufklärung, 10, 11, 24, 27–35. *See also
    under* Catholicism; Judaism
Augustine (Saint), 241
Austria, 28, 29, 43

Baader, Franz von, 76, 78
Bach, Johann Sebastian, 183
Bachofen, Johann Jacob, 122, 239, 290
Bacchus. *See* Dionysus
Baden, 124, 142, 148, 247
Baeumler, Alfred, 290–91
Bakunin, Mikhail, 191
Baur, Ferdinand Christian, 159, 246
Bavaria, 40, 70
Bayle, Pierre, 8, 32
Bayreuth, 2, 259, 266, 270, 274, 279, 292,
    298, 299